RESEARCH GUIDE TO BIOGRAPHY AND CRITICISM

1990 UPDATE

BEACHAM PUBLISHING, INC.

Research Guide to Biography and Criticism

1990 Update

Edited by

Walton Beacham
Jessica Dorman
David W. Lowe
Charles J. Moseley

Library of Congress
  Cataloging-in-Publication Data
Research Guide to Biography and
Criticism: 1990 Update
  Includes bibliographical references.
  Summary: Description and evaluation
of the most important biographical,
autobiographical, and critical sources
published since 1985 about 325 British,
American, and Canadian writers.
  1. English literature—History and
criticism. 2. English literature—Bio-
bibliography. 3. Authors, English—
Biography—Bibliography. 4. American
literature—History and criticism—
Bibliography. 5. American literature—
Bio-bibliography. 6. Authors,
American—Biography—Bibliography.
  I.   Beacham, Walton, 1943
  II. Dorman, Jessica
  III. Lowe, David W.
  IV. Moseley, Charles J.
Z2011.R47 1990 016.82'09 85-2188
(PR85)
ISBN 0-933833-23-7

Printed in the United States of America
First Printing, September 1990

CONTENTS

BEACHAM PUBLISHING RESEARCH TITLES IN LITERATURE AND HISTORY

Research Guide Series

Research Guide to Biography and Criticism: Literature
Volumes I-II: 325 British, American and Canadian poets and novelists from *Beowulf* to the present
Volume III: 139 World dramatists from the Greeks to the present
Volume IV: 1990 Update
Volume V: 117 Contemporary American writers

Research Guide to American Historical Biography
Volumes I-III: 278 Americans in all fields from pre-Colonial times to the present
Volume IV: 127 Black and Native Americans, women, other minorities, explorers, and others

Research Guide to European Historical Biography
Volumes I-IV: 390 Important Europeans in all fields from 1500 to the present

Popular Fiction Series

Beacham's Popular Fiction in America
4 volumes analyze the novels of 185 best-selling American and British writers from 1950 to the present.

Popular World Fiction: 1900-Present
4 volumes analyze the novels of 182 world writers, including best-selling American authors from 1900 to the present and European writers whose books were translated into English and became best sellers.

Popular Fiction 1990 Supplement
Analyzes the novels of the writers contained in both Popular Fiction titles that have been published since 1986, and provides analyses of 65 writers who have become prominent since 1986.

Beacham's Guide to Literature for Young Adults
5 volumes analyze the most important and most popular books for young adults. The first three volumes cover classics, biographies, autobiographies, and non-fiction; Volume 4 covers mythology, mystery, science fiction, and adventure; Volume 5 covers fantasy and gothic novels.

PREFACE

Much has happened since the *Research Guide to Biography and Criticism* first appeared in 1985. We changed our name from Research Publishing to Beacham Publishing, Inc. The *Research Guide* has gone through five printings; has received "best reference" citations from the American Library Association and *Choice* magazine; has been widely reviewed; and has become a standard research tool in thousands of libraries. A companion set, the *Research Guide to American Historical Biography*, published in 1988, received similar attention. Although much has changed, the purpose of these research tools remains the same: to assist students in narrowing and researching topics for term papers and essay exams, and to provide librarians with a tool that will help them lead students to valuable, accessible resources.

In the five years since 1985, scholarship and critical methods have changed considerably, resulting in exciting new books that reflect both social and academic awareness. Some writers, such as Edith Wharton and Ellen Glasgow, have undergone a total reevaluation because of feminist criticism; others, such as D. H. Lawrence and Virginia Woolf, have been given new critical life because of deconstructionist methodology; while still others, such as Emily Brontë, George Orwell, and Frank Norris, have received additional attention because of an anniversary or newly discovered biographical materials. Definitive new biographies and collected letters are providing scholars with rich veins of ideas to mine.

Much new ground has been broken, which the 1900 annotated citations in this supplement reflect. We've attempted to provide a description for each book that will help students understand the different interests and approaches critics have taken during the last five years. For some writers we've been able to include all the critical and biographical works; with those who are the subject of boundless criticism, we selected the sources that are most useful to students who are preparing term papers or studying for comprehensive exams.

New to this *1990 Update* is a guide to the academic level of a critical work. **A** (Academic) designates titles most appropriate for scholars and advanced students; **G** (General) designates titles comprehensible to any interested or dedicated reader; **Y** (Youth) designates titles that will interest younger readers only. The works with a double rating **(A,G)** can be used either for general-purpose studies or by specialists. The purpose of this rating system is simply to help users identify sources that may be most appropriate to their academic interests or level.

On the following pages we have provided an outline which explains how students can use the annotated citations to develop a research topic. Because there are so many different users for the *Research Guide*—from beginning students to librarians and faculty, this outline may be above or below your research level. Our intention is to show students how to begin developing term paper ideas without wasting time or becoming frustrated by a lack of direction or available sources.

Soon to follow this *Research Guide Update* is a fifth volume covering contemporary writers who have received wide critical attention during the last five years. We have included the contents of this volume on page 585.

We hope that you continue to enjoy these research tools, and we welcome your ideas for other reference products. Write to Beacham Publishing, Inc., 2100 S Street, N.W., Washington, D.C. 20008.

Walton Beacham

Researching Term Paper Topics in Literature

Step #1
Narrow the Topic

Analyze the assignment you've been given. Some topics may be very general, others quite specific. Here are two examples; the first is more general.

1. Write a paper on any aspect of frontier literature.

2. Research the image of women in frontier literature.

The more general the topic, the more your teacher is looking for *you* to think about the specifics. Part of your research task is to narrow any topic as quickly as possible *before* you begin to take notes. Otherwise, you will be overwhelmed with material, and have no idea where to go next.

"Frontier" can mean almost anything, so the first step is to define your boundaries. Stories as far ranging as Homer's *Odyssey*, Mark Twain's *Huckleberry Finn*, Herman Melville's *Moby Dick*, and Robert Heinlein's *Stranger in a Strange Land* fall into some definition of "frontier" literature. As soon as you recognize that frontier doesn't necessarily have to include cowboys and Indians, you can think of many interesting ideas, such as "How the frontier of the land compares with the frontier of the sea." "The perils of the unknown in Homer's *Ulysses* and Melville's *Moby Dick*." "The sea captain and the Indian scout as frontier hero." "Wagon trains and space ships: similarities in crossing the wide frontier."

Step #2
Research Main Ideas

Keep asking questions until there are no more to ask. For example, what does "image of women" mean? Is it Huck Finn's image of his Aunt Polly, Mark Twain's idea about the function of women in settling the frontier, or a psychologist's analysis of the family unit?

Let's assume that you have a general idea about your topic but don't know how to proceed. You have decided to work on the second topic: women and frontier literature, which could include anything from mail order brides to Huck Finn not having a mother. What's the next step?

One source designed to help you narrow a topic and locate sources is the *Research Guide to Biography and Criticism*. (Vols. I-II cover poets and novelists; Vol. III covers dramatists; the Update covers the most recent sources for the authors in Vols I-II; and Vol. V covers modern American poets and novelists.) These volumes are probably shelved in the reference section of your library.

Looking quickly at Appendix A beginning on page xi of the *1990 Research Guide Update,* we find a list of important frontier writers under the category "Wilderness/Frontier," including James Fenimore Cooper, Mark Twain, and Willa Cather. Since Cather is a woman, we'll turn to her entry in the *Research Guide Update* to find the following entries (among others). The A,G indicate whether the work is most appropriate for an academic (A) or general (G) audience.

As we look at each entry we'll write down the basic idea(s).

#1
Bloom, Harold, ed. *Willa Cather's "My Ántonia".* New York: Chelsea House, 1987. Illustrating a wide range of critical approaches, these twelve essays address the novel's structure, theme, imagery, mythic elements, and use of time and history. For the most part, these essays question the views of earlier critics who interpreted the novel as a celebration of frontier life and viewed Ántonia as the embodiment of pioneer vitality. (A,G)

Main idea in #1: Previous critics viewed Cather as a frontier writer and her character, Ántonia, as the ideal frontier woman. Modern critics do not think Cather responded so favorably to the frontier.

#2
Callander, Marilyn Berg. *Willa Cather and the Fairy Tale.* Ann Arbor: UMI Research, 1989. This study opens the door to provocative insights about the symbolic reach of many of Cather's novels. Callander persuasively traces elements of fairy tales that "provide the primary symbols of romance," including Cinderella in *The Song of the Lark;* the fairy tale journey in *My Ántonia;* Sleeping Beauty and Snow White in *My Mortal Enemy;* and the archetype of the two brothers in *Death Comes for the Archbishop.* (G)

Main idea in #2: Cather used fairy tales as one source of her stories, especially the 'pure' heroines, Sleeping Beauty, Cinderella, and Snow White.

#3
Donovan, Josephine. *After the Fall: The Demeter-Persephone Myth in Wharton, Cather, and Glasgow.* University Park: The Pennsylvania State University Press, 1989. Persephone represents the "daughters" (feminine consciousness) that are whisked away into "patriarchal captivity" (the male world). This world is related to the women's culture of the Victorian era, characterized by a segregated "male-less" web of romantic female friendships. Of special note is Donovan's discussion of the ritual basis of Cather's *My Ántonia.* (A)

Main idea in #3: In a society where men dominate, women form almost mythic friendships. Questions: who were Demeter and Persephone? What do Glasgow, Wharton, and Cather have in common?

#4
O'Brien, Sharon. *Willa Cather: The Emerging Voice*. New York: Oxford University Press, 1986. In a late Victorian culture that provided few literary role models, Cather first attempted to imitate men, then achieved an identity with women. Initially, she was torn between two culturally opposed identities of art and womanhood but ultimately reconciled them. (A,G)

Main idea in #4: Cather's self-perception changed as she shifted her identity from men to women and accepted her role as a woman artist.

Now, compare the main ideas that you've just extracted and ask as many questions as you can think of, such as:

1. Early critics thought that Cather's early work reflected the characteristics of "frontier" literature. What has caused critics to view her work differently?

2. Fairy tales are often as frightening as they are fanciful. How and why does Cather identify with Sleeping Beauty, Snow White, and Cinderella?

3. How are fairy-tale characters like Cinderella, Snow White, and Sleeping Beauty (who are women without men) like or unlike other mythic women, such as Persephone and Demeter (who are symbols of female bonding?)

4. Is it unusual for women in male-dominated societies (such as the frontier), to first identify with men, then bond with women before achieving their own identity?

Step #3
Form a Thesis Statement and Outline

Any of these questions can become term paper topics. By extracting and combining ideas from our sources, we can write a thesis statement without having read any materials. An example of a thesis statement is:

Once Willa Cather realized that she was unsuccessfully identifying with a masculine, frontier sensibility, she gradually turned to women as role models, friends, and mythic symbols as she searched for her identity through her fiction.

Write several different thesis statements until you find the one that seems most appropriate to your assignment.

Now, using only the questions we generated from the *Research Guide* annotations, we can produce a working outline.

Outline

1. Cather's sense of the frontier as reflected in her novel *My Ántonia* (sources #1 and #2)

2. Cather's increasing dependence on women (source #4)

3. Cather's recognition that frontier women were not allowed to be artists (source #4)

4. Cather's use of female symbols, especially fairy tale heroines, as she seeks her release from men and the frontier (source #3)

We now have four different sources and a direction for beginning the research. However, you should keep several points in mind.

1. It is not necessary to read all four critical books—the function of a research paper is to locate the data that relates specifically to your topic. The table of contents and index in each source will tell you where to find the discussion related to each idea in your outline, and you will study only that portion of the book.

2. Your thesis sentence may change several times as you delve into the research phase. Since you have created your own topic, there is no reason to be stuck with an idea that is too difficult to research. Also, each section of the outline will become more specific as you begin reading the source materials.

3. If your library does not have the books that you have identified as sources for your research, you can ask any college library to borrow them through the inter-library loan system. If you cannot locate any of the books, you can still use the same ideas and adjust your topic to the books you do have.

4. At the very worst, if no books of any kind are available on your topic— Willa Cather, for example—you can scrap the whole idea and start over. This entire process of looking at the resources in the *Research Guide,* extracting the main idea, asking questions about the main ideas, then forming a thesis statement and working outline, should require no more than an hour, so you've lost little time even if you have to abandon your original idea.

APPENDIX A

Writers grouped by themes that are fully explored in one or more of the annotated sources in the *1990 Research Guide Update*. Consult Volumes I-II for additional themes covered by those sources.

Aestheticism
Arnold, Matthew
Beckett, Samuel
Coleridge, Samuel Taylor
Crane, Hart
Cummings, E. E.
Eliot, T. S.
Hopkins, Gerard Manley
James, Henry
Lewis, Wyndham
Pater, Walter
Pound, Ezra
Ruskin, John
Shelley, Percy Bysshe
Steinbeck, John
Stevens, Wallace
Waugh, Evelyn
Williams, William Carlos
Woolf, Virginia
Wordsworth, William
Yeats, W. B.

Alcohol/Drugs
Cheever, John
De Quincey, Thomas
Faulkner, William
Fitzgerald, F. Scott
Ginsberg, Allen
Hemingway, Ernest
Lowry, Malcolm
O'Neill, Eugene
Thomas, Dylan
Waugh, Evelyn

American South
Caldwell, Erskine
Faulkner, William
O'Connor, Flannery
Ransom, John Crowe

Simms, William Gilmore
Tate, Allen
Welty, Eudora
Williams, Tennessee

Art vs. Life
Cather, Willa
Dickinson, Emily

Art, Music, and Literature
Austen, Jane
Blake, William
Brontë, Emily
Burns, Robert
Campion, Thomas
Cather, Willa
Coleridge, Samuel Taylor
Crane, Stephen
Cummings, E. E.
Faulkner, William
Hardy, Thomas
Hughes, Langston
James, Henry
Lanier, Sidney
Lewis, Wyndham
Lindsay, Vachel
Melville, Herman
Morris, William
Pound, Ezra
Ruskin, John
Skelton, John
Taylor, Edward
Williams, William Carlos
Yeats, W. B.

The Bible
Arnold, Matthew
Blake, William
Bradstreet, Anne

Carlyle, Thomas
Dickens, Charles
Eliot, George
Emerson, Ralph Waldo
Herbert, George
Lewis, C. S.
Milton, John
Ruskin, John
Shakespeare, William
Spenser, Edmund
Stevens, Wallace
Tolkien, J. R. R.
Vaughan, Henry

Chauvinism
Austen, Jane
Bierce, Ambrose
Browning, Robert
Faulkner, William
Hardy, Thomas
Hawthorne, Nathaniel
Hemingway, Ernest

Childhood (troubled)
Aiken, Conrad
Berryman, John
Blake, William
Byrd, William
Chatterton, Thomas
Cheever, John
Dickens, Charles
Dreiser, Theodore
Ginsberg, Allen
Lewis, Sinclair
Maugham, Somerset
Shaw, George Bernard
Woolf, Virginia

Christianity
Arnold, Matthew
Beowulf-poet
Blake, William
Bradstreet, Anne
Carlyle, Thomas
Chesterton, G. K.
Clough, Arthur
Conrad, Joseph

Dickinson, Emily
Eliot, T. S.
Faulkner, William
Forster, E. M.
Greene, Graham
Hawthorne, Nathaniel
Herbert, George
Hopkins, Gerard Manley
Jeffers, Robinson
Kipling, Rudyard
Lewis, C. S.
Marvell, Andrew
Merton, Thomas
Milton, John
O'Connor, Flannery
Ransom, John Crowe
Rossetti, Christina
Shakespeare, William
Skelton, John
Spark, Muriel
Spenser, Edmund
Stevens, Wallace
Stowe, Harriet Beecher
Tate, Allen
Taylor, Edward
Tolkien, J. R. R.
Twain, Mark
Vaughan, Henry
Waugh, Evelyn

City and the Writer
Aiken, Conrad
Anderson, Sherwood
Dickens, Charles
Ellison, Ralph
Faulkner, William
O'Connor, Flannery
Ransom, John Crowe
Tate, Allen
Williams, Tennessee
Wolfe, Thomas
Woolf, Virginia
Wordsworth, William

Class Struggle
Bennett, Arnold
Clare, John

Dickens, Charles
Dreiser, Theodore
Gissing, George
Hardy, Thomas
Howells, William Dean
Lawrence, D. H.
McKay, Claude
Steinbeck, John

Commerce/Industry/Capitalism

Chesnutt, Charles
Conrad, Joseph
Defoe, Daniel
Dickinson, Emily
Dos Passos, John
Dreiser, Theodore
Franklin, Benjamin
Gissing, George
Hawthorne, Nathaniel
Howells, William Dean
James, Henry
Melville, Herman
Milton, John
Norris, Frank
Rossetti, Christina
Shakespeare, William
Spenser, Edmund
Twain, Mark
Wharton, Edith
Whitman, Walt

Courtship

Austen, Jane
Brontë, Charlotte
Brontë, Emily

Education/Learning

Austen, Jane
Frost, Robert
Morris, William
Ruskin, John

Existentialism

Beckett, Samuel
Conrad, Joseph
Dickinson, Emily

Ford, Ford Madox
Greene, Graham
James, Henry
Joyce, James
Orwell, George
Twain, Mark

Fate/Fatalism

Defoe, Daniel
Richardson, Samuel
Sterne, Laurence
Wright, Richard

Film and Literature

Agee, James
Faulkner, William
Fitzgerald, F. Scott
Lindsay, Vachel
Maugham, Somerset
Sandburg, Carl
Shakespeare, William
Stowe, Harriet Beecher

Female Friendship

Brontë, Charlotte
Browning, Elizabeth
Cather, Willa
Eliot, George
Gaskell, Elizabeth
Glasgow, Ellen
Rossetti, Christina
Wharton, Edith

Gender Criticism on

Austen, Jane
Baldwin, James
Bishop, Elizabeth
Bogan, Louise
Brontë, Charlotte
Brontë, Emily
Browning, Elizabeth
Browning, Robert
Cable, George Washington
Cather, Willa
Cavendish, Margaret
Chopin, Kate
Dickens, Charles

Dickinson, Emily
Dreiser, Theodore
Eliot, George
Faulkner, William
Fitzgerald, F. Scott
Gaskell, Elizabeth
Gissing, George
Glasgow, Ellen
H. D. (Hilda Doolittle)
Hardy, Thomas
Hawthorne, Nathaniel
Hemingway, Ernest
Hunt, Leigh
James, Henry
Joyce, James
Lawrence, D. H.
Mansfield, Katherine
McCullers, Carson
Milton, John
Moore, Marianne
Murdoch, Iris
Nin, Anais
O'Connor, Flannery
Plath, Sylvia
Pope, Alexander
Richardson, Samuel
Rossetti, Christina
Rowson, Susanna
Scott, Sir Walter
Shakespeare, William
Shelley, Mary
Stead, Christina
Stein, Gertrude
Steinbeck, John
Stowe, Harriet Beecher
Swift, Jonathan
Trollope, Anthony
Updike, John
Welty, Eudora
Wharton, Edith
Williams, William Carlos
Wollstonecraft, Mary

History and Literature
Donne, John
Dos Passos, John
Dryden, John
Ford, Ford Madox

Herrick, Robert
Jonson, Ben
Milton, John
O'Connor, Flannery
Stowe, Harriet Beecher
Tennyson, Alfred Lord
Updike, John

Hypocrisy/Deception
Hawthorne, Nathaniel
Shakespeare, William
Twain, Mark
Waugh, Evelyn
Williams, William Carlos
Woolf, Virginia

Illusion and Reality
Bennett, Arnold
Blake, William
Coleridge, Samuel Taylor
Conrad, Joseph
Defoe, Daniel
Hawthorne, Nathaniel
Keats, John
Langland, William
Shelley, Percy Bysshe
Steinbeck, John
Tennyson, Alfred Lord
Warren, Robert Penn
Wells, H. G.
West, Nathanael
Wordsworth, William

Imagination and the Creative Process
Addison, Joseph
Arnold, Matthew
Cary, Joyce
Coleridge, Samuel Taylor
De Quincey, Thomas
Dickinson, Emily
Hazlitt, William
Hopkins, Gerard Manley
Hughes, Langston
Keats, John
Lamb, Charles
Lewis, Wyndham

Pater, Walter
Steele, Richard
Stevens, Wallace
Woolf, Virginia
Wordsworth, William
Yeats, William Butler

Journalism and Literature
Anderson, Sherwood
Crane, Stephen
Dreiser, Theodore
Hemingway, Ernest
London, Jack
Norris, Frank

Law and Literature
Chaucer, Geoffrey
Collins, Wilkie
Cooper, James Fenimore
Hardy, Thomas
Hawthorne, Nathaniel
Melville, Herman
Stevens, Wallace
Stowe, Harriet Beecher
Trollope, Anthony

Literary Circles and Friendships
Bishop/ Robert Lowell
Bishop/Marianne Moore
Cather/Wharton/Glasgow
Coleridge/Wordsworth
Conrad/Ford
Conrad/Lawrence/Woolf
Dreiser/H. L. Menchen
Durrell/Henry Miller
T. S. Eliot/Joyce/Pound
Ginsberg/Kerouac/Wm. Burroughs
Hardy/Kipling/Haggard
Hellman/Hammett
Howells/Twain
Hughes/Hurston
Hunt/Mary Shelley/Dickens
James/Conrad/Crane/
  Wells/Wharton
James/Ford

Jarrell/Warren/Ransom/Schwartz/
  Berryman/Lowell
Jonson/Philip Sidney
Lawrence/Amy Lowell
Henry Miller/Nin
Pound/Yeats
Sexton/Robert Lowell
Sexton/Maxine Kumin
Tate/Robert Lowell/Ransom
Tate/Andrew Lytle
Yeats/George Russell

Literary Influences
Austen on Forster
Ballantyne on William Golding
Carlyle on Tennyson
Coleridge on Wordsworth
Conrad on Graham Greene
Defoe on Paul Theroux
Dickens on Dostoyevsky/Kafka
Eliot, T. S. on Berryman
Eliot, T. S. on Jarrell
Eliot, T. S. on Lowell
Eliot, T. S. on Schwartz
Goldsmith on Canadian literature
H. D. on Margaret Atwood
H. D. on Robert Duncan
H. D. on Adrienne Rich
Hardy on Anderson
Hardy on Cather
Hardy on Dreiser
Hardy on John Fowles
Hardy on Lawrence
Hardy on George Moore
Hardy on Proust
Hawthorne on Cheever
Hawthorne on Faulkner
Hawthorne on James
Hawthorne on Mailer
Hawthorne on McCullers
Hawthorne on Melville
Hawthorne on Flannery O'Connor
Hawthorne on William Styron
Hawthorne on Updike
Herbert on Meditative poetry
Hispanic culture on Hemingway
Hopkins on Merton
Hopkins on Plath

Hopkins on Dylan Thomas
Joyce on T. S. Eliot
Jung on Olson
Kant/Hegel on Pater
Keats on W. C. Williams
Keats on Amy Lowell
Kierkegaard on Graham Greene
Milton on Keats
Newman on Hopkins
Pater on Eliot
Pater on Joyce
Pater on Pound
Pater on Yeats
Plato on Hopkins
Poe on Doyle
Pound on T. S. Eliot
Shakespeare on Blake
Shakespeare on Byron
Shakespeare on Coleridge
Shakespeare on Doyle
Shakespeare on T. S. Eliot
Shakespeare on Keats
Shakespeare on Wordsworth
Tennyson on Golding
Turgenev on Hemingway
Vergil on Spenser
Vergil on Milton
Whitman on Hart Crane
Whitman on Henry Miller
Whitman on Dos Passos
Wordsworth on P. B. Shelley

Literary Innovators and Theorists

Aldington, Richard
Arnold, Matthew
Austen, Jane
Barth, John
Beckett, Samuel
Beowulf-poet
Blake, William
Brooks, Gwendolyn
Browning, Robert
Burgess, Anthony
Burton, Robert
Campion, Thomas
Chatterton, Thomas

Chaucer, Geoffrey
Chesnutt, Charles
Christie, Agatha
Clare, John
Coleridge, Samuel Taylor
Conrad, Joseph
Cooper, James Fenimore
Crane, Hart
Cynewulf
Defoe, Daniel
Dickinson, Emily
Dryden, John
Durrell, Lawrence
Eliot, T. S.
Faulkner, William
Hemingway, Ernest
James, Henry
Joyce, James
Langland, William
Larkin, Philip
Pound, Ezra
Richardson, Samuel
Sidney, Philip
Swift, Jonathan
Williams, William Carlos

Love (ideal)

Browning, Elizabeth
Coleridge, Samuel Taylor
Dryden, John
Graves, Robert
Malory, Thomas
Moore, George
Swinburne, Algernon

Manners (the Literature of Polite Society)

Austen, Jane
Bennett, Arnold
Brontë, Charlotte
Burney, Fanny
Byron, Lord George
Galsworthy, John
Goldsmith, Oliver
Rochester, Earl of
Shelley, Mary

Marriage/Adultery

Browning, Elizabeth & Robert
Cheever, John
Coleridge, Samuel Taylor
Hawthorne, Nathaniel
James, Henry
London, Jack
Shakespeare, William
Steele, Richard
Updike, John

Moral Decay/Morality

Brooke, Rupert
Scott, Sir Walter

Mystery/Gothic/Occult

Chatterton, Thomas
Christie, Agatha
Collins, Wilkie
Doyle, Arthur Conan
Gaskell, Elizabeth
Hardy, Thomas
Hawthorne, Nathaniel
James, Henry
Kipling, Rudyard
Poe, Edgar Allan
Shelley, Mary
Stevenson, Robert Louis

Myth/Ritual

Beckett, Samuel
Blake, William
Browning, Robert
Burns, Robert
Cather, Willa
Dickey, James
Dickinson, Emily
Eliot, T. S.
Faulkner, William
H. D. (Hilda Doolittle)
Jewett, Sarah Orne
Keats, John
Kipling, Rudyard
Laurence, Margaret
Lawrence, D. H.
Lewis, C. S.
O'Connor, Flannery

Singer, I. B.
Tolkien, J. R. R.
Williams, Tennessee

Nature as Controlling Force

Arnold, Matthew
Brontë, Charlotte
Brontë, Emily
Coleridge, Samuel Taylor
Emerson, Ralph Waldo
Hopkins, Gerard Manley
Langland, William
Pope, Alexander
Thoreau, Henry David
Wordsworth, William

Philosophy and Literature

Arnold, Matthew
Carlyle, Thomas
Clough, Arthur Hugh
Coleridge, Samuel Taylor
Conrad, Joseph
Eliot, George
Eliot, T. S.
Emerson, Ralph Waldo
Gaskell, Elizabeth
Hopkins, Gerard Manley
Melville, Herman
Merton, Thomas
Orwell, George
Pater, Walter
Pound, Ezra
Traherne, Thomas
Waugh, Evelyn

Political Philosophy and Utopia

Coleridge, Samuel Taylor
Godwin, William
Hazlitt, William
Mill, John Stuart
Morris, William
Orwell, George
Pound, Ezra

Shelley, Mary
Shelley, Percy Bysshe
Swift, Jonathan

Psychology and Literature
Chatterton, Thomas
Coleridge, Samuel Taylor
Collins, Wilkie
Conrad, Joseph
Crane, Stephen
Defoe, Daniel
Dickens, Charles
Dickinson, Emily
Eliot, George
Emerson, Ralph Waldo
Forster, E. M.
Gissing, George
Graves, Robert
Hardy, Thomas
Hawthorne, Nathaniel
Hemingway, Ernest
James, Henry
Lawrence, D. H.
Lowell, Robert
Melville, Herman
Merton, Thomas
Mill, John Stuart
Milton, John
Moore, Marianne
Naipaul, V. S.
Orwell, George
Poe, Edgar Allan
Pope, Alexander
Sexton, Anne
Shakespeare, William
Shelley, Mary
Swift, Jonathan
Thoreau, Henry David
Traherne, Thomas
Twain, Mark
Vonnegut, Kurt
Woolf, Virginia
Yeats, W. B.

Puritanism/New England
Bradstreet, Anne
Cooper, James Fenimore

Franklin, Benjamin
Frost, Robert
Hawthorne, Nathaniel
Melville, Herman
Plath, Sylvia
Taylor, Edward

Racial Identity
Baldwin, James
Brooks, Gwendolyn
Cable, George Washington
Cullen, Countée
Hughes, Langston
Hurston, Zora Neale
McKay, Claude
Naipaul, V. S.
Stowe, Harriet Beecher
Toomer, Jean
Wright, Richard

Redemption/Salvation
Aiken, Conrad
Dickey, James
Emerson, Ralph Waldo
Herbert, George
O'Connor, Flannery
Singer, I. B.
Traherne, Thomas
Vaughan, Henry

Revolution/Political Freedom
Blake, William
Byron, Lord George
Clare, John
Emerson, Ralph Waldo
Howells, William Dean
Mill, John Stuart

Satire/Politics
Addison, Joseph
Blake, William
Browne, Thomas
Butler, Samuel
Byron, Lord George
Defoe, Daniel
Dos Passos, John

Dryden, John
Nashe, Thomas
Pope, Alexander
Skelton, John
Swift, Jonathan
Waugh, Evelyn

Science and Literature
Burton, Robert
Chaucer, Geoffrey
Chesterton, G. K.
Dickens, Charles
Doyle, Arthur Conan
Hopkins, Gerard Manley
Moore, Marianne
Stevens, Wallace
Twain, Mark
Williams, William Carlos

Sea
Conrad, Joseph
Crane, Hart
Steinbeck, John
Thoreau, Henry David

Sexual Identity and Independence
Austen, Jane
Baldwin, James
Behn, Aphra
Bellow, Saul
Bishop, Elizabeth
Bogan, Louise
Bradstreet, Anne
Brontë, Charlotte
Brontë, Emily
Browning, Elizabeth
Burney, Fanny
Cather, Willa
Cavendish, Margaret
Chatterton, Thomas
Cheever, John
Chopin, Kate
Collins, Wilkie
Dickens, Charles
Dickinson, Emily
Eliot, George

Fitzgerald, F. Scott
Gaskell, Elizabeth
James, Henry
Kerouac, Jack
Mansfield, Katherine
Maugham, Somerset
McCullers, Carson
O'Connor, Flannery
Rhys, Jean
Richardson, Samuel
Rossetti, Christina
Sexton, Anne
Shakespeare, William
Shelley, Mary
Stead, Christina
Sterne, Laurence
Trollope, Anthony
Twain, Mark
Updike, John
Welty, Eudora
Whitman, Walt
Williams, William Carlos
Woolf, Virginia

Social Criticism
Addison, Joseph
Algren, Nelson
Austen, Jane
Baldwin, James
Blake, William
Butler, Samuel
Byron, Lord George
Caldwell, Erskine
Carlyle, Thomas
Chaucer, Geoffrey
Chesnutt, Charles
Coleridge, Samuel Taylor
Collins, Wilkie
Conrad, Joseph
Dickens, Charles
Dickinson, Emily
Didion, Joan
Dos Passos, John
Dryden, John
Eliot, George
Gaskell, Elizabeth
Golding, William
Hawthorne, Nathaniel

Lewis, Sinclair
Morris, William
Naipaul, V. S.
Orwell, George
Pound, Ezra
Robinson, E. A.
Rossetti, Christina
Roth, Philip
Ruskin, John
Stowe, Harriet Beecher
Updike, John
Wells, H. G.

Suicide

Aiken, Conrad
Berryman, John
Chatterton, Thomas
Plath, Sylvia
Poe, Edgar Allan
Pound, Ezra
Sexton, Anne

Wilderness/Frontier

Bradstreet, Anne
Cather, Willa
Cooper, James Fenimore
Didion, Joan
Emerson, Ralph Waldo
Hawthorne, Nathaniel
Irving, Washington
Twain, Mark

World War I/Paris

Aldington, Richard
Anderson, Sherwood

Brooke, Rupert
Dos Passos, John
Eliot, T. S.
Fitzgerald, F. Scott
Graves, Robert
Hemingway, Ernest
Joyce, James
Owen, Wilfred
Pound, Ezra
Stein, Gertrude

World War II

Dickey, James
Vonnegut, Kurt

Writers between Literary Periods or Cultures

Arnold, Matthew
Bennett, Arnold
Beowulf-poet
Blake, William
Brooke, Rupert
Conrad, Joseph
Dreiser, Theodore
Forster, E. M.
Hardy, Thomas
Hawthorne, Nathaniel
Howells, William Dean
Irving, Washington
James, Henry
Naipaul, V. S.
Wells, H. G.
Wharton, Edith

APPENDIX B

British/Colonial Empire writers in the *Research Guide to Biography and Criticism* grouped by the literary period during which they lived.

Middle Ages
Beowulf-poet
Caedmon
Chaucer, Geoffrey
Cynewulf
Dunbar, William
Gower, John
Henryson, Robert
Langland, William
Layamon
Lydgate, John
Malory, Sir Thomas
Pearl-poet (*Gawain*-poet)
Skelton, John

Elizabethan
Campion, Thomas
Daniel, Samuel
Davies, Sir John
Deloney, Thomas
Drayton, Michael
Gascoigne, George
Greville, Fulke
Jonson, Ben
Lodge, Thomas
Nashe, Thomas
Raleigh, Sir Walter
Shakespeare, William
Sidney, Philip
Spenser, Edmund
Wyatt, Sir Thomas

Restoration/ Seventeenth Century
Behn, Aphra
Browne, Thomas
Burton, Robert
Butler, Samuel
Carew, Thomas
Cavendish, Margaret
Chapman, George
Crashaw, Richard
Davenant, Sir William
Donne, John
Fanshawe, Sir Richard
Herbert, George
Herrick, Robert
Lovelace, Richard
Marvell, Andrew
Milton, John
Oldham, John
Pepys, Samuel
Rochester, Earl of
Southwell, Robert
Suckling, Sir John
Traherne, Thomas
Vaughan, Henry
Waller, Edmund
Walton, Izaak

Neoclassical/ Eighteenth Century
Addison, Joseph
Austen, Jane
Boswell, James
Burney, Fanny
Burns, Robert
Chatterton, Thomas
Collins, William
Crabbe, George
Defoe, Daniel
Dryden, John
Fielding, Henry
Gay, John
Godwin, William
Goldsmith, Oliver
Gray, Thomas
Johnson, Samuel
Lewis, Matthew Gregory
Pope, Alexander

Prior, Matthew
Radcliffe, Ann
Reynolds, Joshua
Richardson, Samuel
Rowson, Susanna
Steele, Richard
Sterne, Laurence
Swift, Jonathan
Warton, Thomas
Watts, Isaac
Wollstonecraft, Mary

Romantic
Blake, William
Byron, Lord George
Clare, John
Clough, Arthur
Coleridge, Samuel Taylor
De Quincey, Thomas
Edgeworth, Maria
Hallam, Arthur Henry
Hazlitt, William
Hunt, Leigh
Keats, John
Lamb, Charles
Landor, Walter Savage
Scott, Sir Walter
Shelley, Mary
Shelley, Percy Bysshe
Wordsworth, William

Victorian/ Nineteenth Century
Arnold, Matthew
Brontë, Charlotte
Brontë, Emily
Browning, Elizabeth
Browning, Robert
Carlyle, Thomas
Collins, Wilkie
De la Mare, Walter
Dickens, Charles
Doyle, Arthur Conan
Eliot, George
Gaskell, Elizabeth
Gissing, George
Hardy, Thomas

Hopkins, Gerard Manley
Housman, A. E.
Kipling, Rudyard
Le Fanu, Joseph
Macaulay, Thomas B.
Mill, John Stuart
Moore, George
Morris, William
Pater, Walter
Patmore, Coventry
Rossetti, Christina
Rossetti, Dante Gabrielle
Ruskin, John
Shaw, George Bernard
Stevenson, Robert Louis
Swinburne, Algernon
Tennyson, Alfred
Thackeray, William
Trollope, Anthony
Wilde, Oscar

Modern British
Acton, Harold
Aldington, Richard
Amis, Kingsley
Auden, W. H.
Beckett, Samuel
Bennett, Arnold
Bowen, Elizabeth
Brooke, Rupert
Buchan, John
Burgess, Anthony
Cary, Joyce
Chesterton, G. K.
Christie, Agatha
Conrad, Joseph
Day-Lewis, Cecil
Durrell, Lawrence
Eliot, T. S.
Empson, William
Forster, E. M.
Galsworthy, John
Golding, William
Graves, Robert
Greene, Graham
Heaney, Seamus
Isherwood, Christopher
James, Henry

Joyce, James
Koestler, Arthur
Lawrence, D. H.
Larkin, Philip
Lavin, Mary
Lewis, C. S.
Lewis, Wyndham
MacNeice, Louis
Mansfield, Katherine
Maugham, Somerset
O'Connor, Frank
Orwell, George
Owen, Wilfred
Rhys, Jean

Richardson, Dorothy
Saki
Sayers, Dorothy
Snow, C. P.
Spender, Stephen
Stead, Christina
Thomas, Dylan
Tolkien, J. R. R.
Waugh, Evelyn
Wilson, Angus
Wells, H. G.
Woolf, Virginia
Yeats, William Butler

APPENDIX C

American writers in the *Research Guide to Biography and Criticism* grouped by the literary period during which they lived, and Canadian writers of all periods.

Colonial
Bradstreet, Anne
Brown, Charles Brockden
Byrd, William
Franklin, Benjamin
Freneau, Philip
Rowson, Susanna
Taylor, Edward
Wheatley, Phillis

American Romanticism
Benét, Stephen Vincent
Bierce, Ambrose
Cable, George Washington
Chesnutt, Charles
Cooper, James Fenimore
Dickinson, Emily
Emerson, Ralph Waldo
Harris, Joel Chandler
Hawthorne, Nathaniel
Irving, Washington
Jewett, Sarah
Lanier, Sidney
Longfellow, Henry W.
Lowell, Amy
Melville, Herman
Poe, Edgar Allan
Simms, William Gilmore
Stowe, Harriet Beecher
Thoreau, Henry David
Twain, Mark
Whitman, Walt

American Realism/Naturalism
Chopin, Kate
Crane, Hart
Crane, Stephen
Dreiser, Theodore

Freeman, Mary Wilkins
Garland, Hamlin
Harte, Bret
Howells, William Dean
James, Henry
Jeffers, Robinson
Lardner, Ring
Lewis, Sinclair
London, Jack
Norris, Frank
O. Henry
Robinson, E. A.
Sinclair, Upton
Wharton, Edith

Modern
Agee, James
Aiken, Conrad
Algren, Nelson
Anderson, Sherwood
Baldwin, James
Barth, John
Bellow, Saul
Berryman, John
Bishop, Elizabeth
Bogan, Louise
Brooks, Gwendolyn
Buck, Pearl
Caldwell, Erskine
Cather, Willa
Cheever, John
Cozzens, James Gould
Cullen, Countée
Cummings, E. E.
Dickey, James
Didion, Joan
Dos Passos, John
Eberhart, Richard
Eliot, T. S.
Farrell, James T.

Faulkner, William
Ferlinghetti, Lawrence
Fitzgerald, F. Scott
Fletcher, John Gould
Ford, Ford Madox
Frost, Robert
Ginsberg, Allen
Glasgow, Ellen
H.D. (Hilda Doolittle)
Hayden, Robert
Hellman, Lillian
Hemingway, Ernest
Hughes, Langston
Hurston, Zora Neale
Jarrell, Randall
Kerouac, Jack
Lindsay, Vachel
Lowell, Robert
MacLeish, Archibald
Malamud, Bernard
Marquand, John P.
McCullers, Carson
McKay, Claude
Merton, Thomas
Millay, Edna St. Vincent
Miller, Arthur
Miller, Henry
Moore, Marianne
Nabokov, Vladimir
Nin, Anais
O'Connor, Flannery
O'Hara, Frank
O'Hara, John
O'Neill, Eugene
Olson, Charles
Plath, Sylvia
Porter, Katherine Anne
Pound, Ezra

Ransom, John Crowe
Roberts, Elizabeth Madox
Roethke, Theodore
Roth, Philip
Sandburg, Carl
Saroyan, William
Sarton, May
Schwartz, Delmore
Sexton, Anne
Singer, I. B.
Stein, Gertrude
Steinbeck, John
Stevens, Wallace
Stuart, Jesse
Tate, Allen
Teasdale, Sara
Thurber, James
Toomer, Jean
Updike, John
Vonnegut, Kurt
Warren, Robert Penn
Welty, Eudora
West, Nathanael
Wilder, Thornton
Williams, Tennessee
Williams, William Carlos
Wolfe, Thomas
Wright, Richard

Canadian

Birney, Earle
Callaghan, Morley
Davies, Robertson
Laurence, Margaret
Lowry, Malcolm
MacLennan, Hugh
Pratt, E. J.
Service, Robert

RESEARCH GUIDE TO BIOGRAPHY AND CRITICISM

1990 UPDATE

JOSEPH ADDISON
1672-1719

Evaluation of Selected Biography and Criticism

Bloom, Edward A., Lillian Bloom, and Edmund Leites. *Educating the Audience: Addison, Steele, and Eighteenth-Century Culture.* Los Angeles: William Andrews Clark Memorial Library, University of California, 1984. In two papers—by the Blooms and Leites—read at a Clark Library Seminar in 1980, the Blooms examine the role of the imagination and contemplation in the life and works of Addison and Steele. Leites focuses on the ethics of Steele on issues of marriage and the civilities of social life. **(A)**

Ketcham, Michael G. *Transparent Designs: Reading, Performance, & Form in the "Spectator" Papers.* Athens: University of Georgia Press, 1985. Ketcham attempts to explain why *The Spectator* was the most successful, polished, and influential periodical of the eighteenth century. Divided into six chapters, this book analyzes *The Spectator* for its style and attitudes, and examines how the periodical's particular readership responded to the editors' social and artistic biases. Although *Transparent Designs* plows some new ground, it is sometimes tedious, sometimes outdated, and demonstrates that additional scholarship is necessary for a full understanding of *The Spectator's* success. Recommended for scholars and advanced students of Addison and the period. **(A)**

McCrea, Brian. *Addison and Steele are Dead: The English Department, Its Canon, and the Professionalization of Literary Criticism.* Newark: University of Delaware Press, 1990. This clever book uses the lives, careers, and works of Addison and Steele to develop a devastating critique of how college English departments were established, how they function, and how they fail. McCrea begins with the simple question—How could the two loudest voices of the eighteenth century, Addison and Steele, be now so stilled? The authors lie neglected, untaught, unread. The reasons are bound up with the formation of a "canon" of books that were considered acceptable to teach and in the formation of a professional cadre of critics who employ fashionable theories to dissect susceptible works. **(A)**

Other Sources

Lannering, J. *Studies in the Prose Style of Joseph Addison.* Reprint [1951]. Millwood, NY: Kraus, 1985.

1

JAMES AGEE
1909-1955

Evaluation of Selected Biography and Criticism
   Ashdown, Paul, ed. *James Agee, Selected Journalism*. Knoxville: University of Tennessee Press, 1985. This is a selection of diverse essays by James Agee published between 1933 and 1947 in *Time* or *Fortune* magazines. This volume includes a bibliography that lists all articles by Agee published in these two magazines. **(A,G)**

   Spears, Ross, and Jude Cassidy, eds. *Agee: His Life Remembered*. New York: Holt, Rinehart, 1985. The editors have collected interviews conducted for a documentary film on Agee, who was himself a highly regarded film critic as well as writer. These portray Agee affectionately and compassionately, and do little to alter the portrait of a hard driving, immoderate writer who lived life fully and died young. **(A,G)**

Other Sources
   Richards, Nancy J. *James Agee: An Annotated Bibliography*. New York: Garland, 1990.

CONRAD AIKEN
1889-1973

Evaluation of Selected Biography and Criticism

Butscher, Edward. *Conrad Aiken: Poet of White Horse Vale.* Athens: University of Georgia Press, 1988. The focus of this first volume of a projected 2-volume biography is the years 1889-1925, in which Aiken struggled to deal with a family tragedy—his father murdered his mother, then committed suicide. Butscher argues that this event is central to all of Aiken's writings, and he applies his theory to some of the works. Amply illustrated and with an indispensable critical bibliography, this is the best treatment of Aiken to date and is essential for understanding the man and his work. (A,G)

Marten, Harry. *The Art of Knowing: The Poetry and Prose of Conrad Aiken.* Columbia: University of Missouri Press, 1988. Focusing on the prose, long fiction, and poetry, Marten explores how Aiken viewed his world. He treats Aiken as both an intellectual observer and literary critic, a creative force in a generation of important American writers. There are complete notes for all the chapters, a selective bibliography, and an index of quotations from Aiken's works. This critical biography will assist students, general readers, and aficionados of Aiken. (A,G)

Spivey, Ted R. *The Writer as Shaman: The Pilgrimages of Conrad Aiken and Walker Percy.* Macon, GA: Mercer University Press, 1986. Spivey incorporates one of his favorite critical themes—the use of myth for cultural renewal—into the particular "quests" that Aiken and Percy undertook in search of their battered psyches. Both suffered a parental suicide when they were young, leaving them alienated and lonely. Spivey contends that both men finally balanced their hearts and minds to become artistic visionaries. Using Aiken's autobiography, *Ushant,* Spivey explores the manic-depressive character of Aiken's poetry and fiction. This interesting thesis offers sensitive insights into Aiken's work, which has been long neglected. (A)

Spivey, Ted R. *Revival: Southern Writers in the Modern City.* Gainesville: University Presses of Florida, 1986. Spivey sets out to correct the belief that southern writers are exclusively steeped in rural culture by selecting a group who came to terms with the modern city. He discusses the attitudes and adaptations of playwright Williams, poets Ransom, Tate, and Aiken, and novelists Faulkner, Wolfe, Ellison, O'Connor, and Percy. Although compelled to address the issues of southern "decadence and decline," Spivey also demonstrates how many of these writers offered a vision of how to integrate old values with new social structures, allowing the past to reanimate the present. (A,G)

3

RICHARD ALDINGTON
1892-1962

Evaluation of Selected Biography and Criticism

Doyle, Charles. *Richard Aldington: A Biography*. Carbondale: Southern Illinois University Press, 1989. Aldington was one of the most respected thinkers of his time, attaining fame as poet, editor, translator, critic, novelist, and biographer. By age nineteen, Aldington had mastered free verse and was an innovator in the form. Under the influence of Pound, he became a leader of the English imagist movement, which he later abandoned. Along with Flint and Eliot, Aldington was influential in presenting the sensibilities of contemporary French poetry to English readers through the journal *Egoist*. In the 1920s, he wrote what he termed his "jazz novel," *Death of a Hero*, which is one of the finest novels about World War I. He wrote important biographies of both D. H. Lawrence and T. E. Lawrence. Through satire and penetrating criticism, Aldington indicted the English caste system, manipulative theologians, and plotting scientists. His last important study examined the life and works of Mistral, a poet of Provence. (A,G)

Other Sources

Barlow, Adrian. *Answers for My Murdered Self*. Francestown, NH: Typographeum, 1988.

NELSON ALGREN
1909-1981

Evaluation of Selected Biography and Criticism

Bruccoli, Matthew J. *Nelson Algren: A Descriptive Bibliography*. Pittsburgh: University of Pittsburgh Press, 1985. This bibliography provides detailed information on all of the editions of Algren's works. This descriptive information is primarily of use to librarians, catalogers, and collectors. **(A)**

Drew, Bettina. *Nelson Algren: A Life on the Wild Side*. New York: Putnam, 1989. Drew's biography draws on a series of interviews with Algren as well as an examination of primary sources and existing scholarship. The novelist and social critic emerges as a rebellious intellectual who always knew what he stood against but rarely what he stood for. Although Drew presents details of Algren's life that other biographers have missed, she neglects nuances of Algren's style and flair that other biographers have detailed. **(A)**

Giles, James R. *Confronting the Horror: The Novels of Nelson Algren*. Kent, OH: The Kent State University Press, 1989. Giles contends that Algren's literary reputation has suffered from the basic misperceptions of critics. This study offers a reevaluation of Algren's significance in an attempt to correct this critical bias. Giles surveys Algren's narrative structures and techniques, and his use of imagery and symbolism in all of the major novels. A selected bibliography is included. **(A,G)**

KINGSLEY AMIS
1922

Author's Recent Bibliography
   The Old Devils, 1987 (novel); *The Crime of the Century*, 1987 (nonfiction); *Difficulties with Girls*, 1988 (novel); *The Folks That Live on the Hill*, 1990 (novel).

Evaluation of Selected Biography and Criticism
   Hassan, Salem K. *Philip Larkin and His Contemporaries: An Air of Authenticity.* New York: St. Martin's, 1988. Larkin is one of modern poetry's most skilled craftsmen, and Hassan's study explores at length how craft affects the meaning. Hassan then compares Larkin's response to the modern world with that of his British contemporaries: Amis, Thom Gunn, D. J. Enright, and John Wain. The second section provides a basic introduction to each of these writers. (A)

   McDermott, John. *Kingsley Amis: An English Moralist.* New York: St. Martin's Press, 1989. McDermott contends that Amis' works are not merely humorous but have a serious, and intentional, moral purpose. He argues that Amis' intentions are primarily to untangle fiction from non-literary issues and to describe the world he sees without undue evaluation. McDermott discusses the novels chronologically as he builds a case for the reassessment of Amis' lagging reputation. He considers Amis "one of the few important novelists writing in his time." (A,G)

Other Sources
   Salwak, Dale. *Kingsley Amis.* Mercer Island, WA: Starmont House, 1990.

SHERWOOD ANDERSON
1876-1941

Autobiographical Sources

Campbell, Hilbert H., ed. *The Sherwood Anderson Diaries, 1936-1941.* Athens: University of Georgia Press, 1987. Although three volumes of Anderson's letters have been published, this collection marks the first time anyone other than select scholars has had an opportunity to read the extensive diaries Anderson kept during the last five years of his life. Campbell believes that the diaries reveal more personal information and introspection than either Anderson's letters or memoirs. **(A)**

Sutton, William A., ed. *Letters to Bab: Sherwood Anderson to Marietta D. Finley, 1916-1933.* Champaign: University of Illinois Press, 1985. These 309 letters portray Anderson in the midst of a prolonged mid-life crisis. He is admittedly self-occupied and carries on an ongoing commentary on himself, his hopes and problems. This emphasis on the self makes this collection particularly valuable for biographical insights. Unfortunately only two of Marietta Finley's letters to Anderson survive. She obviously functioned as a powerful muse in the novelist's life, and he remained indebted to her for much of his inspiration. **(A,G)**

Evaluation of Selected Biography and Criticism

Carpenter, Humphrey. *Geniuses Together: American Writers in Paris in the 1920s.* Boston: Houghton Mifflin, 1988. Carpenter, who has written biographies of Auden and Tolkien, provides a portrait of expatriate life on the Left Bank in post-WWI Paris and surveys the American writers who flocked there for inspiration and camaraderie. The spotlight is primarily on Hemingway and his immediate circle, including Anderson, Fitzgerald, Boyle, Pound, Joyce, and Stein. **(A)**

Townsend, Kim. *Sherwood Anderson.* Boston: Houghton Mifflin, 1987. Townsend has written a well-researched and moving biography that reveals Sherwood Anderson to have been a writer of a profound contemporary sensibility. Townsend's effort is more engaging and comprehensive than earlier biographies by Irving Howe and James Schevill, both published in 1951. Anderson viewed himself as the "quintessential American man" who expressed his nature through a variety of endeavors, drama being only one of many. Townsend's analyses of the writings are always sympathetic and insightful. **(A,G)**

Williams, Kenny J. *A Storyteller and a City: Sherwood Anderson's Chicago.* DeKalb: Northern Illinois University Press, 1988. In a narrowly focused approach, Williams argues that Anderson's work was greatly influenced by his experiences in Chicago as a young man. Far from depicting only the isolated, rural existence of Winesburg, Ohio, Anderson's works reflect the more sophisticated issues of free will, nature, religion, and experimentation with language that he would have learned from the creative force of the city. (A)

Other Sources
Modlin, Charles E., ed. *Sherwood Anderson's Love Letters to Eleanor Copenhaver Anderson*. Athens: University of Georgia Press, 1990.

White, Ray Lewis, ed. *Sherwood Anderson's Early Writings*. Kent, OH: Kent State University Press, 1989.

MATTHEW ARNOLD
1822-1888

Evaluation of Selected Biography and Criticism

Collini, Stefan. *Arnold.* New York: Oxford University Press, 1988. This critical study focuses on the "conversational" quality of the voice and tone in Arnold's prose. For Collini, it is not the theory but the voice that gives Arnold's work permanent significance. This is a compelling introduction to Arnold's prose, particularly to that of the 1860s, and can be considered a complement to W. Stacy Johnson's study of the poetry, *The Voices of Matthew Arnold* (1961). (A,G)

Donoghue, Denis. *England, Their England: Commentaries on English Language and Literature.* New York: Knopf, 1988. Noted literary critic Donoghue offers a collection of over twenty of his essays addressing the accomplishments and significance of selected English authors. Shakespeare is included, of course, along with Defoe, Peter Ackroyd, and Wyndham Lewis (whose works are discussed in some detail). Donoghue writes insightfully about the poetic contributions of Shelley, Eliot, and Hopkins, and considers the criticism of Arnold, Pater, and Leavis. (A,G)

Fraser, Hilary. *Beauty and Belief: Aesthetics and Religion in Victorian Literature.* Cambridge: Cambridge University Press, 1986. In this specialized study in intellectual history, Fraser traces the relationship between religion and aesthetic doctrine from Coleridge and Wordsworth through the aestheticism of Walter Pater and Oscar Wilde. Fraser argues that through concepts propounded by Hopkins, Ruskin, Arnold, and the Oxford aesthetes, Christianity is reduced to a merely subjective religion of art. (A)

Giddings, Robert, ed. *Matthew Arnold: Between Two Worlds.* Totowa, NJ: Barnes & Noble, 1986. Giddings has compiled a collection of essays that addresses Arnold's concerns with education, religion, criticism, culture, and country. Arnold pursued these interests, according to the introduction, because of an ambivalent nostalgia linked with an uncertain hope for the future. (A)

Livingston, James C. *Matthew Arnold and Christianity: His Religious Prose Writings.* Columbia: University of South Carolina Press, 1986. Later in life Arnold became increasingly disenchanted with his "romantic" identity and turned toward religion. In the process, he abandoned poetry to write books and essays on the Bible and Christianity. Livingston traces Arnold's religious ideas, his assessment of the Bible as literature, and his repeated attempts to see experience as the base of faith. T. S. Eliot asserted that Arnold pretended to be a Christian while undermining Christianity's tenets; specifically, that Arnold's works purported that the "emotions of Christianity can be preserved without the belief." Livingston demonstrates that Arnold spent much of his

9

literary life after 1860 attempting to free religion from false dogma. Much of this ground was previously covered by A. Dwight Culler's *Imaginative Reason* (1966), but Livingston occasionally contributes a fresh insight into Arnold's Victorian conception of Christianity. **(A,G)**

Machann, Clinton, and Forrest D. Burt, eds. *Matthew Arnold in His Time and Ours: Centenary Essays.* Charlottesville: University Press of Virginia, 1988. These fourteen essays by renowned Arnold scholars cover such subjects as Arnold's view of America, his poetics, his important distinctions between "culture" and "religion," his lectures on Celtic literature, and future directions for Arnold scholarship. The topics are so specialized as to be of value primarily to scholars and advanced students. **(A)**

Riede, David G. *Matthew Arnold and the Betrayal of Language.* (Virginia Victorian Series). Charlottesville: University Press of Virginia. 1987. Riede's theory is that Arnold struggled to find power and authority in language that could speak to an age which began to apply the methods of scientific inquiry to everyday thought. That is, the beliefs, faith and imagination that characterized the way people thought during the Romantic period were less valued than fact and logic. Arnold, like other Victorian writers, believed that a balance was essential as people experienced a radically changing world. Riede analyzes Arnold's principal works for their use of language to establish imagination as an important societal component. Recommended for students studying Arnold or the Victorian era. **(A)**

Scott, Nathan A. *The Poetics of Belief: Studies in Coleridge, Arnold, Pater, Santayana, Stevens, and Heidegger.* Chapel Hill: University of North Carolina Press, 1985. This collection of Scott's essays on writers and philosophers explores the power of the imagination for evoking religious awareness and transcendence. Examining each writer in turn—Coleridge, Arnold, Pater, Santayana, and Stevens—Scott finds a commonality of purposes and intentions among them that is best articulated by Heidegger. **(A)**

Ullmann, S. O. A., ed. *Matthew Arnold: The Yale Manuscript.* Ann Arbor: University of Michigan Press, 1989. Although long recognized as valuable by scholars, this odds-and-ends collection of Arnold papers—known as the Yale Manuscript—has been collecting dust in Yale's Beinecke Library. Ullmann has now resurrected these forty pages, arranged them chronologically, and published them as an aid to scholarly research. These pages include essays, several poems and fragments, as well as Arnold's random reflections on life and art. Arranged in this manner, the various elements have a surprising coherence. This material could be useful for tracing the development of Arnold's thinking through the critical period 1843-1857. An important contribution to Arnold studies. **(A)**

Other Sources

Allott, Miriam, ed. *Matthew Arnold 1988: A Centennial Review.* Highlands, NJ: Humanities, 1988.

Allott, Miriam, and Robert H. Sugar, eds. *Matthew Arnold.* New York: Oxford University Press, 1987.

Buckler, William E. *Matthew Arnold's Prose: Three Essays in Literary Enlargement.* New York: AMS Press, 1984.

Clubbe, John, and Jerome Meckier, eds. *Victorian Perspectives: Six Essays.* Newark: University of Delaware Press, 1989.

Schnieder, Mary W. *Poetry in the Age of Democracy: The Literary Criticism of Matthew Arnold.* Lawrence: University Press of Kansas, 1989.

W. H. AUDEN
1907-1973

Evaluation of Selected Biography and Criticism

Bold, Alan, ed. *W. H. Auden: The Far Interior*. Totowa, NJ: Barnes & Noble, 1985. While not breaking any new ground, this collection of eight essays on Auden's poetry provides a useful overview of current criticism. Contributors, including Charles Osborne and William Logan, address Auden's poetic techniques and use of images. (A,G)

Johnson, Wendell Stacy. *W. H. Auden*. New York: Continuum, 1990. Johnson provides a short and rather superficial look at the long life of an intricate man. Presenting neither challenges nor surprises, this study provides a chronology and summary useful for introductory studies. (G)

Norse, Harold. *Memoirs of a Bastard Angel*. New York: William Morrow, 1989. In this no-holds-barred autobiography, Norse describes his acquaintance and encounters with many of the major figures of twentieth-century "bohemian" literature—Auden, Tennessee Williams, William Burroughs, Anaïs Nin, James Baldwin and Ezra Pound. This is arresting reading for students of the period. (A,G)

Rowse, A. L. *The Poet Auden: A Personal Memoir*. London and New York: Weidenfeld & Nicolson, 1988. The outspoken Rowse offers his portrait of W. H. Auden in opinionated prose, which reveals as much about himself as about the poet. This is not a vacillating biography but tends to portray Auden's complex personality in stark blacks and whites. Rowse entertains and infuriates as he examines minute details in Auden's poetry and links deduced meanings to incidents in his life. Although many will feel that Rowse often gets in the way of his subject, his opinions are honestly held and have done much to provoke lively debate among literary scholars. (A)

Smith, Stan. *W. H. Auden*. Oxford: Basil Blackwell, 1985. This general survey of Auden's life and works is suited for beginning students but is also recommended to advanced scholars who are interested in a different and insightful perspective. Smith is unmatched in his ability to debunk critical judgments based on faulty assumptions about Auden or his intentions. Highlighted are Auden's struggles with the various ideologies that attracted him. Highly recommended. (A,G)

Other Sources

Bhattacharyya, Binay K. *The Oxford Group: Auden and Others*. New York: Advent, 1989.

JANE AUSTEN
1775-1817

Evaluation of Selected Biography and Criticism

Austen-Leigh, William. *Jane Austen, A Family Record.* Revised edition edited by Deidre Le Faye. Boston: G. K. Hall, 1989. This is a greatly enlarged revised edition of the 1913 biography written by Austen's nephew and grandnephew. Le Faye includes unpublished notes for Austen Le Faye's proposed second edition, archival and parish records, naval log books, and new letters. Although no more readable than Park Honan's 1988 biography based on the same sources, this biography does offer a more complete picture than any other. (A,G)

Burrows, J. F. *Computation into Criticism: A Study of Jane Austen's Novels as an Experiment in Method.* Oxford: Clarendon Press, 1987. Using a computer-based statistical analysis of thirty words Austen most commonly uses in each of the novels, Burrows attempts an explanation of how Austen manipulates language. Of little interest to Austen scholars, per se, this study could shed some light on developing critical methods. (A)

Cottom, Daniel. *The Civilized Imagination: A Study of Ann Radcliffe, Jane Austen, and Sir Walter Raleigh.* Cambridge: Cambridge University Press, 1985. Cottom explores the role of the educated and refined in defining social aesthetics by examining the writings of Radcliffe, Austen, and Raleigh—three writers, he contends, who represent the epitome of "taste." For these individuals, the perceptions of the uneducated were unimportant, and he demonstrates how the class values of the eighteenth century were inextricably connected with aesthetic values. (A)

Evans, Mary. *Jane Austen and the State.* London and New York: Tavistock Publications, 1987. Evans' aim is to show that "Jane Austen advances a radical critique of the morality of bourgeois capitalism and demonstrates a concern for the articulation of women's rights and views whilst bringing out the vulnerability of women in the economic marketplace." Although Evans' reading of the novels sheds no new light, the approach challenges sociological/feminist awareness. (A,G)

Grey, J. David, *et al.* eds. *The Jane Austen Companion: With a Dictionary of Jane Austen's Life and Works by H. Abigail Bok.* New York: Macmillan, 1986. Over forty literary critics, historians, and aficionados have contributed to this remarkable collection of essays, which survey Austen's life and works. The essays range freely over a variety of topics, including architectural motifs, children and servants in the novels, Victorian medicines, Austen's reading list, and her place in literary history. The dictionary lists places, characters, and events—real and invented—from Austen's world. This compilation is an important work of scholarship that is simultaneously entertaining. (A,G)

Grey, J. David, ed. *Jane Austen's Beginnings: The Juvenilia and "Lady Susan"*. Ann Arbor: UMI Research, 1989. Austen's early writings—tales and sketches, "History of England," and *Lady Susan*—have been dismissed as insignificant by many critics. The essays included here, however, argue for their importance for a variety of reasons: biographical insight, social and political commentary, historical context, or clues to structure and form. The extensive bibliography and notes provide guidance for students searching for research topics. (A)

Harris, Jocelyn. *Jane Austen's Art of Memory*. Cambridge: Cambridge University Press, 1989. Harris argues that Austen assimilated the texts of Richardson, Shakespeare, Chaucer, and Milton as she experimented with new techniques and characters. She makes involved comparisons between works: *Clarissa* and *Paradise Lost* to *Sense and Sensibility;* and various sections in Chaucer and Shakespeare to *Emma* and *Persuasion*. Useful for scholars interested in sources or the literary imagination. (A)

Honan, Park. *Jane Austen: Her Life*. New York: St. Martin's/Dunne, 1988. Honan's masterful biography of Austen makes extensive use of family documents, letters, and diaries. In concentrating on Austen's personal life, he is particularly revealing in his treatment of Austen's family life at Steventon, Bath, Chawton, and Winchester. Austen's literary output is examined closely only for the Chawton period, but scholars will note echoes of her fictional characters and plots in many details of her life. Honan expands the story of Austen's brief engagement in 1802, first revealed in the *Encyclopedia Britanica* in 1975, to a wealthy, but colorless, businessman, (A,G)

Johnson, Claudia L. *Jane Austen: Women, Politics, and the Novel*. Chicago: University of Chicago Press, 1988. The debate about Austen's political views continues, and Johnson steps into the controversy with this study. She believes that Austen was not apolitical, as many critics have contended, but that she was skeptical of conservative ideology and that in her own way—through the discourse of social values—she advocated reform. Johnson examines each of the novels to support her thesis. This study provides a useful perspective for students seeking a different approach to interpreting Austen's ideas about society. Recommended for all serious readers of Austen. (A,G)

Lane, Maggie. *Jane Austen's England*. New York: St. Martin's, 1987. Noted Austen aficionado Maggie Lane has produced a well-researched, popular guide to Jane Austen's England. Far from being a recluse (as rumor has it), Austen was widely travelled within her native country. Illustrated with numerous black and white photographs, this delightful narrative is recommended for all Austen lovers. (A,G)

Mooneyham, Laura G. *Romance, Language, and Education in Jane Austen's Novels*. New York: St. Martin's, 1988. From depictions in Austen's novels, Mooneyham examines the relationship between education and language and delineates their combined effect on the formation, reformation, and transformation of character. Austen's characters who speak poorly are generally deficient in character. Proper speech is one result of a correct moral education. Mooneyham concentrates on close readings of the texts, making a more persuasive case than others who have treated this subject. **(A,G)**

Morris, Ivor. *Mr. Collins Considered: Approaches to Jane Austen*. London and New York: Routledge & Kegan Paul, 1987. Morris explicates the character of Mr. Collins as Austen's perfect creation of folly, then compares him to her other male characters. He demonstrates that the fool is not much different from the other males, especially in a courtship ritual governed by wealth and rank. Although Austen's men have been analyzed by many critics, Morris is the first to use this most pompous bore as a yard-stick by which to measure standards of behavior. This study will delight any Austen enthusiast. **(A,G)**

Poovey, Mary. *The Proper Lady and the Woman Writer: Ideology as Style in the Works of Mary Wollstonecraft, Mary Shelley, and Jane Austen*. Chicago: University of Chicago Press, 1984. This was perhaps the first extended feminist study of eighteenth and nineteenth-century fiction to introduce a rigorously applied historical dimension to literary analysis. Poovey reveals the underlying ideological contradictions in the Victorian ideal of the "proper lady" through close readings of works by Wollstonecraft, Shelley, and Austen. **(A,G)**

Sale, Roger. *Closer to Home*. Cambridge: Harvard University Press, 1988. Sale, a critic at home in many literary periods, addresses the treatment of place in the works of five English authors, including Austen, Clare, Crabbe, and Wordsworth. The local landscape and society strongly influenced all five writers and became a principal theme and structural device for their art. Sale contends that these authors broke away from the established pictorial treatment of landscape to produce a psychological response to place and time. This, in turn, set the stage for the realism that would emerge in the writings of the Victorians, especially Hardy, Dickens, and Eliot. For serious students, Sale offers fresh and provocative ideas for interpreting each of these writers. **(A,G)**

Southam, B.C. *Jane Austen: The Critical Heritage; Volume 2, 1870-1940*. London and New York: Routledge & Kegan Paul/Methuen, 1987. In this monograph, Southam examines the "packaging" and marketing of Austen's reputation and works, beginning with Austen-Leigh's *A Memoir of Jane Austen* (1870). He describes how Austen's significance emerged only gradually as critics developed their own theories and standards. The contributions or obfuscation of such critics as William Dean Howells and D. W. Harding are dealt with in intriguing detail. **(A,G)**

Sulloway, Alison G. *Jane Austen and the Province of Womanhood.*
Philadelphia: University of Pennsylvania Press, 1989. This study of Austen's
gender politics contends that "pride and prejudice" are feminist code words for
the arrogance of the Victorian male. Sulloway argues that, unlike the overt
feminists of the time, Austen adopted a covert strategy of pressing for
women's rights and recognition. For her, *Pride and Prejudice* can be best
viewed as a satire on male-centered behaviors. Sulloway's readings of several
of Austen's novels broaden conventional interpretations and are likely to
attract widespread attention. (A,G)

Tanner, Tony. *Jane Austen.* Cambridge: Harvard University Press, 1986.
Tanner, a witty and provocative critic of contemporary fiction, provides a
close reading and interpretation of each of Austen's novels. Although his
views on Austen are fairly traditional, his insights into her work and his clear,
charming prose make this one of the most readable critical books on Austen's
novels. His focus is on the novelist as a member of her society, reflected by
the education and language of her characters. Tanner compares Austen's use
of the role of marriage in earlier and later novels, revealing attitudes that
range from marriage as a mode of reconciliation to marriage as imprisonment.
Austen, Tanner maintains, was not just a critic of manners but of ideology.
Recommended for general readers, students and scholars. (A,G)

Thompson, James. *Between Self and World: The Novels of Jane Austen.*
University Park and London: Pennsylvania State University Press, 1988. Based
on theories developed by critic George Lukács, Thompson attempts to show
how Austen's fiction argues against the priority of social obligation over the
character's inner experience that yearns for emotional seclusion. This involved,
scholarly study compels the academic reader to ask new questions about the
role of women, economics, and courtship in the eighteenth century. (A)

Weldon, Fay. *Letters to Alice: On First Reading Jane Austen.* New York:
Taplinger, 1985. The Alice of the title is a skeptical, first reader of Austen
who, herself, wants to become a novelist. Weldon, the accomplished writer,
explains to her young friend why Austen is such an important writer, especially in her mastery of craft. This is a fascinating, non-scholarly account useful
to both Austen students and aspiring writers. (G)

Wright, Andrew. *Fictional Discourse and Historical Space: Defoe and
Theroux, Austen and Forster, Conrad and Greene.* New York: St. Martin's,
1987. An intelligent approach to fiction and current academic discourse,
Wright's study examines the relationship between the reading of literature and
the study of literary history. By comparing three pairs of books, he attempts
to isolate distinct voices in diverse fiction across time and changing audiences.
Wright compares Defoe's *Robinson Crusoe* with Paul Theroux's *Mosquito
Coast* to reveal Theroux's use of aspects of the Crusoe character. He compares Jane Austen's *Emma* with Forster's *Howard's End* to connect the various voices of class and gender used by both authors. Finally, he examines
Graham Greene's *The Human Factor* in light of Conrad's *The Secret Agent* to

understand the authors' views on anarchy and social control. Wright contends that both closure and history give fiction moral meaning. (A)

Other Sources

Apperson, G. A. *Jane Austen Dictionary*. Brunswick, ME: Bern Porter, 1985.

Butler, Marilyn. *Jane Austen and the War of Ideas*. New York: Oxford University Press, 1988.

Chapman, W. *Jane Austen: Selected Letters, 1796-1817*. New York: Oxford University Press, 1985.

Dhatwalia, H. R. *Familial Relationships in Jane Austen's Novels*. New York: Advent, 1988.

Dussinger, John A. *In the Pride of the Moment: Encounters in Jane Austen's World*. Columbus: The Ohio State University Press, 1989.

Edwards, Anne-Marie. *In the Steps of Jane Austen*. New York: Countryside Books/State Mutual, 1987.

Gard, Roger. *Jane Austen: "Emma" and "Persuasion."* New York: Penguin, 1989.

Hardy, John P. *Jane Austen's Heroines: Intimacy in Human Relationships*. New York: Routledge Chapman and Hall, 1985.

Koppel, Gene. *The Religious Dimension of Jane Austen's Novels*. Ann Arbor: UMI Research, 1987.

Laski, Marghanita. *Jane Austen*. New York: Thames Hudson, 1986.

Modert, Jo. *Jane Austen's Manuscript Letters in Facsimile: Reproductions of Every Known Extant Letter, Fragment, and Autograph Copy*. Carbondale: Southern Illinois University Press, 1989.

Morgan, Susan. *Sisters in Time: Imagining Gender in Nineteenth-Century British Fiction*. New York: Oxford University Press, 1989.

Mukherjee, Meenakshi. *Jane Austen*. Savage, MD: Rowman, 1990.

Williams, Michael J. *Jane Austen: Six Novels and Their Methods*. New York: St. Martin's, 1986.

JAMES BALDWIN
1924-1987

Author's Recent Bibliography
The Price of the Ticket: Collected Nonfiction, 1948-1985, 1985; *Jimmy's Blues: Selected Poems*, 1986.

Evaluation of Selected Biography and Criticism
Harris, Trudier. *Black Women in the Fiction of James Baldwin*. Knoxville: University of Tennessee Press, 1985. Rather than drawing upon the current trend of extremism, Harris's examination of Baldwin's female characters goes out of its way to present a balanced view. From the claustrophobic fundamentalism of *Go Tell It on the Mountain*, Harris argues, Baldwin moves toward creating narrative situations that freed his feminine characters from the domination of men and of traditional religion. **(A,G)**

Porter, Horace A. *Stealing the Fire: The Art and Protest of James Baldwin*. Middletown, CT: Wesleyan University Press, 1989. In this sympathetic evaluation of Baldwin's contribution to modern literature, Porter focuses on the earlier novels and essays, placing them in the context of those he sees as the author's literary precursors—Richard Wright, Harriet Beecher Stowe, and Henry James. Recommended for the general reader interested in how Baldwin's works may fit into the larger literary picture. **(G)**

Weatherby, W. J. *James Baldwin: Artist on Fire*. New York: Donald I. Fine, 1989. Weatherby interweaves a collection of author interviews with observations drawn from published and unpublished sources. Although not an analytical biography, this chronological compilation presents a personal and intimate view of Baldwin, his passions, idealism, and accomplishments. **(G)**

Other Sources
Davis, Ursula B. *Paris Without Regret: James Baldwin, Chester Himes, Kenny Clarke, and Donald Byrd*. Iowa City: University of Iowa Press, 1986.

Rosset, Lisa. *James Baldwin*. New York: Chelsea House, 1989.

Standley, Fred L., and Louis H. Pratt, eds. *Conversations with James Baldwin*. Jackson: University Press of Mississippi, 1989.

Standley, Fred L., and Nancy V. Burt, eds. *Critical Essays on James Baldwin*. Boston: G. K. Hall, 1988.

JOHN BARTH
1930

Author's Recent Bibliography
The Tidewater Tales, 1987 (novel).

Evaluation of Selected Biography and Criticism
Dryden, Edgar A. *The Form of American Romance.* Baltimore: The Johns Hopkins University Press, 1988. In this study, Dryden undertakes an analysis of the structure and development of American Romanticism. He first examines the origins of the novel and its relationship to romance by discussing *Don Quixote* and Scott's *Waverley.* He views Scott's early novel as a "founding text" in the history of the English novel. Dryden then dissects the narrative structures of five American novels—Hawthorne's *The Marble Faun,* Melville's *Pierre,* James's *The Portrait of a Lady,* Faulkner's *Absalom, Absalom!,* and Barth's *LETTERS.* He sees these American novelists responding directly to narrative problems inherited from Scott. **(A)**

Gorak, Jan. *God the Artist: American Novelists in a Post-Realist Age.* Champaign: University of Illinois Press, 1987. Gorak's study attempts to trace the idea of the artist as a "godly" maker of worlds in the work of three twentieth-century novelists: West, Hawkes, and Barth. He argues that the ubiquity of this conception among artists has weakened its force and rendered it little more than an excuse for linguistic gamesmanship. Gorak argues that West's fiction shows the predicament of the artist in modern society: he is "trapped in illusion-making machinery he can no longer control." He develops the idea of the modern artist's preoccupation with world-making in close readings of Hawkes' *Travesty* and Barth's *The Sot-Weed Factor* and *LETTERS.* A valuable critical study for students of the modern novel. **(A,G)**

Safer, Elaine B. *The Contemporary American Comic Epic: The Novels of Barth, Pynchon, Gaddis, and Kesey.* Detroit: Wayne State University Press, 1988. Safer is one of several recent critics who have traced a distinctly American comic tradition, running from Brockden Brown, to Whitman and Melville, through Faulkner, and into the absurd novelists of the 1970s and 1980s. This tradition is characterized by use of black humor, the absurd, stasis, ironic allusiveness, and the grotesque. Safer contends that these writers "combine laughter with pain, farce and horror, causing the reader to recognize the ideal and confront its absence." Safer's is a readable and convincing comparative study. **(A,G)**

Walkiewicz, E. P. *John Barth.* Boston: Twayne, 1986. Books in the Twayne series are designed to provide thorough introductions to the life and works of selected authors. This offering on Barth is comprehensive, carefully documented, and strong in its critical commentaries. However, not enough background is included to allow a new reader to place Barth in proper literary context. Included are a brief chronology and biography. The primary and secondary bibliographies are particularly useful. (A,G)

Young, Thomas Daniel, ed. *Modern American Fiction: Form and Function.* Baton Rouge: Louisiana State University, 1989. Young has collected thirteen critical essays that he believes represent the best current thinking on the modes of expression of American novelists. The essays examine novels by such authors as Crane (*The Red Badge of Courage*), Warren (*All the King's Men*), Barth (*The Floating Opera*), and James (*The Wings of the Dove*). The form of each novel is examined and related to the particular author's "vision of life." Many of these essayists remark that American authors are much more likely to allow the action to unfold without the commentary of an omnipresent narrator than are most British and European authors. This collection provides a thoughtful overview for students of nineteenth- and twentieth-century American literature. (A)

Ziegler, Heide. *John Barth.* London: Metheun, 1987. This short overview enumerates the basic themes of Barth's fiction and concludes that he tends to write pairs of complementary novels, both of which are necessary to complete the theme. This study is too short to develop a complex thesis, but it is helpful as a beginning reference to major ideas in the work. (A,G)

Other Sources
Stonehill, Brian. *The Self-Conscious Novel: Artifice in Fiction from Joyce to Pynchon.* Philadelphia: University of Pennsylvania Press, 1988.

SAMUEL BECKETT
1906-1989

Author's Recent Bibliography

Disjecta, 1984 (miscellaneous writings and drama fragment); *Collected Shorter Plays*, 1984; *Three Plays*, 1984; *Collected Poems, 1930-1978*, 1984; *Happy Days*, 1985 (play); *The Complete Dramatic Works*, 1986; *As the Story Was Told: Uncollected and Late Prose*, 1990.

Evaluation of Selected Biography and Criticism

Ben-Zvi, Linda. *Samuel Beckett*. Boston: Twayne, 1986. Ben-Zvi encompasses Beckett's entire canon in all its varied genres and media to provide an excellent introduction for new readers. Extremely well-researched and up-to-date, this study provides insight into the development of Beckett's style and techniques and describes the thematic unity of individual works. The introduction offers students guidance in the study of Beckett. **(A,G)**

Brater, Enoch. *Beyond Minimalism: Beckett's Late Style in the Theater*. London: Oxford University Press, 1987. Brater analyzes eight plays written by Beckett between 1973-1984, comparing their use of language, movement, sound, costume, stage design, and lighting. He argues that while these plays take their roots from *Waiting for Godot* (1952) and *Endgame* (1957), they move beyond minimalism to create a new subgenre of drama. Brater's scholarship is sound and his notes are excellent. **(A)**

Brienza, Susan D. *Samuel Beckett's New Worlds: Style in Metafiction*. Norman: University of Oklahoma Press, 1987. Beckett's novel, *The Unnamable* (1953) was his last prose work to use complete sentences and standard vocabulary. Brienza undertakes the arduous task of examining and explaining Beckett's fiction since then—works that abandon familiar sentence construction for phrases, skewed grammar, and a new vocabulary. She treats each work separately, analyzing the ground rules for vocabulary and syntax, which will help readers better understand Beckett's intentions and directions. Because Beckett is problematic enough in the original French, to translate his work requires an interpretation of it. Brienza compares the French versions to their English translations in order to illuminate the innovative, if difficult techniques that Beckett pioneered. Recommended for serious students. **(A)**

Burkman, Katherine H., ed. *Myth and Ritual in the Plays of Samuel Beckett*. Rutherford, NJ: Fairleigh Dickinson University Press, 1987. These ten essays are divided into three groupings that address the mythical motif of "journeying," the ritual of storytelling, and the demythification of Beckett's drama. Of particular note is Martha Fehsenfeld's essay on the rhythmic relationship of word and movement. The various critical approaches serve as a useful introduction to Beckett criticism. (A,G)

Cohn, Ruby, ed. *Beckett: "Waiting for Godot," A Selection of Critical Essays.* London: Macmillan, 1987. This anthology of forty-five critical essays on Beckett's *Waiting for Godot* is divided into three sections—theatre critics, armchair critics, and critics at large. A full gamut of critical responses is cataloged here; many are helpful, while others are as obscure as Beckett's pronouncements on his own work. (A)

Connor, Stephen. *Samuel Beckett: Repetition, Theory, and Text.* Oxford: Basil Blackwell, 1988. Connor contends that Beckett's revisions and self-translations were "repetitions," in that they copied the original works, but that they were also "enhancements" of the original texts. Connor examines Beckett's reworkings in detail and discusses recent Beckett criticism. As such, this study provides a useful overview of critical perspectives on Beckett. (A)

Doll, Mary A. *Beckett and Myth: An Archetypal Approach.* Syracuse, NY: Syracuse University Press, 1988. Delving into an area that has had too little attention, Doll traces recurring myths and archetypes through Beckett's "resoundingly mythic" works. Drawing on the theories of Jung, Eliade, and Hillman, Doll discusses three classical myths—Cronus, Narcissus and Echo, and Demeter and Persephone—and shows how Beckett develops them in archetypal figures—the wise old man, the crone, the child. (A,G)

Ellmann, Richard. *Four Dubliners: Wilde, Yeats, Joyce, and Beckett.* New York: Braziller, 1987. With his usual elegance and clarity, Ellmann discusses the lives and works of four Irish writers who shaped the character of twentieth-century literature. Although these authors have significant differences, Ellmann concentrates on their commonalities: the desire to transform language and literature, the need to establish autonomy, a preoccupation with inner conflicts, and an insistence on remaining Irish in spite of living as expatriates. This is a splendid introduction for new readers to the authors' lives and works. Highly recommended. (A,G)

Gontarski, S. E. *On Beckett: Essays and Criticism.* New York: Grove Press, 1986. This collection of essays by renowned critics presents a portrait of Beckett, not as a prophet of doom, but as a lively, multi-egoed personality who is variously an acerbic social critic, light-hearted ham, philosopher, or clown. These essayists, working independently, form a consensus that the aesthetic cynic of *Endgame* represents only one side of a complex personality. This book provides a good balance to criticism that stresses Beckett's philosophical pessimism. (A)

Hale, Jane Alison. *The Broken Window: Beckett's Dramatic Perspective.* West Lafayette, IN: Purdue University Press, 1987. Hale examines the conceptual content of six of Beckett's most notable dramatic works— *Endgame, Cascando, Film, Eh Joe, A Piece of Monologue,* and *Rockaby.* In her analysis,

Beckett's experimentation with new dramatic forms can be more clearly understood by comparison with modern theories of perspective. Hale applies theories of linear perspective, derived from art and epistemology, to Beckett's presentation of time and space. She suggests that Beckett reflects similar developments in his own redefinition of dramatic perspective. This specialized study tries to get at the philosophical underpinnings of Beckett's radical departure from traditional dramatic forms. **(A)**

Kennedy, Andrew K. *Samuel Beckett.* Cambridge: Cambridge University Press, 1989. Kennedy's clear style and informed opinions justify this new study of Beckett's plays and novels. He offers readings of *Waiting for Godot, Endgame, Krapp's Last Tape, Happy Days, Play, Molloy, Malone Dies,* and *The Unnamable.* He describes the elements that make each text unique and original, while setting each in the context of Beckett's work as a whole. According to Kennedy, Beckett adopted "an economy of form that corresponds to an urgency of vision." An ideal guide for the undergraduate or general reader, this study should also interest the specialist with its concise articulation of many of the current issues of Beckett criticism. **(A,G)**

McMillan, Dougald, and Martha Fehsenfeld. *Beckett in the Theatre: The Author As Practical Playwright and Director: From "Waiting for Godot" to "Krapp's Last Tape."* New York: Riverrun Press, 1988. This is the first volume of a multi-volume study focusing on Beckett's own concept of his work. Collecting prompt books, notebooks, production history, letters, photographs, interviews and stage sketches, the authors demonstrate how Beckett altered his concepts from page to stage. This is a very helpful study for serious students researching Beckett's themes and craft. **(A)**

O'Brien, Eoin. *The Beckett Country: Samuel Beckett's Ireland.* London: Faber and Faber, 1986. This "coffee table" book combines photographs, illustrations, quotations, accompanying text, notes, and references to create a collage of Beckett's roots. Unlike other books of this type, which often seem haphazardly thrown together, O'Brien's effort exhibits a basic integrity that attests to his knowledge of Beckett and his world. An informative and entertaining introduction to the life, works, and milieu of the universal Beckett. **(A,G)**

Other Sources
Acheson, James, and Kateryna Arthur. *Beckett's Later Fiction and Drama: Texts for Company.* New York: St. Martin's, 1987.

Barale, Michele A., and Rubin Rabinowitz, eds. *A KWIC Concordance to Samuel Beckett's "Molloy Malone Dies," and "The Unnamable."* New York: Garland, 1988.

Barge, Laura. *God, the Quest, the Hero: Thematic Structures in Beckett's Fiction.* Chapel Hill: The University of North Carolina Press, 1988.

24   *Samuel Beckett*

Brater, Enoch, ed. *Beckett at Eighty: Beckett in Context.* New York: Oxford University Press, 1986.

Calder, John, ed. *As No Other Dare Fail: Festschrifft for Samuel Beckett's 80th Birthday.* New York: Riverrun, 1986.

Culotta-Andonian, Cathleen. *Samuel Beckett: A Reference Guide.* Boston: G. K. Hall, 1988.

Davis, Robin J., and Lance S. Butler, eds. *Make Sense Who May: Essays on Samuel Beckett's Later Works.* Totowa, NJ: Barnes & Noble, 1988.

Fletcher, John, *et al. A Student's Guide to the Plays of Samuel Beckett.* London: Faber and Faber, 1985.

Foster, Paul. *The Zen of Samuel Beckett: A Study of Dilemma in His Novels.* Boston: Wisdom, 1988.

Friedman, Alan W., *et al.,* eds. *Beckett Translating: Translating Beckett.* University Park: The Pennsylvania State University Press, 1987.

Gidal, Peter. *Understanding Beckett: A Study of Monologue and Gesture in the Works of Samuel Beckett.* New York: St. Martin's, 1986.

Graver, Lawrence. *Samuel Beckett: Waiting for Godot.* New York: Cambridge University Press, 1989.

Hart, Clive, and C. George Sandulescu. *Language and Structure in Beckett's Plays.* Chester Springs, PA: Dufour, 1987.

Henning, Sylvie D. *Beckett's Critical Complicity: Carnival, Contestation and Tradition.* Lexington: University Press of Kentucky, 1988.

Kalb, Jonathan. *Beckett in Performance.* New York: Cambridge University Press, 1989.

Knowlson, James, ed. *"Happy Days": Samuel Beckett's Production Notebook.* New York: Grove, 1986.

McCarthy, Patrick A. *Critical Essays on Samuel Beckett.* Boston: G. K. Hall, 1986.

Mayberry, Bob. *Theatre of Discord: Dissonance in Beckett, Albee, and Pinter.* Madison, NJ: Fairleigh Dickinson University Press, 1989.

Megged, Matti. *Dialogue in the Void: Beckett and Giacometti.* Sacramento, CA: Lumen, 1985.

Merrell, Floyd. *Deconstruction Reframed.* Lafayette, IN: Purdue University Press, 1985.

Morrison, Kristin. *Canters and Chronicles: The Use of Narrative in the Plays of Samuel Beckett and Harold Pinter.* Chicago: University of Chicago Press, 1986.

Pountney, Rosemary. *Theatre of Shadows: Samuel Beckett's Drama, 1956-76.* Totowa, NJ: Barnes & Noble, 1988.

Sheringham, Michael. *Beckett: "Molloy."* Dover, NH: Longwood, 1985.

Topsfield, Valerie. *The Humour of Samuel Beckett.* New York: St. Martin's, 1988.

Zurbrugg, Nicholas. *Beckett and Proust.* Totowa, NJ: Barnes & Noble, 1988.

APHRA BEHN
1640?-1689

Evaluation of Selected Biography and Criticism

Burns, Edward. *Restoration Comedy: Crises of Desire and Identity*. New York: St. Martin's, 1987. This ambitious study of Restoration comedy attempts to transcend the typical emphasis on Wycherley, Etherege, and Congreve in order to consider the importance of works by Aphra Behn, Susanna Centlivre, Colley Cibber, John Crowne, Thomas Southerne, and Thomas Shadwell. In Burns' view these comedies have in common plots based on "pastoral intrigues" set in London's parks and pleasure grounds. Characters are typically drawn from the English "leisure class." (A,G)

Mendelson, Sara Heller. *The Mental World of Stuart Women*. Amherst: University of Massachusetts Press, 1987. In this study of women's social history, Mendelson examines the context of the lives of three notable women of the Stuart period—Aphra Behn, Margaret Cavendish (Duchess of Newcastle), and Mary Rich (Countess of Warwick). She analyzes their writings to reveal an underlying conflict between self-identity and social roles. In this era, women struggled to publish against a patriarchal code that demanded them to be silent, modest, obedient, and chaste. (A,G)

SAUL BELLOW
1915

Author's Recent Bibliography
   More Die of Heartbreak, 1987 (novel); *A Theft*, 1989 (novella); *The Bellarosa Connection*, 1989 (novel).

Evaluation of Selected Biography and Criticism
   Kiernan, Robert F. *Saul Bellow*. New York: Crossroad/Continuum/Ungar, 1989. Kiernan undertakes a comprehensive critical analysis of Bellow's fiction that relates plot and characters to events in the author's life. Particularly important is coverage of little-studied works, such as *Him with His Foot in His Mouth* and *More Die of Heartbreak*. Kiernan contends that Bellow's style is more in line with nineteenth-century realism than with a modern tradition. (A)

   Shinn, Thelma J. *Radiant Daughters: Fictional American Women*. Westport, CT: Greenwood, 1986. In this provocative study, Shinn analyzes fictional women characters in a variety of novels from the 1940s through the 1960s. Maintaining that fictional females often reflect "common human social concerns," Shinn extrapolates from her analysis to characterize a changing social climate. The novels of Bellow, Hortense Calisher, Shirley Jackson, John Updike, and Carson McCullers present a series of female characters slowly moving from fragmented identities toward greater maturity. For Shinn, both men and women are searching for community in a dehumanized society.(A,G)

   Wilson, Jonathan. *On Bellow's Planet: Readings from the Dark Side*. Rutherford, NJ: Fairleigh Dickinson University Press, 1985. In this provocative study of Bellow's works, Wilson tries to explain why the once intellectually dazzling author seems to have lost the edge that made his early novels so impressive. He describes Bellow's most recent novels as "insufficiently reprocessed autobiography." Wilson diagnoses Bellow as a preserver of dilemmas; his heroes "dangle" but don't "do." This results in characters who become increasingly detached from their passions. (A,G)

Other Sources
   Goldman, L. H., and Gloria L. Cronin, eds. *Saul Bellow in the 1980s: Critical Essays*. East Lansing: Michigan State University Press, 1989.

   Melbourne, Lucy L. *Double Heart: Explicit and Implicit Texts in Bellow, Camus, and Kafka*. New York: Peter Lang, 1986.

   Wilson, Jonathan. *"Herzog": The Limits of Ideas*. Boston: Twayne, 1990.

ARNOLD BENNETT
1867-1931

Evaluation of Selected Biography and Criticism

Alden, Patricia. *Social Mobility in the English Bildungsroman: Gissing, Hardy, Bennett, and Lawrence.* Ann Arbor: UMI Research, 1986. The expression of a sense of upward social mobility in the late-nineteenth and early twentieth-century bildungsroman differed significantly from previous conceptions in the same genre. Many writers of the time believed that the upward mobility of the individual was a progressive phenomenon. Gissing, Hardy, Bennett, and Lawrence, on the other hand, viewed the process as a regressive disintegration of individual character. As portrayed in their works, the struggle to break out of one's social class leads only to frustration, alienation, and loss of identity. (A,G)

Anderson, Linda R. *Bennett, Wells, and Conrad: Narrative in Transition.* New York: St. Martin's, 1988. Anderson maintains that between 1890 and 1910 ideas about the nature of fiction were undergoing a major change, which led Bennett, Wells, and Conrad to redefine the relationship of the novel to reality. One result of this change was the incorporation of many of the unsavory aspects of life into the novel; another was a growing moral concern over the effects of confronting the darker side of life. Anderson develops this theme through her discussions of the major novels of these writers. This is a valuable study to those interested in the transition from the Victorian to the modern novel. (A,G)

Other Sources

Hepburn, James, ed. *Letters of Arnold Bennett, Vol. IV: Family Letters.* New York: Oxford University Press, 1986.

Lake, Marilyn. *Limits of Hope: Soldier Settlement in Victoria, 1915-1938.* New York: Oxford University Press, 1987.

THE *BEOWULF*-POET
c. 1000

Evaluation of Selected Biography and Criticism

Bloom, Harold, ed. *Beowulf*. New York: Chelsea House, 1987. This is a collection of six essays published since 1983 on the question of Christianity in *Beowulf*. Fred C. Robinson argues that the poet balances Dark Age heroism and Christian regret, and imposes his Christian vision on pagan heroic life. The Christian poet confronts the Germanic past, admires its heroism, and regrets its paganism. J. R. R. Tolkien's traditional reading argues that Hrothgar is a Christian surrounded by pagan companions. T. A. Shippey addresses the "world of the poem," including language, emotions, money, worth and prestige, weapons, symbols, and illusion and reality. Roberta Frank traces the perspective and sense of history, and the poet's intuition for cultural diversity and man's role on earth. Raymond P. Tripp, Jr., explains critical theories about the *Beowulf*-poet's uses of digression. Although there is little unity among these essays, students seeking good criticism about these specific topics will find this collection useful. (A,G)

Dahlberg, Charles. *The Literature of Unlikeness*. Hanover, NH: University Press of New England, 1988. The title of this book derives from a phrase, "Land of Unlikeness," found in St. Augustine's *Confessions*. This study examines the appearance of the land of unlikeness in works of literature, including *Beowulf*. The poet, Dahlberg contends, evokes the motifs of unlikeness to mediate between his pagan material and his Christian audience. Dahlberg develops a lengthy discussion on the nature of kingship as portrayed in the epic. (A)

Fajardo-Acosta, Fidel. *The Condemnation of Heroism in the Tragedy of Beowulf: A Study in the Characterization of the Epic*. Lewiston, Ontario: Edwin Mellen, 1989. Fajardo-Acosta argues that it was the intention of the *Beowulf* poet to speak against the heroic world, not to glorify his heroic heritage, spiritual heirloom, and birthright of his nation, as other critics have argued. This study attempts to illustrate the tragic process by which Beowulf brings about his own destruction and that of his people. Through a comparative analysis of classical and medieval narratives, Fajardo-Acosta argues that the poet's anti-heroic vision belongs to an ancient Indo-European tradition in which the hero and the monsters he battles are essentially indistinguishable and equally condemnable from a moral point of view. *Beowulf*, he concludes, is a lament for the loss of the human being at the hands of the beast. (A,G)

Greenfield, Stanley B. *Hero and Exile: The Art of Old English Poetry*. London: Hambledon Press, 1989. This is a collection of twenty-one essays by noted Old English scholar Greenfield. Eight of these essays directly address *Beowulf* as epic tragedy and poetic art. Of particular note is the discussion entitled "A Touch of the Monstrous in the Hero or Beowulf Re-Marvellized," which seeks to counter recent critics who have tried to reduce Beowulf to more human proportions by stripping away his super-human attributes. (A)

Hoover, David L. *A New Theory of Old English Meter*. New York: Peter Lang, 1985. Hoover argues that alliteration rather than stress is the primary metrical feature of Old English poetry. As a result, Hoover rejects most critical theories that Old English meter is based on rhythm. In the first chapter, he traces the criticism and theories of metrics; thereafter he examines patterns of stress, alliteration, and anacrusis, develops his argument, and explains its application to the poetry, especially to *Beowulf*. (A)

Irving, Edward B., Jr. *Rereading "Beowulf"*. Philadelphia: University of Pennsylvania Press, 1989. In this study, Irving revises his 1969 theory (published as *A Reading of "Beowulf"*). He argues that if *Beowulf* is read like a novel or epic poem, some sections, events, and characters are consistent and provides structured unity, while other elements seem out of place or inappropriate. Irving believes that he and other critics have been applying theories of *either* written or oral poetry, and that a combination of critical theories will crack the mystery of a seemingly flawed poem. The first chapter discusses recent critical approaches, and outlines the poem's "oral" characteristics. The second chapter focuses on oral modes of characterization and the problems they have caused critics. Chapter 3 explains the accepted methods of narrative construction, and the final chapter examines the use of symbol as a unifying factor. Although Irving's study breaks no new ground, its clear prose and sound critical approach provide an excellent overview of the nature of *Beowulf* criticism and a good close reading of the poem. (A,G)

Parker, Mary A. *Beowulf and Christianity*. New York: Peter Lang, 1987. For 150 years scholars have argued about the presence or absence of Christianity in *Beowulf*. Is the poem a secular heroic epic with a Christian veneer or is Christianity an integral part of the work, perhaps even to the extent that the poem is a Christian allegory? The question of Christianity arises because of the poem's specific references to three biblical stories—the Creation, the Flood, and Cain and Abel. However, there are no references to Christ, the Saints, the Trinity, or Salvation. If it is a Christian work, there is no evidence that the poet knew the New Testament. Parker argues that the question of Christianity cannot be answered because too little is known about pre-Christian Anglo-Saxon religion to compare the poem to it. Until documentary and archeological evidence provides a clearer picture of Anglo-Saxon social, political, and religious history, or until scholars can determine who the *Beowulf*-poet was, the overlap between Christian and secular elements will remain conjecture. This doctoral dissertation offers a cautious overview of the problem without attempting answers. (A)

Renoir, Alain. *A Key to Old Poems: The Oral-Formulaic Approach to the Interpretation of West-Germanic Verse*. University Park: Pennsylvania State University Press, 1988. Renoir examines the critical history that argues whether *Beowulf*, the *Hildebrandslied*, and other early Anglo-Germanic poems were originally written or oral creations. Having traced the history and methods of oral-formulaic criticism, Renoir demonstrates how it is applied to specific themes and text. Although he disclaims any originality of ideas, he does draw an interesting, if obvious, conclusion: that the poems "exhibit all kinds of oral-formulaic features [that] could actually have been composed in writing within the context of a society in which preliterate and literate cultures could still interact with each other." Advanced students will find this overview useful for understanding the evolution of *Beowulf* criticism. **(A)**

Robinson, Fred C. *"Beowulf" and the Appositive Style.* Knoxville: University of Tennessee Press, 1985. In order to demonstrate the relationship between theme and style, Robinson examines the "appositive" style, or the use of verse variation in order to accentuate the meaning of words. He believes that the apposition of words provides the simultaneous Christian and pre-Christian themes—the only style by which the poet could communicate his Christian vision of pagan heroic life. The first chapter describes the poet's appositive strategies; the second chapter treats his vocabulary as a way to accommodate his Christian and pre-Christian perspectives. The final chapter argues that the poet used the appositive style not only to convey theme but also to implement his narrative purposes. **(A)**

Russom, Geoffrey. *Old English Meter and Linguistic Theory.* New York: Cambridge University Press, 1987. In order to establish a theory of metrical systems operating in a poem like *Beowulf*, the theorist must identify consistent elements that form a pattern, then identify legitimate deviations from the pattern, and finally show how the deviations are intentional and not simply a result of bad or naive verse. Russom argues that advances in the fields of paleography, textual criticism, philology, and linguistics now make it possible to provide a coherent metrical system for Old English poetry that defines the norm and explains the limits of deviation. Recommended for specialists. **(A)**

Other Sources
Magnuson, Magnus, *et al. Beowulf: An Adaptation by Julian Glover of the Verse Translations of Michael Alexander and Edwin Morgan.* New York: Hippocrene, 1989.

Renoir, Alain, and Ann Hernandez, eds. *Approaches to Beowulfian Scansion.* Lanham, MD: University Press of America, 1985.

Wolff, Hope N. *A Study in the Narrative Structure of Three Epic Poems: "Gilgamesh," "Odyssey," and "Beowulf."* New York: Garland, 1987.

JOHN BERRYMAN
1914-1972

Autobiographical Sources

Kelly, Richard, ed. *We Dream of Honour: John Berryman's Letters to His Mother.* New York: Norton, 1988. Twenty-two of Berryman's letters to his mother, culled from over seven hundred, and nineteen of her letters to him make up this collection. The letters, which span the years from 1928 to 1971, were chosen on the basis of their biographical and literary interest. Berryman's close relationship with his often-difficult mother is revealed through their strikingly frank dialogue. This work also includes twelve of Berryman's previously unpublished poems. Kelly's notes and annotations are extremely useful. (A)

Evaluation of Selected Biography and Criticism

Bawer, Bruce. *The Middle Generation: The Lives and Poetry of Delmore Schwartz, Randall Jarrell, John Berryman, and Robert Lowell.* Hamden, CT: Shoe String Press, Archon Books, 1986. This critical study brings some needed structure to the study of these four poets whose richly textured verse often confuses readers. Bawer examines the influence of T. S. Eliot on the early work of all four poets and shows how each emerged from that influence in the later poetry. Critics may quibble with the interpretations of particular poems, but the overall value of this work is unchallenged, making it essential for the study of these poets at any level. (A,G)

Halliday, Ernest Milton. *John Berryman and the Thirties, A Memoir.* Amherst: University of Massachusetts Press, 1988. Written by Berryman's college friend, this memoir provides an intimate look at a troubled genius. Halliday quotes generously from over fifty of Berryman's letters to him to illustrate the foibles of their youth. An overriding concern of their relationship in its hey-day seems to have been the pursuit of nubile members of the opposite sex. In later life, Halliday became severely disillusioned with his friend and bemoaned his decline into depression and self-betrayal. (A,G)

Mariani, Paul. *Dream Song: The Life of John Berryman.* New York: Morrow, 1990. Mariani's biography of Berryman reveals an intimate understanding of this outrageous and charismatic poet, detailing his obsessions with poetry, women, and alcohol, and the forces behind his tragic suicide at age fifty-eight. Although primarily concerned with Berryman's life, the biographer lays a firm foundation for a deeper reading of the poems. (A,G)

Matterson, Stephen. *Berryman and Lowell: The Art of Losing.* Totowa, NJ: Barnes & Noble, 1988. This short study attempts to trace the "theme of

32

disintegration" in the lives and works of both poets. Matterson raises some interesting parallels and provides a useful reading of some of their poems, but is too brief a treatment to be satisfying. It best serves as an introduction to either poet or as a starting point for comparative research. (A,G)

Thomas, Harry, ed. *Berryman's Understanding: Reflections on the Poetry of John Berryman.* Boston: Northeastern University Press, 1988. This collection includes two interviews with the poet that are among the best he ever gave, as well as memoirs by friends who knew him well: Lowell, Meredith, and Bellow. His first wife, Eileen Simpson, provides insight into Berryman's erratic behavior and dark personality. These memoirs, combined with the essays that cover the various stages of Berryman's poetic development, establish a frame of reference for the remaining essays on Berryman's major works, particularly *The Dream Songs.* A bibliography is included in this readable, useful overview of Berryman and his work. (A, G)

Other Sources
Hyde, Lewis. *Alcohol and Poetry: John Berryman and the Booze Talking.* Dallas: Dallas Institute, 1987.

Mancini, Joseph, Jr. *The Berryman Gestalt: Therapeutic Strategies in the Poetry of John Berryman.* New York: Garland, 1987.

AMBROSE BIERCE
1842-1914?

Evaluation of Selected Biography and Criticism
Saunders, Richard. *Ambrose Bierce: The Making of a Misanthrope*. San Francisco: San Francisco Chronicle, 1985. Saunder's factual biography traces the life and adventures of Bierce, the vituperative newspaper columnist and fiction writer, through the boomtown years of early San Francisco. Saunders' use of quotations from the newspaper columns helps bring Bierce alive for the reader. Bierce, who was strongly opinionated, bitter, and chauvinistic, disappeared without a trace in Mexico in 1914. (A,G)

Other Sources
Berkove, Lawrence, ed. *Skepticism and Dissent: Selected Journalism, 1898-1901*. Ann Arbor: UMI Research, 1986.

ELIZABETH BISHOP
1911-1979

Evaluation of Selected Biography and Criticism

Bloom, Harold, ed. *Elizabeth Bishop.* New York: Chelsea House, 1985. Bloom has collected "the best literary criticism devoted to Elizabeth Bishop," including reviews, critical essays, and readings of individual poems. Although the list of contributors includes such luminaries as John Ashbery, Richard Howard, John Hollander, and Sandra McPherson, these are generally laudatory blurbs that demonstrate how much serious work remains to be done on Bishop. (G)

Kalstone, David. *Becoming A Poet: Elizabeth Bishop with Marianne Moore and Robert Lowell.* New York: Farrar, Straus & Giroux, 1989. Kalstone examines the deep friendship that developed between Bishop and her mentor Moore. Upon Moore's death, Bishop found some of the same support in a relationship with Lowell, who maintained contact with her despite her self-destructive binges and his mental instability. (A)

McCorkle, James. *The Still Performance: Writing, Self, and Interconnection in Five Postmodern American Poets.* Charlottesville: University Press of Virginia, 1989. McCorkle examines the poetics of Elizabeth Bishop, John Ashbery, Adrienne Rich, W. S. Merwin, and Charles Wright to show how each uses American speech in the search for self and the role of art. Each of these poets believes that meaning can be achieved through art. This fairly complex book will not only interest serious students of Bishop but anyone studying the development of contemporary poetry. (A)

Parker, Robert Dale. *The Unbeliever: The Poetry of Elizabeth Bishop.* Champaign: University of Illinois Press, 1988. Parker divides Bishop's career into three stages in which different forms of anxiety influenced the poetry. Parker attempts to show the terror within the poems in each stage, and in close readings, brings to light some of Bishop's self-consciousness about gender that lies beneath the poems' deceptively simple surface. Parker's treatment explicates the poems in light of "the sexual identity [that] is an almost secret subject of a great many Bishop poems." (A,G)

Schwartz, Lloyd. *That Sense of Constant Readjustment.* New York: Garland, 1987. This 1975 doctoral dissertation examines Bishop's first book, *North & South,* in detail to show that the poems form a delicate interaction, so intricate that no poem can be excluded from a discussion, and that they should be read in sequence. Schwartz believes that tone and irony comprise essential elements and greatly influence Bishop's imagery. He argues that irony is developed through the juxtaposition of subjects, images, levels of diction, line length, and rhythmic patterns. (G)

Travisano, Thomas. *Elizabeth Bishop: Her Artistic Development.* Charlottesville: University Press of Virginia, 1988. Travisano has produced one of the
best critical studies of Bishop to date. He unites a thorough, powerful reading
of her major poems with a discussion of the most important events in her life.
Travisano sees Bishop's earlier poems as solitary and confessional and believes the later, more personal poems reflect significant social and historical
concerns. This is an excellent source for all readers coming to Bishop's
poems for the first time as well as for serious researchers. **(A,G)**

Other Sources
  Greenhalgh, Anne M. *A Concordance to Elizabeth Bishop's Poetry.* New
York: Garland, 1984.

WILLIAM BLAKE
1757-1827

Evaluation of Selected Biography and Criticism

Baine, Rodney M. *The Scattered Portions: William Blake's Biological Symbolism*. Athens, GA: Agee Publishers, 1986. This study examines in detail Blake's possible sources for the animal and vegetable representations used in his illustrations. Baine argues that Blake's images are not sexually perverted, as some critics have suggested, but that these biological images were employed in such a way that they would be instantly recognized and interpreted by readers of his day. The book is organized by types of plants and animals, and includes relevant quotations. Scholars may find this text useful as a concordance to the images in Blake's works. **(A)**

Bate, Jonathan. *Shakespeare and the English Romantic Imagination*. Oxford: Oxford University Press, 1986. In this well-written study, Bate examines the influence of Shakespeare on Byron, Coleridge, Wordsworth, Keats, and Blake. He demonstrates how each poet's critical theory developed either out of or as a reaction to Shakespeare's poetic identity. This is a large field to cover, and Bate's study is a creditable overview that should be useful for anyone studying the English romantics. **(A,G)**

Ferber, Michael. *The Social Vision of William Blake*. Princeton: Princeton University Press, 1985. Ferber attempts to locate Blake in a socially radical tradition that stretches from the seventeenth century through Marxism to the present. He is especially concerned with Blake's relationship to seventeenth-century radicals, his vision of women, and his belief in the importance of brotherhood. Ferber combines cultural history with literary criticism to produce an excellent study for serious readers. **(A)**

Gardner, Stanley. *Blake's Innocence and Experience Retraced*. New York: St. Martin's, 1986. Gardner's subject is the complex interrelationship between Blake's etchings and his poems. He divides his study between Blake's concepts of "innocence" and "experience" and provokes the reader into confronting Blake's vision of the two contrary states. He examines the themes and central concepts of this dichotomy explored in *Songs of Innocence and Experience* and reveals how Blake expressed his vision in both words and images. One of the best of recent Blake books, this study requires some familiarity with the works. **(A)**

Hilton, Nelson, and Thomas A. Volger, eds. *Unnam'd Forms: Blake and Textuality*. Berkeley and London: University of California Press, 1986. The contributors apply Derrida's concept of "writing" to *Urizen, The Marriage of Heaven and Hell, Visions of the Daughters of Albion, The Four Zoas*, and *Milton*. For scholars only. **(A)**

Larrissy, Edward. *William Blake*. London: Blackwell, 1985. Drawing on the ideas of Derrida and Frye, Larrissy offers sophisticated critical readings of some of Blake's most important works—*Songs of Innocence and Experience, There is No Natural Religion, Europe, The Marriage of Heaven and Hell, Urizen, The Four Zoas*, and *Jerusalem*. He contends that Blake employed a dialectic of form that is at once inhibitive and expressive. He argues that Blake used the values of the occult tradition in an inverted manner and perceived human beings as constrained by ideologies for which they cannot be made entirely accountable. In Larrissy's view, Blake represents a conjuncture of Christianity and radical rationalism. (A)

Lister, Raymond. *The Paintings of William Blake*. Cambridge: Cambridge University Press, 1986. Although this volume does not displace previous Blake biographies, Lister concisely summarizes the essential knowledge of Blake's life, his craft, and his spiritual quest. His discussions of allegory and symbolism are clear and serve to demystify the subject for newcomers to the field. This book is structured as seventy-five individual essays, which include descriptions of Blake's watercolors, drawings, engravings, and paintings. The text is fully illustrated. (A,G)

Metzger, Lore. *One Foot in Eden: Modes of Pastoral in Romantic Poetry*. Chapel Hill: University of North Carolina Press, 1986. In this study, Metzger traces the influence of classical pastoralism on the works of some of the major romantics—Blake, Coleridge, Wordsworth, and Keats. In the process, he provides an important overview of English romanticism. Drawing upon Schiller's thesis that pastoral innocence must be put to a more practical test, Metzger examines the question of whether individuality and idealism can be truthfully expressed in the same work of art. For the most part, she concludes, the English romantics only intensified the dissonance between the ideal and the real world. This book is recommended for scholars and students of the romantic period. (A)

Pagliaro, Harold. *Selfhood and Redemption in Blake's Songs*. University Park, PA: Pennsylvania State University Press, 1987. Pagliaro argues that each of the poems in the *Songs of Innocence and Experience* is the child's response to a world of pain in which death is an imminent possibility. The development of selfhood is realized through repression and self-deceit as the child transforms reality into innocence. Pagliaro's reading of the poems is clear, insightful, and of real value to anyone reading the poems. (A,G)

Schulz, Max F. *Paradise Preserved: Recreations of Eden in Eighteenth and Nineteenth-Century England*. Cambridge: Cambridge University Press, 1986. Schulz's study explores the idealized gardens and landscapes of the English nobility and relates these miniature Edens to the work of painters and poets of the era. Schulz discusses works of Blake and Coleridge and provides insightful parallels with landscape artists such as Constable and Turner. He also considers Tennyson's view of Eden and anti-Eden within the context of

Whistler and the mid-Victorians. Selected illustrations help amplify many of Schulz's points. This is an important study that seeks to interrelate areas of scholarship that are too often compartmentalized. Highly recommended. (A,G)

Other Sources
Approaches to Teaching Blake's "Songs of Innocence and Experience." New York: Modern Language Association, 1989.

Bentley, G. E., Jr. *Blake Records Supplement: Being New Materials Relating to the Life of William Blake Discovered since the Publication of Blake Records.* New York: Oxford University Press, 1988.

Bidney, Martin. *Blake and Goethe: Psychology, Ontology, Imagination.* Columbia: University of Missouri Press, 1988.

Bindman, David. *The Complete Graphic Works of William Blake.* New York: Thames Hudson, 1986.

Bracher, Mark. *Being Form'd: Thinking through Blake's Milton.* Barrytown, NY: Station Hill Press, 1985.

Butlin, Martin, *et al. William Blake and His Circle.* San Marino, CA: Huntington Library, 1989.

Damon, S. Foster, and Morris Eaves. *A Blake Dictionary: The Ideas and Symbols of William Blake.* Hanover, NH: University Press of New England, 1988.

Essick, Robert N. *William Blake and His Contemporaries and Followers: Selected Works from the Collection of Robert N. Essick.* San Marino, CA: Huntington Library, 1987.

Essick, Robert N. *William Blake and the Language of Adam.* New York: Oxford University Press, 1989.

Ginsberg, Allen. *Your Reason and Blake's System.* Old Chelsea Station, NY: Hanuman Books, 1988.

Gleckner, Robert F. *Blake and Spenser.* Baltimore and London: Johns Hopkins University Press, 1985.

Godard, Jerry C. *Mental Forms Creating: William Blake Anticipates Freud, Jung, and Rank.* Lanham, MD: University Press of America, 1985.

Goslee, Nancy M. *Uriel's Eye: Miltonic Stationing and Statuary in Blake, Keats, and Shelley.* Tuscaloosa: University of Alabama Press, 1985.

Hagstrum, Jean H. *The Romantic Body: Love and Sexuality in Keats, Wordsworth, and Blake.* Knoxville: University of Tennessee Press, 1986.

Hoagwood, Terence A. *Prophecy and the Philosophy of Mind: Traditions of Blake and Shelley.* Tuscaloosa: University of Alabama Press, 1985.

Miller, Dan, *et al.,* eds. *Critical Paths: Blake and the Argument of Method.* Durham, NC: Duke University Press, 1987.

Nesfield-Cookson, Bernard. *William Blake: Prophet of Universal Brotherhood.* New York: Sterling, 1988.

Weiskel, Thomas. *The Romantic Sublime: Studies in the Structure and Psychology of Transcendence.* Baltimore: Johns Hopkins University Press, 1986.

Werner, Bette C. *Blake's Vision of the Poetry of Milton.* Lewisburg, PA: Bucknell University Press, 1986.

Whitlark, James. *Illuminated Fantasy: From Blake's Vision to Recent Graphic Fiction.* Madison, NJ: Fairleigh Dickinson University Press, 1988.

Witke, Joanne. *William Blake's Epic: Imagination Unbound.* New York: St. Martin's, 1986.

Youngquist, Paul. *Madness and Blake's Myth.* University Park: The Pennsylvania State University Press, 1990.

LOUISE BOGAN
1897-1970

Evaluation of Selected Biography and Criticism

Bowles, Gloria. *Louise Bogan's Aesthetics of Limitations.* Bloomington: Indiana University Press, 1987. For Bowles, Bogan was "limited" by a heavily burdened psyche resulting primarily from her gender. She contends that Bogan's poetry has not been appreciated by male readers because of a complex interaction of gender, background, and temperament that establishes her poetic voice. In spite of these restrictive critical views, Bowles shows considerable understanding of Bogan's psychic difficulties, and makes a provocative case for why a major poetic talent can be ignored for so long. (A)

JAMES BOSWELL
1740-1795

Evaluation of Selected Biography and Criticism

Bloom, Harold, ed. *James Boswell's "Life of Samuel Johnson."* New York: Chelsea House, 1986. As part of the "Modern Critical Interpretations" series, Chelsea House has anthologized seven previously published critical essays on Boswell's famous biography. Several of the essays may be found in Vance's *Boswell's "Life of Johnson"* (1986) or Clifford's *Twentieth Century Interpretations of Boswell's "Life of Johnson"* (1970); several others are excerpted from recent book-length studies. Although the contributors are uniformly well-regarded, their essays are presented without notes or references, limiting this anthology's usefulness. **(G)**

Lustig, Irma, and Frederick Pottle, eds. *Boswell: The English Experiment, 1785-1789.* New York: McGraw-Hill, 1986. This volume, the thirteenth in the Yale edition of Boswell's collected private papers, covers the period between the death of Johnson and the death of Boswell's wife. His experiences under the patronage of the ruthless Earl of Lonsdale are described in detail. His comments on the approaching demise of his wife show a sentimental side to Boswell that has often been overlooked. Although this study has the complete scholarly apparatus, it is arranged to have appeal for the casual reader. **(A,G)**

Vance, John A, ed. *Boswell's "Life of Johnson": New Questions, New Answers.* Athens: University of Georgia Press, 1985. This anthology of eleven essays on Boswell's famous biography of Johnson addresses old issues with newer theories. The central conflict among these critics is over the factual accuracy of Boswell's book, which is considered an important but dated document by many, and an unimpeachable standard by others. These essayists attempt to revitalize what they feel has become a stagnant critical climate. **(A)**

Other Sources

Abbott, C. C. *Boswell.* Brunswick, ME: Bern Porter, 1985.

Danziger, Marlies K., and Frank Brady, eds. *Boswell, the Great Biographer, 1789-1795.* New York: McGraw-Hill, 1989.

Quennell, Peter. *Four Portraits: Boswell, Gibbon, Sterne and Wilkes.* New York: David and Charles, 1988.

ELIZABETH BOWEN
1899-1973

Author's Recent Bibliography

The Mulberry Tree: Writings of Elizabeth Bowen, 1987. This collection of the nonfiction writings of the eminent Anglo-Irish author—essays, book reviews, prefaces, letters, radio broadcasts, and autobiographical musings—exhibits considerable intelligence and stylistic elegance.

Evaluation of Selected Biography and Criticism

Craig, Patricia. *Elizabeth Bowen*. London and New York: Penguin, 1987. As part of a series designed to introduce students to the works of modern women writers, this biocritical study examines the life and works of Bowen from an empathetic perspective. Bowen was one of the important writers who expressed in her works the fears of women trapped by proper English society, and Craig appreciatively explains the ground that Bowen broke, her exceptional craft, and her importance in literary history. (A,G)

Sekine, Masaru, ed. *Irish Writers and Society At Large*. Totowa, NJ: Barnes & Noble, 1985. This anthology collects fourteen essays on Anglo-Irish writers, including Bowen, Joyce, Moore, Corkery, and MacNeice. (A,G)

Other Sources

Austin, Allan E. *Elizabeth Bowen*. [Rev. ed.] Boston: Twayne, 1989.

Lassner, Phyllis. *Elizabeth Bowen*. Savage, MD: Rowman, 1989.

ANNE BRADSTREET
1612-1672

Evaluation of Selected Biography and Criticism

Von Frank, Albert J. *The Sacred Game: Provincialism and Frontier Consciousness in American Literature, 1630-1860.* New York: Cambridge University Press, 1985. Von Frank's wide-ranging study examines the reactions of various writers to the wilderness environment of young America. He contends that Anne Bradstreet felt compelled to retain the old culture in order to preserve identity in her new surroundings. He views Washington Irving's works as a reaction to American provincialism, and sees many of the same provincial themes evident in Hawthorne's *The Scarlet Letter.* Von Frank's major thesis is that the wilderness environment accepts immigrants but at the same time rejects the immigrant's culture. He uses Emerson's works to analyze this and other themes. **(A)**

Westbrook, Perry D. *A Literary History of New England.* Bethlehem, PA: Lehigh University Press, 1988. Spanning the years 1620 to 1950, this study of literary New England explains how literature mirrored and influenced the religious, political, social, and cultural forces of the region. Besides the most famous authors—Mather, Plath, Frost, Bradstreet—many lesser-known writers, such as Mercy Warren, Catharine Sedgwick, and Lucy Larcom, are also treated. Detailed enough to provide information for scholars, this lively study may also satisfy a more general audience. **(A,G)**

White, Peter, ed. *Puritan Poets and Poetics: Seventeenth-Century American Poetry in Theory and Practice.* University Park: Pennsylvania State University Press, 1985. This collection of twenty-two essays examines the nature and vocabulary of Puritan poetry during the seventeenth century. Separate essays are devoted to the works of Bradstreet, Taylor, and others. Bradstreet's poetry is examined for its biblically derived prophetic rhetoric; Taylor is examined in the context of his contemporaries. A closing group of essays provides an overview of the various poetic forms of the period. **(A)**

Other Sources

Crowell, Pattie, and Ann Stanford. *Critical Essays on Anne Bradstreet.* Boston: G. K. Hall, 1983.

CHARLOTTE BRONTË
1816-1855

Evaluation of Selected Biography and Criticism

Berg, Maggie. *"Jane Eyre": Portrait of a Life*. Boston: Twayne, 1987. In this contribution to the "Masterwork" series, Berg examines the auto-biographical elements of Brontë's *Jane Eyre*. She points out the often-overlooked fact that Jane is the fictional author of the novel and that the title page reads "An Autobiography." Berg's thesis is that the novel portrays Brontë's own struggle to establish her artistic career. In developing this thesis she challenges many of the established interpretations of events in the novel, and goes on to develop striking parallels with Joyce's *A Portrait of the Artist as a Young Man*. In all, this is a smoothly written, challenging example of critical reading at its best. Recommended highly. (A,G)

Chitham, Edward. *The Brontës' Irish Background*. New York: St. Martin's, 1986. Chitham reopens the controversy of the Brontë sisters' Irish ancestors. As the story goes, Patrick Brontë's father was adopted by an uncle who had himself been adopted by an Irish family named Brunty. The father ran away from home and eventually settled down to have ten children, among them Patrick who in turn begot Charlotte, Emily, and Anne. Patrick passed on stories of his wild Irish ancestors that in turn influenced the "life outlook" of the Brontë sisters. The problem is that the story has been repeatedly debunked by such scholars as Angus MacKay (*The Brontës: Fact and Fiction*), who judged the story a fiction devised by Irish peasants to entertain themselves at the expense of a visiting scholar. In fact, next to nothing is known about the Brontës' family background, and Chitham provides no new evidence. (A,G)

Coslett, Tess. *Woman to Woman: Female Friendship in Victorian Fiction*. Brighton, England: Harvester Press, 1988. Focusing on the Victorian era, Coslett demonstrates how women writers of the time were able to lend special power and significance to female friendships in their fiction. In these works, personal transformation is wrought through "sisterhood," rather than through the conventions of courtship and marriage. Coslett traces the process of individual development in novels by Gaskell, Rossetti, Browning, Eliot, and Charlotte Brontë. (A,G)

Crump, Rebecca W. *Charlotte and Emily Brontë, 1955-1983: A Reference Guide*. G. K. Hall, 1986. This is the most comprehensive bibliography currently available on the Brontë sisters. Its annotated entries extend from 1955 to 1983. Crump's introduction provides an overview of Brontë scholarship and discusses the major critical trends. (A)

Duthie, Enid Lowry. *The Brontës and Nature*. New York: St. Martin's, 1986. This noted Brontë scholar examines the depiction and use of nature in the novels and poems of the Brontë sisters. Duthie's encyclopedic approach collects the allusions, images, and patterns of the "mobility of the human spirit as it recognizes the flux of nature." Duthie discusses Patrick Brontë's understanding of nature, a great influence on all three sisters, and goes on to consider Anne's collections of poetry, *Agnes Grey,* and *The Tenant of Wildfell Hall,* as well as Charlotte's and Emily's better-known novels. Charlotte, who made the greatest use of nature as setting and theme, is by far the star of this study. This study's theme is interesting; its analysis intriguing; and the writing top-notch. It is recommended for students and any others with a general interest in the Brontës or the period. (A,G)

Fraser, Rebecca. *The Brontës: Charlotte Brontë and Her Family.* New York: Crown, 1988. The main focus of this biography is the family milieu that shaped the creative powers of both Charlotte and Emily Brontë. A large portion of Fraser's narrative is devoted to the composition of *Jane Eyre,* its publication, and its reception by a public too quick to praise and to criticize. The scholarly tone does not disguise the biographer's empathy with the suffering of a literary woman who refused to "know her place." (A,G)

Homans, Margaret. *Bearing the Word: Language and Female Experience in Nineteenth-Century Women's Writing.* Chicago: University of Chicago Press, 1986. Delving into the Oedipal propositions of psychoanalytic theory, Homans emerges with an insight into the interaction of language acquisition and the formation of gender identity. Building on the ideas of Jacques Lacan and Nancy Chodorow, she describes a dominant myth of language that identifies the woman with the "literal," and a dominant myth of gender that connects her with nature and matter. To support these theories, Homans provides close readings of excerpts from Dorothy Wordsworth, Mary Shelley, the Brontë sisters, Elizabeth Gaskell, George Eliot, and Virginia Woolf. Homans has produced an important theoretical framework for studying Brontë. (A)

Kucich, John. *Repression in Victorian Fiction: Charlotte Brontë, George Eliot, and Charles Dickens.* Berkeley: University of California Press, 1987. This lengthy study traces the theme of psychological repression through the life and works of Brontë, Eliot, and Dickens. Kucich's thorough scholarship examines in detail the nineteenth-century tendency to "exalt interiority." In the process, he eschews traditional critical terms, such as "self-denial" and "renunciation," in favor of his own vision of "repression." Although at times overburdened with psychoanalytical terminology, this study presents a fresh perspective from which to read the fiction of these authors. (A)

LaBelle, Jenijoy. *Herself Beheld: The Literature of the Looking Glass.* Ithaca, NY: Cornell University Press, 1988. LaBelle examines the importance of the mirror as symbol in the work of nineteenth-century women writers. For her, the mirror's reflection symbolizes introspection and revelation, instead of vanity which is dominant in traditional Christian, male-dominated symbology.

She examines looking-glass episodes in George Eliot, the Brontës, and many of the period's lesser-known works of fiction. This is a fresh feminist look at a common, recurring symbol in fiction. **(A,G)**

Martin, Philip W. *Mad Women in Romantic Writing.* New York: St. Martin's, 1988. Martin examines the ways in which patriarchal culture depicted women in the nineteenth century and explores the stereotype of the "weaker sex." He contends that the rising interest in individual psychology merged with the belief in women's weakness to create a new and important figure in romantic literature—the madwoman. He supports his thesis through discussions of selected novels of the period, among them *Jane Eyre*, *Wuthering Heights, Great Expectations,* and *Sense and Sensibility.* **(A,G)**

Maynard, John. *Charlotte Brontë and Sexuality.* Cambridge: Cambridge University Press, 1984. Maynard's thesis is that Brontë "creates a vision of sexual experience that can rival that of any of her successors in the twentieth century for depth of psychological insight and fidelity to the complex nature of sexuality itself." After first attacking Freudian and feminist critics whose "reductive" analyses depict Brontë as a psychological cripple, Maynard applies his theories of sexuality to Brontë's work, arguing that Victorian readers well understood the intensity of her depiction of sexuality, especially as expressed through her symbolism. He analyzes *Jane Eyre, Villette, The Professor,* and *Shirley* to demonstrate that Brontë's portrayal of sexual relationships underwent a progressive deepening. Maynard provides a serious reassessment that will anger some and challenge others. **(A)**

Myer, Valerie Grosvenor. *Charlotte Brontë: Truculent Spirit.* Totowa, NJ: Barnes & Noble, 1987. In individual essays Myer treats both Brontë's life and works. In lively prose, she lauds or castigates various critics who have interpreted Brontë over the years. She then offers her own observations on the works, particularly *Jane Eyre.* Myer is strongly opinionated, which should stimulate an equally strong reaction in the reader. **(A)**

Nestor, Pauline. *Female Friendships and Communities: Charlotte Brontë, George Eliot, Elizabeth Gaskell.* Oxford: Clarendon Press, 1986. Devoting two chapters to each author, Nestor describes the authors' association with other women, their attitudes toward gender, and their treatment of women in their fiction. In doing so, she enlarges her study to include nineteenth-century attitudes toward single women, female friendship, communal living, sexuality, and the emotions which society elicits from women, including anger, violence, passivity, jealously, and resignation. This provocative study illuminates the fiction of three writers, the context in which they created characters, and the society that would accept or reject both them and their work. **(A,G)**

Nestor, Pauline. *Charlotte Brontë.* Totowa, NJ: Barnes & Noble, 1987. Nestor's critical examination of Charlotte Brontë's fiction provides a concise overview of current critical trends. Nestor writes from a feminist literary perspective and reexamines the cultural attitudes of Victorian writers and critics that sought to keep a woman writer in a "woman's place." This careful social critique does much to explain Brontë's preoccupation with such themes as imprisonment and escape and why in her private life she emphasized education, self-reliance, and rebellion. Nestor enables the reader to assess Brontë within the context of women's literature and to reassess her contribution to the Romantic movement. Highly readable. (A,G)

Neufeldt, Victor, ed. *The Poems of Charlotte Brontë: A New Text and Commentary*. New York: Garland, 1986. Although not the first complete collection of Charlotte Brontë's poetry, Neufeldt's edition lays claims at being the most accurate. Brontë's difficult handwriting has defeated many attempts to correctly transcribe her poetry, particularly early drafts. Neufeldt agrees with other critics who have faulted earlier editions and prints photostats of contested manuscript pages to bolster his readings. His introduction summarizes the challenges of tracking down and comparing manuscripts, an instructive discussion for any student facing a similar task. This edition is likely to become the standard text for Charlotte Brontë's poetry. (A,G)

Williams, Judith. *Perception and Expression in the Novels of Charlotte Brontë*. Ann Arbor: UMI Research, 1988. This scholarly work, which includes a thorough bibliography and excellent index, develops the thesis that imagination and sympathy reveal the character of female protagonists whose worlds are closed spaces. These spaces symbolize the terrors of Brontë's women as they strive to achieve self awareness and sexual independence. Williams fully develops her theme in her discussion of *Villette*, particularly its problematic ending. This specialized book is excellent for Brontë scholars and advanced students. (A)

Winnifrith, Tom. *A New Life of Charlotte Brontë*. New York: St. Martin's, 1988. Little biographical information exists about the Brontës, other than what can be extrapolated from Charlotte's letters and speculation about biographical elements in the novels. Winnifrith's short biography attempts to demonstrate the shortcomings of other biographies, in particular their depictions of the Brontës as having lived romantic, though difficult lives. In criticizing the standard biographies, Winnifrith eliminates much of the mystery, as well as the joy, from the Brontë's lives. General readers will find this an accessible introduction, while more specialized students can read it as a corrective for other biographies. (A,G)

Other Sources

Alexander, Christine. *An Edition of the Early Writings of Charlotte Brontë, Vol. 1: 1826-1832*. Cambridge: Basil Blackwell, 1986.

Bentley, Phyllis. *The Brontës*. New York: Thames Hudson, 1986.

Gates, Barbara Timm, ed. *Critical Essays on Charlotte Brontë*. Boston: G. K. Hall, 1990.

Imlay, Elizabeth. *Charlotte Brontë and the Mysteries of Love: Myth and Allegory in "Jane Eyre"*. New York: St. Martin's, 1989.

Moglen, Helene. *Charlotte Brontë: The Self Conceived*. Madison: University of Wisconsin Press, 1984.

Prentis, Barbara. *The Brontë Sisters and George Eliot: A Unity of Difference*. Totowa, NJ: Barnes & Noble, 1988.

Wilkes, Brian, ed. *The Illustrated Brontës of Haworth: Scenes and Characters from the Novels of the Brontë Sisters*. New York: Facts on File, 1986.

EMILY BRONTË
1818-1848

Evaluation of Selected Biography and Criticism

Chitham, Edward. *The Brontës' Irish Background*. New York: St. Martin's, 1986. Chitham reopens the controversy of the Brontë sisters' Irish ancestors. As the story goes, Patrick Brontë's father was adopted by an uncle who had himself been adopted by an Irish family named Brunty. The father ran away from home and eventually settled down to have ten children, among them Patrick who in turn begot Charlotte, Emily, and Anne. Patrick passed on stories of his wild Irish ancestors that in turn influenced the "life outlook" of the Brontë sisters. The problem is that the story has been repeatedly debunked by such scholars as Angus MacKay (*The Brontës: Fact and Fiction*), who judged the story a fiction devised by Irish peasants to entertain themselves at the expense of a visiting scholar. In fact, next to nothing is known about the Brontë's family background, and Chitham provides no new evidence. **(A,G)**

Chitham, Edward. *A Life of Emily Brontë*. London: Basil Blackwell, 1987. Because the facts of Brontë's life are few but well-known, any new biographer must go beyond merely presenting them and provide interpretations. Chitham is so diligent in excluding any disputable information that he is left with only the bare skeleton of a life story to examine and interpret. This short biography, which includes photographs, is a good introduction to what is definitely known of Brontë's life. **(A,G)**

Crump, Rebecca W. *Charlotte and Emily Brontë, 1955-1983: A Reference Guide*. G. K. Hall, 1986. This is the most comprehensive bibliography currently available on the Brontë sisters. Its annotated entries extend from 1955 to 1983. Crump's introduction provides an overview of Brontë scholarship and discusses the major critical trends. **(A)**

Davies, Stevie. *Emily Brontë*. Bloomington: Indiana University Press, 1988. Davies, a noted feminist critic, rejects psychological literary theory narrowly derived from Freud and attempts to develop a broader psychological perspective for literary criticism. She adapts modern theories of perception (the interaction of the left and right hemispheres of the brain) to the critical process. In an examination of Brontë's literary themes, Davies shows how the author transcended gender distinctions to create characters that reflected an underlying psychic unity. She explores distinctions that have been drawn between "masculine" and "feminine" attitudes as embodied in fiction. The methodology of this study should be of special interest to students of feminist and psychological criticism. **(A)**

Dobyns, Ann. *The Voices of Romance: Studies in Dialogue and Character*. Newark: University of Delaware Press, 1989. For Dobyns, a characteristic element of the romance is the fact that character is of secondary importance and is usually determined by plot necessities. She argues that romance authors use speech characteristics to develop distinct characters that embody themes. In arguing her thesis, she compares parallel characters from Malory's *Le Morte Darthur*, Sydney's *New Arcadia*, and Brontë's *Wuthering Heights*. She demonstrates that although the characters in romance are conventional and sometimes static and abstract, they can at the same time be "complex and richly detailed." Useful to students of the romance. **(A)**

Duthie, Enid Lowry. *The Brontës and Nature.* New York: St. Martin's, 1986. This noted Brontë scholar examines the depiction and use of nature in the novels and poems of the Brontë sisters. Duthie's encyclopedic approach collects the allusions, images, and patterns of the "mobility of the human spirit as it recognizes the flux of nature." Duthie discusses Patrick Brontë's understanding of nature, a great influence on all three sisters, and goes on to consider Anne's collections of poetry, *Agnes Grey,* and *The Tenant of Wildfell Hall,* as well as Charlotte's and Emily's better-known novels. This study's theme is interesting; its analysis intriguing; and the writing top-notch. It is recommended for students and any others with a general interest in the Brontës or the period. **(A,G)**

Fraser, Rebecca. *The Brontës: Charlotte Brontë and Her Family.* New York: Crown, 1988. The main focus of this biography is the family milieu that shaped the creative powers of both Charlotte and Emily Brontë. A large portion of Fraser's narrative is devoted to the composition of *Jane Eyre,* its publication, and its reception by a public too quick to praise and to criticize. The scholarly tone does not disguise the biographer's empathy with the suffering of a literary woman who refused to "know her place." **(A,G)**

Haggerty, George E. *Gothic Fiction/Gothic Form.* University Park: Pennsylvania State University Press, 1989. In this study in reader-response criticism, Haggerty attempts to lift Gothic fiction into the category of serious literature. To do this, he establishes two categories—Gothic novels and Gothic tales. Gothic *novels* fail because the genre is unsuited to the effects generated in the reader by the Gothic impulse. Gothic *tales,* on the other hand, succeed admirably. Indeed, because Haggerty's conception of the tale is represented by such works as Shelley's *Frankenstein,* Brontë's *Wuthering Heights,* Poe's "The Fall of the House of Usher," Hawthorne's "Rappaccini's Daughter," and James' *Turn of the Screw*, it is difficult to argue with the conclusion. Some have questioned Haggerty's categories of novel and tale as artificial. **(A,G)**

Homans, Margaret. *Bearing the Word: Language and Female Experience in Nineteenth-Century Women's Writing.* Chicago: University of Chicago Press, 1986. Delving into the Oedipal propositions of psychoanalytic theory, Homans emerges with an insight into the interaction of language acquisition and the formation of gender identity. Building on the ideas of Jacques Lacan and

Nancy Chodorow, she describes a dominant myth of language that identifies the woman with the "literal," and a dominant myth of gender that connects her with nature and matter. To support these theories, she provides close readings of excerpts from Dorothy Wordsworth, Mary Shelley, the Brontë sisters, Elizabeth Gaskell, George Eliot, and Virginia Woolf. Scholars should acquaint themselves with the theoretical framework that Homans develops here. (A)

LaBelle, Jenijoy. *Herself Beheld: The Literature of the Looking Glass.* Ithaca, NY: Cornell University Press, 1988. LaBelle examines the importance of the mirror as symbol in the work of nineteenth-century women writers. For her, the mirror's reflection symbolizes introspection and revelation, instead of vanity which is dominant in traditional Christian, male-dominated symbology. She examines looking-glass episodes in George Eliot, the Brontës, and many of the period's lesser-known works of fiction. This is a fresh feminist look at a common, recurring symbol in fiction. (A,G)

Pykett, Lyn. *Emily Brontë.* New York: Barnes & Noble, 1989. Pykett's stated goal is to focus on "the relationship of the woman writer to the history and tradition of fiction." Specifically, she explains the basic ideas of feminist criticism as they relate to genre, theme, and character in *Wuthering Heights* and the poems. Included is a basic bibliography on Brontë and women writers. This 147-page book is a good primer for students of Brontë or gender studies. (G)

Wallace, Robert K. *Emily Brontë and Beethoven: Romantic Equilibrium in Fiction and Music.* Athens, GA: University of Georgia Press, 1986. Wallace's study picks up where biographer Winifred Gerin leaves off in discussing Emily Brontë's affinity for Beethoven. Wallace compares Brontë's *Wuthering Heights* with three of Beethoven's sonatas, revealing parallels that serve to illuminate emotional, spiritual, and stylistic aspects of her creative motivations and intentions. Wallace examines both narrative and compositional structures, characterizing the revealed "romantic equilibrium" in terms of internal dynamics and symmetry of form. The technique is similar to that used in his highly praised book, *Jane Austen and Mozart.* As an insightful interdisciplinary analysis, this book is highly recommended to those interested in either the literature or music of the nineteenth century. (A,G)

Other Sources

Barclay, Janet M., ed. *Emily Brontë Criticism, Nineteen Hundred to Nineteen Eighty: An Annotated Check List.* Westport, CT: Meckler, 1984.

Bentley, Phyllis. *The Brontës.* New York: Thames Hudson, 1986.

Crump, R. W. *Emily Brontë: The Artist As a Free Woman.* New York: Carcanet, 1984.

Jacobs, Carol. *Uncontainable Romanticism: Shelley, Brontë, Kleist.* Baltimore: Johns Hopkins University Press, 1989.

Kavanagh, James. *Emily Brontë.* Cambridge: Basil Blackwell, 1985.

Prentis, Barbara. *The Brontë Sisters and George Eliot: A Unity of Difference.* Totowa, NJ: Barnes & Noble, 1988.

Wilkes, Brian, ed. *The Illustrated Brontës of Haworth: Scenes and Characters from the Novels of the Brontë Sisters.* New York: Facts on File, 1986.

RUPERT BROOKE
1887-1915

Autobiographical Sources

Brooke, Rupert. *Letters from America.* New York: Beaufort. 1988. This collection of short letters, written during a year-long journey through the United States, Canada, and the South Pacific, was first printed in the *Westminster Gazette* and later published in book form in London in 1916, along with an adoring preface by Henry James. Compared to Brooke's finest writing, these letters are superficial, overwritten, and offer few personal insights, and while they may be of interest to the specialist, they have little to offer the general reader. (A)

Evaluation of Selected Biography and Criticism

Delany, Paul. *The Neo-Pagans: Rupert Brooke and the Ordeal of Youth.* Free Press, 1987. At the turn of the century, the rejection of Victorian moral values combined with industrial and political upheavals, created an environment characterized by expanded opportunity as well as "moral decay." One circle of young writers became both the voice and the symbol of the youth of this generation. Their rootlessness, their search for sexual adventure, and their play-acting led Virginia Woolf to christen them "Neo-Pagans," much as Gertrude Stein would refer to Hemingway and Fitzgerald as the "Lost Generation." Delany focuses his biographical profile of this generation on Brooke, as representative of their collective sensibility and disillusionment with life on the eve of World War I. While little is said of Brooke's poetry, this is fascinating reading for anyone interested in the period or the personalities. (A,G)

Other Sources

Giddings, Robert. *The War Poets: The Lives and Writings of Rupert Brooke, Siegfried Sassoon, Wilfred Owen, Robert Graves, Edmund Blunden and the Other Great Poets of the 1914-1918 War.* Durango, CO: Orion Books, 1988.

GWENDOLYN BROOKS
1917

Author's Recent Bibliography
The Near-Johannesburg Boy and Other Poems, 1986; *Blacks*, 1987 (prose and poetry); *Winnie*, 1988 (poetry); *Göttschalk and the Grande Tarantelle*, 1988 (poetry).

Evaluation of Selected Biography and Criticism
Carby, Hazel V. *Reconstructing Womanhood: The Emergence of the Afro-American Woman Novelist.* Oxford: Oxford University Press, 1987. In this attempt to place Afro-American women novelists in historical context, Carby focuses on four major themes: ideologies of womanhood, white women writers as part of the racist hierarchy, the nineteenth-century renaissance of black women writers, and the overall literary contributions of black women. In her discussion of the Harlem Renaissance, she describes how the works of Mella Larsen and Jessie Fauset influenced the development of urban-centered fiction, as represented by Brooks, Ann Petry, Dorothy West, and Toni Morrison.(A,G)

Kent, George. *A Life of Gwendolyn Brooks.* Lexington, KY: University Press of Kentucky, 1989. Basing his account on interviews, correspondence, and private papers, Kent examines the development of Brooks' poetry as it moves from formal traditionalism to the looser structure and informal presentation by which she captured a mass audience. His access to the poet's journals and notebooks provides a behind-the-scenes look at her creative processes. Kent chronicles Brooks' life and works up to 1978; a concluding essay by D. H. Melhem summarizes subsequent years. (A,G,Y)

Melhem, D. H. *Gwendolyn Brooks: Poetry and the Heroic Voice.* Lexington, KY: University Press of Kentucky, 1987. Melhem closely examines the themes and techniques of Brooks' poetry and argues that she is truly a "major poet." The case is presented in ten essays focusing on various aspects of the poet's life and art, including her use of language and formal innovations, stylistic influences, and thematic scope. The essays include close readings of *A Street in Bronxville*, *In the Mecca*, and *Maud Martha*. The essays ably describe Brooks' persistence in perfecting her craft. (A,G)

Other Sources
Madhubuti, Haki R., ed. *Say That the River Turns: The Impact of Gwendolyn Brooks.* Chicago: Third World, 1987.

Mootry, Maria K., and Gary Smith, eds. *A Life Distilled: Gwendolyn Brooks, Her Poetry and Fiction.* Champaign: University of Illinois Press, 1989.

CHARLES BROCKDEN BROWN
1771-1810

Evaluation of Selected Criticism

Bennett, Maurice J. *An American Tradition—Three Studies: Charles Brockden Brown, Nathaniel Hawthorne, and Henry James.* New York: Garland, 1987. This dissertation examines and compares three American authors and focuses on a major work by each—Brown's *Ormond, or the Secret Witness*, Hawthorne's *The Scarlet Letter*, and James' *The Portrait of a Lady*. This volume includes an extensive bibliography. (A)

Levine, Robert S. *Conspiracy and Romance: Studies in Brockden Brown, Cooper, Hawthorne, and Melville.* New York: Cambridge University Press, 1989. This study consists of four loosely connected essays. An essay on Brown's *Ormond* focuses on the writer's foreign villains and conspiratorial plots against the integrity of the fledgling United States. Examining Cooper's *The Bravo*, Levine demonstrates that the author's desire was to demystify and oppose the "mysterious power" that directed the state of Venice, which he described as a "soulless corporation." Levine examines the roles of insiders and outsiders in Hawthorne's *The Blithedale Romance*. Finally, he turns his attention to Melville's *Benito Cereno*, where he examines the conflicts between captains and mutineers. (A)

SIR THOMAS BROWNE
1605-1682

Evaluation of Selected Criticism
  Post, Jonathan. *Sir Thomas Browne*. Boston: Twayne, 1987. Rife with
political implications during England's Civil War years, Sir Thomas Browne's
works have since been neglected, in part because of their "peculiar" style.
Post sets out to guide newcomers through Browne's varied riches by evoking
a sense of familiarity that dispels the peculiar. Next to Joan Bennett's *Sir
Thomas Browne* (1962), this is the finest overview of the subject available.
(A,G)

Other Sources
  Finch, Jeremiah S. *A Catalogue of the Libraries of Sir Thomas Browne and
Dr. Edward Browne, His Son: A Facsimile Reproduction with an Introduction,
Notes, and Index.* Leiden, Netherlands: E. J. Brill, 1986.

ELIZABETH BARRETT BROWNING
1806-1861

Autobiographical Sources

Karlin, Daniel. *Robert Browning and Elizabeth Barrett: The Courtship Correspondence, 1845-1846: A Selection.* Oxford: Oxford University Press, 1989. Aimed at a general audience, this selection of letters traces the courtship of Robert and Elizabeth Browning. The letters are briefly introduced, placed in context, and carefully annotated. This edition of selected letters serves admirably as an introduction to the Brownings' courtship. (G)

Raymond, Meredith B., and Mary Rose Sullivan, eds. *Women of Letters: Selected Letters of Elizabeth Barrett Browning and Mary Russell Mitford.* Boston: Twayne, 1987. These letters, selected from the complete correspondence between Browning and her intellectual confidante Mitford, offer a lively, intimate portrait of the minds and lives of two important Victorians. They also provide excellent primary material for the non-scholarly reader. In light of the feminist reevaluation of Browning's poetry, the letters are also relevant for general research on Victorian women and their image in literature. (G)

Evaluation of Selected Biography and Criticism

Cooper, Helen. *Elizabeth Barrett Browning, Woman and Artist.* Chapel Hill: University of North Carolina Press, 1988. In this strict feminist reading of Browning's life and work, Cooper traces how she broke from male poetic dominance to establish her own distinctive voice. Cooper argues for a view of Browning as a model for all women and poets. (A)

Coslett, Tess. *Woman to Woman: Female Friendship in Victorian Fiction.* Brighton: Harvester Press, 1988. Focusing on the Victorian era, Coslett demonstrates how women writers of the time were able to lend special power and significance to female friendships in their fiction. In these works, personal transformation is wrought through "sisterhood," rather than through the conventions of courtship and marriage. Coslett traces the process of individual development in novels by Gaskell, Rossetti, Browning, Eliot, and Charlotte Brontë. (A,G)

Forster, Margaret. *Elizabeth Barrett Browning.* New York: Doubleday, 1989. This biography of Browning presents a wealth of new information, much of it gathered from the Philip Kelley collection of Barrett/Browning letters. Forster, who sizes up Browning's parents and family life with a clear eye, is not shy in drawing provocative conclusions. She examines the psychological blow of the death of the poet's mother and goes on to describe her "playing off" father against lover and fooling them both. For Forster, her dramatic elopement with Robert Browning to Italy was probably unnecessary; her father would have approved of the marriage. The narrative does not end with Elizabeth's death but continues with the relationship of Robert Browning and their son. (A)

Leighton, Angela. *Elizabeth Barrett Browning*. Bloomington: Indiana University Press, 1986. In this study of Browning's poetics, Leighton offers a reassessment of the poet's life and work that elevates her significantly over her contemporaries. Much of the discussion centers on *Aurora Leigh*, but, in the process, over twenty of her other poems are treated. Some may find this sample too narrow, but Leighton's conclusions appear to have broad relevance for all of Browning's work. This book provides an example of feminist methodology at its best. It is recommended for anyone interested in the Victorian era and women writers in general. (A,G)

Meredith, Michael. *Meeting the Brownings*. New York: Armstrong Browning Library, 1986. This is a catalogue of an exhibition of portraits and documents, some rarely seen, which help trace the Brownings' friendships. An introduction and well-informed notes explain the background of each item. (A,G)

Mermin, Dorothy. *Elizabeth Barrett Browning: The Origins of a New Poetry*. Chicago: University of Chicago Press, 1989. Mermin's analysis of Browning's poetry makes claims for its significance but also acknowledges that it is plagued by a literal-mindedness that affected most Victorian poets. In spite of these shortcomings, Mermin contends, Browning broke with convention by acting as the subject, rather than the object, of her love sonnets. Focusing primarily on the ballads, sonnets, and political poems—in particular, *Aurora Leigh*—Mermin makes the case that Browning is deserving of critical attention today. (A,G)

Other Sources
Stephenson, Glennis. *Elizabeth Barrett Browning and the Poetry of Love*. Ann Arbor: UMI Press, 1989.

ROBERT BROWNING
1812-1889

Autobiographical Sources

Karlin, Daniel. *Robert Browning and Elizabeth Barrett: The Courtship Correspondence, 1845-1846: A Selection.* Oxford: Oxford University Press, 1989. Aimed at a general audience, this selection of letters traces the courtship of Robert and Elizabeth Browning. The letters are briefly introduced, placed in context, and carefully annotated. This edition of selected letters serves admirably as an introduction to the Brownings' courtship. **(G)**

Evaluation of Selected Biography and Criticism

Brady, Ann P. *Pompilia: A Feminist Reading of Robert Browning's "The Ring and the Book."* Athens, OH: Ohio University Press, 1988. Brady argues that Pompilia's seduction of the priest in Browning's *The Ring and the Book* was a noble act, and that the love between Caponsacchi and Pompilia was non-sexual and pure. In arguing that Browning supported the equality of women, Brady traces the history of misogyny from classical times, discussing such writers as the Apostle Paul, Aquinas, Dionysius, and Livy. This lively study will provoke new ideas from serious students of Browning. **(A)**

Buckler, William E. *Poetry and Truth in Robert Browning's "The Ring and the Book."* Dover, NH: Croom Helm, 1985. Using Henry James' critical essay on Browning's work, "The Novel in *The Ring and the Book*," Buckler demonstrates that James' approach is entirely suitable for discussing the poem's meaning. Many of Buckler's ideas revise accepted critical opinions and suggest a new perspective on and interpretation of the work. **(A)**

Gibson, Mary Ellis. *History and the Prism of Art: Browning's Poetic Experiments.* Columbus: Ohio State University Press, 1987. Browning has continued to speak more directly to the twentieth century than to his own Victorian audience. His sense of evil and violence, his questions about the process of history, the ways in which individuals are placed in time, and the meaning of success have given him an enduring appeal. Gibson argues that Browning entangles history into the forms of myth. She then closely reads all of the major poems, and some little-known ones, to support her thesis. Although some may find the study over-detailed, Gibson provides a thorough examination of a body of difficult poetry. **(A)**

Martin, Loy. *Browning's Dramatic Monologues and the Post-Romantic Subject.* Baltimore: The Johns Hopkins University Press, 1985. Martin's examination of Browning's dramatic monologues incorporates current critical thinking on style and content within an enlarged framework of Marxist dialectic. Martin's thesis is that Browning's monologue is a formal device which "isolates the ideology of the autonomous bourgeois self to reveal through irony the self's internal contradictions and to point to a communal solidarity inherent in language." In the process of developing his discussion of Browning, Martin suggests ways in which the often divergent psychological and sociological approaches to literature can be seen as complementary. (A)

Meredith, Michael. *Meeting the Brownings.* New York: Armstrong Browning Library, 1986. This is a catalogue of an exhibition of portraits and documents, some rarely seen, which help trace the Brownings' friendships. An introduction and well-informed notes explain the background of each item. (A,G)

Other Sources
Collins, Thomas J., and Richard J. Shroyer. *The Plays of Robert Browning.* New York: Garland, 1988.

Karlin, Daniel. *The Courtship of Robert Browning and Elizabeth Barrett.* New York: Oxford University Press, 1985.

Meredith, Michael C., and Rita S. Humphrey, eds. *More Than Friend: The Letters of Robert Browning to Katharine de kay Bronson.* Winfield, KS: Wedgestone Press, 1985.

Posnock, Ross. *Henry James and the Problem of Robert Browning.* Athens: University of Georgia Press, 1985.

Thomas, Charles F. *Art and Architecture in the Poetry of Robert Browning: An Illustrated Compendium of Sources.* Troy, NY: Whitston, 1989.

Woolford, John. *Browning the Revisionary.* New York: St. Martin's, 1988.

PEARL BUCK
1892-1973

Evaluation of Selected Biography and Criticism
   Rizzon, Beverly. *Pearl S. Buck: The Final Chapter.* Palm Springs, CA: ETC Publications, 1989. In early 1970, when Buck moved to Danby, Vermont, Rizzon became her personal secretary and ultimately "her companion and confidant." Rizzon's memoir describes Buck's final years and, following her death, the bitter fight over her estate. Rizzon's attitude to Buck is reverential, but she gives an inside view of the novelist's last years. (A,G)

Other Sources
   Cwiklik, Robert. *Pearl S. Buck.* New York: Kipling Press, 1988.

   Cwiklik, Robert. *Pearl S. Buck: China's Witness.* New York: Kipling Press, 1989.

ANTHONY BURGESS
1917

Author's Recent Bibliography

Enderby's Dark Lady; Or No End to Enderby, 1984 (novel); *The Kingdom of the Wicked*, 1985 (novel); *Flame into Being: The Life and Work of D. H. Lawrence*, 1985 (critical biography); *The Pianoplayers*, 1986 (novel); *But Do Blondes Prefer Gentlemen?: Homage to QWERT YUIOP and Other Writings*, 1986; *Blooms of Dublin*, 1986 (muscial play); *A Clockwork Orange: New American Edition*, 1987 (novel); *Little Wilson and Big God* (autobiography), 1987; *Any Old Iron*, 1989 (novel).

Evaluation of Recent Bibliography

Burgess, Anthony. *A Clockwork Orange: New American Edition*. New York: Norton, 1987. All American editions since its first publication in 1962 have omitted the crucial final chapter of *A Clockwork Orange* in which the protagonist grows up, marries, and renounces his previous life of violence. This final chapter, and hence this edition, is absolutely essential for understanding the novel's structure and Burgess' intent in writing it. Interestingly, editions published overseas have always included the final chapter; only American editors saw fit to omit it. (A,G)

Burgess, Anthony. *Flame into Being: The Life and Work of D. H. Lawrence*. New York: Arbor House, 1985. Burgess has written influential biographical/critical studies of Joyce and Shakespeare. Here he applies his critical acumen to Lawrence, arguing how the life permeates the work. The pleasure of reading Burgess on Lawrence is twofold; in many ways they are similar men and similar writers. Burgess not only understands Lawrence's fiction, he has lived the creative process behind it. Even if this is not the most scholarly of the many Lawrence studies produced on the centenary of his birth, it is certainly one of the best written and most provocative. (A)

Autobiographical Sources

Burgess, Anthony. *Little Wilson and Big God*. London: Weidenfeld & Nicolson, 1987. Burgess has been variously characterized as obsessive, manic, and self-destructive. He has also emerged as one of the century's best wits and a brilliant master of language. When he was forty, he was diagnosed as having a brain tumor and given less than a year to live. During the succeeding months he wrote five novels, and when he did not die at the end of a year, he just kept on writing. In this, the first volume of a two-volume autobiography, Burgess covers his life from childhood, through his first marriage to an alcoholic wife, his service in World War II in Gibraltar, to his gruelling life in Malaysia. Burgess' autobiography is as full of energy and wit as his novels and criticism, making it vivid reading for anyone who likes biography, and a fascinating resource for students or scholars researching Burgess. (A,G)

Evaluation of Selected Biography and Criticism

Aggeler, Geoffrey. *Critical Essays on Anthony Burgess*. Boston: G.K. Hall, 1986. This collection of fifteen essays provides indispensable coverage of many of Burgess' major works, including *Tremor of Intent*, *A Clockwork Orange*, *The Malayan Trilogy*, and *Napoleon Symphony*. The essays (all but two are reprints) were carefully selected to present a range of critical approaches. Aggeler offers an introductory overview of the critical attention paid to Burgess over the years. The fact that no bibliography is included represents a missed opportunity, since few are available on Burgess. (A,G)

Ghosh-Shellhorn, Martina. *Anthony Burgess: A Study in Character*. Frankfurt-am-Main: Peter Lang, 1986. This specialized study establishes a typology of Anthony Burgess' characters in twenty-seven novels. Burgess protagonists are arrayed as three types of the "representative man"—colonial, Englishman, or creator. In each category a single work is selected for extended analysis. These are *The Malayan Trilogy*, *The Doctor is Sick*, and *Earthly Powers*. The other novels are addressed only in summary form. (A)

Other Sources

Boytinck, P. *Anthony Burgess, Bibliography*. Brunswick, ME: Bern Porter, 1985.

Boytinck, Paul. *Anthony Burgess: A Reference Guide*. New York: Garland, 1985.

FANNY BURNEY
1752-1840

Autobiographical Sources

Troide, Lars E., ed. *The Early Journals and Letters of Fanny Burney: 1768-1773.* Montreal: McGill-Queen's University Press, 1988. This is the first volume of a projected ten- to twelve-volume collection. In addition to Burney's witty and interesting perceptions, these letters and journals provide unusual insight into the writer herself, for Burney censored her own work. Much in these papers had been blacked out and was indecipherable. However, through painstaking scholarship, the editor has restored the censored passages, thus providing an unusual view of Burney's private thoughts. Troide's scholarship may well open the way for a reassessment of Burney. (A)

Evaluation of Selected Biography and Criticism

Devlin, D. D. *The Novels and Journals of Fanny Burney.* New York: St. Martin's, 1987. This short (118 pages) study offers an excellent introduction to the historical and political context of Burney's writing. Devlin believes that Burney's marriage to a French refugee sharpened her political awareness, which worked its way into her fiction. Devlin also demonstrates how the directness of her journal writing technique provided the tone and structure of her early novels. One of the most interesting (but least developed) of Devlin's ideas is that Burney's experiences in the 1780s and 1790s were directly reflected in the work of her contemporaries, especially Mary Shelley. Students coming to Burney for the first time will find Devlin's study a sound basic treatment. (A,G)

Doody, Margaret Anne. *Frances Burney: The Life in the Works.* New Brunswick, NJ: Rutgers University Press, 1988. This exhaustively researched and comprehensive study of Burney's family and her life includes close readings of her novels and plays and is a convincing argument that Burney was not the prudish, weak, insecure woman portrayed by some prior biographers. Doody also maintains that Burney's works are critical in the development of both the English novel and the English comic stage. This definitive biography will reshape Burney scholarship and, no doubt, initiate a flurry of revisionist criticism. Because Doody includes a great deal of information about Burney's associates and the contemporary social customs, this biography is recommended for all readers interested in the eighteenth century. (A,G)

Epstein, Julia. *The Iron Pen: Frances Burney and the Politics of Women's Writing.* Madison: University of Wisconsin Press, 1989. Epstein offers lively readings of Burney's works, demonstrating that her protagonists struggle bravely to maintain a political *status quo* against considerable inner anger. These protagonists, Epstein contends, must continually balance the dangers of asserting their independence with the humiliation of submitting to patriarchal dominance. In this vein, Burney wrote ironically and out of anger, seeking to overthrow outmoded social codes that suppressed women, while pretending to support the patriarchal power structure. She became more obsessed with images of violence and rebellion as time went on, although she maintained a passive authorial persona. Epstein admits that few of Burney's contemporaries would have been able to see the irony in her works. Only now, she believes, can the depth of Burney's feminist position be truly noted and appreciated. (A,G)

Simmons, Judy. *Fanny Burney*. Totowa, NJ: Barnes & Noble, 1987. This study, one of the few to treat all of Burney's novels and plays, examines how feminist sentiments pervade Burney's traditional views. Simmons is strongest in her explications of the works, but some will question her claims for Burney's feminism. This brief study provides a convenient overview of the works and should be used to supplement other critical studies. (A,G)

Straub, Kristina. *Divided Fictions: Fanny Burney and Feminine Strategy*. Lexington: University Press of Kentucky, 1988. In this sophisticated study of a neglected eighteenth-century novelist, Straub combines biography, history, and close textual analysis to survey the major themes in Burney's novels. Straub believes that through her characters, Burney consistently presented an "ideology" of romantic love that was in conflict with an "ideology" of female powerlessness. This conflict was played out within the restricted female social role as reflected in the strictures of clothing and the social ambivalence toward women's work and working women. Straub argues convincingly for a reevaluation of Burney's literary significance. (A,G)

Other Sources
Daugherty, Tracy E. *Narrative Techniques in the Novels of Fanny Burney*. New York: Peter Lang, 1989.

Hemlow, Joyce. *Fanny Burney: Selected Letters and Journals*. New York: Oxford University Press, 1986.

Wallace, Tara G., ed. *A Busy Day: Fanny Burney*. New Brunswick, NJ: Rutgers University Press, 1984.

ROBERT BURNS
1759-1796

Autobiographical Sources

Ferguson, J. DeLancey, ed. *The Letters of Robert Burns: Vol. I, 1780-1789; Vol. II, 1790-1796.* Oxford: Clarendon Press, 1985. Drawing on new material, this new edition adds to and corrects former collections published in 1931. One important new section reprints summaries of 302 letters from the 1800 edition. Since many of the letters have since been lost, these summaries provide the only source of information. (A)

Evaluation of Selected Biography and Criticism

Bentman, Raymond. *Robert Burns.* Boston: G. K. Hall/Twayne, 1987. Bentman outlines the literary, linguistic, cultural, and psychological contexts in which Burns worked, then argues that Scotland was ripe for poetry during Burns' time because the language was unspoiled by the intellectual demands of the English Enlightenment. He believes that Burns is "perhaps the age's most typical and articulate spokesman" who has best preserved the rituals and customs of the Scots. This readable book argues convincingly for a reassessment of Burns' declining literary reputation. (A,G)

Brown, Mary Ellen. *Burns and Tradition.* Champaign: University of Illinois Press, 1984. Brown argues that Burns became a folk model because he uses so much of the Scottish tradition, including narratives, songs, anecdotes, stories, and jokes. She discusses the bawdy tradition and places Burns in the center of it because of his sexual exploits and excessive drinking. Although Brown does not provide sustained close readings of the poems, readers can extrapolate the influence of folk culture on them. (A,G)

Low, Donald A. *Robert Burns.* Edinburgh: Scottish Academic Press, 1986. Low begins with an account of Burns' life; follows with four chapters covering most of the major works, including the corpus of songs; and ends with a short bibliography. The biographical details are analyzed for their bearing on the poems, and Low quotes from Burns' contemporaries to demonstrate cultural influences. This general study will be of little value to scholars but provides a good introduction for students and non-specialists. (G)

McGuirk, Carol. *Robert Burns and the Sentimental Era.* Athens: The University of Georgia Press, 1985. McGuirk's study seeks to reassess the place of Burns in literary history. She questions the common critical conceptions about the structure and content of his works and strives to remove the stigma of sentimentality that clings to his poetry. In later life, Burns failed to live up to the expectations of his public and turned to writing songs. McGuirk reveals the poet's close relationship with folk songs and lyrics. (A,G)

ROBERT BURTON
1577-1640

Evaluation of Selected Biography and Criticism

Conn, Joey. *Robert Burton and "The Anatomy of Melancholy": An Annotated Bibliography of Primary and Secondary Sources.* Westport, CT: Greenwood Press, 1988. This bibliography offers a comprehensive listing of critical sources, including theses and dissertations. The entries are briefly annotated. (A)

Heusser, Martin. *The Gilded Pill: A Study of the Reader-Writer Relationship in Robert Burton's "Anatomy of Melancholy."* Tübingen, Germany: Stauffenburg Verlag, 1987. Heusser contends that the reader of Burton's *Anatomy of Melancholy* is subjected to an artfully structured array of authorial techniques that are disguised by the book's apparent shapelessness. For example, Burton creates paradox in a variety of unothrodox ways, such as through the density of imagery. Heusser goes on to argue that Burton's prose resembles his poetry in the use of techniques, and differs in that it is structured as a compendium of information that more closely resembles an encyclopedia than a poem or essay. The reader is forced to continually change his frame of reference in response to the shifting perspective of the text. Heusser takes issue with many of Burton's critics, while developing an analysis of his style, techniques, and methodologies of generating paradoxes. (A)

O'Connell, Michael. *Robert Burton.* Boston: Twayne, 1986. This is the most comprehensive biography of Burton currently in print. Burton's works--in particular, *Anatomy of Melancholy*—are explicated in the context of his life. O'Connell contends that Burton forged his own "macaronic prose," laden with Latin which he translates, elaborates, and makes puns on in turn. He also treats Burton's minor poems and his play, *Philosophaster*. Included is a very detailed selected bibliography of sources and criticism. (A,G)

SAMUEL BUTLER
1612-1680

Evaluation of Selected Biography and Criticism
Wasserman, George. *Samuel Butler and the Earl of Rochester: A Reference Guide*. Boston: G. K. Hall, 1986. This reference guide provides selected annotated citations of writings by and about authors Butler and Rochester. A list of recent dissertations is included. The purpose of this guide is to provide scholars with up-to-date assessments of the available sources. (A)

Wasserman, George. *Samuel "Hudibras" Butler: Updated Edition*. Boston: Twayne, 1989. Restoration satirist Samuel Butler has been the subject of renewed critical attention in recent years. Wasserman has updated his previous edition to consider current perspectives of the works, particularly those that address his most famous poem, *Hudibras*. Wasserman is concerned with delineating Butler's role as a thinker within his social context. This volume includes a thorough bibliography of primary and secondary sources. (A)

Other Sources
Norrman, Ralf. *Samuel Butler and the Meaning of Chiasmus*. New York: St. Martin's, 1986.

WILLIAM BYRD II
1674-1744

Evaluation of Selected Biography and Criticism
Lockridge, Kenneth A. *The Diary and Life of William Byrd of Virginia, 1674-1744*. Chapel Hill: University of North Carolina Press, 1987. Based on his interpretations of the diaries, Lockridge extrapolates a psychological portrait of Byrd. He argues that Byrd's childhood was filled with rejection and a sense of failure that stemmed from fears of not living up to his father's expectations. His insecurities followed him into manhood and greatly affected his political and social ambitions. When he was about forty years old, Byrd shed himself of this burden and became a mature Virginia gentleman. Lockridge stresses that there is so much material about Byrd that is obscure, undated, or unobtainable that his is merely one attempt to tell Byrd's story. (A,G)

Other Sources
Wenger, Mark R., ed. *The English Travels of Sir John Percival and William Byrd II: The Percival Diary of 1701*. Columbia: University of Missouri Press, 1989.

GEORGE GORDON, LORD BYRON
1788-1824

Evaluation of Selected Biography and Criticism

Bate, Jonathan. *Shakespeare and the English Romantic Imagination.* Oxford: Oxford University Press, 1986. In this well-written study, Bate examines the influence of Shakespeare on Byron, Coleridge, Wordsworth, Keats, and Blake. He examines how each poet's critical theory developed either out of or as a reaction to Shakespeare's poetic identity. This is a large field to cover, and Bate's study is a creditable overview that should be useful for anyone studying the English romantics. (A,G)

Beaty, Frederick L. *Byron the Satirist.* De Kalb: Northern Illinois University Press, 1985. Beaty demonstrates the parallels of Byron's satire to Latin texts; discusses Byron's personal and social motives for writing satire; analyzes the viewpoints taken by the various satiric narrators; and discusses satiric form and the themes which evolve from a satiric mode. (A)

Kelsall, Malcolm. *Byron's Politics.* New York: Barnes & Noble, 1987. Although Byron took up political causes in Italy and Greece that made him seem liberal to a romantic age, Kelsall argues effectively that Byron was a conservative who believed in the stability that the aristocracy ensured. Although his language suggests otherwise, he was, in fact, anti-revolutionary. Kelsall examines Byron's parliamentary speeches, long poems, and Venetian tragedies as he explains Byron's political philosophy and his impact on European intellectuals. This is a fresh, provocative study for advanced students. (A)

McGann, Jerome J., ed. *Byron.* Oxford: Oxford University Press, 1986. This anthology of selected poetry, prose, letters, and journal entries provides a useful starting point for studying Byron. McGann's introduction ably places Byron in historical and literary perspective for the student and general reader. McGann is completing the seven-volume Oxford English Texts edition of Byron's *Complete Poetical Works,* of which this anthology is but a sampler. (A,G)

Shilstone, Frederick W. *Byron and the Myth of Tradition.* Lincoln: University of Nebraska Press, 1988. Taking a biographical approach, Shilstone presents Byron's poetry as a journey of self-exploration in which the "autonomous" self conflicts with tradition as expressed through religious and family values. Shilstone contends that Byron moves further away from tradition in his satires and becomes submerged in an exclusive subjective experience. He quotes extensively from Byron's letters and journals to support his thesis. (A,G)

Other Sources
Beatty, Bernard, and Vincent Newey, eds. *Byron and the Limits of Fiction.* Totowa, NJ: Barnes & Noble, 1988.

Corbett, Martyn. *Byron and Tragedy.* New York: St. Martin's, 1988.

Garber, Frederick. *Self, Text, and Romantic Irony: The Example of Byron.* Princeton: Princeton University Press, 1988.

Page, Norman. *A Byron Chronology.* Boston: G. K. Hall, 1988.

Polito, Robert. *At the Titan's Breakfast: Three Essays on Byron's Poetry.* New York: Garland, 1987.

Storey, Mark. *Byron and the Eye of Appetite.* New York: St. Martin's, 1986.

Watkins, Daniel P. *Social Relations in Byron's Eastern Tales.* Madison: Fairleigh Dickinson, 1987.

GEORGE WASHINGTON CABLE
1844-1925

Evaluation of Selected Biography and Criticism
Elfenbein, Anna Shannon. *Women on the Color Line: Evolving Stereotypes and the Writings of George Washington Cable, Grace King, Kate Chopin.* Charlottesville: University Press of Virginia, 1989. Elfenbein examines the way in which three post-Civil War southern writers used and modified the stereotype of the mixed-race female. After reviewing the social and fictional history of the stereotype, she turns to Cable's *The Grandissimes*, King's "Monsieur Motte," and Chopin's *The Awakening*. She concludes that their treatment of the stereotype indicts the "social masquerades that inscribe race, class, and gender difference, thereby fixing an individual's life chances from birth." **(A)**

Petry, Alice Hall. *A Genius in His Way: The Art of Cable's "Old Creole Days."* Madison, NJ: Fairleigh Dickinson University Press, 1988. Long admired for his story-telling gifts, Cable has evolved as an important literary figure more for his opposition to Black oppression after Reconstruction than for his literary achievements. In this study, Petry focuses only on the work in an effort to demonstrate its superb craftsmanship. Although she accomplishes this goal, her interpretations seem incomplete since she chooses not to relate Cable's craft to its social implications. If scholars doubt Petry's methodology, students and teachers should appreciate her incisive comments on various stories. **(A,G)**

ERSKINE CALDWELL
1903-1987

Author's Recent Bibliography

With All My Might, 1987 (autobiography); *Midsummer Passion and Other Tales of Maine Cussedness,* 1990 (stories).

Autobiographical Sources

Arnold, Edwin T., ed. *Conversations with Erskine Caldwell.* Columbia: University of Missouri Press, 1988. During the late 1930s Caldwell had more books in print than any other writer in the world and was considered to be one of America's most prominent literary lights. He and his wife, photographer Margaret Bourke-White, toured Europe on the eve of World War II recording their experiences in words and pictures. His novels *Tobacco Road* (1932) and *God's Little Acre* (1933) scandalized America with their portrayal of sex and poverty. In this collection of interviews, Caldwell candidly discusses his life, his career, his work, and his place in literature. Arranged chronologically, these interviews cover the years 1929, when he first began to publish, until just before his death in 1987. They provide excellent primary material for anyone researching Caldwell's life. **(A,G)**

Caldwell, Erskine. *With All My Might: An Autobiography.* Atlanta: Peachtree Publishers, 1987. Although Caldwell wrote his autobiography, *Call It Experience,* in 1951, this new account of his life starts again at the beginning, sometimes covering the same material, sometimes adding new material, and sometimes interpreting the same events differently. In 1951 Caldwell was still considered a major American writer and his critical reputation rivaled that of Faulkner. But by 1987 Caldwell was remembered for only three novels and the stage production of *Tobacco Road. With All My Might,* however, does not address his declining reputation, nor does it place in perspective how major events in his life, such as his four marriages, affected his thinking or his art. In spite of Caldwell's reluctance to become personal with his reader, he tells his story with the usual Caldwell flair and offers tantalizing tidbits for anyone who has enjoyed the novels. **(A,G)**

Other Sources

Devlin, James E. *Erskine Caldwell.* Boston: Twayne, 1984.

McIver, Ray, ed. *The Black and White Stories of Erskine Caldwell.* Atlanta: Peachtree, 1984.

THOMAS CAMPION
1567-1620

Evaluation of Selected Biography and Criticism

Davis, Walter R. *Thomas Campion*. Boston: Twayne, 1987. Campion is considered one of the two great masters of rhymed lyric poetry, and the only important writer who was both a poet and composer. Davis' purpose is to explain how Campion's music and verse interact, showing how influential Campion was in every field he touched: Latin poetry; metrical theory (as champion of classical verse); English poetry (where he changed the direction of the Renaissance lyric); and music (where he replaced the madrigal with the ayre). Framed by chapters tracing Campion's life and reputation, the heart of this study analyzes Campion's poetry and music within the historical context of his time, then fuses the two with an excellent analysis of Campion's use of the court masque, where he joined music and poetry with stage spectacle, dance, and drama. This short, readable work provides an excellent introduction for the serious student. (A,G)

Lindley, David. *Thomas Campion*. Leiden, Netherlands: E. J. Brill, 1986. Lindley's four chapters cover Campion's poetry, music, poetry and music together, and his masques. His focus is on the structure of the poetry and the relationship among poems. Lindley's assumption is that the architecture of the poems resembles that of the music. He proceeds by arguing how the shared qualities of poetry and music reflect significant aesthetic movements within a period. Having established his groundwork, he demonstrates how Campion's masques are the ultimate social statement. This is a short, readable study for serious students of Campion or music. (A,G)

THOMAS CARLYLE
1795-1881

Autobiographical Sources

Ryals, Clyde de L., and Kenneth J. Fielding. *The Collected Letters of Thomas and Jane Welsh Carlyle, Vol. 13, 1841; Vol. 14, January-July 1842; Vol. 15, August-December 1842.* Durham, NC: Duke University Press, 1987. Now at fifteen volumes, this major contribution to Carlyle scholarship is only half complete. The letters offer both an intimate portrait of two of the most remarkable Victorians and an unrivaled portrait of Britain at the time. These witty letters will delight anyone interested in the period. (A,G)

Evaluation of Selected Biography and Criticism

apRoberts, Ruth. *The Ancient Dialect: Thomas Carlyle and Comparative Religion.* Berkeley: University of California Press, 1988. Carlyle developed very personal concepts of God and religion, which figure prominently into his ideas on the wonder and the mystery of the universe. In order to fully understand Carlyle's thought, it is necessary to trace his break with orthodox thought and his abiding interest in comparative religion. apRoberts skillfully traces and explains Carlyle's views and the influences that led to their development. Recommended for serious students and scholars of Carlyle. (A)

Rosenberg, John D. *Carlyle and the Burden of History.* Cambridge: Harvard University Press, 1985. In this fresh, lively study, Rosenberg explores Carlyle's poetic view of history. He believed that history had "a human voice" and that, in order to be understood, this voice had to be recreated from the smothering historical materials. For Carlyle, Rosenberg argues, the journey into history is a journey into the self; it is "the only Poetry." The poet-historian serves as an oracle and prophet as he performs "his ancient bardic role of singer and preserver of the deeds of the noble dead." Rosenberg connects Carlyle's historical theories with works of world literature to demonstrate Carlyle's responses to the burden of history. (A)

Timko, Michael. *Carlyle and Tennyson.* Iowa City: University of Iowa Press, 1988. Timko's study traces the complex history of mutual influence between Carlyle and Tennyson. Carlyle opened Tennyson's eyes to the multitude of Victorian social problems. Tennyson envisioned solutions that were gradualist, while Carlyle became apocalyptic in his outlook. As a result, Tennyson was more generally received, while Carlyle became increasingly more isolated. Unfortunately, this edition is an example of good ideas put into a shoddy package. Careless, if any, proofreading has left the text laced with errors that even distort the integrity of the quotations. (A,G)

Williams, A. Susan. *The Rich Man and the Diseased Poor in Early Victorian Literature*. Atlantic Highlands, NJ: Humanities, 1987. Williams begins her study with a discussion of the widespread incidence of disease and high mortality rates in the Victorian era. She then traces the use of the disease metaphor in the writings of Carlyle, Dickens, and Kingsley. The metaphor is split in its application to the upper classes and the lower classes, which suffered from poor sanitation and the lack of health care. Williams then shifts to the potential for social upheaval generated by the separation of the "two nations." While it is difficult to see how the last part of the discussion contributes to the first, her discussion of disease as metaphor is highly rewarding. (A,G)

Other Sources
Clubbe, John, and Jerome Meckier, eds. *Victorian Perspectives: Six Essays*. Newark: University of Delaware Press, 1989.

Cumming, Mark. *A Disimprisoned Epic: Form and Vision in Carlyle's French Revolution*. Philadelphia: University of Pennsylvania Press, 1988.

Helmling, Steven. *The Esoteric Comedies of Carlyle, Newman, and Yeats*. New York: Cambridge University Press, 1988.

La Bossiere, Camille R. *The Victorian Sage: Comparative Readings on Carlyle, Emerson, Melville and Conrad*. Lewisburg, PA: Bucknell University Press, 1988.

JOYCE CARY
1888-1957

Evaluation of Selected Biography and Criticism
Bishop, Alan. *Gentleman Rider: A Life of Joyce Cary*. London: Michael Joseph, 1988. This is the most comprehensive biography of Cary in print and may well prove definitive. Bishop divides Cary's life and career into two parts—"Man of Action/Writer" (1887-1919) and "Writer/Man of Action" (1920-1957). Cary's military career dominates the first part but his hunger for adventure is gradually tamed by an increasing devotion to his writing. Bishop makes extensive use of Cary's letters, autobiographical sketches, and unpublished works. These materials have been augmented by public interviews and personal conversations. Cary's works are discussed in the context of his life. A thorough bibliography is included. (A,G)

Christian, Edwin Ernest. *Joyce Cary's Critical Imagination*. New York: Peter Lang, 1988. In this study of Cary's novels, Christian attempts to trace the many expressions the novelist gave to his lifelong theme: how "creative imagination" shapes our response to life. For Christian, Cary's idea of creative imagination informed everything that he wrote and grew more subtle and complex over his career. His detailed examination of all of Cary's fiction should interest those who would like to explore Cary's work beyond *The Horse's Mouth*. (A,G)

Fisher, Barbara. *The House as a Symbol: Joyce Cary and The Turkish House*. Atlantic Highlands, NJ: Rodopi/Humanities, 1986. Fisher examines Cary's use of the house—in particular, the Turkish house—as a theme and symbol in his fiction. The working title for his first novel, *Prisoner of Grace,* was, in fact, "The Turkish House." Fisher examines the influences of Tolstoy and Dostoevsky and she documents influences at specific periods of Cary's career. Although Fisher tends to over-extend her arguments, moving from documented thoughts to educated guessing, the technique does provoke the reader to reconsider many assumptions about Cary's work. (A,G)

Fisher, Barbara, ed. *Joyce Cary Remembered in Letters and Interviews by His Family and Others*. Totowa, NJ: Barnes & Noble, 1988. This collection of sixty-seven short pieces offers many personal insights into Cary's life, his methods of composition, and the significance of his works. The reminiscences by those who were close to Cary have been grouped according to his family background and early years, his career, and his critical reputation. Included are tributes from several of Cary's more famous contemporaries, such as Iris Murdoch and Alec Guiness. Also included is a detailed chronology of Cary's life. (A,G)

Vander Closter, Susan. *Joyce Cary and Lawrence Durrell: A Reference Guide*. Boston: G. K. Hall, 1985. This guide to the critical response to two twentieth-century British authors consists of separate chronologically arranged annotated bibliographies. The Cary section covers the period 1932 until 1981; the Durrell bibliography begins with a 1937 review of *Panic Spring* and continues into 1983. The annotations are descriptive rather than evaluative and give a flavor of the work through a liberal use of quotations. Short introductions provide an overview of critical opinion on each writer. A useful resource for the student or researcher. (A)

WILLA CATHER
1873-1947

Autobiographical Sources

Bohlke, L. Brent, ed. *Willa Cather in Person: Interviews, Speeches, and Letters*. Lincoln: University of Nebraska Press, 1987. Most of the material in this collection consists of interviews that Cather gave to newspapers. These reveal not only her opinions but how they were viewed by the public. Since Cather's will forbade the publication of her letters, the ones included here have been previously published. Although the selections lack a coherent critical rationale, Bohlke has added to our knowledge of Cather by gathering these scattered fragments into a well-organized and thoroughly indexed volume. (A,G)

Evaluation of Selected Biography and Criticism

Ambrose, Jamie. *Willa Cather: Writing at the Frontier*. New York: Berg, 1989. Ambrose provides a concise critical introduction to the life and works of Willa Cather. Solidly researched and ably directed, the narrative examines the interrelations between Cather's life and fiction. (A,G,Y)

Arnold, Marilyn, ed. *Willa Cather: A Reference Guide*. G. K. Hall, 1986. This bibliography is a much-needed guide to the growing scholarship on Willa Cather. Concisely annotated citations are arranged chronologically from 1895 to 1984. Citations include biographical works as well as articles, book reviews, and criticism. Author and subject indexes provide easy access to the material. In an introduction, Arnold reliably surveys the trends in Cather biography and criticism. (A,G)

Bloom, Harold, ed. *Willa Cather's "My Ántonia."* New York: Chelsea House, 1987. This anthology reprints many of the best modern essays on Cather's *My Ántonia*. Illustrating a wide range of critical approaches, these twelve essays address the novel's structure, themes, imagery, mythic elements, and use of time and history. Contributors include David Daiches, Wallace Stegner, James E. Miller, Jr., Robert Scholes, Dorothy VanGhent, Blanche Gelfant, and Terence Martin. For the most part, these essays question the views of earlier critics, who interpreted the novel as a celebration of frontier life and viewed Ántonia as the embodiment of pioneer vitality. This is an excellent contribution to the study of Cather's novel that could also serve to introduce readers to a variety of critical perspectives. (A,G)

Callander, Marilyn Berg. *Willa Cather and the Fairy Tale*. Ann Arbor: UMI Research, 1989. Although brief (66 pages), this study opens the door to provocative insights about the symbolic reach of many of Cather's novels. Callander persuasively traces elements of fairy tales that "embroider the fabric of Cather's work" and provide the "primary symbols of romance." She limits her discussion to those novels with clear fairy tale allusions: Cinderella in *The Song of the Lark*; the fairy tale journey in *My Ántonia*; Sleeping Beauty and Snow White in *My Mortal Enemy*; the archetypes of the two brothers in *Death Comes for the Archbishop*; and Cather's own fairy tale in *Shadows on the Rock*. General readers will see a new dimension of Cather's work in this clearly written book. (G)

Donovan, Josephine. *After the Fall: The Demeter-Persephone Myth in Wharton, Cather, and Glasgow*. University Park: Pennsylvania State University Press, 1989. Donovan contends that the "Demeter-Diana-Persephone script" is preeminent in the literature of American women writers of the late nineteenth and early twentieth centuries. For Donovan, Persephone represents the "daughters" (feminine consciousness) that are whisked away into "patriarchal captivity." The Demeter-Diana world is related to the women's culture of the Victorian era, characterized by a marginal, segregated, "male-less" web of romantic female friendships. Donovan explores her thesis by devoting a section to each of these writers she feels most fully express the myth— Wharton, Cather, and Glasgow. Of special note is Donovan's discussion of the ritual basis of Cather's *My Ántonia*. (A)

Fryer, Judith. *Felicitous Space: The Imaginative Structures of Edith Wharton and Willa Cather*. Chapel Hill: University of North Carolina Press, 1986. Fryer's thesis is that because men have been given dominion over physical space and women relegated to "enclosure," the use of space as a structural device reflects the cultural responses of novelists to their society. Thus, Fryer examines the works of both writers to discover Wharton's "meticulously conceived interiors" and Cather's "unfurnished rooms" and "vast, empty landscapes." This insightful work is a good introduction to a French critical approach that has only recently managed to cross the Atlantic. (A)

Nelson, Robert J. *Willa Cather and France: In Search of the Lost Language*. Champaign: University of Illinois Press, 1988. Despite its title, this book is not about Cather's travels but rather an application of French deconstructive criticism to her novels. In applying this method, Nelson reveals the multiplicity of imagery, the richness of proper names, and the stripping of language that helps explain even Cather's sexual ambiguities. This complex critical approach may be of value to some scholars. (A)

O'Brien, Sharon. *Willa Cather: The Emerging Voice*. New York: Oxford University Press, 1986. This first book of a 2-volume biography covers the years 1873 from Cather's birth until 1913, when she published her first important novel, *O Pioneers*. O'Brien provides a fresh approach to Cather's years of growth and apprenticeship, a period neglected by other biographers and critics. In a late-Victorian culture that provided few literary role models, Cather first attempted to imitate men, then achieved an identity with women through an acceptance of her lesbianism. Initially, she was torn between two culturally opposed identities of art and womanhood but ultimately reconciled them. Besides offering considerable insight into Cather's personality, O'Brien's study is a valuable contribution to the study of gender and creativity. (A,G)

Rosowski, Susan J. *The Voyage Perilous: Willa Cather's Romanticism*. Lincoln: University of Nebraska Press, 1986. Rosowski's study divides Cather's fiction into distinct stages, each defined by a dominant theme or narrative mode. In her examination of the individual works she discusses fictional precedents and Cather's evolving style. Her schema works best with such works as *My Mortal Enemy* and *Sapphira and the Slave Girl*, but less well with *The Professor's House* or *My Ántonia*, where Cather's dominant themes become indistinct. Rosowski's approach, however, provides a handy way to compare and contrast Cather's earlier "pastoral" and later "gothic" fiction. Cather's recurrent themes—anguish of loss, the schism between life and art, the injuries caused by the abuse of personal power—are skillfully highlighted. This analysis is especially accessible to new readers of Cather. (A,G)

Thomas, Susie. *Willa Cather*. New York: Barnes & Noble, 1989. Thomas looks at Cather's work from a European perspective and argues that one of Cather's achievements was to "transcend the limitations of gender and nationality." She is particularly original in her analysis of Cather's response to European literature, music, and painting. This refreshing study provides a complement to the many recent feminist studies by American critics. (A)

Wagner-Martin, Linda. *The Modern American Novel, 1914-1945: A Critical History*. Boston: Twayne, 1989. Wagner-Martin presents a densely compact overview of modernist writers that flies in the face of the traditional critique that the modernists were a uniformly angst-ridden lot. Besides Faulkner, some of the authors treated are Cather, Stein, Hemingway, Norris, and Agee. This study goes beyond the traditional pantheon to treat many writers highly regarded during their times but nearly forgotten now—Nella Larsen, Meridel Le Sueur, Martha Gellhorn, and Henry Brown, among others. Black and woman modernists are "dusted off" and given their fair place on the shelf. This study is intended for a scholarly audience. (A)

Woodress, James. *Willa Cather: A Literary Life*. Lincoln: University of Nebraska Press, 1987. Until this biography, Cather scholars were hampered by the lack of information about certain periods of Cather's life. Woodress, editor of *American Literary Scholarship*, tackles the difficult task of filling in these voids and succeeds admirably. Using primary source material and the work of preceding scholars, he narrates the story of a strong-willed, prodigiously talented woman who put art before all else in her life. Woodress follows the perpetual traveler from season to season, explaining when and why she settled. As the story unfolds, the reader comes to realize how closely the novels reflect her real-life experiences. Woodress addresses and answers some of the continuing questions about Cather's celibacy and her disap- pointment with the reception of her novel *One of Ours*. The issue of Cather's ambivalent sexuality is examined with discretion. This is a readable, important biography for both the new facts uncovered and its sensitive interpretation of them. (A,G)

Other Sources
Lewis, Edith. *Willa Cather Living: A Personal Record.* Athens: Ohio University Press, 1989.

Murphy, John J. *"My Ántonia": The Road Home.* Boston: Twayne, 1989.

Rosnowski, Susan J. *Approaches to Teaching Cather's "My Ántonia".* New York: Modern Language Association, 1989.

Welsch, Roger L., and Linda K. Welsch. *Cather's Kitchens: Foodways in Literature and Life.* Lincoln: University of Nebraska Press, 1987.

MARGARET CAVENDISH
DUCHESS OF NEWCASTLE
1623-1673

Evaluation of Selected Biography and Criticism

Jones, Kathleen. *A Glorious Fame: The Life of Margaret Cavendish, Duchess of Newcastle, 1623-1673*. London: Bloomsbury, 1989. Jones focuses on Cavendish's personality, an almost schizophrenic duality of pathological shyness and flamboyance. She places Cavendish in the context of changing feminist ideas in Europe and England, and demonstrates her importance in asserting the rights of women, their individual emotions, and their ability to handle fame, wealth, professional careers, and humiliation. This is a short, readable biography that includes a bibliography. (A,G)

Mendelson, Sara Heller. *The Mental World of Stuart Women*. Amherst: University of Massachusetts Press, 1987. In this study of women's social history, Mendelson examines the context of the lives of three notable women of the Stuart period—Aphra Behn, Margaret Cavendish (Duchess of Newcastle), and Mary Rich (Countess of Warwick). She analyzes their writings to reveal an underlying conflict between self-identity and social roles. In this era, women struggled to publish against a patriarchal code that demanded them to be silent, modest, obedient, and chaste. (A,G)

GEORGE CHAPMAN
1559?-1634

Evaluation of Selected Biography and Criticism

Farley-Hills, David. *Jacobean Drama: A Critical Study of the Professional Drama, 1600-1625*. New York: St. Martin's, 1988. In this study Farley-Hills surveys English drama from 1600 to the death of James I, excluding Shakespeare. He divides his attention evenly among Marston, Jonson, Middleton, Chapman, Webster, and Fletcher. In most cases the focus is on the circumstances of production and related questions. In his treatment the playwrights and their works curiously appear to exist in a vacuum that is beyond the influence of the considerable political machinations of Jacobean England. Farley-Hills' contention seems to be that politics rarely intruded onto the professional stage. The approach is similar to Ann Jennalie Cook's study of Jacobean audiences, *The Privileged Playgoers of Shakespeare's London* (1981). (A,G)

Holaday, Allan, ed. *The Plays of George Chapman: The Tragedies with Sir Gyles Goosecappe. A Critical Edition*. Cambridge: D. S. Brewer, 1987. This much-needed critical edition supersedes all other collections, and should provide new material for Chapman scholars. This edition supplies textual introductions to each play; a table of press-variants; a collation of emendations made by the editor in deriving his critical text from his copy-text; a historical collation of variants from earlier editions; and textual notes dealing with cruxes. This volume contains all of Chapman's tragedies plus a comedy, which completes publication of all the plays now attributed to Chapman. (A)

Snare, Gerald. *The Mystification of George Chapman*. Durham, NC: Duke University Press, 1989. Snare argues that scholars have made Chapman's work unnecessarily obscure and difficult by creating theories which they, themselves, hardly understand. Snare examines the history of these theories and demonstrates why they are unnecessary to a correct (and fulfilling) understanding of Chapman. Whether or not critics agree with his combative views, both students and scholars will find much to discuss in this study. (A,G)

Other Sources

Corballis, Richard. *George Chapman's Minor Translations*. Dover, NH: Longwood, 1984.

Cummings, L. A. *Studies in the Autograph of George Chapman*. Dover, NH: Longwood, 1985.

THOMAS CHATTERTON
1752-1770

Evaluation of Selected Biography and Criticism

Ackroyd, Peter. *Chatterton*. New York: Grove, 1987. Chatterton, whose father died three months before his birth, was fascinated with the ancient church where his father had worked as a chorister. When his mother gave him scraps of a manuscript found in the church, Chatterton began writing; his mother said that he had fallen in love with antiquity. By sixteen, he had composed the "Rowley" sequence; at seventeen he moved to London to become a writer; a few months later he was dead of suicide. Shrouded in mystery, Chatterton's life has captured many imaginations. This fictionalized biography brings the few facts to life and serves as pleasurable reading for Chatterton enthusiasts. **(G)**

Haywood, Ian. *The Making of History: A Study of the Literary Forgeries of James MacPherson and Thomas Chatterton in Relation to Eighteenth-Century Ideas of History and Fiction*. Madison, NJ: Farleigh Dickinson University Press, 1986. Haywood examines the neglected literary forgeries of MacPherson and Chatterton within the context of the eighteenth-century debate about the relationship between history and fiction. He argues that the methods and techniques used by these authors had a basis in the historiographical theory of the time. Haywood sees the forgeries as anticipating the historical novel as it was later shaped by Sir Walter Scott. This is a detailed study useful to scholars of the period. **(A)**

Kaplan, Louise J. *The Family Romance of the Imposter-Poet Thomas Chatterton*. New York: Atheneum, 1987. Kaplan, a clinical psychologist, has published widely on adolescent behavior. One of her theories is that "when the exalted maternal ideal of masculinity replaces or overshadows the masculine ideal as represented by the father, this produces the emotional hothouse in which manifest perversions and character perversions, including certain failures of identification such as impostureness, seem to flourish." This disorder of "impostureness," totally absent in female behavior, is the male equivalent of anorexia, which is rare in males. The fatherless Chatterton, whose teenage years were legendary for sexual promiscuity and alleged perversity, seemed to fall directly into Kaplan's theory, but during the course of her investigation she discovered new wrinkles in her theory and Chatterton's life. Kaplan's well-documented psychoanalysis is fascinating and her explanation of his suicide plausible. This study will interest students of Chatterton, literary biography, and psychology. **(A,G)**

GEOFFREY CHAUCER
1343?-1400

Evaluation of Selected Biography and Criticism

Aers, David. *Chaucer: An Introduction.* Atlantic Highlands, NJ: Humanities, 1986. Aers examines many of Chaucer's major themes in this introductory study, including his representations of society, religion, marriage, and sexual relations. He takes a broadly humanistic approach. His goal is to stimulate readers to follow their own instincts when studying Chaucer, to generate their own questions, and to pursue the answers by a variety of critical methods, rather than narrowing their interpretation according to a particular critical school. This is a fine introduction to Chaucer for newcomers to the field or for those with a general interest in the subject. **(A,G)**

Benson, C. David. *Chaucer's Drama of Style: Poetic Variety and Contrast in the Canterbury Tales.* Chapel Hill, NC: University of North Carolina Press, 1986. Benson's study seeks to go beyond what he terms the "increasingly outdated" dramatic theory approach to Chaucer's work. In his examination of the individual tales, Benson isolates significant oppositions, discrepancies, and variations to build his case against dramatic theory. The uniqueness of each tale, according to Benson, does not derive from the individualized narrators but from Chaucer's use of differing narrative principles. This is a provocative thesis in Chaucer criticism and certainly not the last word in this ongoing debate. **(A)**

Blamires, Alcuin. *"The Canterbury Tales."* Atlantic Highlands, NJ: Humanities, 1987. Blamires offers a concise and balanced overview of the last twenty years of critical scholarship on Chaucer's *The Canterbury Tales.* The first section provides a survey of critical perspective that makes such distinctions as "Old New Criticism" and "Brand New Critical Theory." The second section, an appraisal of the state of current scholarship, discusses topics such as Chaucer's "play of mind," "narrative resonance," and "audacity." The annotated bibliography is as comprehensive and useful as any in print. This study is recommended for those who already have some acquaintance with Chaucer and who are seeking to broaden their perspective. **(A)**

Boitani, Piero and Jill Mann, eds. *The Cambridge Chaucer Companion.* Cambridge: Cambridge University Press, 1986. This is a manageable companion whose expressed intention is to help readers enjoy Chaucer, not intimidate them with Chaucerian scholarship. Both students and scholars will find a wealth of information in these essays by renowned critics. Topics range from influences on Chaucer to his style and contribution to developing Middle English. **(A,G)**

Hornsby, Joseph Allen. *Chaucer and the Law*. Norman, OK: Pilgrim Books, 1988. Chaucer's works are full of legal references, especially to contract and criminal law, and scholars have long assumed that Chaucer had some legal training. Hornsby offers an explanation of Chaucer's law knowledge, where he might have acquired it, and what the laws mean in the context of his work. As one might expect, this study is dry, though illuminating and important to Chaucer scholars. **(A)**

Howard, Donald R. *Chaucer: His Life, His Works, His World*. New York: Dutton, 1987. This encyclopedic work recreates every aspect of Chaucer's life and world, from his personality to his travels. All that is known about Chaucer is included here, and Howard's excellent scholarly conjecture fills in the gaps. This readable study will fascinate anyone interested in the poet or the period. **(A,G)**

Jordan, Robert M. *Chaucer's Poetics and the Modern Reader*. Berkeley: University of California Press, 1987. This book follows Jordan's important study, *Chaucer and the Shape of Creation* (1967). Here, he approaches several critical issues, especially Chaucerian techniques as they relate to postmodern critical theories. Jordan argues that Chaucer mistrusted language as a means to convey truth, that he developed a rhetorically based aesthetic, and that he was self-consciously aware of language. Recommended for scholars. **(A)**

Knight, Stephen Thomas. *Geoffrey Chaucer*. Oxford: Basil Blackwell, 1986. In this factually sound but strongly opinionated work, Knight delves into the underlying social and political forces at work in Chaucer's poetry. His tone is by turns serious and playful as he takes on the "establishment" critics over such issues as the sexuality and symbolism in the "Wife of Bath's Tale." Knight's analysis is often excessively narrow but his eccentricity and enthusiasm are enough to recommend it to students of Chaucer. **(A,G)**

Leyerle, John. *Chaucer: A Bibliographical Introduction*. Toronto: University of Toronto Press, 1986. This compilation of Chaucer citations, the first in recent years, surveys all material before 1980. The entries are classified into three sections—materials with which to study Chaucer's works, criticism of individual works, and materials descriptive of the time period. Coverage is broad, but the annotations are often too brief to be very useful. **(A)**

Lindahl, Carl. *Earnest Games: Folkloric Patterns in The Canterbury Tales*. Bloomington: Indiana University Press, 1987. This study is an ambitious attempt to show that Chaucer adopted the stance of "folk poet" to protect himself from the wrath of royal censors. Lindahl includes a survey of slander laws and legal actions during the reign of Richard II which is thorough and useful. This study should interest folklorists as well as Chaucerians. **(A)**

North, J. D. *Chaucer's Universe*. Oxford: Clarendon Press, 1988. Scholars have long known that Chaucer was fascinated with astrology, and that the stars were tangentially connected to the structure of his verse and the personalities of his characters. North, however, takes Chaucer's interest in the universe light years beyond previous criticism, arguing that Chaucer's knowledge of astronomy far surpassed what has been believed. North presents medieval principles of astronomy, the nature and use of an astrolabe and Chaucer's *Treatise on the Astrolabe,* the astronomical tables of John Somer and Nicholas Lynn, the nature and use of an equatory, and the theory and rules of astrology. He concludes that Chaucer's poems were meticulously planned around the universal structure. **(A)**

Olson, Paul A. *The Canterbury Tales and the Good Society.* Princeton: Princeton University Press, 1987. Olson details Chaucer's society and argues that his comedy is derived from the dynamics of the social structure and realities of his times. This is a highly specialized book intended for scholars. **(A)**

Rowe, Donald. *Through Nature to Eternity: Chaucer's "Legend of Good Women."* Lincoln: University of Nebraska Press, 1988. Scholars have maintained that *The Legend of Good Women* is so dull that Chaucer abandoned his effort to finish it, and although the Prologue has been praised for its lyric beauty, little serious attention has been paid to the nine legends. In this study, Rowe establishes a thesis that may open new readings. Noting the references to "heaven" and "hell" in the Prologue, Rowe argues that these are catchwords which provide keys to understanding the descent into and out of hell, a journey that parallels Dante's *Inferno.* Serious students of Chaucer will find much to celebrate in this important revisionist study. **(A)**

Traversi, Derek. *Chaucer: The Earlier Poetry.* Newark: University of Delaware Press, 1987. Traversi offers an excellent analysis of *The Book of the Duchess, The House of Fame, The Parliament of Fowls,* and *Trolius and Criseyde* to demonstrate how Chaucer was dissatisfied with the limitations of verse techniques. Traversi convincingly explains why Chaucer was driven to experiment with themes, rhythms, language, and techniques to produce the first original poetry in English, *The Canterbury Tales.* Good students will find much of interest here, as well as fresh ideas for interpreting Chaucer. **(A)**

Williams, David. *The Canterbury Tales: A Literary Pilgrimage.* Boston: Twayne, 1987. Within the tales themselves, says Williams, Chaucer was carrying on a debate between nominalism and realism. He contends that beneath the surface of the narrative there is a structure that reveals the nature of fiction itself. In his view, Chaucer, the audience, the characters, and the tales become interchangeable commodities that reveal underlying "market forces." What promises to be a sweeping revelation of Chaucer's profound insight into his own work is hampered by the brevity of this provocative study. **(A,G)**

Other Sources
Anderson, David, ed. *Sixty Bokes Olde and Newe: Manuscripts and Early Printed Books from Libraries in and Near Philadelphia Illustrating Chaucer's Sources, His Works, and Their Influence.* Charlottesville: University Press of Virginia, 1986.

Baird-Lange, Lorrayne Y., and Hildegard Schnuttgen, eds. *A Bibliography of Chaucer, 1974-1985.* Hamden, CT: Archon, 1988.

Birney, Earle. *Essays on Chaucerian Irony.* Toronto: University of Toronto Press, 1985.

Bowden, Betsy. *Chaucer Aloud: The Varieties of Textual Interpretation.* Philadelphia: University of Pennsylvania Press, 1987.

Daichman, Graciela. *Wayward Nuns in Medieval Literature.* Syracuse, NY: Syracuse University Press, 1986.

Davenport, W. A. *Chaucer: Complaint and Narrative.* Dover, NH: Longwood, 1988.

De Weever, Jacqueline. *A Chaucer Name Dictionary: Guide to Astrological, Biblical, Historical, Literary, and Mythological Names in the Works of Geoffrey Chaucer.* New York: Garland, 1988.

Ellis, Roger. *Patterns of Religious Narrative in the Canterbury Tales.* London: Croom Helm, 1986.

Ferster, J. *Chaucer on Interpretation.* New York: Cambridge University Press, 1985.

Fisher, John H., and Mark Allen. *The Essential Chaucer: An Annotated Bibliography of Major Modern Studies.* Boston: G. K. Hall, 1987.

Holloway, Julia B. *The Pilgrim and the Book: A Study of Dante, Langland and Chaucer.* New York: Peter Lang, 1987.

Kendrick, Laura. *Chaucerian Play: Comedy and Control in the Canterbury Tales.* Berkeley: University of California Press, 1988.

Knapp, Peggy. *Chaucer and the Social Contest.* New York: Routledge Chapman and Hall, 1989.

Koff, Leonard M. *Chaucer and the Art of Storytelling.* Berkeley: University of California Press, 1988.

Lawton, David. *Chaucer's Narrators.* Cambridge: D.S. Brewer, 1985.

McBride, M. F. *Chaucer's Physician and Fourteenth Century Medicine: A Compendium for Students.* Bristol, IN: Wyndham Hall, 1985.

Mehl, Dieter. *Geoffrey Chaucer: An Introduction to His Narrative Poetry.* New York: Cambridge University Press, 1986.

Mitchell, Jerome. *Scott, Chaucer, and Medieval Romance: A Study in Sir Walter Scott's Indebtedness to the Literature of the Middle Ages.* Lexington: University Press of Kentucky, 1987.

Rogers, William E. *Upon the Ways: The Structure of "The Canterbury Tales."* Victoria: University of Victoria Press, 1986.

Sandved, Arthur O. *Introduction to Chaucerian English.* Dover, NH: Longwood, 1985.

Sklute, Larry. *Virtue of Necessity: Inconclusiveness and Narrative Form in Chaucer's Poetry.* Columbus: The Ohio State University Press, 1985.

Smith, Jeremy J. *The English of Chaucer.* Elmsford, NY: Pergamon, 1989.

Stone, Brian. *Chaucer.* New York: Penguin, 1989.

Taylor, Karla. *Chaucer Reads "The Divine Comedy."* Stanford, CA: Stanford University Press, 1989.

Wallace, David. *Chaucer and the Early Writings of Boccaccio.* Dover, NH: Longwood, 1985.

Wasserman, Julian, and Robert Blanch, eds. *Chaucer in the Eighties.* Syracuse, NY: Syracuse University Press, 1986.

Weiss, Alexander. *Chaucer's Native Heritage.* New York: Peter Lang, 1985.

JOHN CHEEVER
1912-1982

Autobiographical Sources
Cheever, Benjamin, ed. *The Letters of John Cheever*. New York: Simon & Schuster. 1988. Although not intended as literary works, Cheever's letters to John Updike, Saul Bellow, Josephine Herbst, Malcolm Cowley, Frederick Exley, and Philip Roth exhibit both his unmistakable wit and bristling scorn. Benjamin Cheever, the author's son, tells his own story through commentaries interwoven with the letters and describes the passions and faults of his alcoholic father. A must for the scholar of Cheever's work, this collection of letters reveals the dark contradictions inherent in his life. **(A)**

Donaldson, Scott, ed. *Conversations with John Cheever*. Jackson: University Press of Mississippi, 1987. This anthology collects published interviews, magazine articles, and radio and television interviews with Cheever between 1940 and 1985. Most of them were conducted after 1975, following his successful treatment for alcoholism. After his cure, Cheever became "entirely forthright about his alcoholism and his marriage and very nearly so about his sexual orientation." Donaldson has reprinted the published interviews in full and has only slightly edited the audio interviews for intelligibility. A useful collection of hard to find material for the Cheever reader and critic. **(A,G)**

Evaluation of Selected Biography and Criticism
Donaldson, Scott. *John Cheever: A Biography*. New York: Random House, 1988. Donaldson, who has written biographies of Fitzgerald and Hemingway, produces the first in-depth look at Cheever and his works. Donaldson explores the premise that as an adolescent, Cheever suffered from emotional neglect and guilt over his bisexuality. He shows the relation of the writer's manic-depressive personality to the thematic structure of his work. With a deft touch, Donaldson also examines the author's various affairs and deepening alcoholism that eventually lead to problems in his career and the collapse of his marriage. A sensitive reappraisal of Cheever's work—particularly his short stories—is interwoven into the narrative, but the literary side of the man often takes a back seat to his troubled personality. Combined with *The Letters of John Cheever*, edited by his son, and two other biographies written by Cheever's son and daughter, Donaldon's book provides a rounded portrait of an esteemed writer whose personal life was dark and scandalous. **(A,G)**

O'Hara, James E. *John Cheever: A Study of the Short Fiction*. Boston: Twayne, 1989. In this study O'Hara gives an overview of the 154 short stories written by Cheever between 1930 and 1981. He believes that Cheever's short fiction written after World War II established him as an accomplished master. On the heels of popular success, Cheever entered a period of personal

92

decline culminating in an alcoholic crisis at the age of 63. O'Hara believes that following his cure, Cheever was able "to recover the sense of spiritual balance that characterizes the best work of his earlier years." In addition to a critical analysis of the short fiction, O'Hara has included a short selection from Cheever's correspondence, two brief interviews, and five short critical excerpts. A valuable addition to Cheever criticism. (A,G)

CHARLES WADDELL CHESNUTT
1858-1932

Evaluation of Selected Biography and Criticism

Callahan, John F. *In the African-American Grain: The Pursuit of Voice in Twentieth-Century Black Fiction.* Champaign: University of Illinois Press, 1988. This thematic study of narrative voice links aspects of folk culture to the works of several generations of black writers. Callahan focuses on the folk tradition of call and response and how it influenced the narrative voice. He compares the tales of Joel Chandler Harris and Chesnutt to show how the authors used folk expressions to articulate democratic ideals. Callahan explores the lyrical qualities of Jean Toomer's *Cane*, which is expressed in a "musical" rather than rhetorical voice. Examining Zora Hurston's *Their Eyes Were Watching God* and the *Autobiography of Jane Pittman,* he shows how the conventions of storytelling are used to establish an interactive relationship with the reader. Turning to Ralph Ellison's *Invisible Man*, Callahan traces the emotional development of the narrator through a careful analysis of the speeches. Callahan stresses the essential "Americanness" of these works, placing them in the line of Emerson and democratic idealism. (A,G)

Schulman, Robert. *Social Criticism and Nineteenth-Century American Fictions.* Columbia: University of Missouri Press, 1987. Schulman examines the political psychology of capitalism and its influence on the lives and works of some of the most famous American authors—Chesnutt, Franklin, Twain, Melville, Hawthorne, Whitman, Wharton, Howells, and Dreiser. His study pursues three main themes—the fragmentation of community, the impact of social change, and the styles of American individualism. This is truly a new and refreshing reevaluation of nineteenth-century American literature. (A,G)

G. K. CHESTERTON
1874-1936

Evaluation of Selected Biography and Criticism

Coren, Michael. *Gilbert: The Man Who Was G. K. Chesterton.* New York: Paragon, 1990. Coren's biography is an adoring look at this prolific poet, novelist, and essayist. While attempting a carefully balanced treatment of controversial aspects of Chesterton's writing, Coren glosses over his strongly held opinions—the very core of Chesterton's power and personality. While this book is generally entertaining, the researcher must yet await the definitive Chesterton biography. (A,G)

Ffinch, Michael. *G.K. Chesterton.* New York: Harper & Row, 1987. Chesterton, a widely celebrated novelist and thinker in his day, is best remembered now for his Father Brown detective stories. In this biography, Ffinch presents the known facts and offers an interpretation that strays little from the middle ground. One of the central events of Chesterton's life was his conversion to Catholicism, which is described by Ffinch as his solution to inner turmoil. Beneath Chesterton's jolly exterior lurked a few dark demons, but Ffinch describes them only from a distance. (A,G)

Jaki, Stanley L. *Chesterton, A Seer of Science.* Champaign: University of Illinois Press, 1986. Chesterton has been described in previous studies as a Seer of Philosophy and a Seer of Theology. Now, Jaki presents a case for Chesterton as Seer of Science. Chesterton, the unabashed genius who astonished the Thomists with his book on Aquinas and overwhelmed the philosophers with his extraordinary intuitions, now startles us with his perceptions of the sciences and scientific method. This detailed approach might overwhelm the average reader were the topic not so aptly and succinctly set forth by Jaki. (A,G)

Other Sources

Dale, Alzina S. *The Art of G. K. Chesterton.* Chicago: Loyola, 1985.

Lauer, Quentin. *G. K. Chesterton: Philosopher Without Portfolio.* New York: Fordham University Press, 1988.

MacDonald, Michael H., ed. *G. K. Chesterton and C. S. Lewis: The Riddle Joy.* Grand Rapids, MI: Eerdmans, 1989.

KATE CHOPIN
1851-1904

Evaluation of Selected Biography and Criticism

Elfenbein, Anna Shannon. *Women on the Color Line: Evolving Stereotypes and the Writings of George Washington Cable, Grace King, Kate Chopin.* Charlottesville: University Press of Virginia, 1989. Elfenbein examines the way in which three post-Civil War southern writers used and modified the stereotype of the mixed-race female. After reviewing the social and fictional history of the stereotype, she turns to Cable's *The Grandissimes,* King's "Monsieur Motte," and Chopin's *The Awakening.* She concludes that their treatment of the stereotype indicts the "social masquerades that inscribe race, class, and gender difference, thereby fixing an individual's life chances from birth." (A)

Koloski, Bernard, ed. *Approaches to Teaching Chopin's "The Awakening."* New York: Modern Language Association, 1988. These twenty-one essays have been contributed by faculty members in English, philosophy, history, and women's studies departments across the country. Designed to assist the college classroom instructor, the suggested approaches to Chopin's *The Awakening* would also be useful to the advanced student or interested reader who is looking for new ways to approach this complex work. (A,G)

Martin, Wendy, ed. *New Essays on "The Awakening."* Cambridge: Cambridge University Press, 1988. Much of the critical work done on Chopin's *The Awakening* has been grounded in the New Criticism. Martin has collected essays that expand the focus to include other approaches and methodologies. Contributions by Michael Gilmore, Andrew Delbanco, and Cristina Giorcelli relate the work to modernism, examine the role of the heroine, or provide a European critical perspective. The editor's introduction provides information on the novel's composition, publication history, and popular reception. This anthology is nicely complimentary to the Norton critical edition. (A)

Skaggs, Peggy. *Kate Chopin.* Boston: G. K. Hall/Twayne, 1985. Chopin has been variously characterized by critics ever since the publication of her famous novel, *The Awakening,* in 1899. According to Skaggs, she has been viewed as "a feminist, a local colorist, a regionalist, a romantic, a neotranscendentalist, an antiromantic, a realist, a naturalist, and an existentialist." Skaggs explicates all of Chopin's works, including those unpublished or unfinished, to demonstrate the richness and complexity of a writer whom critics have only recently begun to recognize. (A,G)

Taylor, Helen. *Gender, Race, and Region in the Writings of Grace King, Ruth McEnery Stuart, and Kate Chopin.* Baton Rouge: Louisiana State University Press, 1989. Taylor studies the relationship between racism and feminism in the works of three nineteenth-century white women writers. Her thesis is that gender alters cultural assumptions to provide an essential alternative perspective to historical and cultural events. Taylor examines Chopin for her relations to European male realists and feminists, and explains some of the reasons behind these writers' ideology of "southern local color." **(A)**

Other Sources

Bonner, Thomas, Jr. *Kate Chopin Dictionary*. New York: Garland, 1985.

Bonner, Thomas, Jr. *The Kate Chopin Companion: With Chopin's Translations from French Fiction*. Westport, CT: Greenwood, 1988.

Toth, Emily. *Kate Chopin*. New York: Atheneum/Macmillan, 1988.

AGATHA CHRISTIE
1890-1976

Evaluation of Selected Biography and Criticism

Gill, Gillian. *Agatha Christie*. New York: Free Press, 1990. Harvard professor Gill conducts her own impressive sleuthing to turn up clues about the elusive Christie. She believes Christie concealed her personality in her fiction, and she sets out to analyze the personality of a woman whom critics have often portrayed as a proper Victorian but whom Gill discovers is lusty and adventuresome. This enjoyable biography brings out the detective instincts in the reader and affirms why Christie is, herself, a master sleuth. (A,G)

Hart, Anne. *The Life and Times of Miss Jane Marple*. New York: Dodd, Mead, 1985. Analyzing a mystery writer's detective character who appears in a great number of novels presents a challenge to the critic. Hart solves this problem by fashioning a fictional biography of Christie's fictional character. Hart's book is less a critical analysis than an appreciation, but is a testament to the devotion that legions of Christie fans have for Miss Marple. (G)

Hart, Anne. *The Life and Times of Hercule Poirot*. New York: Putnam, 1990. Hart has followed her "biography" of Miss Jane Marple, with one chronicling Christie's famous detective, Hercule Poirot. She traces the shrewd dandy from his first appearance in *The Mysterious Affair at Styles* (1921) to his demise in *Curtain* (1975), which may spur a closer look at Christie's methods of characterization. Contains a useful bibliography of all Poirot's appearances. (G)

Wagoner, Mary S. *Agatha Christie*. Boston: Twayne, 1986. Following a brief discussion of Christie's life, Wagoner examines the novels in chronological order. She sees Christie's power as that of a master storyteller who excelled at keeping literary formulas fresh despite repeated use. For Wagoner, Christie variously combined four different kinds of writing: formulas, romantic treatment of fairy-tale motifs, supernaturalism, and comedy of manners. She discusses Christie's considerable body of work, including the plays, romances, spy thrillers, and autobiographical writings. The bibliography gives a list of Christie's works and annotated secondary sources. (A,G)

Other Sources

Morselt, Ben. *An A to Z of the Novels and Short Stories of Agatha Christie*. New York: David and Charles, 1985.

Sanders, Dennis. *The Agatha Christie Companion: The Complete Guide to Agatha Christie's Life and Work*. New York: Delacorte, 1984.

JOHN CLARE
1793-1864

Author's Recent Bibliography

Clare, John. *The Parish*. New York: Viking Penguin, 1985. Over a century and a half after it was originally composed, Clare's satirical poem, *The Parish*, is printed in this edition at its complete length of 2200 lines. Editor Eric Robinson has added a critical introduction that discusses biographical elements in the poem and clarifies the poem's textual history. David Powell provides notes to clarify obscure passages. Previously, only about 1190 lines of the poem had been published in Feinstein's *Selected Poems* (1968). (A,G)

Evaluation of Selected Biography and Criticism

Clare, Johanne. *John Clare and the Bounds of Circumstance*. Montreal: McGill-Queen's University Press, 1987. Clare's life was a struggle against class prejudice, poverty, hard labor, and haggles with patrons and publishers. It ended in a complete mental breakdown. Johanne Clare moves between biography and criticism as she chronicles the persistence of an undereducated laborer in striving for a life of the imagination. Clare's is a story of courage and defeat, whose ultimate victory is attested to by his critics. (A,G)

Sale, Roger. *Closer to Home*. Cambridge: Harvard University Press, 1988. Sale, a critic at home in many literary periods, addresses the treatment of place in the works of five English authors, including Austen, Clare, Cragge, and Wordsworth. The local landscape and society strongly influenced all five writers and became became a principal theme and structural device for their art. Sale contends that these authors broke away from the established pictorial treatment of landscape to produce a psychological response to place and time. This, in turn, set the stage for the realism that would emerge in the writings of the Victorians, especially Hardy, Dickens, and Eliot. Sale offers fresh and provocative ideas for interpreting each of these writers. (A,G)

Williams, Merryn, and Raymond Williams. *John Clare, Selected Poetry and Prose*. London and New York: Methuen, 1986. The editors, who note that Clare is attracting more readers with each decade of the twentieth century, provide the social, cultural, historical, and critical contexts for understanding his life and works. The selected poems are mostly concerned with the theme of freedom. This readable edition with notes is valuable to all students. (A,G)

Other Sources

Storey, Mark, ed. *The Letters of John Clare*. New York: Oxford University Press, 1986.

ARTHUR HUGH CLOUGH
1819-1861

Evaluation of Selected Biography and Criticism
   Kenny, Anthony. *God and Two Poets: Arthur Hugh Clough and Gerard Manley Hopkins*. London: Sidgwick & Jackson, 1988. Kenny, a philosopher rather than literary critic, believes that Clough and Hopkins are the two most significant English religious poets of the nineteenth century, and it is their philosophy, not their poetry, that draws them together. Kenny begins by establishing the basic biographies of both poets, tracing their education in philosophy at Oxford. He discusses Clough's move from Anglicanism to agnosticism and Hopkins' conversion to Catholicism. He presents a lucid comparison of their beliefs on prayer, scripture, original sin, the sacramental system, and the relation of religion and politics. (A)

SAMUEL TAYLOR COLERIDGE
1772-1834

Evaluation of Selected Biography and Criticism

Barth, J. Robert. *Coleridge and the Power of Love.* Columbia: University of Missouri Press, 1989. This study by a noted scholar of Romanticism, examines a single theme—Coleridge and the power of love. Consciously indebted to Anthony John Harding's work on the same topic (*Coleridge and the Idea of Love*), Barth examines Coleridge's ideal of love as expressed in his life and art. A developing image of love is traced through the conversation poems, the poems of high imagination, and the penultimate poem—"Dejection: An Ode." Barth's insightful observations of Coleridge can also be extrapolated to other romantic poets obsessed with the ideal. (A,G)

Bate, Jonathan. *Shakespeare and the English Romantic Imagination.* Oxford: Oxford University Press, 1986. In this well-written study, Bate examines the influence of Shakespeare on Byron, Coleridge, Wordsworth, Keats, and Blake. He examines how each poet's critical theory developed either out of or as a reaction to Shakespeare's poetic identity. This is a large field to cover, and Bate's study is a creditable overview that should be useful for anyone studying the English romantics. (A,G)

Coleman, Deirdre. *Coleridge and "The Friend" (1809-1810).* New York: Oxford University Press, 1989. Between 1809 and 1810 Coleridge issued a periodical philosophical journal, entitled *The Friend,* which he considered a "well-kept secret." Coleman provides the first full-length study of the journal that most other scholars have dismissed as inconsequential and finds it full of intimations of the poet's future development. The influence of Kant on Coleridge's political thinking at this time is evident. (A)

Engell, James. *Forming the Critical Mind: Dryden to Coleridge.* Cambridge: Harvard University Press, 1989. Engell presents a lucid discussion of the origins and theories of eighteenth-century literary criticism with special emphasis on Dryden, Johnson, and Hume. After dividing criticism into its component preoccupations—genre, canon, refinement, and form—he then attempts to relate these to modern critical theories. This book is recommended to students for its methodology as well as for its argument. (A)

Fraser, Hilary. *Beauty and Belief: Aesthetics and Religion in Victorian Literature.* Cambridge: Cambridge University Press, 1986. In this specialized study in intellectual history, Fraser traces the relationship between religion and aesthetic doctrine from Coleridge and Wordsworth through the aestheticism of Walter Pater and Oscar Wilde. Fraser argues that through concepts propounded by Hopkins, Ruskin, Arnold, and the Oxford aesthetes, Christianity is reduced to a merely subjective religion of art. (A)

Greenberg, Martin. *The Hamlet Vocation of Coleridge and Wordsworth.* Iowa City: University of Iowa Press, 1986. The separation of mind and action, according to Greenburg, represents the current situation of modern civilization. Shakespeare's Hamlet is described as the prototypical character whose attitude revealed a preoccupation with the inner world that worked to defeat the outer man. Both Coleridge and Wordsworth were "called" to adopt inward lives of reflection unsuited to the practical life. Thus, the work of both poets—through inner reflection and outward "defeat"—provides insight into the current human condition. **(A)**

Holmes, Richard. *Coleridge: Early Visions.* New York: Viking, 1990. Drawing from the voluminous letters, journals, and poetry, Holmes renders Coleridge's early years in a style that gives the sense that Coleridge is narrating his own life. This humorous, readable biography traces the growth of Coleridge's imagination until he sets sail for Malta at age 31. First published in Great Britain in 1989, this first of a two-part biography won England's prestigious Whitbread Prize. The second volume, *Coleridge: Later Reflections* will cover the last thirty-five years. These two accounts will supersede previous biographies. **(A,G)**

Leask, Nigel. *The Politics of Imagination in Coleridge's Critical Thought.* New York: St. Martin's, 1988. In the Prefaces to each edition of the *Lyrical Ballads* Coleridge and Wordsworth addressed the power of poetry to shape social awareness and action. Both poets drew on social change for the subject matter of their work, but Coleridge went on to develop his ideas about art, knowledge, and the imagination in his mammoth, unfinished *Biographia Literaria.* In this study, Leask begins by examining Wordsworth's developing aesthetics and how Coleridge altered or modified them. He goes on to explain the impact of Kant and Schelling on Coleridge's thought and to define the relationship between Coleridge's politics and imagination. **(A)**

Lefebure, Molly. *The Bondage of Love: A Life of Mrs. Samuel Taylor Coleridge.* New York: Norton, 1987. Drawing upon previously unavailable sources, Lefebure constructs a revised image of Sara Fricker Coleridge, the much maligned wife of Samuel Taylor Coleridge. Lefebure richly renders their relationship and explores the couple's curious interactions with the Wordsworths, the Southeys, Sarah Hutchinson, and others. Of special interest are Lefebure's observations on the nature and progression of Coleridge's addiction to laudanum. With his family torn asunder, his career in decline, he finally achieved a reconciliation with his wife in the last 18 months of his life. **(A,G)**

Magnuson, Paul. *Coleridge and Wordsworth: A Lyrical Dialogue.* Princeton: Princeton University Press, 1988. Magnuson's assumption is that it is more important to see the connections between the poems of these two poets than it is to study the integral unity of individual poems. He argues that Wordsworth and Coleridge were so influenced by each other that their poems result in a dialogue that reveals a process of negation, interrogation, and interruption. Individual poems, therefore, are most revealingly seen as fragments of a long lyrical sequence. Magnuson argues his points carefully, and the result is an intriguing study for scholars and students of Romanticism. (A)

McKusick, James C. *Coleridge's Philosophy of Language.* New Haven: Yale University Press, 1986. McKusick sets out to describe Coleridge as a coherent linguistic philosopher and for the most part succeeds. A highlight of this study is an overview of debates over the naturalness of language from Classical times to the present. The task of applying modern linguistic theory to Coleridge is not easy, but McKusick's prose is always lucid and informative. Recommended as a model for making a difficult subject accessible. (A,G)

Metzger, Lore. *One Foot in Eden: Modes of Pastoral in Romantic Poetry.* Chapel Hill, NC: University of North Carolina Press, 1986. In this study, Metzger traces the influence of classical pastoralism on the works of some of the major romantics—Blake, Coleridge, Wordsworth, and Keats. In the process, he provides an important overview of English romanticism. Drawing upon Schiller's thesis that pastoral innocence must be put to a more practical test, Metzger examines the question of whether individuality and ideality can be truthfully expressed in the same work of art. For the most part, she concludes, the English romantics only intensified the dissonance between the ideal and the real world. This book is recommended for scholars and students of the romantic period. (A)

Modiano, Raimonda. *Coleridge and the Concept of Nature.* Gainesville: University Presses of Florida, 1985. Modiano argues that Coleridge came to believe that people rather than nature were the appropriate means for communicating with God. This, she believes, integrates Coleridge's ideas about love with his concerns about a personal God. This rich, complex study explores the relation of Coleridge's philosophical thinking about God and nature to his literary work. (A)

Newlyn, Lucy. *Coleridge, Wordsworth, and the Language of Allusion.* Oxford: Oxford University Press, 1986. Newlyn examines the early poetry of Coleridge and Wordsworth to reveal an intricate structure of similar allusions in each poet's work. According to Newlyn's reading, Coleridge dominated Wordsworth intellectually and artistically, particularly in the first six months of their association. Her assessment of the relationship is part of an ongoing critical controversy that shows little sign of waning. Although this is primarily a book for scholars, the style and tone are accessible to any student of English romanticism. (A,G)

Piper, H. W. *The Singing of Mount Abora: Coleridge's Use of Biblical Imagery and Natural Symbolism in Poetry and Philosophy.* Madison, NJ: Fairleigh Dickinson University Press, 1987. Piper is the author of *The Active Universe* (1962), a critically acclaimed appraisal of the significance of Wordsworth and Coleridge. In this clear and concise study that combines a close reading of the poems with biography, Piper distills the results of a lifetime of scholarship. His reevaluation of the role of Unitarian doctrines in Coleridge's early life and works makes this a work of importance. (A,G)

Roe, Nicholas. *Wordsworth and Coleridge: The Radical Years at Oxford.* New York: Oxford University Press, 1988. From 1789 to 1798 the winds of revolution were so strong in England and France that Wordsworth and Coleridge moved to Germany. Roe's detailed research focuses on Romanticism as a political and social movement, rather than a literary response to nature, and places these poets squarely in the center of political upheaval. This is an exciting narrative of two fascinating men. (A,G)

Rzepka, Charles J. *The Self as Mind: Vision and Identity in Wordsworth, Coleridge, and Keats.* Cambridge: Harvard University Press, 1986. Rzepka's thesis is that visionary egocentricity can lead to isolation, driving the poet into prolific and creative periods in which he tests the reality of self against others. He argues that these three poets attempted to reintegrate their confused selves into historical and social reality by seeking recognition from others. Rzepka explores the psychological dimensions of romanticism and the ways the isolated self communicates with the outside world. Rzepka examines the nature of the visionary self, its expression, and the role of the reading public in providing external affirmation of the internal experience. This complex study is recommended for scholars of literature or psychology. (A)

Schulz, Max F. *Paradise Preserved: Recreations of Eden in Eighteenth and Nineteenth-Century England.* Cambridge: Cambridge University Press, 1986. Schulz's study explores the idealized gardens and landscapes of the English nobility and relates these miniature Edens to the work of painters and poets of the era. Schulz discusses works of Blake and Coleridge and provides insightful parallels with landscape artists such as Constable and Turner. He also considers Tennyson's view of Eden and anti-Eden within the context of Whistler and the mid-Victorians. Selected illustrations help amplify many of Schulz's points. This is an important study that seeks to interrelate areas of scholarship that are too often compartmentalized. Highly recommended. (A,G)

Scott, Nathan A. *The Poetics of Belief: Studies in Coleridge, Arnold, Pater, Santayana, Stevens, and Heidegger.* Chapel Hill: University of North Carolina Press, 1985. This collection of Scott's essays on writers and philosophers explores the power of the imagination for evoking religious awareness and transcendence. Examining each writer in turn—Coleridge, Arnold, Pater, Santayana, and Stevens—Scott finds a commonality of purposes and intentions among them that is best articulated by Heidegger. (A)

Taylor, Anya. *Coleridge's Defense of the Human.* Columbus: Ohio State University Press, 1986. Taylor argues that it is important to recognize that Coleridge's themes are, in part, based on a dichotomy between humans and animals. Humans are empowered with different knowledge and understanding, which gives them a personal identity and leads them to look for continuity between the human and the spiritual. Being neither fully a part of the natural world or of the spiritual world, people must bridge the gap through a leap of faith. In building her argument, Taylor rejects both the philosophy of Hume —Coleridge's archenemy—and modern deconstructionists. (A)

Other Sources

Austin, Frances. *The Language of Wordsworth and Coleridge.* New York: St. Martin's, 1989.

Cutsinger, James S. *The Form of Transformed Vision: Coleridge and the Knowledge of God.* Macon, GA: Mercer University Press, 1987.

Gallant, Christine, ed. *Coleridge's Theory of the Imagination Today.* New York: AMS Press, 1987.

Goodson, A. C. *Verbal Imagination: Coleridge and the Language of Modern Criticism.* New York: Oxford University Press, 1988.

Gravil, Richard, and Lucy Newlyn, eds. *Coleridge's Imagination: Essays in Memory of Pete Laver.* New York: Cambridge University Press, 1985.

Harding, Anthony John. *Coleridge and the Inspired Word.* Montreal: McGill-Queen's University Press, 1985.

Hodgson, John A. *Coleridge, Shelley and Transcendental Inquiry: Rhetoric, Argument, Metapsychology.* Lincoln: University of Nebraska Press, 1989.

Jackson, H. J., ed. *Samuel Taylor Coleridge: Selected Letters.* New York: Oxford University Press, 1987.

Jasper, David, ed. *The Interpretation of Belief: Coleridge, Schleiermacher, and Romanticism.* New York: St. Martin's, 1986.

Jasper, David. *Coleridge as Poet and Religious Thinker.* New York: Macmillan, 1985.

Mudge, Bradford Keyes. *Sara Coleridge, a Victorian Daughter: Her Life and Essays.* New Haven, CT: Yale University Press, 1989.

Ruoff, Gene W. *Wordsworth and Coleridge: The Making of the Major Lyrics, 1802-1804.* New Brunswick: Rutgers University Press, 1989.

Wylie, Ian. *Young Coleridge and the Philosophers of Nature.* New York: New York: Oxford University Press, 1989.

WILKIE COLLINS
1824-1889

Evaluation of Selected Biography and Criticism

O'Neill, Philip. *Wilkie Collins: Women, Property, and Propriety*. New York: Barnes & Noble, 1988. In this study of Collins' novels O'Neill examines the roles of gender, women, and sexuality. While the readings are generally illuminating, the prose often bogs down with critical-theory and Marxist-derived jargon. There is little doubt that the lives of Victorian women were in many ways delineated by attitudes toward property and propriety. O'Neill's study clarifies an accepted wisdom and occasionally enlarges upon it. (A)

Taylor, Jenny Bourne. *In the Secret Theatre of Home: Wilkie Collins, Sensation Narrative, and Nineteenth-century Psychology*. London: Routledge & Keagan Paul, 1988. This fascinating book examines nineteenth-century theories about insanity, traces their influence on "sensation fiction" popular from 1850-1870, and demonstrates how Collins incorporated it into his own work. Taylor argues that Collins' characters were not merely figures in a suspenseful plot but were masterfully drawn psychological figures. Particularly interesting is how Collins shifted from the gothic tradition to science fiction in his later novels. Taylor provides full analyses of *Basil, The Woman in White, No Name, Armadale, The Moonstone, The Law and the Lady*, and *Heart and Science*. This study is useful for students of Victorian thought, psychological fiction, or the development of the novel, as well as for serious students of Collins. (A,G)

Trodd, Anthea. *Domestic Crime in the Victorian Novel*. New York: St. Martin's, 1989. Trodd uses the patterns of domestic crime in fiction as a barometer of changing Victorian attitudes and social values. Early Victorian households cleaved to the rights of privacy and autonomy, no matter what the internal abuse. This gradually gave way to a belief in the right of the public to expose and punish domestic crimes. Trodd's cross-disciplinary approach provides fruitful insights into the roles of women and crimes against them, the roles of servants as perpetrators and victims, and the sensationalism of the courtroom. Offering impressive scope, this study examines fiction by such diverse authors as Kipling, Collins, Hardy, and Gaskell. (A,G)

JOSEPH CONRAD
1857-1924

Autobiographical Sources

Karl, Frederick, and Laurence Davies, ed. *The Collected Letters of Joseph Conrad: Volume 2, 1898-1902*. Cambridge: Cambridge University Press, 1986. This collection of letters covers the period when Conrad produced some of his finest works—*Youth, Heart of Darkness*, and *Lord Jim*. Conrad's letters while writing *Lord Jim* and the responses are especially detailed. Revealed in this correspondence are Conrad's strong sense of self-confidence, his frustration at the slow pace of his writing, and his chronic shortage of money. Conrad's concerns for his family and assessment of the Boer War are also highlighted. The high editorial standards of this volume should attract the critical praise afforded *Volume 1*. This is an essential reference work for study of Conrad. (A,G)

Karl, Frederick, and Laurence Davies, eds. *The Collected Letters of Joseph Conrad: Volume 3, 1903-1907*. Cambridge: Cambridge University Press, 1988. *Volume 3* of the collected letters of Conrad picks up in 1903 when the writer is suffering from numerous financial and health-related problems. In spite of these handicaps, he produces *Nostromo* and *The Secret Agent* and begins work on *Under Western Eyes*. This edition continues the high scholarly stardards of previous volumes. (A)

Evaluation of Selected Biography and Criticism

Adelman, Gary. *Heart of Darkness: Search for the Unconscious*. Boston: G. K. Hall/Twayne, 1987. In this specialized study, Adelman focuses on Freudian psychology and British imperialism as thematic forces in *Heart of Darkness*. (A)

Anderson, Linda R. *Bennett, Wells, and Conrad: Narrative in Transition*. New York: St. Martin's, 1988. Anderson maintains that between 1890 and 1910 ideas about the nature of fiction were undergoing a major change, which led Bennett, Wells, and Conrad to redefine the relationship of the novel to reality. One result of this change was the incorporation of many of the unsavory aspects of life into the novel; another was a growing moral concern over the effects of confronting the darker side of life. Anderson develops this theme through her discussions of the major novels of these writers. This is a valuable study to those interested in the transition from the Victorian to the modern novel. (A,G)

Armstrong, Paul B. *The Challenge of Bewilderment: Understanding and Representation in James, Conrad, and Ford*. Ithaca, NY: Cornell University Press, 1987. Armstrong distills the thematic and philosophical concerns of

James, Conrad, and Ford to a single existential essence—bewilderment. Focusing on Conrad's narrators and characters in *Lord Jim* and *Nostromo*, he examines their shifting and often contradictory explanations of the reality of events. Comparing these viewpoints with the purposeful blurring of real life and illusion accomplished by James and the temperamental inconsistencies of Ford Madox Ford, Armstrong finds a strong basis for claiming that the expression of "bewilderment" was the source of many of their obscurities. **(A)**

Batchelor, John. *Lord Jim*. Boston: Unwin Hyman, 1988. In this study, Batchelor provides a careful critical reading of Conrad's *Lord Jim*. In his introductory chapters, Batchelor examines the novel's literary context and critical reception. He then divides the book into four sections and discusses each in turn, providing insights derived from his thorough knowledge of all Conrad's novels. Batchelor's emphasis is on the novel's themes and characters, rather than its form or fictional techniques. **(A,G)**

Bradbury, Malcolm. *The Modern World: Ten Great Writers*. New York: Viking, 1989. Bradbury's study consists of essays on ten modern writers who he believes have shaped twentieth-century literature—Eliot, Conrad, Woolf, Joyce, Kafka, Pirandello, Mann, Proust, Ibsen, and Dostoevsky. He examines these writers' underlying themes of alienation, rage, and disaffection and describes how their work influenced contemporary authors. **(A)**

Brebach, Raymond. *Joseph Conrad, Ford Madox Ford, and the Making of "Romance."* Ann Arbor: UMI Research, 1985. Conrad and Ford worked together on two novels, and this study analyzes the interaction between the two writers in terms of the "rules" they established for their collaboration. For example, they agreed that a character's speech should never directly reply to an immediately preceding speech. Conrad was drawn to the collaboration because of the chance to develop certain political themes, which he thought would be ironic within the context of *Romance*. Ford was more-or-less coerced into the collaboration since it was a difficult way of working for him. Brebach attempts to show how the collaboration influenced the works of both men. **(A)**

Brown, Dennis. *The Modernist Self in Twentieth-Century English Literature: A Study in Self-Fragmentation*. New York: St. Martin's, 1989. In this study of major British writers of the twentieth century, Brown develops the thesis that the convention of unitary selfhood was the heart of narrative perspective until challenged by the modernists. Drawing heavily on such writers as Conrad, Joyce, Pound, David Jones, and Ford Madox Ford, Brown masses material from writers who depicted the self as fragmentary and heterogeneous, rather than unitary. He examines the roles of inner conflict and self-deception in shaping the form of the novel. Fragmentation of self, in Brown's view, could be depicted negatively—leading to various forms of disintegration—or positively—allowing a restricted selfhood to expand and diversify. **(A,G)**

Fogel, Aaron. *Coercion to Speak: Conrad's Poetics of Dialogue.* Cambridge: Harvard University Press, 1985. According to Fogel, Conrad devised a technique of dialogue that was non-cooperative and non-conversational. In this context, Fogel equates the writer's use of speech and dialogue with coercion and force. He applies this observation to the body of Conrad's work and shows the consequences for modern theories of the novel. (A)

Fraser, Gail. *Interweaving Patterns in the Works of Joseph Conrad.* Ann Arbor: UMI Research, 1988. Fraser argues that for most of Conrad's novels there is a corresponding shorter work that can be used to interpret the novel. She believes that the themes are clearer in the short fiction, making it easier to understand his intentions in the novels. Some of the pairs she explicates are: "An Outpost of Progress" and *The Secret Agent*; "Youth" and *Lord Jim*; "The Secret Sharer"and *Under Western Eyes.* This interesting study is useful for understanding both Conrad's fiction and techniques. (A,G)

Graham, Kenneth. *Indirections of the Novels: James, Conrad, and Forster.* London: Cambridge University Press, 1988. Graham argues that while all three writers rejected the literary directions of the Victorian era, none quite advanced into modernism and, as a result, developed common themes of isolation. Faced with a world of uncertainty, they employed similar language, narrative form, and an ambiguity toward society. The novels that Graham uses to develop his thesis include James' *The Bostonians, The Europeans, What Maisie Knew,* and *The Golden Bowl;* Conrad's *Heart of Darkness, Lord Jim, Nostromo, The Secret Agent, Under Western Eyes,* and *The Shadow Line;* and Forster's *A Passage to India* and *Howard's End.* (A)

Lester, John. *Conrad and Religion.* New York: St. Martin's, 1988. From his childhood in Poland to his life at sea, Conrad was exposed to a wide variety of religious beliefs. From his father's "religiosity" to his knowledge of Islam and Buddhism, Conrad fused theologies and made them part of the rich texture of his work. Lester admirably explicates the sources and meaning of Conrad's use of religion in his fiction, and suggests that this is a major reason why it has elicited so much archetypal criticism. The annotations, index, and bibliography make this a useful resource for serious students of Conrad. (A)

Milbauer, Asher Z. *Transcending Exile: Conrad, Nabokov, I. B. Singer.* Gainesville: University Presses of Florida, 1985. In this narrowly focused study, Milbauer, an emigré himself, examines the issue of literary transplantation in the works of Conrad, Nabokov, and Singer. Each of these authors experienced cultural displacement or created their finest works in a language other than their native tongue. (A)

Raval, Suresh. *The Art of Failure: Conrad's Fiction.* Boston: Allen & Unwin, 1986. Raval argues that Conrad's fiction "is almost always concerned with problems of a social, historical, and moral nature, and with institutions that constitute, sustain, and complicate forms of life in society." In critiquing the institutions of Western culture, Conrad placed his fictional protagonists in extreme social environments, subjected them to certain failure, and forced them to contemplate their social responsibilities. Although this is a detailed study, it is appropriate for any good student who is familiar with Conrad's major novels. (A,G)

Ressler, Steve. *Joseph Conrad: Consciousness and Integrity*. New York: New York University Press, 1988. Although this critical reading of Conrad's major novels offers few new insights, it is well written and well organized, and can be considered a basic book for entry-level research. (A,G)

Seymour, Miranda. *A Ring of Conspirators: Henry James and His Literary Circle, 1895-1915*. Boston: Houghton Mifflin, 1989. The godfather of literature during the opening decades of the twentieth century, James attracted the best and the brightest writers to his estate in Rye. He especially attracted Americans who were either expatriates or temporarily enchanted by the wonders of the European intelligentsia. Seymour recreates this world and the band of gypsy writers who inhabited it, including Joseph Conrad, H.G. Wells, Ford Madox Ford, Edith Wharton, and Stephen Crane. This delightful and readable biography is sound in scholarship and is valuable to anyone studying any of these writers, the period, or the development of modern fiction. (A,G)

Whiteley, Patrick J. *Knowledge and Experimental Realism in Conrad, Lawrence, and Woolf*. Baton Rouge: Louisiana State University Press, 1987. Whiteley offers a good analysis of all three writers' works as he explains how each writer thought people perceived reality, and how they embodied this perceptual process in their fiction. The quest for self-knowledge and its implications for people's relationships is, in Whiteley's opinion, the important thread that ties these three writers together and establishes the groundwork for the modern psychological novel. (A)

Winner, Anthony. *Culture and Irony: Studies in Joseph Conrad's Major Novels*. Charlottesville: University Press of Virginia, 1988. Winner argues that Conrad could not accept faith that demanded the acceptance of a mystery, and he used irony to question moral codes and values. According to Winner, readers can be certain that to take any situation or character in a Conrad novel at face value is to fall into a trap of illusion. At the same time, Conrad believed that certain illusions were a nurturing element, and Winner closely examines four novels—*Lord Jim*, *Nostromo*, *Under Western Eyes*, and *The Secret Sharer*—to demonstrate how Conrad plays culture against irony and illusion. This brilliant study will provoke new ideas from scholars and advanced students. (A)

Wright, Andrew. *Fictional Discourse and Historical Space: Defoe and Theroux, Austen and Forster, Conrad and Greene*. New York: St. Martin's, 1987. An intelligent approach to fiction and current academic discourse, Wright's study examines the relationship between the reading of literature and the study of literary history. By comparing three pairs of books, he attempts to isolate distinct voices in diverse fiction across time and changing audiences. Wright compares Defoe's *Robinson Crusoe* with Paul Theroux's *Mosquito Coast* to reveal Theroux's use of aspects of the Crusoe character. He compares Jane Austen's *Emma* with Forster's *Howard's End* to connect the various voices of class and gender used by both authors. Finally, he examines Greene's *The Human Factor* in light of Conrad's *The Secret Agent* to understand the authors' views on anarchy and social control. Wright contends that both closure and history give fiction moral meaning. (A)

Other Sources
Billy, Ted. *Critical Essays on Joseph Conrad.* Boston: G. K. Hall, 1987.

Dobrinsky, Joseph. *The Artist in Conrad's Fiction: A Psychocritical Study.* Ann Arbor: UMI Research, 1989.

Hamner, Robert D., ed. *Joseph Conrad: Third World Perspectives.* Washington: Three Continents, 1989.

La Bossiere, Camille R. *The Victorian Sage: Comparative Readings on Carlyle, Emerson, Melville and Conrad.* Lewisburg, PA: Bucknell University Press, 1988.

Land, Stephen K. *Paradox and Polarity in the Fiction of Joseph Conrad.* New York: St. Martin's, 1985.

Lothe, Jakob. *Conrad's Narrative Method.* New York: Oxford University Press, 1989.

Page, Norman. *A Conrad Companion.* New York: St. Martin's, 1986.

Pecora, Vincent P. *Self and Form in Modern Narrative.* Baltimore: Johns Hopkins University Press, 1989.

Schwarz, Daniel R. *The Transformation of the English Novel, 1890-1930.* New York: St. Martin's, 1989.

Secor, Robert, and Debra Moddelmog, eds. *Joseph Conrad and American Writers: A Bibliographical Study of Affinities, Influences and Relations.* Westport, CT: Greenwood, 1985.

Watts, Cedric. *The Deceptive Text: An Introduction to Covert Plots.* Totowa, NJ: Barnes & Noble, 1984.

Wilson, Robert B. *Conrad's Mythology.* Troy, NY: Whitston, 1987.

JAMES FENIMORE COOPER
1789-1851

Evaluation of Selected Biography and Criticism

Levine, Robert S. *Conspiracy and Romance: Studies in Brockden Brown, Cooper, Hawthorne, and Melville.* New York: Cambridge University Press, 1989. This study consists of four loosely connected essays. An essay on Brown's *Ormond* focuses on the writer's foreign villains and conspiratorial plots against the integrity of the fledgling United States. Examining Cooper's *The Bravo*, Levine demonstrates that the author's desire was to demystify and oppose the "mysterious power" that directed the state of Venice, which he described as a "soulless corporation." Levine examines the roles of insiders and outsiders in Hawthorne's *The Blithedale Romance*. Finally, he turns his attention to Melville's *Benito Cereno* where he examines the conflicts between captains and mutineers. (A)

Morse, David. *American Romanticism.* New York: Barnes & Noble, 1987. With cool, critical detachment, Morse examines the ethic of "excessiveness" which he feels underlies the early literature of the new American nation. He traces this theme through eleven authors from Cooper and Melville to James. Nineteenth-century American authors, he argues, were driven by an impulse to extravagance in order to create a fitting symbol of national significance. (A,G)

Motley, Warren. *The American Abraham: James Fenimore Cooper and the Frontier Patriarch.* New York: Cambridge University Press, 1987. Cooper's fiction is rich with frontier patriarchs—surrogate fathers who guide the uninitiated through the primeval Garden of Eden. Motley provides a rich biographical and historical context for psychological studies of these father figures. Motley suggests that Cooper's literary creations are indebted to his vision of his father, who carved the settlement of Cooperstown out the Otsego Wilderness. Motley offers a fresh approach to understanding why Cooper's novels are considered important steps in developing the cultural characteristics of the American novel. Recommended for all researchers of Cooper. (A,G)

Tanner, Tony. *Scenes of Nature, Signs of Men.* Cambridge: Cambridge University Press, 1987. For the sheer ingenuity and brilliance of comparative thinking, Cambridge professor Tanner is one of the best critics of our time. In this collection of essays, Tanner works out his idea of the profound influence on American fiction of the Puritans' obsession with signs. He contends that this obsession set the tone for all subsequent American fiction for it established the need for American writers to find a special significance in their landscape and history. Tanner elaborates his insight in discussions of individual American writers from Cooper to the contemporary novelist William Gass. (A,G)

Thomas, Brook. *Cross-Examinations of Law and Literature: Cooper, Hawthorne, Stowe, and Melville.* Cambridge: Cambridge University Press, 1987. In this specialized study in cultural history, Thomas examines the early nineteenth-century tradition of combining the study of law and literature. He uses selected works of writers of the American Renaissance—Cooper, Hawthorne, Stowe, and Melville—to define the fictional presentation of legal issues of the times. He pairs these writers with prominent contemporary lawyers with whom they had a personal or professional connection. For example, he relates Stowe's work to litigation over slavery. **(A)**

Wallace, James D. *Early Cooper and His Audience.* New York: Columbia University Press, 1986. In this award-winning study, Wallace examines the literary context faced by the young Cooper: the potential market for American writers, the stranglehold of European literature on American tastes, and the failure of other American writers with a similar vision, such as Charles Brockden Brown. Wallace analyzes the character of the American reading public and shows how Cooper consciously shaped his work to appeal to them. What emerges is the portrait of a serious artist attuned to the interests and needs of his time and capable of transforming the literary tastes and values of his readers. This is an innovative work that should be read by anyone interested in the history of American literature. **(A,G)**

Other Sources

Kelly, William P. *Plotting America's Past: Fenimore Cooper and the Leatherstocking Tales.* Carbondale: Southern Illinois University Press, 1984.

Ringe, Donald A. *James Fenimore Cooper.* [Rev. ed.] Boston: Twayne/ G. K. Hall, 1988.

Summerlin, Mitchell. E. *A Dictionary to the Novels of James Fenimore Cooper.* Greenwood, FL: Penkevill, 1990.

GEORGE CRABBE
1754-1832

Author's Recent Bibliogrpahy

Dalrymple-Champneys, Norma, and Arthur Pollard. *The Complete Poetical Works of George Crabbe*. Oxford: Clarendon Press, 1988. These three volumes, totaling 2,400 pages, contain the most complete, scholarly collection of Crabbe's poetical works, including a few tales, fragments, and occasional poems. Some of the occasional poems hold biographical interest since they address Crabbe's romantic interests after the death of his wife. His working notes for his tales shed light on his methods of composition. The editors focus more on the early works than those published after 1834. The notes, such as those explaining Crabbe's use of epigraphs and personal names, provide scholars with an excellent source. (A)

Autobiographical Sources

Faulkner, Thomas C. *Selected Letters and Journals of George Crabbe*. Oxford: Clarendon Press, 1985. Crabbe's letters are scattered throughout sixty libraries in Britain, and a collection of them is welcomed. This collection contains 154 letters and journals from 1776 to 1832—from the American Revolution to the enactment of the first Reform Bill. These tumultuous times gave rise to various pronouncements by Crabbe on theology, botany, agriculture, politics, and literary history. Of special interest are his observations on social and economic conditions in England during the Industrial Revolution. (A)

Evaluation of Selected Biography and Criticism

Sale, Roger. *Closer to Home*. Cambridge: Harvard University Press, 1988. Sale, a critic at home in many literary periods, addresses the treatment of place in the works of five English authors, including Austen, Clare, Crabbe, and Wordsworth. The local landscape and society strongly influenced all five writers and became a principal theme and structural device for their art. Sale contends that these authors broke away from the established pictorial treatment of landscape to produce a psychological response to place and time. This, in turn, set the stage for the realism that would emerge in the writings of the Victorians, especially Hardy, Dickens, and Eliot. For serious students, Sale offers fresh and provocative ideas for interpreting each of these writers. (A,G)

HART CRANE
1899-1932

Evaluation of Selected Biography and Criticism

Bennett, Maria F. *Unfractioned Idiom: Hart Crane and Modernism.* New York: Peter Lang, 1987. Bennett has produced a study of modernism that ranges from Cubism and Vorticism, to the use of the color white by Mallarme, to syncopation in jazz music. Having developed the thesis that fragmentation is both a strategy and theme for modernist artists, Bennett goes on to examine similarities in the works of Crane, Rimbaud, and Baudelaire, concentrating on their poetic use of the voyage, the figure of Helen of Troy, and the sea as the emblem of life. Although Crane is the subject of considerable discussion, Bennett's study is most interesting when comparing art forms. **(A)**

Berthoff, Warner. *Hart Crane: A Re-Introduction.* Minneapolis: University of Minnesota Press, 1989. Berthoff believes that because of the volatile nature of Crane's psyche, most biographers have misjudged their subject and have in turn wrongly influenced critical interpretations of his poetry. This fresh and lively "corrective" convincingly challenges accepted critical theories about Crane and is a valuable addition to Crane scholarship. **(A)**

Brunner, Edward. *Splendid Failure: Hart Crane and the Making of "The Bridge."* Champaign: University of Illinois Press, 1985. For years Crane had thought of writing a civic-minded poem based on historical themes—a Whitmanesque portrait of America for his time. During the summer of 1926, in an outpouring of poetic inspiration, Crane produced a poem that was more personal than historical, which Brunner argues is a more compelling poem than the finished version published in 1930. Drawing on Crane's letters and other biographical materials, Brunner examines the conditions which led to the inspired summer, explains the differences between the two poems, and provides a sensitive reading of the final version. **(A)**

Dickie, Margaret. *On the Modernist Long Poem.* Iowa City: University of Iowa Press, 1986. Dickie contends that by extending their "personal imagist pieces" into the extended "public" long poem, modernist poets redefined the shape and direction of their movement. In this study, which is, in effect, a history of the development of modernism, Dickie examines the formal problems faced by Crane (*The Bridge*), Williams (*Paterson*), Eliot (*The Waste Land*), and Pound (*The Cantos*). This study would be most useful for teachers and students who are seeking a framework for discussion of these complex works. **(A)**

Edelman, Lee. *Transmemberment of Song: Hart Crane's Anatomies of Rhetoric and Desire.* Stanford: Stanford University Press, 1987. According to

115

Edelman, Crane's poetic strategy utilizes three recurrent rhetorical gestures—
anacoluthon (conscious violation of grammar and syntax), *chiasmus* (reversal
and negation), and *catechresis* (an effort to extend the domain of poetry). Of
particular note is the discussion of Crane's response to the demands of Whitman's ideas and techniques on poetry. Although it is difficult to read at times,
the Crane enthusiast should not overlook this important study. (A)

Giles, Paul. *Hart Crane: The Contexts of "The Bridge."* Cambridge: Cambridge University Press, 1986. Giles analyzes Crane's poetic technique in *The
Bridge* and rejects a large body of criticism based on hermeneutics. Rather
than finding "inflated rhetoric," Giles discovers a complex texture built up
from double entendre, puns, echoes, signals, and purposeful ambiguity. Giles
demonstrates that through these devices Crane is able to pack simple words
and phrases with additional meaning and provide "bridges" from idea to idea
within the body of the poem. Giles ranks Crane's *The Bridge* with *Finnegan's
Wake* as a successful experiment with the "revolution of the word." This book
is highly recommended for any student of American modernism. (A,G)

Simon, Marc, ed. *The Poems of Hart Crane.* New York: Liveright, 1986.
Simon's edition of Crane's complete poems supersedes all previous editions,
including the 1958 Frank edition. The editor's notes supply authoritative
textual and publication information, making this text essential for any critical
work on Crane. (A,G)

Other Sources
  Walker, Jeffrey. *Bardic Ethos and the American Epic Poem: Whitman,
Pound, Crane, Williams, Olson.* Baton Rouge: Louisiana State University
Press, 1989.

STEPHEN CRANE
1871-1900

Autobiographical Sources

Wertheim, Stanley and Paul Sorrentino, eds. *The Correspondence of Stephen Crane*. New York: Columbia University Press, 1988. Although the editors have uncovered much new primary material, the new letters bring to light few new facts about the life of this elusive writer. Rather, they tend to confirm the more sordid rumors, and as such do little to improve Crane's reputation. Still, for scholars and serious students of Crane, the letters with their careful annotations offer an important primary source. (A)

Evaluation of Selected Biography and Criticism

Clark, Lee, ed. *New Essays on "The Red Badge of Courage."* New York: Cambridge University Press, 1987. This collection of essays offers substantial new insight into Crane's most famous work. Topics include the vast differences between Crane's original manuscript and the published novel as a result of changes demanded by the publisher; the religious and social elements that embody the moral struggle in the novel; the influence on Crane of his minister father; and the novel's ironic structure. This is an ambitious collection, full of new ideas for advanced researchers. (A)

Fried, Michael. *Realism, Writing, Disfiguration: On Thomas Eakins and Stephen Crane*. Chicago: University of Chicago Press, 1987. Fried applies a formalistic and Freudian analysis to Eakins' great painting *The Gross Clinic* to extrapolate its themes. He then turns to Crane and applies the same critical approach. (A)

Gibson, Donald B. *"The Red Badge of Courage": Redefining the Hero*. Boston: Twayne, 1988. Twayne's "Masterwork" series has consistently high standards of scholarship, and this volume is no exception. Gibson's introduction sets Crane firmly in historical context and provides a chronology of his life and works. He then gives a solid reading of the text, interpreting *The Red Badge of Courage* as a psychological study of a protagonist in the crisis of war. Gibson demonstrates Crane's theme that consciousness separates humans from nature. He then examines the conflicts that develop in the novel between the narrator and the protagonist. Gibson contends that although the protagonist feels he has matured in combat, from the narrator's perspective he has made little progress. A highly recommended introduction to this classic work. (A,G)

Knapp, Bettina L. *Stephen Crane*. New York: Crossroad/Ungar/Continuum, 1987. Part of Ungar's series of "Literature and Life," this volume provides standard biographical information, plot outlines, and straightforward analyses

117

of Crane's major works. Knapp attempts to define Crane's significance in terms of the epic tradition. (A,G)

Lindberg-Seyersted, Brita. *Ford Madox Ford and His Relationship to Stephen Crane and Henry James.* Atlantic Highlands, NJ: Humanities Press, 1987. The purpose of this study is to provide an exhaustive analysis of the contacts and mutual influences of Ford and James. In spite of the title's emphasis, Crane is addressed only in one short chapter. (A)

Mitchell, Lee Clark, ed. *New Essays on "The Red Badge of Courage."* Cambridge: Cambridge University Press, 1986. This collection of six essays gives a representative view of recent critical approaches to Crane's *The Red Badge of Courage.* The strength of this collection is in its breadth of coverage, ranging from textual and historical criticism to deconstructive analysis. Mitchell's introduction provides an overview of Crane's life and discusses the popular and critical reception of the novel. Hershel Parker traces the torturous publication history and argues that the original manuscript was superior to the Appleton version. Andrew Delbanco places the novel in its cultural and historical context. Other contributors include Amy Kaplan, Howard Horsford, and Christine Brooke-Rose. This is an excellent presentation of current critical perspectives. (A,G)

Seymour, Miranda. *A Ring of Conspirators: Henry James and His Literary Circle, 1895-1915.* Boston: Houghton Mifflin, 1989. The godfather of literature during the opening decades of the twentieth century, James attracted the best and the brightest writers to his estate in Rye. He especially attracted Americans who were either expatriates or temporarily enchanted by the wonders of the European intelligentsia. Seymour recreates this world and the band of gypsy writers who inhabited it, including Joseph Conrad, H. G. Wells, Ford Madox Ford, Edith Wharton, and Stephen Crane. This delightful and readable biography is sound in scholarship and is valuable to anyone studying any of these writers, the period, or the development of modern fiction. (A,G)

Tanner, Tony. *Scenes of Nature, Signs of Men.* Cambridge: Cambridge University Press, 1987. For the sheer ingenuity and brilliance of comparative thinking, Cambridge professor Tanner is one of the best critics of our time. In this collection of essays, Tanner works out his idea of the profound influence on American fiction of the Puritans' obsession with signs. He contends that this obsession set the tone for all subsequent American fiction for it established the need for American writers to find a special significance in their landscape and history. Tanner elaborates his insight in discussions of individual American writers from Cooper and Crane to the contemporary novelist William Gass. (A,G)

Wolford, Chester L. *Stephen Crane: A Study of the Short Fiction.* Boston: Twayne, 1989. This study of Crane's shorter fiction offers a new look at some neglected masterpieces, many published only after his death. Wolford begins his coverage with the early *Sullivan County Sketches* and ends with the *Whilomville Stories*. In addition, he reprints and discusses an 1896 interview in which Crane discusses his literary philosophy, and, in a final section of the book, collects a group of critical essays by noted Crane scholars. This is a useful study that can serve to introduce new readers to an author who made an important contribution to literary impressionism. **(A,G)**

Young, Thomas Daniel, ed. *Modern American Fiction: Form and Function.* Baton Rouge: Louisiana State University Press, 1989. This anthology of thirteen critical essays examines how novelists achieve form in their best novels and how this form allows the writers to express a philosophy of life. These contributors seem to have reached a consensus that modern American novelists tend to use an objective narrative stance, allowing the action to unfold, in contrast to the more subjective narrators of the nineteenth century. Henry James' *Wings of a Dove*, Stephen Crane's *The Red Badge of Courage*, John Barth's *The Floating Opera*, and Robert Penn Warren's *All the King's Men* are singled out for special attention. In all, this is a useful introduction to the criticism of American literature. **(A,G)**

Other Sources
Haliburton, David. *The Color of the Sky: A Study of Stephen Crane.* New York: Cambridge University Press, 1989.

RICHARD CRASHAW
c. 1612-1649

Evaluation of Selected Biography and Criticism
Roberts, John R. *Richard Crashaw. An Annotated Bibliography of Criticism, 1632-1980*. Columbia: University of Missouri Press, 1985. This extensive bibliography (478 pages) provides descriptive annotations of all items, except modern reviews and doctoral dissertations, related to Crashaw. The fullness of the annotations make them especially valuable. (A)

Other Sources
Healy, Thomas F. *Richard Crashaw*. Leiden, Netherlands: E. J. Brill, 1986.

COUNTÉE CULLEN
1903-1946

Evaluation of Selected Biography and Criticism
Baker, Houston A., Jr. *Afro-American Poetics: Revisions of Harlem and the Black Aesthetic.* Madison: University of Wisconsin Press, 1988. Noted African-American literature scholar Houston Baker began as a student of Victorian literature. This collection of Baker's essays is as much about his personal transition to the study of black literary forms as about the development of the Black Arts movement of the 1960s and 1970s. As such, it is part literary criticism and part autobiography. Four of these essays have been previously published—on Countée Cullen, Jean Toomer, Amiri Baraka, and Larry Neal. For this collection, Baker has added essays on Hoyt Fuller and "The Afro-American Spirit Work," as well as critical introductions for each piece. (A,G)

Other Sources
Shucard, Alan R. *Countée Cullen.* Boston: Twayne/G. K. Hall, 1984.

E. E. CUMMINGS
1894-1962

Evaluation of Selected Criticism
  Cohen, Milton A. *Poet and Painter: The Aesthetics of E. E. Cummings'*
Early Work. Detroit: Wayne State University Press, 1987. Cummings considered himself as much a painter as poet, and in fact his estate included over sixteen hundred oils and watercolors. Cohen compares Cummings to his contemporary artists and explains the development of his visual style. Although Cohen does not relate Cummings' poems to his paintings, he suggests that this is an appropriate next step. (A)

CYNEWULF
775-825?

Evaluation of Selected Criticism
   Olsen, Alexandra Hennessey. *Speech, Song, and Poetic Craft: The Artistry of the Cynewulf Canon.* New York: Peter Lang, 1984. In this, her doctoral dissertation, Olsen argues for the importance of speeches in understanding Cynewulf. She focuses on "the nouns that describe speech acts and the verbs of speech that introduce them" in order to examine the original versions of the legends and the heroic tradition that reinforces the Christian elements. Recommended for linguists and Cynewulf specialists. (A)

SIR WILLIAM DAVENANT
1606-1668

Evaluation of Selected Biography and Criticism

Edmond, Mary. *Rare Sir William Davenant: Poet Laureate, Playwright, Civil War General, Restoration Theatre Manager.* New York: St. Martin's, 1987. Edmond has uncovered new information about Davenant's family and education. For the first time we have a detailed and evocative account of his father's unknown life in London in the 1590s. She goes on to chronicle how Davenant's fortunes rose and fell with those of the royal family, and explains how the times shaped his life and career. This well-researched biography will please both general readers and specialists and supersedes all previous biographies. (A)

Other Sources

Blaydes, Sophia B., and Philip Bordinat. *Sir William Davenant: An Annotated Bibliography.* New York: Garland, 1986.

ROBERTSON DAVIES
1913

Author's Recent Bibliography
What's Bred in the Bone, 1985 (novel); *The Papers of Samuel Marchbanks*, 1985 (novel); *The Lyre of Orpheus*, 1989 (novel).

Autobiographical Sources
Davis, J. Madison, ed. *Conversations with Robertson Davies*. Jackson: University Press of Mississippi, 1989. These twenty-nine interviews and musings by Davies reveal several common themes, including his belief in the importance of mystery, his shift from Freudianism to Jungianism, and the importance of Canadian identity and heritage. Davies, who is always thoughtful, crusty, and forthright, reveals much about himself and the sources of his art. (A,G)

Evaluation of Selected Biography and Criticism
Stone-Blackburn, Susan. *Robertson Davies, Playwright: A Search for the Self on the Canadian Stage*. Vancouver: University of British Columbia, 1985. Davies wrote and produced over forty plays over a twenty-year span, yet his work as a playwright has been largely neglected by the critical community. This study examines the similarities between Davies' fiction and plays. Stone-Blackburn contends that, against the dangers of puritanical excess, Davies upholds an ideal of humanistic wholeness. (A,G)

THOMAS DE QUINCEY
1785-1859

Evaluation of Selected Criticism

McFarland, Thomas. *Romantic Cruxes: The English Essayists and the Spirit of the Age.* Oxford: Clarendon, 1987. This concise study addresses romanticism as expressed by the English essayists Hazlitt, Lamb, and De Quincey. These writers emphasized nature, imagination, egotism, medieval imagining, and dreams. McFarland reveals Lamb to have been a more influential cultural figure than is currently appreciated. He examines Hazlitt's standing debate with Coleridge over the workings of the imagination for its political and social implications. McFarland attempts to recapture the importance of these essayists and remove them from the shadow of the major romantic poets. (A,G)

Snyder, Robert Lance, ed. *Thomas de Quincey: Bicentenary Studies.* Norman: University of Oklahoma Press, 1986. De Quincey continues to languish in the shadow of Coleridge and Wordsworth despite his prodigious output of finely crafted works. This anthology of sixteen essays addresses the full breadth of De Quincey's works, including *The Confessions of an English Opium-Eater*, for which he is best remembered. The diversity of critical perspectives presented offers an intelligent introduction to the life and works. (A,G)

Other Sources

Whale, John C. *Thomas De Quincey's Reluctant Autobiography.* Totowa, NJ: Barnes & Noble, 1984.

DANIEL DEFOE
1660?-1731

Evaluation of Selected Biography and Criticism

Backscheider, Paula R. *Daniel Defoe: His Life*. Baltimore: The Johns Hopkins University Press, 1989. By the time Defoe published *Robinson Crusoe* at age fifty-nine he had been through enough harrowing experiences to fill several biographies. He had survived the plague, London's Great Fire, imprisonment for debt, and political persecution. He went on to build a controversial reputation as a scathing satirist and effective propagandist. Backscheider sets out to recreate the social and political turmoil of Restoration England and to place Defoe securely within this roiling context. She analyzes not only the novels for which Defoe is most remembered, but also the poetry, satires, and political pamphlets. Defoe is often omitted from standard anthologies of the period, perhaps because no biography of this caliber existed for critics to measure the meaning and merit of his works. (A,G)

Backscheider, Paula R. *Daniel Defoe: Ambition and Innovation*. Lexington: University Press of Kentucky, 1986. Backscheider's depth of acquaintance with Defoe's enormous output enables her to place each work in historical, literary, and intellectual context. She is equally adept with the fiction, the poetry, and the political and religious pamphlets. The book presents a convincing argument that Defoe was the most influential propagandist of his time and champions the view that he was indeed "the indisputable father of the English novel." This is the most comprehensive and detailed treatment of Defoe's work in print. (A,G)

Bell, Ian A. *Defoe's Fiction*. Totowa, NJ: Barnes & Noble, 1985. Bell sees Defoe as "a fantasist rather than a realist," whose work is "sufficiently grounded in the details of day-to-day life that it otherwise contradicts." The fantasy lures readers "with the absorbing issues of danger and escape, in a manner that is at once plausible and strange, simultaneously drawn to earth and dreamlike." Bell believes that Defoe may forever be relegated to the ranks of popular writers, but that he deliberately avoided creating high art, believing that irony was the greatest teacher of all. (A,G)

Curtis, Laura A. *The Elusive Daniel Defoe*. Totowa, NJ: Barnes & Noble, 1984. Curtis argues that Defoe masks not only his life but his works as he manipulates vocabulary, imagery, rhythms, and the structure of episodes. She focuses on how Defoe's texts shape the reader's response, and how he juxtaposes an ideal world with the disorder of the real world. Curtis believes that this clash created the nightmare horror in *Robinson Crusoe* and *Roxanna*, but that Defoe subjugated this horror to the higher purpose of comedy and fantasy. This thoughtful study skillfully treats Defoe's non-fiction as well as novels; Curtis explains the complexity of Defoe's personality in light of the masks of his fiction. (A,G)

Dijkstra, Bram. *Defoe and Economics: The Fortunes of "Roxanna" in the History of Interpretation.* New York: St. Martin's, 1987. Dijkstra presents Defoe's *Roxanna* as a "celebration of economic individualism" in which the heroine overcomes all obstacles to succeed as a merchant. In the process of his critique, Dijkstra argues against most of the accepted critical opinions about Defoe in general and of this novel in particular. Interpretations that ignore historical and political contexts, he suggests, are little more than "critical fictions." (A)

Erickson, Robert A. *Mother Midnight: Birth, Sex, and Fate in Eighteenth-Century Fiction: Defoe, Richardson, and Sterne.* New York: AMS, 1986. Erickson examines the ambiguous character of the midwife in eighteenth-century fiction to shed light on the philosophical attitudes toward fate prevalent during the period. The "representation of fate," as examined in *Moll Flanders, Pamela, Clarissa,* and *Tristram Shandy* extends to a discussion of "spiritual midwives" who appear at crisis points in a character's life to assist an emotional and spiritual rebirth. Erickson's discussion of the governess in *Moll Flanders* is especially rich and provocative. Although the reader may sense that the midwife metaphor is occasionally strained, this in no way undermines the overall value of this book. (A,G)

Meier, Thomas Keith. *Defoe and the Defense of Commerce.* Victoria, B.C.: University of Victoria, 1987. Before wholesale exploitation of workers turned many nineteenth-century writers against business, progressive thinkers extolled the virtues of industry, trade, and commerce. Writing in the eighteenth century, Defoe was clearly ahead of his time, and it is interesting to see the sort of world he imagined business and commerce would create. Meier explores the subject with clarity and grace and gives close readings of Defoe's non-fiction, such as *A Tour Through the Whole Island of Great Britain.* Discussion of the fiction has been purposely omitted. (A,G)

Richetti, John J. *Daniel Defoe.* Boston: G.K. Hall/Twayne. 1987. Richetti's thesis is that all Defoe's novels "challenge the notion of simple or stable identity. His characters record nothing less than the fluid and dynamic nature of personality, a matter of changing roles, wearing masks, responding to the circumstances, and discovering new possibilities of self-expression." Defoe's career as a political journalist reveals a man who was ambitious, shrewd, realistic, devious, and passionate. Richetti explores the psychological process by which personality is formed in *The Family Instructor,* and explicates *Robinson Crusoe, Moll Flanders,* and *Roxanna.* He argues that the continued best-selling status of Defoe's novels confirm his status as "a great innovator of realistic fiction." This readable, informative study is recommended for both beginning and advanced students of Defoe. (A,G)

Roosen, William. *Daniel Defoe and Diplomacy.* Cranbury, NJ: Susquehanna University Press, 1986. Over a period of four decades, Daniel Defoe wrote innumerable pamphlets and essays in a persistent effort to influence public opinion about British foreign affairs. Although this facet of Defoe has often been overlooked, Roosen contends that it should be examined to arrive at a full understanding of Defoe, both as writer and politician. This study examines Defoe's views on political issues such as the European balance of power, the War of Spanish Succession, and the Peace of Utrecht. Roosen also attempts to measure the impact of Defoe's writings on public opinion, but here the documentation is too sparse to support more than informed speculation. This is a well-written, ground-breaking study. **(A)**

Wright, Andrew. *Fictional Discourse and Historical Space: Defoe and Theroux, Austen and Forster, Conrad and Greene.* New York: St. Martin's, 1987. An intelligent approach to fiction and current academic discourse, Wright's study examines the relationship between the reading of literature and the study of literary history. By comparing three pairs of books, he attempts to isolate distinct voices in diverse fiction across time and changing audiences. Wright compares Defoe's *Robinson Crusoe* with Paul Theroux's *Mosquito Coast* to reveal Theroux's use of aspects of the Crusoe character. He compares Jane Austen's *Emma* with Forster's *Howard's End* to connect the various voices of class and gender used by both authors. Finally, he examines Greene's *The Human Factor* in light of Conrad's *The Secret Agent* to understand the authors' views on anarchy and social control. Wright contends that both closure and history give fiction moral meaning. **(A)**

Other Sources
Peterson, Spiro. *Daniel Defoe: A Reference Guide.* Boston: G. K. Hall, 1987.

Stoler, John A. *Daniel Defoe: An Annotated Bibliography of Modern Criticism, 1900-1980.* New York: Garland, 1984.

THOMAS DELONEY
1543?-1600

Evaluation of Selected Biography and Criticism
Reuter, O. R. *Proverbs, Proverbial Sentences and Phrases in Thomas Deloney's Works.* Helsinki: The Finnish Society of Sciences and Letters, 1986. This specialized study looks at Deloney's use of proverbs and proverbial lore in his writings. Each proverb or suggested source is listed and annotated in a format that quotes Deloney's use of the material, cites the work and chapter, and offers references to the proverb's use by other contemporary authors. (A)

CHARLES DICKENS
1812-1870

Evaluation of Selected Biography and Criticism

Ackroyd, Peter. *Dickens' London: An Imaginative Vision*. London: David & Charles, 1988. Ackroyd, a noted British novelist, has recreated the working class London of Charles Dickens. Descriptions of the Thames, the streets and byways, and famous and less than famous buildings are interspersed with quotations from Dickens. The text is amply illustrated with period photographs. This is good background material for new or younger readers of Dickens' novels. (G,Y)

Allen, Michael. *Charles Dickens' Childhood*. New York: St. Martin's, 1988. By consulting rent books, newspapers, maps, street directories, and other topographical tools available during Dickens' boyhood, Allen has discovered that Dickens lived in fifteen different houses from 1812-1827. Then, by analyzing the types of houses and neighborhoods, he is able to project the Dickens' social standing and speculate as to how Dickens developed his ideas about class structure. Allen offers new information about Dickens' father, John, and argues that father and son had a better relationship than most biographers have thought. Allen also believes that Dickens spent thirteen months working in a blacking warehouse, three times longer than previously thought. With street maps indicating the sites of twelve Dickens' residences (now demolished), and a comprehensive index and bibliography, this study offers more new information and scholarly apparatus than any book on Dickens in a long time. (A,G)

Chittick, Kathryn. *The Critical Reception of Charles Dickens, 1833-1841*. New York: Garland, 1989. If, as Chittick insists in her introduction to this bibliography, the reviews published during Dickens' lifetime influenced the shape and content of his novels, then the evidence should certainly be found in this list of 120 reviews, culled from contemporary magazines, newspapers, and journals. The first part of this three-section bibliography is a chronological listing of articles on literary criticism published between 1814 and 1841. (Articles specifically addressing Dickens are separate.) A second section lists reviews by the novel discussed. A third section lists these same citations according to the source along with a note about reviewer practices and prejudices. A large number of influential citations from the later nineteenth and twentieth centuries are included in an appendix. (A)

Connor, Steven. *Charles Dickens*. New York and Oxford: Basil Blackwell, 1985. Connor provides three different kinds of theoretical readings of Dickens' work: structuralist, post-structuralist, and "a blend of Marxist and psycho-analytic approaches." (A)

Cotsell, Michael. *The Companion to "Our Mutual Friend."* London: Allen & Unwin, 1986. This study, one of a series that will offer direction for readers of Dickens' major works, examines the dense narrative texture of *Our Mutual Friend*. The approach is straight-forward, factual, and less theoretical than similar works. Cotsell has organized a series of mini-essays that link biographical, literary, historical, social, and cultural information with relevant passages of Dickens' novel. The range of topics is broad, and Cotsell uses material from Dickens' letters and journals to expand his context. The sheer amount of information and the easy-to-use format make this book an excellent tool to accompany a serious reading of *Our Mutual Friend*. (A,G)

Daldry, Graham. *Charles Dickens and the Form of the Novel: Fiction and Narrative in Dickens' Work*. New York: Barnes & Noble, 1987. This analysis of Dickens' fiction attempts to restate the traditional form-versus-content argument in the updated version of "narrative versus fictive." Daldry's argument is hampered by what often seems an arbitrary classification of particular novels. (A)

Flint, Kate. *Dickens*. Atlantic Highlands, NJ: Humanities Press, 1986. This short critical biography attempts to apply contemporary critical methods (gender, feminist, deconstruction) to reconsider more traditional social and historical readings of Dickens' novels. Although this study is much too short (130 pages) to be complete, Flint does provide some smart ideas for astute students. (A,G)

Hawthorn, Jeremy. *"Bleak House"*. Atlantic Highlands, NJ: Humanities, 1987. In this study, Hawthorn has effectively summarized Dickens scholarship as it relates to a particular work, *Bleak House*. He cogently examines the elements of Dickens' fiction—characterization, narrative form, and social representation—and provides an assessment of the various critical interpretations the novel has attracted, including traditional, historicist, and feminist critiques. He pays particular attention to the ideological content of the novel and convincingly argues his own view from a neo-Marxist perspective. (A,G)

Hornback, Bert G. *"Great Expectations": A Novel of Friendship*. Boston: Twayne, 1987. This fine introduction to Dickens' novel examines both its context and content. Although biographical material is scanty, Hornback excels in his discussion of Pip's role as narrator, Dickens' use of language, and the interplay of ideals and guilt. The character of Joe is seen as the book's central imaginative artist, who seeks to reveal truth in relationships as well as art. The novel's imagery as a unifying narrative element is also well presented. Recommended for those with a general interest in Dickens' work. (A,G)

Jacobson, Wendy S. *The Companion to "The Mystery of Edwin Drood."* London: Allen & Unwin, 1986. Jacobson has collected factual information on the biographical details, and historical and social events that underlie Dickens' novel *The Mystery of Edwin Drood.* The emphasis is factual, rather than critical. These annotations, which are more like small essays, provide the answers to questions most readers don't even know to ask. This highly recommended book is part of a series of companion guides that will eventually annotate all of Dickens' major works. **(A,G)**

Kaplan, Fred. *Dickens: A Biography.* New York: Morrow, 1988. Kaplan, a biographer of Thomas Carlyle, has produced a skillful look at the personal life of Dickens based on the accumulated scholarship. A careful examination of the novels reveals previously undetected autobiographical details. For its detail, chronology, and critical judgments, Kaplan's work is dependable and precise. **(A,G)**

Kucich, John. *Repression in Victorian Fiction: Charlotte Brontë, George Eliot, and Charles Dickens.* Berkeley: University of California Press, 1987. This lengthy study traces the theme of psychological repression through the life and works of Brontë, Eliot, and Dickens. Kucich's thorough scholarship examines in detail the nineteenth-century tendency to "exalt interiority." In the process, he eschews traditional critical terms, such as "self-denial" and "renunciation," in favor of his own vision of "repression." Although at times overburdened with psychoanalytical terminology, this study presents a fresh perspective from which to read the fiction of these authors. **(A)**

Larson, Janet L. *Dickens and the Broken Scripture.* Athens: University of Georgia Press, 1986. Larson argues that Dickens both used the Bible, and undermined it, as he developed fictional themes. She views him as a religious writer, especially in *Bleak House,* where his interpretations of the Bible directly influenced his rhetoric, allusions, and ironies. **(A)**

Lynch, Tony. *Dickens' England.* New York: Facts on File, 1986. This gazetteer locates and describes the many towns and parts of London that appear in Dickens' works. Quotations from the novels are matched with photographs and descriptions of the site as it is today. This study is aimed at the Dickens enthusiast and could be used to plan a fascinating vacation. **(A,G)**

Magnet, Myron. *Dickens and the Social Order.* Philadelphia: University of Pennsylvania Press, 1985. Magnet examines four novels of the late 1830s and early 1840s—*Nicholas Nickleby, Barnaby Rudge, American Notes,* and *Martin Chuzzlewit*—and argues that these were the works through which Dickens began to understand the nature and function of society. Here, Dickens developed the social assumptions that led to the complex social order of his major novels. This well-written, well-argued study provides new insights into Dickens' artistic development, purpose, and achievement. **(A)**

Martin, Philip W. *Mad Women in Romantic Writing.* New York: St. Martin's, 1988. Martin examines the ways in which patriarchal culture depicted women in the nineteenth century and explores the stereotype of the "weaker sex." He contends that the rising interest in individual psychology merged with the belief in women's weakness to create a new and important figure in romantic literature—the madwoman. He supports his thesis through discussions of selected novels of the period, among them *Jane Eyre*, *Wuthering Heights*, *Great Expectations*, and *Sense and Sensibility*. (A,G)

McMaster, Juliet. *Dickens the Designer*. New York: Barnes & Noble, 1987. By his own account, Dickens used principles derived from physiognomy and phrenology to show the relation of appearance and character. This study examines the physical appearance of the figures in his fiction. The first part is organized around body parts and uses characters from the novels to illustrate Dickens' technique. The second part of the study analyzes six major novels. McMaster's study will help all students understand the physical nature of Dickens' work, the world from which it came, and its relation to theme. (A,G)

Meckier, Jerome. *Hidden Rivalries in Victorian Fiction: Dickens, Realism, and ReEvaluation*. Lexington: University Press of Kentucky, 1987. In the mid-nineteenth century novelists not only questioned the means of depicting reality but disagreed about the nature of reality itself. According to Meckier, this resulted in a literary era of "competing secular realisms." Although the spotlight in this study is on Dickens, his novelistic rivals step on and off the stage. Trollope detests Dickens' radicalism in *The Warden*. George Eliot expounds a vision of unfolding social good, while dismissing Trollope's tendency toward "spontaneous combustion." Gaskell challenges the angry despair in *Hard Times* with a romance of industrial progress, which Wilkie Collins, in turn, parodies through overt sensationalism. Whether or not these authors were conscious rivals or not is almost beside the point. Meckier is able to use one to shed light upon another in this well-written and entertaining book. (A,G)

Page, Norman. *A Dickens Chronology*. Boston: G. K. Hall, 1988. This comprehensive log of Dickens' life follows him day by day through his writings, travels, friendships, social and family events, and the publication of his works. The information is scrupulously researched, primarily from Dickens' letters and journals, and should provide scholars with a wealth of useful detail. (A,G)

Sadrin, Anny. *Great Expectations*. Winchester, MA: Unwin Hyman, 1988. Much of this study consists of an up-to-date review of the most important scholarly criticism of *Great Expectations*. To this Sadrin adds discussions of Victorian attitudes toward gentlemen and convicts, the transportation and incarceration of Australian convicts, and the complexity of Pip's character. According to Sadrin, Pip is the most autobiographical of the characters, reflecting Dickens' sense of alienation. An appendix details the publishing history of the novel. (A,G)

Stone, Harry, ed. *Dickens' Working Notes for His Novels.* Chicago: University of Chicago Press, 1987. Dickens kept extensive notes as he planned and wrote his novels, and this volume reproduces and transcribes notes for ten of them. In his introduction, Stone details the relationship between the notes and novels, and gives an account of the circumstances under which each novel was produced. For anyone interested in the process of composition or in textual studies, this is an essential source. (A)

Storey, Graham. *Charles Dickens: Bleak House.* Cambridge: Cambridge University Press, 1987. Storey has produced a full and useful handbook to Dickens' *Bleak House.* It provides excellent cultural and literary background and gives an extensive account of the novel's structure. Dickens' social criticism and use of irony are fully covered, as is his influence on later writers, such as Dostoyevsky and Kafka. The book contains a chronology and bibliography. (A,G)

Watkins, Gwen. *Dickens in Search of Himself: Recurrent Themes and Characters in the Work of Charles Dickens.* New York: Barnes & Noble, 1987. Watkins develops a complex analysis of Dickens by tracing recurrent themes in his novels. She isolates themes, such as death of a child, the empty heart, the double self, and the murder of the self, and concludes that these are Dickens' attempts to come to terms with his childhood feelings of abandonment by his parents. Watkins writes for a reader who has a firm grasp of the details of Dickens' life and works. (A,G)

Welsh, Alexander. *From Copyright to Copperfield: The Identity of Dickens.* Cambridge: Harvard University Press, 1987. Welsh contends that Dickens' copyright dispute during his first trip to America (1842) influenced his life as much as his well-documented childhood traumas. He contends that Dickens' involvement in the copyright debate enabled him to define his identity as an author. The change is evident in *Martin Chuzzlewit,* which is viewed as a mocking, Molière-influenced *Paradise Lost. Dombey and Son,* according to Welsh, was produced in imitation of *King Lear.* Relying heavily on biographical materials, Welsh offers a fresh perspective on Dickens that is sure to stimulate debate. (A,G)

Williams, A. Susan. *The Rich Man and the Diseased Poor in Early Victorian Literature.* Atlantic Highlands, NJ: Humanities Press, 1987. Williams begins her study with a discussion of the widespread incidence of disease and high mortality rates in the Victorian era. She then traces the use of the disease metaphor in the writings of Carlyle, Dickens, and Kingsley. The metaphor is split in its application to the upper classes and the lower classes, which suffer from poor sanitation and the lack of health care. Williams then shifts to the potential for social upheaval generated by the separation of the "two nations." While it is difficult to see how the last part of the discussion contributes to the first, her discussion of disease as metaphor is highly rewarding. (A,G)

Other Sources

Adrian, Arthur A. *Dickens and the Parent-Child Relationship.* Athens: Ohio University Press, 1984.

Bolton, H. Philip. *Dickens Dramatized.* Boston: G. K. Hall, 1987.

Brooks-Davies, Douglas. *Fielding, Dickens, Gosse, Iris Murdoch and Oedipal Hamlet.* New York: St. Martin's, 1989.

Collins, Philip. *Charles Dickens.* New York: Routledge, 1987.

Davies, James A. *Characterization in Dickens.* Totowa, NJ: Barnes & Noble, 1988.

Den Hartog, Dink. *Dickens and the Romantic Psychology: The Self in Time in Nineteenth-Century Literature.* New York: St. Martin's, 1987.

Donovan, John A. *The Dogs Found in the Writings of Charles Dickens.* Fairfax, VA: Denlingers, 1989.

Ericsson, Catarina. *A Child Is a Child, You Know: The Inversion of Father and Daughter in Dickens' Novels.* Stockholm: Almquist and Wiksell, 1986.

Frank, Lawrence. *Charles Dickens and the Romantic Self.* Lincoln: University of Nebraska Press, 1984.

Gilbert, Elliot L. *Critical Essays on Charles Dickens' "Bleak House."* Boston: G. K. Hall, 1989.

Glancy, Ruth F. *Dickens' Christmas Books, Christmas Stories and Other Short Fiction: An Annotated Bibliography.* New York: Garland, 1985.

Golding, William R. *Idiolects in Dickens: The Major Techniques and Chronological Development.* New York: St. Martin's, 1985.

Goodman, Marcia R. *Mothering and Authorship in Dickens.* Ann Arbor: UMI Research, 1990.

Goodman, Nancy. *Charles Dickens: Master Storyteller.* New York: Kipling Press, 1989.

Hardy, Barbara. *The Moral Art of Dickens.* Highlands, NJ: Humanities, 1985.

Hollington, Michael. *Dickens and the Grotesque.* Totowa, NJ: Barnes & Noble, 1984.

Lettis, Richard. *The Dickens Aesthetic.* New York: AMS Press, 1989.

Martin, Graham. *"Great Expectations."* New York: Open University Press/Taylor and Francis, 1985.

Moss, Sidney P. *Charles Dickens' Quarrel with America.* Troy, NY: Whitston, 1984.

Newcomb, Mildred. *The Imagined World of Charles Dickens.* Columbus: The Ohio State University Press, 1989.

Oppenlander, Ann. *Dickens' All Year Round: An Index.* Troy, NY: Whitston, 1985.

Page, Norman. *A Dickens Companion.* New York: Schocken, 1984.

Pluckrose, H. *A Dickens Anthology.* Brunswick, ME: Bern Porter, 1985.

Raina, Badri. *Dickens and the Dialectic of Growth.* Madison: University of Wisconsin Press, 1986.

Rotkin, Charlotte. *Deception in Dickens' "Little Dorrit."* New York: Peter Lang, 1989.

Sanders, Andrew. *The Companion to "A Tale of Two Cities."* Winchester, MA: Unwin Hyman, 1988.

Schlicke, Paul. *Dickens and Popular Entertainment.* London: Allen & Unwin, 1985.

Shatto, Susan. *The Companion to "Bleak House."* Winchester, MA: Unwin Hyman, 1988.

Sorensen, Knud. *Charles Dickens: Linguistics Innovator.* Aarhus: Arkona, 1985.

Timko, Michael, *et al.,* eds. *Dickens Studies Annual: Essays on Victorian Fiction, Vol. 18.* New York: AMS Press, 1989.

Trotter, David. *Circulation: Defoe, Dickens and the Economies of the Novel.* New York: St. Martin's, 1988.

JAMES DICKEY
1923

Author's Recent Bibliography
Bronwen, the Traw, and the Shape-Shifter, 1986 (children's poetry); *Alnilam*, 1987 (novel); *From the Green Horseshoe*, 1987 (poems by Dickey's students); *Wayfarer*, 1988 (travel); *The Eagle's Mile*, 1990 (poems).

Evaluation of Selected Biography and Criticism
Baughman, Ronald. *Understanding James Dickey*. Columbia: University of South Carolina Press, 1985. Baughman believes that Dickey's World War II experience in the Army Air Corps left him with a guilt that first punished him, then led to reconciliation. From his first published collection of poetry in 1960 to the publication of his novel, *Deliverance* in 1970, Dickey's principal theme was psychological survival. The setting of *Deliverance* is a war zone in which the participants are finally able to bury their tormentors. Dickey, like his characters, is delivered from evil. After 1970, Baughman believes that Dickey was free to experiment with both form and meaning, and he gives a sound close reading of the poems, showing their interrelationships and tracing the evolving themes of transformation and death. (A,G)

Bowers, Neal. *James Dickey: The Poet as Pitchman*. Columbia: University of Missouri Press, 1985. Dickey was a shrewd businessman and knew how to promote his own reputation to secure financial security. This study examines his techniques for self-promotion with a slightly cynical eye. (A,G)

Kirschten, Robert. *James Dickey and the Gentle Ecstasy of Earth: A Reading of the Poems*. Baton Rouge: Louisiana State University Press, 1988. Kirschteng's study enumerates the influences he finds in Dickey's poetry—mysticism, Neoplatonism, Romanticism, and ritual—then explicates a number of the poems to illustrate these elements. His enthusiastic, appreciative reading will help students understand Dickey's contribution to modern American poetry, as well as broaden their understanding of Romanticism. (A,G)

Weigl, Bruce, and T. R. Hummer, eds. *The Imagination as Glory: The Poetry of James Dickey*. Champaign: University of Illinois Press, 1984. These thirteen essays by well-known critics deal with Dickey's personality and the problems of experimentation in the poems. The most interesting is Joyce Carol Oates' summation of Dickey's themes. (A)

Other Sources
Baughman, Ronald. *The Voiced Connections*. Columbia: University of South Carolina Press, 1989.

EMILY DICKINSON
1830-1886

Evaluation of Selected Biography and Criticism

Barker, Wendy. *Lunacy of Light: Emily Dickinson and the Experience of Metaphor*. Carbondale: Southern Illinois University Press, 1987. In this two-part study Barker first traces the use of light and dark imagery in Western literature and culture. She then analyzes the patterns of light and darkness in Dickinson's poetry. Barker argues that light has been traditionally associated with energy, reason, God, and male authority while darkness has been associated with death, chaos, Satan, and women. She continues her argument by showing how Dickinson, well aware of these traditional uses, countered them with new patterns. In developing her theory, Barker explicates many of Dickinson's best-known poems, providing a fresh approach and provocative ideas. Recommended for both students and specialists. **(A)**

Benfey, Christopher, ed. *Emily Dickinson: Lives of a Poet*. New York: Braziller, 1986. This elegantly produced selection of Dickinson's poetry includes a lengthy introduction that surveys the poet's life and examines her critical reputation. Current critical controversies and areas for research areas are suggested for students. This edition should accomplish its intended purpose--to attract new readers to Dickinson's work. **(G)**

Berg, Temma F., ed. *Engendering the Word: Feminist Essays in Psychosexual Poetics*. Champaign: University of Illinois Press, 1989. This collection of twelve essays focuses on the psychosexual aspects of women's writing, using perspectives derived from Cixous, Lacan, Chodorow, and Freud. Divided into three sections, this book first examines theory and then introduces a cross-cultural view by examining how writers address racially and economically marginal groups. Finally, the essays delve into linguistic analysis with particular emphasis on the works of Dickinson and Moore. This is a recommended introduction to feminist methodology. **(A,G)**

Briggs, John. *Fire in the Crucible: The Alchemy of Creative Genius*. St. Martin's, 1988. Briggs adopts alchemy as a metaphor for the transformation of emotions and ideas into products of the creative genius. Against this backdrop, he examines the creative processes of scientists, artists, and authors, among them Emily Dickinson and Virginia Woolf. This study is recommended for those who are generally interested in the author's creative act. **(A, G)**

Budick, E. Miller. *Emily Dickinson and the Life of Language: A Study in Symbolic Poetics*. Baton Rouge: Louisiana State University Press, 1985. Budick contends that Dickinson abandoned traditional poetics in order to find a language that would restore the individual to nature and to God. Many critics have found Dickinson to be theologically skeptical and anti-idealist, but

Budick can find no animating force in barren skepticism to account for the lively tone of her poems. Instead Budick describes how Dickinson transforms "false" Christian symbology into "true" and meaningful, living symbols. (A)

Dandurand, Karen. *Dickinson Scholarship: An Annotated Bibliography, 1969-1985.* New York: Garland, 1988. This comprehensive bibliography of Dickinson criticism picks up where Buckingham's *Emily Dickinson: An Annotated Bibliography* (1970) leaves off. Nearly 760 books, articles, and dissertations are cited and annotated. For the most part, the notes tend toward the descriptive, rather than the evaluative, and are generally useful. The subject index can be used to develop research themes. (A,G)

Dickinson, Donna. *Emily Dickinson.* Dover, NH: Berg, 1986. This concise summary of the poet's life, major literary themes, and critical reputation is aimed at the general reader. It provides a needed bridge between more specialized scholarly studies and older biographies. Dickinson closely examines the poet's professional identity and argues that public recognition, and not a lover, was the central loss in her life. Although presenting nothing that is unfamiliar to scholars, Dickinson does an admirable job of drawing a well-balanced and believable portrait of the poet for those with an interest in her life and works. (A,G)

Donoghue, Denis. *Reading America: Essays on American Literature.* New York: Knopf, 1987. Noted Irish literary critic Donoghue turns his critical eye on American writers in this collection of nine essays and seventeen book reviews. Each of the longer pieces—on Dickinson, Thoreau, Trilling, Whitman, Henry Adams, Emerson, Henry James, and Stevens—is prefaced by a discussion of the writer's moral and rhetorical intentions. Donoghue has a dedicated following of serious-minded readers who swear by his awesome insights. Others may have difficulty working through the details to reach the payoff. (A)

Eberwein, Jane Donahue. *Dickinson: Strategies of Limitation.* Amherst: University of Massachusetts Press, 1985. According to Eberwein, Emily Dickinson relied upon the poetic imagination as a means to overcome the limitations of social role, cultural expectations and, ultimately, of death. She chose a path of personal renunciation, constricting her life as a means to develop her art. Further, she developed specific strategies to constrict her art in order to distill the essence of her meaning. Eberwein examines in detail fictive roles expressed in Dickinson's writing—among them, "boy-child," "distanced queen," and "exultant bride." In the final section of the book, Eberwein explores the poet's "vision-quest" for spiritual fulfillment which led to Dickinson ultimately sacrificing herself as a martyr to her art. (A,G)

Johnson, Greg. *Emily Dickinson: Perception and the Poet's Quest.* University: University of Alabama Press, 1985. Arguably, what drove Emily Dickinson to create poetry was a quest for salvation. In this disciplined study, Johnson examines the spiritual impulses that directed the poet's life and career. The goal of immortality hung huge before her as she wrote. Johnson traces her quest with a closely reasoned explication of well-selected poems. This is an intelligent look at Dickinson's mind at work. **(A,G)**

Leder, Sharon, and Andrea Abbott. *The Language of Exclusion. The Poetry of Emily Dickinson and Christina Rossetti.* New York: Greenwood. 1987. For much of their critical history, both these poets have been examined with regard to the reclusive, sheltered lives they seem to have led, but revisionist and gender critics have radically altered that perception during the last few years. These two critics set out to prove that Dickinson and Rossetti were "public poets" very aware of and engaging in the issues of their day. They argue that Dickinson's and Rossetti's gender exclusions in historical, economic, and political terms led to their use of complex language to critique the industrial world around them. Specifically, Leder and Abbott discuss these poets' views on war and marriage to demonstrate their interaction with a changing society. This study should inspire new views of both poets, as well as validate the importance of gender criticism. **(A)**

Loving, Jerome. *Emily Dickinson: The Poet on the Second Story.* New York: Cambridge University Press, 1986. Loving teases out many levels of symbolic meaning from the second story bedroom where Emily Dickinson composed her poetry. Loving blends biography and an interiorized form of literary criticism to explicate the poetry as "psychic states" of the poet rather than as texts. Loving's vivid descriptions of the literary, historical, and cultural context in which Dickinson wrote are, perhaps, his most valuable contribution. **(A,G)**

McNeil, Helen. *Emily Dickinson.* New York: Pantheon, 1986. With so much new work on Dickinson available, this slight critical biography gets lost in the shuffle. Still, it is an accessible account whose thesis is that Dickinson led a double life: that of the Belle of Amherst, who agreeably played the submissive role that society assigned women and that of the revolutionary poet who broke new ground in both style and content. McNeil groups a selection of Dickinson's poems around selected themes and explicates their biographical references. The result is a good general introduction for students. **(A,G)**

Miller, Christanne. *Emily Dickinson: A Poet's Grammar.* Cambridge: Harvard University Press, 1987. Miller examines five poems in full, and portions of others, to show how Dickinson employed syntactical doubling, recurring deletions, parataxis, and upper/lower cases to establish her linguistic freedom, which Miller believes was necessary, in part, to disguise the poet's gender. She then traces some of the books that might have instructed Dickinson in her linguistic revolt, one which opened the door for modern verse. As much a study in gender politics as poetic craft, this book will interest a variety of readers who take their art and politics seriously. **(A)**

Phillips, Elizabeth. *Emily Dickinson: Personae and Performance*. University Park: Pennsylvania State University Press, 1988. Because Dickinson led what was once seen as a solitary, isolated, chaste life, it was presumed that her poetry must have relied solely on introspection and imagination. Phillips argues that Dickinson's poetry is far more universal than personal and constitutes "a haunting record of human experience." Phillips examines Dickinson's letters, as well as the poetry, to support her position. (A)

Stocks, Kenneth. *Emily Dickinson and the Modern Consciousness*. New York: St. Martin's, 1988. Stocks argues that Dickinson was the first English-speaking poet (not simply American) to examine "the heart of darkness" in a truly modern way, thus establishing herself as the first modern poet. In his examination of her work for its philosophy and relation to existentialism he argues that she was a "guide" into the twentieth-century psyche. Stocks is principally concerned with broadening the view of Dickinson from that of simply an American poet to a "lantern" that anticipated a modern world. Because Stocks refuses to admit that Dickinson was influenced by her gender, his reading of the works provides a provocative contrast for students interested in gender criticism. (A,G)

Wolff, Cynthia Griffin. *Emily Dickinson*. Knopf, 1986. Wolff covers the same ground as previous Dickinson biographers, Johnson and Sewell, but then strikes out on her own to redefine the poet's relationship to her work. The critical readings she undertakes for many of the poems are thought-provoking, even controversial. Wolff isolates Dickinson's poetic themes and examines each in light of the poet's family and religious context. This study is carefully crafted and offers new insight into a poet who has attracted the attention of several gifted biographers in recent years. This book is highly recommended for students or anyone interested in Dickinson's life and works. (A,G)

Other Sources

St. Armand, Barton Levi. *Emily Dickinson and Her Culture: The Soul's Society*. New York: Cambridge University Press, 1985.

Stonum, Gary Lee. *The Dickinson Sublime*. Madison: University of Wisconsin Press, 1990.

JOAN DIDION
1934

Author's Recent Bibliography
Miami, 1987 (travel).

Evaluation of Selected Biography and Criticism
Loris, Michelle Carbone. *Innocence, Loss, and Recovery in the Art of Joan Didion*. New York: Peter Lang, 1989. Loris argues that the common thread uniting Didion's novels, essays, and reportage is the joining of a western wilderness narrative, which emphasizes personal perseverance and hope, to a vision of a fallen and morally bankrupt modern culture. In commenting on Didion's reportage in *Salvador* and *Miami*, Loris sees them as "parables of how we relinquish the promise of personal dignity and cultural prosperity to human arrogance and greed. She devotes a chapter to each of Didion's novels, one to her essays, and another to her reportage. A useful overview of Didion's career to date. (A,G)

Winchell, Mark Royden. *Joan Didion, Revised Edition*. Boston: Twayne, 1989. For this new edition of his 1980 critical biography of Didion, Winchell has expanded and substantially revised the text. A short biographical introduction leads directly into a prolonged discussion of Didion's most noted nonfiction works, *Slouching Towards Bethlehem* and *The White Album*. These works are treated thematically, according to arts, morality, social classes, lifestyles, politics, people, and places. Winchell then examines the short fiction and concludes with a discussion of several recent works, *Salvador*, *Miami*, and *Democracy*. (A,G)

JOHN DONNE
1572-1631

Evaluation of Selected Biography and Criticism
Guibbory, Achsah. *The Map of Time: Seventeenth-Century English Literature and Ideas of Pattern in History.* Champaign: University of Illinois Press, 1986. Guibbory reveals the conceptions of time and history that underlie seventeenth-century thought in this closely reasoned study of six major writers—Donne, Bacon, Jonson, Herrick, Milton, and Dryden. Guibbory divines three such conceptions: degeneration and decay since the Garden of Eden; cycles of generation and decay; and the advance of civilization. He then shows how these three patterns of historical perspective influence poetry, drama, scientific and religious prose, and the writing of history. In every case, Guibbory relates history to genre, structure, imagery, and theme. Highly recommended. (A,G)

Larson, Deborah Aldrich. *John Donne and Twentieth-Century Criticism.* Madison, NJ: Fairleigh Dickinson University Press, 1989. Larson discusses the key points of modern literary criticism of Donne's poetry. Each of the five chapters addresses a critical argument, such as T. S. Eliot's reassessment in terms of New Criticism. By analyzing the critical heritage and reception, Larson shows why Donne seems more like a modern poet than an antique one. Recommended for advanced students and scholars. (A)

Marotti, Arthur F. *John Donne: Coterie Poet.* Madison: University of Wisconsin Press, 1986. This is a well-researched critique of Donne's work based on revisionist history, psychoanalytic theory, and post-structuralist criticism. Marotti seeks to identify a particular rhetorical audience for individual works. The force of this socio-historical analysis is weakened by an ambiguous definition of audience. The bibliography can give students an indication of the genesis of Marotti's theoretical perspective. Recommended for graduate students and researchers who are looking for alternative critical approaches. (A)

Summers, Claude, and Ted-Larry Pebworth, eds. *The Eagle and the Dove: Reassessing John Donne.* Athens: University of Georgia Press, 1986. This collection of fifteen wide-ranging essays presents an overview of critical opinion on Donne's poetry. Contributors, such as Dennis Flynn, Stella Revard, and John Shawcross, examine Donne's satires, epigrams, epithamalia, sermons, and characteristic style. This is a useful introduction to the current state of Donne scholarship. (A,G)

Waller, Gary. *English Poetry of the Sixteenth Century.* White Plains, NY: Longman, 1986. Using the theories of Eagleton, Greenblatt, Sinfield, and Greenberg, Waller's study is a revisionist history of English Renaissance poetry. Waller develops a parallel chronological overview and critical reevaluation. Chapters cover sixteenth-century literary theory, the ideology of the Elizabethan court, Petrarch, and Protestantism. Several authors are given prolonged treatment—Dunbar, Wyatt, Raleigh, Greville, Sidney, Spenser, Shakespeare, and Donne. This book was meant to, but does not, supplant C. S. Lewis' *English Literature of the Sixteenth Century* (1954). (A)

Warnke, Frank J. *John Donne.* Boston: Twayne, 1987. This short critical biography depicts Donne's life and times and analyzes his poetry in relation to baroque culture. Warnke explores the reasons why Donne faded into critical oblivion and how he was rediscovered during the 1920s, largely as a result of T. S. Eliot's brilliant criticism. This excellent introduction will serve advanced students well. (A)

Other Sources

Bald, R. C. *John Donne: A Life.* New York: Oxford University Press, 1986.

Clements, Arthur. *Poetry of Contemplation: John Donne, George Herbert, Henry Vaughan, and the Modern Period.* Albany: State University of New York Press, 1989.

Docherty, Thomas. *John Donne, Undone.* London: Methuen, 1986.

Elimimian, Issac I. *A Study of Rhetorical Patterns in John Donne's Epicedes and Obsequies.* New York: Vantage, 1987.

Sellin, Paul R. *So Doth, So Is Religion: John Donne and Diplomatic Contexts in the Reformed Netherlands, 1619-1620.* Columbia: University of Missouri Press, 1988.

Sloane, Thomas O. *Donne, Milton, and the End of Humanist Rhetoric.* Berkeley: University of California Press, 1985.

Stanwood, Paul G., and Heather Asals. *John Donne and the Theology of Language.* Columbia: University of Missouri Press, 1986.

Willmott, Richard. *Four Metaphysical Poets: An Anthology of Poetry by Donne, Herbert, Marvell, and Vaughan.* New York: Cambridge University Press, 1985.

JOHN DOS PASSOS
1896-1970

Evaluation of Selected Criticism

Clark, Michael. *Dos Passos's Early Fiction, 1912-1938*. Cranbury, NJ: Susquehanna University Press, 1987. Clark's study traces the development of Dos Passos' style and thematic concerns through the period of the *U.S.A.* trilogy, pointing out his affinities with other American authors, such as Walt Whitman and William James. The 1920s served as a period of gestation for Dos Passos, who eventually developed the coherent philosophy expressed in his later novels. Dos Passos worked to expose the fragmentation of the modern world and viewed nature as a healing force, capable of mitigating the effects of an accelerating social alienation. Clark's prose is clear and to the point, and his readings of the works well-reasoned. (A)

Pizer, Donald, ed. *John Dos Passos: The Major Nonfictional Prose*. Detroit: Wayne State University Press, 1988. Pizer has selected over eighty examples of Dos Passos' articles, reviews, and interviews to represent the novelist's nonfictional output. Arranged chronologically, these pieces document Dos Passos' considerable shift in political views from his college days to later years. His opinions on fellow novelists, especially Hemingway, are disappointingly undeveloped. The selections are thoroughly indexed, adding to the value of the collection. (A)

Pizer, Donald. *Dos Passos' "U.S.A.": A Critical Study*. Charlottesville: University Press of Virginia, 1988. Pizer examines Dos Passos' *U.S.A.* trilogy as a modernist American epic in the tradition of Walt Whitman's *Leaves of Grass*. In an overview of Dos Passos' earlier works, Pizer examines the process of growth and refinement that lead to production of the trilogy. He then turns his attention to the trilogy to reveal that the extended work was created in four modes, each a distinctive literary form. Each mode is intricately intertwined with the others. The four modes depend for unity upon Dos Passos' overall satiric vision. (A)

Other Sources

Maine, Barry, ed. *Dos Passos*. New York: Routledge Chapman and Hall, 1988.

Sanders, David. *John Dos Passos: A Comprehensive Bibliography*. New York: Garland, 1987.

SIR ARTHUR CONAN DOYLE
1859-1930

Autobiographical Sources

Gibson, John and Richard Lancelyn Green, eds. *Arthur Conan Doyle: Letters to the Press.* Iowa City: University of Iowa Press, 1986. Doyle was a firm believer in airing his opinions about almost anything in the press. This selection of letters, arranged chronologically, shows the creator of Sherlock Holmes ranging freely from global politics to spiritualism. His arguments are so well-reasoned and persuasive that one cannot help but sense the Holmesian mind at work. This is an intellectual treat for those who have loved Doyle's fiction. (A,G)

Evaluation of Selected Biography and Criticism

Accardo, Pasquale. *Diagnosis and Detection: The Medical Iconography of Sherlock Holmes.* Madison, NJ: Fairleigh Dickinson University Press, 1987. This study explores Arthur Conan Doyle's medical and literary sources to shed light on aspects of the Sherlock Holmes stories. While talking about sources, Accardo touches upon many points that will interest Holmes fans, including astute comparisons of Holmes with mythic and epic heroes, and Watson with Shakespeare's Falstaff. That Accardo moves quickly from insight to insight may irritate some scholars but can stimulate a student who is searching for topics to explore more fully. (A,G)

Hardwick, Michael. *The Complete Guide to Sherlock Holmes.* New York: St. Martin's, 1987. Beginning with the debut of Holmes in *A Study in Scarlet,* Hardwick treats the stories in chronological order. He discusses influences, subject matter, and characters; relates plot complications; and summarizes each story (without disclosing the endings). The stories are linked by an ongoing discussion of Doyle's life. Also included are illustrations from *Strand Magazine,* where the stories first appeared. Hardwick's guide is a useful introduction for the Holmes neophyte and a mine of background information for the long-time reader. (A,G)

Harrison, Michael. *Immortal Sleuth: Sherlockian Musings and Memories.* Dubuque, IA: Gasogene Press, 1987. In this study, Harrison offers wide-ranging thoughts on Doyle's fiction: how the stories should be dramatized, the influence of Poe on Doyle's plots and landscapes, political events that Doyle incorporated into his fiction, and tidbits about Doyle's personal life. The book includes illustrations, a bibliography, and index. In all this is a collection of interesting minor material for Doyle enthusiasts. (G)

Jaffe, Jacqueline A. *Arthur Conan Doyle.* Boston: Twayne, 1987. Jaffe's approach treats Doyle's writings in chronological order, classifying them by genre. She extracts from the stories a Victorian code of honor that she claims animated Doyle's life, as well as his works. Unlike many treatments that examine Doyle's work in isolation, this balanced study places the famous stories within the context of literary history. (A,G)

Lellenberg, Jon L., ed. *The Quest for Sir Arthur Conan Doyle: Thirteen Biographers in Search of a Life.* Carbondale: Southern Illinois University Press, 1987. This anthology brings together the work of a number of scholars to assess the value of existing biographies of Doyle and to discuss the problems inherent in studying his life. In his autobiographical writings, Doyle clearly presented only those aspects of his life that he wanted the public to see. To compound the problem, his unpublished memoirs and letters are currently closed to scholars by legal restrictions. Only a few biographers have been granted limited access to the Doyle family archives. This has resulted in a situation where a small number of facts and many falsehoods are in constant circulation. (A,G)

Stavert, Geoffrey. *A Study in Southsea: The Unrevealed Life of Doctor Arthur Conan Doyle.* Cincinnati, OH: Seven Hills, 1988. Stavert investigates Doyle's life during the eight years he lived in Southsea, Portsmouth. During this period he established his medical practice and, more importantly, created the character of Sherlock Holmes. For Holmes' enthusiasts, this book turns up many new details, though they may be of little interest to general readers. (A,G)

Symons, Julian, *Conan Doyle: Portrait of an Artist.* New York: Mysterious Press, 1987. Mystery writer and critic Julian Symons has produced a knowledgeable and discerning biography of Doyle, the physician turned mystery writer. Symons makes perceptive comments on the Sherlock Holmes stories but also gives needed attention to Doyle's other writings, which he preferred over his mysteries. The anecdotes involving the various mediums and spiritualists that targeted Doyle as an easy mark are particularly entertaining. (A,G)

Tracy, Jack, ed. *Strange Studies from Life and Other Narratives: The Complete True Crime Writing of Sir Arthur Conan Doyle.* Bloomington, IN: Gaslight, 1988. From time to time Doyle wrote magazine articles based on true crimes. Not content with just the facts, he embellished his accounts by developing characters and speculating on the circumstances of the crimes. Because of this, these articles, "which examined grisly crimes from the past," have some of the flavor of short stories. Not only do they provide intriguing reading for Doyle fans, but they are a valuable resource for those researching the development of his fictional techniques. (G)

Other Sources
Cox, Don R. *Arthur Conan Doyle.* New York: Ungar, 1985.

Goodrich, William D. *Good Old Index: The Sherlock Holmes Reference Guide.* Dubuque, IA: Gasogene Press, 1988.

Harper, Leslie V., ed. *The Secret Conan Doyle Correspondence.* Hascom, 1986.

Harrison, Michael. *London by Gaslight.* Dubuque, IA: Gasogene Press, 1987.

Nown, Graham. *Elementary, My Dear Watson: Sherlock Holmes Centenary, His Life and Times.* Salem House, 1986.

THEODORE DREISER
1871-1945

Autobiographical Sources

Riggio, Thomas, ed. *Dreiser-Mencken Letters: The Correspondence of Theodore Dreiser and H. L. Mencken, 1907-1945.* Philadelphia, University of Pennsylvania Press, 1987. Riggio, who edited Dreiser's *American Diaries*, sets out to illuminate the relationship that existed between Dreiser and H. L. Mencken. Of over 1,200 letters and notes they exchanged, Riggio has selected all but about two hundred for this volume, the remainder being deemed trivial or repetitive. The letters are arranged chronologically and are carefully annotated to identify obscure names and references. Two appendixes are included, one containing Mencken's letters to Helen Dreiser after her husband's death, the other reprinting the two men's published criticisms of each other's work. (A,G)

Evaluation of Selected Biography and Criticism

Bowlby, Rachel. *Just Looking: Consumer Culture in Dreiser, Gissing, and Zola.* New York: Methuen, 1985. Combining recent critical theory, history, and economics with a feminist perspective, Bowlby analyzes the novels of Dreiser, Gissing, and Zola in terms of the emerging consumer culture of the late nineteenth century. She contends that during this period poetry became "more pure" and the novel became a "commodity." Changing economic conditions prompted a change both in gender-based roles and in the concepts of masculinity and femininity. The "naturalistic" novel functioned as a critique of these social forces. (A,G)

Griffin, Joseph. *The Small Canvas: An Introduction to Dreiser's Short Stories.* Madison, NJ: Fairleigh Dickinson University Press, 1985. Most treatments of Dreiser's fiction contend with the critical problems produced by the author's "behemoth" qualities. For example, the two-volume *An American Tragedy* was cut by Dreiser's editors from about one million words to a mere 300,000. Griffin has avoided this issue by focusing on Dreiser's thirty-one short stories, which vary significantly in technique, genre, and quality. Each is presented with a full publishing history and a discussion of its critical acceptance. Griffin then examines the revisions that each story underwent from drafts to serial and book publication. Although tame by modern standards, many of these stories were considered "racy" by publishers of the time. This introduction provides an insightful look at a neglected body of Dreiser's work. (A,G)

Hakutani, Yoshinobu, ed. *Selected Magazine Articles of Theodore Dreiser: Life and Art in the American 1890s.* Madison, NJ: Fairleigh Dickinson University Press, 1985, 1987. This two-volume collection of magazine articles contains about half of the hundred or so essays Dreiser wrote before the success of his first novel. Few of these essays are currently in print, and they have never been collected in this manner before. In Dreiser's broad range of topics and themes, Hakutani finds a reflection of American life and art in the 1890s. More specifically, these essays provide a benchmark for measuring Dreiser's developing intellect and sense of aesthetics. In them, for example, he passes judgment upon such noted contemporary figures as Howells, Stieglitz, Sonntag, Carnegie, and Edison. The essays are carefully introduced and annotated. (A,G)

Kaplan, Amy. *The Social Construction of American Realism.* Chicago: University of Chicago Press, 1988. In this study of American realists, Kaplan focuses on the works of Howells, Wharton, and Dreiser and stresses their relation to the social changes of the late-1800s. Kaplan challenges recent feminist criticism by describing Wharton as a professional writer in conflict with women writers with a more popular appeal. She examines Dreiser's conception of art as commodity. Kaplan's arguments are well-documented and persuasively developed. (A,G)

Lingeman, Richard R. *Theodore Dreiser: At the Gates of the City, 1871-1907* (Volume 1); *Theodore Dreiser: An American Journey* (Volume 2). New York: Putnam, 1986, 1990. This first volume takes Dreiser from his traumatic childhood in Indiana through his work as a journalist and the publication of his first novel, *Sister Carrie.* A major mental breakdown then follows leading to a temporary abandonment of his work. The volume ends in 1907, when Dreiser has largely recovered and is ready to launch the most productive phase of his career. The second volume picks up with Dreiser making drastic life changes: he leaves his wife and his conservative job as an editor for a bohemian writer's life in New York's Greenwich Village. It was a gamble that paid handsomely. *An American Tragedy* was hailed by critics and readers alike as one of the most important novels in American literature. At this point Lingeman steps back from his subject, evaluates the politics and social conditions of the time, then attempts to explain Dreiser's forays into Stalinism. Lingeman's approach is almost novelistic in its descriptions of people, places, and events. This first-rate biography, which uses material unavailable to earlier biographers, provides insights for Dreiser scholars and a vividly told life story for the more general reader. (A,G)

Mills, Nicolaus. *The Crowd in American Literature.* Baton Rouge: Louisiana State University Press, 1986. Mills explicates the use of "crowds" by American writers from Jefferson to Steinbeck. For colonial writers crowds were a "force for democracy;" for the classical American novelists—Twain, Hawthorne, and Melville—they were a force for national unity. Mills examines the "noble" working-class masses of such writers as Howells, Dreiser, and Steinbeck. Finally, he turns to Norman Mailer and Ralph Ellison for an examination of post-war crowds, the repository of intellectual and moral power contrasted with brute force. This is a fascinating thematic social history drawn from American literary works. (A,G)

Mukherjee, Arun. *The Gospel of Wealth in the American Novel: The Rhetoric of Dreiser and Some of His Contemporaries.* London: Croom Helm, 1987. About half this study is devoted to Dreiser, whom Mukherjee depicts as a reformed materialist. Mukherjee claims that after 1894, when Dreiser encountered the writings of Herbert Spencer, he abandoned the American dream of wealth for everyone and turned to the naturalistic fiction that made him famous. Mukherjee attempts to show how the materialist and the minister wear the same cloth but ultimately are strangers in the quest of the American Dream. This study draws heavily on historical context through which Dreiser would have developed his naturalistic/materialistic ideas. (A)

Nostwich, T. D., ed. *Theodore Dreiser: Journalism.* Volume 1. This is a collection of Dreiser's newspaper stories written between 1892-1895 when he worked as an apprentice on seven newspapers in Chicago, St. Louis, Cleveland, Toledo, Pittsburgh, and New York. During his stint as a cub reporter, Dreiser was exposed to murders, train wrecks, con men, executions, séances, and many other seedy elements of urban life. These experiences combined with his training as a reporter, offer excellent insights into the novelist's attitudes, themes, and style. Readers will enjoy the journalism and learn much about Dreiser's sensibility. (A,G)

Schulman, Robert. *Social Criticism and Nineteenth-Century American Fictions.* Columbia: University of Missouri Press, 1987. Schulman examines the political psychology of capitalism and its influence on the lives and works of some of the most famous American authors—Franklin, Twain, Melville, Hawthorne, Chesnutt, Whitman, Wharton, Howells, and Dreiser. His study pursues three main themes—the fragmentation of community, the impact of social change, and the styles of American individualism. In his discussion of Franklin's *Autobiography*, Schulman describes the costs of success and upward mobility as emotional deadening, increased isolation, and personal fragmentation. A truly new and refreshing reevaluation of nineteenth-century American literature. (A,G)

Other Sources
Boswell, Jeanetta. *Theodore Dreiser and the Critics, 1911-1982: A Bibliography with Selective Annotations.* Metuchen, NJ: Scarecrow, 1986.

Nostwich, T. D. *Theodore Dreiser's "Heard in the Corridors" Articles and Related Writings.* Iowa City: Iowa State University Press, 1988.

West, James L., III. *A "Sister Carrie" Portfolio.* Charlottesville: University Press of Virginia, 1985.

JOHN DRYDEN
1631-1700

Evaluation of Selected Biography and Criticism

Anderson, James. *John Dryden and His World*. New Haven and London: Yale University Press, 1987. Anderson explores the relations between Dryden's literary, political, and religious themes, and shows how the period's sense of decorum influenced his stylistic choices. (A)

Engell, James. *Forming the Critical Mind: Dryden to Coleridge*. Cambridge: Harvard University Press, 1989. Engell presents a lucid discussion of the origins and theories of eighteenth-century literary criticism with special emphasis on Dryden, Johnson, and Hume. After dividing criticism into its component preoccupations—genre, canon, refinement, and form—he then relates these to modern critical theories. This book is recommended to students for its methodology as well as for its argument. (A)

Guibbory, Achsah. *The Map of Time: Seventeenth-Century English Literature and Ideas of Pattern in History*. Champaign: University of Illinois Press, 1986. Guibbory reveals the conceptions of time and history that underlie seventeenth-century thought in this closely reasoned study of six major writers—Donne, Bacon, Jonson, Herrick, Milton, and Dryden. Guibbory divines three such conceptions: degeneration and decay since the Garden of Eden; cycles of generation and decay; and the advance of civilization. He then shows how these three patterns of historical perspective influence poetry, drama, scientific and religious prose, and the writing of history. In every case, Guibbory relates history to genre, structure, imagery, and theme. Highly recommended. (A,G)

Guilhamet, Leon. *Satire and the Transformation of Genre*. Philadelphia: University of Pennsylvania Press, 1987. Using selected works of Dryden, Pope, and Swift, Guilhamet dissects and analyzes satiric form. He divides satire into three types—demonstrative, deliberative, and judicial—and then shows how these types interact within the complex structures devised by the authors. Great satire, he contends, emerges with the belief that the past is superior to the present and that innovation is destructive of important institutions. (A)

Hopkins, David. *John Dryden*. Cambridge: Cambridge University Press, 1986. Hopkins provides a selective introduction to Dryden for new readers. Dryden's later studies and translations of classical writers are emphasized, while his plays, criticism, and panegyrics are briefly summarized in a single chapter. The poems *Mac Flecknoe* and *Absalom and Achitophel* are only discussed to compare their inferior quality with his classical poetic translations.

153

This is useful as a supplementary introduction to Dryden's work but hardly tells the whole story. (A,G)

Reverand, Cedric D. III. *Dryden's Final Poetic Mode: The "Fables."* Philadelphia: University of Pennsylvania Press, 1988. Once Dryden's most popular work, The *Fables* has long been neglected. Reverand examines the work's thematic structure, including Dryden's treatment of the heroic ideal and the various forms of love and kinship. He emphasizes the poet's concern about the political stability of England upon the accession of William III. Reverand interprets the reasons for Dryden's departures from his staple sources of inspiration and material: Homer, Boccaccio, Ovid, and Chaucer. Recommended for scholars. (A)

Winn, James Anderson. *John Dryden and His World.* New Haven: Yale University Press, 1987. C. E. Ward's 1961 biography cleared up some of the ambiguities surrounding Dryden's life; Winn's biography details everything else that is ever likely to be known. Winn sees the central forces in Dryden's life as politics, the court, religion, and morality, and he explains how these four elements affect Dryden's poetry. This account includes appendixes on the Dryden family, his Westminster school curriculum, payments to the poet, and details of his mistress, Anne Reeves. The endnotes and index are valuable for research. This readable biography is likely to become definitive. (A,G)

Other Sources
Frost, William. *John Dryden: Dramatist, Satirist, Translator.* New York: AMS Press, 1988.

Hall, James M. *John Dryden: A Reference Guide.* Boston: G. K. Hall, 1984.

McHenry, Robert, ed. *Contexts 3: Absalom and Achitophel.* Hamden, CT: Archon Books/Shoe String Press, 1986.

Sloman, Judith. *Dryden: The Poetics of Translation.* Toronto: University of Toronto Press, 1985.

Walker, Keith, ed. *Dryden.* New York: Oxford University Press, 1987.

Zwicker, Steven N. *Politics and Language in Dryden's Poetry.* Princeton: Princeton University Press, 1984.

WILLIAM DUNBAR
c. 1455-1517

Evaluation of Selected Criticism

Scheps, Walter, and J. Anna Looney. *Middle Scots Poets: A Reference Guide to James I of Scotland, Robert Henryson, William Dunbar, and Gavin Douglas.* Boston: G. K. Hall, 1986. The first section provides a general bibliography, followed by one chapter on each of the four poets. For most bibliographical entries a descriptive account is offered. (A)

LAWRENCE DURRELL
1912

Author's Recent Bibliography

Antrobus Complete, 1985 (stories); *Quinx, or the Ripper's Tale*, 1985 (novel).

Autobiographical Sources

MacNiven, Ian S., ed. *The Durrell-Miller Letter, 1935-1980*. New York: New Directions, 1988. Durrell initiated a correspondence with Miller in 1935 that continued until Miller's death in 1980. The two authors developed a lively relationship through the mail, and these letters sparkle with mischievous wordplay. Each comments frankly on the other's works and works-in-progress and offers sometimes-brutal commentary on the books of other writers. Both men discuss their theoretical approaches to the purpose and structure of the novel and often describe their work habits. At one point Durrell entices Miller to visit him in France, extolling the virtues of his village's "medieval" atmosphere. Miller responds that life in America has spoiled him, that "medieval" has little appeal, but that he will be content if the little bistro Durrell described serves decent wine. This is an invaluable primary source for the study of both Miller and Durrell. MacNiven provides unobtrusive annotations to the letters and a useful introduction to each section. **(A,G)**

Evaluation of Selected Biography and Criticism

Friedman, Alan Warren, ed. *Critical Essays on Lawrence Durrell*. Boston: G. K. Hall, 1987. Durrell is best known for *The Alexandria Quartet*, but he has produced works in a variety of genres. This anthology contains ten reviews of Durrell's books, nineteen critical essays, and a parody. Friedman purports to have collected the best thinking on Durrell to lay to rest the controversy over his critical significance. Some insist he is a genius; others contend that he is at best a minor writer. In all, this is an excellent anthology that is confident enough to poke fun at its subject by including a parody. **(A,G)**

Kums, Guido. *Fiction, or the Language of Our Discontent: A Study of the Built-in Novelist in Novels by Angus Wilson, Lawrence Durrell, and Doris Lessing*. New York: Peter Lang, 1985. Kums contends that the use of the novelist as a character in a novel allows the author to comment theoretically on the process of writing in a way that is unique. He examines three works that feature novelist characters—Wilson's *No Laughing Matter*, Durrell's *Alexandria Quartet*, and Lessing's *The Golden Notebook*—finding parallels in the authors' perspectives on writing. This is a specialized study that attempts a radical reevaluation of the form and definition of the modern novel. **(A)**

Pine, Richard. *The Dandy and the Herald: Manners, Mind, and Morals from Brummell to Durrell.* New York: St Martin's, 1988. In this study of literary forms, Pine examines the role played by Durrell, Miller, and Nin in tearing down the outmoded narrative structures they inherited. For Pine, the "dandy" represents the pompous and shallow conventions of fiction. In rebellion against this figure, Miller, Nin, and Durrell, in particular, set up the image of the artist as "herald," a prophetic announcer of the literary future. Pine finds parallels of this process in literary history, tracing the struggle of innovation and tradition through the English Renaissance, romanticism, and early twentieth-century writers. After establishing the context in which "dandies," like Wilde, Beardsley, and Jarry flourished, Pine goes on to examine the failure of modern literature to solve or transcend the dandy/herald dichotomy. (A)

Vander Closter, Susan. *Joyce Cary and Lawrence Durrell: A Reference Guide.* Boston: G. K. Hall, 1985. This guide to the critical response to two twentieth-century British authors consists of separate chronologically arranged annotated bibliographies. The Cary section covers the period 1932 until 1981; the Durrell bibliography begins with a 1937 review of *Panic Spring* and continues into 1983. The annotations are descriptive rather than evaluative and give a flavor of the work through a liberal use of quotations. Short introductions provide an overview of critical opinion on each writer. A useful resource for the student or researcher. (A)

Weigel, John A. *Lawrence Durrell.* Boston: Twayne, 1989. This critical study (part of the English Authors series) examines Durrell's works, including his less-studied dramas and humorous sketches. The bulk of the book focuses on the novels—*The Alexandria Quartet, The Revolt of Aphrodite,* and *The Avignon Quintet.* In his analysis, Weigel suggests that Durrell has moved away from his earlier psychological preoccupations into themes influenced by the "ineffables" of Buddhism. Weigel also dissects the many, often-conflicting critical responses that Durrell's books seem to arouse. Biographical materials are concisely presented. This volume includes a chronology and selected bibliography and should serve as a useful guide through the complexities of Durrell's novels. (A,G)

MARIA EDGEWORTH
1767-1849

Evaluation of Selected Criticism

Owens, Cóilin, ed. *Family Chronicles: Maria Edgeworth's "Castle Rackrent."* Totowa, NJ: Barnes & Noble, 1987. This is an anthology of fourteen critical essays that address aspects of Edgeworth's *Castle Rackrent*, including discussions of the book's narrator, didacticism, use of folklore, and the author's politics and biography. John Cronin provides a biographical introduction. Marilyn Butler examines the work's sources and the circum- stances of its composition, while Ernest Boher places it in the context of the English novel. W. B. Cooley discusses Edgeworth's role as an early Irish novelist. Other contributors include Thomas Flanagan, Roger McHugh, Maurice Colgan, Johann Altieri, and Elizabeth Harden. A bibliography of additional Edgeworth criticism is provided. **(A,G)**

GEORGE ELIOT
1819-1880

Autobiographical Sources

Haight, Gordon S., ed. *Selections from George Eliot's Letters*. New Haven: Yale University Press, 1985. Haight has selected letters that relate most directly to Eliot's biography and literary interests. Although Eliot was a partial recluse, primarily because of her illicit relationship with George Henry Lewes, she carried on a vigorous, intelligent correspondence with the literary luminaries of her day. These lively letters, more accessible than the collected letters, should enlarge the readership of her correspondence. (A,G)

Evaluation of Selected Biography and Criticism

Beer, Gillian. *George Eliot*. Bloomington: Indiana University Press, 1986. In this enterprising study of George Eliot, Beer makes a distinction between feminist politics and the literary criticism of women's writing. She defends Eliot against charges by feminist critics that claim the author fails to "liberate" her protagonists. Beer concludes her defense by showing that Eliot's feminism was more subtle than critics have acknowledged. Beer is persuasive in her discussion of the problems of ideologically driven literary criticism and in her analyses of *Middlemarch* and *Daniel Deronda*. (A,G)

Berg, Temma F., ed. *Engendering the Word: Feminist Essays in Psychosexual Poetics*. Champaign: University of Illinois Press, 1989. This collection of twelve essays focuses on the psychosexual aspects of women's writing, using perspectives derived from Cixous, Lacan, Chodorow, and Freud. Divided into three sections, this book first examines theory, then examines how women writers address race and economically marginal groups. Finally, the essays delve into linguistic analyses with particular emphasis on the works of Dickinson and Moore. (A,G)

Carpenter, Mary Wilson. *George Eliot and the Landscape of Time-Narrative Form and Protestant Apocalyptic History*. Chapel Hill: University of North Carolina Press, 1986. Underlying much of George Eliot's writing, Carpenter contends, is a preoccupation with the forms and imagery of Christian apocalyptic writings found in the books of *Revelation, and Daniel,* and in other more obscure works. Eliot relies heavily on numerology to structure her chapters and in the design of her narratives. Of particular interest is Carpenter's treatment of *Adam Bede, Mill on the Floss, Romola, Daniel Deronda,* and *The Legend of Jubal*. The study contains extensive notes and a bibliography that includes works on millenarianism, as well as those by and about Eliot. Carpenter succeeds in making a difficult subject accessible to a range of readers. (A,G)

Coslett, Tess. *Woman to Woman: Female Friendship in Victorian Fiction.* Brighton: Harvester Press, 1988. Focusing on the Victorian era, Coslett demonstrates how women writers of the time were able to lend special power and significance to female friendships in their fiction. In these works, personal transformation is wrought through "sisterhood," rather than through the conventions of courtship and marriage. Coslett traces the process of individual development in novels by Eliot, Gaskell, Rossetti, Browning, and Charlotte Brontë. (A,G)

Dentith, Simon. *George Eliot.* Boston: Humanities Press, 1986. Dentith's short work on Eliot is intended to provide a rereading of the author for a student audience. Dentith establishes the thesis that Eliot is a realist writer, then defends it with an interpretation of her novels. (G)

Ermarth, Elizabeth. *George Eliot.* Boston: Twayne, 1985. Ermarth opens with a short biography of Eliot, then proceeds to trace her intellectual development, showing how her translations of theological and philosophical works influenced the moral vision of her fiction. Ermarth argues that Eliot's primary theme is individual freedom restricted by social customs. (A,G)

Freadman, Richard. *Eliot, James, and the Fictional Self.* New York: St. Martin's, 1986. Freadman offers a comparative study of the presentation of characters in novels of Eliot and James. Early chapters discuss both authors' theories of the novel: its structure, purpose, and intent. This is a specialized study useful to scholars. (A,G)

Homans, Margaret. *Bearing the Word: Language and Female Experience in Nineteenth-Century Women's Writing.* Chicago: University of Chicago Press, 1986. Delving into the Oedipal propositions of psychoanalytic theory, Homans emerges with an insight into the interaction of language acquisition and the formation of gender identity. Building on the ideas of Jacques Lacan and Nancy Chodorow, she describes a dominant myth of language that identifies the woman with the "literal," and a dominant myth of gender that connects her with nature and matter. To support these theories, Homans provides close readings of excerpts from Eliot, Dorothy Wordsworth, Mary Shelley, the Brontë sisters, Elizabeth Gaskell, and Virginia Woolf. Scholars should acquaint themselves with the theoretical framework that Homans develops. (A)

Hornback, Bert G. *"Middlemarch": A Novel of Reform.* Boston: Twayne, 1988. In this volume of the Twayne Masterworks Series, Hornback provides an introduction to Eliot's famous novel for high school and undergraduate audiences. The study is strongest when discussing the roles and complexities of the characters. In spite of the subtitle's implication, Eliot's political beliefs and the political context of the novel are not fully developed. (G,Y)

Kucich, John. *Repression in Victorian Fiction: Charlotte Brontë, George Eliot, and Charles Dickens.* Berkeley: University of California Press, 1987. This lengthy study traces the theme of psychological repression through the life and works of Brontë, Eliot, and Dickens. Kucich's thorough scholarship examines in detail the nineteenth-century tendency to "exalt interiority." In the process, he eschews traditional critical terms, such as "self-denial" and "renunciation," in favor of his own vision of "repression." Although at times overburdened with psychoanalytical terminology, this study presents a fresh perspective from which to read the fiction of these authors. (A)

LaBelle, Jenijoy. *Herself Beheld: The Literature of the Looking Glass.* Ithaca, NY: Cornell University Press, 1988. LaBelle examines the importance of the mirror as symbol in the work of twentieth-century women writers. For her, the mirror's reflection symbolizes introspection and revelation instead of vanity, which is dominant in traditional Christian, male-dominated symbology. She examines looking-glass episodes in the novels of Eliot and the Brontës, as well as many of the period's lesser-known works of fiction. This is a fresh feminist look at a common, recurring symbol in fiction. (A,G)

McKee, Patricia. *Heroic Commitment in Richardson, Eliot, and James.* Princeton, NJ: Princeton University Press, 1986. This demanding theoretical excursion into the works of Samuel Richardson, George Eliot, and Henry James derives its critical stance from the works of Derrida and the French feminist school. Comparing the structures, characterization, and thematic preoccupations of the authors, McKee offers insightful, open-ended readings of major works. Women characters are seen as drawn into relationships of heroic commitment made possible by an indeterminacy that negates the determinacy of power. (A,G)

Nestor, Pauline. *Female Friendships and Communities: Charlotte Brontë, George Eliot, Elizabeth Gaskell.* Oxford: Clarendon Press, 1985. Devoting two chapters to each author, Nestor describes the writers' association with other women, their attitudes toward gender, and their treatment of women in their fiction. In doing so, Nestor enlarges her study to include nineteenth-century attitudes toward single women, female friendship, communal living, sexuality, and the emotions which society elicits from women, including anger, violence, passivity, jealously, and resignation. This provocative study illuminates the fiction of three writers, the context in which they created characters, and the society that would accept or reject both them and their work. (A,G)

Thomas, Jeanie. *Reading "Middlemarch": Reclaiming the Middle Distance.* Ann Arbor: UMI Research, 1987. This reading of Eliot's novel will anger feminist critics and seem critically restrictive to others. Its approach is a psychoanalytical reading of character motivation and interaction that addresses the moral questions of Victorian thought. Thomas believes, as Eliot did, that the novel should provide moral therapy, and she demonstrates how *Middlemarch* fulfills this purpose. (A,G)

Uglow, Jennifer. *George Eliot.* Virago/Pantheon, 1987. Uglow has produced an impressive critical biography of Eliot that focuses on the paradoxes of her life and work. In Uglow's view, Eliot struggled to reconcile her sense of duty with a desire to avenge women wronged by society. When analyzing the works, Uglow focuses on themes that reflect Eliot's life—her ambivalent relationship to the feminism of her day, her focus on relationships of power between men and women, and her attempt to reconcile the traditional masculine and feminine modes of expression and spheres of influence. Written with style and aplomb, Uglow's work merits serious attention from students of Eliot. (A,G)

Welsh, Alexander. *George Eliot and Blackmail.* Cambridge: Harvard University Press, 1985. In this involved study, Welsh argues that Eliot was especially sensitive to the complexities of concealment. Her own illicit relationship with George Henry Lewes, which was an open secret, forced her to publish under the pseudonym, Marian Evans, a well-guarded secret. Welsh continues his argument with an analysis of English society in 1860, observing that because information was more readily available than in the past, concealment became more difficult. Society itself became an unwitting blackmailer, and Eliot's plots dramatize the effects of the blackmailer upon public and private lives. Welsh examines the characters who are blackmailers—Dunstan Cass in *Silas Marner*, Baldassare in *Romola*, Jermyn, Christian, and Johnson in *Felix Hall, the Radical*, Raffles in *Middlemarch*, and Grandcourt in *Daniel Deronda*—but the importance of this study is the theme of the responsibility of society to individuals. (A)

Other Sources

Barrett, Dorothea. *Vocation and Desire: George Eliot's Heroines.* London: Routledge and Kegan Paul, 1989.

Brady, Kristin. *George Eliot.* Savage, MD: Rowman, 1990.

Cottom, Daniel. *Social Figures: George Eliot, Social History and Literary Representation.* Minneapolis: University of Minnesota Press, 1987.

Dodd, Valerie A. *George Eliot: An Intellectual Life.* New York: St. Martin's, 1989.

Gray, Beryl. *George Eliot and Music.* New York: St. Martin's, 1989.

Hands, Timothy. *A George Eliot Chronology.* Boston: G. K. Hall, 1988.

Marshall, David. *The Figure of Theater: Shaftesbury, Defoe, Adam Smith, and George Eliot.* New York: Columbia University Press, 1986.

Perlis, Alan D. *A Return to the Primal Self: Identity in the Fiction of George Eliot.* New York: Peter Lang, 1989.

Taylor, Ina. *A Woman of Contradictions: The Life of George Eliot.* New York: Morrow, 1990.

T. S. ELIOT
1888-1965

Autobiographical Sources

Eliot, Valerie. *The Letters of T. S. Eliot: Volume I, 1898-1922*. San Diego: Harcourt Brace Jovanovich, 1988. Until now, Eliot's second wife, Valerie, has been ferocious in protecting the privacy of her famous husband. In her preface, she says that he authorized her to publish some of his letters, but only if she, and she alone, selected them. The six hundred letters contained here provide the first direct glimpse into Eliot's autobiography, though the picture could well be incomplete or distorted. Many of the letters deal with the writing and publication of *The Waste Land* in 1922. This volume is particularly good in its depiction Eliot's American background. (A,G)

Evaluation of Selected Biography and Criticism

Ali, Agha Shahid. *T. S. Eliot as Editor*. Ann Arbor: UMI Research, 1986. This study focuses exclusively on Eliot's tenure at the *Criterion* between 1922 and 1939. Although Ali does provide some sense of Eliot's aesthetic judgments reflected in his editing, Ali neglects a large body of Eliot's correspondence that directly addresses his views on the role of the editor. (A,G)

Bedient, Calvin. *He Do the Police in Different Voices: "The Waste Land" and Its Protagonist*. Chicago: University of Chicago Press, 1986. Taking its title from the character, Sloppy, in Dickens' *Our Mutual Friend*, Bedient argues that the poem's fundamental message is reflected in the narrator's chameleon-like voice. Bedient argues that Eliot's own proclivity to juxtapose extreme faith with irony fingerprints the character of the poem's unidentified narrator. This study offers a slightly different perspective to modernism's most discussed poem. (A)

Beehler, Michael. *T. S. Eliot, Wallace Stevens, and the Discourses of Difference*. Baton Rouge: Louisiana State University Press, 1987. Beehler relates the work of both Eliot and Stevens to a single theme—the need of the human mind for unity in a pluralistic world. Chapters alternate between Eliot and Stevens as Beehler attempts to define how each poet treats diversity and the instinct for wholeness. (A)

Bloom, Harold, ed. *T. S. Eliot's "The Waste Land"*. New York: Chelsea House, 1986. These nine essays each treat different aspects of *The Waste Land*, including its literary antecedents. None attempts an overview of the full work. The contributors are all well-known in the field—Bernard Dick, Eleanor Cook, Richard Ellmann, Grover Smith, Hugh Kenner, and C. Kearns. Biographical insights abound. This anthology brings together some of the best available commentary on the poem. (A,G)

Bradbury, Malcolm. *The Modern World: Ten Great Writers.* New York: Viking, 1989. Bradbury's study consists of essays on ten modern writers who he believes have shaped twentieth-century literature—Eliot, Conrad, Woolf, Joyce, Kafka, Pirandello, Mann, Proust, Ibsen, and Dostoevsky. He examines these writers' underlying themes of alienation, rage, and disaffection and describes how their work influenced contemporary authors. (A)

Calder, Angus. *T. S. Eliot.* Boston: Humanities Press, 1987. Calder's examination of Eliot's non-dramatic poetry situates it firmly within its twentieth-century context and provides a convincing view of its literary significance. According to Calder, three modernist tendencies heavily influenced Eliot's verse—French symbolism, Pound's imagery, and the burst of creative innovation evident in European art at the time. Calder's premises are clearly stated and his readings of the poems enlightening. (A,G)

Cooper, John Xiros. *T. S. Eliot and the Politics of Voice: The Argument of "The Waste Land."* Ann Arbor: UMI Research, 1987. This interpretation of Eliot's master poem, *The Waste Land,* analyzes the differences in the metonymic and metaphoric voices of the poem. Cooper attempts to "immerse" the poem in its historical context to reveal the narrative's didactic character. (A)

Crawford, Robert. *The Savage and the City in the Work of T. S. Eliot.* New York: Oxford University Press, 1988. Crawford examines Eliot's fascination for ritual in primitive religions to explain the presence of opposites in his poetry. Although narrowly focused, this study provides a good research tool for students seeking specialized topics. (A)

Dale, Alzina Stone. *T. S. Eliot, the Philosopher-Poet.* Wheaton, IL: Shaw, 1988. Eliot's second wife, Valerie, vowed not to allow Eliot's biography to be written and has been less than cordial to would-be chroniclers of his life. However, believing that critics have failed to appreciate Eliot's spiritual growth, she cooperated fully with Dale, an Episcopalian scholar. Dale divides Eliot's spiritual journey into four phases: Puritan (1889-1914, when he left Harvard for England); Pilgrim (his English years up to publishing "Ash-Wednesday" in 1930); Preacher (1930-1945); and Prophet. In tracing Eliot's religious journey, Dale necessarily incorporates the biography, the poetry, and the intellectual influences on Eliot's theological ideas, especially those of Dante. General readers as well as students will find this an instructive study of one of the twentieth century's most influential poets. (A,G)

Davidson, Harriet. *T. S. Eliot and Hermeneutics: Absence and Interpretation in "The Waste Land."* Baton Rouge: Louisiana State University Press, 1985. In this treatment of Eliot's classic poem, "The Waste Land," most of the actual textual analysis takes place in the last chapter. The bulk of this study consists of discussions of Heidegger and other excursions into critical theory. (A,G)

Dickie, Margaret. *On the Modernist Long Poem.* Iowa City: University of Iowa Press, 1986. Dickie contends that by extending their "personal imagist pieces" into the extended "public" long poem, modernist poets redefined the shape and direction of their movement. In this study, which is, in effect, a history of the development of modernism, Dickie examines the formal problems faced by Eliot (*The Waste Land*), Hart Crane (*The Bridge*), Williams (*Paterson*), and Pound (the *Cantos*). This study would be most useful for teachers and students who are seeking a framework for discussion of these complex works. **(A)**

Douglass, Paul. *Bergson, Eliot, and American Literature.* Lexington: University Press of Kentucky, 1986. In this admirably researched and well-written study, Douglass evaluates the influence of Henri Bergson on the works of Eliot and other American writers, including Faulkner, Williams, Wolfe, Stein, Frost, and Henry Miller. Douglass considers Eliot to be the prime disseminator of Bergson's ideas to the American literary community. **(A)**

Ellman, Maud. *The Poetics of Impersonality: T. S. Eliot and Ezra Pound.* Cambridge: Harvard University Press, 1988. Eliot and Pound were central to the twentieth-century aesthetic principal, which held that the writer must disassociate himself from his work—that the narrator be impersonal and distinct from the author himself. Ellman attacks this much-heralded theory, arguing that the poets were merely disguising their anti-semitic and fascist politics. She examines the poetry in light of Eliot's own notes about Henri Bergson, and links both Eliot and Pound to Bergsonian ideas of time and memory. Recommended for scholars. **(A)**

Gish, Nancy K. *"The Waste Land": A Poem of Memory and Desire.* Boston: Twayne, 1988. In this model guide to a difficult poem, Gish focuses on the narrator as a "central consciousness" that unites the seemingly disparate pieces of the poem. Extremely well organized, this book proceeds through Eliot's complexities with precision and style. The bibliography is excellent. Highly recommended for all readers. **(A,G,Y)**

Gordon, Lyndall. *Eliot's New Life.* New York: Farrar, Straus & Giroux, 1988. This is the sequel to Gordon's previous biographical treatment of Eliot, *Eliot's Early Years* (1977). Here he covers the mature phase of Eliot's career, the loss of his wife to mental illness, and his attachments to women who served as muses or nursemaids. Gordon is the first biographer to tackle Eliot's problematic relationship with Emily Hale, whom the poet adopted as his "guardian spirit." Previously unavailable letters reveal new connections between Eliot's personal life and the characters and events of his poems and plays. **(A,G)**

Hastings, Michael. *Tom and Viv.* London: Penguin, 1985. This is the text of a successful play about the lives of T. S. and Vivienne Eliot, who were married for eighteen years before Tom had her committed to an asylum. In a lengthy introduction, playwright Hastings explains how he was opposed at every turn by the Eliot estate, and how most of his intimate information was provided by Vivienne's brother. Sensational and scandalous, the play nonetheless explores the psyche of a poet who psychoanalyzed modern society through his art. (A,G)

Kearns, Cleo McNelly. *T. S. Eliot and the Indic Tradition: A Study in Poetry and Belief.* Cambridge: Cambridge University Press, 1987. Kearns traces the influence of Indian mysticism and metaphysics on Eliot, and the manner in which he assimilated it into his own cultural thinking. This is a rich study for scholars. (A)

Leeming, Glenda. *Poetic Drama.* New York: St. Martin's, 1988. This concise look at twentieth-century British poetic drama is a useful introductory study. Significant portions of the book are devoted to Eliot and Yeats. This study is valuable for understanding how Eliot used British theatrical conventions to create drama in both his poetry and plays. (A,G)

Menand, Louis. *Discovering Modernism. T. S. Eliot and His Context.* Oxford: Oxford University Press, 1987. Menand looks at Eliot's poetry, criticism, and philosophy to examine why his influence dominated an entire literary period. Menand argues that most of Eliot's philosophy can be traced to nineteenth-century values and that his later criticism contradicted his earlier judgments. If the effect of Menand's theory is to reduce Eliot's reputation, it also does him a service by placing him in the context of nineteenth- and early twentieth-century literary movements. Menand concludes that while Eliot might not have been such an original thinker, or the sole creator of modernism, he certainly was one of the wisest interpreters of the *avant-garde.* Clearly written with grace and wit, this study is appropriate for all researchers interested in Eliot, aesthetics, or modernism. (A,G)

Pinion, F. B. *A T. S. Eliot Companion: Life and Works.* New York: Barnes & Noble, 1986. Pinion is a veteran "companion" writer who now has the format down to a science. Eliot's life and works are treated in separate sections, and the biography is accurate and sympathetic, particularly when discussing Eliot's religious convictions. The reading of each play, poem, or critical essay is carefully conservative, designed to provide solid direction for new students of Eliot. Pinion is effective in his treatment of Eliot's sources. Photographs and a chronology enhance this package. (A,G)

Ross, Andrew. *The Failure of Modernism: Symptoms of American Poetry.* New York: Columbia University Press, 1986. Ross examines the works of Eliot, Charles Olson, and John Ashberry to conclude that modernism as a poetic movement was an unabashed failure. The cause of this failure, he contends, was a confusion between subjectivism and subjectivity, a confusion that he believes continues to plague the work of critics who address modernist poets. (A)

Scofield, Martin. *T. S. Eliot: The Poems*. London: Cambridge University Press, 1988. Perhaps more now than during the heyday of Eliot worship, the meaning of his poetry is even less accessible to students. Thus, this lucidly written, carefully explained guide to the poems will help almost anyone who is genuinely interested in understanding the complexities of the century's most celebrated poet. Scofield presents a short biography, then goes on to show how Eliot's poetic theory reflects his personal beliefs about life. Combined with good close readings of the major poems, this approach demonstrates why Eliot may emerge historically as a more important critic than poet. (A,G)

Sharma, Kumar. *Time and T. S. Eliot: His Poetry, Plays, and Philosophy*. New York: APT, 1985. Sharma's thesis is that Eliot's work is so all-encompassing and awe-inspiring that it can only be understood within the context of the philosophies of India. Although Sharma offers a different and interesting perspective, critics may fault his premise—that because Eliot's works transcend Christianity the meaning can be found only in the context of another culture. (A,G)

Skaff, William. *The Philosophy of T. S. Eliot: From Skepticism to a Surrealist Poetic, 1909-1927*. Philadelphia: University of Pennsylvania Press, 1986. This literary, philosophical, and biographical synopsis of Eliot's life moves from his graduate studies at Harvard to his baptism into the Church of England. Carefully laid out and logically developed, Skaff's exposition traces Eliot's gradual abandonment of intellectualism for mystical experience and religious vision. (A)

Stead, Christian Karlson. *Pound, Yeats, Eliot, and the Modernist Movement*. New Brunswick, NJ: Rutgers University Press, 1986. Stead's study surveys the origins of the modernist movement, with particular attention to Pound, Yeats, and Eliot. He argues that Pound's influence on Yeats and Eliot has not been adequately acknowledged. To demonstrate this Stead scrutinizes the manuscript of *The Waste Land*, pointing out those sections where Pound dominated over Eliot's more conventional approach. In his discussion of politics and modernism, he claims that Eliot's conservative views had a deadening effect on the work, holding "Burnt Norton" an abject failure. The result of Pound's bout with fascism is noted in the structures of the *Cantos*. Stead's study is solid and well-written, and provides an enlightening account of the causes and effects of modernism. (A,G)

Sultan, Stanley. *Eliot, Joyce, and Company*. London and New York: Oxford University Press, 1987. One of the most valuable aspects of this study is Sultan's explanation of the modernist movement. He examines how Eliot, Pound, and Joyce contributed to the movement and argues that Joyce and Pound exerted considerable influence on Eliot, especially in *The Waste Land* and "The Love Song of J. Alfred Prufrock." This readable book will assist anyone researching the development of modern literature. (A,G)

Svarny, Erik. *The Men of 1914: T. S. Eliot and Early Modernism.* Philadelphia: Open University, 1988. The subject of this densely argued study is the influence of Pound upon Eliot's poetic development from 1914 through 1922 when *The Waste Land* was published. During his years of close cooperation with Pound, Eliot relied heavily on tradition which was incompletely reconciled with his modernist tendencies. In later works, Eliot would master his use of tradition and become more accessible to his audience. During the course of the discussion, Svarny describes the influences of Joyce, C. S. Lewis, and T. E. Hulme on both Pound and Eliot. (A)

Warren, Charles. *T. S. Eliot on Shakespeare.* Ann Arbor: UMI Research, 1987. This is a general bibliographic survey of Eliot's criticism on Shakespeare. Excerpts from BBC interviews as well as published pieces are included. In Warren's summations of each entry he manages to elucidate Eliot's vision of Shakespeare's art. This volume is more valuable for its insights into Eliot and the influences on his work than for Eliot's insights of Shakespeare. (A,G)

Other Sources

Bagchee, Shyamal, ed. *T. S. Eliot Annual, No 1.* Highlands, NJ: Humanities Press, 1989.

Brooker, Jewel S., ed. *Approaches to Teaching T. S. Eliot's Poetry and Plays.* New York: Modern Language Association, 1988.

Christ, Carol T. *Victorian and Modern Poetics.* Chicago: University of Chicago Press, 1986.

Cookson, William, and Peter Dale, eds. *T. S. Eliot.* Redding Ridge, CT: Black Swan Books, 1988.

D'Ambrosio, Vinnie-Marie. *Eliot Possessed: T. S. Eliot and Fitzgerald's "Rubáiyát."* New York: New York University Press, 1989.

Dickens, David B. *Negative Spring: Crisis Imagery in the Works of Brentano, Lenau, Rilke and T. S. Eliot.* New York: Peter Lang, 1989.

Eder, Doris L. *Three Writers in Exile: Eliot, Pound, and Joyce.* Troy, NY: Whitston, 1985.

Freadman, Richard. *Eliot, James and the Fictional Self: A Study in Character and Narration.* New York: St. Martin's, 1986.

Gilbert, Sandra. *T. S. Eliot.* Highlands, NJ: Humanities Press, 1990.

Gunner, Eugenia M. *T. S. Eliot's Romantic Dilemma.* New York: Garland, 1985.

Hinchliffe, Arnold P. *The Waste Land and Ash Wednesday.* Highlands, NJ: Humanities Press, 1987.

Jha, Ashok K. *Oriental Influences in T. S. Eliot.* New York: Advent, 1988.

Manganiello, Dominic. *T. S. Eliot and Dante.* New York: St. Martin's, 1989.

Mayer, John. *T. S. Eliot's Silent Voices: The Psychic Monologues.* New York: Oxford University Press, 1989.

Morgan, John H., ed. *Celebrating T. S. Eliot: On the Centennial of His Birth A Collection of Poems.* Bristol, IN: Wyndham Hall, 1988.

Niesen de Abruno, Laura E. *The Refining Fire: Herakles and Other Heroes in T. S. Eliot's Works.* New York: Peter Lang, 1988.

Olney, James, ed. *T. S. Eliot: Essays from the Southern Review.* New York: Oxford University Press, 1988.

Raffel, Burton, ed. *Possum and Ole Ez in the Public Eye: Contemporaries and Peers on T. S. Eliot and Ezra Pound.* Hamden, CT: Archon/Shoe String, 1985.

Reeves, Gareth. *T. S. Eliot: A Virgilian Poet.* New York: St. Martin's, 1989.

Ricks, Christopher. *T. S. Eliot and Prejudice.* Berkeley: University of California Press, 1988.

Roby, Kinley E. *Critical Essays on T. S. Eliot: The Sweeney Motif.* Boston: G. K. Hall, 1985.

Schwarz, Robert L. *Broken Images: A Study of The Waste Land.* Lewisburg, PA: Bucknell University Press, 1988.

Shusterman, Richard M. *T. S. Eliot and the Philosophy of Criticism.* New York: Columbia University Press, 1988.

Sigg, Eric. *The American T. S. Eliot: A Study of the Early Writings.* New York: Cambridge University Press, 1989.

Singh, Ranjit K. *Heroes of T. S. Eliot's Plays.* New York: Advent, 1988.

Srivastava, S. B. *Imagery in T. S. Eliot's Poetry.* New York: Advent, 1985.

Takacs, T. *T. S. Eliot and the Language of Poetry.* Highlands, NJ: Humanities Press, 1989.

RALPH WALDO EMERSON
1803-1882

Autobiographical Sources

Orth, Ralph, *et al.*, eds. *The Poetry Notebooks of Ralph Waldo Emerson.*
Columbia: University of Missouri Press, 1986. More than 1,300 pages of
poems and fragments are presented in this edition of Emerson's nine poetry
notebooks. The notebooks from the collection of Harvard's Houghton Library
are arranged in chronological order and accurately reproduce Emerson's creative process. Deletions, insertions, and alternate readings are included with the
main text. Various transcription symbols enable the student to trace individual
poems through their many drafts and revisions. This edition also contains a
valuable section that analyzes each poem and fragment in terms of its production, intent, and significance. These notebooks and accompanying material,
including Emerson's own indexes, should do much to encourage a comprehensive study of the development of Emerson's techniques, style, and thematic
emphasis. (A)

Von Frank, Albert J., ed. *The Complete Sermons of Ralph Waldo Emerson,
Volume 1.* Columbia: University of Missouri Press, 1989. Most of Emerson's
180 sermons have never been published, and in this first volume von Frank
collects forty-two sermons delivered between 1826 and 1838. Arranged chronologically, they clearly illustrate Emerson's developing power of language
and his increased attention to the importance of virtue and character. An introduction and detailed chronology place Emerson's ministerial career within an
historical context. This is an important source for understanding Emerson's
philosophical development. (A,G)

Evaluation of Selected Biography and Criticism

Carpenter, Delores Bird, ed. *The Selected Letters of Lidian Jackson
Emerson.* Columbia: University of Missouri Press, 1987. This book contains a
selection of letters sent to Emerson by his second wife. Sometimes the subject
of the letters is trivial, sometimes reflective of Emerson's mature career. All
are of some interest to serious students of Emerson. (A)

Donoghue, Denis. *Reading America: Essays on American Literature.* New
York: Knopf, 1987. Noted Irish literary critic Donoghue turns his critical eye
on American writers in this collection of nine essays and seventeen book
reviews. Each of the longer pieces—on Emerson, Dickinson, Thoreau, Trilling,
Whitman, Henry Adams, Henry James, and Stevens—is prefaced by a discussion of the writer's moral and rhetorical intentions. Donoghue has a
dedicated following of serious-minded readers who swear by his awesome
insights. Others may have difficulty working through the details to reach the
payoff. (A)

Gonnaud, Maurice. *An Uneasy Solitude: Individual and Society in the Work of Ralph Waldo Emerson*. Translated by Lawrence Rosenwald. Princeton, NJ: Princeton University Press, 1987. Originally published in French, this spiritual biography fills a significant niche in Emerson scholarship. Gonnaud argues convincingly that Emerson was not the self-absorbed individualist, as he was popularly portrayed, but a concerned individual who struggled with the social and political issues of his time. Emerson's primary internal conflict was reconciling freedom and fate as acted out through the dialectic of society and self. Under Gonnaud's guiding hand, this dialectical process can be followed through Emerson's initial identification with Unitarianism, his subsequent withdrawal from the ministry, his embrace of Transcendentalism, and his increasing concern over the implications of slavery. After the onset of the Civil War, Emerson began to balance his dual outlook as individual and citizen. **(A)**

Hodder, Alan D. *Emerson's Rhetoric of Revelation: "Nature," the Reader, and the Apocalypse Within*. University Park: Pennsylvania State University Press, 1989. In biblical prophecy Emerson found a model for poetic inspiration. Emerson's work *Nature*, composed shortly after he left the ministry, is clearly influenced by the Scriptures. Hodder contends that Emerson's Transcendentalist rhetoric has a scriptural basis, and by focusing on allusions to the book of *Revelation*, Hodder examines Emerson's concept of "apocalypse" as individual revelation. When an individual grasps the true significance of an "event" or "appearance," the old order of self-identity passes and a new order is created. **(A)**

Michael, John. *Emerson and Skepticism: The Cipher of the World*. Baltimore: The Johns Hopkins University Press, 1988. Michael argues that Emerson's radical change from optimism and aspiration to skepticism has not been fully analyzed or evaluated. Emerson's changing view of nature and his relationship to his brother Charles partly account for his skeptical outlook, combined with his growing admiration of Hume's philosophy. This study is required reading for Emerson scholars. **(A)**

Rosenwald, Lawrence. *Emerson and the Art of the Diary*. New York: Oxford University Press, 1988. Scholars have never thought that Emerson's sixteen volumes of journals revealed very much about his mastery of the essay form. In this study Rosenwald argues brilliantly, though not always convincingly, that the form of the journals rather than the essays best accommodates Emerson's aesthetics. A consummate Emerson scholar, Rosenwald raises interesting new possibilities for Emerson studies. **(A,G)**

Steele, Jeffrey. *The Representation of the Self in the American Renaissance*. Chapel Hill: University of North Carolina Press, 1987. Steele draws on modern psychological theories to explore the concept of the self as portrayed in major works of the American Renaissance. He makes illuminating comparisons between the orientations of writers and psychologists/philosophers—for example, Emerson and Jung, Thoreau and Medard Boss, Hawthorne and Freud, and Melville and Nietzsche. (A,G)

Toulouse, Teresa. *The Art of Prophesying: New England Sermons and the Shaping of Belief.* Athens: University of Georgia Press, 1987. Toulouse's thesis is that Puritan ministers fragmented the sermon tradition for the purpose of evoking spiritual beliefs from the congregation. She then extrapolates from this technique of fragmentation to explain how congregations would have responded differently to each man's sermons. She also explains how Emerson used these same techniques in his essays, which he usually delivered to large audiences—an interweaving of imagery and argument that required the audience to supply the emotion. Toulouse's book is clear and well-written but the subject requires familiarity with the sermonizers and the period. (A)

Van Leer, David. *Emerson's Epistemology: The Argument of the Essays.* Cambridge: Cambridge University Press, 1986. Many years have passed since the American Transcendentalists were taken seriously as philosophers. Van Leer conducts a reexamination of Emerson as a systematic thinker and shows how he contributed to the philosophical discipline of his time. Van Leer carves out a niche for Emerson in the Kantian tradition of epistemological thought. (A)

Von Frank, Albert J. *The Sacred Game: Provincialism and Frontier Consciousness in American Literature, 1630-1860.* New York: Cambridge University Press, 1985. Von Frank's wide-ranging study examines the reactions of various writers to the wilderness environment of young America. He contends that Anne Bradstreet felt compelled to retain the old culture in order to preserve identity in her new surroundings. He views Washington Irving's works as a reaction to American provincialism, and sees many of the same provincial themes evident in Hawthorne's *The Scarlet Letter.* Von Frank's major thesis is that the wilderness environment accepts immigrants but at the same time rejects the immigrant's culture. He uses Emerson's works to analyze this and other themes. (A)

Other Sources
Albee, J. *Remembrances of Emerson.* Brunswick, ME: Bern Porter, 1985.

Burkholder, Robert E., and Joel Myerson. *Emerson: An Annotated Secondary Bibliography.* Pittsburgh: University of Pittsburgh Press, 1985.

Cady, Edwin H., and Louis J. Budd, eds. *On Emerson.* Durham, NC: Duke University Press, 1988.

Carton, Evan. *The Rhetoric of American Romance: Dialectic and Identity in Emerson, Dickinson, Poe, and Hawthorne.* Baltimore: The Johns Hopkins University Press, 1985.

Cayton, Mary Kupiec. *Emerson's Emergence: Self and Society in the Transformation of New England, 1800-1845.* Chapel Hill: The University of North Carolina Press, 1990.

Donadio, Stephen, *et al.*, eds. *Emerson and His Legacy: Essays in Honor of Quentin Anderson.* Carbondale: Southern Illinois University Press, 1986.

Hudson, Yeager. *Emerson and Tagore, the Poet as Philosopher.* Notre Dame, IN: Cross Cultural Press, 1988.

Hughes, Gertrude R. *Emerson's Demanding Optimism.* Baton Rouge: Louisiana State University Press, 1984.

La Bossiere, Camille R. *The Victorian Sage: Comparative Readings on Carlyle, Emerson, Melville and Conrad.* Lewisburg, PA: Bucknell University Press, 1988.

Lange, Lou A. *The Riddle of Liberty: Emerson on Alienation, Freedom and Obedience.* Decatur, GA: Scholars Press, 1986.

Leer, David V. *Emerson's Epistemology: The Argument of the Essays.* New York: Cambridge University Press, 1986.

Loewenberg, Robert J. *An American Idol: Emerson and the "Jewish Idea."* Lanham, MD: University Press of America, 1984.

Marr, David. *American Worlds Since Emerson.* Amherst: University of Massachusetts Press, 1988.

Mott, Wesley T. *"The Strains of Eloquence": Emerson and His Sermons.* University Park: Pennsylvania State University Press, 1989.

Steele, Jeffrey. *Unfolding the Mind: The Unconscious in American Romanticism and Literary Theory.* New York: Garland, 1987.

WILLIAM FAULKNER
1897-1962

Evaluation of Selected Biography and Criticism

Blotner, Joseph, Thomas McHaney, Michael Millgate, and Noel Polk, eds. *William Faulkner Manuscripts*. New York: Garland, 1986-1987. This set of forty-four volumes reproduces Faulkner's fiction manuscripts held in the collections of the Alderman Library at the University of Virginia and the New York Public Library. The texts are thoughtfully arranged and include ample introductory information and commentary. The editorial standards are uniformly high. The result is an invaluable source for the study of Faulkner's compositional methods, the development of his techniques and style, and his collaboration with editors. These volumes are essential for Faulkner studies. (A)

Brooks, Cleanth. *On Prejudices, Predilections, and Firm Beliefs of William Faulkner*. Baton Rouge: Louisiana State University Press, 1987. This collection of twelve previously published essays by Cleanth Brooks sums up the views of this noted critic on Faulkner's achievements and significance. In such essays as "Faulkner and the Community," "Faulkner and Christianity," and "Faulkner and the Fugitive-Agrarians," Brooks presents his case with finesse. His strongly held opinions have been influential in shaping the critical climate surrounding Faulkner. Whether one agrees or disagrees with Brooks, he is a force to be reckoned with. This is required reading for students of Faulkner. (A)

Carothers, James B. *William Faulkner's Short Stories*. Ann Arbor: UMI Research, 1985. Had Faulkner never written a novel, argues Carothers, his short stories alone would rank him high among twentieth-century American writers. This study is particularly valuable for its analysis of the Snopes tales, which Carothers traces from their conception through revision to finished work. Many of Carothers' discussions focus on points of critical controversy, limiting its appeal to the general reader, but enhancing it for serious Faulkner students. (A,G)

Crane, John Kenny. *The Yoknapatawpha Chronicle of Gavin Stevens*. Cranbury, NJ: Susquehanna University Press, 1988. In this witty, engaging work, the fictitious persona of Gavin Stevens narrates a history of William Faulkner's famous Mississippi county. Reconstructing its history from Faulkner's works, this chronological account and interpretation of Faulkner's fiction make it easy to see how his cast of characters interrelates. This work is enormously valuable for researchers or for students trying to make their way through the convoluted maze of Yoknapatawpha County. (A,G)

Dardis, Tom. *The Thirsty Muse: Alcohol and the American Writer.* London: Ticknor & Fields, 1989. Dardis applies the results of current addiction research to the lives and careers of American writers. Of eight authors who won the Nobel Prize, five were alcoholics. The popular theory that alcohol liberates the creative impulse, however, is thoroughly debunked. These were addicted men whose addictions got in the way of their creativity. Close-up views of O'Neill, Faulkner, Fitzgerald, Hemingway, and others are fraught with binges, black-outs, wife-beatings, delirium, disease, and untimely death. (A, G)

Dryden, Edgar A. *The Form of American Romance.* Baltimore: The Johns Hopkins University Press, 1988. In this study, Dryden undertakes an analysis of the structure and development of American Romanticism. He first examines the origins of the novel and its relationship to romance by discussing *Don Quixote* and Scott's *Waverley*. He views Scott's early novel as a "founding text" in the history of the English novel. Dryden then dissects the narrative structures of five American novels—Hawthorne's *The Marble Faun*, Melville's *Pierre*, James's *The Portrait of a Lady*, Faulkner's *Absalom, Absalom!*, and Barth's *LETTERS*. He sees these American novelists responding directly to narrative problems inherited from Scott. (A)

Fowler, Doreen, and Ann Abadie, eds. *Faulkner and Yoknapatawpha Conference: Faulkner and Women.* Jackson: University Press of Mississippi, 1987. The role of women in Faulkner's fiction is a challenging theme for scholars, offering a wide range of possible perspectives. Faulkner has often been portrayed as an out-and-out misogynist, yet the gender situations in his fiction often reflect real-life attitudes and relationships that existed in the Old South. This collection of essays attempts to get behind simplistic assessments of Faulkner's attitudes toward women to arrive at a more complex analysis of the social and cultural structures that shaped the role of women in Faulkner's world. (A,G)

Gladstein, Mimi Reisel. *The Indestructible Woman in Faulkner, Hemingway, and Steinbeck.* Ann Arbor: UMI Research, 1986. "Indestructible" women are those who are generally defined by men as "other." Because they are essentially unknown quantities, men tend to project upon them idealized traits of strength and perseverance. Such is the case, argues Gladstein, with the few women characters that appear in the fiction of Faulkner, Steinbeck, and Hemingway. This feminist critique is handled with well-balanced precision and lays bare the personal dependencies of a group of male writers who leaned too heavily on the women in their lives. (A,G)

Gray, Richard. *Writing the South: Ideas of an American Region.* Cambridge: Cambridge University Press, 1986. Gray begins his examination of southern themes in literature by isolating thematic contrasts—rural versus urban, farm versus factory, paternalism versus populism, region versus tradition. He then demonstrates how writers developed a myth of meaning for the South by exploring those contrasts. The South created these writers, and the writers, in turn, recreated the southern identity. Excluded from the many themes he discusses is the race issue. In all, he presents a strong case that the last "southern novel" has not yet been written. (A,G)

Grimwood, Michael. *Heart in Conflict: Faulkner's Struggles with Vocation.* Athens: University of Georgia Press, 1987. Conflict is the heart and genius of Faulkner's fiction, so it should come as no surprise that a critic has identified yet another conflict in Faulkner's life: his uncertainty that he could be, or wanted to be a writer. From accusations that he plagiarized his brother John's work, to admitting that he wrote his short stories to be "pot-boilers," to his exploits as a Hollywood screenwriter, some critics have suspected that Faulkner was not a "pure" artist. Grimwood examines these ideas, and applies them to a reading of four novels: *The Wild Palms, The Hamlet, Knight's Gambit,* and *Go Down Moses.* (A)

Hoennighausen, Lothar. *William Faulkner: The Art of Stylization.* Cambridge: Cambridge University Press, 1987. Hoennighausen examines Faulkner's early prose poems, his drawings, his early one-act play, and the influence of various artistic movements to demonstrate the forces that shaped the mature fiction. He traces the profound influence that symbolism, modernism, the Pre-Raphaelites, the *fin de siècle,* and *art nouveau* exerted on his work. This is an ambitious, fascinating work for anyone interested in the relationship of art to poetry or in the stylistic development of an accomplished writer. (A)

Karl, Frederick R. *William Faulkner: American Writer.* London: Weidenfeld & Nicolson. 1988. This hefty critical biography by a noted Conrad scholar, meticulously and pleasurably examines every detail of Faulkner's life, from his obsession with the Civil War to his artistic indebtedness to Conrad, Eliot, Joyce, and Camus. Karl is especially insightful on Faulkner's suicidal disposition, revealing the complexities of the man both at his peak and during his decline. He provides an excellent assessment of the fiction, and demonstrates the nature and power of Faulkner's myth-making capabilities. Karl closely scrutinizes plot and character to reveal the personal anguish and peculiar idealism of the novelist. This biography is required reading for any serious student of Faulkner, or any general reader looking for an in-depth portrait of a great writer and troubled man. (A,G)

Kreyling, Michael. *Figures of the Hero in Southern Narrative.* Baton Rouge: Louisiana State University Press, 1987. In Kreyling's exposition, the "hero" is less dependent on personality than upon a set of culturally conditioned responses to the alternatives proposed by history. He begins his analysis with George Tucker's *The Valley of the Shenanadoah* and follows with discussions of Gilmore Simms' and Richard Watson's evolving attempts to "nationalize" the southern hero. He examines the portrayal of the hero by Ellen Glasgow, Faulkner, and Allen Tate, and concludes with Richard Watson Gilder's efforts to lift the hero to universal importance, independent of historical context. Of note is Kreyling's discussion of the difficulty of black southern writers to identify with or fit into this tradition. This is an excellent assessment of a critical theme that underlies many aspects of this rich regional literature. (A,G)

Millgate, Michael. *New Essays on "Light in August."* New York: Cambridge University Press, 1987. The most valuable aspect of this collection is the evaluation of the importance of *Light in August* in the context of both Faulkner's canon and the history of the American novel. Millgate's introduction provides an overview of the novel and critical responses to it. Other essays, which deal with structure and interpretation, will be of value to scholars and advanced students. (A)

Montauzon, Christine de. *Faulkner's "Absalom, Absalom!" and Interpretability: The Inexplicable Unseen.* New York: Peter Lang, 1985. All critical theories, de Montauzon contends, are reductive by virtue of their strategies to achieve closure and completeness. This specialized study examines the insufficiency of reductive theories when applied to the open, indeterminate text of *Absalom, Absalom!.* (A)

Oates, Stephen B. *William Faulkner: The Man and the Artist: A Biography.* New York: Harper & Row, 1987. Oates, a master stylist and a prominent practitioner of the "New Biography," combines meticulous attention to detail with a balanced portrait of the man and his work. Of particular interest is Oates' discussion of women in Faulkner's life, from his mother and black "mammy", to his wife, lovers, and friends. Oates, who has written important biographies on Martin Luther King and Abraham Lincoln, has produced the standard biography that supersedes Laurance Thompson's in detail, and Joseph Blotner's in style. Recommended for general readers, all students, and scholars. (A,G)

Parker, Robert Dale. *Faulkner and the Novelistic Imagination.* Champaign: University of Illinois Press, 1985. Parker analyzes four of Faulkner's major novels—*As I Lay Dying, Sanctuary, Light in August,* and *Absalom, Absalom!* His focus is on Faulkner's insistence on withholding information from his readers and how this narrative strategy shaped the structure of his novels. Faulkner used a variety of other methods in shaping his novels. He created discontinuous sections that could not be comprehended without reference to the whole. He experimented with withholding various categories of information to create a state of "epistemological uncertainty." This skillfully written critique reveals *Absalom, Absalom!* as "one of the most elaborately and precisely structured novels" in the English language. Recommended for Faulkner enthusiasts. (A)

Phillips, Gene D. *Fiction, Film, and Faulkner: The Art of Adaptation.* Knoxville: University of Tennessee Press, 1988. This study provides some insight into how a popular audience responds to an immensely complicated writer. Phillips compares the fiction with film adaptations to explore how and why they are different. (G)

Putzel, Max. *Genius of Place: William Faulkner's Triumphant Beginnings.* Baton Rouge: Louisiana State University Press, 1985. Putzel reconstructs the chronology of all of Faulkner's notes, journals, and drafts, to trace the development of his art. Putzel's focus is the influence of place on the settings, characters, and themes of Faulkner's work. He analyzes the major novels and short stories, particularly, "A Rose for Emily," "Father Abraham," "Dry September," and "The Hound." (A,G)

Ragan, David Paul. *William Faulkner's "Absalom, Absalom!": A Critical Study.* Ann Arbor: UMI Research, 1987. Ragan has produced a comprehensive treatment of Faulkner's complex novel. He examines in turn the perspectives of the novel's four narrators to identify the "facts" about the protagonist, Thomas Sutpen. He then goes beyond Sutpen to look at the cultural and psychological motivations of the narrators. His comparisons of *The Sound and the Fury* and *Absalom, Absalom!* are compelling and controversial. Although some students will find the arguments intriguing, this is primarily a book for the Faulkner scholar. (A)

Ross, Stephen M. *Fiction's Inexhaustible Voice: Speech and Writing in Faulkner.* Athens: University of Georgia Press, 1989. Faulkner's fiction teems with voices, and Ross attempts to analyze their significance within the body of Faulker's fiction. Through close examination of *The Sound and the Fury*, *As I Lay Dying*, *Absalom, Absalom!*, and *Light in August*, Ross isolates four types of voices—phenomenal, mimetic, psychic, and oratorical. Of particular interest is his discussion of the role of oratory in southern culture. (A,G)

Ruzicka, William T. *Faulkner's Fictive Architecture: The Meaning of Place in the Yoknapatawpha Novels.* Ann Arbor: UMI Research, 1987. Ruzicka applies the twin concepts of fictive landscape and fictive architecture to Faulkner's works. He demonstrates that the way the author delineates a character's space often adds additional meaning to the character's actions. The architecture of the American South and its classical models are used to enlarge upon Faulkner's descriptions and comment upon his characters. Fully annotated, this study is recommended for serious students of Faulkner. (A)

Schwartz, Lawrence. *Creating Faulkner's Reputation: The Politics of Modern Literary Criticism.* Knoxville: University of Tennessee Press, 1988. Schwartz contends that Faulkner owes his reputation not to the artistic merit of his fiction but to the various commercial and ideological interests that found his work useful for their own purposes. Much of the book examines a "conspiracy" of New Critics and East Coast intellectuals to capitalize on the introduction of the twenty-five-cent paperback that boosted Faulkner's readership from thousands to millions. At the time, Schwartz maintains, the "literary establishment" sought an ideologically conservative champion to counter the effects of subversive, socialist writers. (A,G)

Snead, James A. *Figures of Division: William Faulkner's Major Novels.* New York: Methuen. 1986. Snead's study is an elaboration of the idea that humans need to classify and name feared occurrences in order to combat them. This need inevitably leads to social classification, which in turn leads to racism and violence. Snead believes that Faulkner has created his major characters to reflect this process, and he explicates the important novels published between 1929 and 1942 to prove his case. Faulkner, according to Snead, is opposed to "binary" thinking, and this study attempts to show how the writer uses rhetoric and narrative structure to overcome division. Recommended for serious students of Faulkner. (A)

Spivey, Ted Ray. *Revival: Southern Writers in the Modern City.* Gainesville: University Presses of Florida, 1986. Spivey sets out to correct the belief that southern writers are exclusively steeped in rural culture by selecting a group who came to terms with the modern city. He discusses the attitudes and adaptations of playwright Williams, poets Ransom, Tate, and Aiken, and novelists Faulkner, Wolfe, Ellison, O'Connor, and Percy. Although compelled to address the issues of southern "decadence and decline," Spivey also demonstrates how many of these writers offered a vision of how to integrate old values with new social structures, allowing the past to reanimate the present. (A,G)

Wadlington, Warwick. *Reading Faulknerian Tragedy.* Ithaca, NY: Cornell University Press, 1987. Wadlington contends that in Faulkner's fiction "reciprocating voices," or a kind of cosmic dialogue, constitutes what amounts to a tragic dramatic performance. He concentrates on four novels: *The Sound and the Fury*, *As I Lay Dying*, *Light in August*, and *Absalom, Absalom!*. Although the focus may seem narrow, Wadlington's study is lively, fresh criticism, and some critics have praised it as the best Faulkner study of the decade. (A)

Wagner-Martin, Linda. *The Modern American Novel, 1914-1945: A Critical History.* Boston: Twayne, 1989. Wagner-Martin presents a densely compact overview of modernist writers that flies in the face of the traditional critique that the modernists were a uniformly angst-ridden lot. Besides Faulkner, some of the authors treated are Cather, Stein, Hemingway, Norris, and Agee. This study goes beyond the traditional pantheon to treat many writers highly regarded during their times but nearly forgotten now—Nella Larsen, Meridel Le Sueur, Martha Gellhorn, and Henry Brown, among others. Black and woman modernists are "dusted off" and given their fair place on the shelf. This study is intended for a scholarly audience. (A)

Watson, James G. *William Faulkner: Letters & Fictions.* Austin: University of Texas Press, 1987. Faulkner, a prolific letter writer in his personal life, often used letters as fictional devices. Watson attempts to show how the personae in the fiction are drawn from his personal letters. There are no revelations in this study, but it does provide a convenient source for considering one small facet of Faulkner's complicated fiction. (A)

Zender, Karl F. *The Crossing of the Ways: William Faulkner, the South, and the Modern World*. New Brunswick, NJ: Rutgers University Press, 1989. Zender's thesis is that during mid-life Faulkner lost his poetic power because of passing youth, financial obligations, and the changing character of the Old South. The study opens with an overview of Faulkner's career, comparing images from the early, middle, and later novels. Zender considers the themes of money and materialism in *Pylon* and *The Wild Palms* and discusses Faulkner's growing dependence on his income from Hollywood. The remainder of the study examines novels from different stages of Faulkner's career to demonstrate that Faulkner lost, then regained his fictional power. Recommended for Faulkner enthusiasts. (A)

Other Sources
Bloom, Harold, ed. *"Caddy Compson": Critical Essays*. New York: Chelsea House, 1990.

Connolly, Thomas E. *Faulkner's World: A Directory of His People and Synopses of Actions in His Published Works*. Lanham, MD: University Press of America, 1988.

Dowling, David. *William Faulkner*. New York: St. Martin's, 1989.

Faulkner, Jim. *Across the Creek: Faulkner Family Stories*. Jackson: University Press of Mississippi, 1986.

Ford, Dan, ed. *Heir and Prototype*. Conway: University of Central Arkansas Press, 1988.

Fowler, Doreen. *Faulkner and the Craft of Fiction*. Jackson: University Press of Mississippi, 1989.

Friedman, Alan W. *William Faulkner*. New York: Frederick Ungar, 1985.

Gresset, Michel, and Noel Polk, eds. *Intertextuality in Faulkner*. Jackson: University Press of Mississippi, 1985.

Gresset, Michel. *Fascination: Faulkner's Fiction, 1919-1936*. Durham: Duke University Press, 1989.

Gwin, Minrose. *The Feminine and Faulkner: Reading (Beyond) Sexual Difference*. Knoxville: University of Tennessee Press, 1990.

Hall, Constance H. *Incest in Faulkner: A Metaphor for the Fall*. Ann Arbor: UMI Research Press, 1985.

Harrison, Robert. *Aviation Lore in Faulkner*. Philadelphia: John Benjamins, 1985.

Haynes, Jane I. *William Faulkner: His Tippah County Heritage.* Dearborn, MI: Seajay Society, 1985.

Keating, Bern. *Faulkner's Seacoast of Bohemia.* Memphis: White Rose Press, 1989.

Kinney, Arthur F. *Critical Essays on William Faulkner: The Sartoris Family.* Boston: G. K. Hall, 1985.

Kreiswirth, Martin. *William Faulkner: The Making of a Novelist.* Athens: University of Georgia Press, 1984.

Millgate, Michael. *The Achievement of William Faulkner.* Athens: University of Georgia Press, 1989.

Morris, Wesley, and Barbara A. Morris. *Reading Faulkner.* Madison: University of Wisconsin Press, 1989.

Oates, Stephen B. *William Faulkner: Storyteller of the Heart.* New York: Harper & Row, 1987.

Ohashi, Kenzaburo, and Kiyoyuki Ono, eds. *Faulkner Studies in Japan.* Athens: University of Georgia Press, 1985.

Polk, Noel, and John D. Hart, eds. *"Absalom, Absalom!": A Concordance to the Novel.* Ann Arbor: UMI Research Press, 1989.

Sensibar, Judith L. *Faulkner's Poetry: A Bibliographical Guide to Texts and Criticism.* Ann Arbor: UMI Research Press, 1988.

Urgo, Joseph R. *Faulkner's Apocrypha: "A Fable," "Snopes," and the Spirit of Human Rebellion.* Jackson: University Press of Mississippi, 1989.

Wilhelm, James J., and Richard Saez, eds. *Religious Feeling and Religious Commitment in Faulkner, Dostoevsky, Werfel and Bernanos.* New York: Garland, 1988.

LAWRENCE FERLINGHETTI
1919

Author's Recent Bibliography

Over All the Obscene Boundaries, 1984 (poems); *Seven Days in Nicaragua Libre*, 1984 (diaries and photos); *European Poems and Translations*, 1988; *Love in the Days of Rage*, 1988 (novel); *Wild Dreams of a New Beginning*, 1988 (poems); *When I Look at Pictures*, 1990 (poems about paintings).

Evaluation of Selected Biography and Criticism

Silesky, Barry. *Ferlinghetti: The Artist in His Time*. New York: Warner, 1990. Although times have changed enormously since the coffee-house days of the 1950s when Allen Ginsberg and Lawrence Ferlinghetti were arrested for walking barefoot through the posh Mark Hopkins Hotel in San Francisco, Ferlinghetti has not, and it is remarkable that his messages still interest people of social conscience, but they do. In this sympathetic biography, Silesky argues that Ferlinghetti's life and poetry have been shaped by how "the outsider was an inextricable part of his identity." Orphaned at age two and abandoned at six, Ferlinghetti has led the life of a loner, not one of a rebel, and Silesky attempts to explain why Ferlinghetti became a sensitive social barometer for our times. Silesky had access to Ferlinghetti's journals, papers, and personal comments in compiling his work. Includes photographs. (A,G)

Skau, Michael. *"Constantly Risking Absurdity": The Writings of Lawrence Ferlinghetti*. Troy, NY: Whitston, 1989. The main drawback of this collection of essays is that it is excessively annotated with bibliographic citations, quotations, and references. It is perhaps best read for the meticulous notes. (A,G)

HENRY FIELDING
1707-1754

Evaluation of Selected Biography and Criticism

Battestin, Martin C. *Henry Fielding: A Life*. London and New York: Routledge, 1990. This important new biography delves into Fielding's childhood and the shadow of his reckless father to portray a man who was continually angry about the social status and authority which he was denied. Battestin vividly depicts a young Henry whose mother died when he was eleven years old, leaving him in the company of five sisters, a caring grandmother, and a father who wasted money and marriages. This biography clearly shows how Fielding created his literary material and developed his themes based on class; the puzzle is how such an embittered man could produce such lovable characters as Joseph Andrews and Tom Jones. **(A,G)**

Lewis, Peter. *Fielding's Burlesque Drama: Its Place in the Tradition*. Edinburgh: Edinburgh University Press, 1988. In this well-paced study, Lewis examines the burlesque tradition of English drama. English burlesque, which was used to parody and criticize heroic drama, tragedy, and opera, was heir to an extensive Restoration and Augustan tradition. Lewis discusses Fielding's lesser-known contemporaries, such as Duke of Buckingham, Thomas Duffet, and John Gay. Lewis then examines Fielding's eight plays, particularly *The Author's Farce*, *The Tragedy of Tragedies*, and *The Covent-Garden Tragedy*. **(A,G)**

McDermott, Hubert. *Novel and Romance: The "Odyssey" to "Tom Jones."* Totowa, NJ: Barnes & Noble, 1989. This study seeks to isolate the elements that constitute the romance tradition of the eighteenth-century novel and to examine their classical origins. He examines the narrative structures of the *Odyssey* and several Greek romances, then turns his attention to comic Latin works, such as *Satyricon* and *The Golden Ass*, and the medieval romances. He then demonstrates how the novels of Fielding and Richardson continue this tradition. Anyone interested in the origins of the novel and eighteenth-century literature, in particular, should find this study provocative and enlightening. **(A,G)**

Rivero, Albert J. *The Plays of Henry Fielding: A Critical Study of His Dramatic Career*. Charlottesville: University Press of Virginia, 1989. Rivero examines nine of Fielding's plays that have been "written off" by most critics as mere "prologue" to the novels. He contends that the plays are valuable in themselves and are an important part of Fielding's canon. Particular attention is paid to *Love in Several Masques*, *The Temple Beau*, *Pasquin*, and *The Historical Register*. Anyone approaching the study of Fielding's plays would find this volume an essential tool. **(A)**

Simpson, K. G., ed. *Henry Fielding: Justice Observed*. Totowa, NJ: Barnes & Noble, 1985. This collection of nine essays examines Fielding's moral sensibility and his use of judicial concepts in his fiction. Contributor Donald Low traces parallels between Fielding's dual careers as judge and writer. Morris Golding explores the influence of Fielding's politics on his writings. Donald Fraser examines the theme of deception in Fielding's last novel, *Amelia*. (A)

Varey, Simon. *Henry Fielding*. Cambridge: Cambridge University Press, 1986. Varey has produced a thorough critical reading of all of Fielding's work. He surveys the state of Fielding scholarship and incorporates the best of it into his analyses. Although there are no critical surprises and the account of Fielding's life is brief, no comparable volume on Fielding's works exists. This is a good starting point for any examination of Fielding's significance. (A,G)

Other Sources

Brooks-Davies, Douglas. *Fielding, Dickens, Gosse, Iris Murdoch and Oedipal Hamlet*. New York: St. Martin's, 1989.

Cleary, Thomas. *Henry Fielding: Political Writer*. Waterloo, Ontario: Wilfrid Laurier University Press/Humanities, 1984.

Hume, Robert D. *Henry Fielding and the London Theatre, 1728-1737*. New York: Oxford University Press, 1988.

Lynch, James J. *Henry Fielding and the Heliodoran Novel: Romance, Epic and Fielding's New Provenience of Writing*. Madison, NJ: Fairleigh Dickinson University Press, 1986.

Smallwood, Angela J. *Fielding and the Woman Question: Henry Fielding's Novels and Feminist Debate, 1700-1750*. New York: St. Martin's, 1989.

F. SCOTT FITZGERALD
1896-1940

Evaluation of Selected Biography and Criticism

Bloom, Harold, ed. *F. Scott Fitzgerald's "The Great Gatsby."* New York: Chelsea House, 1988. The eight essays collected here include topics such as Fitzgerald's criticism of America, mythic and structural elements, and point of view. Each of the topics will lead students to ideas for research. (A,G)

Carpenter, Humphrey. *Geniuses Together: American Writers in Paris in the 1920s.* Boston: Houghton Mifflin, 1988. Carpenter, who has written biographies of Auden and Tolkien, provides a portrait of expatriate life on the Left Bank in post-WWI Paris and surveys the American writers who flocked there for inspiration and comraderie. The spotlight is primarily on Hemingway and his immediate circle. Carpenter traces the evolution of Hemingway's "bare bones" writing style and recounts a number of unflattering anecdotes. Also making appearances are Anderson, Fitzgerald, Boyle, Pound, Joyce, and Stein. (A)

Dardis, Tom. *The Thirsty Muse: Alcohol and the American Writer.* London: Ticknor & Fields, 1989. Dardis applies the results of current addiction research to the lives and careers of American writers. Of eight authors who won the Nobel Prize, five were alcoholics. The popular theory that alcohol liberates the creative impulse, however, is thoroughly debunked. These were addicted men whose addictions got in the way of their creativity. Close-up views of O'Neill, Faulkner, Fitzgerald, Hemingway, and others are fraught with binges, black-outs, wife-beatings, delirium, disease, and untimely death. (A,G)

Dixon, Wheeler Winston. *The Cinematic Vision of F. Scott Fitzgerald.* Ann Arbor: UMI Research, 1986. Dixon contends that Fitzgerald's last years as a screenwriter (1937-1940) represent a previously unrecognized development of his artistic expression. Comparing his screenplays (in particular, *Three Comrades*) with his final novels, Dixon shows how the novelist mastered the techniques and language of film. He demonstrates how this work, in turn, influenced the structure and language of the unfinished novel, *The Last Tycoon.* (A,G)

Fryer, Sarah Beebe. *Fitzgerald's New Women: Harbingers of Change.* Ann Arbor: UMI Research Press, 1988. Fryer argues that Fitzgerald's female characters, though not modern women, were in a transitional state. They were victims of a patriarchal system which left them powerless without a male protector. Far from being dismantled by the sexual revolution of the 1920s, the system was strengthened by the redoubling of women's interest in romance and marriage. Fryer examines Fitzgerald's fictional females to

185

demonstrate how they are women in transition, even though they are victims of oppression. (A,G)

Lee, A. Robert. *Scott Fitzgerald: The Promises of Life*. New York: St. Martin's, 1989. Nine essays, all written by noted British critics, make up this new anthology of Fitzgerald criticism. Together, these essayists manage to cover many of Fitzgerald's short stories and all five novels, including *The Last Tycoon*. Of special interest is the Aldrich essay on women as depicted in the novels. Lee's introduction is a useful overview of Fitzgerald's place in literary history. (A,G)

Ring, Frances Kroll. *Against the Current: As I Remember F. Scott Fitzgerald*. Berkeley: Creative Arts, 1985. Frances Kroll interviewed for a secretarial position in 1939 with a slipped-into-obscurity novelist named F. Scott Fitzgerald. After passing several tests of her honesty and discretion, she was hired and remained with him until his death in December 1940. Fitzgerald's obsessions in his last years were money, gin, and writing, not necessarily in that order. In offering this memoir, Kroll has in many ways remained true to her employer to the last. She is confessedly biased in his favor, and her intent seems to be to pass on a little of that good will to readers and harsher critics. Fitzgerald's secrets—the ones he asked her to keep—seem still to be in good hands. In one revealing scene, Kroll sneaks out of the house to dispose of a burlap bag full of empty gin bottles to preserve her employer's "dignity." This image sums up the attitude of this memoir, but most readers would prefer a closer look inside the burlap bag. (A,G)

Other Sources
Bruccoli, Matthew J. *New Essays on "The Great Gatsby."* New York: Cambridge University Press, 1985.

Chambers, John B. *The Novels of F. Scott Fitzgerald*. New York: St. Martin's, 1989.

Lehan, Richard. *The Great Gatsby: The Limits of Wonder*. Boston: Twayne, 1990.

Metzger, Charles R. *F. Scott Fitzgerald's Psychiatric Novel: Nicole's Case, Dick's Case*. New York: Peter Lang, 1989.

Phillips, Gene. *Fiction, Film and F. Scott Fitzgerald*. Chicago: Loyola University Press, 1986.

Seiters, Dan. *Image Patterns in the Novels of F. Scott Fitzgerald*. Ann Arbor: UMI Research Press, 1985.

JOHN GOULD FLETCHER
1886-1950

Evaluation of Selected Criticism
  Carpenter, Lucas, ed. *Selected Essays of John Gould Fletcher.* Fayetteville: University of Arkansas Press, 1989. This anthology of nineteen of Fletcher's essays provides a useful overview of his contributions to literary criticism. Fletcher commandingly explicates the styles and works of such authors as Blake, Whitman, Hardy, Pound, Amy Lowell, Ransom, and Tate. His extended essay, "Some Contemporary American Poets" first published in 1920, is still considered a definitive statement on the imagist school. A few of his observations seem dated, but Carpenter has carefully selected essays that provide critical insights as useful today as when they first appeared. (A,G)

FORD MADOX FORD
1873-1939

Author's Recent Bibliography

Ford, Ford Madox. *A History of Our Own Times*. Bloomington: Indiana University Press, 1988. This interesting volume, written by Ford but never published, was to be the first in a three-volume treatment of world history. This was the only volume he completed. It covers England, Europe, and the United States, from 1870 to 1895. As history, this book is competent and readable, but Ford scholars will undoubtedly find it interesting for what it reveals about the writer's views on politics, economics, arts and literature, and the significance of the events of his time. **(A,G)**

Evaluation of Selected Criticism

Armstrong, Paul B. *The Challenge of Bewilderment: Understanding and Representation in James, Conrad, and Ford*. Ithaca: Cornell University Press, 1987. Armstrong distills the thematic and philosophical concerns of James, Conrad, and Ford to a single existential essence—bewilderment. Focusing on Conrad's narrators and characters in *Lord Jim* and *Nostromo*, he examines their shifting and often contradictory explanations of the reality of events. Comparing these viewpoints with the purposeful blurring of real life and illusion accomplished by James and the temperamental inconsistencies of Ford Madox Ford, Armstrong finds a strong basis for claiming that the expression of "bewilderment" was the source of many of their obscurities. **(A)**

Brebach, Raymond. *Joseph Conrad, Ford Madox Ford, and the Making of "Romance."* Ann Arbor: UMI Research, 1985. Conrad and Ford worked together on two novels, and this study analyzes the interaction between the two writers in terms of the "rules" they established for their collaboration. For example, they agreed that a character's speech should never directly reply to an immediately preceding speech. Conrad was drawn to the collaboration because of the chance to develop certain political themes, which he thought would be ironic within the context of *Romance*. Ford was more-or-less coerced into the collaboration since it was a difficult way of working for him. Brebach attempts to show how the collaboration influenced the works of both men. **(A)**

Cassell, Richard A., ed. *Critical Essays on Ford Madox Ford*. Boston: G. K. Hall, 1987. This collection offers essays and reviews of Ford's work, a great help to students in understanding and appreciating his life and times, as well as the themes of his novels. Ford, who co-authored novels with Joseph Conrad and was friends with American expatriates in Paris during the 1920s, is benefiting from a growing critical reputation. **(A,G)**

Dawson, Carl. *Prophets of Past Time: Seven British Autobiographers, 1880-1914*. Baltimore: Johns Hopkins University Press, 1988. This group of essays on seven autobiographers—Ford, W. H. White, George Tyrell, Samuel Butler, Edmund Goss, George Moore, and W. B. Yeats—goes beyond the typical concerns of nonfictional and fictional presentation of the self. It also examines the nature of memory, its role in creativity, its unconscious influences, and the anxiety of forgetting. Dawson draws upon these autobiographies to explore the interplay of past, present, and future in literary lives. He quotes extensively from philosophers, psychologists, and authors to enhance the context of his approach. A major contribution to the history of turn-of-the-century thought. (A,G)

Lindberg-Seyersted, Brita. *Ford Madox Ford and His Relationship to Stephen Crane and Henry James*. Atlantic Highlands, NJ: Humanities Press, 1987. The purpose of this study is to provide an exhaustive analysis of the contacts and mutual influences of Ford and James. In spite of the title's emphasis, Crane is addressed only in one short chapter. (A)

Seymour, Miranda. *A Ring of Conspirators: Henry James and His Literary Circle, 1895-1915*. Boston: Houghton Mifflin, 1989. The godfather of literature during the opening decades of the twentieth century, James attracted the best and the brightest writers to his estate in Rye. He especially attracted Americans who were either expatriates or temporarily enchanted by the wonders of the European intelligentsia. Seymour recreates this world and the band of gypsy writers who inhabited it, including Joseph Conrad, H. G. Wells, Ford Madox Ford, Edith Wharton, and Stephen Crane. This delightful and readable biography is sound in scholarship and is valuable to anyone studying any of these writers, the period, or the development of modern fiction. (A,G)

Other Sources
Radell, Karen M., ed. *Affirmation in a Moral Wasteland: A Comparison of Ford Madox Ford and Graham Greene*. New York: Peter Lang, 1987.

Snitow, Ann Barr. *Ford Madox Ford and the Voice of Uncertainty*. Baton Rouge: Louisiana State University Press, 1984.

E. M. FORSTER
1879-1970

Evaluation of Selected Criticism

Beer, John, ed. *"A Passage to India": Essays in Interpretation.* Totowa, NJ: Barnes & Noble, 1986. The collection of essays accurately presents the changing emphasis in Forster studies since similar collections appeared in 1970. The essayists—among them Gillian Beer, Molly Tinsley, G. K. Das, Wilfred Stone, and John Drew—examine the construction, themes, and critical reputation of Forster's justifiably famous novel of India. John Beer's conclusion provides a concise overview of the current state of scholarship and points to areas for future work. This collection is recommended to students as the first place to begin further research into the novel. (A,G)

Bloom, Harold, ed. *E. M. Forster's "A Passage to India."* New York: Chelsea House, 1987. The seven essays collected here deal with specific topics, such as "Forster as Victorian and Modern," while Bloom provides a provocative analysis of Forster's religious beliefs. Both the introduction and the essays will lead students to a deeper understanding of Forster's novels and offer good ideas for additional research. (A,G)

Graham, Kenneth. *Indirections of the Novels: James, Conrad, and Forster.* London: Cambridge University Press, 1988. Graham argues that while all three writers rejected the literary directions of the Victorian era, none quite advanced into modernism and, as a result, developed common themes of isolation. Faced with a world of uncertainty, they employed similar language, narrative form, and an ambiguity toward society. The novels that Graham uses to develop his thesis include James' *The Bostonians, The Europeans, What Maisie Knew,* and *The Golden Bowl;* Conrad's *Heart of Darkness, Lord Jim, Nostromo, The Secret Agent, Under Western Eyes,* and *The Shadow Line;* and Forster's *A Passage to India* and *Howard's End.* (A)

Herz, Judith Scherer. *The Short Narratives of E. M. Forster.* New York: St. Martin's, 1988. Herz argues that four building blocks emerge from Forster's short fiction and essays: transforming the past, myth and history, the private vs. the public self, and the creator as critic. She also traces the writers and philosophers who influenced Forster, and in doing so offers new readings for the stories. (A)

Page, Norman. *E. M. Forster.* New York: St. Martin's, 1988. This study of Forster follows a similar format to other books in the Modern Novelists Series. The opening sections are biographical. These are followed by a concise analysis of the author's work, and an annotated bibliography of criticism. Page's prose is lively and interesting and should serve to introduce students to Forster's fiction. (A,G)

Wilde, Alan, ed. *Critical Essays on E. M. Forster.* Boston: G. K. Hall, 1985. In various ways, these essayists delve into the intellectual, moral, philosophical, artistic, and sexual elements in Forster's works. In treating the meaning and significance of the novels, they evolve a consensus that Forster was devoted to his moral vision and its realistic presentation in his fiction. (A)

Wright, Andrew. *Fictional Discourse and Historical Space: Defoe and Theroux, Austen and Forster, Conrad and Greene.* New York: St. Martin's, 1987. An intelligent approach to fiction and current academic discourse, Wright's study examines the relationship between the reading of literature and the study of literary history. By comparing three pairs of books, he attempts to isolate distinct voices in diverse fiction across time and changing audiences. Wright compares Defoe's *Robinson Crusoe* with Paul Theroux's *Mosquito Coast* to reveal Theroux's use of aspects of the Crusoe character. He compares Jane Austen's *Emma* with Forster's *Howard's End* to connect the various voices of class and gender used by both authors. Finally, he examines Greene's *The Human Factor* in light of Conrad's *The Secret Agent* to understand the authors' views on anarchy and social control. Wright contends that both closure and history give fiction moral meaning. (A)

Other Sources

Dowling, David. *Bloomsbury Aesthetics and the Novels of Forster and Woolf.* New York: St. Martin's, 1985.

Kirkpatrick, B. J. *A Bibliography of E. M. Forster.* Oxford: Clarendon Press, 1985.

Lago, Mary, ed. *Calendar of the Letters of E. M. Forster.* Bronx, NY: Mansell, 1985.

Land, Stephen K. *Challenge and Conventionality in the Fiction of E. M. Forster.* New York: AMS Press, 1987.

BENJAMIN FRANKLIN
1706-1790

Evaluation of Selected Biography and Criticism

Breitwieser, Mitchell Robert. *Cotton Mather and Benjamin Franklin: The Price of Representative Personality.* Cambridge: Cambridge University Press, 1984. Breitwieser explores the transition from Puritanism to the Enlightenment in colonial America by comparing the lives of two prominent individuals—Benjamin Franklin and Cotton Mather. The two men were acquainted in Boston, when Mather's influence was declining and Franklin's was increasing. The story is that of two conflicting views of the universe—one based on reason, the other on divine will. (A,G)

Buxbaum, Melvin H. *Critical Essays on Benjamin Franklin.* Boston: G. K. Hall, 1987. Among the essays collected in this anthology are four new ones by Ormond Seavey, William Willcox, Tracy Mott and George Zinke, and Donald Meyer. A diverse range of topics is addressed from a variety of critical perspectives. (A)

Lemay, J. A. Leo *The Canon of Benjamin Franklin, 1722-1776: New Attributions and Reconsiderations.* Newark: University of Delaware Press, 1986. Lemay's extensive, systematic gleaning of eighteenth-century periodicals has resulted in a reassessment of the diverse writings of Franklin. Through painstaking scholarship Lemay has recovered nearly eighty Franklin pieces that were published anonymously or misattributed. In addition, he has discarded over twenty items from the "Collected Papers" that he claims are falsely attributed to Franklin. These writings are arranged chronologically and introduced with a history of their publication. Lemay relates his role as literary "detective" with obvious relish, and following him as he tracks clues of authorship is an education in itself. This is a valuable resource for the study of colonial American writers and a contribution to a critical reassessment of Franklin's role in literary history. (A)

Randall, Willard. *A Little Revenge: Benjamin Franklin and His Son.* Boston: Little, Brown, 1984. In spite of the innumerable contributions William Franklin made to the career of his famous father, Benjamin Franklin nearly succeeded in wiping the memory of his son from the face of history. Fortunately, Randall has located documents that reinstate William to his rightful place next to his father. More interesting, he speculates on the Oedipal urges and the political intrigues that drove a wedge between father and son and contributed to years of animosity. Benjamin installed William as postmaster of Philadelphia and later was influential in securing his position as Royal Governor of New Jersey. Because of his English education, William believed strongly in the loyalist cause and disagreed with his father's radical views on colonial independence. Forgiveness, even long after the issue was settled, was not forthcoming. (A,G)

Schulman, Robert. *Social Criticism and Nineteenth-Century American Fictions*. Columbia: University of Missouri Press, 1987. Schulman examines the political psychology of capitalism and its influence on the lives and works of some of the most famous American authors—Franklin, Twain, Melville, Hawthorne, Chesnutt, Whitman, Wharton, Howells, and Dreiser. His study pursues three main themes—the fragmentation of community, the impact of social change, and the styles of American individualism. In his discussion of Franklin's *Autobiography*, Schulman describes the costs of success and upward mobility as emotional deadening, increased isolation, and personal fragmentation. A truly new and refreshing reevaluation of nineteenth-century American literature. (A,G)

Seavey, Ormond. *Becoming Benjamin Franklin: The Autobiography and the Life*. University Park: Pennsylvania State University Press, 1988. Seavey uses the *Autobiography* to discern Benjamin Franklin's "pattern of inner life." He examines the vast differences between the life Franklin created for himself in the *Autobiography* and his real life and explores Franklin's motivations for fictionalizing himself. After detailing how questions of tone, audience, reader expectations, and philosophical framework shaped his narrative, Seavey argues that the Franklin who is popularly known existed only on paper. Seavey then treats episodes of Franklin's "real" life to emphasize the fictions of the *Autobiography*. The questions raised here will undoubtedly influence future directions in Franklin scholarship. (A,G)

Wright, Esmond. *Franklin of Philadelphia*. Cambridge: Harvard University Press, 1986. Wright bases his biography on the premise that Franklin built an image of himself that both concealed and revealed his life and personality. Famous for his alter-ego personae, such as Poor Richard and Silence Dogood, the myths and stories surrounding Franklin were legendary, even in his own time. Especially interesting is Wright's account of Franklin in Paris, where he was suspected of being a double agent, and where he led an affluent private life. The only fully comprehensive biography of the last fifty years, this book is a model of historical scholarship and lively prose. (A,G)

Other Sources

Sayre, Robert F. *The Examined Self: Benjamin Franklin, Henry Adams, Henry James*. Madison: University of Wisconsin Press, 1988.

Tanford, Charles. *Ben Franklin Stilled the Waves: An Informal History of Pouring Oil on Water with Reflections on the Ups and Downs of Scientific Life in General*. Durham: Duke University Press, 1989.

White, Charles W. *Benjamin Franklin: A Study in Self-Mythology*. New York: Garland, 1987.

MARY E. WILKINS FREEMAN
1852-1930

Autobiographical Sources
Kendrick, Brent L., ed. *The Infant Sphinx: Collected Letters of Mary E. Wilkins Freeman.* Metuchen, NJ: Scarecrow Press, 1985. Surprisingly, this is the first collection of Mary E. Wilkins Freeman's correspondence. This edition of 510 letters, spanning the years 1875 to 1930, provides new information and should stimulate renewed biographical efforts. There are unfortunately large gaps in the record where letters have been deliberately or carelessly destroyed. More than a hundred are addressed to her publishers and editors and reveal a marked business sense. Kendrick provides an excellent biographical introduction that outlines the contours of Freeman's literary career and reputation. (A,G)

Other Sources
Westbrook, Perry D. *Mary Wilkins Freeman.* [Rev. ed.] Boston: Twayne, 1988.

PHILIP MORIN FRENEAU
1752-1832

Evaluation of Selected Criticism
Hiltner, Judith. *The Newspaper Verse of Philip Freneau: An Edition and Bibliographical Survey.* Troy, NY: Whitson Publishing, 1986. This scholarly study consists of an introduction, which discusses attributions to Freneau, a chronology of his verse published in periodicals, and appendices listing uncollected poems. Of these poems, Hiltner categorizes them as "probable," "less probable," and "unlikely" candidates to have been written by Freneau. She discusses the characteristics of his poetry, including his English mentors, Pope, Gray, Collins, and Goldsmith. By comparing variants of the same poems, she raises questions about Freneau's creative process. **(A)**

ROBERT FROST
1874-1963

Evaluation of Selected Biography and Criticism

Burnshaw, Stanley. *Robert Frost Himself.* New York: Braziller, 1986. Using previously unpublished material, combined with personal reminiscence, Burnshaw provides a judiciously complex view of the elusive poet. Frost's generosity and humor are presented as a counterweight to the moody, angry outbursts emphasized by previous biographers. The last section compiles tributes to Frost by his fellow poets. **(A)**

Holland, Norman N. *The Brain of Robert Frost: A Cognitive Approach to Literature.* New York: Routledge, 1988. Holland maintains that structural balance and metaphor in both Frost's poems and his reading of other poets offers a good example of how cognitive science can be applied to literary criticism. Although Frost only provides a means to Holland's end, his interpretation of Frost is provocative. **(A,G)**

Monteiro, George. *Robert Frost and the New England Renaissance.* Lexington: University of Kentucky Press, 1988. Monteiro, an established Frost scholar, argues that Frost adopted many of his ideas from other New England writers. He shows the influence of Hawthorne, Thoreau, William Dean Howells, Dickinson and others on specific poems. Monteiro's careful scholarship lends credence to his theory, and will interest serious students of Frost and other New England writers. **(A)**

Walsh, John E. *Into My Own: The English Years of Robert Frost, 1912-1915.* New York: Grove, 1988. Walsh argues two major points about Frost's biography: that not enough attention has been devoted to the importance of Frost's years in England, and too much attention has been devoted to, and thus distorted, the dark side of Frost's personality. Walsh convincingly demonstrates how Frost's experience in England led him to write, in a span of only two years, most of the poems for which he was to be remembered. During the English years he also developed a critical theory that would give his poetry credibility and make him a critical, as well as popular success. Recommended for scholars and students studying Frost biography. **(A)**

Westbrook, Perry D. *A Literary History of New England.* Bethlehem, PA: Lehigh University Press, 1988. Spanning the years 1620 to 1950, this study of literary New England explains how literature mirrored and influenced the religious, political, social, and cultural forces of the region. Besides the most famous authors—Mather, Plath, Frost, Bradstreet—many lesser-known writers, such as Mercy Warren, Catharine Sedgwick, and Lucy Larcom, are also treated. Detailed enough to provide information for scholars, this lively study may also satisfy a more general audience. **(A,G)**

Other Sources

Dierkes, Henry. *Robert Frost: A Friend to a Younger Poet.* Notasulga, AL: Armstrong Press, 1984.

Hadas, Rachel. *Form, Cycle, Infinity: Landscape Imagery in the Poetry of Robert Frost and George Seferis.* Lewisburg, PA: Bucknell University Press, 1985.

Hall, Dorothy J. *Robert Frost: Contours of Belief.* Athens: Ohio University Press, 1986.

Pritchard, William H. *Frost: A Literary Life Reconsidered.* New York: Oxford University Press, 1984.

Wakefield, Richard. *Robert Frost and the Opposing Lights of the Hour.* New York: Peter Lang, 1984.

JOHN GALSWORTHY
1867-1933

Evaluation of Selected Biography and Criticism

Gindin, James. *John Galsworthy's Life and Art: An Alien's Fortress.* Ann Arbor: University of Michigan Press, 1987. Galsworthy has attracted little critical attention in recent years. Gindin describes the playwright as being rooted in earlier traditions and "out of step" with the modernism of his own times. Drawing on family papers and other archival materials, Gindin has produced a biography of Galsworthy that attempts to carve an appropriate niche for him in literary history. He paints his portrait detail by detail, allowing the evidence to slowly accumulate before drawing conclusions. (A,G)

Sternlicht, Sanford. *John Galsworthy.* Boston: Twayne, 1987. This is a thorough and interesting introduction to the life and works of John Galsworthy, who was considered the "most accessible" writer of his generation. His descriptions of the Edwardian upper class shaped the image of the "Briton" for thousands of readers. Sternlicht provides a biographical introduction followed by individual assessments of the major novels—*The Forsyte Saga* and *End of the Chapter*—and the short stories, including *Five Tales*. (A,G)

HAMLIN GARLAND
1860-1940

Evaluation of Selected Criticism

Murphy, Brenda. *American Realism and American Drama, 1880-1940.* Cambridge: Cambridge University Press, 1987. Murphy clarifies the relationship between literary realism and dramatic realism in this study of the works of Howells and James, culminating in the plays of O'Neill. Several plays by Hamlin Garland and James A. Herne are examined to demonstrate the impact of realistic theory on dramatic practice. Murphy sees the works of Odets and Hellman leading, via the cultural impact of Freud, to O'Neill, who reigns as undisputed master of the American stage. A valuable overview of the antecedents of twentieth-century American drama. **(A,G)**

Silet, Charles, Robert Welch, and Richard Boudreau, eds. *The Critical Reception of Hamlin Garland, 1891-1978.* Troy, NY: Whitston, 1985. This anthology compiles thirty-three selections, ranging from general reviews to sophisticated critical essays. Garland's career is divided into four phases, and the selections are grouped to illuminate the public and critical reception of his works during each of these periods. A full range of responses is recorded. Garland is hailed as an "unqualified genius," on one hand, or derided as a "pedestrian talent," on the other. Contributors include Howells, Mencken, Parrington, Hicks, Kazin, Walcutt, Pizer, and Ziff. **(A)**

ELIZABETH GASKELL
1810-1865

Evaluation of Selected Biography and Criticism

Brodetsky, Tessa. *Elizabeth Gaskell.* New York: Berg, 1987. Part of Berg's "Women's Series," this volume reassesses the literary accomplishments of Elizabeth Gaskell. Brodetsky presents Gaskell as a traditional, middle-class, Victorian woman who wrote seven intriguing social novels. She devotes a chapter to each novel and includes a section on the shorter fiction. Well-indexed with a useful chronology, this work can serve as an introduction to Gaskell for new readers. (A,G)

Coslett, Tess. *Woman to Woman: Female Friendship in Victorian Fiction.* Brighton: Harvester Press, 1988. Focusing on the Victorian era, Coslett demonstrates how women writers of the time were able to lend special power and significance to female friendships in their fiction. In these works, personal transformation is wrought through "sisterhood," rather than through the conventions of courtship and marriage. Coslett traces the process of individual development in novels by Gaskell, Rossetti, Browning, Eliot, and Charlotte Brontë. (A,G)

Nestor, Pauline. *Female Friendships and Communities: Charlotte Brontë, George Eliot, Elizabeth Gaskell.* Oxford: Clarendon Press, 1985. Devoting two chapters to each author, Nestor describes their association with other women, their attitudes toward gender, and their treatment of women in their fiction. In doing so, she enlarges her study to include nineteenth-century attitudes toward single women, female friendship, communal living, sexuality, and the emotions which society elicits from them, including anger, violence, passivity, jealously, and resignation. This provocative study illuminates the fiction of three writers, the context in which they created characters, and the society that would accept or reject both them and their work. (A,G)

Stoneman, Patsy. *Elizabeth Gaskell.* Bloomington: Indiana University Press, 1987. Stoneman's theoretical perspective is grounded in feminism, psycho-analysis, and political analysis. She argues that, behind her traditional facade, Gaskell was a radical revisionist intent on exposing the inequalities of gender and class. This is revealed in her rebellion against "male-dominated" literary themes and the adoption of a style based on themes of motherhood and family life. The narrow reading of Gaskell's work, however, reduces the depth of Gaskell's achievements to little more than the fiction of nurturing. This volume in Indiana's "Key Women Writers" series is recommended for serious students of Gaskell and feminist philosophy. (A)

Trodd, Anthea. *Domestic Crime in the Victorian Novel.* New York: St. Martin's, 1989. Trodd uses the patterns of domestic crime in fiction as a barometer of changing Victorian attitudes and social values. Early Victorian households cleaved to the rights of privacy and autonomy, no matter what the internal abuse. This gradually gave way to a belief in the right of the public to expose and punish domestic crimes. Trodd's cross-disciplinary approach provides fruitful insights into the roles of women and crimes against them, the roles of servants as perpetrators and victims, and the sensationalism of the courtroom. Offering impressive scope, this study examines fiction by such diverse authors as Kipling, Collins, Hardy, and Gaskell. **(A,G)**

Other Sources

Chapple, J. A., and J. G. Sharps. *Elizabeth Gaskell: A Portrait in Letters.* New York: St. Martin's, 1988.

Spencer, Jane. *Mrs. Gaskell.* Savage, MD: Barnes & Noble/Rowman, 1990.

JOHN GAY
1685-1732

Evaluation of Selected Criticism

Bloom, Harold, ed. *John Gay's "The Beggar's Opera."* New York: Chelsea House, 1988. This anthology of criticism on *The Beggar's Opera* reprints eight articles by a variety of scholars including William Empson, Martin Price, Patricia Meyer Spacks, and John Full, the editor of Gay's plays. Bloom provides a brief introduction which gives an overview of the essays. A convenient compilation of high-quality criticism for students. (A)

Lewis, Peter, and Nigel Wood, eds. *John Gay and the Scriblerians.* New York: St. Martin's, 1989. The ten essays cover the subject of Gay's patronage, politics, life style, his world of theatre and opera, and his attitudes toward sex and gender. Included are close readings of sections taken from Gay's poetry and drama. (A)

ALLEN GINSBERG
1926

Author's Recent Bibliography
White Shroud: Poems 1980-1985, 1986; *Howl: Original Draft Facsimile*, 1987 (poetry).

Ginsberg, Allen. *Howl: Original Draft Facsimile*. New York: Harper & Row, 1987. This anniversary edition reprints the original typescripts of each revision of this highly regarded and extremely influential poem. Taken together, this material provides a behind-the-scenes look at the composition of a complex poem. Revealed almost unintentionally are the eccentricities of Ginsberg's creative process. This is a unique compilation, useful for students at all levels. (A,G)

Evaluation of Selected Biography and Criticism
Cassady, Carolyn. *Off the Road: My Years with Cassady, Kerouac, and Ginsberg*. New York: William Morrow, 1990. The famous literary and sexual ménage-à-quatre, Neal, Carolyn, Jack, and Allen, is authentically and touchingly rendered by the educated, beautiful upper middle-class woman who thought she could tame charismatic Neal Cassady, convicted automobile thief and self-proclaimed wild man. Married to Neal, Carolyn was lover to Jack and friend to Allen, and she tells all their stories of love and literary ambition, bringing to life the counterculture that turned Kerouac and Ginsberg into heroes. (A,G)

Hyde, Lewis, ed. *On the Poetry of Allen Ginsberg*. Ann Arbor: University of Michigan Press, 1984. Hyde's anthology on Ginsberg's poetry contains several notable essays—James Breslin on the origins of "Howl" and "Kaddish," and Diane Trilling's "A Report from the Academy," among them. Also included are a variety of curiosities, such as a facsimile of Ginsberg's FBI records. The introduction summarizes the current state of Ginsberg scholarship. (A,G)

Miles, Barry. *Ginsberg: A Biography*. New York: Simon & Schuster, 1989. Miles has written a detailed account of Ginsberg's rise from obscurity to become what he terms "the most famous living poet on earth." Seemingly every event from the poet's life is included: his eccentric childhood, drug-enhanced adventures with Timothy Leary, world travels, relationships with Kerouac, Burroughs, and Orlovsky, and meditation. (A)

Other Sources
Merril, Thomas F. *Allen Ginsberg*. [Rev. ed.] Boston: Twayne, 1988.

GEORGE GISSING
1857-1903

Evaluation of Selected Biography and Criticism

Alden, Patricia. *Social Mobility in the English Bildungsroman: Gissing, Hardy, Bennett, and Lawrence.* Ann Arbor: UMI Research, 1986. The expression of a sense of upward social mobility in the late-nineteenth and early twentieth-century bildungsroman differed significantly from previous conceptions in the same genre. Many writers of the time believed that the upward mobility of the individual was a progressive phenomenon. Gissing, Hardy, Bennett, and Lawrence, on the other hand, viewed the process as a regressive disintegration of individual character. As portrayed in their works, the struggle to break out of one's social class leads only to frustration, alienation, and loss of identity. **(A,G)**

Bowlby, Rachel. *Just Looking: Consumer Culture in Dreiser, Gissing, and Zola.* New York: Methuen, 1985. Combining recent critical theory, history, and economics with a feminist perspective, Bowlby analyzes the novels of Dreiser, Gissing, and Zola in terms of the emerging consumer culture of the late nineteenth century. She contends that during this period poetry became "more pure" and the novel became a "commodity." Changing economic conditions prompted a change both in gender-based roles and in the concepts of masculinity and femininity. The "naturalistic" novel functioned as a critique of these social forces. **(A,G)**

Grylls, David. *The Paradox of Gissing.* Winchester, MA: Allen & Unwin, 1986. According to Grylls, the central paradox of Gissing's life was a deep-rooted pessimism that continually undermined his aspirations. The conflicts in his psyche abound: sympathy for the poor but disgust for their behavior, a sense of superiority inevitably giving way to self-loathing, his glorification of the "pure" woman but delight in lustfulness. Grylls skillfully builds an entertaining discussion of Gissing's personal extremes into an understanding of his internal dynamics. He then relates these conflicts to the fluctuating themes of Gissing's fiction. The study's socio-psychological approach yields ample insight into Gissing's often contradictory personality. **(A,G)**

Other Sources

Coustillas, Pierre, and Patrick Bridgewater. *George Gissing at Work: A Study of His Notebook "Extracts from My Reading."* Greensboro, NC: ELT Press, 1988.

Sloan, John. *George Gissing: The Cultural Challenge.* New York: St. Martin's, 1989.

ELLEN GLASGOW
1874-1945

Evaluation of Selected Criticism

Donovan, Josephine. *After the Fall: The Demeter-Persephone Myth in Wharton, Cather, and Glasgow.* University Park: The Pennsylvania State University Press, 1989. Donovan contends that the "Demeter-Diana-Persephone script" is preeminent in the literature of American women writers of the late nineteenth and early twentieth centuries. For Donovan, Persephone represents the "daughters" (feminine consciousness) that are whisked away into "patriarchal captivity." The Demeter-Diana world is related to the women's culture of the Victorian era, characterized by a marginal, segregated, "male-less" web of romantic female friendships. Donovan explores her thesis by devoting a section on each of the writers she feels most fully express the myth—Wharton, Cather, and Glasgow. Of special note is Donovan's discussion of the ritual basis of Cather's *My Ántonia.* **(A)**

MacDonald, Edgar E., and Tonette Bond Inge. *Ellen Glasgow: A Reference Guide.* Boston: G. K. Hall, 1986. This guide consists of a comprehensive annotated bibliography of writings about Glasgow. In addition to the usual books and journal articles, newspaper reviews and doctoral dissertations have been included. The entries, which are arranged chronologically, use short quotes to give the flavor of the original. A useful anthology for the student or researcher. **(A)**

Rowan, Julius, ed. *Ellen Glasgow's Reasonable Doubts: A Collection of Her Writings.* Baton Rouge: Louisiana State University Press, 1988. This volume collects Glasgow's nonfiction prose into a convenient study source, which should increase interest in Glasgow scholarship, especially for biographers and feminist critics. **(A,G)**

Saunders, Catherine E. *Writing the Margins: Edith Wharton, Ellen Glasgow, and the Literary Tradition of the Ruined Woman.* Cambridge: Harvard University English Department, 1987. This 73-page monograph is another in the series that Harvard's English Department occassionally awards to outstanding honors students. Saunders places Wharton and Glasgow within their restrictive societies, then demonstrates how they both use the archetypal "ruined woman" to attack social injustice and inequality. This single-thesis discussion may serve as a model for undergraduate writing and research.

Other Sources

Raper, Julius R., ed. *Ellen Glasgow's Reasonable Doubts: A Collection of Her Writings.* Baton Rouge: Louisiana State University Press, 1988.

WILLIAM GODWIN
1756-1836

Evaluation of Selected Biography and Criticism

Philip, Mark. *Godwin's "Political Justice."* Ithaca, NY: Cornell University Press, 1986. When Godwin's treatise outlining a scheme of Utopian anarchism—*Political Justice*—was published in 1793, it immediately catapulted him to notoriety and fame. Philp offers a clear interpretation of this watershed work and an explanation of why Godwin so quickly slipped back into obscurity. The social and political contexts for the composition and subsequent critical reception of the book are examined in detail. The appendixes and bibliography are useful for guiding further research. (A,G)

Rosen, Frederick. *Progress and Democracy: William Godwin's Contribution to Political Philosophy.* New York: Garland, 1987. This volume reprints the author's 1965 doctoral thesis, which examines the nature of Godwin's political thought. "Godwin was able at the same time to be a Whig, Republican, and Philosopher," contends Rosen—a combination that reflects a division between his theoretical and practical works. This thesis has not been updated to consider more recent critical perspectives. (A)

St. Clair, William. *The Godwins and the Shelleys: The Biography of a Family.* New York: Norton, 1989. Meeting the highest standards of research and analysis, this biography interweaves the lives and works of four of the most influential literary minds of the nineteenth century. St. Clair examines the origin and impact of William Godwin's *Political Justice*, Mary Wollstonecraft's *Vindication of the Rights of Women*, Mary Shelley's *Frankenstein*, and Percy Bysshe Shelley's poetry. The interplay of radical political beliefs, divergent moral standards, and literary achievement makes for intriguing and thought-provoking reading. This book is highly recommended for the scholar and for the general reader. (A,G)

WILLIAM GOLDING
1911

Author's Recent Bibliography

An Egyptian Journal, 1985; *Close Quarters*, 1987 (novel); *Fire Down Below*, 1989 (novel).

Evaluation of Selected Biography and Criticism

Baker, James R., ed. *Critical Essays on William Golding*. Boston: G. K. Hall, 1988. Golding has received little critical attention for a decade, and this collection of essays provides a much-need update. Nine previously published and three new essays are included, along with Golding's Nobel Prize acceptance speech, an interview with the writer, and a substantial introduction, "Three Decades of Criticism." Although Baker fails to include some of the most important criticism written during Golding's heyday, this collection provides an excellent view of current criticism. **(A,G)**

Boyd, S. J. *The Novels of William Golding*. New York: St. Martin's, 1988. Boyd analyzes the social, moral, and religious themes in six of Golding's novels, explaining the writer's views of society, human nature, and spiritual decline. Although scholars will disagree with some of Boyd's assumptions and conclusions, there are many good ideas here for students. **(A,G)**

Dick, Bernard. *William Golding*. Twayne, 1987. This revision of Dick's 1967 critical study of Golding provides a context for understanding his place in literary history. Dick's penetrating analysis answers some of the most frequently asked questions about the much maligned author, such as why he was awarded a Nobel Prize. Although concentrating primarily on the early works, Dick extends his coverage to 1980 by examining *Darkness Visible* and *Rites of Passage*. The brevity and clarity of this work make it a suitable critical introduction to Golding. **(A,G)**

Gindin, James. *William Golding*. New York: St. Martin's, 1988. Gindin begins this excellent assessment with Golding's biography, focusing particularly on the literary career, and the critical reception of *Lord of the Flies*. He then traces the literary influences on the novel, arguing that R.B. Ballantyne's *The Coral Island* (1858), which Golding admired, inspired the setting, while Alfred Lord Tennyson's moralism led Golding to create his cast of characters. Gindin also explores the novel's mythic dimensions. **(A,G)**

Redpath, Philip. *William Golding: A Structural Reading of His Fiction*. Totowa, NJ: Barnes & Noble, 1987. To explore the techniques used by Golding "to create meaning" in his fiction, Redpath takes a close critical look at the novels, notably *The Paper Men* (1984). The methodology of this study should make it interesting for advanced students. (A)

Subbarao, V. V. *William Golding: A Study.* New York: Envoy, 1987. As a scholar working in India, Subbarao brings a different social perspective to a writer whose major work dealt with society. Subbarao's examination of Golding's novels reveals the consistent theme of the human struggle for order in an uncertain universe. This readable study is useful for its explication of the novels, the extended references, and the index. General readers will appreciate Subbarao's straight-forward treatment. (A,G)

Other Sources
Carey, John, ed. *William Golding: The Man and His Books.* New York: Farrar, Straus & Giroux, 1987.

Singh, Satyanarain, *et al.,* eds. *William Golding: An Indian Response: A Collection of Critical Essays on the Fiction of William Golding.* New Delhi: Arnold Heinemann, 1987.

OLIVER GOLDSMITH
1730?-1774

Autobiographical Sources
Myatt, Wilfrid E., ed. *Autobiography of Oliver Goldsmith: A Chapter in Canada's Literary History*. Hantsport, Nova Scotia: Lancelot Press, 1985. This is an edition of the only non-fiction prose work composed by Goldsmith, an autobiographical sketch that was never intended for publication. According to Myatt, Goldsmith is not known so much for the quality of his poetry as for his contribution to the embryonic Canadian literature of the early nineteenth century. A brief introduction focuses primarily on the origins and history of Goldsmith's manuscript. **(A)**

Evaluation of Selected Criticism
Bloom, Harold, ed. *Oliver Goldsmith*. New York: Chelsea House, 1987. Another in the Modern Critical Views series, this book contains eleven essays which offer excellent critical readings of *The Vicar of Wakefield*, *The Citizen of the World*, *The Good Natur'd Man*, *The Deserted Village*, *The Traveller*, and *She Stoops to Conquer*, together with essays on Goldsmith's poetry and a general introduction to the novel of manners. Recommended for advanced students and critics. **(A)**

Other Sources
Swarbrick, Andrew, ed. *The Art of Oliver Goldsmith*. Savage, MD: Barnes & Noble, 1984.

JOHN GOWER
c. 1330-1408

Evaluation of Selected Criticism

Pickles, J. D. and J. L. Dawson, eds. *A Concordance to John Gower's "Confessio Amantis."* Woodbridge, Suffolk Wolfeboro, NH: D. S. Brewer. A publication of The John Gower Society, 1987. This computer generated concordance, based on G. C. Macaulay's edition of the *Complete Works,* provides an indispensable research tool for the study of language and style. Recommended for scholars. (A)

Other Sources

Nicholson, Peter. *An Annotated Index to the Commentary on John Gower's Confessio Amantis.* New York: Medieval & Renaissance, 1989.

Pearsall, Derek, *et al., A Descriptive Catalogue of the Manuscripts of the Works of John Gower.* New York: Garland, 1989.

ROBERT GRAVES
1895-1985

Author's Recent Bibliography
Collected Poems, 1975, 1988; *Poems about War*, 1990.

Evaluation of Selected Biography and Criticism
Bryant, Hallman Bell. *Robert Graves: An Annotated Bibliography*. New York: Garland Publishing, 1986. This bibliography is designed for students but should prove useful to anyone pursuing an interest in Graves' life and work. It is divided into two sections: the primary sources lists all of the fiction, poetry, mythography, and miscellaneous writings; secondary sources include citations of biographies, critical studies, reviews, and dissertations. **(A)**

Carter, D. N. G. *Robert Graves: The Lasting Poetic Achievement*. Totowa, NJ: Barnes & Noble, 1989. Carter examines the underlying integrity of themes in Graves' poetry. Through close readings of the poems, he explores the various incarnations of the love theme which culminated in Graves' self-generated "monomyth," the White Goddess. Carter contends that Graves was obsessed with "poetically right conduct" in both structure and prosody, while at the same time he was intrigued with varieties of "unreason" as expressed through more anarchic poetic forms. **(A,G)**

Graves, Richard Perceval. *Robert Graves: The Assault Heroic, 1895-1926* (Volume 1); *Robert Graves: The Years with Laura, 1926-1940* (Volume 2). New York: Viking, 1987, 1990. Robert Graves' nephew Richard had access to unpublished family papers that allow him to speak with authority on the life and work of the novelist, poet, and mythographer. Examined in some detail are Graves' often-excessive personal attachments, his strong sense of morality, his marriage to Nancy Nicholson, his war experiences, and his life-long interest in psychology. His copious creative successes resulted from a prolonged period of relative poverty and obscurity. **(A,G)**

Kersnowski, Frank, ed. *Conversations with Robert Graves*. Jackson: University Press of Mississippi, 1989. This collection of short interviews provides enough diversity to complement biographies of Graves. Most of the interviewers are writers or journalists, but even Gina Lolabrigida gets the chance to ask a few questions. **(G)**

Other Sources
O'Prey, Paul, ed. *In Broken Images: Selected Correspondence of Robert Graves* and *Between Man and Moon: Selected Letters of Robert Graves*. Mount Kisco, NY: Moyer Bell Limited, 1988, 1990.

THOMAS GRAY
1716-1771

Evaluation of Selected Criticism

Bloom, Harold, ed. *Thomas Gray's "Elegy Written in a Country Churchyard."* New York: Chelsea House, 1987. This collection of nine in-depth essays examines the literary significance of Gray's well-known poem. Frank Brady discusses structure and meaning in the *Elegy*. Roger Lonsdale surveys the full context of Gray's "versions of the self." Howard Weinbrot offers a moral reading, while W. Hutchings analyzes how Gray creates an audience for his poem inside the poem itself. Jean-Pierre Milheur compares the work to the "high romantic anxieties" of Wordsworth and Shelley. Other contributors include Thomas Carper, Eric Smith, Anne Williams, and Peter Sacks. Bloom provides a brief critical introduction. **(A)**

Golden, Morris. *Thomas Gray.* Boston: Twayne, 1988. In this updated edition of his 1964 study, Golden provides a short biography, a discussion of Gray's theories of literary composition, an explanation of the basic qualities of neoclassicism and romanticism, and a general reading of Gray's chief poems, incidental pieces, fragments, and posthumously published works. Recommended for beginning students of Gray or the eighteenth century. **(G)**

GRAHAM GREENE
1904

Author's Recent Bibliography
Getting to Know the General, 1984 (non-fiction); *The Tenth Man*, 1985 (novel); *The Captain and the Enemy*, 1988 (novel).

Evaluation of Selected Biography and Criticism
Couto, Maria. *Graham Greene: On the Frontier: Politics and Religion in the Novels*. New York: St. Martin's, 1988. Greene himself divided his novels into two types: fictions and entertainments, and critics have usually acknowledged that some of his novels are more serious than others. Thus, critics who often discuss the religious theme of redemption in *The Power and the Glory*, seldom find much to explicate in *Our Man in Havanna*. Couto's thesis is that politics forms the basis for all of Greene's work—not a startling discovery since Greene is famous for travelling to the center of political upheavals: in Vietnam, Nicaragua, Cuba, Northern Ireland. Couto attempts to unify what Greene himself divided. **(A)**

DeVitis, A. A. *Graham Greene*. Boston: Twayne, 1986. This is an updated and revised edition of an earlier study examining Greene's impressive literary career. DeVitis tackles the complex tangle of attitudes bound up with Greene's conversion to Catholicism in a short section that conveys more information than several existing books on the subject. His analyses of *Brighton Rock, The Power and the Glory*, and *The End of the Affair*, are perceptive and valuable. The study has been updated to include Greene's newest plays and *The Tenth Man* (1985), which was originally produced as a film script for MGM in 1948. The annotated bibliography is up-to-date. Highly recommended for anyone interested in Greene's work. **(A,G)**

Erdinast-Vulcan, Daphna. *Graham Greene's Childless Fathers*. New York: St. Martin's, 1988. This rather specialized study examines Greene's concept of fatherhood as portrayed in the characters of his novels. In fact, for Erdinast-Vulcan, biological, mental, emotional, and spiritual "fatherhood" becomes the theme which ties Greene's many disparate novels together. **(A)**

Kelly, Richard Michael. *Graham Greene*. New York: Ungar, 1985. In this critical study, Kelly makes a detailed examination of Greene's novels, short stories, and plays. According to Kelly, the underlying themes of these works cluster around issues of guilt, anxiety, spiritual quest, grace, and redemption. Of particular interest is Kelly's discussion of Greene's technique of blending mystery and adventure with spiritual and political analysis. A concise biographical introduction is provided. **(A,G)**

213

Meyer, Michael. *Words Through a Windowpane: A Life in London's Literary and Theatrical Scenes.* New York: Grove Weidenfeld, 1989. Meyer's entertaining reminiscences of postwar British literary circles touches upon his association with Shaw, Orwell, Graham Greene, and poet Sidney Keys, among others. The amusing anecdotes seem to spring from an inexhaustible source. (A,G)

Salvatore, Anne T. *Greene and Kierkegaard: The Discourse of Belief.* University: University of Alabama Press, 1988. In this complex study, Salvatore focuses on the rhetorical strategies that link Greene to Kierkegaard, rather than on their religious or philosophical affinities. Both writers use indirect exposition to hint at existential truth and the possibility for spiritual harmony. Because Greene approaches experience from a position of radical and negative skepticism, Salvatore contends, he should be considered a Kierkegaardian existentialist. (A)

Sherry, Norman. *The Life of Graham Greene: Volume 1, 1904-1939.* New York: Viking, 1989. Sherry's work on Greene amounts to an "official biography" but fortunately suffers few of the pitfalls of the genre. Author Greene selected biographer Sherry on the basis of his previous work on Joseph Conrad. Greene granted Sherry access to a prodigious volume of private papers and correspondence and allowed himself to be interviewed for the project. Sherry has used these advantages to produce a first-rate, even-handed account. Sherry expands upon many of the details first introduced in Greene's autobiographical writings. Volume one covers the formative years and early manhood, including Greene's conversion to Catholicism, which was eventually to reshape the wild, raw material of his youth into a more thoughtful maturity. (A)

Thomas, Brian. *An Underground Fate: The Idiom of Romance in the Later Novels of Graham Greene.* Athens: University of Georgia Press, 1988. Thomas explicates Greene's novels published between 1950 and 1973 from the perspective that romanticism is the dominant theme. Whether this thesis is true, the definition of romance leads to a provocative new approach for understanding how Greene fuses travels in exotic, often deadly places with freeing the spirit from the shackles of society, church, and conformity. In developing his thesis, Thomas compares Greene's novels with those of other romantic writers, such as Conrad. Although scholars may question Thomas' methodology and conclusions, students will find this a fascinating approach. (A,G)

Wolfe, Peter, ed. *Essays in Graham Greene: An Annual Review, Volume 1.* Greenwood, FL: Penkevill, 1987. This periodical compilation of essays provides a valuable new source for criticism of Greene's long, prolific career. Essays in this volume examine Greene's dislike of Hitchcock's films, his religious beliefs and their influence on his work, his use of sex as a theme and narrative device, and the critical interpretation of his works. There is also a section of reviews of biographical and critical books on Greene. (A,G)

Wright, Andrew. *Fictional Discourse and Historical Space: Defoe and Theroux, Austen and Forster, Conrad and Greene.* New York: St. Martin's, 1987. An intelligent approach to fiction and current academic discourse, Wright's study examines the relationship between the reading of literature and the study of literary history. By comparing three pairs of books, he attempts to isolate distinct voices in diverse fiction across time and changing audiences. Wright compares Defoe's *Robinson Crusoe* with Paul Theroux's *Mosquito Coast* to reveal Theroux's use of aspects of the Crusoe character. He compares Jane Austen's *Emma* with Forster's *Howard's End* to connect the various voices of class and gender used by both authors. Finally, he examines Greene's *The Human Factor* in light of Conrad's *The Secret Agent* to understand the authors' views on anarchy and social control. Wright contends that both closure and history give fiction moral meaning. (A)

Other Sources

Adamson, Judith. *Graham Greene and Cinema.* Norman, OK: Pilgrim, 1984.

Falk, Quentin. *Travels in Greeneland: The Cinema of Graham Greene.* London: Quartet Books/Salem House, 1984.

Gaston, Georg M. *The Pursuit of Salvation: A Critical Guide to the Novels of Graham Greene.* Troy, NY: Whitston, 1984.

Lamba, B. P. *Graham Greene: His Mind and Art.* New York: Apt Books, 1987.

McEwan, Neil. *Graham Greene.* New York: St. Martin's, 1988.

Radell, Karen M., ed. *Affirmation in a Moral Wasteland: A Comparison of Ford Madox Ford and Graham Greene.* New York: Peter Lang, 1987.

Smith, Grahame. *The Achievement of Graham Greene.* Savage, MD: Barnes & Noble, 1986.

SIR FULKE GREVILLE
1554-1628

Evaluation of Selected Criticism

Gouws, John. *The Prose Works of Fulke Greville, Lord Brooke*. Oxford: Clarendon Press, 1986. Gouws provides carefully edited texts of Greville's life of Sidney, and an unfinished epistle, *A Letter to an Honorable Lady*. Written a quarter of a century after Sidney's death, Greville's *Dedication to Sir Philip Sidney* (in *The Life of the Renowned Sir Philip Sidney*, 1652) served not only to provide a detailed biography but to confirm Sidney's reputation as a courtier, writer, and patron. Gouws explains the circumstances under which Greville would have composed this work, including his use of material that was originally written for a history of Queen Elizabeth I. Gouws argues that the theme underlying Greville's prose works was the irreconcilable opposition of "the moral and spiritual private life to the life of public responsibility and action." This carefully edited edition raises numerous questions for scholarly consideration. (A)

Klemp, P. J. *Fulke Greville and Sir John Davies: A Reference Guide*. Boston: G. K. Hall, 1985. In this bibliography, writings by and about Fulke Greville and Sir John Davies are listed chronologically with brief summaries of their contents. The entries range in date from 1581 to 1982, although the last two years are not covered comprehensively. (A)

Waller, Gary. *English Poetry of the Sixteenth Century*. White Plains, NY: Longman, 1986. Using the theories of Eagleton, Greenblatt, Sinfield, and Greenberg, Waller's study is a revisionist history of English Renaissance poetry. Waller develops a parallel chronological overview and critical reevaluation. Chapters cover sixteenth-century literary theory, the ideology of the Elizabethan court, Petrarch, and Protestantism. Several authors are given prolonged treatment—Dunbar, Wyatt, Raleigh, Greville, Sidney, Spenser, Shakespeare, and Donne. This book was meant to, but does not supplant C. S. Lewis' *English Literature of the Sixteenth Century* (1954). (A)

H. D.
1886-1961

Evaluation of Selected Biography and Criticism

DiPace-Fritz, Angela. *Thought and Vision: A Critical Reading of H. D.'s Poetry.* Washington, DC: Catholic University of America, 1988. DiPace Fritz explicates each of H. D.'s collections in order to examine her quest for a "synthesis between objective reality and spirituality." H. D.'s themes of myth and love began to emerge in *Collected Poems* (1925), develop through *Red Roses for Bronze* (1931), and culminate in the second *Collected Poems* (1944), in which she develops a voice that moves her work from "fragmentation to integration." In *Helen in Egypt* (1961) she creates a new mythology based on self-transforming powers. Though complicated, this study provides one of the best explications of H. D.'s themes and accomplishments. **(A)**

DuPlessis, Rachel Blau. *H. D.: The Career of That Struggle.* Bloomington: Indiana University Press, 1986. DuPlessis reviews the varied career of H. D. and attempts to establish how her works can be regarded as feminist. Her argument revolves around H. D.'s response to four areas of authority, which she judges to be at the center of feminist concerns—cultural, gender, sexual/ erotic, and the authority of otherness. Although this short work does not deal with this thesis in detail, DuPlessis outlines topics and issues that require further inquiry. As such, students should consult this book for thesis ideas. **(A,G)**

King, Michael, ed. *H. D., Woman and Poet.* Orono: National Poetry Foundation, University of Maine, 1986. This collection opens with memorial tributes to Hilda Doolittle by her daughter, friends, and fellow writers, including Silvia Dobson and May Sarton. The next two sections address H.D.'s continuing importance in the modern and post-modern periods, including the meaning of her work to women writers and for gender critics. Another section includes a selection of poems by younger writers influenced by her, including Adrienne Rich, Robert Duncan, and Margaret Atwood. The final chapters outline H. D.'s career as a poet, prose writer, photographer, and film-maker. These varied accounts of her life and art offer many potential ideas for research topics. **(G)**

Kloepfer, Deborah Kelly. *The Unspeakable Mother: Forbidden Discourses in Jean Rhys and H. D.* Ithaca, NY: Cornell University Press, 1989. Using a psychosexual/linguistic approach, Kloepfer provides an analysis of four of Rhys' novels and five prose works by Hilda Doolittle. Applying feminist critical theory, Kloepfer cleverly demonstrates how much more there is to the works of these writers than meets the eye. **(A)**

THOMAS HARDY
1840-1928

Autobiographical Sources

Purdy, Richard, and Michael Millgate, eds. *The Collected Letters of Thomas Hardy: Volume 6, 1920-1925*. New York: Oxford University Press, 1987. During the years covered by these letters, Hardy was occupied with two volumes of poetry—*Late Lyrics and Earlier*, and *Human Shows, Far Phantasies, Songs, and Trifles*—and two plays—*The Famous Tragedy of the Queen of Cornwall* and an updated, dramatic version of *Tess of the D'Urbervilles*. As he moved into his eighties, Hardy spent much of his time fending off would-be biographers and trying to control what was being written about him by supplying "autobiographical" stories that were often only outrageous lies. The letters, however, reveal many of his underlying attitudes. For example, he viewed the mass of his readers as "consumers of goods." And many of the letters are about money—getting it, dividing it up, holding on to it. (A,G)

Evaluation of Selected Biography and Criticism

Alden, Patricia. *Social Mobility in the English Bildungsroman: Gissing, Hardy, Bennett, and Lawrence*. Ann Arbor: UMI Research, 1986. The expression of a sense of upward social mobility in the late-nineteenth and early twentieth-century bildungsroman differed significantly from previous conceptions in the same genre. Many writers of the time believed that the upward mobility of the individual was a progressive phenomenon. Gissing, Hardy, Bennett, and Lawrence, on the other hand, viewed the process as a regressive disintegration of individual character. As portrayed in their works, the struggle to break out of one's social class leads only to frustration, alienation, and loss of identity. (A,G)

Alexander, Anne. *Thomas Hardy: The "Dream-Country" of His Fiction*. Totowa, NJ: Barnes & Noble, 1987. Drawing on Jungian psychology and archetypal criticism, Alexander examines the "dream country" of Thomas Hardy's fiction. This revised thesis does not have the staying power to adequately address its provocative subject. (A,G)

Bullen, J. B. *The Expressive Eye: Fiction and Perception in the Work of Thomas Hardy*. Oxford: Oxford University Press, 1986. Bullen brings the perspective of art-criticism to Hardy's fiction. He examines Hardy's references to paintings, architecture, and other visual media in notes, letters, and diaries to identify a definite visual perspective for each novel. The discussions are convincing, and Hardy scholars should find Bullen's methodology stimulating and enlightening. (A,G)

Casagrande, Peter J. *Hardy's Influence on the Modern Novel.* Totowa, NJ: Barnes & Noble, 1987. Casagrande traces Hardy's influence on a wide array of modern writers, including George Moore, Lawrence, Fowles, Proust, Alain-Fournier, Dreiser, Sherwood Anderson, Cather, and perhaps even Faulkner. In building his case, he relies heavily on the criticism of Harold Bloom, T. S. Eliot, and Henry James. The perspective is unusually broad, and the specifics are compressed. The staying power of Hardy's prose is reaffirmed throughout. **(A,G)**

Draper, Jo, and John Fowles, eds. *Thomas Hardy's England.* Boston: Little, Brown, 1984. Using period photographs, most of which were taken by Hardy's friend Hermann Lea, the editors explain many details of life and landscape during Hardy's time. Hardy guided Lea through his country, Dorset, which appears in the novels as Wessex, showing him the places that inspired his fiction. Novelist John Fowles, who has himself drawn heavily on English landscape, explains how a novelist might be influenced by places. This is an informative supplement for students of Hardy or nineteenth century England. **(A,G)**

Gatrell, Simon. *Hardy the Creator: A Textual Biography.* Oxford: Clarendon Press, 1988. Gatrell seeks to illuminate Hardy's creative life by documenting his changing attitudes towards the Victorian literary market. The book is organized chronologically and begins in 1868 when Hardy sent his first manuscript to Macmillan publishers. Displaying a breadth of scholarship, Gatrell examines subsequent manuscripts, serializations, and revisions to reveal Hardy's shifting priorities and emphases. Gatrell concludes with a detailed analysis of *Two on a Tower*, which sheds light on Hardy's attitudes in his later years. A comprehensive chronology of the writing and revising of the prose fiction is included as an appendix. **(A)**

Harvey, Geoffrey. *The Romantic Tradition in Modern English Poetry: Rhetoric and Experience.* New York: St. Martin's, 1986. Harvey fashions a framework of rational sympathy and rhetorical balance to gather Wordsworth, Hardy, Betjeman, and Larkin within a single poetic tradition. He then discusses the complex relationship between the "native English tradition" and emerging modernism. **(A,G)**

Jekel, Pamela L. *Thomas Hardy's Heroines: A Chorus of Priorities.* Troy, NY: Whitston, 1986. Jekel's all-inclusive study sheds some light on the increasing complexity of Hardy's heroines. **(G)**

Lucas, John. *Modern English Poetry from Hardy to Hughes: A Critical Survey.* Totowa, NJ: Barnes & Noble, 1986. The study uses socialist theory to select those modern English poets whose stance is communal rather than personal. As such it is not really a survey. For example, Lucas neglects Lawrence, Pound, and women poets, while giving extended attention to Eliot, Yeats, Larkin, and Igor Gurney. The value of this study suffers from its narrow ideological focus. **(A)**

Millgate, Michael, ed. *The Life and Work of Thomas Hardy,* by Thomas
Hardy. Athens: University of Georgia Press, 1985. Hardy's second wife
published what she alleged was a two-volume biography of her husband. Over
time, scholars determined that Hardy wrote most of the work himself, and that
it contained many deceptions. Millgate has endeavored to reconstruct the text
"as it stood at the time of Hardy's death, after receiving its last reading and
revision at his hands." Scholars will appreciate having a reliable annotated
edition. **(A)**

Morgan, Rosemarie. *Women and Sexuality in the Novels of Thomas Hardy.*
London and New York: Routledge, 1988. Morgan examines five of Hardy's
strongest female characters—Elfride Swancourt, Bathsheba Everdene, Eustacia
Vye, Tess Dubeyfield, and Sue Bridehead—and defines their activities,
vitality, ingenuity, passion, and honesty to show how Hardy attempted to
"demolish the doll of English fiction." He portrayed women of "less-than-
perfect natures in a less-than-perfect world," and in doing so liberated them
from the conventional mold of feminine perfection. Morgan explains why
Hardy was attacked as a misogynist, primarily by critics threatened by his
portrayal of women as triumphant pioneers. Ironically, Morgan is so laudatory
of the imperfect heroines that she turns them into ideals. Students will find
much to cheer about in this modern reading of an avant garde novelist. **(A,G)**

Orel, Harold. *The Unknown Thomas Hardy: Lesser-Known Aspects of
Hardy's Life and Career.* New York: St. Martin's, 1987. Compiled from a
series of public lectures, these essays by Orel examine major elements of
Hardy's life which remain unfamiliar to the general public. Orel delves into
Hardy's fascinations with architecture, archeology, theater, and law. Hardy
seemed obsessed with the details of murders, executions, prisoners, smuggling,
and poorhouses. Orel describes Hardy's unusual friendships with literary men
and women, particularly Kipling and Haggard. While targeted for a general
audience, there are many details in this book that the Hardy scholar may have
overlooked. **(A,G)**

Schweik, Robert, ed. *"Far From the Madding Crowd": An Authoritative
Text, Backgrounds, Criticism.* New York: Norton, 1986. To produce this
critical edition of Hardy's masterwork, Schweik collated twelve texts using the
1912 Wessex text as his base. To this he compared the manuscript and
Hardy's own 1912 edition, which contains handwritten corrections. To the
carefully annotated text, he appends Hardy's Wessex map, an essay on the
biographical and social contexts of the novel, and a selection of reviews and
essays that reveal the critical reception and subsequent modern scholarship.
This edition is a virtual textbook on *Far from the Madding Crowd.* **(A,G)**

Trodd, Anthea. *Domestic Crime in the Victorian Novel.* New York: St.
Martin's, 1989. Trodd uses the patterns of domestic crime in fiction as a
barometer of changing Victorian attitudes and social values. Early Victorian
households cleaved to the rights of privacy and autonomy, no matter what the
internal abuse. This gradually gave way to a belief in the right of the public

to expose and punish domestic crimes. Trodd's cross-disciplinary approach provides fruitful insights into the roles of women and crimes against them, the roles of servants as perpetrators and victims, and the sensationalism of the courtroom. Offering impressive scope, this study examines fiction by such diverse authors as Kipling, Collins, Hardy, and Gaskell. (A,G)

Wright, Terence. *"Tess of the D'Urbervilles."* Atlantic Highlands, NJ: Humanities Press, 1987. This book is an overview of critical perspectives that have been applied to Hardy's *Tess of the D'Urbervilles*. All of the major critics are represented—Tony Tanner, Dorothy Van Ghent, David DeLaura, Arnold Kettle, and Lionel Johnson. Wright groups them into critical "schools" —those who focus on social elements, on characterization, on themes, or structure. His approach is satisfyingly "holistic" in that it acknowledges the individual strengths of each school and then demonstrates how the approaches are complementary when applied to the work itself. This concise work is recommended as an accurate, unbiased introduction to Hardy criticism—both useful for the scholar and accessible to the student. (A,G)

Other Sources

Bjork, Lennart. *The Literary Notebooks of Thomas Hardy.* New York: New York University Press, 1985.

Butler, Lance St. John, ed. *Alternative Hardy.* New York: St. Martin's, 1989.

Danon, Ruth. *Work in the English Novel: The Myth of Vocation.* Savage, MD: Barnes & Noble, 1986.

Elliott, Ralph W. *Thomas Hardy's English.* Cambridge: Basil Blackwell, 1986.

Giordano, Frank R., Jr. *"I'd Have My Life Unbe": Thomas Hardy's Self-Destructive Characters.* Tuscaloosa: University of Alabama Press, 1984.

Goode, John. *Thomas Hardy.* Cambridge: Basil Blackwell, 1988.

Hands, Timothy. *Thomas Hardy, Distracted Preacher?: Hardy's Religious Biography and Its Influence on His Novels.* New York: St. Martin's, 1989.

Hardy, Thomas. *An Autobiography in Verse.* Chester Springs, PA: Dufour/Shepheard-Walwyn UK, 1984.

Ingham, Patricia. *Thomas Hardy.* Atlantic Highlands, NJ: Humanities Press, 1989.

Schur, Owen. *Victorian Pastoral: Tennyson, Hardy, and the Subversion of Forms.* Columbus: The Ohio State University Press, 1989.

Schwarz, Daniel R. *The Transformation of the English Novel, 1890-1930.* New York: St. Martin's, 1989.

Taylor, Dennis. *Hardy's Metres and Victorian Prosody: With a Metrical Appendix of Hardy's Stanza Forms.* New York: Oxford University Press, 1989.

Widdowson, Peter. *Hardy in History.* New York: Routledge Chapman & Hall, 1989.

Wotton, George. *Thomas Hardy: Towards a Materialist Criticism.* Savage, MD: Barnes & Noble, 1985.

Wright, T. R. *Hardy and the Erotic.* New York: St. Martin's, 1989.

JOEL CHANDLER HARRIS
1848-1908

Evaluation of Selected Biography and Criticism

Bikley, R. Bruce, Jr. *Joel Chandler Harris.* Athens: University of Georgia Press, 1987. This biography of Harris is a reprint of the G. K. Hall edition first published in 1977. The annotated bibliography has been updated and expanded to include more recent secondary sources. (A,G)

Callahan, John F. *In the African-American Grain: The Pursuit of Voice in Twentieth-Century Black Fiction.* Champaign: University of Illinois Press, 1988. This thematic study of narrative voice links aspects of folk culture to the works of several generations of black writers. Callahan focuses on the folk tradition of call and response and how it influenced the narrative voice. He compares the tales of Joel Chandler Harris and Charles Chesnutt to show how the authors used folk expressions to articulate democratic ideals. Callahan explores the lyrical qualities of Jean Toomer's *Cane*, which is expressed in a "musical" rather than rhetorical voice. Examining Zora Hurston's *Their Eyes Were Watching God* and the *Autobiography of Jane Pittman,* he shows how the conventions of storytelling are used to establish an interactive relationship with the reader. Turning to Ralph Ellison's *Invisible Man*, Callahan traces the emotional development of the narrator through a careful analysis of the speeches. Callahan stresses the essential "Americanness" of these works, placing them in the line of Emerson and democratic idealism. (A,G)

NATHANIEL HAWTHORNE
1804-1864

Autobiographical Sources

Woodson, Thomas, *et al.*, eds. *The Centenary Edition of the Works of Nathaniel Hawthorne: The Letters, 1813-1843* (Vol. 15), *1843-1853* (Vol. 16). Columbus: Ohio State University Press, 1984, 1985. These are the first two volumes of letters in this definitive edition of the collected works. They are to be followed by two more volumes of personal letters and one of consular items from Liverpool. Volumes fifteen and sixteen together comprise over 650 letters, the first written when Hawthorne was but nine years old. The literary and biographical quality of these letters is generally superb. The editors have provided a fine introduction and meticulously researched notes. (A,G)

Evaluation of Selected Criticism

Abel, Darrel. *The Moral Picturesque: Studies in Hawthorne's Fiction.* Lafayette, IN: Purdue University Press, 1988. These essays, published between 1953-1974, contain valuable Hawthorne criticism. Abel uses the term "moral picturesque" to describe Hawthorne's technique for depicting the psychological tension between characters as he explores the differences between the real and ideal worlds. *The Scarlet Letter* is Abel's centerpiece, though he explores many of the other novels and stories. This is an excellent introduction for students and general readers. (A,G)

Auerbach, Jonathan. *The Romance of Failure: First-Person Fictions of Poe, Hawthorne, and James.* New York: Oxford University Press, 1989. Auerbach examines the first-person narratives of Poe, Hawthorne, and James to better understand the writers' relationship to their works. Auerbach believes the first-person perspective is revealing because it provides less of a grammatical barrier to mediation between author and text. Poe is shown to display a contradiction between his personal and public identities. In *The Blithedale Romance*, Hawthorne preserves his artistic integrity by hiding behind a "clownish" persona. In *The Sacred Fount*, James drives his narrator into madness in order to maintain his own sanity. (A)

Baym, Nina. *"The Scarlet Letter": A Reading.* Boston: Twayne, 1986. In this study, the first of a projected series of readings of English and American classics, Baym provides a masterful summary and critique of Hawthorne's *The Scarlet Letter*. She thoroughly covers the major elements of author, text, and critical reception in a way that makes the material accessible to nearly all readers. This is an excellent introduction for new Hawthorne readers. (A,G,Y)

Bennett, Maurice J. *An American Tradition—Three Studies: Charles Brockden Brown, Nathaniel Hawthorne, and Henry James.* New York:

Garland, 1987. This dissertation examines and compares three American authors and focuses on a major work by each—Brown's *Ormond, or the Secret Witness,* Hawthorne's *The Scarlet Letter,* and James' *The Portrait of a Lady.* This volume includes an extensive bibliography. (A)

Brodhead, Richard H. *The School of Hawthorne.* New York: Oxford University Press, 1986. Hawthorne's fiction has survived evolving tastes in literature, new critical theories, and a world that has changed dramatically since Hawthorne's time. Brodhead attempts to trace the influence that Hawthorne has exerted on American literature in both the nineteenth and twentieth centuries, and his importance to such writers as Melville, James, and Faulkner. Brodhead provides a valuable overview of the American tradition in literature and the common denominators of American fiction. Recommended for all serious researchers. (A,G)

Coale, Samuel Chase. *In Hawthorne's Shadow: American Romance from Melville to Mailer.* Lexington: University Press of Kentucky, 1985. Undoubtedly, Hawthorne's influence on the shape of American fiction has been immense. In this study, Coale isolates what he considers to be the essential elements of Hawthorne's fiction and traces their dissemination through the works of his literary heirs, including Melville, Faulkner, Mailer, McCullers, O'Connor, Styron, Cheever, Updike, Gardner, and many others. In Coale's view, Hawthorne's fiction embodies radical dualisms: mind/matter, spirit/substance, and imagination/nothingness. The shadow he casts, says Coale, is from his "own dark vision of himself and his country." (A,G)

DeSalvo, Louise. *Nathaniel Hawthorne.* Atlantic Highlands, NJ: Humanities Press, 1987. DeSalvo argues that literature is too often taught as high culture rather than as a reflection of the social oppression it embodies. She thinks that racism, classism, and misogyny are expressed by many American writers, and that Hawthorne is no exception in his denial of women their historic role. This strongly feminist study is more interesting for its social criticism than for its interpretation of Hawthorne. (A)

Donohue, Agnes McNeill. *Hawthorne: Calvin's Ironic Stepchild.* Kent, OH: Kent State University Press, 1985. Hawthorne considered himself a "Puritan," and in many ways the Calvinistic doctrine of "damnation" inspired many of his most important works. Calvin's vision of a New Jerusalem on earth, however, had been proven to be just another illusion. Donohue argues that Hawthorne's novels retell the tale of the fall of man in the New World. His characters fall from "Grace" and fail to find happiness or salvation in their fallen state. As such, she reads *The Scarlet Letter* as an exercise in bitter irony. The protagonists appear to have achieved an assurance of salvation, while in reality there is no way to return to the lost Eden. Hawthorne's later sojourn in Europe and exposure to Anglicanism and Roman Catholicism, argues Donohue, paralyzed him as a writer by confusing his sources of dramatic tension. (A,G)

Dryden, Edgar A. *The Form of American Romance*. Baltimore: Johns Hopkins University Press, 1988. In this study, Dryden undertakes an analysis of the structure and development of American Romanticism. He first examines the origins of the novel and its relationship to romance by discussing *Don Quixote* and Scott's *Waverley*. He views Scott's early novel as a "founding text" in the history of the English novel. Dryden then dissects the narrative structures of five American novels—Hawthorne's *The Marble Faun*, Melville's *Pierre*, James' *The Portrait of a Lady*, Faulkner's *Absalom, Absalom!*, and Barth's *LETTERS*. He sees these American novelists responding directly to narrative problems inherited from Scott. (A)

Greenwald, Elissa. *Realism and the Romance: Nathaniel Hawthorne, Henry James, and American Fiction*. Ann Arbor: UMI Research Press, 1989. Greenwald argues that Hawthorne's romances directly influenced the development of James' realism, which opened the door to modernist fiction. She provides excellent close readings of some of the fiction of both writers, linking *The Scarlet Letter* with *The Portrait of a Lady*, and *The Blithedale Romance* with *The Bostonians*. She demonstrates an important connection in the development of the American novel, and the road which romanticism traveled to survive in the modernist mind. This is a valuable study for any serious reader of either writer. (A,G)

Greiner, Donald J. *Adultery in the American Novel: Updike, James, and Hawthorne*. Columbia: University of South Carolina Press, 1985. This narrowly focused study examines the relationship between the depiction of adultery in Updike's novels and the narrative models provided by his predecessors, Hawthorne and James. Greiner believes that Updike's essentially religious outlook inhibits a full development of the adultery theme, and his work suffers in comparison with the past masters. (A)

Haggerty, George E. *Gothic Fiction/Gothic Form*. University Park: Pennsylvania State University Press, 1989. In this study in reader-response criticism, Haggerty attempts to lift Gothic fiction into the category of serious literature. To do this, he establishes two categories—Gothic novels and Gothic tales. Gothic *novels* fail because the genre is unsuited to the effects generated in the reader by the Gothic impulse. Gothic *tales*, on the other hand, succeed admirably. Indeed, because Haggerty's conception of the tale is represented by such works as Shelley's *Frankenstein*, Brontë's *Wuthering Heights*, Poe's "The Fall of the House of Usher," Hawthorne's "Rappaccini's Daughter," and James' *Turn of the Screw*, it is difficult to argue with the conclusion. Some have questioned Haggerty's categories of novel and tale as artificial. (A,G)

Harris, Kenneth Marc. *Hypocrisy and Self-Deception in Hawthorne's Fiction*. Charlottesville: University Press of Virginia. 1988. Harris traces the influence of New England theologians' concerns with detecting spiritual impostors on Hawthorne's creation of character, and argues how hypocrisy and self-deception affect the themes and structure of the major works. Recommended for serious students. (A)

Hunter, Gordon. *Secrets and Sympathy: Forms of Disclosure in Hawthorne's Novels.* Athens: University of Georgia Press, 1988. In this ambitious study, Hunter postulates that Hawthorne created a "rhetoric of secrecy" that gives the novels an aura of psychological, as well as thematic, mystery. Relying on reader-response criticism, Hunter demonstrates how Hawthorne uses secrecy to disrupt the reader's or the character's progress toward discovery. Hunter is insightful on why Hawthorne deliberately fails to explain events in his fiction. (A)

Levine, Robert S. *Conspiracy and Romance: Studies in Brockden Brown, Cooper, Hawthorne, and Melville.* New York: Cambridge University Press, 1989. This study consists of four loosely connected essays. An essay on Brown's *Ormond* focuses on the writer's foreign villains and conspiratorial plots against the integrity of the fledgling United States. Examining Cooper's *The Bravo*, Levine demonstrates that the author's desire was to demystify and oppose the "mysterious power" that directed the state of Venice, which he described as a "soulless corporation." Levine examines the roles of insiders and outsiders in Hawthorne's *The Blithedale Romance.* Finally, he turns his attention to Melville's *Benito Cereno* where he examines the conflicts between captains and mutineers. (A)

McIntosh, James, ed. *Nathaniel Hawthorne's Tales: Authoritative Texts, Backgrounds, Criticism.* New York: Norton, 1987. As part of the Norton Critical Editions Series, this compact volume provides authoritative texts of twenty-one of Hawthorne's most important tales and sketches, introduced with textual information, background materials, and a discussion of critical issues. Scrupulous notes are provided. Appended is a selection of modern critical essays that express a broad range of interpretations. The bibliography is invaluable. Highly recommended. (A)

Mills, Nicolaus. *The Crowd in American Literature.* Baton Rouge: Louisiana State University Press, 1986. Mills explicates the use of "crowds" by American writers from Jefferson to Steinbeck. For colonial, political writers crowds were a "force for democracy;" for the classical American novelists—Hawthorne, Melville, and Twain—they were a force for national unity. Mills examines the "noble" working-class masses of such writers as Howells, Dreiser, and Steinbeck. Finally, he turns to Norman Mailer and Ralph Ellison for an examination of post-war crowds, the repository of intellectual and moral power contrasted with brute force. This is a fascinating thematic social history drawn from American literary works. (A,G)

Newberry, Frederick. *Hawthorne's Divided Loyalties: England and America in His Works.* Rutherford, NJ: Fairleigh Dickinson University Press, 1987. Newberry's thesis is that Hawthorne was a genuinely democratic individual who was at the same time drawn to the pomp and traditions of the Old Country. Newberry's analysis of these conflicting urges helps explain why Hawthorne was never able to complete his last narrative projects. He was unable to reconcile his American identity and English sympathies, the extent of which have not been previously documented by researchers. Recommended for serious readers of Hawthorne. **(A)**

Pahl, Dennis. *Architects of the Abyss: The Indeterminate Fictions of Poe, Hawthorne, and Melville.* Columbia: University of Missouri Press, 1989. Drawing on the theories of Nietzsche, Derrida, and de Man, Pahl explores the nature of the "abyss of signification" generated by a writer's problematic notions of "truth." Using Poe's short stories and *The Narrative of Arthur Gordon Pym*, Pahl examines categories of "the uncanny," "recuperation," and "authority" as they relate to narration. Using Hawthorne's "Rappaccini's Daughter," he dissects the contradictory nature of the perspective on which the reader is forced to rely. Turning to Melville's "Billy Budd," Pahl develops the full complexity of his theoretical paradigms. This is a specialized study that should be of interest to scholars of critical theory and American literature. **(A)**

Schulman, Robert. *Social Criticism and Nineteenth-Century American Fictions.* Columbia: University of Missouri Press, 1987. Schulman examines the political psychology of capitalism and its influence on the lives and works of some of the most famous American authors—Franklin, Twain, Melville, Hawthorne, Chesnutt, Whitman, Wharton, Howells, and Dreiser. His study pursues three main themes—the fragmentation of community, the impact of social change, and the styles of American individualism. In his discussion of Franklin's *Autobiography*, Schulman describes the costs of success and upward mobility as emotional deadening, increased isolation, and personal fragmentation. A truly new and refreshing reevaluation of nineteenth-century American literature. **(A,G)**

Steele, Jeffrey. *The Representation of the Self in the American Renaissance.* Chapel Hill: University of North Carolina Press, 1987. Steele draws on modern psychological theories to explore the concept of the self as portrayed in major works of the American Renaissance. He makes illuminating comparisons between the orientations of writers and psychologists/philosophers—for example, Emerson and Jung, Thoreau and Medard Boss, Hawthorne and Freud, and Melville and Nietzsche. **(A,G)**

Sutherland, Judith. *The Problematic Fictions of Poe, James, and Hawthorne.* Columbia: University of Missouri Press, 1984. Sutherland focuses on three texts that "force romantic premises to the breaking point"—*The Narrative of Arthur Gordon Pym, The Sacred Fount,* and *The Marble Faun.* According to Sutherland, each of these works resists thematic interpretation and represents the writer's confrontation with the schism between the world and its representation, a theme developed by the modernist writers who followed. This study in deconstructive methodology provides new insights into the relationship between the modernists and their predecessors. **(A)**

Tanner, Tony. *Scenes of Nature, Signs of Men.* Cambridge: Cambridge University Press, 1987. For the sheer ingenuity and brilliance of comparative thinking, Cambridge professor Tanner is one of the best critics of our time. In this collection of essays, Tanner works out his idea of the profound influence on American fiction of the Puritans' obsession with signs. He contends that this obsession set the tone for all subsequent American fiction for it established the need for American writers to find a special significance in their landscape and history. Tanner elaborates his insight in discussions of individual American writers from Cooper and Hawthorne to the contemporary novelist William Gass. (A,G)

Thomas, Brook. *Cross-Examinations of Law and Literature: Cooper, Hawthorne, Stowe, and Melville.* Cambridge: Cambridge University Press, 1987. In this specialized study in cultural history, Thomas examines the early nineteenth-century tradition of combining the study of law and literature. He uses selected works of writers of the American Renaissance—Cooper, Hawthorne, Stowe, and Melville—to define the fictional presentation of legal issues of the times. He pairs these writers with prominent contemporary lawyers with whom they had a personal or professional connection. For example, he relates Stowe's work to litigation over slavery. (A)

Von Frank, Albert J. *The Sacred Game: Provincialism and Frontier Consciousness in American Literature, 1630-1860.* New York: Cambridge University Press, 1985. Von Frank's wide-ranging study examines the reactions of various writers to the wilderness environment of young America. He contends that Anne Bradstreet felt compelled to retain the old culture in order to preserve identity in her new surroundings. He views Washington Irving's works as a reaction to American provincialism, and sees many of the same provincial themes evident in Hawthorne's *The Scarlet Letter.* Von Frank's major thesis is that the wilderness environment accepts immigrants but at the same time rejects the immigrant's culture. He uses Emerson's works to analyze this and other themes. (A)

Wagenknect, Edward. *Nathaniel Hawthorne: The Man, His Tales and Romances.* New York: Ungar, 1989. Wagenknect, who wrote a biography in 1961 focusing on Hawthorne's psychological characteristics, complements his earlier work with this biographical/critical reading of the short fiction, plus the five completed romances and the fragments. Relating the facts of Hawthorne's life to his fiction, Wagenknect offers a reading of "The Gray Champion," "Endicott and the Red Cross," "The Maypole of Merry Mount," "The Gentle Boy," "Legends of the Province House," "The Birthmark," "Ethan Brand," "Rappaccini's Daughter," "Young Goodman Brown," and "My Kinsman, Major Molineux." This study is organized into chapters on Hawthorne's life, his character, the short stories, and the novels, and provides an excellent biographical and critical introduction for all readers. (A,G)

Other Sources
Carton, Evan. *The Rhetoric of American Romance: Dialectic and Identity in Emerson, Dickinson, Poe, and Hawthorne.* Baltimore: Johns Hopkins University Press, 1985.

Colacurcio, Michael J. *Province of Piety: Moral History in Hawthorne's Early Tales.* Cambridge: Harvard University Press, 1984.

Colacurcio, Michael J., ed. *New Essays on "The Scarlet Letter."* New York: Cambridge University Press, 1985.

Cole, Phyllis. *The American Writer and the Condition of England, 1815-1860.* New York: Garland, 1987.

Erlich, Gloria C. *Family Themes and Hawthorne's Fiction: The Tenacious Web.* New Brunswick: Rutgers University Press, 1986.

Gollin, Rita K. *Portraits of Nathaniel Hawthorne: An Iconography.* De Kalb: Northern Illinois University Press, 1984.

Kesterton, David B. *Critical Essays on Hawthorne's "The Scarlet Letter."* Boston: G. K. Hall, 1988.

Lloyd-Smith, Allan G. *Eve Tempted: Writing and Sexuality in Hawthorne's Fiction.* Savage, MD: Barnes & Noble, 1984.

Luedtke, Luther S. *Nathaniel Hawthorne and the Romance of the Orient.* Bloomington: Indiana University Press, 1989.

Person, Leland S., Jr. *Aesthetic Headaches: Women and a Masculine Poetics in Poe, Melville, and Hawthorne.* Athens: University of Georgia Press, 1988.

Scharnhorst, Gary. *Nathaniel Hawthorne: An Annotated Bibliography of Comment and Criticism Before 1900.* Metuchen, NJ: Scarecrow, 1988.

Wrege, Charles D. *Facts and Fallacies of Hawthorne: A Historical Study of the Origins, Procedures and Results of the Hawthorne Illumination Tests and Their Influence upon the Hawthorne Studies.* New York: Garland, 1986.

ROBERT HAYDEN
1913-1980

Author's Recent Bibliography
Collected Prose, 1984; *Collected Poems*, 1985.

Evaluation of Selected Biography and Criticism
Hatcher, John. *From the Auroral Darkness: The Life and Poetry of Robert Hayden.* Oxford: George Ronald, 1984. This in-depth biography examines the life and works of Hayden, who wrote both as a black American and as a member of the Baha'i faith. Above all, the poetic art was his mistress, and he refused to bow to political fashion in order to attract a wider audience. Hatcher provides sensitive readings of the poetry and is particularly strong in his analysis of Hayden's symbols and images. (A,G)

Williams, Pontheolla T. *Robert Hayden: A Critical Analysis of His Poetry.* Champaign: University of Illinois Press, 1987. Robert Hayden has been called the poet with "perfect pitch," and this study examines the significance of his life and works. Williams uses a strongly biographical approach to the poems and reveals many useful details of Hayden's life and career. The material here could be used to supplement study of the recently published *Collected Poetry* (1985) and *Collected Prose* (1984). (A,G)

WILLIAM HAZLITT
1778-1830

Evaluation of Selected Biography and Criticism

Bloom, Harold, ed. *Modern Critical Views: William Hazlitt.* New York: Chelsea House, 1986. This anthology of eight critical essays is introduced by Bloom, who establishes the historical and literary context for understanding Hazlitt. Contributors to this volume include Tave, Salvesen, Ready, Kinnaird, Foot, and Mahoney. Of particular note is David Bromwich's essay on the "egotistical sublime," which compares the views of Hazlitt with those of Wordsworth and Rousseau. A chronology and selected bibliography are included. (A,G)

Jones, Stanley. *Hazlitt: A Life: From Winterslow to Frith Street.* Oxford: Clarendon Press, 1989. This biography, researched for twenty-five years, contains extensive notes, chronology, and a complete, useful index. Chapters focus on Hazlitt's withdrawal from and return to London, his apprenticeship days as a parliamentary reporter, his career as an art and drama critic, and his association with other writers, including Leigh Hunt, Charles Lamb, Keats, and especially Wordsworth, who attempted to turn Lamb and Hunt against him. Jones attempts to debunk the image of Hazlitt as a sinister, scowling misanthrope and explain the harsh criticism as a tactic by his political enemies. Jones skillfully weaves the details of Hazlitt's personal life with the political intrigue that made him so threatening and persuasive. (A,G)

McFarland, Thomas. *Romantic Cruxes: The English Essayists and the Spirit of the Age.* Oxford: Clarendon, 1987. This concise study addresses romanticism as expressed by the English essayists Hazlitt, Lamb, and De Quincey. These writers emphasized nature, imagination, egotism, medieval imagining, and dreams. McFarland reveals Lamb to have been a more influential cultural figure than is currently appreciated. He examines Hazlitt's standing debate with Coleridge over the workings of the imagination for its political and social implications. McFarland attempts to recapture the importance of these essayists and remove them from the shadow of the major romantic poets. (A,G)

Uphaus, Robert W. *William Hazlitt.* Boston: Twayne, 1985. Uphaus places Hazlitt's career squarely within the dissenting tradition and compares his works with those of Samuel Johnson and such political thinkers as Godwin, Malthus, Burke, and Scott. Uphaus focuses primarily on selected political and literary essays, which he feels are representative of Hazlitt's views. The result is a study that underscores Hazlitt's distinctive genius and claims a larger significance for his ideas than has been previously accepted. (A)

SEAMUS HEANEY
1939

Author's Recent Bibliography

The Haw Lantern, 1987 (poetry); *The Government of the Tongue: Selected Prose, 1978-1987*, 1988; *The Place of Writing*, 1989 (criticism); *The Redress of Poetry*, 1990 (address at Oxford Univ.); *Selected Poems 1966-1987*, 1990.

Evaluation of Selected Criticism

Corcoran, Neil. *Seamus Heaney*. London: Faber and Faber, 1986. This sophisticated critical examination of Heaney's poetry is perceptive but requires a rather solid background in contemporary poetry. The most receptive reader will probably be the graduate student, while others may lack sufficient background to fully follow Corcoran's arguments. **(A,G)**

Johnston, Dillon. *Irish Poetry after Joyce*. South Bend, IN: Notre Dame, 1985. This study provides an overview of Irish poetry since the death of Joyce. Johnston, director of the Wake Forest University Press, which specializes in contemporary Irish verse, has had personal and professional contact with many of the poets of whom he writes. He compares contemporary poets and their responses to Joyce with the successors of Yeats, showing similar or divergent poetic reactions. He compares Heaney with Kavanagh, and Mahon with MacNeice. Other poets afforded careful treatment are Kinsella, Longley, Montague, Muldoon, and Murphy. This is considered an essential text for those interested in the study of Irish poetry. **(A,G)**

Sekine, Masaru, ed. *Irish Writers and Society At Large*. Totowa, NJ: Barnes & Noble, 1985. This anthology collects fourteen essays on Anglo-Irish writers. In addition to contributions on Joyce, Moore, and Corkery, Alasdair Macrae writes on the autobiographical elements in Heaney's *Station Island*. Two other pieces are devoted to the works of Bowen and MacNeice. **(A,G)**

LILLIAN HELLMAN
1905-1984

Evaluation of Selected Biography

Bryer, Jackson R., ed. *Conversations with Lillian Hellman.* Jackson: University Press of Mississippi, 1986. Forty-five years of interviews portray Hellman as candid, intriguing, and insightful. Among the topics she covers in these transcribed talks are the theater, her craft, controversial aspects of her career, and her relationship with Dashiell Hammett. The list of interviewers is long and varied, including Bill Moyers, Rex Reed, and Nora Ephron. (A,G)

Feibleman, Peter. *Lilly: Reminiscences of Lillian Hellman.* New York: Morrow. 1988. This is an intimate view of Hellman by a man who was her lover and a friend for forty-three years. He lovingly depicts their early years together, especially their time on Martha's Vineyard when they were both struggling writers. Although Feibleman is straightforward about Hellman's anger, impatience, and acerbic tongue, he also chronicles her honesty, pride, and vulnerability. Not intended to be an academic study, this memoir might, in fact, improve the reputation of a playwright who alienated almost everyone with whom she came in contact. (A,G)

Wright, William. *Lillian Hellman: The Image, the Woman.* New York: Simon & Schuster, 1986. Wright argues that Hellman was a liar about herself, and that the public image of her tirades, rages, love affairs, and lurid social life cannot be taken at face value. Nor can her denials about belonging to the Communist Party. Wright has spun an intriguing tale about a colorful life that will not only fascinate readers but shed light on the plays. (A,G)

ERNEST HEMINGWAY
1899-1961

Author's Recent Bibliography
The Dangerous Summer, 1985 (travel); *Dateline Toronto*, 1985 (journalism); *The Garden of Eden*, 1986 (novel).

White, William, ed. *Dateline Toronto: The Complete Toronto Star Dispatches, 1920-1924*. New York: Scribner's, 1985. Hemingway began his career as a journalist, and he continued to write stories for the *Star* even after he published some of his best-known short stories. These dispatches clearly show the relationship between Hemingway's style and subject matter in his journalism and fiction. Anyone with an interest in Hemingway or journalism will profit from comparing the dispatches to the stories. **(A,G)**

Evaluation of Selected Biography and Criticism
Beegel, Susan F. *Hemingway's Craft of Omission: Four Manuscript Examples*. Ann Arbor: UMI Press, 1988. Critical opinion has long proclaimed that what Hemingway left out of his fiction was as important as what he put in. In this work, Beegel examines unpublished material which Hemingway cut from "Fifty Grand," "A Natural History of the Dead," the final chapter of *Death in the Afternoon*, and three versions of "After the Storm." She analyzes these deleted texts focusing on both their isolated characteristics and the reasons they might have been cut, then explains them in context of the completed work. Beegel's astute judgments challenge readers to reconsider these three often neglected stories. In an introduction, she also argues that scholars should reexamine all of Hemingway's works in light of the recently available unpublished material. **(A,G)**

Brian, Denis. *True Gen: An Intimate Portrait of Ernest Hemingway by Those Who Knew Him*. New York: Grove, 1988. Brian has compiled over one hundred interviews with those who knew or studied Hemingway. The interviewees include wives, sons, writers, critics, artists, as well as his drinking, hunting, and fishing cronies. Brian has arranged the material chronologically but in a way that simulates an ongoing colloquium on Hemingway's life and creative drive. Recent biographers, many with unflattering views of the author, are confronted and asked to justify their opinions. Psychiatrists have been invited to discuss their views of Hemingway's psychological problems. In all, a surprisingly rounded and pleasing portrait of the author emerges. The book's title, "true gen," derives from military slang for "a fact you can bet your life on." Critics have described this book as a "marvelous" oral biography, and it should appeal to both academic and general audiences. **(A,G)**

236   *Ernest Hemingway*

Bruccoli, Matthew J. *Conversations with Ernest Hemingway.* Jackson: University Press of Mississippi, 1986. These interviews, reprinted from major magazines, cover the period from the 1940s until Hemingway's death in 1961 and present a full picture of a writer whose life was as famous as his novels. Hemingway addresses numerous subjects familiar from his work—prizefighting, the bull ring, his travels. Eavesdroppers on these conversations will quickly identify the narrator's voice of the novels. This is less a research tool than an enjoyable snapshot of a colorful writer. **(G)**

Capellan, Angel. *Hemingway and the Hispanic World.* Ann Arbor: UMI Research Press, 1985. Ernest Hemingway set most of his fiction in exotic locales and seemed hesitant to use American settings. In this study, Capellan contends that in Spain and Cuba Hemingway found a culture and sensibility that matched his own needs. He examines the writer's fascination with Hispanic culture and traces the influence of Hispanic writers on his work. **(A,G)**

Carpenter, Humphrey. *Geniuses Together: American Writers in Paris in the 1920s.* Boston: Houghton Mifflin, 1988. Carpenter, who has written biographies of Auden and Tolkien, provides a portrait of expatriate life on the Left Bank in post-WWI Paris and surveys the American writers who flocked there for inspiration and comraderie. The spotlight is primarily on Hemingway and his immediate circle. Carpenter traces the evolution of Hemingway's "bare bones" writing style and recounts a number of unflattering anecdotes. Also making appearances are Anderson, Fitzgerald, Boyle, Pound, Joyce, and Stein. **(A)**

Dardis, Tom. *The Thirsty Muse: Alcohol and the American Writer.* London: Ticknor & Fields, 1989. Dardis applies the results of current addiction research to the lives and careers of American writers. Of eight authors who won the Nobel Prize, five were alcoholics. The popular theory that alcohol liberates the creative impulse, however, is thoroughly debunked. These were addicted men whose addictions got in the way of their creativity. Close-up views of O'Neill, Faulkner, Fitzgerald, Hemingway, and others are fraught with binges, black-outs, wife-beatings, delirium, disease, and untimely death. **(A, G)**

Fellner, Harriet. *Hemingway as Playwright: The Fifth Column.* Ann Arbor: UMI Research, 1986. Hemingway's only drama, *The Fifth Column*, was produced in 1938. Fellner examines the play's creation, structure, staging, and popular reception. Concluding that it was not one of his most successful pieces, she finds interest in the play's mood and effective use of symbolism. Hemingway's journalism is examined against the background of the Spanish Civil War. **(A,G)**

Fuentes, Norberto, *et al. Ernest Hemingway Rediscovered.* New York: Scribner's, 1988. Although not truly a "rediscovery," this book gives a disarming look at Hemingway as seen through the camera of one of his good friends, Sotolongo. Hundreds of photographs of Hemingway, taken in Cuba, at the Florida Bar, and aboard his boat display a personal side of Hemingway often missing from the public persona. The text by Fuentes, author of *Hemingway in Cuba*, provides the needed context. **(G)**

Garcia, Wilma. *Mothers and Others: Myths of the Females in the Works of Melville, Twain, and Hemingway.* New York: Peter Lang, 1984. Garcia's study of female characters of Melville, Twain, and Hemingway promises a complex archetypal analysis of feminine imagery. It delivers significantly less, however. Although the study contains a useful overview of archetypal theory and criticism, it is flawed by a confusion over the differences between "archetype" and "stereotype." **(A,G)**

Gladstein, Mimi Reisel. *The Indestructible Woman in Faulkner, Hemingway, and Steinbeck.* Ann Arbor: UMI Research, 1986. "Indestructible" women are those who are generally defined by men as "other." Because they are essentially unknown quantities, men tend to project upon them idealized traits of strength and perseverance. Such is the case, argues Gladstein, with the few women characters that appear in the fiction of Faulkner, Steinbeck, and Hemingway. This feminist critique is handled with well-balanced precision and lays bare the personal dependencies of a group of male writers who leaned too heavily on the women in their lives. **(A,G)**

Griffin, Peter. *Hemingway: The Early Years.* New York: Oxford University Press, 1985. Griffin makes good use of new archival materials, in particular the letters Hadley Johnson wrote to her new husband, to reveal a rather naive young Hemingway whose ambition led him to Paris. In Paris, the Hemingways began mixing with the literary set, and a different Ernest began to emerge, one beset by bearish moods and fierce competitiveness. He had affairs with Agnes von Kurowsky and Katy Smith, who later married John Dos Passos, and produced *A Farewell to Arms* against a background of infidelity and emotional instability. If there is a problem with this first of a projected multi-volume biography, it is that Hemingway's extreme complexity seems to emerge all at once. A drastic change of personality did occur during the sojourn in Paris, but the elements that forced it are still unclear. **(A,G)**

Johnson, Paul. *Intellectuals.* Harper & Row, 1989. Johnson exercises his caustic wit in a critical look at some of the world's most famous, and often self-proclaimed, intellectuals. Coming under the gun are Marx, Rousseau, Sartre, Brecht, Bertrand Russell, Hellman, Shelley, and Hemingway. Hemingway is described as an immature rebel who adopted an ethic of violent action to oppose his parents' stifling religiosity. Although colored by a readily admitted "anti-intellectual" bias, Johnson's profiles are thought-provoking, entertaining, and useful as an antidote to hero worship. **(A,G)**

Johnston, Kenneth G. *The Tip of the Iceberg: Hemingway and the Short Story.* Greenwood, FL: Penkevill, 1987. This collection of twenty-one short essays by Johnston examines various aspects of Hemingway's short stories.

The analyses often seem to proceed by "free association" rather than by systematic methodology. (A,G)

Lynn, Kenneth S. *Hemingway: The Life and the Work.* New York: Simon & Schuster, 1987. Hemingway emerges from the pages of this biography as a deeply disturbed, neurotic individual who was able to forge a writing career almost in spite of himself. Lynn supports the view of "Papa" as a competitive man, who was at the same time insecure. Rather than decrying the neuroses, however, Lynn views them as the wellspring of Hemingway's literary creativity. Well-researched and written, this biography tells a riveting tale of great virtue in the midst of vice. (A,G)

Meyers, Jeffrey. *Hemingway: A Biography.* New York: Harper & Row, 1985. Meyers' biography is dominated by a Hemingway who looms larger than life. Meyers depicts every blemish—the affairs, temper tantrums, and alcoholic binges. Ironically, this only seems to enhance the stature of his subject. While offering insightful readings of some of Hemingway's works (in particular, *A Moveable Feast*), Meyers never seems to get at the essential unity of the man and writer. The actual process of writing always seems to be occurring offstage, while more important events like hunting, fishing, and other forms of "male bonding" are pushed up front. Ultimately, Hemingway comes off looking more like a caricature than a fully rounded human being. (A,G)

Reynolds, Michael. *Hemingway, the Paris Years.* London: Basil Blackwell, 1989. Although not exactly a sequel to Reynolds' *The Young Hemingway*, in that it does not pick up where the first book stopped, this well-written, engrossing biography provides the same sharp, uncompromising assessment of Hemingway's personality and career. Covering the years 1922 to 1925, when Paris was the most exciting intellectual city in the world, Reynolds recounts how Hemingway developed from ambitious reporter to literary genius. Reynolds combines meticulous scholarship with a novelistic style, making this one of the best studies for both scholars and general readers. Includes notes, photographs, and index. (A,G)

Reynolds, Michael S. *"The Sun Also Rises," A Novel of the Twenties.* Boston: Twayne, 1988. This short analysis argues that the novel must be read in context of its times to understand why it does not contain a hero. In this regard, *The Sun Also Rises* is truly a "modernist" novel, establishing yet another of Hemingway's innovations. Various chapters discuss the novel's structural unity, signs, motifs, themes, geography, history, values, and critical reception. This is an excellent overview for general readers. (G)

Reynolds, Michael. *The Young Hemingway.* New York: Basil Blackwell, 1986. This study chronicles Hemingway's life up to his marriage and departure for Paris. According to Reynolds, the key to understanding the man and his writing is to appreciate his ability to "reinvent" himself as he matured, always embroidering and embellishing his experiences, a habit he continued throughout his life. Reynolds is perceptive on the relationships within the Hemingway family. The father is shown to be less strong and more neurotic than one might assume from Hemingway's fictional fathers. His mother is portrayed as a strong woman with an artistic nature who is impatient with the role of housekeeper. Reynolds also details Hemingway's earliest attempts at writing fiction for the *Saturday Evening Post*. (A,G)

Villard, Henry S., Agnes Von Kurowsky, and James Nagel, eds. *Hemingway in Love and War: The Lost Diary of Agnes von Kurowsky, Her Letters and Correspondence of Ernest Hemingway*. Boston: Northeastern University, 1989. Kurowsky was the American nurse courted by Hemingway in a Milan hospital as he recovered from his war wounds. Villard was a fellow patient, who offers his own reminiscences of the time. Many of the materials in this book have never before been published and offer essential background for Hemingway's war experiences and his novel, *A Farewell to Arms*. Nagel supplies a well-documented essay that contradicts many of the accepted views on Hemingway's war record. (A)

Wagner-Martin, Linda. *The Modern American Novel, 1914-1945: A Critical History*. Twayne, 1989. Wagner-Martin presents a densely compact overview of modernist writers that flies in the face of the traditional critique that the modernists were a uniformly angst-ridden lot. Besides Faulkner, some of the authors treated are Cather, Stein, Hemingway, Norris, and Agee. This study goes beyond the traditional pantheon to treat many writers highly regarded during their times but nearly forgotten now—Nella Larsen, Meridel Le Sueur, Martha Gellhorn, and Henry Brown, among others. Black and woman modernists are "dusted off" and given their fair place on the shelf. This study is intended for a scholarly audience. (A)

Wagner-Martin, Linda. *New Essays on "The Sun Also Rises."* New York: Cambridge University Press, 1987. The six essays cover the topics: the 1920s influence on the novel; humor in an otherwise serious novel; the historical context; Brett Ashley as a "new woman;" and the Hemingway hero. While the topics of most of the essays have been covered in full-length studies, this collection provides a useful beginning for general readers and students. (A,G)

Wilkinson, Myler. *Hemingway and Turgenev: The Nature of Literary Influences*. Ann Arbor: UMI Research, 1986. Hemingway read Turgenev extensively, and Wilkinson examines Turgenev's influence on his literary style. Borrowing heavily from Harold Bloom's work on poetry, Wilkinson shows how Hemingway's style paralleled Turgenev's, then sharply diverged in reaction. Although many of the arguments are inconclusive, particularly in the analysis of *The Sun Also Rises*, the methodology shows promise for further work. Very useful as an introduction to defining literary influences. (A)

Other Sources

Beegel, Susan F., ed. *Hemingway's Neglected Short Fiction: New Perspectives.* Ann Arbor: UMI Research, 1989.

Brenner, Gerry. *Concealments in Hemingway's Works.* Columbus: The Ohio State University Press, 1984.

Cooper, Stephen. *The Politics of Ernest Hemingway.* Ann Arbor: UMI Research Press, 1987.

Gaggin, John R. *Hemingway and Nineteenth-Century Aestheticism.* Ann Arbor: UMI Research Press, 1987.

Hardy, Richard E., and John G. Cull. *Hemingway: A Psychological Portrait.* New York: Irvington, 1987.

Hemingway, Jack. *Misadventures of a Fly Fisherman: My Life with and without Papa.* New York: McGraw-Hill, 1987.

Kobler, J. F. *Ernest Hemingway: Journalist and Artist.* Ann Arbor: UMI Research Press, 1984.

Naessil, Anders. *Rites and Rhythms: Hemingway, a Genuine Character.* New York: Vantage, 1988.

Nagel, James, ed. *Ernest Hemingway: The Writer in Context.* Madison: University of Wisconsin Press, 1984.

Noble, Donald R. *Hemingway: A Revaluation.* Troy, NY: Whitston, 1984.

Phillips, Larry W., ed. *Ernest Hemingway on Writing.* New York: Charles Scribner, 1984.

Samuelson, Arnold. *With Hemingway: A Year in Key West and Cuba.* New York: Random House, 1984.

Smith, Paul. *Reader's Guide to the Short Stories of Ernest Hemingway.* Boston: G. K. Hall, 1989.

Stanton, Edward F. *Hemingway and Spain: A Pursuit.* Seattle: University of Washington Press, 1989.

Whitlow, Roger. *Cassandra's Daughters: The Women in Hemingway.* Westport, CT: Greenwood, 1984.

ROBERT HENRYSON
c. 1425-1505

Evaluation of Selected Criticism

Gopen, George D. *Robert Henryson, Moral Fables: A New Edition of the Middle Scots Text with a Facing Prose Translation.* Edinburgh: Scottish Academic Press, 1987. This book consists of a prose translation of Henryson's *Fables,* a lengthy introduction, end notes, bibliography, and appendixes, one of which is devoted to Henryson's use of proverbs. The introduction provides insights into Henryson's career, the political and social context of his writings, the fable genre, and the construction of the *Fables.* Scholars may find constructive ideas not published elsewhere. (A)

Scheps, Walter, and J. Anna Looney. *Middle Scots Poets: A Reference Guide to James I of Scotland, Robert Henryson, William Dunbar, and Gavin Douglas.* Boston: G. K. Hall, 1986. The first section provides a general bibliography, followed by one chapter on each of the four poets. For most bibliographical entries a descriptive account is offered. (A,G)

GEORGE HERBERT
1593-1633

Evaluation of Selected Criticism

Bloch, Chana. *Spelling the Word: George Herbert and the Bible*. Berkeley: University of California Press, 1985. Bloch admirably demonstrates Herbert's indebtedness to the Bible, especially in his vocabulary, didacticism, aphorisms, images, and hymns. Of special interest is his reliance on the Book of Psalms for images, diction, and motifs. **(A)**

Dickson, Donald R. *The Fountain of Living Waters: The Typology of the Waters of Life in Herbert, Vaughan, and Traherne*. Columbia: University of Missouri Press, 1987. Dickson traces the use of water by medieval writers and theologians to explain the process of salvation. Dickson then applies these theories to the three poets. Good footnotes, index, and bibliography make this study especially useful to scholars. **(A)**

Roberts, John R. *George Herbert: An Annotated Bibliography of Modern Criticism, 1905-1984*. Columbia: University of Missouri Press, 1988. This is a revised edition of Roberts' definitive 1978 bibliography. Over two hundred items published between 1905 and 1978 have been added, as well as over 450 entries from 1975 to 1984. These additions nearly double the work's size. Subject headings have been revised and updated. The often-lengthy annotations (several pages for major works) continue to be descriptive rather than evaluative to serve the needs of advanced scholars. Dissertations are not referenced. **(A)**

Sherwood, Terry G. *Herbert's Prayerful Art*. Toronto: University of Toronto Press, 1989. Using Herbert's *The Temple* as the vehicle for analyzing Herbert's poetic craft, Sherwood focuses on the character of the narrator, who believes that language, rather than theology or professed belief, is the key to winning the Lord's approval. Sherwood argues that Herbert, having established his power to formulate language that could speak directly to God, then became aware of his power to win his own salvation through direct contact with the Deity. This in turn made him self-conscious about his poetry and of his progress toward salvation. This original, provocative thesis is highly recommended for scholars and any student of Herbert. **(A,G)**

Singleton, Marion White. *God's Courtier: Configuring a Different Grace in George Herbert's "Temple."* Cambridge: Cambridge University Press, 1988. The thesis of this innovative study is that the self-perception and unfolding self-image, as revealed in *The Temple*, are grounded in the Renaissance image of aristocratic courtliness. Providing insight into the themes, structures, and voices of this masterwork, Singleton demonstrates how Herbert intentionally transformed the courtly ideal of secular service into an ideal of serving God.

The sequencing of poems is more readily explained in terms of relational structure, rather than of a more traditional narrative structure. Singleton's observations often provide intriguing glimpses into Herbert's inner self. Highly recommended. (A,G)

Stewart, Stanley. *George Herbert*. Boston: Twayne, 1986. This carefully reasoned study deserves a place on the shelf next to other definitive works on the religious poetry of the 17th century. Stewart's stated purpose is to correct "distortions" of the poet's life, historical context, and poetic intent that have crept into established critical opinion. Those familiar with the issues will enjoy the lively debate that ensues. His thesis is that Herbert's Protestant or Puritan associations have been over-emphasized, causing a misleading "drift" in subsequent criticism. Stewart reexamines the influence of medieval sources on Herbert's poetry and is particularly lucid when discussing Herbert's influence on forms of meditative poetry which followed. (A)

Todd, Richard. *The Opacity of Signs: Acts of Interpretation in George Herbert's "The Temple"*. Columbia: University of Missouri Press, 1987. Todd attempts to show how Herbert's understanding of the tension between the separate but related worlds of "things" and "words" is developed into a theory of poetic expression embedded in *The Temple*. He argues that Herbert believed that for fallen man "opacity" is a fact of life, and that absolute clarity is not God's will. The communication that does occur through opacity is derived from signs, and Herbert constructed *The Temple* to imitate the concealment of the world. Therefore, Todd concludes, "Herbert's interpretation of his experience of relationship to God is revealingly analogous to the act of interpretation performed by the reader of his verse." Recommended for specialists only. (A)

Wall, John N. *Transformations of the Word: Spenser, Herbert, Vaughan*. Athens: University of Georgia Press, 1988. Wall contends that the works of Spenser, Herbert, and Vaughan are best understood within the context of the sixteenth and seventeenth-century tenets of the Church of England. The post-Reformation Church had distinctive characteristics that have been obscured, causing the modern reader to lose the meaning of these writers' works. This dense book is divided into sections that treat each of the authors individually against a backdrop of theological concepts and liturgical practices. While certainly offering valuable information, the plodding prose makes the argument difficult to follow for the uninitiated. (A)

Other Sources
Clements, Arthur. *Poetry of Contemplation: John Donne, George Herbert, Henry Vaughn, and the Modern Period*. Albany: State University of New York Press, 1989.

Di Cesare, Mario A. *George Herbert, The Temple: An Edition of the Bodleian Manuscript*. New York: Medieval and Renaissance, 1988.

Kumar, Kailash. *George Herbert: Heart in Pilgrimage.* New Delhi: Mercer & Aitchison/Arundel Press, 1989.

Martz, Louis L., ed. *George Herbert and Henry Vaughan.* New York: Oxford University Press, 1986.

Miller, Edmund, and Robert DiYanni. *Like Season'd Timber: New Essays on George Herbert.* New York: Peter Lang, 1988.

Pahlka, William H. *St. Augustine's Meter and George Herbert's Will.* Kent, OH: Kent State University Press, 1987.

Strier, Richard. *Love Known: Theology and Experience in George Herbert's Poetry.* Chicago: University of Chicago Press, 1986.

Willmott, Richard. *Four Metaphysical Poets: An Anthology of Poetry by Donne, Herbert, Marvell, and Vaughan.* New York: Cambridge University Press, 1985.

ROBERT HERRICK
1591-1674

Evaluation of Selected Criticism

Coiro, Ann Baynes. *Robert Herrick's "Hesperides" and the Epigram Book Tradition*. Baltimore: Johns Hopkins University Press, 1988. The Renaissance valued epigrams and epigram collections highly, although this genre has received little modern critical attention. In this specialized study, Coiro examines Herrick's epigrammatic collection, *Hesperides*, in its cultural, political, and generic contexts, isolating themes in the epigrams themselves and offering extensive commentary on Herrick's style, structure, and intent. **(A)**

Gertzman, Jay A. *Fantasy, Fashion, and Affection: Editions of Robert Herrick's Poetry for the Common Reader, 1810-1968*. Bowling Green, OH: Bowling Green State University Press, 1986. Gertzman examines the many editions of Herrick's *Hesperides* that have been published over the last two centuries to determine the reasons for the book's appeal to a changing popular audience. He is particularly informed on the contributions of the book's many illustrators. Included as an appendix is a comprehensive descriptive bibliography of Herrick editions. **(A)**

Guibbory, Achsah. *The Map of Time: Seventeenth-Century English Literature and Ideas of Pattern in History*. Champaign: University of Illinois Press, 1986. Guibbory reveals the conceptions of time and history that underlie seventeenth-century thought in this closely reasoned study of six major writers—Donne, Bacon, Jonson, Herrick, Milton, and Dryden. Guibbory divines three such conceptions: degeneration and decay since the Garden of Eden; cycles of generation and decay; and the advance of civilization. He then shows how these three patterns of historical perspective influence poetry, drama, scientific and religious prose, and the writing of history. In every case, Guibbory relates history to genre, structure, imagery, and theme. Highly recommended. **(A,G)**

GERARD MANLY HOPKINS
1844-1889

Evaluation of Selected Criticism

Deane, Sheila. *Bardic Style in the Poetry of Gerard Manley Hopkins, W. B. Yeats, and Dylan Thomas.* Ann Arbor: UMI Research Press, 1989. Deane examines the poetry of Hopkins, Yeats, and Thomas in terms of the poets' use of traditional bardic sources and rhetorical devices. Deane finds close parallels among these authors who were "suspicious" of one another during their lifetimes. Each thought the other "obscure" due to the "subjective haze" of their romantic and metaphysical affectations—all of which, according to Deane, derive from a "bardic style." (A)

Donoghue, Denis. *England, Their England: Commentaries on English Language and Literature.* New York: Knopf, 1988. Noted literary critic Donoghue offers a collection of over twenty of his essays addressing the accomplishments and significance of selected English authors. Shakespeare is here, of course, along with Defoe, Peter Ackroyd, and Wyndham Lewis (whose works are discussed in some detail). Donoghue writes insightfully about the poetic contributions of Shelley, Eliot, and Hopkins, and considers the criticism of Arnold, Pater, and Leavis. (A,G)

Downes, David Anthony. *Hopkins' Sanctifying Imagination.* Lanham, MD: University Press of America, 1985. Downes contends that Hopkins followed a similar imaginative process as Wordsworth and Coleridge, allowing direct experience of natural beauty to stimulate inner meditation which leads to spiritual experiences. Downes examines the influences of Plato and Newman on Hopkins' conceptions of the reality of inner experiences. After establishing a fairly complex theoretical context, he then applies his ideas to poems and groups of poems, paying particularly close attention to "The Wreck of the Deutschland" and Hopkins' God-in-nature poems. (A)

Fraser, Hilary. *Beauty and Belief: Aesthetics and Religion in Victorian Literature.* Cambridge: Cambridge University Press, 1986. In this specialized study in intellectual history, Fraser traces the relationship between religion and aesthetic doctrine from Coleridge and Wordsworth through the aestheticism of Walter Pater and Oscar Wilde. Fraser argues that through concepts propounded by Hopkins, Ruskin, Arnold, and the Oxford aesthetes, Christianity is reduced to a merely subjective religion of art. (A)

Giles, Richard F., ed. *Hopkins Among the Poets: Studies in Modern Responses to Gerard Manley Hopkins.* Hamilton, Ontario: International Hopkins Association, 1985. This anthology of twenty-six critical essays addresses the impact of Hopkins on twentieth-century poetry and, in particular, how individual modern poets accepted, incorporated, or abandoned different aspects of

Hopkins' poetry. The modernist poets are given deserving attention, but the essayists also examine Hopkins' influence on a variety of other poets. Merton, Jones, Plath, and Thomas are found to be heavily influenced; Heaney, Roethke, Lowell, and Crane are found to be hardly influenced, if at all. Yeats and Eliot both disliked Hopkins' poetry but registered a reaction to it in their own poetry. (A)

Kenny, Anthony. *God and Two Poets: Arthur Hugh Clough and Gerard Manley Hopkins.* London: Sidgwick & Jackson, 1988. Kenny, a philosopher rather than literary critic, believes that Clough and Hopkins are the two most significant English religious poets of the nineteenth century, and it is their philosophy, not their poetry, that draws them together. Kenny begins by establishing the basic biographies of both poets, tracing their education in philosophy at Oxford. He discusses Clough's move from Anglicanism to agnosticism and Hopkins' conversion to Catholicism. He presents a lucid comparison of their beliefs on prayer, scripture, original sin, the sacramental system, and the relation of religion and politics. (A)

Lichtmann, Maria R. *The Contemplative Poetry of Gerard Manley Hopkins.* Princeton, NJ: Princeton University Press, 1989. According to Lichtmann, the key to unraveling Hopkins' poetry relies on his use of parallelism. In reaction to what he considered a shapeless romanticism, Hopkins returned to early poetry for formal principles. He found his answer in the use of parallels. To support her case, she discusses several of Hopkins' early, unpublished essays on classical poets. Individual chapters focus on "The Wreck of Deutschland," and the "terrible sonnets." Lichtmann offers a fruitful approach for further study of Hopkins' work. (A,G)

Ong, Walter J. *Hopkins, the Self, and God.* Toronto: University of Toronto Press, 1986. This book is a collection of lectures on Hopkins' ability to differentiate elements of the internal and external worlds. Hopkins, a product of the Victorian age, was steeped in the Catholic tradition. For Ong, Hopkins' knowledge of academic philosophy and theology allowed him to develop a strong consciousness of self. Of special interest is Hopkins' rationale for affirming his faith in the face of scientific progress. (A,G)

Roberts, Gerald. *Gerard Manley Hopkins: The Critical Heritage.* London: Routledge & Kegan Paul, 1987. Roberts traces the critical reception through the various phases of interest in Hopkins: his metrics, the dichotomy of priest and poet, content, and influences. (A)

Zaniello, Tom. *Hopkins in the Age of Darwin.* Iowa City: University of Iowa Press, 1988. In Zaniello's view, Hopkins was not only a gifted poet, but an excellent scientist, naturalist, and philosopher who was fascinated by the social transformations being wrought by Darwinian theory. Zaniello carefully documents Hopkins' reactions to the major cultural events of his time. Though primarily of interest to Victorian scholars, this volume provides useful contextual material for students of Hopkins' poetry. (A)

Other Sources
  Ellsberg, Margaret R. *Created to Praise: The Language of Gerard Manley Hopkins.* London: Oxford University Press, 1987.

  Loomis, Jeffrey B. *Dayspring in Darkness: Sacrament in Hopkins.* Lewisburg, PA: Bucknell University Press, 1988.

  MacKenzie, Norman H., ed. *The Early Poetic Manuscripts and Notebooks of Gerard Manley Hopkins in Facsimilie.* New York: Garland, 1989.

  Plotkin, Cary H. *The Tenth Muse: Victorian Philology and the Genesis of the Poetic Langauge of Gerard Manley Hopkins.* Carbondale: Southern Illinois University Press, 1989.

  Sulloway, Alison, G., ed. *Critical Essays on Gerard Manley Hopkins.* Boston: G. K. Hall, 1990.

WILLIAM DEAN HOWELLS
1837-1920

Autobiographical Sources

Fischer, William, and Christoph Lohmann, eds. *Selected Letters of W. D. Howells: 1902-1911* (Vol. 5); *1912-1920* (Vol. 6). Boston: Twayne, 1983. Howells wrote more than ten thousand letters in his lifetime, most of which have survived. These two volumes bring to completion an annotated edition of over 1,700 of these letters. Chosen for biographical and literary interest, this selection reveals the many facets of Howells as editor, critic, novelist, and social commentator. The editors have maintained the highest standards in compiling and annotating this definitive edition, providing an essential primary source for the study of Howells. **(A,G)**

Evaluation of Selected Biography and Criticism

Borus, Daniel H. *Writing Realism: Howells, James, and Norris in the Mass Market.* Chapel Hill: University of North Carolina Press, 1989. Borus examines the economic and social conditions following the Civil War and their effect on concepts of realism. He then analyzes how the effects of commercial publishing, printing innovations, and popular magazines established a new class of readers who regarded writers more as newscasters and celebrities than prophets. The result bred a new generation of writers who regarded both their purpose and their work differently than preceding generations. This fascinating thesis is impressively documented by the letters, records, and the literary criticism of its subjects. Recommended for advanced students and scholars. **(A)**

Cady, Edwin H. *Young Howells and John Brown: Episodes in a Radical Education.* Columbus: Ohio State University Press, 1985. Cady argues that John Brown played a central role in Howells' "radical education." Cady examines the relationship of the Howells family with Brown and his conspirators and concludes that Howells was probably aware of the plans to raid Harper's Ferry. Such knowledge adds depth and immediacy to a reading of Howells' "Old Brown." Howells was a poet whose entire work was infused with the passion of reform. He argued for racial equality, women's suffrage, the rights of laborers and socialists, and even supported the cause of the Haymarket Anarchists. As a fitting climax to this study, Cady examines the image of John Brown as portrayed in *A Chance Acquaintance.* Highly recommended. **(A,G)**

Crowley, John W. *The Black Heart's Truth: The Early Career of W. D. Howells.* Chapel Hill: University of North Carolina Press, 1985. Restricting himself in this volume to Howells' early years, Crowley creates a portrait of the writer that is not particularly attractive. But black heart or no, Howells was a dynamic and prolific writer whose significance Crowley clearly reveals. The highlight of this study is a contextual analysis of *A Modern Instance*. Though certainly not the last word, this biography may be the best to date and is suitable for a range of readers. (A,G)

Eble, Kenneth E. *Old Clemens and W. D. H.: The Story of a Remarkable Friendship.* Baton Rouge: Louisiana State University Press, 1985. In this thorough study, Eble traces the forty-one-year friendship of two transplanted midwesterners—Mark Twain and William Dean Howells. The two met in 1869 when both men were in their early thirties; they remained close friends until Twain's death in 1910. As both grew older they suffered the gradual loss of those closest to them and turned increasingly to each other for support. Their relationship is offered here as a model friendship. Eble provides a biographical perspective that sheds light on the career and writings of both men. (A,G)

Kaplan, Amy. *The Social Construction of American Realism.* Chicago: University of Chicago Press, 1988. In this study of American realists, Kaplan focuses on the works of Howells, Wharton, and Dreiser and stresses their relation to the social changes of the late-1800s. Kaplan challenges recent feminist criticism by describing Wharton as a professional writer in conflict with women writers with a more popular appeal. She examines Dreiser's conception of art as commodity. Kaplan's arguments are well-documented and persuasively developed. (A,G)

Merrill, Ginette, and George Arms, eds. *If Not Literature: Letters of Elinor Mead Howells.* Columbus: Ohio State University Press, 1988. Most of these 130 letters written by the wife of William Dean Howells are published here for the first time. Mostly directed to family members, their significance lies in what they reveal about social life in Cambridge in the years after the Civil War and the comments on aquaintances such as Mark Twain and Henry James. Those interested in Howells, nineteenth-century American culture, or women's history should find this carefully edited and annotated collection invaluable. (A,G)

Murphy, Brenda. *American Realism and American Drama, 1880-1940.* Cambridge: Cambridge University Press, 1987. Murphy clarifies the relationship between literary realism and dramatic realism in this study of the works of Howells and James, culminating in the plays of O'Neill. Several plays by Hamlin Garland and James A. Herne are examined to demonstrate the impact of realistic theory on dramatic practice. Murphy sees the works of Odets and Hellman leading, via the cultural impact of Freud, to O'Neill, who reigns as undisputed master of the American stage. A valuable overview of the antecedents of twentieth-century American drama. (A,G)

Nettles, Elsa. *Language, Race, and Social Class in Howells' America.* Lexington: University Press of Kentucky, 1988. Nettles' thesis is that as the foremost voice for literary realism, Howells used speech and language to show cultural distinctions, which were in conflict with his professed ideal of equality. Instead of using speech simply to characterize people, he used it to deepen class divisions. **(A)**

Schulman, Robert. *Social Criticism and Nineteenth-Century American Fictions.* Columbia: University of Missouri Press, 1987. Schulman examines the political psychology of capitalism and its influence on the lives and works of some of the most famous American authors—Franklin, Twain, Melville, Hawthorne, Chestnutt, Whitman, Wharton, Howells, and Dreiser. His study pursues three main themes—the fragmentation of community, the impact of social change, and the styles of American individualism. In his discussion of Franklin's *Autobiography*, Schulman describes the costs of success and upward mobility as emotional deadening, increased isolation, and personal fragmentation. A truly new and refreshing reevaluation of nineteenth-century American literature. **(A,G)**

Tanner, Tony. *Scenes of Nature, Signs of Men.* Cambridge: Cambridge University Press, 1987. For the sheer ingenuity and brilliance of comparative thinking, Cambridge professor Tanner is one of the best critics of our time. In this collection of essays, Tanner works out his idea of the profound influence on American fiction of the Puritans' obsession with signs. He contends that this obsession set the tone for all subsequent American fiction for it established the need for American writers to find a special significance in their landscape and history. Tanner elaborates his insight in discussions of individual American writers from Cooper and Howells to the contemporary novelist William Gass. **(A,G)**

LANGSTON HUGHES
1902-1967

Evaluation of Selected Biography and Criticism

Harris, Trudier, and Thadious Davis, eds. *Afro-American Writers From the Harlem Renaissance to 1940*. Detroit: Gale, 1987. This welcome addition to Gale's "Dictionary of Literary Biography" series contains essays on thirty-four carefully selected black writers, including Langston Hughes, Arna Bontemps, Zora Neale Hurston, James Weldon Johnson, Jessie R. Fauset, and Willis Richardson. Photographs accompany each of the articles, which consist of a checklist of the author's work, a biographical/critical essay, and a bibliography of secondary sources. (A)

Miller, R. Baxter. *The Art and Imagination of Langston Hughes*. Lexington: University Press of Kentucky, 1989. Miller's biographical criticism of Hughes' poems and stories provides a perfect complement to Rampersad's recently published biography. Miller deftly reveals characteristic themes and examines how black folk culture influenced Hughes' style and fired his imagination. (A,G)

Mullen, Edward J., ed. *Critical Essays on Langston Hughes*. G.K. Hall, 1986. Along with several critical essays, this book also collects thirty-five reviews of Hughes's work published between 1936 and 1968. Mullen's introduction argues for a view of Hughes as a major poet. Others—Arthur P. Davis, Walter Daniel, and Baxter Miller—establish the elements of social and critical context that define his significance. The reviews provide a quick way to survey the poet's critical reception. Taken together, this material provides a useful introduction to the critical opinions about an influential Harlem poet, dramatist, and prose stylist. (A,G)

Rampersad, Arnold. *The Life of Langston Hughes: Volume I, 1902-1941: I Too Sing America*. Oxford: Oxford University Press, 1986. This first volume of Rampersad's biography of Hughes skillfully interweaves life events and astute critical commentary on the works. Drawing on interviews and previously unavailable papers, he describes Hughes' childhood and family background, his education and travels, and the early development of his writing career. The study details Hughes' involvement in leftist politics and the Harlem Renaissance during the 1920s, as well as his professional and personal relationships with Zora Neale Hurston and Charlotte Mason. Highly recommended. (A,G)

Rampersad, Arnold. *The Life of Langston Hughes: Volume II, 1941-1967: I Dream a World*. Oxford: Oxford University Press, 1988. The concluding volume of Rampersad's biography follows the writer beyond the discouraging 1940s through two decades of hope and creative activity. Hughes drew inspiration from the civil rights movement yet could never overcome his sense of alienation from younger authors, such as James Baldwin and LeRoi Jones. This engrossing critical biography is at the same time an astute description of the experience of American blacks in the twentieth century. **(A)**

Tracy, Steven C. *Langston Hughes and the Blues*. Champaign: University of Illinois Press, 1988. Tracy explicates the nuances and structures of the blues and relates their importance to the Harlem Renaissance. He also examines the importance of the musical form to Hughes' poetry. This very readable study is important to all readers researching topics on Hughes' poetry, the blues, or black culture. **(A,G)**

LEIGH HUNT
1784-1859

Evaluation of Selected Biography and Criticism

Blainey, Ann. *Immortal Boy: A Portrait of Leigh Hunt.* New York: St. Martin's, 1985. Leigh Hunt, one of the most influential literary critics of his time, produced a large number of astute essays and polemics. He was regarded by contemporary critics as the equal of Byron, Shelley, or Keats. He accumulated huge debts, and received large gifts of money from his friends, including Mary Shelley and Charles Dickens. The portrait of Hunt that emerges from Blainey's biography is of a man of staggering impracticality and self-absorption. Although more concerned with contemporary rumor than with documented facts, this study should add to a growing interest in Hunt's life and literary significance. **(G)**

Lulofs, Timothy J., and Hans Ostrom. *Leigh Hunt: A Reference Guide.* Boston: G. K. Hall, 1985. Nearly every writer of importance in the nineteenth century turned critical attention to Hunt as his reputation evolved from revolutionary to man of letters. The twentieth century has relegated Hunt to a supporting role. This reference guide provides a precise account of each bibliographical entry, making the books easy to locate and at the same time providing a history of Hunt criticism. Researchers will find this book an indispensable tool. **(A,G)**

McCown, Robert A., ed. *The Life and Times of Leigh Hunt.* Iowa City: Friends of the University of Iowa Libraries, 1985. This is a collection of papers delivered at the University of Iowa to celebrate the 200th anniversary of Hunt's birth. Topics include: Charles Dickens' portrayal of Hunt as Harold Stimpole in *Bleak House;* gender criticism—specifically how Hunt connected female beauty to "innocent incest," and how this affects the way women read him; his success on the stage; his personal essays; his contribution to cultural influence during the high Victorian age; and his association with libraries. Because these papers were intended to be heard by an audience, they are more chatty and less academic than serious students demand, but still interesting in their appreciation of a writer of declining reputation. **(A,G)**

Other Sources

Waltman, John L., and Gerald G. McDaniel. *Leigh Hunt: A Comprehensive Bibliography.* New York: Garland, 1985.

ZORA NEALE HURSTON
1901?-1960

Evaluation of Selected Criticism

Awkward, Michael. *Inspiriting Influences: Tradition, Revision and Afro-American Women's Novels.* New York: Columbia University Press, 1989. In this specialized study, Awkward examines the inter-textual relationships among novels by four black women writers—Hurston, Morrison, Naylor, and Walker. He contends that each of these writers utilizes similar expressive elements of Afro-American culture. Consistent use of these expressive elements allows the critic to identify these writers with a specific tradition that has contributed new elements to the Western novel. (A)

Bloom, Harold, ed. *Zora Neale Hurston.* New York: Chelsea House, 1986. An introduction by Harold Bloom places Zora Neale Hurston in critical context. The twenty essays discuss important themes and issues in Hurston's works and represent a range of theories and perspectives. This collection is useful as an introduction to Hurston's critical reputation. (A,G)

Braxton, Joanne M. *Black Women Writing Autobiography: A Tradition Within a Tradition.* Philadelphia: Temple University Press, 1990. Braxton contends that black women have been slighted in most studies of autobiographical writers and sets out to rectify this situation by looking at the writings of Harriet Tubman, Maya Angelou, Susie King Taylor, Charlotte Forten Grimke, Ida Wells, and Zora Neale Hurston. Black and feminist issues are addressed within the contexts of culture and politics. (A,G)

Callahan, John F. *In the African-American Grain: The Pursuit of Voice in Twentieth-Century Black Fiction.* Champaign: University of Illinois Press, 1988. This thematic study of narrative voice links aspects of folk culture to the works of several generations of black writers. Callahan focuses on the folk tradition of call and response and how it influenced the narrative voice. He compares the tales of Joel Chandler Harris and Chesnutt to show how the authors used folk expressions to articulate democratic ideals. Callahan explores the lyrical qualities of Jean Toomer's *Cane*, which is expressed in a "musical" rather than rhetorical voice. Examining Zora Hurston's *Their Eyes Were Watching God* and the *Autobiography* of Jane Pittman, he shows how the conventions of storytelling are used to establish an interactive relationship with the reader. Turning to Ralph Ellison's *Invisible Man*, Callahan traces the emotional development of the narrator through a careful analysis of the speeches. Callahan stresses the essential "Americanness" of these works, placing them in the line of Emerson and democratic idealism. (A,G)

Holloway, Karla F. C. *The Character of the Word: The Texts of Zora Neale Hurston.* Westport, CT: Greenwood. 1987. Holloway examines Hurston's shift from standard English to black dialect in order to give her narratives a voice that identifies their journeys toward self awareness. Holloway argues that Hurston's literary precedent is the folk tale, in which the narrator shifts from story teller to participant during the course of the story. This general study is appropriate for all serious readers of Hurston. (A,G)

Newson, Adele S. *Zora Neale Hurston: A Reference Guide.* G. K. Hall, 1987. During the Harlem Renaissance, Hurston was extremely popular as a folklorist and novelist. She died impoverished and unknown in 1960. But recent scholarship has revived her reputation and is seeking to define her place in the history of Afro-American literature. This excellent bibliography of critical sources—books and book chapters, reviews, articles, and dissertations—follows the ups and downs of her popularity from 1931 to 1986. Entries are grouped by year and then arranged alphabetically by author. Newson has carefully annotated each citation and provided an introductory overview of Hurston's accomplishments. Although not comprehensive, this bibliography contains most of the important works. (A,G)

Walker, Nancy, and Zita Dresner, eds. *Redressing the Balance: American Women's Literary Humor from Colonial Times to the 1980s.* Jackson: University Press of Mississippi, 1988. This collection gathers samples of wit and humorous verse from about sixty American women writers, including Sarah Kemble Knight, Phoebe Cary, Mary Roberts Rinehart, Zora Neale Hurston, Nora Ephron, and Fran Lebowitz. A well-written introduction places the collection in historical and literary context. (A,G)

Other Sources
Sheffey, Ruthe T., ed. *Zora Neale Hurston Forum.* Baltimore: Morgan State University Press, 1990.

WASHINGTON IRVING
1783-1859

Evaluation of Selected Criticism

Bowden, Edwin T., ed. *Washington Irving Bibliography*. Boston: Twayne, 1989. This extensive bibliography catalogs and describes in detail all of the books and other publications printed about Washington Irving during his lifetime (before 1860). The physical appearance of the books, as well as the contents, are described; the printer's name and the lineation of selected pages are given—the kind of details useful to librarians, catalogers, and book collectors. **(A)**

Rubin-Dorsky, Jeffrey. *Adrift in the Old World: The Psychological Pilgrimage of Washington Irving*. Chicago: University of Chicago Press, 1988. Through close readings of the fiction Rubin-Dorsky brings into focus Irving's sense of what it meant to be an American. Irving's internal struggle was between the cultural pressures of the "Old World"—in particular, English values—and the bewildering potential of the New. In many ways, Irving's psychological conflict reflects the formative throes of the young American nation. Rubin-Dorsky's analysis of "Rip Van Winkle" and "The Legend of Sleepy Hollow" reaffirms the significance of these works and alone would justify reading this book. Highly recommended. **(A,G)**

Von Frank, Albert J. *The Sacred Game: Provincialism and Frontier Consciousness in American Literature, 1630-1860*. New York: Cambridge University Press, 1985. Von Frank's wide-ranging study examines the reactions of various writers to the wilderness environment of young America. He contends that Anne Bradstreet felt compelled to retain the old culture in order to preserve identity in her new surroundings. He views Washington Irving's works as a reaction to American provincialism, and sees many of the same provincial themes evident in Hawthorne's *The Scarlet Letter*. Von Frank's major thesis is that the wilderness environment accepts immigrants but at the same time rejects the immigrant's culture. He uses Emerson's works to analyze this and other themes. **(A)**

Other Sources

Brodwin, Stanley, ed. *The Old and New World Romanticism of Washington Irving*. Westport, CT: Greenwood, 1986.

CHRISTOPHER ISHERWOOD
1904-1986

Author's Recent Bibliography
Mr. Norris Changes Trains; and Goodbye to Berlin, 1985 (history); *Lions and Shadows: An Education in the Twenties,* 1985 (nonfiction); *The Wishing Tree,* 1987 (non-fiction).

Evaluation of Selected Biography and Criticism
Lehmann, John. *Christopher Isherwood: A Personal Memoir.* Orlando, FL: Holt, 1988. Lehmann, who was Isherwood's editor at Hogarth Press in England, looks back over his thirty-five-year friendship and professional association with the author. With an insider's view, he describes Isherwood's rebellion against his family, his passion for yoga, his pacifism, and the techniques Isherwood used to maintain his mental equilibrium. Of particular interest to scholars are Isherwood's letters to Lehmann, which are copiously quoted. (A, G)

Schwerdt, Lisa M. *Isherwood's Fiction: The Self and Technique.* New York: St. Martin's, 1989. Schwerdt examines Isherwood's fiction to describe the various stages of his emotional and spiritual development, using the scheme of maturation developed by Erik Erickson. Biographical details are related to Isherwood's works to reveal a significant interpenetration of life and art. In this approach, Schwerdt owes much to Isherwood's previous biographers, Alan Wilde and Brian Finney. The bibliography is exceptionally thorough. (A)

Other Sources
Ferres, Kay. *Christopher Isherwood.* Mercer Island, WA: Starmont House, 1990.

HENRY JAMES
1843-1916

Autobiographical Sources

Edel, Leon, and Lyall Powers, eds. *The Complete Notebooks of Henry James.* New York: Oxford University Press, 1987. Starting with the same nine notebooks first published in 1947 (*The Notebooks of Henry James*, Matthiessen and Murdock, eds.), Edel and Powers add a wealth of additional information, including pocket diaries, plot outlines, pages of notes for unfinished novels, and a scenario for an unfinished play. Most of this new material has never before been published and enhances the reader's understanding of the writer's creative process—his inspirations, working methods, techniques, and intentions. The pocket diaries provide many biographical details that have previously been unavailable. The editors' introduction gives an overview of the current status of James scholarship. **(A)**

Edel, Leon, ed. *Henry James Letters: Volume 4, 1895-1916.* Cambridge: Harvard University Press, 1984. All of the power and passion of James' correspondence comes through in this concluding volume of the *Letters.* This phase of his life begins rather dismally with the failure of *Guy Domville*, but James soon finds his stride and produces some of his most famous works— *The Ambassadors* and *The Wings of the Dove.* His life is animated through a new relationship with Hendrik Andersen, expatriate American sculptor. He generates new friendships with Edith Wharton and Stephen Crane and maintains his close ties with William Dean Howells. The letters are carefully annotated and several important appendixes are included—"The Deathbed Dictation," for example. This highly recommended edition of the letters is more than a supplement to recent biographies; it has a literary life of its own. **(A,G)**

Powers, Lydall H. *Henry James and Edith Wharton: Letters 1900-1915.* New York: Scribner's, 1990. In periods of deep depression in 1909 and again in 1915, a year before his death, James burned his personal papers, including much of his voluminous correspondence. Wharton, however, kept hers, and of the estimated 400 letters that passed between them, the 180 that are known to exist are collected in this volume. The subjects range from literary analysis of James' novels to Wharton's seeking advice about her ill-fated marriage to William Morton Fullerton. The letters display a rich and complex exchange of frank views and tempered passions. James played the confidant for Wharton, who provided the writer with sustained and intimate friendship. Here is a glimpse of the mutually supportive relationship that existed between these two expatriates. **(A,G)**

Evaluation of Selected Biography and Criticism

Anesko, Michael. *"Friction with the Market": Henry James and the Profession of Authorship.* New York: Oxford University Press, 1986. Anesko's ground-breaking study examines James' literary marketplace to discover the socio-economic context within which he wrote his fiction. The myth of James as an "ivory-tower novelist" evaporates under Anesko's scrutiny, which contends that James wrote with one eye on the imagination and one on the marketplace. His finished works were shaped by a constructive friction between these two forces. (A,G)

Armstrong, Paul B. *The Challenge of Bewilderment: Understanding and Representation in James, Conrad, and Ford.* Ithaca, NY: Cornell University Press, 1987. Armstrong distills the thematic and philosophical concerns of James, Conrad, and Ford to a single existential essence—bewilderment. Focusing on Conrad's narrators and characters in *Lord Jim* and *Nostromo*, he examines their shifting and often contradictory explanations of the reality of events. Comparing these viewpoints with the purposeful blurring of real life and illusion accomplished by James and the temperamental inconsistencies of Ford Madox Ford, Armstrong finds a strong basis for claiming that the expression of "bewilderment" was the source of many of their obscurities. (A)

Auchard, John. *Silence in Henry James: The Heritage of Symbolism and Decadence.* University Park: Pennsylvania State University Press, 1986. This specialized study examines the various aspects of silence in the narrative fiction. Auchard adapts the views of modern critics Sartre, Steiner, and Arendt to his brief critical readings of *Roderick Hudson, The American, The Portrait of a Lady, The Wings of the Dove,* and others. (A)

Auerbach, Jonathan. *The Romance of Failure: First-Person Fictions of Poe, Hawthorne, and James.* New York: Oxford University Press, 1989. Auerbach examines the first-person narratives of Poe, Hawthorne, and James to better understand the writers' relationship to their works. Auerbach believes the first-person perspective is revealing because it provides less of a grammatical barrier to mediation between author and text. Poe is shown to display a contradiction between his personal and public identities. In *The Blithedale Romance,* Hawthorne preserves his artistic integrity by hiding behind a "clownish" persona. In *The Sacred Fount,* James drives his narrator into madness in order to maintain his own sanity. (A)

Beidler, Peter G. *Ghosts, Demons, and Henry James: "The Turn of the Screw" at the Turn of the Century.* Columbia: University of Missouri Press, 1989. Beidler examines over one hundred nineteenth-century accounts of ghosts, demons, and mediums that were available to James when he wrote *The Turn of the Screw.* Quoting extensively from these accounts, Beidler builds a case for the "real" rather than symbolic nature of the ghosts and reveals that at some points James considers the two children to be literally possessed by demons. Many of the ghost accounts contain details that are astonishingly similar to details in the novel. (A,G)

Bennett, Maurice J. *An American Tradition—Three Studies: Charles Brockden Brown, Nathaniel Hawthorne, and Henry James.* New York: Garland, 1987. This dissertation examines and compares three American authors and focuses on a major work by each—Brown's *Ormond, or the Secret Witness,* Hawthorne's *The Scarlet Letter,* and James' *The Portrait of a Lady.* This volume includes an extensive bibliography. **(A)**

Bishop, George. *When the Master Relents: The Neglected Short Fictions of Henry James.* Ann Arbor, MI: UMI Research, 1988. Bishop examines six of James' neglected tales, some of which have only recently been published. To explain the significance of these stories and the reasons for their neglect, Bishop turns to James' voluminous notebooks and cites his own ideas about the contradictions of art. **(A)**

Bloom, Harold, ed. *Henry James' "The Portrait of a Lady".* New York: Chelsea House, 1987. All seven of these essays focus on the issue of marriage in *The Portrait of a Lady.* Although this focus seems single-minded, the theme brings up an array of questions that leads to a clearer understanding of character and plot. Recommended for any serious student of James. **(A)**

Borus, Daniel H. *Writing Realism: Howells, James, and Norris in the Mass Market.* Chapel Hill: University of North Carolina Press, 1989. Borus examines the economic and social conditions following the Civil War and their effect on concepts of realism. He then analyzes how the effects of commercial publishing, printing innovations, and popular magazines established a new class of readers who regarded writers more as newscasters and celebrities than prophets. The result bred a new generation of writers who regarded both their purpose and their work differently than preceding generations. This fascinating thesis is well wrought and impressively documented by the letters, records, and literary criticism of its subjects. Recommended for advanced students and scholars. **(A)**

Dryden, Edgar A. *The Form of American Romance.* Baltimore: Johns Hopkins University Press, 1988. In this study, Dryden undertakes an analysis of the structure and development of American Romanticism. He first examines the origins of the novel and its relationship to romance by discussing *Don Quixote* and Scott's *Waverley.* He views Scott's early novel as a "founding text" in the history of the English novel. Dryden then dissects the narrative structures of five American novels—Hawthorne's *The Marble Faun,* Melville's *Pierre,* James' *The Portrait of a Lady,* Faulkner's *Absalom, Absalom!,* and Barth's *LETTERS.* He sees these American novelists responding directly to narrative problems inherited from Scott. **(A)**

Edel, Leon. *Henry James: A Life.* New York: Harper & Row, 1985. This one-volume abridgement of Edel's two-volume biography published in 1977, continues the academic controversy over Edel's treatment of James' life. **(A,G)**

Freadman, Richard. *Eliot, James, and the Fictional Self.* New York: St. Martin's, 1986. Freadman offers a comparative study of the presentation of characters in novels of Eliot and James. Early chapters discuss both authors' theories of the novel: its structure, purpose, and intent. A rather specialized study, this book is useful for scholars of either Eliot or James. **(A)**

Gage, Richard P. *Order and Design: Henry James' Titled Story Sequences.* New York: Peter Lang. 1988. Gage believes that James structured the stories in his seven collections so that they form meaningful sequences. Although the theory is inviting, Gage does little to effectively argue his case, and so this study is more interesting to scholars who might want to pursue the thesis. **(A,G)**

Goetz, William R. *James and the Darkest Abyss of Romance.* Baton Rouge: Louisiana State University Press, 1986. Goetz' study examines James' use of autobiographical elements in his fiction and non-fiction. Of particular note are Goetz's discussions of James' relationship with his brother William, and the doubling of characters in "The Beast in the Jungle" and *The Ambassadors.* Although Goetz adopts a structuralist orientation, his complex arguments are developed without distracting jargon. While many of the study's conclusions will be familiar to the specialist, Goetz's insight into the overall unity of James' work is new and intriguing. **(A)**

Graham, Kenneth. *Indirections of the Novels: James, Conrad, and Forster.* London: Cambridge University Press, 1988. Graham argues that while all three writers rejected the literary directions of the Victorian era, none quite advanced into modernism and, as a result, developed common themes of isolation. Faced with a world of uncertainty, they employed similar language, narrative form, and an ambiguity toward society. The novels that Graham uses to develop his thesis include James' *The Bostonians, The Europeans, What Maisie Knew,* and *The Golden Bowl;* Conrad's *Heart of Darkness, Lord Jim, Nostromo, The Secret Agent, Under Western Eyes,* and *The Shadow Line;* and Forster's *A Passage to India* and *Howard's End.* **(A)**

Greenwald, Elissa. *Realism and the Romance: Nathaniel Hawthorne, Henry James, and American Fiction.* Ann Arbor: UMI Research Press, 1989. Greenwald argues that Hawthorne's romances directly influenced the development of James' realism, which opened the door to modernist fiction. She provides excellent close readings of some of the fiction of both writers, linking *The Scarlet Letter* with *The Portrait of a Lady,* and *The Blithedale Romance* with *The Bostonians.* She demonstrates an important connection in the development of the American novel, and the road which romanticism traveled to survive in the modernist mind. This is a valuable study for any serious reader of either writer. **(A,G)**

Greiner, Donald J. *Adultery in the American Novel: Updike, James, and Hawthorne.* Columbia: University of South Carolina Press, 1985. This narrowly focused study examines the relationship between the depiction of

adultery in Updike's novels and the narrative models provided by his predecessors, Hawthorne and James. Greiner believes that Updike's essentially religious outlook inhibits a full development of the adultery theme, and his work
suffers in comparison with the past masters. (**A**)

Habegger, Alfred. *Henry James and the "Woman Business"*. Cambridge:
Cambridge University Press, 1989. Habegger applies a Freudian reading to the
women in James' novels, particularly *The Portrait of a Lady* and *The
Bostonians,* and analyzes James' response to women writers who were his
contemporaries. What emerges is a new, interesting conception of James' idea
of female psyches that illuminates his fiction and expands the importance of
women writers at the turn of the century. (**A**)

Haggerty, George E. *Gothic Fiction/Gothic Form*. University Park:
Pennsylvania State University Press, 1989. In this study in reader-response
criticism, Haggerty attempts to lift Gothic fiction into the category of serious
literature. To do this, he establishes two categories—Gothic novels and Gothic
tales. Gothic *novels* fail because the genre is unsuited to the effects generated
in the reader by the Gothic impulse. Gothic *tales,* on the other hand, succeed
admirably. Indeed, because Haggerty's conception of the tale is represented by
such works as Shelley's *Frankenstein*, Brontë's *Wuthering Heights*, Poe's "The
Fall of the House of Usher," Hawthorne's "Rappaccini's Daughter," and
James' *Turn of the Screw*, it is difficult to argue with the conclusion. Some
have questioned Haggerty's categories of novel and tale as artificial. (**A,G**)

Heller, Terry. *"The Turn of the Screw": Bewildered Vision*. Boston:
Twayne, 1989. Heller succinctly applies the psychoanalytic theories of Jacques
Lacan to the narrative ambiguities of Henry James' famous ghost-story. This
brief study reopens several older critical debates but is not able to address
them adequately. Still, Heller's work is useful for provoking questions about
James' artistic techniques and intentions. (**A,G**)

Johnson, Courtney. *Henry James and the Evolution of Consciousness: A
Study of "The Ambassadors."* East Lansing: Michigan State University Press,
1987. In James' *The Ambassadors*, the protagonist achieves a transcendence of
the type popularly associated with meditation. This transcendence imparts the
freedom needed to pursue his own destiny. By analyzing relevant passages,
Johnson is able to relate the novel's themes to current psychological theories
and, in particular, transcendental meditation. The bulk of this study is grounded in twentieth-century preoccupations and neglects the historical context and
James' religious background. (**G**)

Jones, Vivian. *James the Critic*. New York: St. Martin's, 1985. In this
study, Jones traces the course of James' career as a literary critic. She devotes
considerable attention to his American background, his exposure to French
realism, his participation in English critical debates, and his role as a critic of
his own works. James' critical perspective stemmed largely from his own self-
imposed criteria for successful writing, which Jones analyzes in detail. The

result is a surprisingly consistent critical methodology. Jones argues that many of James' insights prefigured the preoccupations of recent criticism. **(A)**

Lindberg-Seyersted, Brita. *Ford Madox Ford and His Relationship to Stephen Crane and Henry James.* Atlantic Highlands, NJ: Humanities Press, 1987. The purpose of this study is to provide an exhaustive analysis of the contacts and mutual influences of Ford and James. In spite of the title's emphasis, Crane is addressed only in one short chapter. **(A)**

Macnaughton, William R. *Henry James: The Later Novels.* Boston: Twayne, 1987. Macnaughton analyzes James' last six novels, addressing the problems each presents, and treats his work in the theatre and his last, unfinished novel. Written in clear prose and complete with excellent notes and selected bibliography, this study is both a guide to beginning students and a good resource for scholars. **(A,G)**

McKee, Patricia. *Heroic Commitment in Richardson, Eliot, and James.* Princeton: Princeton University Press, 1986. This demanding theoretical excursion into the works of Samuel Richardson, George Eliot, and Henry James derives its critical stance from the works of Derrida and the French feminist school. Comparing the structures, characterization, and thematic preoccupations of the authors, McKee offers insightful, open-ended readings of major works, focusing most closely on James' *The Golden Bowl.* Women characters are seen as drawn into relationships of heroic commitment made possible by an indeterminacy that negates the determinacy of power. **(A,G)**

McWhirter, David. *Desire and Love in Henry James: A Study of the Late Novels.* Cambridge: Cambridge University Press, 1989. McWhirter examines three of James' major novels—*The Ambassadors, The Wings of the Dove,* and *The Golden Bowl*—from what is essentially a Freudian perspective. Through these novels, James' conception of love gradually develops from dilatory relationships that are doomed to repetition because they cannot be truly consummated to an acknowledgement that relationships can come to embody love. McWhirter contends that through repetition James awakened into the "possibility of a more productive and fulfilling life." Once he achieved this insight in *The Golden Bowl,* James lost the drive to express himself through the novel form and abandoned subsequent attempts. **(A)**

Morse, David. *American Romanticism.* New York: Barnes & Noble, 1987. With cool, critical detachment, Morse examines the ethic of "excessiveness" which he feels underlies the early literature of the new American nation. He traces this theme through eleven authors from Cooper and Melville to James. Nineteenth-century American authors, he argues, were driven by an impulse to extravagance in order to create a fitting symbol of national significance. **(A,G)**

Murphy, Brenda. *American Realism and American Drama, 1880-1940.* Cambridge: Cambridge University Press, 1987. Murphy clarifies the relationship between literary realism and dramatic realism in this study of the works of

Howells and James, culminating in the plays of O'Neill. Several plays by Hamlin Garland and James A. Herne are examined to demonstrate the impact of realistic theory on dramatic practice. Murphy sees the works of Odets and Hellman leading, via the cultural impact of Freud, to O'Neill, who reigns as undisputed master of the American stage. A valuable overview of the antecedents of twentieth-century American drama. (A,G)

Putt, S. Gorley. *A Preface to Henry James.* White Plains, NY: Longman, 1987. Cambridge professor S. Gorley Putt has written a useful introduction to the life and works of Henry James. Focusing on James' technical mastery and complex thematic structures, Putt examines the major works, injecting biographical details where appropriate. For those who have found James intimidating in the past, this study should provide guidance. (A,G)

Schwarz, Daniel R. *The Humanistic Heritage: Critical Theories of the English Novel from James to Hillis Miller.* Philadelphia: University of Pennsylvania Press, 1986. This ambitious work organizes and discusses the diverse approaches and theoretical assumptions of the major critics of the twentieth-century Anglo-American novel. Schwarz describes the critical attitudes of Henry James, Dorothy Van Ghent, Northrop Frye, Frank Kermode, and many others. He classifies their theories along two axes: formalist-aesthetic and humanist-empiricist. Schwarz has produced a powerful analysis of the modes of literary perception. The bibliography is extensive and well-annotated. (A,G)

Seymour, Miranda. *A Ring of Conspirators: Henry James and His Literary Circle, 1895-1915.* Boston: Houghton Mifflin, 1989. James was a close neighbor and associate of Crane, Conrad, and Ford during the two decades covered by this social biography. Did these men conspire to transform the face of English literature as H. G. Wells suggested? Seymour examines the Wells hypothesis by analyzing the personalities and works of James and his circle. (A)

Sutherland, Judith. *The Problematic Fictions of Poe, James, and Hawthorne.* Columbia: University of Missouri Press, 1984. Sutherland focuses on three texts that "force romantic premises to the breaking point"—*The Narrative of Arthur Gordon Pym, The Sacred Fount,* and *The Marble Faun.* According to Sutherland, each of these works resists thematic interpretation and represents the writer's confrontation with the schism between the world and its representation, a theme developed by the modernist writers who followed. This study in deconstructive methodology provides new insights into the relationship between the modernists and their predecessors. (A)

Tanner, Tony. *Scenes of Nature, Signs of Men.* Cambridge: Cambridge University Press, 1987. For the sheer ingenuity and brilliance of comparative thinking, Cambridge professor Tanner is one of the best critics of our time. In this collection of essays, Tanner works out his idea of the profound influence on American fiction of the Puritans' obsession with signs. He contends that this obsession set the tone for all subsequent American fiction, for it established the need for American writers to find a special significance in their landscape and history. Tanner elaborates his insight in discussions of individual American writers from Cooper and Hawthorne to the contemporary novelist William Gass. (A,G)

Tanner, Tony. *Henry James: The Writer and His Work.* Amherst: University of Massachusetts Press, 1985. This concise biography of Henry James is a useful introduction for the general reader. Tanner writes of James' creative process with authority and direction. In explaining how James was able to achieve such deep insights in his novels, he describes James' "curious combination of empathy and detachment"—a balance of perspectives that enabled subjective participation and objective observation. Although short, this study is long on substance. (A,G)

Tintner, Adeline R. *The Book World of Henry James: Appropriating the Classics.* Ann Arbor: UMI Research, 1987. Henry James' two greatest literary sources were Shakespeare and Balzac, yet he incorporated language, imagery, and situations from many other sources, among them Milton, Pater, the English Romantics, Victorian novelists, Poe, and Hawthorne. In this collection of previously published essays, Tintner examines these sources and the use to which James puts them. Tinter provides a wealth of meticulously researched detail and demonstrates the role of literary appropriation throughout James' career. Highly recommended. (A,G)

Tintner, Adeline R. *The Museum World of Henry James.* Ann Arbor: UMI Research, 1986. James was as fascinated by art museums as Hemingway was by bullfighting. James packs an entire museum of art objects into his twenty novels and a hundred short stories. In her study of James and art, Tintner lovingly analyzes these art objects. Of all the books that treat this subject, Tintner's is easily the most comprehensive. She provides considerable insight into James' aesthetic sensibilities and how these translated into fiction. The profusely illustrated text helps the reader visualize many of James' references. Highly recommended. (A,G)

Varnado, S. L. *Haunted Presence: The Numinous in Gothic Fiction.* Tuscaloosa: University of Alabama Press, 1987. Drawing upon Rudolph Otto's concept of the "numinous," Varnado examines the subjective experience of the supernatural as revealed in the major gothic texts. In Walpole he sees the harmony of contrasts, in Radcliff the sublime raised to numinosity. Lewis presents the demonic, while Stoker evokes the rational-nonrational paradigm. Separate chapters are devoted to Mary Shelley's sacred and profane theme and Poe's mysticism. This is an intriguing application of a useful theory that applies directly to James' gothic fiction. (A,G)

Young, Thomas Daniel, ed. *Modern American Fiction: Form and Function.* Baton Rouge: Louisiana State University Press, 1989. This anthology of thirteen critical essays examines how novelists achieve form in their best novels and how this form allows the writers to express a philosophy of life. These contributors seem to have reached a consensus that modern American novelists tend to use an objective narrative stance, allowing the action to unfold, in contrast to the more subjective narrators of the nineteenth century. Henry James' *Wings of a Dove*, Stephen Crane's *The Red Badge of Courage*, John Barth's *The Floating Opera*, and Robert Penn Warren's *All the King's Men* are singled out for special attention. In all, this is a useful introduction to the criticism of American literature. (A,G)

Other Sources

Allen, Elizabeth E. *A Woman's Place in the Novels of Henry James.* New York: St. Martin's, 1984.

Banta, Martha, ed. *New Essays on "The American."* New York: Cambridge University Press, 1987.

Bell, Ian F., ed. *Henry James: Fiction As History.* Savage, MD: Barnes & Noble, 1985.

Bellringer, Alan W. *Henry James.* New York: St. Martin's, 1988.

Bender, Todd K. *A Concordance to Henry James' "The Awkward Age."* New York: Garland, 1989.

Bender, Todd K., *et al. A Concordance to James' "Daisy Miller" and the American Reference Books on Literature.* New York: Garland, 1987.

Bender, Todd K. *A Concordance to Henry James' "Turn of the Screw."* New York: Garland, 1988.

Bender, Todd K., and Leon D. Higdon. *A Concordance to Henry James' "The Spoils of Poynton".* New York: Garland, 1988.

Bogardus, Ralph F. *Pictures and Texts: Henry James, A. L. Coburn, and New Ways of Seeing in Literary Culture.* Ann Arbor: UMI Research Press, 1984.

Boren, Lynda S. *Eurydice Reclaimed: Language, Gender, and Voice in Henry James.* Ann Arbor: UMI Research Press, 1989.

Cameron, Sharon. *Thinking in Henry James.* Chicago: University of Chicago Press, 1989.

Cowdery, Lauren T. *The Nouvelle of Henry James in Theory and Practice.* Ann Arbor: UMI Research Press, 1985.

Davis, Lloyd. *Sexuality and Textuality in Henry James: Reading Through the Virginal*. New York: Peter Lang, 1989.

Fogel, Daniel Mark. *"Daisy Miller": A Dark Comedy of Manners*. Boston: Twayne, 1990.

Fowler, Virginia C. *Henry James' American Girl: The Embroidery on the Canvas*. Madison: University of Wisconsin Press, 1984.

Gale, Robert. *A Henry James Encyclopedia*. Westport, CT: Greenwood, 1989.

Gard, Roger. *Henry James*. New York: Routledge Chapman & Hall, 1987.

Gargano, James W., ed. *Critical Essays on Henry James: The Early Novels*. Boston: G. K. Hall, 1987.

Kaston, Carren. *Imagination and Desire in the Novels of Henry James*. New Brunswick: Rutgers University Press, 1984.

MacDonald, Bonney. *Henry James's "Italian Hours": Revelation and Resistant Impression*. Ann Arbor: UMI Research, 1990.

Margolis, Anne T. *Henry James and the Problem of Audience: An International Act*. Ann Arbor: UMI Press, 1985.

McEwen, Fred B. *A Biographical Dictionary of the Characters in the Fiction of Henry James*. New York: Garland, 1986.

Moore, Rayburn S., ed. *Selected Letters of Henry James to Edmund Gosse, 1882-1915: A Literary Friendship*. Baton Rouge: Louisiana State University Press, 1988.

Morgan, Susan. *Sisters in Time: Imagining Gender in Nineteenth-Century British Fiction*. New York: Oxford University Press, 1989.

Page, Norman, ed. *Henry James: Interviews and Recollections*. New York: St. Martin's, 1984.

Pecora, Vincent P. *Self and Form in Modern Narrative*. Baltimore: Johns Hopkins University Press, 1989.

Posnock, Ross. *Henry James and the Problem of Robert Browning*. Athens: University of Georgia Press, 1985.

Przybylowicz, Donna. *Desire and Repression: The Dialectic Between Self and Other in the Late Works of Henry James*. Tuscaloosa: University of Alabama Press, 1986.

Rowe, John C. *The Theoretical Dimensions of Henry James.* Madison: University of Wisconsin Press, 1984.

Sayre, Robert F. *The Examined Self: Benjamin Franklin, Henry Adams, Henry James.* Madison: University of Wisconsin Press, 1988.

Seltzer, Mark. *Henry James and the Art of Power.* Ithaca, NY: Cornell University Press, 1984.

Singh, Amritjit, and Ayyappa Paniker, eds. *The Magic Circle of Henry James.* New York: Envoy Press, 1989.

Smit, David W. *The Language of a Master: Theories of Style and the Late Writing of Henry James.* Carbondale: Southern Illinois University Press, 1988.

Stowe, William W. *Balzac, James and the Realistic Novel.* Princeton: Princeton University Press, 1986.

Tintner, Adeline. *The Pop World of Henry James.* Ann Arbor: UMI Press, 1989.

Torgovnick, Marianna. *The Visual Arts, Pictorialism and the Novel: James, Lawrence, and Woolf.* Princeton: Princeton University Press, 1985.

Wagenknecht, Edward. *The Tale of Henry James.* New York: Frederick Ungar, 1984.

RANDALL JARRELL
1914-1965

Autobiographical Sources

Jarrell, Mary, ed. *Randall Jarrell's Letters: An Autobiographical and Literary Selection*. Boston: Houghton Mifflin, 1985. Jarrell's wife has collected and annotated the letters of a man both loved and feared for his wit, intelligence, and conversational acumen. A leading poet, critic, and prose stylist of his day, Jarrell developed friendships with other leading writers, including Robert Penn Warren, John Crowe Ransom, Delmore Schwarz, John Berryman, Robert Lowell, and many others. These letters record the events, personality, and innermost thoughts of a remarkable man. However they shed no light on the circumstances of his mysterious death. Every serious student of Jarrell or modern poetry will profit from these meticulously researched and edited letters. (A,G)

Evaluation of Selected Biography and Criticism

Bawer, Bruce. *The Middle Generation: The Lives and Poetry of Delmore Schwartz, Randall Jarrell, John Berryman, and Robert Lowell*. Hamden, CT: Shoe String Press, Archon Books, 1986. This critical study brings some needed structure to the study of these four poets whose richly textured poetry often confuses readers. Bawer examines the influence of T. S. Eliot on the early work of all four poets and shows how each emerged from that influence in their later poetry. Critics may quibble with the interpretations of particular poems, but the overall value of this work is unchallenged, making it essential for the study of these poets at any level. (A,G)

Bryant, Joseph Allen. *Understanding Randall Jarrell*. Columbia: University of South Carolina Press, 1986. This handbook is the fifth volume in the "Understanding Contemporary American Literature" series. Bryant provides a chapter on the poet's career and two chapters on the structure and content of the poetry before examining individual poems. Bryant's interpretations are unconventional and should stimulate debate. For this reason students should accept his readings with caution and refer to other sources for a balanced view. (A,G)

Griswald, Jerome. *The Children's Books of Randall Jarrell*. Athens: University of Georgia Press, 1988. During the last three years of his life, Jarrell wrote four books for children that have been neglected by the critics. In this study, Griswald contends that the content and form of these books make them worthy of adult attention, as well. Mary Jarrell contributes a biographical introduction to this book that should be read by any student of her husband's works. (A,G)

Pritchard, William H. *Randall Jarrell: A Literary Life.* New York: Farrar, Straus & Giroux, 1990. Jarrell's place in the history of American literature is still being debated, and this biography may tilt the argument in his favor. As an undergraduate Jarrell got to know such literary notables as John Crowe Ransom, Allen Tate, Robert Penn Warren, and Yvor Winters. Pritchard's familiarity with the careers of these poets allows him to discuss Jarrell's contribution with authority. This is a fine addition to Jarrell studies and should interest the scholar as well as the general public. (A,G)

Other Sources
Wright, Stuart. *Randall Jarrell: A Descriptive Bibliography 1929-1983.* Charlottesville: University Press of Virginia, 1986.

ROBINSON JEFFERS
1887-1962

Author's Recent Bibliography
The Collected Poetry of Robinson Jeffers: 1928-1938 (Volume 2), 1989.

Evaluation of Selected Criticism
Boswell, Jeanetta. *Robinson Jeffers and the Critics, 1912-1983: A Bibliography of Secondary Sources with Selective Annotations.* Metuchen, NJ: Scarecrow Press, 1986. Boswell catalogs 830 books, articles, essays, and reviews that address the life and works of Robinson Jeffers. The items are presented in chronological order and most are briefly described in terms of content. (A)

Everson, William. *The Excesses of God: Robinson Jeffers as a Religious Figure.* Stanford, CA: Stanford University Press, 1988. It is a rare treat when a poet of Everson's accomplishments turns his creative efforts to the criticism of a subject with whom he has so much affinity. Everson, formerly a Dominican lay Brother, argues that Jeffers was a religious poet, contrary to the commonly held view that he was a nihilist. Everson believes that Jeffers' seeming indifference to humankind positioned him as a healer capable of confronting an uncaring universe. Recommended for both theologians and serious students of Jeffers. (A)

Other Sources
Klein, Mina C., and J. Arthur Klein. *Jeffers Observed.* Lombard, IL: Quintessence, 1986.

SARAH ORNE JEWETT
1849-1909

Evaluation of Selected Biography and Criticism

Keyworth, Cynthia. *Master Smart Woman: A Portrait of Sarah Orne Jewett.* Utica, NY: North Country Books, 1988. This pictorial biography of Jewett was derived from an award-winning film of the same name. The popular format features over ninety black-and-white photos by Peter Narmuth with accompanying text from the filmscript. This well-designed book should contribute to Jewett's growing reputation as a portraitist of small-town and rural life in New England. It is recommended as an accessible introduction to the author's life and works. **(G,Y)**

Magowan, Robin, and James J. Wilhelm. *Narcissus and Orpheus: Pastoral in Sand, Fromentin, Jewett, Alain-Fournier and Dinesen.* New York: Garland, 1988. Magowan defines the pastoral tradition in the first chapter, then devotes one chapter to each of her subjects, in which she examines the principal works for their pastoral qualities. **(G)**

Nagel, Gwen L., ed. *Critical Essays on Sarah Orne Jewett.* G. K. Hall, 1984. Nagel opens this collection of critical essays with an excellent summary of the current state of Jewett scholarship. The remainder of the essays are grouped into three sections—reviews by Jewett's nineteenth-century contemporaries (Howells, Alice Brown, Scudder), essays reprinted from the *Colby Library Quarterly*, and eight new essays. Of the new essays, those by Richard Cary and Josephine Donovan are of particular note. This volume is valuable for its breadth of coverage and diversity of topics. **(A,G)**

Sherman, Sarah Way. *Sarah Orne Jewett, an American Persephone.* Hanover, NH: University Press of New England, 1989. Sherman uses the Demeter-Persephone myth to illuminate Jewett's development as a writer from her earliest works to her acknowledged masterpieces—"A White Heron" and *The Country of the Pointed Firs.* Sherman builds her theoretical approach on the structuralism of Lévi-Strauss, the philosophy of James, and the work of such critics as De Beauvoir and Chodorow. She contends that Jewett's sophisticated use of the myth served to feminize and humanize her writings, especially when contrasted with the "patriarchal Protestantism" of her contemporaries Stowe and Cooke. **(A)**

SAMUEL JOHNSON
1709-1784

Evaluation of Selected Criticism

Brownell, Morris. *Samuel Johnson's Attitude to the Arts*. Oxford: Oxford University Press, 1989. Brownell reviews previous Johnson biographers and critics, exposing literary prejudice and misconception at every turn. This survey is highly recommended for students of eighteenth-century literature and the arts. (A)

Davis, Philip. *In Mind of Johnson: A Study of Johnson the Rambler*. Athens: University of Georgia Press, 1989. In this loosely connected series of essays, Davis examines the "mind" of Samuel Johnson, his influence on his contemporaries, and his place in literary history. He covers ground that is familiar to Johnson scholars but his pace is lively and his phrasing fresh and inviting. This is an affectionate introduction to his life and works and should be recommended to students coming to Johnson for the first time. (A,G)

DeMaria, Robert. *Johnson's "Dictionary" and the Language of Learning*. Chapel Hill: University of North Carolina Press, 1986. DeMaria provides a reading of the quotes in Johnson's famous *Dictionary* that serves as an analysis of the mind of the compiler. Impressive in scope and in its familiarity with Johnson's sources, this study provides a useful introduction to eighteenth-century thought. (A,G)

Engell, James. *Forming the Critical Mind: Dryden to Coleridge*. Cambridge: Harvard University Press, 1989. Engell presents a lucid discussion of the origins and theories of eighteenth-century literary criticism with special emphasis on Dryden, Johnson, and Hume. After dividing criticism into its component preoccupations—genre, canon, refinement, and form—Engell then attempts to apply these to modern critical theories. This book is recommended to students for its methodology as well as for its argument. (A)

Grundy, Isobel. *Samuel Johnson and the Scale of Greatness*. Athens: University of Georgia Press, 1986. Scholars and advanced students will find Grundy's analysis of Johnson's central theme informative and provocative. Grundy demonstrates how Johnson's concept of greatness and his "sliding scale" of measuring it underlies much of his thought and work. The text is meticulously documented and the arguments are developed with subtle complexity. A highly recommended work on Johnson and the eighteenth century. (A)

Harp, Richard, ed. *Dr. Johnson's Critical Vocabulary: A Selection from His "Dictionary."* Lanham, MD: University Press of America, 1986. Harp's selection from Samuel Johnson's *Dictionary* focuses on literary criticism, rhetoric, prosody, and literature. Both the definitions and illustrative quotations are included under each entry. The selection is appropriate for introducing students to the use and study of Johnson's *Dictionary*. (A,G)

Hudson, Nicholas. *Samuel Johnson and Eighteenth-Century Thought.* London and New York: Oxford University Press, 1988. Boswell's biography of Johnson portrayed its subject so brilliantly that any other portrait seems heretical. Hudson avoids this problem by analyzing the ideas that shaped Johnson's personality and work, thus letting the reader construct his own image. Hudson discusses such ideas as free will, faith, optimism, and religious freedom, then explains Johnson's views of them. This study is not only useful to students of Johnson, but for anyone attempting to study the period. (A)

Johnson, Samuel. *Selections from Johnson on Shakespeare*. Edited by Bertrand Bronson. New Haven: Yale University Press, 1986. Johnson remains one of the most respected critics of Shakespeare who ever lived. A selection of his writings on the Bard has been judiciously compiled by Bronson in this one-volume abridgement of a previous Yale collection. Bronson's introduction provides some detail of Johnson's life, but it is too brief to encompass the full significance of his neoclassical critical position. (A)

Kaminski, Thomas. *The Early Career of Samuel Johnson*. Oxford: Oxford University Press, 1987. By confining his study to the years from 1737, when Johnson first arrived in London, to 1746, when he signed a contract for the dictionary, Kaminski can concentrate on Johnson's endeavors as a magazine editor, translator, and library cataloguer. He shows Johnson's early writing in the light of contemporary journalistic and publishing practices, and while he presents no new facts about the life, he nicely fills out a piece of literary history. This is a very useful study for Johnsonians and students of the period. (A,G)

Korshin, Paul J., ed. *Johnson After Two Hundred Years*. Philadelphia: University of Pennsylvania Press, 1986. These fourteen essays are collected from a 1984 Johnson conference at Pembroke College, Oxford, and cover the full range of current debate among Johnson scholars. Many heretofore unknown biographical facts emerge from these pages. Of particular note is Bertram Davis's essay on "Johnson's 1764 Visit to Percy," which debunks the event. Contributor Thomas Curley writes on the relationship between Johnson and Sir Robert Chambers, who later became Chief Justice of the Supreme Court of British India. (A)

Maner, Martin. *The Philosophical Biographer: Doubt and Dialectic in Johnson's "Lives of the Poets"*. Athens: University of Georgia Press, 1989. This study examines Johnson's dialectical approach to biography in his *Lives of the Poets*. In his narratives Johnson first instilled doubt then used dialectic to "educate the reader's judgement" on moral questions. Maner focuses particular attention on Johnson's lives of Savage, Swift, Milton, and Pope. This is a scholarly study, written specifically for an academic audience. (A)

Nath, Prem, ed. *Fresh Reflections on Samuel Johnson: Essays in Criticism.* Troy, NY: Whitson, 1987. The essayists in this collection bring new ideas and wit to treatments of Johnson as critic, his style, his sources, and his pleasures. Recommended for graduate students. (A)

Page, Norman, ed. *Dr. Johnson.* Totowa, NJ: Barnes & Noble, 1987. Too often modern interpretations of Johnson are derived from Boswell, as Page points out in his introduction to this anthology of Johnsoniana. Although brilliantly written, Boswell's portrait is not without prejudices and distortions. This collection of contemporary interviews, recollections, and observations seeks to provide a corrective to Boswell's inaccuracies. This is a useful sourcebook for anyone interested in the study of Johnson. (A,G)

Wheeler, David, ed. *Domestick Privacies: Samuel Johnson and the Art of Biography.* Lexington: University of Kentucky Press, 1987. Johnson was not only the subject of one of the most famous biographies of all time but also the author of a dozen brief biographies and the first critic to codify the form. The nine essays in this volume deal exclusively with Johnson's biographies without any reference to Boswell. About half deal with *Lives of the Poets*; the other four deal with Johnson's interest in the effects of literature on emotions, beliefs, and the lives of readers. One essay even speculates on how to make Johnson's writings more popular among American students. (A)

Other Sources
Engell, James, ed. *Johnson and His Age.* Cambridge: Harvard University Press, 1984.

Hinnant, Charles H. *Samuel Johnson: An Analysis.* New York: St. Martin's, 1988.

Kernan, Alvin. *Printing Technology, Letters, and Samuel Johnson.* Princeton: Princeton University Press, 1987.

Olson, Robert C. *Motto, Context, Essay: The Classical Background of Samuel Johnson's "Rambler" and "Adventurer" Essays.* Lanham, MD: University Press of America, 1985.

Temmer, Mark. *Samuel Johnson and Three Infidels: Rousseau, Voltaire, Diderot.* Athens: University of Georgia Press, 1988.

Tomarken, Edward. *Johnson, "Rasselas," and the Choice of Criticism.* Lexington: University Press of Kentucky, 1989.

Vance, John A. *Samuel Johnson and the Sense of History.* Athens: University Press of Georgia, 1984.

BEN JONSON
1572?-1637

Evaluation of Selected Biography and Criticism

Farley-Hills, David. *Jacobean Drama: A Critical Study of the Professional Drama, 1600-1625.* New York: St. Martin's, 1988. In this study Farley-Hills surveys English drama from 1600 to the death of James I, excluding Shakespeare. He divides his attention evenly among Marston, Jonson, Middleton, Chapman, Webster, and Fletcher. In most cases the focus is on the circumstances of production and related questions. In his treatment of the playwrights, Farley-Hills observes that the works curiously occur in a vacuum that is beyond the influence of the considerable political machinations of Jacobean England. Farley-Hills' contention seems to be that politics rarely intruded onto the professional stage. The approach is similar to Ann Jennalie Cook's study of Jacobean audiences, *The Privileged Playgoers of Shakespeare's London* (1981). (A,G)

Guibbory, Achsah. *The Map of Time: Seventeenth-Century English Literature and Ideas of Pattern in History.* Champaign: University of Illinois Press, 1986. Guibbory reveals the conceptions of time and history that underlie seventeenth-century thought in this closely reasoned study of six major writers—Donne, Bacon, Jonson, Herrick, Milton, and Dryden. Guibbory divines three such conceptions: degeneration and decay since the Garden of Eden; cycles of generation and decay; and the advance of civilization. He then shows how these three patterns of historical perspective influence poetry, drama, scientific and religious prose, and the writing of history. In every case, Guibbory relates history to genre, structure, imagery, and theme. Highly recommended. (A,G)

Miles, Rosalind. *Ben Jonson: His Life and Work.* London: Routledge & Kegan Paul, 1987. Although this biography is thorough and detailed, it is not as readable as its predecessors. Miles shifts between discussions of Jonson's life, works, and times without developing sufficient connections. Its strength is that people and events are more fully explained than in the other biographies, which makes it a useful addition for serious students. (A)

Riggs, David. *Ben Jonson: A Life.* Cambridge: Harvard University Press, 1989. Jonson was one of the first writers to consider himself part of a distinct literary profession, and as such calculated and plotted his career. Riggs uses Jonson's literary ambitions as a framework for analyzing his character. (A)

Van den Berg, Sara J. *The Action of Ben Jonson's Poetry.* Newark: University of Delaware Press, 1987. Van den Berg argues that Jonson's poetry is a dramatic response to the people and events in his life, and to prove her thesis she examines the relation of love and friendship in his life and work.

Of particular interest is Jonson's friendship with the Sidneys. This study develops some complicated theories about Jonson's aesthetics, but for the most part it is suitable for any serious student. The notes, bibliography, and index make it a valuable research tool. (A)

Watson, Robert N. *Ben Jonson's Parodic Strategy: Literary Imperialism in the Comedies.* Cambridge: Harvard University Press, 1987. Watson reexamines Jonson's comedies to argue that they are much more than satire or morality plays. He believes that Jonson established a strategy in which the characters elicit unauthentic responses from their experiences, and thus mock both audience and critics who demand conventional theatre. The plays Watson analyzes are *Every Man in His Humor, Every Man Out of His Humor, Volpone, Epicoene, The Alchemist, Bartholomew Fair, The Devil Is an Ass,* and *The New Inn.* (A)

Womack, Peter. *Ben Jonson.* New York: Basil Blackwell, 1987. This study attempts to show how Marxism, feminism, and deconstructionist criticism open new and exciting ways of reading Jonson's work. (A)

Other Sources
Craig, D. H. Ven *Jonson: The Critical Heritage.* New York: Routledge Chapman & Hall, 1989.

Donaldson, Ian, ed. *Ben Jonson.* New York: Oxford University Press, 1985.

Evans, Robert C. *Ben Jonson and the Poetics of Patronage.* Lewisburg, PA: Bucknell University Press, 1988.

Jensen, Ejner J. *Ben Jonson's Comedies on the Modern Stage.* Ann Arbor: UMI Research Press, 1985.

Loewenstein, Joseph. *Responsive Readings: Versions of Echo in Pastoral, Epic, and the Jonsonian Masque.* New Haven: Yale University Press, 1984.

McDonald, Russ. *Shakespeare and Jonson; Jonson and Shakespeare.* Lincoln: University of Nebraska Press, 1988.

Mebane, John S. *Renaissance Magic and the Return of the Golden Age: The Occult Tradition and Marlowe, Jonson, and Shakespeare.* Lincoln: University of Nebraska Press, 1989.

Rowe, George E. *Distinguishing Jonson: Imitations, Rivalry, and the Direction of a Dramatic Career.* Lincoln: University of Nebraska Press, 1988.

Wiltenberg, Robert. *Ben Jonson and Self-Love: The Subtlest Maze of All.* Columbia: University of Missouri Press, 1989.

JAMES JOYCE
1882-1941

Autobiographical Sources

Banta, Melissa, and Oscar A. Silverman, eds. *James Joyce's Letters to Sylvia Beach, 1921-1940*. Bloomington: Indiana University Press, 1987. Most of the 210 letters and short messages included in this volume are cryptic comments on business-related matters, conveyed from Joyce to his French publisher, Sylvia Beach. If it were not for the editors' painstaking research and diligent annotations, many of these letters would be unintelligible. A useful complement to other collections of Joyce's correspondence. (A,G)

Evaluation of Selected Criticism

Begnal, Michael H. *Dreamscheme: Narrative and Voice in "Finnegans Wake."* Syracuse, NY: Syracuse University Press, 1988. Arguing that *Finnegans Wake* is a traditional novel in that it has plot, character, and theme, Begnal goes on the demonstrate how Joyce restructures the reader's relationship to events so they can be experienced simultaneously, much as a cubistic painting is experienced. Thus, there is structure, though the "dreamscheme" may seem as disjointed as a nightmare. Readers will appreciate the excellent close reading Begnal offers, making this study a good choice for beginning Joyceans as well as scholars. (A)

Beja, Morris, and Shari Benstock, eds. *Coping with Joyce: Essays from the Copenhagen Symposium*. Columbus: Ohio State University Press, 1989. The bulk of this collection of 18 essays examines *Finnegans Wake* from a variety of angles. Of particular interest is K. Devlin's discussion of "dialectical logic" that reveals an underlying structure for the novel. Robert Scholes turns the spotlight on biography in his essay on modernist ideology and finds surprising parallels among the early lives and thought of Mussolini, George Lukacs, and Joyce. Carrying the analysis further, he puts his finger on the points where the lives diverged and examines the consequences. This collection provides a fine introductory sampling of current critical opinion. (A,G)

Benstock, Bernard, ed. *James Joyce: The Augmented Ninth*. Syracuse: Syracuse University Press, 1988. Derived partly from the 1984 Joyce symposium in Frankfurt, this collection of essays combines traditional criticism with avant-garde and feminist contributions. (A,G)

Bishop, John. *Joyce's Book of the Dark: "Finnegans Wake."* Madison: University of Wisconsin Press, 1987. Bishop's excursion into the heart of *Finnegans Wake* is a self-proclaimed "funferall." He succeeds where more plodding explicators fail because of a quick wit and droll humor. Rather than attempting a linear explication, Bishop sets out to reveal spatial relationships within the novel's structure, which is a dream where space and time meta-morphose according to the author's unique "dream logic." If Bishop's spritely approach and love for the subject do not persuade students to tackle this great "unread classic," it is not clear what will. (A,G)

Brown, Dennis. *The Modernist Self in Twentieth-Century English Literature: A Study in Self-Fragmentation.* New York: St. Martin's, 1989. In this study of major British writers of the twentieth century, Brown develops the thesis that the convention of unitary selfhood was the heart of narrative perspective until challenged by the modernists. Drawing heavily on such writers as Conrad, Joyce, Pound, David Jones, and Ford Madox Ford, Brown masses material from writers who depicted the self as fragmentary and heterogeneous, rather than unitary. He examines the roles of inner conflict and self-deception in shaping the form of the novel. Fragmentation of self, in Brown's view, could be depicted negatively—leading to various forms of disintegration—or posi-tively—allowing a restricted selfhood to expand and diversify. (A,G)

Cahalan, James M. *The Irish Novel: A Critical History.* Boston: Twayne, 1988. Cahalan's work, the first in the series "Critical History of the Novel," is a competent survey of nineteenth- and twentieth-century Irish novels. Cahalan examines only those novels actually set in Ireland. His intention is to dis-entangle many deserving Irish novelists from the web of criticism spun around Joyce. Without a doubt, Joyce was a decisive formative influence—Cahalan devotes a full chapter to him—but later Irish novelists are presented in a new and more positive light. The book is recommended for any serious student of the Irish novel. (A)

Carpenter, Humphrey. *Geniuses Together: American Writers in Paris in the 1920s.* Boston: Houghton Mifflin, 1988. Carpenter, who has written biog-raphies of Auden and Tolkien, provides a portrait of expatriate life on the Left Bank in post-WWI Paris and surveys the American writers who flocked there for inspiration and comraderie. Although the spotlight is primarily on Hemingway and his immediate circle, Carpenter weaves the story of the expa-triate coterie that inspired and gave courage to the brilliant experimental writers of the twentieth century, including Joyce, Anderson, Fitzgerald, Boyle, Pound, and Stein. (A)

Deane, Seamus. *A Short History of Irish Literature.* South Bend, IN: University of Notre Dame Press, 1986. Noted Irish scholar Deane develops a number of themes in this survey of Irish literature: the allegiance of Irish literature to history and politics; the struggle of authors to champion acceptance of Irish ideals; and the interplay of art and political polemic. The approach is primarily historical, but Deane offers concise and useful readings of works by Joyce, Yeats, and others. The volume is divided into chronolog-ical sections: Gaelic background, Anglo-Irish tradition, Celtic revival, nine-teenth-century fiction and drama, and Irish modernism. This book has been recommended as a supplement to McHugh's *Short History of Anglo-Irish Lit-erature.* (A,G)

Ellmann, Richard. *Four Dubliners: Wilde, Yeats, Joyce, and Beckett.* New York: Braziller, 1987. With his usual elegance and clarity, Ellmann discusses the lives and works of four Irish writers who shaped the character of twentieth-century literature. Although these authors have significant differences, Ellmann concentrates on their commonalities: the desire to transform language and literature, the need to establish autonomy, a preoccupation with inner conflicts, and an insistence on remaining Irish in spite of living as expatriates. This is a splendid introduction for new readers to their lives and works. Highly recommended. (A,G)

Gaiser, Gottlieb, ed. *International Perspectives on James Joyce.* Troy, NY: Whitston, 1986. This volume compiles fifteen essays from a cast of contributors who represent seven European countries and the U.S. Ten of the essays analyze texts, mostly *Ulysses.* The remaining studies examine Joyce's international literary reputation. Well-known Joyce scholars—Henke, Levitt, and Senn—are represented. Students of Joyce should find this volume worth examining. (A)

Garratt, Robert F. *Modern Irish Poetry: Tradition and Continuity from Yeats to Heaney.* Berkeley: University of California Press, 1986. Beginning with the romanticism of Yeats, Garratt follows the developing themes of Irish poets since the grudging acceptance of Joyce's modernism. Following an introductory chapter that establishes the poetic tradition of Yeats, Garrett examines in turn the revivalists, Joyce, Austin Clarke, Patrick Kavanagh, Thomas Kinsella, John Montague, Seamus Heaney, and some of the Ulster poets, such as Tom Paulin, Paul Muldoon, and Derek Mahon. This book is indispensable for anyone with an interest in twentieth-century Irish poetry. (A,G)

Gordon, John. *"Finnegans Wake": A Plot Summary.* Syracuse, NY: Syracuse University Press, 1987. Despite the title, Gordon's study goes beyond plot summary to probe the nature and use of Joyce's language in *Finnegans Wake.* As such, he contributes significantly to an understanding of the meaning of this complex book. Gordon contends that Joyce is as wedded to realism in *Finnegans Wake* as in many of his earlier works. The difference is that Joyce has become increasingly skilled at protraying the outside world through the "prison" of an individual narrative perspective. Gordon's assessments differ on many points with most contemporary criticism, and he, therefore, provides a useful counter-balance to prevailing views. (A)

Herr, Cheryl. *Joyce's Anatomy of Culture.* Champaign: University of Illinois Press, 1986. Herr's aim is to show how Joyce modeled his work on Irish popular culture, including newspapers, pantomime, music, and sermons, which he uses to oppose institutional ideology. (A)

Herring, Philip F. *Joyce's Uncertainty Principle.* Princeton: Princeton University Press, 1987. In this specialized study, Herring attempts to go beyond riddle-solving to examine the difficulties of Joyce's arcane narrative approach as an artistic strategy. Herring proposes several new categories of

difficulty, including "gnomonic" thinking, which requires the reader to construct a portion of a novel's structural design. The discussion leads to an
analysis of Joyce's existentialist and nihilist perspectives. (A)

Kershner, R. B. *Joyce, Bakhtin, and Popular Literature: Chronicles of
Disorder.* Chapel Hill: University of North Carolina Press, 1989. Kershner's
study continues the trend started by other critics of placing Joyce more fully
in a social and cultural context. Building on theories of political and cultural
criticism—Bakhtin, Barthes, and Althusser—Kershner rejects the exclusive
view that Joyce represented the "elite artist" and attempts to account for the
Babel of popular voices he incorporated into his writings. These voices, of
course, derived from Joyce's immediate social and cultural environment. (A,G)

Maddox, Brenda. *Nora: The Real Life of Molly Bloom.* Boston: Houghton
Mifflin, 1988. For years Joyce biographers and scholars have believed little
information about Nora Barnacle existed. Maddox's impressive biography has
proven them wrong. She contends not only that Nora was a stabilizing influence on a restless and troubled man, but that she also served as the inspiration for Molly Bloom and Anna Livia Plurabelle. Maddox gleaned her data
from Joyce's unpublished letters, from public documents, and from the memoirs of people who knew the Joyces intimately. Maddox changes the picture
of Nora from country bumpkin to essential literary partner. Her work is so
well documented and indexed that even skeptical scholars will have to take a
closer look. For anyone interested in Joyce or the marital relationships of
writers, this enthusiastic biography offers interesting reading. (A,G)

Mahaffey, Vicki. *Reauthorizing Joyce.* Cambridge: Cambridge University
Press, 1988. Mahaffey's study scrutinizes Joyce's use of duality and his belief
that opposites balance and complement, rather than cancel each other. The
duality of language and experience allows Stephen Dedalus to be at once aesthetic and pragmatic, romantic and realist, or savior and demon. Joyce
combines extremes into a single all-embracing concept. In Mahaffey's scheme,
Stephen, Leopold, and Molly form a dynamic triad of complementary forces.
Despite the complexity of the ideas, the prose is clear and convincing. (A,G)

O'Sullivan, J. Colm. *Joyce's Use of Colors: "Finnegans Wake" and Earlier
Works.* Ann Arbor: UMI Research, 1987. O'Sullivan plots the occurrences and
discusses the importance of the colors that appears in Joyce's work, then
explains their contribution to thematic development. Color patterns are
particularly important in *Finnegans Wake*, and O'Sullivan's analysis opens
new understanding of Joyce's artistry. Rather than simplifying any understanding of this complicated novel, however, O'Sullivan adds layers to its
complexity, making this a study for scholars and graduate students. It contains
a comprehensive bibliography, and a thorough awareness of recent Joyce
criticism. (A)

Schwarz, Daniel R. *Reading Joyce's "Ulysses."* New York: St. Martin's,
1986. Although Stuart Gilbert's and Anthony Burgess' explications of *Ulysses*

have successfully guided readers through one of the most convoluted, difficult novels in English, Schwarz' is the first book-length study based on the controversial 1984 emended edition of the novel. Employing the elements of formal criticism, Schwarz explores how Joyce creates relationships between metaphor and allusion. He contends that Joyce consciously refused to allow every word to develop a coherent structural pattern, and thus demanded the reader to reconsider the tensions being developed as Leopold Bloom goes through his day. **(A)**

Scott, Bonnie Kime, ed. *New Alliances in Joyce Studies: "When It's Aped to Foul a Delfian."* Newark: University of Delaware Press, 1988. This anthology of recent feminist critical responses to the works of Joyce was compiled from the Philadelphia conference of 1984. The editor contends that most feminist scholarship on Joyce was produced in reaction to the critical establishment. These essays attempt to break out of the reactionary mode. **(A,G)**

Scott, Bonnie Kime. *James Joyce.* Atlantic Highlands, NJ: Humanities, 1987. Building on her previous work on the historical and biographical backgrounds of major female characters, Scott expands her feminist treatment of the women in Joyce's fiction. Going beyond simple character analyses, she applies several newer critical approaches, including neo-Marxist, lesbian, and poststructuralist. Her treatment of the myths of female origins is provocative. Of special note is her summary chart and discussion of contemporary feminist critical practices, which amounts to a useful critique of feminist criticism. **(A,G)**

Sultan, Stanley. *Eliot, Joyce, and Company.* London and New York: Oxford University Press, 1987. One of the most valuable aspects of this study is Sultan's explanation of the modernist movement. He examines how Eliot, Pound, and Joyce contributed to the movement and argues that Joyce and Pound exerted considerable influence on Eliot, especially in *The Waste Land* and "The Love Song of J. Alfred Prufrock." This readable book will assist anyone researching the development of modern literature. **(A,G)**

Torchiana, Donald T. *Backgrounds for Joyce's "Dubliners."* Winchester, MA: Allen & Unwin, 1986. Torchiana has meticulously researched the numerous place names, historical and literary references, religious saints and relics, and family names referred to by Joyce in *Dubliners.* Torchiana's scholarship is sound, and his efforts should provide students and scholars with new insights into Joyce's elusive meanings. **(A)**

Werner, Craig H. *"Dubliners": A Pluralistic World.* Boston: Twayne, 1988. Werner examines the historical context of *Dubliners* and it relationship to Joyce's other works. Part of this context includes the evolution of the critical reception of this collection of stories, which was the work that first introduced and defined Joyce's themes that would recur throughout his career. Werner ably explicates these themes and explains how they fit into various critical approaches: autobiographical, political, socio-historical, symbolic, and deconstructive. Werner not only provides an excellent guide to the stories and a good annotated bibliography, but he has also written a solid introduction for anyone beginning the difficult voyage into the works of Joyce since understanding the themes in *Dubliners* paves the way for understanding the novels. (A,G)

Other Sources

Attridge, Derek, and Daniel Ferrer, eds. *Post-Structuralist Joyce: Essays from the French.* New York: Cambridge University Press, 1985.

Beja, Morris, *et al.*, eds. *James Joyce: The Centennial Symposium.* Champaign: University of Illinois Press, 1986.

Ben-Merre, Diana A., and Maureen Murphy, eds. *James Joyce and His Contemporaries: A Centenary Tribute.* Westport, CT: Greenwood, 1989.

Benstock, Bernard, ed. *Critical Essays on James Joyce's "Ulysses."* Boston: G. K. Hall, 1989.

Benstock, Bernard, ed. *Critical Essays on James Joyce.* Boston: G. K. Hall, 1985.

Bowen, Zack R., and James F. Carens, eds. *A Companion to Joyce Studies.* Westport, CT: Greenwood, 1984.

Bowen, Zack. *"Ulysses" as a Comic Novel.* Syracuse: Syracuse University Press, 1989.

Brivic, Sheldon R. *Joyce the Creator.* Madison: University of Wisconsin Press, 1985.

Brown, Richard. *James Joyce and Sexuality.* New York: Cambridge University Press, 1989.

Card, James Van Dyck. *An Anatomy of Penelope.* Madison, NJ: Fairleigh Dickinson University Press, 1984.

Eckley, Grace. *Children's Lore in "Finnegans Wake."* Syracuse, NY: Syracuse University Press, 1985.

Eder, Doris L. *Three Writers in Exile: Eliot, Pound and Joyce.* Troy, NY: Whitston, 1985.

Freund, Gisele. *Three Days with Joyce.* Translated by Peter Ginna. New York: Persea Books, 1989.

Gaskell, Philip. *"Ulysses": A Review of Three Texts: Proposals for Alterations to the Texts of 1922, 1961, and 1984.* Totowa, NJ: Barnes & Noble, 1989.

Harkness, Marguerite. *The Aesthetics of Dedalus and Bloom.* Lewisburg, PA: Bucknell University Press, 1984.

Harkness, Marguerite. *"A Portrait of the Artist As a Young Man": Voices in the Text.* Boston: Twayne, 1990.

Hayashi, Tetsumaro, ed. *James Joyce: Research Opportunities and Dissertation Abstracts.* Jefferson, NC: McFarland, 1985.

Houston, John Porter. *Joyce and Prose: An Exploration of the Language of "Ulysses."* Lewisburg, PA: Bucknell University Press, 1989.

Keane, Patrick J. *Terrible Beauty: Yeats, Joyce, Ireland, and the Myth of the Devouring Female.* Columbia: University of Missouri Press, 1988.

Kelly, Dermot. *Narrative Strategies in Joyce's "Ulysses."* Ann Arbor: UMI Research Press, 1988.

Lanters, Jose. *Missed Understandings: A Study of the Stage Adaptations of the Works of James Joyce.* Atlantic Highlands, NJ: Humanities, 1988.

Lobner, Corinna del Greco. *James Joyce's Italian Connection: The Poetics of the Word.* Iowa City: University of Iowa Press, 1989.

Loss, Archie K. *Joyce's Visible Art: The Work of Joyce and the Visual Arts, 1904-1922.* Ann Arbor: UMI Research Press, 1984.

McCarthy, Patrick A. *"Ulysses"—Portals of Discovery.* Boston: Twayne, 1989.

Mikhail, E. H., ed. *James Joyce: Interviews and Recollections.* New York: St. Martin's, 1989.

Nadel, Ira B. *Joyce and the Jews: Culture and Texts.* Iowa City: University of Iowa Press, 1989.

Nelson, James G. *Elkin Mathews: Publisher to Yeats, Joyce, Pound.* Madison: University of Wisconsin Press, 1989.

O'Shea, Michael J. *James Joyce and Heraldry.* Albany: State University of New York Press, 1986.

Palencia-Roth, Michael. *Myth and the Modern Novel: Garcia Marquez, Mann, and Joyce.* New York: Garland, 1987.

Restuccia, Frances L. *Joyce and the Law of the Father*. New Haven: Yale University Press, 1989.

Sandulescu, C. George. *The Language and the Devil: Texture and Archetype in "Finnegans Wake."* Chester Springs, PA: Dufour, 1988.

Sandulescu, C. George, and Hart Clive, eds. *Assessing the Nineteen Eighty-Four "Ulysses."* Savage, MD: Barnes & Noble, 1986.

Schlossman, Beryl. *Joyce's Catholic Comedy of Language*. Madison: University of Wisconsin Press, 1985.

Schwarz, Daniel R. *The Transformation of the English Novel, 1890-1930*. New York: St. Martin's, 1989.

Scott, Bonnie K. *Joyce and Feminism*. Bloomington: Indiana University Press, 1984.

Staley, Thomas F., ed. *An Annotated Critical Bibliography of James Joyce*. New York: St. Martin's, 1989.

Stonehill, Brian. *The Self-Conscious Novel: Artifice in Fiction from Joyce to Pynchon*. Philadelphia: University of Pennsylvania Press, 1988.

SUNY at Buffalo Editorial Staff. *The Complete James Joyce Catalog*. Boston: G. K. Hall, 1987.

Theoharis, C. *Joyce's "Ulysses": An Anatomy of the Soul*. Chapel Hill: University of North Carolina Press, 1988.

Van Caspel, Paul. *Bloomers on the Liffey: Eisegetical Readings of Joyce's "Ulysses."* Baltimore: Johns Hopkins University Press, 1986.

Weir, Lorraine. *Writing Joyce: A Semiotics of the Joyce System*. Bloomington: Indiana University Press, 1989.

Wilhelm, James J., and Richard Saez, eds. *Death and Marriage: Self-Reflective Images of Art in Joyce and Mallarmé*. New York: Garland, 1988.

JOHN KEATS
1795-1821

Evaluation of Selected Criticism

Aske, Martin. *Keats and Hellenism: An Essay.* New York: Cambridge University Press, 1985. Aske's contention is that Keats was foredoomed to fail with his epic poems, *Endymion* and *Hyperion*, because he sought single-handedly to revive the classical forms of Hellenism. A suitable overview of the existing attitudes of contemporary historians, antiquarians, and the literati to classical literature is provided. Aske analyzes Keats' "Ode on a Grecian Urn" with special fervor. The tone of this study seems geared to create as much disturbance as possible among Keats scholars. (A)

Baker, Jeffrey. *John Keats and Symbolism.* St. Martin's, 1986. This study of Keats' major poetry is an important look at the poet's use of symbolism. Baker attributes the developing complexity of Keats' symbols to his "growing awareness of the nature and workings of the human mind." Keats uses symbolism to reveal underlying conflicts and contradictions—the problem of appearance and reality in the love poems, the conflict of aspiration and limitation in *Hyperion*, the creation of order from chaos in the great odes. Because of the clarity of Baker's prose, his book may be recommended for both graduate and undergraduate students. (A,G)

Barnard, John. *John Keats.* Cambridge: Cambridge University Press, 1987. Barnard's intent is to relate the text of the poems to the context in which they were conceived. He follows Keats from the radical poet of 1817, to the philosophic idealism and hedonism of *Endymion,* to the myth-maker of *Hyperion,* to the erotic stylist of the narrative poems, to the "spacious confines" of the odes. Barnard's solid criticism provides good insights for intermediate students. (A,G)

Bate, Jonathan. *Shakespeare and the English Romantic Imagination.* Oxford: Oxford University Press, 1986. In this well-written study, Bate examines the influence of Shakespeare on Byron, Coleridge, Wordsworth, Keats, and Blake. He examines how each poet's critical theory developed either out of or as a reaction to Shakespeare's poetic identity. This is a large field to cover, and Bate's study is a creditable overview that should be useful for anyone studying the English romantics. (A,G)

Metzger, Lore. *One Foot in Eden: Modes of Pastoral in Romantic Poetry.* Chapel Hill: University of North Carolina Press, 1986. Metzger traces the influence of classical pastoralism on the works of some of the major romantics—Blake, Coleridge, Wordsworth, and Keats. In the process, he provides an important overview of English romanticism. Drawing upon Schiller's thesis that pastoral innocence must be put to a more practical test, Metzger examines the question of whether individuality and idealism can be truthfully expressed in the same work of art. For the most part, she concludes, the English romantics only intensified the dissonance between the ideal and the real world. This book is recommended for scholars and students of the romantic period. (A)

Rzepka, Charles J. *The Self as Mind: Vision and Identity in Wordsworth, Coleridge, and Keats.* Cambridge: Harvard University Press, 1986. This award-winning study of the Romantic mind examines Coleridge, Wordsworth, and Keats as they struggled to create a place for their "visionary selves" in the external world. Rzepka examines the nature of the visionary self, its expression, and the role of the reading public in providing external affirmation of the internal experience. A thorough overview of relevant scholarship is provided through extensive documentation. (A)

Steinhoff, Stephen T., ed. *Keats's "Endymion": A Critical Edition.* Troy, NY: Whitston, 1987. This edition of Keats' poem *Endymion* has received praise for its high standard of scholarship. The book is divided into four parts—an introduction which includes a thoughtful critical analysis; the text of the poem; extensive interpretive notes; and a compilation of four reviews that appeared when Keats first published the poem (1818). In the introduction, the influence on Keats of the Elizabethans, Milton, and the early romantics are examined. Steinhoff sees Keats' poem as a theoretical bridge between romance as embodied by Spenser and the more self-conscious works of Shelley and Wordsworth. (A)

Waldoff, Leon. *Keats and the Silent Work of Imagination.* Champaign: University of Illinois Press, 1985. Waldoff examines "the crucial role of repetition of similar characters, objects, quests, themes and recognition scenes" in order to identify the unconscious workings of Keats' imagination in the major poems. Waldoff offers excellent close readings of the poems, and if his study falls prey to speculation about the imaginative process, that is the nature of romantic criticism. (A)

White, R. S. *Keats as a Reader of Shakespeare.* Norman: University of Oklahoma Press, 1987. In an empirical study of Keats's admiration for Shakespeare, White systematically documents the influence on Keats's works. He argues that the reading process is the bridge between passive reflection and active creation. This study is recommended for advanced students of Keats. (A)

Other Sources
Barth, J. Robert, and S. J. Mahoney, eds. *Coleridge, Keats, and the Imagination: Romanticism and Adam's Dream.* Columbia: University of Missouri Press, 1989.

Fleming, Ray. *Keats, Leopardi, and Holderlin: The Poet As Priest of the Absolute.* New York: Garland, 1987.

Goellnicht, Donald C. *The Poet-Physician: Keats and Medical Science.* Pittsburgh: University of Pittsburgh Press, 1984.

Goslee, Nancy M. *Uriel's Eye: Miltonic Stationing and Statuary in Blake, Keats, and Shelley.* University: University of Alabama Press, 1985.

Hagstrum, Jean H. *The Romantic Body: Love and Sexuality in Keats, Wordsworth, and Blake.* Knoxville: University of Tennessee Press, 1986.

Jugurtha, Lillie B. *Keats and Nature.* New York: Peter Lang, 1985.

Marquess, William H. *Lives of the Poet: The First Century of Keats Biography.* University Park: The Pennsylvania State University Press, 1985.

Plooard, David. *The Poetry of Keats: Language and Experience.* New York: Barnes & Noble, 1985.

Rhodes, Jack W. *Keats' Major Odes: An Annotated Bibliography of the Criticism.* Westport, CT: Greenwood, 1984.

Ricks, Christopher. *Keats and Embarrassment.* New York: Oxford University Press, 1984.

Ward, Aileen. *John Keats: The Making of a Poet.* [Rev. ed.] New York: Farrar, Straus & Giroux, 1986.

Watkins, Daniel P. *Keats' Poetry and the Politics of the Imagination.* Madison, NJ: Fairleigh Dickinson University Press, 1989.

Wolfson, Susan. *The Questioning Presence: Wordsworth, Keats and the Interrogative Mode in Romantic Poetry.* Ithaca, NY: Cornell University Press, 1986.

Yost, George. *Keats's Apprenticeship.* New York: Peter Lang, 1988.

JACK KEROUAC
1922-1969

Evaluation of Selected Biography and Criticism
Cassady, Carolyn. *Off the Road: My Years with Cassady, Kerouac, and Ginsberg*. New York: William Morrow, 1990. The famous literary and sexual ménage-à-quatre, Neal, Carolyn, Jack, and Allen, is authentically and touchingly rendered by the educated, beautiful upper middle-class woman who thought she could tame charismatic Neal Cassady, convicted automobile thief and self-proclaimed wild man. Married to Neal, Carolyn was lover to Jack and friend to Allen, and she tells all their stories of love and literary ambition, bringing to life the counterculture that turned Kerouac and Ginsberg into heroes. She possesses genuine insight into their personalities and is able to explain why each man was possessed by genius. **(A,G)**

French, Warren. *Jack Kerouac*. Boston: Twayne, 1986. As part of Twayne's United States Authors series, this study offers a more serious view of Kerouac's life and works than is typically presented. French views Kerouac as a visionary writer who tried to live a self-generated legend. Going beyond *On the Road*, French examines many of the lesser-known works, including the series known as the "Duluoz Legend." This is a thoughtful work that attempts to change the tenor of Kerouac criticism. **(A,G)**

Kerouac, Jan. *Trainsong*. Orlando, FL: Holt, 1988. This autobiographical account by the restless daughter of Jack Kerouac reveals her desire to discover the father she never really knew. Jan's travels over the globe are full of parallels, even allusions, to her father's writings. **(G)**

Weinreich, Regina. *The Spontaneous Poetics of Jack Kerouac: A Study of the Fiction*. Carbondale: Southern Illinois University Press, 1987. Weinreich examines Kerouac's nineteen volumes in terms of style and thematic content, exploring the thesis that each is merely a single element of "one vast book." Weinreich's intent is to draw critical attention away from a focus on Kerouac's biography so that the novels can be viewed in a more objective light. **(A,G)**

Other Sources
Clark, Tom. *Kerouac's Last Word: Jack Kerouac in Escapade*. Sudbury, MA: Water Row Press, 1987.

Knight, Kit, and Arthur Knight, eds. *Kerouac and the Beats: A Primary Sourcebook*. New York: Paragon House, 1988.

RUDYARD KIPLING
1865-1936

Evaluation of Selected Biography and Criticism

Cortazzi, Hugh, and George Webb, eds. *Kipling's Japan: Collected Writings*. Atlantic Highlands, NJ: Athlone Press, 1987. Kipling's journalistic accounts of his travels are often as interesting, if less read, than his fiction. The editors have recovered accounts of his Japanese adventure from 1889-1892, including published journalism, letters, stories, and some previously unpublished poems and lectures. The editors carefully annotate their sources, explaining terms and connotations, and providing the context for these works. Recommended for serious Kipling students and scholars. **(A)**

Crook, Nora. *Kipling's Myths of Love and Death*. New York: St. Martin's, 1990. Crook argues that Kipling derived the "mythic resonances" that are reflected in his plot, characters, and language from other writers: the Pre-Raphaelites, Dante, Chaucer, and Swinburne. The result of her academic sleuthing into sources breaks some new ground in understanding Kipling's intentions. Includes scholarly apparatus. **(A)**

Kemp, Sandra. *Kipling's Hidden Narratives*. London: Blackwell, 1988. Kemp uses the guiding theme of "divided identity" to explore over one hundred of Kipling's stories and tales. For Kemp, this divided identity comprises four parts: subjective self versus cultural codes, the ambivalence of narrative voice, equivocation and silence, and madness. Kemp is particularly insightful in her assessment of the role of religion and the influence of women on Kipling's writings. Six chapters of the study deal with Kipling's subject matter: India, the occult, fantasy, modernism, war, and Christianity. Recommended at the graduate level. **(A,G)**

Laski, Marghanita. *From Palm to Pine: Rudyard Kipling Abroad and At Home*. New York: Facts on File, 1987. Derived from a BBC series on Kipling, this abundantly illustrated book is a survey of the author's life and accomplishments. Laski relates individual works to the geography of Kipling's extensive travels. Focusing on India, Africa, and North America, she quotes liberally from his writings, revealing how his experiences influenced his view of himself and the human condition. A well-rounded portrait of the author and man emerges. This is a highly recommended work of popular literary criticism. **(A,G)**

Mallett, Phillip, ed. *Kipling Considered*. New York: St. Martin's, 1989. The nine essays include topics on Kipling's language, use of names, and his world view. The argument over Kipling's morality continues, with some contributors still clinging to Orwell's pronouncement that Kipling was "morally insensitive" and "aesthetically disgusting." Although nothing links these essays except the subject, students may find the individual topics enlightening. (A,G)

Moore-Gilbert, B. J. *Kipling and "Orientalism"*. New York: St. Martin's, 1986. This book offers an informative excursion into Kipling's place in Anglo-Indian literature. Moore-Gilbert traces shared themes among Anglo-Indian writers, such as "domestic instability" and "the white man's grave," and presents a much fuller picture of Kipling's attitudes toward Indian literature than has previously been available. (A,G)

Paffard, Mark. *Kipling's Indian Fiction*. New York: St. Martin's, 1989. As with most Kipling critics with a social orientation, Paffard rejects Kipling as a critic of India's colonial society. He argues that Kipling's knowledge of India was already commonplace in England and that he merely used the culture to manipulate his own values. On the other hand, Paffard admires Kipling's craft and this study is a clearly stated, if unoriginal, analysis of Kipling's failures and achievements. (A)

Seymour-Smith, Martin. *Rudyard Kipling*. New York: St. Martin's, 1990. Seymour-Smith's thesis is that Kipling was a repressed homosexual with sadomasochistic tendencies. This study caused controversy in Britain because of its portrayal of Kipling as a self-loathing, petty-spirited imperialist. Seymour-Smith is much more generous with his treatment of Kipling's lesser known stories, many of which are examined closely here for the first time. This work is purposely provocative but not overly persuasive. (A)

Trodd, Anthea. *Domestic Crime in the Victorian Novel*. New York: St. Martin's, 1989. Trodd uses the patterns of domestic crime in fiction as a barometer of changing Victorian attitudes and social values. Early Victorian households cleaved to the rights of privacy and autonomy, no matter what the internal abuse. This gradually gave way to a belief in the right of the public to expose and punish domestic crimes. Trodd's cross-disciplinary approach provides fruitful insights into the roles of women and crimes against them, the roles of servants as perpetrators and victims, and the sensationalism of the courtroom. Offering impressive scope, this study examines fiction by such diverse authors as Kipling, Collins, Hardy, and Gaskell. (A,G)

Other Sources
Orelan, Harold, ed. *Critical Essays on Rudyard Kipling*. Boston: G. K. Hall, 1989.

ARTHUR KOESTLER
1905-1983

Evaluation of Selected Criticism

Day, Frank. *Arthur Koestler: A Guide to Research.* New York: Garland, 1987. This compact research guide provides annotated citations of both primary and secondary sources for the study of Koestler's life and works. The entries are arranged chronologically within various subgroupings. Koestler's writings are organized by novels, drama, autobiography, essays, contributions to books and periodicals, interviews, and lectures. The secondary sources include biographies, critical works, essays, and reviews. The short introduction provides basic biographical information and an overview of Koestler's fiction and nonfiction. **(A)**

Goodman, Celia, ed. *Living with Koestler: Mamaine Koestler's Letters, 1945-51.* London: Weidenfeld & Nicolson, 1985. Between 1945 and 1951, Mamaine Koestler corresponded frequently with her twin sister, Celia Goodman, who is the compiler and editor of this collection of letters and diary extracts. Goodman expands the contexts of the letters in annotations derived from interviews with Arthur Koestler, who separated from Mamaine in 1951. The tone of these letters is personal, ususally addressing the incidentals of daily life. The content is also suggestive of Koestler's attitudes, preoccupations, and publication dealings during these years. This is a useful, if unexciting, primary source for biographical information. **(A,G)**

CHARLES LAMB
1775-1834

Evaluation of Selected Criticism

McFarland, Thomas. *Romantic Cruxes: The English Essayists and the Spirit of the Age*. Oxford: Clarendon, 1987. This concise study addresses romanticism as expressed by the English essayists Hazlitt, Lamb, and De Quincey. These writers emphasized nature, imagination, egotism, medieval imagining, and dreams. McFarland reveals Lamb to have been a more influential cultural figure than is currently appreciated. He examines Hazlitt's standing debate with Coleridge over the workings of the imagination for its political and social implications. McFarland attempts to recapture the importance of these essayists and remove them from the shadow of the major romantic poets. (A,G)

Other Sources

Monsman, Gerald. *Confessions of a Prosaic Dreamer: Charles Lamb's Art of Autobiography*. Durham: Duke University Press, 1984.

WILLIAM LANGLAND
1330?-1390?

Evaluation of Selected Criticism

Alford, John A., and M. Teresa Tavormina, eds. *The Yearbook of Langland Studies, Volumes 1-3*. East Lansing, MI: Colleagues Press, 1987, 1988, 1989. This series of books compiles significant articles, notes, reviews, and bibliographical references that address Langland, *Piers Plowman* and closely related subjects. Most of the important aspects of Langland scholarship will be addressed in the pages of these books, which are scheduled to be published annually. **(A)**

Bowers, John M. *The Crisis of Will in "Piers Plowman."* Washington, DC: Catholic University of America Press, 1986. By examining the thought of Scotus, Ockham, and Holcot, Bowers establishes the intellectual context within which Langland composed his masterwork, *Piers Plowman.* Langland, a theological conservative, responded to the religious turmoil of his era by creating the character of Will, an idealistic dreamer, who failed to recognize his spiritual potential due to sloth. Langland's poem has long been considered difficult, but Bowers provides dependable guidance through its themes, images, and intentions. **(A)**

Davlin, Mary Clemente. *A Game of Heuene: Word Play and the Meaning of "Piers Plowman" B*. Cambridge: D.S. Brewer, 1989. In one passage of the poem, the character Wit describes human speech as "a game of heuene"—an ambiguous metaphor that might mean "heavenly game," "divine jest," or "pleasing to god." Langland probably intended to communicate all of these intentions at once, thus creating a complex layering of meanings and structures that make the poem difficult to interpret. For example, Davlin contends that "the structural strangeness of *Piers Plowman* causes the reader to enter into a particular way of looking at experience, perceiving all forms of poverty and, at the same time, the faithful presence of God *within* this poverty." **(A)**

Godden, Malcolm. *The Making of "Piers Plowman"*. London: Longman, 1990. *Piers Plowman* exists in four versions that Langland composed throughout his lifetime. Godden argues that the poem in all of its versions represents the dreamer-poet's lifelong quest; the poem is a dialectic that Langland conducted with himself, and which he wrote down so that he could more fully understand his thoughts. Each of the versions is a record of the stages of Langland's quest, which explains why the poem contains contradictions. This fascinating thesis is for any serious reader. **(A,G)**

Griffiths, Lavinia. *Personification in "Piers Plowman."* Cambridge: D.S. Brewer, 1985. Griffiths examines Langland's use of allegory and personification in *Piers Plowman* within the context of the literary conventions of the age. She finds that the rhetorical device of personification is employed differently—both in frequency and range—by Langland than by other medieval writers, such as Boethius, Bernard Sylvester, Alain de Liffle, Guillaume de Lorris, or Chaucer. **(A)**

Schmidt, A.V.C. *The Clerkly Maker: Langland's Poetic Art.* Cambridge: D.S. Brewer, 1987. In this narrowly focused study, Schmidt examines three areas of Langland's poetic art—versecraft, diction, and wordplay. Schmidt contends that Langland partook of the "makerly" qualities of the alliterative tradition, yet was deeply colored by his "clerkly" culture, that is, by his role as a clergyman. This study is appropriate for specialists. **(A)**

Simpson, James. *"Piers Plowman": An Introduction to the B-Text.* New York: Longman, 1990. The purpose of this guide to Langland's *Piers Plowman*, is to make this difficult work more accessible to undergraduate students of early English literature. Simpson contends that the major theme of the poem is the dynamic relationship between justice and mercy. Meaning in the poem is generated less from character than from the interweaving of various genres of writing that constitute the work. Chapters are devoted to unravelling each of the eight visions. **(A,G)**

White, Hugh. *Nature and Salvation in "Piers Plowman."* Cambridge: D.S. Brewer, 1988. In this specialized study, White examines Langland's use of the word *kynde* (nature) and related concepts in *Piers Plowman*. Langland's idea of the natural encompasses not only the natural world but also the idea of human kindness. As developed in the poem, the term is eventually identified with God and is seen to play an important role in the salvation of humankind. **(A)**

Other Sources
Holloway, Julia B. *The Pilgrim and the Book: A Study of Dante, Langland and Chaucer.* New York: Peter Lang, 1987.

SIDNEY LANIER
1842-1881

Evaluation of Selected Criticism
   Gabin, Jane S. *A Living Minstrelsy: The Poetry and Music of Sidney Lanier*. Macon, GA: Mercer University Press, 1985. In this study, Gabin examines how Lanier's passion for music and poetry infused his life and works. Without his musical experiences, she argues, his poetry would never have been created. Gabin reexamines the biographical events, focusing on the trauma of the Civil War and Lanier's experience as a prisoner of war during which he contracted tuberculosis. Following the war he rejected a career in law for music and, ultimately, literature. His development as a professional musician allowed him to create "musical" poems of increasing complexity and texture. This is a pleasing biography of Lanier that casts light upon the lush qualities of his poetry. (A,G)

PHILIP LARKIN
1922-1985

Evaluation of Selected Criticism

Day, Roger. *Larkin*. Milton Keynes: Open University Press, 1987. This introduction to Larkin is in effect a tutorial that asks basic questions, such as the uses for metaphor and absence of rhyme, about the poems in Larkin's first three collections. Day's book, which may be difficult to find in the U.S., does not address Larkin's place among modern poets. (G)

Harvey, Geoffrey. *The Romantic Tradition in Modern English Poetry: Rhetoric and Experience*. New York: St. Martin's, 1986. Harvey fashions a framework of rational sympathy and rhetorical balance to gather Wordsworth, Hardy, Betjeman, and Larkin within a single poetic tradition. He then discusses the complex relationship between the "native English tradition" and emerging modernism. (A,G)

Hassan, Salem K. *Philip Larkin and His Contemporaries: An Air of Authenticity*. New York: St. Martin's, 1988. Larkin is one of modern poetry's most skilled craftsmen, and Hassan's study explores at length how craft affects the meaning. This is a ponderous explication for all but Larkin scholars and critics. The remainder of the study compares Larkin's response to the modern world with that of his British contemporaries: Thom Gunn, D. J. Enright, Kingsley Amis, and John Wain. The second section provides a basic introduction to each of these writers. (A)

Lucas, John. *Modern English Poetry from Hardy to Hughes: A Critical Survey*. Totowa, NJ: Barnes & Noble, 1986. The study uses socialist theory to select those modern English poets whose stance is communal rather than personal. As such it is not really a survey. For example, Lucas neglects Lawrence, Pound, and women poets, while giving extended attention to Eliot, Yeats, Larkin, and Igor Gurney. The value of this study suffers from its narrow ideological focus. (A)

Salwak, Dale, ed. *Philip Larkin: The Man and His Work*. Iowa City: University of Iowa Press, 1988. Larkin's quiet, unassuming life as a librarian, combined with his talent and wit, won him many admirers and friends, including Kingsley Amis, John Bayley, David Lodge, and X. J. Kennedy. In this collection of essays and memoirs, they offer an affectionate insider's view of a private man who loved jazz and valued his friends. (A,G)

MARGARET LAURENCE
1926-1987

Author's Recent Bibliography
Dance on the Earth, 1987 (novel).

Evaluation of Selected Criticism
   Buss, Helen M. *Mother and Daughter Relationships in the Manawaka Works of Margaret Laurence.* Victoria: English Literary Studies, University of Victoria, 1985. Adopting an "archetypal" approach, Buss considers Laurence's depiction of mothers and daughters as a manifestation of unconscious energy along the lines of the Demeter-Kore prototype. Buss contends that Laurence is a pioneer and the greatest practitioner in the contemporary movement of Canadian women writing about women. (A,G)

   York, Lorraine M. *"The Other Side of Dailiness": Photography in the Works of Alice Munro, Timothy Findley, Michael Ondaathe, and Margaret Laurence.* Toronto: ECW Press, 1988. York examines the blend of photography and storytelling that come together in the works of Margaret Laurence, a "photographic novelist." York contends that the influence of photography and films led Laurence away from more traditional forms of narrative, culminating in her two most visual works *The Fire Dwellers,* and *The Diviners.* She construes Laurence's works as confrontations between the present and the past. (A,G)

DAVID HERBERT LAWRENCE
1885-1930

Autobiographical Sources

Healey, E. Claire, and Keith Cushman, eds. *The Letters of D. H. Lawrence and Amy Lowell, 1914-1925*. Santa Barbara, CA: Black Sparrow Press, 1985. Lowell and Lawrence met in 1914 in London at a dinner she contrived for imagist poets. Over the next ten years, they corresponded frequently. Eighty-four of their letters survive, fifty-three from Lawrence's pen. The two vastly different personalities found that they had a common devotion to poetry. Lawrence became Lowell's critic, prowling through her verse, as he said, "like a beast of prey." His criticisms, however, reveal considerable tact. Lowell, for her part, promoted Lawrence's work in the U.S. **(A,G)**

Evaluation of Selected Biography and Criticism

Alden, Patricia. *Social Mobility in the English Bildungsroman: Gissing, Hardy, Bennett, and Lawrence*. Ann Arbor: UMI Research, 1986. The expression of a sense of upward social mobility in the late-nineteenth and early twentieth-century bildungsroman differed significantly from previous conceptions in the same genre. Many writers of the time believed that the upward mobility of the individual was a progressive phenomenon. Gissing, Hardy, Bennett, and Lawrence, on the other hand, viewed the process as a regressive disintegration of individual character. As portrayed in their works, the struggle to break out of one's social class leads only to frustration, alienation, and loss of identity. **(A,G)**

Black, Michael. *D. H. Lawrence: The Early Fiction, A Commentary*. Cambridge: Cambridge University Press, 1986. After providing a concise overview of the state of Lawrence criticism in England, Black looks more closely at the writings before *Sons and Lovers*. Because Lawrence was not a systematic thinker, Black examines his use of language and imagery to reveal his fictional themes. He concludes that the key to Lawrence's work is his "ethic of fidelity to the instinctual self." This clearly written study is recommended as an introduction to Lawrence's critical reputation. **(A,G)**

Bonds, Diane. *Language and the Self in D. H. Lawrence*. Ann Arbor: UMI Research, 1987. Bonds applies the theories of Paul de Man and J. Hillis Miller to *Sons and Lovers*, *The Rainbow*, and *Women in Love*. In his use of language, she concludes, Lawrence has devised a means "both to liberate and imprison the self." She then turns to several of his essays on psychoanalysis to piece together Lawrence's (unconscious) theory of language. **(A)**

Britton, Derek. *"Lady Chatterley": The Making of the Novel*. Boston: Unwin Hyman, 1988. In this, Britton's third book on *Lady Chatterley's Lover*, he relies on interviews and ordnance survey maps as he traces the novel's biographical background, local geography, and revisions, as well as to explore Lawrence's final days. The result is a masterful explanation of how Lawrence's social, psychological, and medical circumstances were transformed into art. Britton reveals how Lawrence's tuberculosis, his wife's infidelity, his return to the Midlands, and his response to the miner's strike contributed to making his last novel his boldest. (A,G)

Burgess, Anthony. *Flame into Being: The Life and Work of D. H. Lawrence.* New York: Arbor House, 1985. Burgess has written influential biographical/critical studies of Joyce and Shakespeare. Here he applies his critical acumen to Lawrence, arguing how the life permeates the work. The pleasure of reading Burgess on Lawrence is twofold; in many ways they are similar men and similar writers. Burgess not only understands Lawrence's fiction, he has lived the creative process behind it. Even if this is not the most scholarly of the many Lawrence studies produced on the centenary of his birth, it is certainly one of the best written and most provocative. (A)

Ellis, David, and Howard Mills. *D. H. Lawrence's Non-Fiction: Art, Thought, and Genre.* Cambridge: Cambridge University Press, 1988. Recent years have seen a reassessment of Lawrence's gifts as a writer of non-fiction. This collection of six essays by Ellis and Mills examines Lawrence's travel books, memoirs and sketches, reviews, and essays. The authors contend that Lawrence's non-fiction displays a creativity and originality that match his fiction. The authors explain their choice of texts in the introduction and analyze selected works in depth. (A)

Harris, Janice Hubbard. *The Short Fiction of D. H. Lawrence.* New Brunswick, NJ: Rutgers University Press, 1984. In Harris' view, Lawrence's early short stories showed an acceptance of Continental realism and were a radical break from the form of the traditional English tale. She argues that he later turned to the use of fables and exemplars to provide spiritual illumination. (A,G)

Heywood, Christopher. *D. H. Lawrence: New Studies.* New York: St. Martin's, 1987. This is a collection of papers presented at a recent Lawrence conference. Colin Holmes' essay on Lawrence's working-class background and R. P. Draper's survey of his poetry should be of particular interest to Lawrence scholars. (A)

Jackson, Dennis, and Felda Brown Jackson. *Critical Essays on D. H. Lawrence.* Boston: G. K. Hall, 1988. The Jacksons provide a lengthy introduction that traces the editions and critical studies of Lawrence's works from the 1930s to 1985. The essays that follow cover twelve novels, four plays, the first volume of the letters, and one poem. The final essay is especially useful in explaining how Lawrence developed as a poet. (A,G)

Kalnins, Mara, ed. *D. H. Lawrence: Centenary Essays.* Cransberry, NJ: Classical Press, 1986. This is a collection of nine excellent essays by noted

scholars on the writer's significance. Among the topics examined are
Lawrence's attachment to his birthplace, the errors of feminist attacks on
Lawrence, his view of the nature of the mind, and his marriage themes.
Essayists include Kalnins, John Worthen, Laurence Lerner, David Ellis, John
Turner, Mark Kinkead-Weekes, George Donaldson, and Michael Black on the
progress of the Cambridge edition of the collected works. This anthology
provides a good overview of the author's reputation at the beginning of a
second hundred years. **(A)**

Laird, Holly A. *Self and Sequence: The Poetry of D. H. Lawrence.*
Charlottesville: University Press of Virginia, 1988. Laird analyzes the
published order and revisions of Lawrence's poetry to develop ideas about his
"nostalgic" voice, dramatic engagement with the poem's moment, and attack
on the concept of Christian self-sacrifice. Laird also explores the power of
animals as reflections of the mysterious force of sexuality and the alien nature
of women—themes that dominate all of Lawrence's work. She argues with
clarity and intelligence that Lawrence did not intend for his poems to be
regarded as individual lyrics but as part of a verse cycle. Laird's ideas are
new, and invaluable to advanced students and scholars. **(A)**

Lawrence, D. H. *Memoir of Maurice Magnus.* Edited by Keith Cushman.
Santa Rosa, CA: Black Sparrow, 1987. Lawrence feuded with Norman
Douglas over this memoir, and this volume contains the original text, the
correspondence between Lawrence and Douglas, and excerpts from Magnus'
book *Memoir of the Foreign Legion.* Of interest are Lawrence's passages
dealing with homosexuality, not published in the original edition, as well as
beautiful character sketches. **(A)**

Lockwood, M. J. *A Study of the Poems of D. H. Lawrence: Thinking in
Poetry.* New York: St. Martin's, 1987. Lockwood convincingly argues that
Lawrence first worked out his principal ideas through his poetry, then expanded them in his fiction. The value of this study to students is the clear
manner in which Lockwood discusses the kernels of Lawrence's philosophy
that are developed into fictional themes. It also demonstrates the importance
of studying the poetry and fiction together. **(A)**

MacLeod, Shelia. *Lawrence's Men and Women.* London: Heinemann, 1985.
MacLeod argues that Lawrence saw himself as self-consciously male, and that
his most important relationships were with strong women whom he found
both attractive and threatening. She applies this thesis to Lawrence's
characters and postulates that their emotional uncertainty comes from
Lawrence's own psychic imbalance. **(A)**

Miliaras, Barbara A. *Pillar of Flame: The Mythological Foundations of
D. H. Lawrence's Sexual Philosophy.* New York: Peter Lang, 1987. Lawrence
enriched his fiction through his knowledge of Nordic, Celtic, and Oriental
mythology. In this study, Miliaras examines his use of myth in *Women in
Love, The Rainbow,* and earlier novels. She goes beyond Lawrence's fiction to

describe his tendency to mythologize his world, himself, and especially women. She suggests that Lawrence's mythologizing of women— together with his ambivalent attitude toward his mother—prevented him from ever establishing a mature relationship. (A,G)

Murfin, Ross C. *"Sons and Lovers": A Novel of Division and Desire.* Boston: Twayne, 1987. Murfin provides a clear analysis of themes and characters, developing a thesis that the novel derives its power from the motif of the "divided self." This is a good general introduction for students. (G)

Sagar, Keith. *D. H. Lawrence: Life into Art.* Athens, GA: University of Georgia Press, 1985. Sagar, author of *The Art of D. H. Lawrence* and *The Life of D. H. Lawrence*, has produced a critical study that stakes out a middle ground between documentary biography and orthodox literary criticism. Beginning with the thesis that a writer's work is firmly grounded in his life, Sagar examines Lawrence's readings, travels, and relationships to explain his creative development. He focuses on "breakthrough" moments: the discipline of the working-class dramas, the discovery of ironic perspective, the emphasis on emotional pattern rather than form in the poetry, and Lawrence's use of the novel to explore deeper layers of the human psyche. This book is of interest to both academic and general readers. (A,G)

Schneider, Daniel J. *The Consciousness of D. H. Lawrence: An Intellectual Biography.* Lawrence: University Press of Kansas, 1986. According to Schneider, Lawrence was a Ghandi-like religious figure who believed, among other things, that contact with women weakened his visionary purpose. This study unpacks Lawrence's acknowledged neuroses, rationalizes them, then repackages them into a sanitized image of Lawrence the passionate "monk." (A,G)

Whelan, P.T. *D. H. Lawrence: Myth and Metaphysic in "The Rainbow" and "Women in Love."* Ann Arbor: UMI Research, 1988. In this complex study of *The Rainbow* and *Women in Love*, Whelan examines the underlying intellectual concepts embodied in Lawrence's fiction. For Whelan, these two novels are in essence a single work linked by identifiable "structure and laws." Drawing upon the theories of Harrison, Frazer, and Jung, Whalen isolates mythic motifs of the hero in *The Rainbow*, and shows how they are developed in *Women in Love*. Whalen delves into the metaphysical aspects of the novels and concludes that Lawrence reworked elements of theosophy, mysticism, and the occult arts, incorporating them into the characters, structure, and plot. (A,G)

Whiteley, Patrick J. *Knowledge and Experimental Realism in Conrad, Lawrence, and Woolf.* Baton Rouge: Louisiana State University Press, 1987. Whiteley offers a good analysis of all three writers' works as he explains how each writer thought people perceived reality, and how they embodied this perceptual process in their fiction. The quest for self-knowledge and its implications on people's relationships is, in Whiteley's opinion, the important thread that ties these three writers together and established the groundwork for the modern psychological novel. (A)

Worthen, John. *D. H. Lawrence: A Literary Life*. New York: St. Martin's, 1989. Worthen's study of Lawrence emphasizes the economic hardship of the revolutionary novelist and poet. Lawrence writes an explicit novel, *The Rainbow*, and suffers ostracism and economic oppression as a result. The coal-miner's son turned serious author refuses to give up and continues to create his art for coal miner's wages. (A,G)

Other Sources

Balbert, Peter, and Philip L. Marcus, eds. *D. H. Lawrence: A Centenary Consideration*. Ithaca: Cornell University Press, 1985.

Balbert, Peter. *D. H. Lawrence and the Phallic Imagination: Essays on Sexual Identity and Feminist Misreading*. New York: St. Martin's, 1989.

Cowan, James C., ed. *D. H. Lawrence: An Annotated Bibliography of Writings about Him, Vol. 2*. De Kalb: Northern Illinois University Press, 1985.

Daleski, H. M. *The Forked Flame: A Study of D. H. Lawrence*. Madison: University of Wisconsin Press, 1987.

Das, G. K., and Gamini Salgado, eds. *The Spirit of D. H. Lawrence: Centenary Studies*. Totowa, NJ: Barnes & Noble, 1988.

Gertzman, Jay A. *A Descriptive Bibliography of "Lady Chatterly's Lover": With Essays Toward a Publishing History of the Novel*. Westport, CT: Greenwood, 1989.

Harvey, Geoffrey. *"Sons and Lovers": An Introduction to the Variety of Criticism*. Atlantic Highlands, NJ: Humanities, 1986.

Holderness, Graham. *"Women in Love."* New York: Open University Press/Taylor & Francis, 1986.

Lawrence, D. H. *Movements in European History*. Edited by Philip Crumpton. New York: Cambridge University Press, 1989.

Lebolt, Gladys. *D. H. Lawrence: The True Redeemers?* Tuscaloosa: Portals Press, 1985.

Mackey, Douglas A. *D. H. Lawrence: The Poet Who Was Not Wrong*. San Bernardino: Borgo Press, 1986.

Mandell, Gail P. *The Phoenix Paradox: A Study of Renewal Through Change in the "Collected Poems" and "Last Poems" of D. H. Lawrence.* Carbondale: Southern Illinois University Press, 1984.

Meyers, Jeffrey, ed. *D. H. Lawrence and Tradition.* Amherst: University of Massachusetts Press, 1985.

Meyers, Jeffrey. *The Legacy of D. H. Lawrence.* New York: St. Martin's, 1987.

Meyers, Jeffrey. *D. H. Lawrence: A Biography.* New York: Knopf, 1990.

Milton, Colin. *Lawrence and Nietzsche: A Study in Influence.* Elmsford, NY: Pergamon, 1987.

Nixon, Cornelia. *Lawrence's Leadership Politics and the Turn Against Women.* Berkeley: University of California Press, 1986.

Padhi, Bibhu. *D. H. Lawrence: Modes of Fictional Style.* Troy, NY: Whitston, 1988.

Preston, Peter, and Peter Hoare, eds. *D. H. Lawrence in the Modern World.* New York: Cambridge University Press, 1989.

Scheckner, Peter. *Class, Politics, and the Individual: A Study of the Major Works of D. H. Lawrence.* Madison, NJ: Fairleigh Dickinson University Press, 1985.

Schwarz, Daniel R. *The Transformation of the English Novel, 1890-1930.* New York: St. Martin's, 1989.

Sinha, Radha K. *Literary Influences on D. H. Lawrence.* Columbia, MO: Chanakya India/South Asia Books, 1985.

Squires, Michael, and Dennis Jackson, eds. *D. H. Lawrence's "Lady": A New Look at "Lady Chatterly's Lover."* Athens: University of Georgia Press, 1985.

Stevens, C. J. *Lawrence at Tregerthen.* Troy, NY: Whitston, 1988.

Templeton, Wayne. *States of Estrangement: The Novels of D. H. Lawrence, 1912-1917.* Troy, NY: Whitston, 1989.

Worthen, John. *D. H. Lawrence: A Literary Life.* New York: St. Martin's, 1989.

LAYAMON
fl. 1200

Evaluation of Selected Criticism

Baron, W. R. J. and S. C. Weinberg, eds. and trans. *Layamon's Arthur: The Arthurian Section of Layamon's "Brut."* Austin: University of Texas Press, 1989. This, the second translation of *Brut* in the same year, serves a different purpose than Donald Bzdyl's. This edition contains the original text with a facing page translation that is more literal than Bzdyl's more readable, poetic, and modern verse. The editors provide an extensive introduction explaining the poem's social, cultural, and linguistic contexts; narrative style; and characterization of Arthur. More narrowly focused than Bzdyl and thus more detailed, this edition offers a promising tool for medieval scholars. **(A)**

Bzdyl, Donald G., ed. and trans. *Layamon's "Brut": A History of the Britons.* Binghamton: Medieval & Renaissance Texts & Studies, 1989. Layamon's *Brut*, a sixteen-thousand-line poem composed in Middle English, recounts the mythical history of the kings of Britain. It is considered vital for an understanding of the origins of English literature, yet has been largely unavailable for study because of the lack of a modern translation. This edition of the poem, newly translated by Bzdyl, will make the poem more accessible to students. Bzdyl's introduction provides a context for the poem's composition, transmission, and translation. The text is presented without annotations to encourage reading for interest and pleasure. A useful index to the poem is provided. **(A,G)**

SHERIDAN LE FANU
1814-1873

Evaluation of Selected Criticism

    Melada, Ivan. *Sheridan Le Fanu*. Boston: Twayne, 1987. In this volume in Twayne's English Authors Series, Melada discusses the entire range of Le Fanu's fiction. A prolific writer, Le Fanu published thirteen three-volume novels, a two-volume and one-volume novel, forty-three stories, and a book of poetry. In separate chapters Melada discusses the early fiction, historical novels, suspense novels, the late short fiction, serial fiction, and poetry. He gives an excellent close reading to Le Fanu's major work, *Uncle Silas* (1864). Like the other titles in the series, this study includes a chronology and an annotated bibliography of secondary sources, making it a good introductory treatment for students. (A,G)

C. S. LEWIS
1898-1963

Evaluation of Selected Biography and Criticism

Christopher, Joe R. *C. S. Lewis.* Boston: Twayne, 1987. Christopher opens with Lewis' biography, then proceeds to analyze the book-length works, including Lewis' autobiography, criticism, and romances. He argues that even though Lewis denounced biographical criticism, there are passages in the work that have biographical roots; he also argues that if one reads Lewis as literature rather than as religion or philosophy, he is one of the best writers of his time. In formulating this argument, Christopher provides interesting interpretations of theme and style. Because this study is so clearly written, it can be profitably used by all students. **(A,G)**

Edwards, Bruce L., ed. *The Taste of the Pineapple: Essays on C. S. Lewis as Reader, Critic, and Imaginative Writer.* Bowling Green, OH: Bowling Green Popular Press, 1988. These fourteen essays examine Lewis' critical theories, his rhetorical strategies, and the relationship of his criticism to his imaginative work. This readable, useful book will give readers a good understanding of a writer who is both loved and neglected for the wrong reasons. **(A,G)**

Gresham, Douglas H. *Lenten Lands: My Childhood with Joy Davidman and C. S. Lewis.* New York: Macmillan, 1988. Gresham was Lewis' stepson, and he provides an affectionate portrait of a literary master who was as loyal to family and friends as to his art. The coverage here is particularly good for Lewis' later and most productive years. **(A,G)**

Griffin, William. *Clive Staples Lewis: A Dramatic Life.* New York: Harper & Row, 1986. The facts of Lewis' life are all here, but the disjointed presentation makes it difficult for the reader to tell how Lewis thinks and feels about his interactions with the world. Griffin leaves connections between events mostly unstated, presumably to encourage the reader to draw his own conclusions. **(A,G)**

Manlove, C. N. *C. S. Lewis: His Literary Achievement.* New York: St. Martin's, 1987. Manlove examines all of Lewis' book-length fiction, excluding *The Screwtape Letters.* He analyzes image and plot patterns to reveal the richness and complexity of Lewis' fictional creations. Of particular note is the illuminating discussion of *The Pilgrim's Regress.* **(A,G)**

Sammons, Martha C. *A Better Country: The Worlds of Religious Fantasy and Science Fiction.* Westport, CT: Greenwood Press, 1988. Sammons begins with an analytical discussion of the fantasy works of Tolkien and Lewis and pursues the religious themes revealed there through a range of modern science fiction/fantasy writers. She examines the nature and depiction of evil, the description of the struggle of good and evil, and ultimately how evil may be overcome. Of particular note, is her discussion of the biblical and mythological sources of these works. (A,G)

Wilson, A. N. *C. S. Lewis: A Biography*. New York: Norton, 1990. This is probably the best biography to date on Lewis. Although steeped in psychoanalytic theory, Wilson avoids much of the reductionism and jargon of other "psychobiographies." His use of previously untapped primary sources yields new insights into Lewis' involvement with the Oxford Circle, the Inklings, and Tolkien. Lewis' reworking of myths and childhood fables is firmly placed in the English romantic tradition of Wordsworth and Yeats. A thoughtful, tempered treatment of Lewis that gives an intimate knowledge of the author. (A, G)

Other Sources
Barratt, David. *C. S. Lewis and His World*. Grand Rapids, MI: Eerdmans, 1987.

Donaldson, Mara E. *Holy Places Are Dark Places: C. S. Lewis and Paul Ricoeur on Narrative Transformation*. Lanham, MD: University Press of America, 1989.

Dorsett, Lyle W. *The Essential C. S. Lewis*. New York: Macmillan, 1988.

Freshwater, Mark E. *C. S. Lewis and the Truth of Myth*. Lanham, MD: University Press of America, 1988.

Kreeft, Peter. *C. S. Lewis: A Critical Essay*. [Rev. ed.] Front Royal, VA: Christendom College Press, 1988.

Lewis, C. S. *Bosen: The Imaginary World of the Young C. S. Lewis*. Edited by Walter Hooper. Orlando, FL: Harcourt Brace Jovanovich, 1985.

Lindskoog, Kathryn. *C. S. Lewis Hoax*. Portland, OR: Multnomah, 1988.

McLaughlin, Sara P., and Mark O. Webb. *A Word Index to the Poetry of C. S. Lewis*. Cornwall, CT: Locust Hill Press, 1988.

Sayer, George B. *Jack: C. S. Lewis and His Times*. New York: Harper & Row, 1988.

SINCLAIR LEWIS
1885-1951

Evaluation of Selected Criticism

Bloom, Harold, ed. *Sinclair Lewis*. New York: Chelsea House, 1987. This volume collects what the editor considers "the best criticism available on Sinclair Lewis." Bloom's introduction and an essay by Charles E. Rosenberg discuss *Arrowsmith*, Mark Schorer examines *Elmer Gantry*, T. K. Whipple writes on *Babbitt*, and Martin Light analyzes *Dodsworth*. Other essays discuss Lewis' satire, his serialized fiction, and his treatment of female characters. The collection also contains a chronology of Lewis' life, an unannotated bibliography of secondary sources, and an excellent index. A useful anthology for students of Lewis' fiction. **(A)**

Bloom, Harold, ed. *Sinclair Lewis's "Arrowsmith."* New York: Chelsea House, 1988. Bloom has collected a selection of what he considers the best critical interpretations of *Arrowsmith*. He considers the novel "a romance of science with allegorical overtones" and believes it to be Lewis' most enduring novel. The essays, written between 1955 and 1985, cover the genesis of the novel, characterization, and Lewis' conception of the literary mode of romance. An excellent companion to the study of the novel. **(A,G)**

Bucco, Martin, ed. *Critical Essays on Sinclair Lewis*. Boston: G.K. Hall, 1986. This collection of essays reexamines the work of this often neglected American writer. James Lundquist's essay describes in detail the deplorable conditions Lewis was exposed to in his youth. While the worst of this shocking material never made it into Lewis' work, it was fundamental to its creation. Bucco's introduction and his judicious selection of contributors has produced a useful survey of critical opinion which should encourage others to reassess Lewis' work. **(A,G)**

WYNDHAM LEWIS
1884-1957

Evaluation of Selected Criticism
Campbell, SueEllen. *The Enemy Opposite: The Outlaw Criticism of Wyndham Lewis*. Athens: Ohio University Press, 1988. Lewis, who founded and published a journal called *The Enemy*, became a self-proclaimed renegade critic who managed to attack about all of the best minds of his time, including Pound, Eliot, Bergson, and Joyce, as well as his own work and philosophy. Campbell analyzes Lewis' voice, stance, and critical tactics to show why he became Critical Enemy Number One. (A)

Dasenbrock, Reed Way. *The Literary Vorticism of Ezra Pound & Wyndham Lewis*. Baltimore: Johns Hopkins University Press, 1985. Dasenbrock traces the influence of painting on the modernist literary imagination as revealed in the work of Pound and Lewis. He concentrates on the Vorticist movement, describing its history and philosophy. He analyzes Lewis' *Enemy of the Stars*, *Tarr*, and the *Apes of God*; and Pound's poetry, including the *Cantos*. A useful study of the modernist imagination. (A)

Donoghue, Denis. *England, Their England: Commentaries on English Language and Literature*. New York: Knopf, 1988. Noted literary critic Donoghue offers a collection of over twenty of his essays addressing the accomplishments and significance of selected English authors. Shakespeare is here, of course, along with Defoe, Peter Ackroyd, and Wyndham Lewis (whose works are discussed in some detail). Donoghue writes insightfully about the poetic contributions of Shelley, Eliot, and Hopkins, and considers the criticism of Arnold, Pater, and Leavis. (A,G)

Other Sources
Pound, Ezra, and Wyndham Lewis. *Pound-Lewis: The Letters of Ezra Pound and Wyndham Lewis*. Edited by Timothy Materer. New York: New Directions, 1985.

VACHEL LINDSAY
1879-1931

Evaluation of Selected Biography and Criticism

Camp, Dennis, ed. *The Prose of Vachel Lindsay: Complete and with Lindsay's Drawings, Volume 1*. Peoria, IL: Spoon River Poetry, 1989. This prose collection may go far to revive the declining critical fortunes of Vachel Lindsay. Included here are some of the earliest film criticism ever published, ranging from silent films in 1915 through the introduction of the "talkies." Lindsay's Kerouac-esque outlook is amply represented by his "Handy Guide for Beggars," "Adventures While Preaching the Gospel of Beauty," or "Roughing It," which has echoes of the rustic Mark Twain. Spoon River recently completed an edition of Lindsay's poetry in three volumes, which this prose collection is intended to complement. (A,G)

Weston, Mildred. *Vachel Lindsay: Poet in Exile*. Fairfield, WA: Ye Galleon Press, 1987. This concise biography presents the basic facts and events of Lindsay's life. It provides brief excerpts from his correspondence and is illustrated with the poet's own woodcuts. The works themselves are mentioned only in passing. (A,G)

JACK LONDON
1876-1916

Autobiographical Sources

Labor, Earle, Robert C. Leitz III, and I. Milo Shepard, eds. *The Letters of Jack London*. Stanford: Stanford University Press, 1988. The one-volume *Letters from Jack London* (1965) selected only 1,557 letters from over four thousand; this three-volume edition now makes them all available. London's second wife, Charmian typed all his letters and kept copies throughout their eleven-year marriage, assuring the survival and accuracy of his correspondence. Some of his early letters are lost, notably letters to his first love, Mabel Applegarth and early love letters to Charmian. (A,G)

Evaluation of Selected Biography and Criticism

Hamilton, David Mike. *"The Tools of My Trade": The Annotated Books in Jack London's Library*. Seattle: University of Washington Press, 1987. London's personal library contained over 15,000 volumes, each lovingly read and carefully annotated. Hamilton has poured over the library page by page, compiling London's annotations. The result is an unparalleled look at the writer's resources and his attitude toward his reading. The collection includes works by Bergson, Freud, Jung, William James, Nietzsche, and countless others. Jung's *Psychology of the Unconscious*, for example, alone contained over 300 notations. London read about everything from prison reform to agricultural techniques. Beyond providing material for London biographers and critics, this book offers insight into one man's love for books. (A,G)

Lundquist, James. *Jack London: Adventures, Ideas, and Fiction*. New York: Ungar, 1987. In the first half of this study, Lundquist describes the background, raw adventure, and "uplook" of Jack London's life. He then turns his attention to the fiction and develops four themes that intertwine in London's best works. This is a well-written and insightful study that gives a clear portrait of London and a concise interpretation of his more noted writings. (A,G)

Staz, Clarice. *American Dreamers: Charmian and Jack London*. New York: St. Martin's, 1988. Determined to create an equal-partner marriage during the late Victorian period, the Londons brought different dynamics to their life together. Charmian devoted herself to helping Jack fulfill his high-spirited career and ever-demanding professional and psychological needs. He was a hard-driving, heavy-drinking man of the world, and realizing their dream of an equal partnership wasn't easy. Staz, a sociologist and feminist critic, is more sympathetic to Charmian and Jack's mother than previous biographers, and she offers a unique, balanced perspective on one of the most intriguing literary marriages since the Brownings. (A,G)

313

HENRY WADSWORTH LONGFELLOW
1807-1882

Evaluation of Selected Criticism

Tucker, Edward L. *The Shaping of Longfellow's "John Endicott."* Charlottesville: University Press of Virginia, 1985. This specialized bibliographical study documents the history of Longfellow's play *John Endicott* from its first prose version in 1856 until it reached its final blank verse form in 1872. This is the first publication of these early versions and allows scholars to study how Longfellow moved his material from prose to verse. The study includes an historical introduction, the texts of the two versions, a scene-by-scene comparison, explanatory notes, and a full textual apparatus. Intended for serious Longfellow scholars and bibliographers only. (A)

Wagenknecht, Edward. *Henry Wadsworth Longfellow: His Poetry and Prose.* New York: Crossroad/Ungar/Continuum, 1986. Longfellow scholar Wagenknecht has produced a comprehensive critical-biographical introduction to the poet's works. Besides the famous narrative poems, he treats many lesser known works, such as "The Building of the Ship," "My Lost Youth," and "Divina Commedia," as well as the prose works and drama. Wagenknecht's appraisal suggests that Longfellow's flagging reputation is overdue for a reassessment. (A,G)

AMY LOWELL
1874-1925

Autobiographical Sources
Healey, E. Claire, and Keith Cushman, eds. *The Letters of D. H. Lawrence and Amy Lowell, 1914-1925*. Santa Barbara: Black Sparrow Press, 1985. Lowell and Lawrence met in 1914 in London at a dinner she contrived for imagist poets. Over the next ten years, they corresponded frequently. Eighty-four of their letters survive, fifty-three from Lawrence's pen. The two vastly different personalities found that they had a common devotion to poetry. Lawrence became Lowell's critic, prowling through her verse, as he said, "like a beast of prey." His criticisms, however, reveal considerable tact. Lowell, for her part, promoted Lawrence's work in the U.S. **(A,G)**

Evaluation of Selected Criticism
Benvenuto, Richard. *Amy Lowell*. Boston: Twayne, 1985. In this critical study of the poetry of modernist Amy Lowell, Benvenuto presents a concise biographical introduction that establishes a context for Lowell's literary career. He pronounces Lowell a controversial poet, whose early notoriety was due more to her flamboyant personality than appreciation of her work. The early poetry is found to have strong echoes from Keats, Tennyson, and Browning. In later years, Lowell was proclaimed the leading free-verse practitioner, yet she has slipped steadily into obscurity, because, Benvenuto contends, her works have not been given serious critical attention. This is an attempt to remedy that shortcoming. **(A)**

ROBERT LOWELL
1917-1977

Evaluation of Selected Criticism

Bawer, Bruce. *The Middle Generation: The Lives and Poetry of Delmore Schwartz, Randall Jarrell, John Berryman, and Robert Lowell.* Hamden, CT: Shoe String Press, Archon Books, 1986. This critical study brings some needed structure to the study of these four poets whose richly textured poetry often confuses readers. Bawer examines the influence of T. S. Eliot on the early work of all four poets and shows how each emerged from that influence in their later poetry. Critics may quibble with the interpretations of particular poems, but the overall value of this work is unchallenged, making it essential for the study of these poets at any level. (A,G)

Giroux, Robert, ed. *Robert Lowell: Collected Prose.* Farrar, Straus & Giroux, 1987. Robert Lowell is not well known for his prose writings, which were often tentative and experimental in nature. Giroux, however, has collected the poet's many disparate prose works, which reveal the workings of a penetrating and often wise mind. Not all are equally enlightening, but Lowell's views on Frost, Eliot, Jarrell, and Berryman are perceptive. His measured discussions of ethical and literary questions and his frightening exposure of his own mental disorder, are first-rate endeavors. (A,G)

Kalstone, David. *Becoming A Poet: Elizabeth Bishop with Marianne Moore and Robert Lowell.* Farrar, Straus & Giroux, 1989. Kalstone examines the deep friendship that developed between Bishop and her mentor Moore. Upon Moore's death, Bishop found some of the same support in a relationship with Lowell who maintained contact with her despite her self-destructive binges and his mental instability. (A)

Matterson, Stephen. *Berryman and Lowell: The Art of Losing.* Totowa, NJ: Barnes & Noble, 1988. This short study attempts to trace the "theme of disintegration" in the lives and works of both poets. Matterson raises some interesting parallels and provides a useful reading of some of their poems, but this is too brief a treatment to be satisfying. It best serves as an introduction to either poet or as a starting point for comparative research. (A,G)

Meyers, Jeffrey, ed. *Robert Lowell, Interviews and Memoirs.* Ann Arbor: University of Michigan Press, 1988. This collection spans Lowell's career, and includes early interviews and conversations that are difficult to find. But for the most part, the bulk of the book falls into literary chit-chat that is of more interest than value. (G)

Meyers, Jeffrey. *Manic Power: Robert Lowell and His Circle.* New York: Arbor House, 1987. Meyers' theme, in this study of Lowell, Berryman,

Jarrell, and Roethke, is the interplay of destructive and creative forces in their lives. A sensitive and moving portrait of men who translated tragic impulses into art. (A,G)

Wallingford, Katharine. *Robert Lowell's Language of the Self*. Chapel Hill: University of North Carolina Press, 1988. Wallingford argues that Lowell incorporates into much of his poetry four psychoanalytical techniques: free association, repetition compulsion, the "deliberate concentration" on the relationship of the patient to others, and the use of memory. She shows, for example, how Lowell understands himself by confronting others, and how the recurrent image of the photograph serves as memory that can be reexamined. This study offers an alternative approach to understanding a poet whose emotional traumas solidified and legitimized the "confessional" school of mid-century poets. (A)

Other Sources

Axelrod, Steven, and Helen Deese, eds. *Robert Lowell: Essays on the Poetry*. New York: Cambridge University Press, 1987.

Axelrod, Steven G., and Renee Kilmer. *Robert Lowell: A Descriptive Bibliography*. Westport, CT: Meckler, 1989.

Ramakrishnan, E. V. *Crisis and Confession: Studies in the Poetry of Theodore Roethke, Robert Lowell and Sylvia Plath*. Columbia, MO: Chanakya India/South Asia Books, 1988.

MALCOLM LOWRY
1909-1957

Autobiographical Sources
Tiessen, Paul, ed. *The Letters of Malcolm Lowry and Gerald Noxon, 1940-1952*. Vancouver: University of British Columbia Press, 1988. This volume collects over eighty letters and messages that passed between Lowry and Gerald Noxon, whom Lowry described as "one of the only real friends I have." Tiessen's introduction provides the context for understanding the relationship that developed between these two men, and each chronological section is introduced by a short essay. The letters reveal a facet of Lowry's personality that is more enthusiastic and humane than shown elsewhere. The letters are indexed but not annotated. (A,G)

Evaluation of Selected Biography and Criticism
Bareham, Tony. *Malcolm Lowry*. London: Macmillan, 1989. In his introduction, Bareham confronts the difficulties of constructing a biography of Lowry from inadequate and conflicting sources. He also discusses the problems created by posthumous publication of Lowry novels, which were spliced together from drafts and notes. The two novels published during his lifetime (*Ultramarine* and *Under the Volcano*) are analyzed for thematic continuity, narrative structure, and their imagery. (A,G)

Bowker, Gordon, ed. *Malcolm Lowry: "Under the Volcano": A Casebook*. London: Macmillan, 1987. This anthology offers nine previously published critical essays and a variety of reviews that address Lowry's most famous novel, *Under the Volcano*. Malcolm Bradbury writes on Lowry as a modernist, Richard Cross on his fusion of symbolism and mimesis. Other contributors include Stephen Spender, Victor Doyen, Dale Edmonds, Andrew Pottinger, Barry Wood, Sherril Grace, and Ronald Binns. The editor provides a brief but useful overview of critical perspectives on Lowry's achievement. (A)

Bowker, Gordon, ed. *Malcolm Lowry Remembered*. London: BBC/Ariel Books, 1985. This compilation, extracted from published memoirs, letters, and interviews, provides a humane and intriguing introduction to Lowry's life and career, told in the words of those who knew him, loved him, or detested him. These reminiscences are grouped chronologically. (A,G)

Salloum, Sheryl. *Malcolm Lowry: Vancouver Days*. Madeira Park, BC: Harbour Publishing, 1987. This popular biography examines the writer's "twin daemons"—alcohol and writing—as they alternately ruled his life. Salloum devotes most of her attention to Lowry's life in the Vancouver area from 1939 to 1954. Included as appendixes are maps identifying Lowry's haunts in Vancouver, at Dollarton and Deep Cove, and on Gariola Island. (G)

JOHN LYDGATE
c. 1370-1449

Evaluation of Selected Criticism

Ebin, Lois A. *John Lydgate*. Boston: Twayne, 1985. Ebin undertakes the daunting task of introducing new readers to the breadth of Lydgate's poetic works. She provides useful analyses for *Troy Book*, *Siege of Thebes*, *Fall of Princes*, and many others. Lydgate's florid style in his religious poems, Ebin contends, is justified in that it contributes to the overall "spirit of celebration" expressed by the works. Detailed summaries of such courtly poems as "The Complaint of the Black Knight," and *Temple of Glass*, are presented. Her final chapter sketches out what she feels is Lydgate's proper place in literary history. **(A,G)**

THOMAS BABINGTON MACAULAY
1800-1859

Evaluation of Selected Criticism

Chainey, Graham. *A Literary History of Cambridge.* Ann Arbor: University of Michigan Press, 1986. This behind-the-scenes look at the literary stories and scandals of Cambridge University makes for enjoyable voyeurism. The gossip is truly on an epic scale—spread over eight hundred years of Cambridge history and featuring anecdotes on nearly every notable British writer, including Milton, Wordsworth, Macaulay, and Sylvia Plath. Love affairs, drinking habits, duels, rivalries—all are paraded forth in often humorous detail. This is a very entertaining book that in its own way reveals the immense contribution Cambridge has made to the literary world. **(G)**

Edwards, Owen Dudley. *Macaulay.* New York: St. Martin's, 1988. Edwards provides a useful critical introduction to the major works of Macaulay. Included are a chronology, a lengthy biographical section, and an annotated bibliography. **(A,G)**

ARCHIBALD MACLEISH
1892-1982

Evaluation of Selected Criticism

Drabeck, Bernard, and Helen Ellis, eds. *Archibald MacLeish: Reflections.* Amherst: University of Massachusetts Press, 1986. This is a compilation of interviews with MacLeish conducted between 1976 and 1981. MacLeish called these discussions the autobiography of his professional life. In the absence of the authorized biography, which is in progress, this compilation offers the greatest breadth of biographical detail currently available. MacLeish's assessment of his life and career seem quite objectively balanced and insightful. The interviews touch on all of the major events of his career—his Paris years, his work as an editor at *Fortune*, his curatorship at Harvard and the Library of Congress, government and political work, the writing of his poetry and plays, and receipt of the Pulitzer Prize. This collection is highly recommended for scholars, students, and a general audience. **(A,G)**

Drabeck, Bernard A., *et al*, eds. *The Proceedings of the Archibald MacLeish Symposium, May 7-8, 1982.* Greenfield, MA: University Press of America, 1988. This collection of twenty papers and twenty short tributes offers a personal portrait of MacLeish as writer and former Librarian of Congress. Anecdotal and laudatory in tone, these pieces quote heavily from MacLeish's poetry and offer testimonials as to what the works "mean to me." **(G)**

LOUIS MACNEICE
1907-1963

Evaluation of Selected Criticism

Heuser, Alan, ed. *Selected Literary Criticism of Louis MacNeice*. London: Oxford University Press, 1987. MacNeice wrote with verve about the turbulent literary scene during the first half of the century but his writings were typically eclipsed by his close friends, Auden and Dylan Thomas. This anthology of fifty-six articles and reviews urges a reassessment of the importance of MacNeice's critical voice. A complete bibliography of MacNeice's short prose is included. **(A,G)**

Johnston, Dillon. *Irish Poetry after Joyce*. South Bend, IN: University of Notre Dame Press, 1985. This study provides an overview of Irish poetry since the death of Joyce. Johnston, director of the Wake Forest University Press, which specializes in contemporary Irish verse, has had personal and professional contact with many of the poets of whom he writes. He compares contemporary poets and their responses to Joyce with the successors of Yeats, showing similar or divergent poetic reactions. He compares Heaney with Kavanagh, and Mahon with MacNeice. Other poets afforded careful treatment are Kinsella, Longley, Montague, Muldoon, and Murphy. This is considered an essential text for those interested in the study of Irish poetry. **(A,G)**

Sekine, Masaru, ed. *Irish Writers and Society At Large*. Totowa, NJ: Barnes & Noble, 1985. This anthology collects fourteen essays on Anglo-Irish writers. In addition to contributions on Joyce, Moore, and Corkery, Alasdair Macrae writes on the autobiographical elements in Heaney's *Station Island*. Two other pieces are devoted to the works of Bowen and MacNeice. **(A,G)**

Other Sources

Bhattacharyya, Binay K. *The Oxford Group: Auden and Others*. New York: Associated/Advent, 1989.

Longley, Edna. *Louis MacNeice: A Study*. Winchester, MA: Faber & Faber, 1989.

BERNARD MALAMUD
1914-1986

Evaluation of Selected Criticism

Bloom, Harold, ed. *Bernard Malamud*. New York: Chelsea House, 1986. Harold Bloom's introductory essay places Malamud in critical context and gives an overview of the twenty essays in this anthology. These essays, which discuss themes and issues in Malamud's work, represent a wide range of theories and perspectives. Useful as an introduction to Malamud's critical reputation. **(A,G)**

Helterman, Jeffrey. *Understanding Bernard Malamud*. Columbia: University of South Carolina Press, 1985. This concise study of the Malamud is designed to provide guidance for students and general readers. Themes, imagery, and characterization are discussed for the major works. Although some will find the interpretations overly simplistic, most newcomers to Malamud should find much of the information helpful. **(A,G)**

Solotaroff, Robert. *Bernard Malamud: A Study of the Short Fiction*. Boston: Twayne, 1989. Solotaroff combines biography with an explication of forty-five stories to demonstrate Malamud's craft and themes, the most important of which is the meaning of being human in an inhumane universe. This book also contain interviews with Malamud, excerpts from critical reviews, a chronology of Malamud's life, bibliography, and index. This is a good, basic resource for studying Malamud at any level. **(A,G)**

Salzberg, Joel, ed. *Critical Essays on Bernard Malamud*. Boston, G. K. Hall, 1987. Similar to other volumes in this series, this anthology offers reprints of important critical essays, original essays, and an introduction that provides an overview of the writer's reputation and place in literary history. Contributors include Harvey Swados writing on *The Natural*, Alfred Kazin on *The Assistant*, and James Mellard on *Dubin's Lives*. Salzberg's introduction points out the tasks confronting Malamud scholars and suggests directions for further research. Helpful notes and an index are included. **(A,G)**

Other Sources

Malamud, Bernard. *Long Work, Short Life*. Bennington, VT: Bennington College, 1985.

Rajagopalachari, M. *The Novels of Bernard Malamud*. New York: Prestige New Delhi/Advent, 1988.

Salzberg, Joel. *Bernard Malamud: A Reference Guide*. Boston: G. K. Hall, 1985.

THOMAS MALORY
fl. 1470

Evaluation of Selected Criticism

Dobyns, Ann. *The Voices of Romance: Studies in Dialogue and Character.* Newark: University of Delaware Press, 1989. For Dobyns, a characteristic element of the romance is the fact that character is of secondary importance and is usually determined by plot necessities. She argues that romance authors use speech characteristics to develop distinct characters that embody themes. In arguing her thesis, she compares parallel characters from Malory's *Le Morte Darthur*, Sydney's *New Arcadia*, and Brontë's *Wuthering Heights*. She demonstrates that although the characters in romance are conventional and sometimes static and abstract, they can at the same time be "complex and richly detailed." Useful to students of the romance. **(A)**

Kennedy, Beverly. *Knighthood in "Le Morte Darthur."* Wolfboro, NH: Boydell & Brewer, 1986. In this study, Kennedy isolates three separate but interdependent traditions of the knight in European history and literature. The "heroic knight," as embodied by Gawain in *Le Morte Darthur*, ultimately derives from the traditions of Beowulf and Roland. The "worshipful knight," represented by Lancelot, is traced back to the French prose romances. The "true knight," embodied by Arthur himself, derived from fifteenth-century treatises on knighthood designed to inculcate the qualities of chivalry. After establishing these categories, Kennedy proceeds to relate the scheme to Malory's tales, describing how each tale tests knightly qualities. **(A,G)**

Lenz, Joseph M. *The Promised End: Romance Closure in the Gawain-poet, Malory, Spenser, and Shakespeare.* New York: Peter Lang, 1986. Lenz examines the particular ways romances end as a defining characteristic of the genre. To do this, he examines *Sir Gawain and the Green Knight*, Malory's *Le Morte Darthur*, and two Renaissance texts, *The Faerie Queen* and *The Winter's Tale*. This is a limited but useful study for medieval and Renaissance scholars. **(A)**

Parins, Marylyn Jackson. *Malory: The Critical Heritage.* New York: Routledge, 1989. This compilation of sixty-nine texts gathers together over four hundred years of critical work on *Le Morte Darthur*. Coverage begins in 1485 with William Caxton's "Preface" and ends with George Saintsbury's 1912 essay, written before the discovery of the Winchester manuscript. Students and scholars can now conveniently trace the evolution of the critical debates over sources, narrative structure, and moral stance. The introduction addresses textual history, themes, and imagery and describes the nature of twentieth-century scholarship. **(A,G)**

Riddy, Felicity. *Sir Thomas Malory*. Leiden: E. J. Brill, 1987. Malory's *Le Morte Darthur* was created at a time when handwritten manuscripts were giving over to the printed page, and both kinds of copies of the text exist. Several handwritten manuscripts were even marked up for use as printer's copy. This relationship of script to print is symbolic of the unique transitional time when Malory composed his works. Riddy conducts a thorough analysis of Malory's world view, placing it in historical and social context, and giving close readings of passages of the text. **(A)**

Spisak, James W. *Studies in Malory*. Kalamazoo: Western Michigan University, 1985. This anthology of current critical writing on Malory collects fifteen essays on all facets of Malory's work. Spisak contributes an overview of recent trends in Malory studies as well as an essay on Malory's "lost" source. Terence McCarthy writes on "Malory and the Alliterative Tradition" Stephen C. B. Atkinson examines "Malory's Lancelot and the Quest of the Grail." Elizabeth Kirk focuses on Caxton and Muriel Whitaker examines the history of the illustrations to *Le Morte Darthur*. A useful collection for the specialist. **(A)**

Other Sources

Gaines, Barry. *Sir Thomas Malory: An Anecdotal Bibliography of Editions, 1485-1985*. New York: AMS Press, 1986.

Goodman, Jennifer R. *Malory and Caxton's Prose Romances of 1485*. New York: Garland, 1987.

Merrill, Robert. *Sir Thomas Malory and the Cultural Crisis of the Late Middle Ages*. New York: Peter Lang, 1987.

Whitaker, Muriel. *Arthur's Kingdom of Adventure: The World of Malory's "Morte D'Arthur."* Savage, MD: Barnes & Noble, 1984.

KATHERINE MANSFIELD
1888-1923

Autobiographical Sources

O'Sullivan, Vincent, ed. *The Collected Letters of Katherine Mansfield, 1918-1919*. Oxford: Clarendon Press, 1987. This is the second volume of a projected five, covering a year when Mansfield was battling the lung disease that would kill her. Because of her health, she travelled, seeking warmer climates. Separated from her husband, frequently alone, often in pain and ill-temper, she continued to write stories. These eloquent letters reveal much of the emotion behind the art, and for serious readers help explain the themes. Highly recommended for anyone researching Mansfield, twentieth-century literature, or the creative process. **(A,G)**

Evaluation of Selected Biography and Criticism

Boddy, Gillian. *Katherine Mansfield: The Woman and the Writer*. New York: Penguin, 1988. This is considered one of the essential books for understanding the life and works of New Zealand's Katherine Mansfield. It is divided into four sections: a biographical portrait; a selection of letters and journal entries; an essay on the stories; and a chronological selection from the stories themselves. Boddy characterizes Mansfield as often difficult or immature, but her literary genius is never challenged. This material is supplemented by photographs of Mansfield and the important places and people in her life. **(A,G)**

Fullbrook, Kate. *Katherine Mansfield*. Bloomington: Indiana University Press, 1986. The first part of this study bemoans the "neglect" of Mansfield's work. However, over twenty books have appeared on her life and work since 1970, and she is widely acknowledged as one of the foremost English masters of the short story. Once this puzzling introduction is over, Fullbrook settles into an intelligent analysis of individual stories in terms of Mansfield's literary technique and use of symbolism. This volume is part of the Key Women Writers Series that stresses a feminist critical perspective. **(A,G)**

Hanson, Clare, ed. *The Critical Writings of Katherine Mansfield*. New York: St. Martin's, 1987. This complilation of extracts from letters, journals, essays, and reviews provides a useful view of Mansfield's attitudes toward the writers of her day. Many of them quickly slipped into obscurity and are not likely to return, but she discusses the methods and personalities of Woolf, Conrad, and Lawrence. Rejecting conventional feminism, she developed her own view of the interactive natures of "masculine" and "feminine" prose. The juxtaposition of interviews with later remarks from journals allows the reader to trace the development of Mansfield's attitudes and critical stances. **(A,G)**

Tomalin, Claire. *Katherine Mansfield: A Secret Life.* New York: Knopf, 1988. Although Mansfield's life story has been told in Alpers' biography, Tomalin questions some of his interpretations. She believes that he underestimated the importance of Mansfield's medical history, the blackmail attempt by a former lover, and especially her relationship to D. H. Lawrence, who used their relationship for parts of *Women in Love.* Tomalin is especially good in depicting Mansfield's tension with a feminine role which was denied the male privilege of "recklessness." This readable biography is provocative for students of literature or culture. (A,G)

Other Sources

Crone, Nora. *A Portrait of Katherine Mansfield.* London and New York: Stockwell/State Mutual Book, 1986.

DeBell, Diane. *Katherine Mansfield.* Savage, MD: Barnes & Noble/ Rowman, 1990.

Kirkpatrick, B. J. *A Bibliography of Katherine Mansfield.* New York: Oxford University Press, 1989.

Nathan, Rhoda B. *Katherine Mansfield.* New York: Frederick Ungar, 1988.

ANDREW MARVELL
1621-1678

Evaluation of Selected Criticism

Stocker, Margarita. *Apocalyptic Marvell: The Second Coming in Seventeenth-Century Poetry.* Athens: Ohio University Press, 1987. This comprehensive survey of Marvell's poetry pays special attention to the more difficult works, such as "Upon Appleton House," "An Horatian Ode," "To His Coy Mistress," and "The Garden." Instead of dividing the works into the separate genres, i.e., satires, lyrics, odes, Stocker stresses the overall unity of the poems. Marvell interpreted the English Civil War and Reformation in terms of Protestant apocalyptic ideology, and his expectation of the Second Coming is a theme that pervades his poetry. Clearly written and well-researched, this book is a highly recommended analysis of a major seventeenth-century poet. (A)

Wilcher, Robert. *Andrew Marvell.* Cambridge: Cambridge University Press, 1985. This lucid, well-written book is a beginner's guide. The opening chapter provides an account of Marvell's life and times. Wilcher then analyzes the poems, offering explanations of seventeenth-century poetic conventions and traditions. For example, he discusses the relationship between the perceiver and the perceived, the pastoral tradition, and Restoration politics. A very helpful guide for all students. (A,G)

Other Sources

Klause, John. *The Unfortunate Fall: Theodicy and the Moral Imagination of Andrew Marvell.* Hamden, CT: Shoe String Books/Archon, 1984.

Willmott, Richard. *Four Metaphysical Poets: An Anthology of Poetry by Donne, Herbert, Marvell, and Vaughan.* New York: Cambridge University Press, 1985.

W. SOMERSET MAUGHAM
1874-1965

Evaluation of Selected Biography and Criticism

Calder, Robert. *Willie: The Life of W. Somerset Maugham.* New York: St. Martins, 1990. Calder's biography was fashioned with the cooperation of Alan Searle—Maugham's lover, companion, and personal secretary. The resulting view of Maugham is discreet, sympathetic, and perhaps overly gentle. Calder thoroughly analyzes Maugham's relationships—with his wife and male companions—concludes he was "a man without roots," and relates this theme to his novels, plays, and short stories. The scholarly tone is a welcome departure from previous biographies that emphasized emotional melodrama. Calder tries to offset the more negative stance of previous biographies by stressing Maugham's kindness and charity, but this strategy hardly dilutes Maugham's acerbic personality. Homosexuality, as a theme of Maugham's life and work, is handled in a direct but sensitive manner. **(A,G)**

Curtis, Anthony, and John Whitehead, eds. *W. Somerset Maugham: The Critical Heritage.* New York: Routledge & Kegan Paul, 1987. This anthology provides a useful survey of the critical responses to Maugham's works. The 150 reviews, essays, and excerpts from longer works reprinted here span the years 1897 to 1965. The biographical and introductory notes supplied by the editors enhance this antholgy's usefulness. **(A)**

Loss, Archie K. *"Of Human Bondage": Coming of Age in the Novel.* Boston: Twayne, 1990. This short analysis provides brief background about the historical context, importance, and critical reception of the novel, then discusses the major themes (bondage and troubled grace) as he analyzes Philip's childhood, education, profession, sexuality, and philosophy. One of the appendixes shows the parallels of Philip's fictional life with Maugham's biography, while a second compares the novel with the film adaptation. Included are notes and a bibliography. **(G)**

Loss, Archie K. *W. Somerset Maugham.* New York: Ungar, 1987. This short, general introduction to Maugham's life and work begins with a biographical sketch focusing on the disorder and sorrows of his early life, then devotes one chapter each to *Of Human Bondage*, *The Moon and Sixpence* and *Cake and Ale*, *The Razor's Edge*, the short fiction, the drama, and the essays. Included are a chronology, notes, and bibliography. **(G)**

CARSON MCCULLERS
1917-1967

Evaluation of Selected Criticism

Bloom, Harold, ed. *Carson McCullers: Modern Critical Views.* New York: Chelsea House, 1986. This anthology of McCullers criticism reprints essays by Tennessee Williams and Gore Vidal, among others. There are twelve essays in all, with Bloom supplying a brief introduction. Two of McCullers' five novels are well explicated—*Reflections in a Golden Eye* and *Clock Without Hands.* M. McDowell provides an overview of McCullers' lesser known poems and short fiction. (A,G)

Carr, Virginia Spencer. *Understanding Carson McCullers.* Columbia: University of South Carolina Press, 1990. This introduction to McCullers' work is written by her brilliant biographer, and thus it is full of interesting and important connections between the life and works. Carr relates each of Mc-Cullers' works to her bizarre, troubled life so that in addition to identifying the sources of her material Carr also reveals the creative process. Nonspecialists will find this an intriguing and enlightening beginning to a fascinating writer. (G)

Westling, Louise. *Sacred Groves and Ravaged Gardens: The Fiction of Eudora Welty, Carson McCullers, and Flannery O'Connor.* Athens: University of Georgia Press, 1985. Original and provocative interpretations characterize this study of the fiction of three prominent southern women writers. Focusing on problems of identity, relationships with mothers and with men, and the use of symbolism, Westling argues that Welty "celebrates" her feminine identity while both McCullers and O'Connor struggle against it. By accepting her identity, Welty gains access to the depths of her emotional and psychological resources, while McCullers and O'Connor become increasingly disconnected from feminine wholeness. (A,G)

CLAUDE MCKAY
1889-1948

Evaluation of Selected Biography

Cooper, Wayne F. *Claude McKay, Rebel Sojourner in the Harlem Renaissance: A Biography.* Baton Rouge: Louisiana State University Press, 1987. Cooper tells the lively story of a gifted West Indian writer who emigrated to America in 1912 to find a new life. By 1934, after travelling in Europe and Africa, he returned to America with shattered dreams and in broken health. Doggedly, he picked up the pieces of his life and became a champion of the black working class. Overbearing and demanding of friends, outspoken and direct with issues, and caustic with enemies, McKay had a profound influence on the Harlem Renaissance. Cooper's biography is an essential work for anyone interested in McKay or in Afro-American thought in the first half of this century. (A,G)

HERMAN MELVILLE
1819-1891

Evaluation of Selected Criticism

Brodhead, Richard, ed. *New Essays on "Moby Dick."* Cambridge, Cambridge University Press, 1987. These six new essays survey the current status of scholarship on *Moby Dick*. Of special note are Bryan Wolf's comparison of Melville's imagery and the landscapes portrayed by the Hudson River school of painters, and James McIntosh's structural breakdown of the "quest" theme. Brodhead's judicious selection of essays has kept the discussion focused on the novel itself, rather than the state of Melville criticism. **(A)**

Bryant, John, ed. *A Companion to Melville Studies.* Westport, CT: Greenwood Press, 1986. This helpful "companion" brings together twenty-five distinguished Melville scholars to examine all facets of the man and his art. The text is divided into separate sections on Melville's world, work, thought, art, and legacy. Although of primary value to Melville scholars, it provides a ready-reference to many aspects of the writer's achievements. **(A)**

Coale, Samuel Chase. *In Hawthorne's Shadow: American Romance from Melville to Mailer.* Lexington: University Press of Kentucky, 1985. Undoubtedly, Hawthorne's influence on the shape of American fiction has been immense. In this study, Coale isolates what he considers to be the essential elements of Hawthorne's fiction and traces their dissemination through the works of his literary heirs, including Melville, Faulkner, Mailer, McCullers, O'Connor, Styron, Cheever, Updike, Gardner, and many others. In Coale's view, Hawthorne's fiction embodies radical dualisms: mind/matter, spirit/substance, and imagination/nothingness. The shadow he casts, says Coale, is from his "own dark vision of himself and his country." **(A,G)**

Dillingham, William B. *Melville's Later Novels.* Athens: University of Georgia Press, 1986. Dillingham gives a close reading to Melville's later works from *Moby Dick* to *Billy Budd* and isolates the central theme of survival through self-knowledge. His comparison of *Moby Dick* and *Pierre* reveals an underlying narrative structure that has been overlooked by less observant critics. This study complements Dillingham's other works on Melville—*An Artist in the Rigging* and *Melville's Short Fiction, 1853-1856.* **(A,G)**

Dimock, Wai-chee. *Empire for Liberty: Melville and the Poetics of Individualism.* Princeton, NJ: Princeton University Press, 1989. This ambitious study relates Melville's major works to concepts of Jacksonian and Emersonian individualism. Dimock focuses on the ideologies of the expanding American "empire" as embodied in idea of "manifest destiny" and the rationale for Indian extinction. He argues that, for Melville, politics and poetics are

inextricably intertwined and supports this theory by close readings of *Redburn,
White-Jacket, The Confidence-Man,* and *Moby Dick.* Ahab is another American
"candidate for extinction" because he clings to the past as the nation sweeps
forward into the future. This difficult but intriguing book is recommended for
Melville scholars. **(A)**

Dryden, Edgar A. *The Form of American Romance.* Baltimore: Johns Hopkins University Press, 1988. In this study, Dryden undertakes an analysis of
the structure and development of American Romanticism. He first examines
the origins of the novel and its relationship to romance by discussing *Don
Quixote* and Scott's *Waverley.* He views Scott's early novel as a "founding
text" in the history of the English novel. Dryden then dissects the narrative
structures of five American novels—Hawthorne's *The Marble Faun,* Melville's
Pierre, James's *The Portrait of a Lady,* Faulkner's *Absalom, Absalom!,* and
Barth's *LETTERS.* He sees these American novelists responding directly to
narrative problems inherited from Scott. **(A)**

Garcia, Wilma. *Mothers and Others: Myths of the Females in the Works of
Melville, Twain, and Hemingway.* New York: Peter Lang, 1984. Garcia's study
of female characters of Melville, Twain, and Hemingway promises a complex
archetypal analysis of feminine imagery. It delivers significantly less, however.
Although the study contains a useful overview of archetypal theory and criticism, it is flawed by a confusion over the differences between "archetype"
and "stereotype." **(A,G)**

Higgins, Brian. *Herman Melville: A Reference Guide, 1931-1960.* G. K.
Hall, 1987. This fully annotated research bibliography makes an effort to
include all secondary sources relating to Melville, including books, journal and
magazine articles, reviews, and dissertations. In spite of differing titles, this
volume is actually the continuation of Higgins' *Herman Melville: An
Annotated Bibliography, Volume 1, 1846-1930* published in 1978. Citations are
grouped by year, subdivided into books and shorter works, and then
alphabetized by author or by date. **(A,G)**

Levine, Robert S. *Conspiracy and Romance: Studies in Brockden Brown,
Cooper, Hawthorne, and Melville.* New York: Cambridge University Press,
1989. This study consists of four loosely connected essays. An essay on
Brown's *Ormond* focuses on the writer's foreign villains and conspiratorial
plots against the integrity of the fledgling United States. Examining Cooper's
The Bravo, Levine demonstrates that the author's desire was to demystify and
oppose the "mysterious power" that directed the state of Venice, which he
described as a "soulless corporation." Levine examines the roles of insiders
and outsiders in Hawthorne's *The Blithedale Romance.* Finally, he turns his
attention to Melville's *Benito Cereno* where he examines the conflicts between
captains and mutineers. **(A)**

Martin, Robert K. *Hero, Captain, and Stranger: Male Friendship, Social Critique, and Literary Form in the Sea Novels of Herman Melville.* Chapel Hill: University of North Carolina Press, 1986. Martin examines the sexually charged relationships between men in Melville's novels in terms of their political significance in a world dominated by patriarchal-capitalist-hetero-sexual-aggressors. *Typee, Redburn, White-Jacket, Moby-Dick,* and *Billy Budd* are subjected to this relentless treatment. This picture of Melville is one of a radical homoerotic mythographer. (A,G)

McSweeney, Kerry. *Moby-Dick: Ishmael's Mighty Book.* Boston: Twayne, 1986. This latest volume in Twayne's Masterwork Studies offers a new reading of Melville's novel. Along the way McSweeney presents useful insights into the novelist's narrative strategies and techniques. The main thesis is hidden in the last chapter, so read the ending before starting chapter one. (A,G)

Mills, Nicolaus. *The Crowd in American Literature.* Baton Rouge: Louisiana State University Press, 1986. Mills explicates the use of "crowds" by American writers from Jefferson to Steinbeck. For colonial, political writers crowds were a "force for democracy;" for the classical American novelists —Hawthorne, Melville, and Twain—they were a force for national unity. Mills examines the "noble" working-class masses of such writers as Howells, Dreiser, and Steinbeck. Finally, he turns to Norman Mailer and Ralph Ellison for an examination of post-war crowds, the repository of intellectual and moral power contrasted with brute force. This is a fascinating thematic social history drawn from American literary works. (A,G)

Morse, David. *American Romanticism.* New York: Barnes & Noble, 1987. With cool, critical detachment, Morse examines the ethic of "excessiveness" which he feels underlies the early literature of the new American nation. He traces this theme through eleven authors from Cooper and Melville to James. Nineteenth-century American authors, he argues, were driven by an impulse to extravagance in order to create a fitting symbol of national significance. (A,G)

Pahl, Dennis. *Architects of the Abyss: The Indeterminate Fictions of Poe, Hawthorne, and Melville.* Columbia: University of Missouri Press, 1989. Drawing on the theories of Nietzsche, Derrida, and de Man, Pahl explores the nature of the "abyss of signification" generated by a writer's problematic notions of "truth." Using Poe's short stories and *The Narrative of Arthur Gordon Pym,* Pahl examines categories of "the uncanny," "recuperation," and "authority" as they relate to narration. Using Hawthorne's "Rappaccini's Daughter," he dissects the contradictory nature of the perspective on which the reader is forced to rely. Turning to Melville's *Billy Budd,* Pahl develops the full complexity of his theoretical paradigms. This is a specialized study that should be of interest to scholars of critical theory and American literature. (A)

Richardson, William D. *Melville's "Benito Cereno": An Interpretation with Annotated Text and Concordance.* Durham, NC: Carolina Academic, 1987.

This edition contains an annotated text of the story, an interpretative essay, an account of differences between the two published versions, a concordance locating key words, endnotes, bibliography, and illustrations. The interpretative essay will help undergraduates understand the work more fully, while the annotated text and rear matter will interest scholars and advanced students. (A)

Sealts, Merton M., Jr. *Melville's Reading.* Columbia: University of South Carolina Press, 1988. Not since Walker Cowen's 1965 dissertation entitled *Melville's Marginalia* has any significant study been made of what Melville read and how it influenced him. Examining the Melville family papers now in the New York Public Library, and other books that have turned up since 1965, Sealts demonstrates the impressive range of Melville's erudition. (A)

Stelle, Jeffrey. *The Representation of the Self in the American Renaissance.* Chapel Hill: University of North Carolina Press, 1987. Steele draws on modern psychological theories to explore the concept of the self as portrayed in major works of the American Renaissance. He makes illuminating comparisons between the orientations of writers and psychologists/ philosophers—for example, Emerson and Jung, Thoreau and Medard Boss, Hawthorne and Freud, and Melville and Nietzsche. (A,G)

Tanner, Tony. *Scenes of Nature, Signs of Men.* Cambridge: Cambridge University Press, 1987. For the sheer ingenuity and brilliance of comparative thinking, Cambridge professor Tanner is one of the best critics of our time. In this collection of essays, Tanner works out his idea of the profound influence on American fiction of the Puritans' obsession with signs. He contends that this obsession set the tone for all subsequent American fiction for it established the need for American writers to find a special significance in their landscape and history. Tanner elaborates his insight in discussions of individual American writers from Cooper and Melville to the contemporary novelist William Gass. (A,G)

Thomas, Brook. *Cross-Examinations of Law and Literature: Cooper, Hawthorne, Stowe, and Melville.* Cambridge: Cambridge University Press, 1987. In this specialized study in cultural history, Thomas examines the early nineteenth-century tradition of combining the study of law and literature. He uses selected works of writers of the American Renaissance—Cooper, Hawthorne, Stowe, and Melville—to define the fictional presentation of legal issues of the times. He pairs these writers with prominent contemporary lawyers with whom they had a personal or professional connection. For example, he relates Stowe's work to litigation over slavery. (A)

Tolchin, Neal L. *Mourning, Gender, and Creativity in the Art of Herman Melville.* New Haven: Yale University Press, 1988. Tolchin opens this study with a history of grief in the nineteenth century and analyzes the process of mourning. He then examines *Typee, Pierre,* and *Moby Dick* to construct yet another theory of Melville's psyche. Although Tolchin's theory may seem a little strained, it does open another road for traveling to Melville. (A)

Other Sources

Bercaw, Mary K. *Melville's Sources.* Evanston: Northwestern University Press, 1987.

Bickman, Martin. *Approaches to Teaching Melville's "Moby Dick."* New York: Modern Language Association, 1985.

Budd, Louis J., and Edwin H. Cady, eds. *On Melville.* Durham: Duke University Press, 1988.

Coffler, Gail H. *Melville's Classical Allusions: A Comprehensive Index and Glossary.* Westport, CT: Greenwood, 1985.

Cowen, Walker. *Melville's Marginalia.* New York: Garland, 1965, 1988.

Greenberg, Bruce L. *Some Other World to Find: Quest and Negation in the Works of Herman Melville.* Champaign: University of Illinois Press, 1989.

Hamilton, William. *Reading "Moby Dick" and Other Essays.* New York: Peter Lang, 1989.

La Bossiere, Camille R. *The Victorian Fol Sage: Comparative Readings on Carlyle, Emerson, Melville and Conrad.* Lewisburg, PA: Bucknell University Press, 1988.

McCall, Dan. *The Silence of Bartleby.* Ithaca, NY: Cornell University Press, 1989.

Milder, Robert. *Critical Essays on Melville's "Billy Budd."* Boston: G. K. Hall, 1989.

Moses, Carole. *Melville's Use of Spenser.* New York: Peter Lang, 1989.

Person, Leland S., Jr. *Aesthetic Headaches: Women and a Masculine Poetics in Poe, Melville, and Hawthorne.* Athens: University of Georgia Press, 1988.

Reeve, F. D. *The White Monk: An Essay on Dostoevsky and Melville.* Nashville: Vanderbilt University Press, 1990.

Samson, John. *White Lies: Melville's Narratives of Facts.* Ithaca, NY: Cornell University Press, 1989.

Trimpi, Helen P. *Melville's Confidence Men and American Politics in the 1850's.* Hamden, CT: Shoe String, 1987.

Wegener, Larry E. *A Concordance to Herman Melville's "The Confidence Man, His Masquerade."* New York: Garland, 1987.

THOMAS MERTON
1915-1968

Evaluation of Selected Criticism

Cooper, David D. *Thomas Merton's Art of Denial: The Evolution of a Radical Humanist.* Athens: The University of Georgia Press, 1989. In this critical biography, Cooper traces the origins and development of Merton's conflicting roles as contemplative monk and successful writer. Merton was disappointed with *The Seven Storey Mountain,* which he later considered an over-romanticized view of an heroic convert fleeing to the monastery. Increasingly, he turned from autobiography to social criticism. Fearing that writing would get in the way of his spiritual advancement, yet unable to stop, Merton devised a humanistic philosophy that enabled him to bridge the inner and outer worlds. (A,G)

Giles, Richard F., ed. *Hopkins Among the Poets: Studies in Modern Responses to Gerard Manley Hopkins.* Hamilton, Ontario: International Hopkins Association, 1985. This anthology of twenty-six critical essays addresses the impact of Hopkins on twentieth-century poetry and, in particular, how individual modern poets accepted, incorporated, or abandoned different aspects of Hopkins' poetry. The modernist poets are given deserving attention, but the essayists also examine Hopkins' influence on a variety of other poets. Merton, Jones, Plath, and Thomas are found to be heavily influenced; Heaney, Roethke, Lowell, and Crane are found to be hardly influenced, if at all. Yeats and Eliot both disliked Hopkins' poetry but registered a reaction to it in their own poetry. (A)

Grayston, Donald. *Thomas Merton: The Development of a Spiritual Theologian.* Lewiston, NY: Mellen, 1985. Grayston collates the five existing versions of Merton's masterwork, *Seeds of Contemplation,* from the initial typescript to the final 1961 revision. By analyzing the changes, Grayston maps the gradual unfolding of Merton's vision as he becomes more world-affirming and ecumenical in his thinking. Scholars will find this book thoroughly engaging. Students and the general reader would be better served on this topic by consulting Michael Mott's biography, *The Seven Mountains of Thomas Merton* (1985). (A)

Hawkins, Anne Hunsaker. *Archetypes of Conversion: The Autobiographies of Augustine, Bunyan, and Merton.* Lewisburg, PA: Bucknell University Press, 1985. Hawkins explores the phenomenon of religious conversion by examining the spiritual autobiographies of three notable converts--Augustine, Bunyan, and Merton. This study takes a decidedly Jungian approach in its search for an archetypal basis for conversion. Students of Merton will undoubtedly find the discussion of his spiritual awakening thought-provoking and insightful. (A,G)

337

Kramer, Victor A. *Thomas Merton*. Boston: Twayne, 1984. This biography of Merton examines his life as a man of letters who chose to be a monk. Kramer contends that Merton's writing revealed an inner paradox: accepting the world while simultaneously moving toward greater solitude. Kramer conceives of Merton's life as a spiritual journey, and he analyzes the works within this context. (A,G)

Pennington, M. Basil. *Thomas Merton, Brother Monk: The Quest for True Freedom*. New York: Harper & Row, 1987. Fellow American Cistercian Pennington has produced an informal, yet penetrating portrait of Merton, the writer and the monk. Revealed are the details of daily routine within the monastery, Merton's relationships with other monks, his dealings with superiors within the monastery and with friends outside, and his influence on reform within the Cistercian order. It is Pennington's contention that Merton was able to achieve a sense of "pure freedom" only within the supporting confines of tradition and religious discipline. (A,G)

Other Sources
Carr, Anne E. *A Search for Wisdom and Spirit: Thomas Merton's Theology of the Self*. Notre Dame: University of Notre Dame Press, 1988.

Daggy, Robert E., et al, eds. *The Merton Annual: Studies in Thomas Merton, Religion, Culture, Literature, and Social Concerns, vol. 2*. New York: AMS Press, 1988.

Grayston, Donald. *Thomas Merton's Rewriting: The Five Versions of Seeds—"New Seeds of Contemplation" as A Key to the Development of His Thought*. Lewiston, NY: Edwin Mellen, 1987.

Hart, Patrick, ed. *The Legacy of Thomas Merton*. Kalamazoo, MI: Cistercian, 1985.

Shannon, William H., ed. *The Hidden Ground of Love: The Letters of Thomas Merton on Religious Experience and Social Concerns*. New York: Farrar, Straus & Giroux, 1985.

JOHN STUART MILL
1806-1873

Evaluation of Selected Biography and Criticism

Glassman, Peter. *J. S. Mill: The Evolution of a Genius.* Gainesville: University of Florida Press, 1985. Glassman contends that Mill suffered from an inverted Oedipus complex—he was erotically attracted to his father and violently jealous of his mother. He channeled these unholy desires into his marriage to Harriet Taylor, a stand-in for the father. According to this theory and in spite of contrary appearances, Mill's works on society, government, education, and the improvement of mankind were actually sublimated efforts to seduce and unite with his father, and this conflict is reflected in both style and content. When Glassman is done, Mill's works have been reduced to psychosexual fantasy. **(A)**

Hollander, Samuel. *The Economics of John Stuart Mill: Volume 1, Theory and Method; Volume 2, Political Economy.* Toronto: University of Toronto Press, 1985. Hollander, who has produced studies of two other classical economists, Smith and Ricardo, now turns his attention to the economic and political theories of Mill. His purpose is to provide a more positive assessment of the works than currently exists. Although his emphasis is more on methodology than upon technical economics, Hollander's arguments are densely developed, and a reader who is unfamiliar with Mill's basic tenets may indeed become hopelessly lost. **(A)**

Loesburg, Jonathan. *Fictions of Consciousness: Mill, Newman, and the Reading of Victorian Prose.* New Brunswick, NJ: Rutgers University Press, 1986. Loesburg uses the autobiographies of Mill and Newman to discuss nineteenth-century concepts of consciousness. He traces the relationship between these prose narratives of the time and the contemporary debate as to the nature of consciousness. He contends that autobiography is the genre which transforms philosophy into narrative and compares Mill and Newman with Carlyle and Arnold. **(A)**

Rees, J. C. *John Stuart Mill's "On Liberty."* Edited by G. L. Williams. Oxford: Oxford University Press, 1986. Williams has compiled the unpublished writings of noted Mill scholar J. C. Rees to produce a volume of useful if unsystematic criticism of *On Liberty.* Rees explores Mill's intellectual indebtedness to writers and political theorists such as Coleridge, Comte, and Carlyle. He stresses the essential continuity of Mill's libertarian ideas and discredits the "Two-Mill" theory that has him reversing or contradicting himself in later works. Using textual and historical evidence, Rees demonstrates that "On Social Freedom" has been falsely attributed to Mill. **(A)**

339

Other Sources
Blanshard, Brand. *Four Reasonable Men: Aurelius, Mill, Renan, Sidgwick.* Middletown, CT: Wesleyan University Press, 1984.

Gouinlock, James. *Excellence in Public Discourse: John Stuart Mill, John Dewey, and Social Intelligence.* New York: Teachers College, 1986.

Riley, Jonathan. *Liberal Utilitarianism: Social Choice Theory and J. S. Mill's Philosophy.* New York: Cambridge University Press, 1988.

Scarre, Geoffrey F. *Logic and Reality in the Philosophy of John Stuart Mill.* Norwell, MA: Kluwer Academic, 1989.

Semmel, Bernard. *John Stuart Mill and the Pursuit of Virtue.* New Haven: Yale University Press, 1984.

Skorupski, John. *John Stuart Mill.* New York: Routledge Chapman and Hall, 1989.

Thomas, William. *Mill.* New York: Oxford University Press, 1985.

Thornton, Neil. *The Problem of Liberalism in the Thought of John Stuart Mill.* New York: Garland, 1986.

ARTHUR MILLER
1915

Autobiographical Sources

Miller, Arthur. *Timebends: A Life*. New York: Grove, 1987. In Miller's searching account of his own artistic, political, and domestic lives he lingers over memories with a brooding melancholy that often produces flashes of insight and discovery. He talks of his parents, Marilyn Monroe, *Death of a Salesman*, and communism. He relates encounters with Ronald Reagan, Saul Bellow, and even the state of Nevada, where he lived for six weeks while awaiting a divorce. On the defensive, he discusses why some of his plays failed. A clever and revealing autobiography from a giant of the American theater. (A,G)

Roudane, Matthew C. *Conversations with Arthur Miller*. Jackson: University Press of Mississippi, 1987. This collection of thirty-nine interviews with Miller is drawn from scholarly journals and popular publications. They reveal Miller's considerable commitment to social change and his preoccupation with tragedy and fate in human life. He examines the myth of the American dream and offers considerable insight into the financial and cultural problems of American theater. Although the interviews are spread over forty years, Roudane proves a reliable guide, establishing a context for the interviews and drawing our attention to important themes as they emerge. (A,G)

HENRY MILLER
1891-1980

Autobiographical Sources

MacNiven, Ian S., ed. *The Durrell-Miller Letters, 1935-1980*. New York: New Directions, 1988. Durrell initiated a correspondence with Miller in 1935 that continued until Miller's death in 1980. The two authors developed a lively relationship through the mail, and these letters sparkle with mischievous wordplay. Each comments frankly on the other's works and works-in-progress and offers sometimes-brutal commentary on the books of other writers. Both men discuss their theoretical approaches to the purpose and structure of the novel and often describe their work habits. At one point Durrell entices Miller to visit him in France, extolling the virtues of his village's "medieval" atmosphere. Miller responds that life in America has spoiled him, that "medieval" has little appeal, but that he will be content if the little bistro Durrell described serves decent wine. This is an invaluable primary source for the study of both Miller and Durrell. MacNiven provides unobtrusive annotations to the letters and a useful introduction to each section. **(A,G)**

Miller, Henry. *Dear, Dear Brenda: The Love Letters of Henry Miller*. New York: Morrow, 1986. At the age of 84, Henry Miller fell in love with a young actress named Brenda Venus. Between 1976 and 1980, they exchanged an incredible fifteen hundred letters in which Miller declares himself the "slave of love" and "Venus" his goddess. Unfortunately only Miller's letters are included in this collection. Henry Miller fans should enjoy once again riding the curve of his passion. **(A,G)**

Stuhlmann, Gunther, ed. *A Literate Passion: Letters of Anaïs Nin and Henry Miller, 1932-1953*. Orlando, FL: Harcourt Brace Jovanovich, 1987. This collection of letters evokes the supportive friendship that Nin and Miller sustained over the years despite entangling affairs and emotional disappointments. Stuhlmann describes the relationship that developed between the two authors after they met in France in 1931. Their critiques of each other's life and works are especially interesting. This book has a strong appeal for literary scholars, as well as for the growing popular audiences of both authors. **(A,G)**

Wickes, George, ed. *Letters to Emil*. New York: New Directions, 1989. This is a short but delightful collection of Miller's letters to his friend Emil Schnellock. Miller himself planned this collection nearly forty years ago but never carried it out. Written during Miller's formative years from 1922 to 1935 when he was learning his art and finding his voice, the letters bubble over with plans for the future, witticisms, observations, and general creative mayhem. **(A)**

Evaluation of Selected Biography and Criticism

Brown, James D. *Henry Miller*. New York: Crossroad/Continuum, 1986. This literary biography examines the bohemian life and career of Henry Miller, whom Brown considers the major literary innovator of the 1930s. This study traces the development of Miller's autobiographical "ravings" through his Paris and Greek sojourns, his ongoing battles with the censors, and his relationships with Anaïs Nin, Lawrence Durrell, and others. Brown examines Miller's surprising affinities with Walt Whitman and concludes by placing him in the tradition of American transcendentalism. Highly recommended for students or general readers. (A,G)

Lewis, Leon. *Henry Miller: The Major Writings*. New York: Schocken, 1986. This study takes on the difficult task of mapping the relative significance of Miller's works. In treating Miller's sexual obsessions—as well as the themes of love, art, degradation, and modern life—Lewis deftly portrays the complexity of Miller's images, ranging from the blatantly physical to the sublimely mystical. He is particularly poignant when discussing Miller's musings on the degradation of the male. As major works Lewis nominates *The Tropic of Cancer*, *The Tropic of Capricorn*, *Black Spring*, *The Colossus of Maroussi*, *Big Sur and the Oranges of Hieronymus Bosch*, *Sexus*, and *Nexus*. (A,G)

Nin, Anaïs. *Henry and June: From the Unexpurgated Diary of Anaïs Nin*. San Diego: Harcourt Brace Jovanovich, 1986. The Henry-June-Anaïs triangle is chronicled here from the pages of Nin's journals. Creative passions, man-to-woman passions, and woman-to-woman passions flow together in a swirling account of these now-legendary sexploits. Nin is notably self-reflective and considers this affair one of the turning points of her life and career. (A,G)

Pine, Richard. *The Dandy and the Herald: Manners, Mind, and Morals from Brummell to Durrell*. New York: St Martin's, 1988. In this study of literary forms, Pine examines the role played by Durrell, Miller, and Nin in tearing down the outmoded narrative structures they inherited. For Pine, the "dandy" represents the pompous and shallow conventions of fiction. In rebellion against this figure, Miller, Nin, and Durrell, in particular, set up the image of the artist as "herald," a prophetic announcer of the literary future. Pine finds parallels of this process in literary history, tracing the struggle of innovation and tradition through the English Renaissance, romanticism, and early twentieth-century writers. After establishing the context in which "dandies," like Wilde, Beardsley, and Jarry flourished, Pine goes on to examine the failure of modern literature to solve or transcend the dandy/herald dichotomy. (A)

Winslow, Kathryn. *Henry Miller: Full of Life*. New York: Tarcher/St. Martin's, 1986. Winslow was one of the many writers and artists who continued to support Miller in his wild ways and controversial writing when others had fallen away. Miller and Winslow met in 1944 when he settled in Big Sur. She opened a bookstore and gallery to provide a secure outlet for his writings and watercolors. Her disarmingly unstudied reminiscences of Miller provide details of his personal life, his trips to Paris, and his relationships with such writers as Anaïs Nin and Lawrence Durrell. Included are many photographs of Miller and useful reference notes. (A,G)

Other Sources
   Howard, Joyce, ed. *Letters By Henry Miller to Hoki Tokuda Miller.* New York: Freundlich, 1987.

JOHN MILTON
1608-1674

Evaluation of Selected Criticism

Belsey, Catherine. *John Milton: Language, Gender, Power*. London: Black-well, 1988. Drawing on new historicist, feminist, Marxist, and post-struc-turalist theories, Belsey offers brief critical assessments of Milton's major texts. She locates the power of his verse in its ambiguity and seeming contra-dictions. Her analysis of the themes of voice, authority, gender, and narrative concludes that Milton represents the culmination of Renaissance "poetic sub-jectivity." **(A,G)**

Blessington, Francis C. *"Paradise Lost": Ideal and Tragic Epic*. Boston: Twayne, 1988. This useful introduction to Milton's great epic skillfully addresses a new reader's difficulties with the poem and offers a satisfying overview of the scope and ambition of the work. He describes Milton's liter-ary risks in attempting portrayals of God, Christ, Satan, and an unfallen Adam and Eve. A biographical sketch and a chronology of Milton's life and works is included. **(A,G)**

Chainey, Graham. *A Literary History of Cambridge*. Ann Arbor: University of Michigan Press, 1986. This behind-the-scenes look at the literary stories and scandals of Cambridge University makes for enjoyable voyeurism. The gossip is truly on an epic scale—spread over eight hundred years of Cam-bridge history and featuring anecdotes on nearly every notable British writer, including Milton, Wordsworth, Macaulay, and Sylvia Plath. Love affairs, drinking habits, duels, rivalries—all are paraded forth in often humorous detail. This is a very entertaining book that in its own way reveals the im-mense contribution Cambridge has made to the literary world. **(G)**

Danielson, Dennis, ed. *The Cambridge Companion to Milton*. Cambridge: Cambridge University Press, 1989. For this anthology, Danielson invited noted Milton scholars to address various aspects of Milton's works in a manner that would interest the serious student approaching Milton for the first time. The essays by Shawcross, Lewalski, McColley, Radzinowicz, and Bennett, among others, provide the kind of intelligent guidance that is indispensable for under-standing Milton. At the same time, the essays do not fall into the trap of other, similar companion guides; the scholars do not "talk down" to the reader but offer challenging commentary and insightful direction. This is probably the best guide to Milton currently in print. **(A,G)**

Grose, Christopher. *Milton and the Sense of Tradition*. New Haven: Yale University Press, 1988. Grose's psychobiography presents a Milton whose art enabled him to achieve emotional integration. Grose humanizes Milton as he explores the psychodynamics of a poet who attempted to revive the Reformation. **(A)**

Guibbory, Achsah. *The Map of Time: Seventeenth-Century English Literature and Ideas of Pattern in History.* Champaign: University of Illinois Press, 1986. Guibbory reveals the conceptions of time and history that underlie seventeenth-century thought in this closely reasoned study of six major writers—Donne, Bacon, Jonson, Herrick, Milton, and Dryden. Guibbory outlines three such conceptions: degeneration and decay since the Garden of Eden; cycles of generation and decay; and the advance of civilization. He then shows how these three patterns of historical perspective influence poetry, drama, scientific and religious prose, and the writing of history. In every case, Guibbory relates history to genre, structure, imagery, and theme. Highly recommended. **(A,G)**

Kendrick, Christopher. *Milton: A Study in Ideology and Form.* London: Methuen, 1986. This Marxist reading of *Paradise Lost*, termed the "epic of emergent capitalism," makes a number of valuable critical points. Kendrick describes how romance and pastoral, epic posture and tragic drama, interact to produce major paradoxical moments in the poem. His discussion of utopian motives is particularly insightful. However, long stretches of the book suffer from an exasperating dependence on Marxist economic analysis. **(A)**

Lewalski, Barbara Kiefer. *"Paradise Lost" and the Rhetoric of Literary Forms.* Princeton: Princeton University Press, 1985. This study pulls together the insights of many critics on Milton's poetic rhetoric in *Paradise Lost*. Lewalski reveals the complex layering of literary analogues and genres in passages of the poem and provides a clear interpretation of the work as a whole. A rewarding source for students interested in the wide range of critical opinions that have been brought to bear on the poem. **(A)**

MacCallum, Hugh. *Milton and the Sons of God: The Divine Image in Milton's Epic Poetry.* Toronto: University of Toronto Press, 1986. Drawing upon his extensive knowledge of Reformed dogmatics and church history, MacCallum illuminates the theological dimensions of *Paradise Lost* and *Paradise Regained.* He examines Milton's concept of the Trinity, the intercessional role of the Son, and the evolving image of man in relation to the godhead. This is a finely wrought study of a difficult topic. **(A)**

MacDonald, Ronald R. *The Burial-Places of Memory: Epic Underworlds in Vergil, Dante, and Milton.* Amherst: University of Massachusetts Press, 1987. MacDonald admirably examines how Dante based his epic vision of the Underworld on an understanding of Vergil and how Milton incorporated images of and allusions to both poets. The ghost-inhabited "burial-places" of the title is a shadow land where classical influences meet and intermingle with Christian sensibilities. MacDonald pays special attention to issues of primacy, precedence, legitimacy, and origins in the texts. **(A)**

Myers, William. *Milton and Free Will: An Essay in Criticism and Philosophy.* London: Methuen, 1987. Written for a very specialized audience, this study attempts to "reconstructualize" Milton by appealing to an odd assortment of writers, including Pope John Paul II and Cardinal John Henry Newman. (A)

Radzinowicz, Mary Ann. *Milton's Epics and the Book of Psalms.* Princeton: Princeton University Press, 1989. Milton read and translated the Psalms throughout his life. In this study, Radzinowicz traces the biblical sources that animated Milton's masterworks—*Paradise Lost* and *Paradise Regained.* (A)

Rumrich, John Peter. *Matter of Glory: A New Preface to Paradise Lost.* Pittsburgh: University of Pittsburgh Press, 1987. Rumrich has used C. S. Lewis's important *A Preface to Paradise Lost* as a steppingstone for a reevaluation of Milton. He views the concept of "glory" as the poet's unifying principle and traces the idea through the Scriptures and earlier epics. He examines Milton's conception of God and analyzes the fateful triangle of Adam, Eve, and Satan. His discussion of the differences between angels and humans leads into an insightful analysis of Adam's and Eve's individual decisions to sin. Written in clear and informative prose Rumrich's "preface" is a sound introduction to Milton's masterwork. (A,G)

Stavely, Keith W. *Puritan Legacies: "Paradise Lost" and the New England Tradition, 1630-1890.* Ithaca, NY: Cornell University Press, 1987. Stavely analyzes *Paradise Lost* for its presentation of authority and power, the relationship of Adam and Eve, and the portrayal of Satan to show how the disintegration of English Puritanism foreshadowed a similar decline in New England a century later. His thesis is that Puritan ideas of authority and power led to nineteenth-century American imperialism and capitalism. Although this book is more about politics and feminist philosophy than Milton, the conjectured connections are interesting for students of Milton or American Puritanism. (A)

Wittreich, Joseph. *Interpreting "Samson Agonistes."* Princeton, NJ: Princeton University Press, 1986. Wittreich offers a revisionist interpretation of Milton's *Samson Agonistes* as a paradigm of the "failed hero." The Samson portrayed in these pages is not a savior figure, not "heroic" in the classical sense, and does not undergo regeneration as the body of current criticism insists. Wittreich's case is built upon a thorough survey of Puritan literature, Scriptural commentary, and English political thought. The most telling evidence, in the author's view, are the circumstances of publication. *Samson Agonistes* was first published as a companion piece to *Paradise Regained* in 1671. Interpreted as part of the author's overall design, this edition juxtaposed two types of heroic figures—one who succeeds, another who fails. This well-written study is certain to arouse controversy among traditional Milton scholars. (A,G)

Wittreich, Joseph. *Feminist Milton*. Ithaca, NY: Cornell University Press, 1988. Wittreich selectively chooses passages from Milton's poetry that, when read out of context, show Milton as a precursor of feminism. But even though Milton believed in equal adversaries, both theologically and politically, he did not ascribe to equality as such, and Wittreich stretches many points to give Milton feminist credentials. (A)

Other Sources
Agar, H. *Milton and Plato*. Brunswick, ME: Bern Porter, 1985.

Angelo, Peter G. *Fall to Glory: Theological Reflections on Milton's Epics*. New York: Peter Lang, 1988.

Bauman, Michael. *A Scripture Index to John Milton's "De Doctrina."* New York: Medieval and Renaissance, 1989.

Bennett, Joan S. *Reviving Liberty: Radical Christian Humanism in Milton's Great Poems*. Cambridge: Harvard University Press, 1989.

Brown, Cedric C. *John Milton's Aristocratic Entertainments*. New York: Cambridge University Press, 1985.

Budick, Sanford. *The Dividing Muse: Images of Sacred Disjunction in Milton's Poetry*. New Haven: Yale University Press, 1985.

Crump, Galbraith M., ed. *Approaches to Teaching Milton's Paradise Lost*. New York: Modern Language Association, 1986.

DuRocher, Richard J. *Milton and Ovid*. Ithaca, NY: Cornell University Press, 1985.

Entzminger, Robert L. *Divine Word: Milton and the Redemption of Language*. Pittsburgh: Duquesne University Press, 1985.

Etchells, Ruth, ed. *Milton*. Scarsdale, NY: Lion USA, 1988.

Fallon, Robert T. *Captain or Colonel: The Soldier in Milton's Life and Art*. Columbia: University of Missouri Press, 1985.

Ferguson, Margaret, and Mary Nyquist, eds. *Remembering Milton: Essays on the Texts and Traditions*. New York: Routledge Chapman and Hall, 1988.

Goslee, Nancy M. *Uriel's Eye: Miltonic Stationing and Statuary in Blake, Keats, and Shelley*. Tuscaloosa: University of Alabama Press, 1985.

Gregory, E. Richard. *Milton and the Muses*. Tuscaloosa: University of Alabama Press, 1989.

Griffin, Dustin. *Regaining Paradise: Milton and the Eighteenth Century.* New York: Cambridge University Press, 1986.

Grossman, Marshall. *Authors to Themselves: Milton and the Revelation of History.* New York: Cambridge University Press, 1988.

Henry, Nathaniel H. *The True Wayfaring Christian: Studies in Milton's Puritanism.* New York: Peter Lang, 1988.

Hunter, William B. *Milton's English Poetry: Being Entries from a Milton Encyclopedia.* Lewisburg, PA: Bucknell University Press, 1986.

Hunter, William B. *The Descent of Urania: Studies in Milton, 1946-1988.* Lewisburg, PA: Bucknell University Press, 1989.

Kerrigan, William. *The Sacred Complex on the Psychogenesis of "Paradise Lost."* Cambridge: Harvard University Press, 1983.

Labriola, Albert C., and Edward Sichi, Jr., eds. *Milton's Legacy in the Arts.* University Park: The Pennsylvania State University Press, 1988.

Lieb, Michael. *The Sinews of Ulysses: Form and Convention in Milton's Works.* Pittsburgh: Duquesne, 1988.

Macaulay, Thomas B. *John Milton and the Growth of British Literature.* Albuquerque, NM: American Classical College Press, 1985.

Martindale, Charles. *John Milton amd the Transformation of Ancient Epic.* London: Croom Helm, 1986.

McGuire, Maryann C. *Milton's Puritan Masque.* Athens: University of Georgia Press, 1984.

Merrill, Thomas F. *Epic God-Talk: "Paradise Lost" and the Grammar of Religious Language.* Jefferson, NC: McFarland, 1986.

Moyles, R. G. *The Text of "Paradise Lost": A Study in Editorial Procedure.* Toronto: University of Toronto Press, 1985.

Mustazza, Leonard. *Such Prompt Eloquence: Language As Agency and Character in Milton's Epics.* Lewisburg, PA: Bucknell University Press, 1988.

Patrides, C. A. *An Annotated Critical Bibliography of Milton.* New York: St. Martin's, 1987.

Schindler, Walter L. *Voice and Crisis: Invocation in Milton's Poetry.* Hamden, CT: Archon/Shoe String, 1984.

Schwartz, Regina M. *Remembering and Repeating: Biblical Creation in Paradise Lost.* New York: Cambridge University Press, 1989.

Shawcross, John T. *The Collection of the Works of John Milton and Miltoniana in the Margaret I. King Lexington Library.* Lexington: University of Kentucky Libraries, 1985.

Shawcross, John T. *A Bibliography for the Years 1624-1700.* New York: Medieval and Renaissance, 1984.

Shoaf, R. A. *Milton, Poet of Duality: A Study of Semiosis in the Poetry and the Prose.* New Haven: Yale University Press, 1985.

Simms, James H., and Leland Ryken, eds. *Milton and Scriptural Tradition: The Bible into Poetry.* Columbia: University of Missouri Press, 1984.

Sloane, Thomas O. *Donne, Milton, and the End of Humanistic Rhetoric.* Berkeley: University of California Press, 1985.

Steadman, John M. *Milton and the Paradoxes of Renaissance Heroism.* Baton Rouge: Louisiana State University Press, 1987.

Steadman, John M. *The Hill and the Labyrinth: Discourse and Certitude in Milton and His Near-Contemporaries.* Berkeley: University of California Press, 1984.

Steadman, John M. *The Wall of Paradise: Essays on Milton's Poetics.* Baton Rouge: Louisiana State University Press, 1985.

Steadman, John M. *Milton's Biblical and Classical Imagery: Poetry and Exegetical Tradition.* Pittsburgh: Duquesne, 1984.

Sterne, Laurence, and Harold Kollmeier, eds. *A Concordance to the English Prose of John Milton.* New York: Medieval and Renaissance, 1985.

Stevens, Paul. *Imagination and the Presence of Shakespeare in Paradise Lost.* Madison: University of Wisconsin Press, 1985.

Swaim, Kathleen. *Before and After the Fall: Contrasting Modes in "Paradise Lost."* Amherst: University of Massachusetts Press, 1986.

Toliver, Harold. *Transported Styles in Shakespeare and Milton.* University Park: The Pennsylvania State University Press, 1989.

Travers, Michael E. *The Devotional Experience in the Poetry of John Milton.* Lewiston, NY: Edwin Mellen, 1987.

Walker, Julia M., ed. *Milton and the Idea of Woman.* Champaign: University of Illinois Press, 1988.

Werner, Bette C. *Blake's Vision of the Poetry of Milton.* Lewisburg, PA: Bucknell University Press, 1986.

Willis, Gladys J. *The Penalty of Eve: John Milton and Divorce.* New York: Peter Lang, 1985.

GEORGE MOORE
1852-1933

Autobiographical Sources

Eakin, David B., and Robert Langenfeld, eds. *George Moore's Correspondence with the Mysterious Countess*. Victoria: English Literary Studies, University of Victoria, 1984. From 1903 to 1906, George Moore corresponded with an admirer, whose identity has not been firmly established. She was known variously as "Gabrielle, Countess von Hoenstadt," "Gabrielle Vassal," "Cecile," "Baronne Franzi Ripp" or simply the "Baronne." These twelve, long, and well-written letters by Moore to the countess reveal all the symptoms of an epistolary love affair. Her twenty-two letters to him reveal a flirtatious and capricious nature. Although there is no evidence that they ever met face-to-face, Moore based his play *The Coming of Gabrielle* (1920) on a fantasy of just such a meeting. (A,G)

Gerber, Helmut E. *George Moore on Parnassus: Letters (1900-1933) to Secretaries, Publishers, Printers, Agents, Literati, Friends, and Acquaintances.* Newark: University of Delaware Press, 1988. Gerber introduces this collection of over twelve hundred letters with a biographical essay that describes Moore's life and career and identifies the many recipients of his correspondence. The fully annotated letters are arranged chronologically by recipient. This is an indispensable primary source for Moore scholars. (A)

Evaluation of Selected Criticism

Davis, W. Eugene. *The Celebrated Case of "Esther Waters": The Collaboration of George Moore and Barrett H. Clark on "Esther Waters: A Play."* Lanham, MD: University Press of America, 1984. In a lengthy introduction, Davis describes the collaboration of Moore and Clark to adapt Moore's novel *Esther Waters* for the stage. In one sense, the collaboration was a failure. Each emerged with a different version of the play. In a larger sense, the collaboration succeeded in that both versions embody innovations introduced by both writers. The introduction is followed by the full text of Moore's version of the play. (A)

Langenfeld, Robert. *George Moore: An Annotated Secondary Bibliography of Writings About Him*. New York: AMS Press, 1987. This fully annotated bibliography of over 2,350 secondary sources provides a comprehensive overview of Moore's life, career, and critical reputation. The citations, which are arranged chronologically, span the years 1878 to 1987. Langenfeld's introduction surveys Moore's critical reception. The materials are fully indexed. (A)

MARIANNE MOORE
1887-1972

Evaluation of Selected Criticism

Berg, Temma F., ed. *Engendering the Word: Feminist Essays in Psychosexual Poetics.* Champaign: University of University of Illinois Press, 1989. This collection of twelve essays focus on the psychosexual aspects of women's writing, using perspectives derived from Cixous, Lacan, Chodorow, and Freud. Divided into three sections, this book first examines theory and then introduces a cross-cultural view by examining how writers address racially and economically marginal groups. Finally, the essays delve into linguistic analysis with particular emphasis on the works of Dickinson and Moore. This is a recommended introduction to feminist methodology. (A,G)

Holley, Margaret. *The Poetry of Marianne Moore: A Study in Voice and Value.* New York: Cambridge University Press, 1987. Dividing Moore's canon chronologically into creative periods, Holley argues that Moore's poems divide themselves between the "narrative and the pictorial" and the "temporal and the spatial." Holley examines a wide range of Moore's work under these categories and provides excellent close readings. (A,G)

Kalstone, David. *Becoming A Poet: Elizabeth Bishop with Marianne Moore and Robert Lowell.* Farrar, Straus & Giroux, 1989. Kalstone examines the deep friendship that developed between Bishop and her mentor Moore. Upon Moore's death, Bishop found some of the same support in a relationship with Lowell who maintained contact with her despite her self-destructive binges and his mental instability. (A)

Martin, Taffy. *Marianne Moore: Subversive Modernist.* Austin: University of Texas Press, 1987. Martin argues that Moore rejected the masculine dominance of her time, and redirected her strongly feminist individualism into her poetry, not as a political voice but through her innovative poetics. In arguing for Moore's "modernism," Martin clearly demonstrates the sources of beauty and imagination in the poetry. Though grounded in feminism, Martin's insightful study clearly addresses the poetry, not the politics, of Moore's career. (A,G)

Molesworth, Charles. *Marianne Moore: A Literary Life.* New York: Atheneum, 1990. In this first full-length biography, Molesworth was given access to Moore's private papers on the condition he not quote from them. The result is an account of the events of her narrow, literary life and an excellent analysis of her works, but a timid psychological portrait of a writer and editor who was instrumental in founding modernism. Includes photographs. (A,G)

Schulman, Grace. *Marianne Moore: The Poetry of Engagement.* Champaign: University of Illinois Press, 1987. Schulman's study provides a comprehensive catalog of Moore's rhetorical figures. These are divided into two types: those that speak to a personified human quality or a perceived social type, and those that participate in an interior dialectic. According to Schulman, who draws on the theories of Freud and Valery, Moore's creative process required the contradictions and contraries embodied in this dialectic. **(A,G)**

Slatin, John M. *The Savage's Romance: The Poetry of Marianne Moore.* University Park: Pennsylvania State University Press, 1986. This insightful study is the first to analyze the struggle for poetic form of a poet whose greatest meanings often seem projected through the fewest words. Slatin provides an excellent treatment of the early poems by viewing them within the context of the magazines in which they appeared. Recommended for students and scholars of modern poetry. **(A)**

Steinman, Lisa M. *Made in America: Science, Technology, and American Modernist Poets.* New Haven: Yale University Press, 1987. This study examines how modernist poets—specifically, Williams, Moore, and Stevens—set out to rejuvenate poetry by redefining its relationship with the developing world of technology and commerce. To justify the virtues of "genteel verse," modernists stressed poetry's "technical" structure and virtues (its efficiency, for example) or associated poetry with the values of pure scientific research. This study is a valuable contribution to understanding the modernists, their cultural context, and their theories of poetics. **(A,G)**

Willis, Patricia C., ed. *The Complete Prose of Marianne Moore.* New York: Viking, 1986. This collection of Moore's prose includes many long unavailable gems such as her 1921 review of Eliot's *The Sacred Wood*, in which she examines the connection between poetic criticism and the creation of poetry. Her essays on writers, such as Wallace Stevens and Ezra Pound, demonstrate her critical acumen and poetic sensibility, while more general essays shed light on her personality. Critically acclaimed only for her poetry, Moore's fiction is rich in striking images and cadences. This is an essential primary source for students interested in understanding Moore's poetry. **(A,G)**

Willis, Patricia C. *Marianne Moore: Vision into Verse.* Philadelphia: Rosenbach Museum & Library, 1987. The Marianne Moore Collection at the Rosenbach Library in Philadelphia may well be the most complete record we have of any literary career. This catalog of memorabilia is a striking testament to the power of Moore's imagination to transform the objects of everyday life into poetry. Much of this material—newspaper clippings, curiosities, artifacts, and assorted odds-and-ends—is illustrated here for the first time. "Dear St. Nicklus," written at the age of twelve, begins the collection, and "Prevalent at One Time," written in 1970 at age eighty-seven and her last poem, ends it. The collection is introduced by Willis' sensitive essay on Moore's life and poetry. **(A,G)**

WILLIAM MORRIS
1834-1896

Autobiographical Sources

Kelvin, Norman, ed. *The Collected Letters of William Morris. Vol 1: 1848-1880*. Princeton, NJ: Princeton University Press, 1984. Of the 2,400 letters collected here, 1,500 have not been published before. Kelvin, a knowledgeable scholar, provides extensive notes, a chronology, and an introduction covering Morris' friendships and career. The letters themselves reveal much about Morris, especially his use of myth and legend, prose style, knowledge of painting, and attitudes toward his contemporaries, such as Shelley and Ruskin. This is the most important resource for Morris scholarship published in decades. **(A)**

Evaluation of Selected Criticism

Aho, Gary L. *William Morris: A Reference Guide*. Boston: G. K. Hall, 1985. Every book, article, and review that referred to Morris between 1897 and 1982 is cited in this annotated bibliographical guide. A separate section lists doctoral dissertations. A chronology and a bibliography of bibliographies are included, making this an essential research tool for Morris scholars. **(A)**

Boris, Eileen. *Art and Labor: Ruskin, Morris, and the Craftsman Ideal in America*. Philadelphia: Temple University Press, 1986. Boris undertakes a general history of the American Arts and Crafts Movement of the late nineteenth century. Using William Morris and John Ruskin as the focal points of her discussion, Boris examines the relationship of the movement to education, religion, architecture, the revival of folk traditions, immigration, and the developing factory system of production. This book is probably of most interest to students of social history, although literature is seen as an integral part of the movement. **(A)**

Stansky, Peter. *Redesigning the World: William Morris, the 1880s, and the Arts and Crafts*. Princeton: Princeton University Press, 1985. The Arts and Crafts movement of the 1880s was born at a time when its spiritual founder, William Morris, had begun to doubt its usefulness. In 1883, Morris threw himself behind the cause of socialism after becoming convinced that only political change could bring about a significant reform in the arts. In this study, Stansky focuses primarily on the Arts and Crafts movement. **(A)**

Other Sources

Banham, Joanna, and Jennifer Harris, eds. *William Morris and the Middle Ages*. New York: St. Martin's, 1988.

Hodgson, Amanda. *The Romances of William Morris.* New York: Cambridge University Press, 1987.

Naylor, Gillian, ed. *William Morris by Himself: Designs and Writings.* Boston: Bulfinch Press, 1988.

Peterson, William S. *The Kelmscott Press: A History of William Morris's Typographical Adventure.* Berkeley: University of California Press, 1989.

IRIS MURDOCH
1919

Author's Recent Bibliography

The Philosopher's Pupil, 1983 (novel); *The Good Apprentice*, 1986 (novel); *Acastos: Two Platonic Dialogues*, 1987; *The Book and the Brotherhood*, 1987 (novel); *The Message to the Planet*, 1989 (novel).

Evaluation of Selected Criticism

Begnal, Kate. *Iris Murdoch: A Reference Guide*. Boston: G. K. Hall, 1987. Spanning the years 1953 to 1983, this research guide contains a wealth of citations on Murdoch, including dissertations. Well-written annotations provide detailed descriptions of the books, articles, reviews, and notices to direct researchers. The citations are arranged chronologically. Although not fully comprehensive, this bibliography has considerable breadth and depth. (A)

Bove, Cheryl Browning. *A Character Index and Guide to the Fiction of Iris Murdoch*. New York: Garland, 1986. This guide to Murdoch's fiction is arranged for easy use by either students or general readers. Following a chapter on Murdoch's approach to characterization, Bove provides an index of Murdoch's characters—both named and unnamed. Entries include a description, documentation, literary and historical references, and relevant geographical names. The characters are listed in their order of appearance in Murdoch's fiction, which allows the reader to examine trends of character development across Murdoch's entire body of fiction. A comprehensive general index allows the reader to cross-reference characters, works, and themes. (A,G)

Johnson, Deborah. *Iris Murdoch*. Bloomington: Indiana University Press, 1987. In this short study, Johnson applies feminist theory to Iris Murdoch's fiction, a body of work that stiffly resists such an attempt. Murdoch is known for her strong male narrators; her female characters are most often relegated to peripheral roles where they have little bearing on theme or plot. Johnson's study never really clarifies Murdoch's stance relative to feminism. (A,G)

Todd, Richard. *Iris Murdoch*. New York: Methuen, 1985. This study examines the artistic, social, and moral assumptions in Murdoch's novels. Todd reviews all of the novels to date and briefly considers several of her plays and essays. He argues that Murdoch's writings emerge from deeply held beliefs about the role of art in society. (A,G)

Other Sources

Brooks-Davies, Douglas. *Fielding, Dickens, Gosse, Iris Murdoch and Oedipal Hamlet*. New York: St. Martin's, 1989.

357

Conradi, Peter J. *Iris Murdoch: The Saint and the Artist.* New York: St. Martin's, 1986.

Kane, Richard C. *Iris Murdoch, Muriel Spark, and John Fowles: Didactic Demons in Modern Fiction.* Madison, NJ: Fairleigh Dickinson University Press, 1988.

Mackey, Douglas A. *Iris Murdoch: A Sea of Contingency.* San Bernardino: Borgo Press, 1990.

VLADIMIR NABOKOV
1899-1977

Author's Recent Bibliography
The Enchanter, 1986 (novel).

Autobiographical Sources
Nabokov, Dimitri, and Matthew Bruccoli. *Vladimir Nabokov: Letters, 1940-1977*. Orlando, FL: Harcourt Brace Jovanovich. 1989. This comprehensive collection of letters, written primarily to publishers, editors, and literary friends, sheds light on the multi-faceted Nabokov. The letters cover the period from Nabokov's arrival in America to his death. Full of wit and intimate revelations, this collection is essential for a close understanding of Nabokov's life at the height of his literary career. **(A)**

Evaluation of Selected Biography and Criticism
Clancy, Laurie. *The Novels of Vladimir Nabokov*. New York: St. Martin's, 1985. Clancy examines the themes and techniques of each novel in an attempt to reduce the difficulty and mystery of Nabokov's fiction. She nicely illustrates Nabakov's development from a Russian sensibility to a truly international intellect. **(A,G)**

Field, Andrew. *VN: The Life and Art of Vladimir Nabokov*. New York: Crown, 1986. Nabokov died in 1977, leaving instructions in his will that his private papers not be published until fifty years after the death of his wife and son. Despite this handicap, Field draws on many previously unavailable sources and illuminates the complex and intriguing life of one of the twentieth century's most acclaimed novelists. He focuses on the biographical events but never fails to discuss the works as they shed light on his subject. A powerful and highly recommended biography for all audiences. **(A,G)**

Green, Geoffrey. *Freud and Nabokov*. Lincoln: University of Nebraska Press, 1988. In this exercise in postmodernist fragmentation, Green juxtaposes quotations from these two men, both obsessed with the power and art of memory. Structured as a series of twenty vignettes, their views are presented in dialogue form. Interesting parallels emerge from what at first glance seemed a mere pastiche. **(A)**

Milbauer, Asher Z. *Transcending Exile: Conrad, Nabokov, I. B. Singer*. Gainesville: University Presses of Florida, 1985. In this narrowly focused study, Milbauer, an emigré himself, examines the issue of literary transplantation in the works of Conrad, Nabokov, and Singer. Each of these authors experienced cultural displacement or created their finest works in a language other than their native tongue. (A)

Parker, Stephen Jan. *Understanding Vladimir Nabokov*. Columbia: University of South Carolina Press, 1987. From this study by one who knew him, Nabokov emerges with his self-invented persona intact. Parker competently introduces the new reader or student to Nabakov's entire canon, moving with confidence through a complicated literary landscape. (A,G)

Salomon, Roger B. *Desperate Story-Telling: Post-Romantic Elaborations of the Mock-Heroic Mode*. Athens, GA: University of Georgia Press, 1987. The most important feature of the mock-heroic mode is the attempt to maintain "golden" virtues in an "iron" age. Working to more clearly define the mock-heroic, Salomon traces Nabokov's themes back through literary tradition to Cervantes. The study also examines the works of Stendhal, Byron, Joyce, Stevens, Williams, and others. (A)

Other Sources
Boyd, Brian. *Nabokov's "Ada": The Place of Consciousness*. Ann Arbor: Ardis, 1985.

Rydel, Christine. *A Nabokov Who's Who: A Complete Guide to Characters and Proper Names in the Works of Vladimir Nabokov*. Ann Arbor: Ardis, 1989.

Stonehill, Brian. *The Self-Conscious Novel: Artifice in Fiction from Joyce to Pynchon*. Philadelphia: University of Pennsylvania Press, 1988.

Toker, Leona. *Nabokov*. Ithaca, NY: Cornell University Press, 1985.

Toker, Leona. *Nabokov: The Mystery of Literary Structure*. Ithaca, NY: Cornell University Press, 1989.

V. S. NAIPAUL
1932

Author's Recent Bibliography
   The Loss of El Dorado: A History, 1984 (nonfiction); *The Enigma of Arrival*, 1987 (novel); *A Turn in the South*, 1989 (travel nonfiction).

Evaluation of Selected Criticism
   Cudjoe, Selwyn R. *V. S. Naipaul: A Materialist Reading*. Amherst: University of Massachusetts Press, 1988. As both an important twentieth-century writer and a representative of his native West Indies, Naipaul has long troubled some critics who accuse him of racist attitudes. Cudjoe draws on psychoanalytic and literary theories to explain how Naipaul first absorbed, then rejected, his culture. In building his argument, he provides excellent close readings of Naipaul's work and cites many authorities to explain Naipaul's social attitudes. **(A)**

   Hassan, Dolly Zulakha. *V. S. Naipaul and the West Indies*. New York: Peter Lang, 1989. Hassan examines the body of West Indian literature within which Naipaul expresses his insights on culture and colonialism. Hassan contends that Naipaul is not the Eurocentric "prophet of doom" as described by so many West Indian critics. Instead, she sees Naipaul's novels as accurate descriptions of a culturally sterile society that forces many of its writers into exile. Naipaul's harsh criticism of Caribbean societies masks a "disguised concern" that goes to the root of many social problems but stops short of proposing solutions. The very elements of his works that most alienate his critics are, themselves, a commentary on a colonial society that alienates its most intellectual and objective observers. **(A,G)**

   Hughes, Peter. *V. S. Naipaul*. New York: Routledge, 1988. A volume in the Contemporary Writers Series, this book provides a concise critical introduction to Naipaul's works for the general reader. **(G)**

   Kelly, Richard. *V. S. Naipaul*. New York: Ungar/Continuum, 1989. This critical introduction provides a biographical and sociohistorical perspective on Naipaul's works. Kelly contends that Naipaul is impelled to write because of his sense of cultural marginality. His writing acts to construct a "psychological defense against the world." He considers *A House for Mr. Biswas* the central novel of Naipaul's career, symbolizing as it does his need for psychological shelter. **(A,G)**

Nightingale, Peggy. *Journey Through Darkness: The Writings of V. S. Naipaul.* New York: University of Queensland Press, 1987. This study is a detailed critical analysis of Naipaul's fiction and nonfiction. For Nightingale, Naipaul "discerns the forces that shaped the human sensibility as lurking in the social structure—particularly that left by colonialism." She demonstrates how Naipaul's nonfiction inspires and shapes his fiction and traces selected themes throughout his works. (A,G)

THOMAS NASHE
1567-1601?

Evaluation of Selected Criticism

Hilliard, Stephen S. *The Singularity of Thomas Nashe*. Lincoln: University of Nebraska Press, 1986. Little is known of the life of Nashe, but much can be inferred from the response of the Elizabethan audience to his inflammatory writings. In 1589 Nashe was hired by two clerics, Bancroft and Whitgift, to defend the views of the established church. By 1599, he had so alienated his patrons that they issued an edict banning his works. Nashe's satirical wit fed upon the exploitative mentality of Londoners, and on a perception of rampant injustice in England. Hilliard situates Nashe firmly in the social and political milieu of the 1590s before examining more closely the rhetoric and logic of his essays and satires. (A)

Hutson, Lorna. *Thomas Nashe In Context*. Oxford: Clarendon Press, 1989. This revised doctoral thesis concentrates on Nashe's works. Hutson gives an introductory overview of critical perspectives on Nashe before setting out the various contexts of the writings—Elizabethan economics, the business of publishing, and the activities of social work and leisure. Nashe viewed writing as a "festive" discourse and, in many ways, played the fool for the entertainment of his audience. Through close examination of the works, Hutson demonstrates that beneath the jovial surface was serious intent, as his contemporaries certainly recognized. (A)

Posluszny, Patricia. *Thomas Nashe's "Summer's Last Will and Testament."* New York: Peter Lang, 1989. Nashe, who is known for the racy, pungent style of his prose works *The Unfortunate Traveller* (1594) and *Pierce Penniless* (1592), wrote one play to be performed before the Archbishop of Canterbury at Croydon Castle in 1592. *Summer's Last Will and Testament* is an inventive blend of allegorical pageantry, satire, farce, and morality play. This edition (in modern spelling) collates all eighteen extant copies of the text and the 1600 quarto. Included are a critical introduction, glossary, and explanatory notes. (A,G)

ANAÏS NIN
1903-1977

Autobiographical Sources

Nin, Anaïs. *The Early Diary of Anaïs Nin. Volume 4, 1927-1931.* This volume covers the years of Nin's marriage, her early career as an actress, her love affairs, and her friendships. Still more narcissistic than introspective, these early diaries begin to reveal how she is moving toward the woman in the more profound later diaries. As always, she provides fascinating reading. (A,G)

Nin, Anaïs. *Henry and June: From the Unexpurgated Diary of Anaïs Nin.* San Diego: Harcourt Brace Jovanovich, 1986. The Henry-June-Anaïs triangle is chronicled here from the pages of Nin's journals. Creative passions, man-to-woman passions, and woman-to-woman passions flow together in a swirling account of these now-legendary sexploits. Nin is notably self-reflective and considers this affair one of the turning points of her life and career. (A,G)

Stuhlmann, Gunther, ed. *A Literate Passion: Letters of Anaïs Nin and Henry Miller, 1932-1953.* Orlando, FL: Harcourt Brace Jovanovich, 1987. This collection of letters evokes the supportive friendship that Nin and Miller sustained over the years despite entangling affairs and emotional disappointments. Stuhlmann describes the relationship that developed between the two authors after they met in France in 1931. Their critiques of each other's life and works are especially interesting. This book has a strong appeal for literary scholars, as well as for the growing popular audiences of both authors. (A,G)

Evaluation of Selected Criticism

Benstock, Shari. *Women of the Left Bank: Paris, 1900-1940.* Austin: University of Texas Press, 1986. Benstock sets out to reshape the conventional perception of pre-World War II literary Paris, arguing that what has been called "the Pound era" was actually "the Gertrude Stein era." Included in Benstock's survey of notable women writers of the period are H. D., Anaïs Nin, and Djuna Barnes. Many lesser known female writers are given their proper due, among them: Barney, Beach, Boyle, Colette, Cumard, Flanner, Jolas, Monnier, Solano, Toklas, and Wharton. The result of Benstock's reevaluation of these authors is a redefinition of literary modernism. (A,G)

Pine, Richard. *The Dandy and the Herald: Manners, Mind, and Morals from Brummell to Durrell.* New York: St Martin's Press, 1988. In this study of literary forms, Pine examines the role played by Durrell, Miller, and Nin in tearing down the outmoded narrative structures they inherited. For Pine, the "dandy" represents the pompous and shallow conventions of Edwardian fiction.

In rebellion against this figure, Miller, Nin, and Durrell, in particular, set up the image of the artist as "herald," a prophetic announcer of the literary future. Pine finds parallels of this process in literary history, tracing the struggle of innovation and tradition through the English Renaissance, romanticism, and early twentieth-century writers. After establishing the context in which "dandies," like Wilde, Beardsley, and Jarry flourished, Pine goes on to examine the failure of modern literature to solve or transcend the dandy/herald dichotomy. (A)

Other Sources

Spencer, Sharon, ed. *Anaïs Nin, Art and Artists: A Collection of Essays.* Greenwood, FL: Penkevill, 1987.

FRANK NORRIS
1870-1902

Autobiographical Sources

Crisler, Jesse S., comp. *Frank Norris: Collected Letters*. San Francisco: The Book Club of California, 1986. In 1956 the Book Club of California published the definitive, scholarly edition of Norris' sixty-eight extant letters. Most of Norris' manuscripts and correspondence has disappeared even though he was one of the most popular and critically acclaimed writers of his day. Since 1956 interest in Norris has increased, new materials uncovered, and errors about his life corrected. This handsome new edition contains 124 letters, forty inscriptions, and new or corrected notes. Much of this material is previously unpublished, and this collection is a welcome addition to Norris scholarship. Particularly useful are the extensive notes that introduce each letter, placing it in the context of Norris' life and writing. **(A,G)**

Evaluation of Selected Criticism

Borus, Daniel H. *Writing Realism: Howells, James, and Norris in the Mass Market*. Chapel Hill: University of North Carolina Press, 1989. Borus examines the economic and social conditions following the Civil War and their effect on concepts of realism. He then analyzes how the effects of commercial publishing, printing innovations, and popular magazines established a new class of readers who regarded writers more as newscasters and celebrities than prophets. The result bred a new generation of writers who regarded both their purpose and their work differently than preceding generations. This fascinating thesis is well wrought and impressively documented by the letters, records, and literary criticism of its subjects. **(A)**

Hochman, Barbara. *The Art of Frank Norris, Storyteller*. Columbia: University of Missouri Press, 1988. Hochman's study is an attempt to reevaluate and resurrect Norris' reputation. She devotes one chapter to each of his four major novels—*Vandover and the Brute, McTeague, The Octopus*, and *The Pit*—examining the works for their stylistic devices, images, and narrative techniques. The result is a useful, close reading that will assist both scholars and students in their research. **(A,G)**

FLANNERY O'CONNOR
1925-1964

Autobiographical Sources

Stephens, C. Ralph, ed. *The Correspondence of Flannery O'Connor and the Brainard Cheneys*. Jackson: University Press of Mississippi, 1986. O'Connor corresponded with the Cheneys for eleven years, from 1953 until her death in 1964. This collection includes 117 of her letters and seventy-one of Brainard's; his wife's letters are lost. O'Connor provides insightful advice to improve Brainard's writing. He, in turn, provides lengthy descriptions of many planned novels that were never written or written and never published. The gentle friendship revealed in these letters serves to underscore O'Connor's craving for companionship. O'Connor contributes many anecdotes of southern life, some of which were eventually incorporated into her novels. **(A,G)**

Evaluation of Selected Criticism

Baumgartner, Jill P. *Flannery O'Connor: A Proper Scaring*. Wheaton, IL: Harold Shaw, 1988. Critics have produced more books explaining O'Connor's religious symbolism than most people would want to read, yet more valid work seems to appear, including this one. Baumgartner provides excellent background about Roman Catholicism as interpreted by a writer whose characters are molded by southern Protestant fundamentalism. Baumgartner convincingly argues that O'Connor developed "emblematic moments" to signal encounters with the Divine. By connecting the known and unknown through the device of the emblem, O'Connor creates a mysticism that has haunted her readers and critics. Not related to his thesis but of real curiosity are nine cartoons which O'Connor drew for college publications, plus several photographs of O'Connor.

Brinkmeyer, Robert H. *The Art and Vision of Flannery O'Connor*. Baton Rouge: Louisiana State University Press, 1990. Using four stories and two novels to illustrate his thesis, Brinkmeyer explains the importance of O'Connor's Catholic world view within the narrow confines of southern fundamentalism. Along the way he also compares O'Connor to Eudora Welty and Anton Chekhov; if these are not wildly imaginative sources, they nonetheless provide a framework that will help students understand the tradition and direction of short fiction. **(A,G)**

Coles, Robert. *That Red Wheelbarrow: Selected Literary Essays*. Iowa City: University of Iowa Press, 1988. Harvard professor Coles brings psychiatric insights to bear upon a selection of his favorite authors. Often pedantic in tone, the essays nevertheless are well constructed. Several pieces examine the anti-intellectual tendencies that were shared by Flannery O'Connor, William

Carlos Williams, and James Agee. Also included is a rather clinical assessment of Ezra Pound's supposed insanity. **(A)**

Desmond, John F. *Risen Sons: Flannery O'Connor's Vision of History.* Athens: University of Georgia Press, 1987. Desmond argues that O'Connor's vision of history is reflected in her fictional techniques, and that she attempts to reenact Christ's Incarnation in all her fictional incarnations. He believes that *Wise Blood* marks O'Connor's full recognition of this theme. From this work on, O'Connor's genius lay in her ability to incorporate layer upon layer of reality into one image or situation, which takes the story one step closer to resurrection. This study is provocatively different from the many works that address O'Connor's Christian themes. **(A)**

Fickett, Harold, and Douglas Gilbert. *Flannery O'Connor: Images of Grace.* Grand Rapids, MI: Eerdman's, 1986. In this brief study, the authors trace the literary lineage of O'Connor back through Hawthorne to a foundation in Christian humanism. O'Connor responded to the loss of the Christian mythos in this era with bitter humor, yet she moves her readers away from reason toward a recognition of divinity. **(A,G)**

Gentry, Marshall Bruce. *Flannery O'Connor's Religion of the Grotesque.* Jackson: University Press of Mississippi, 1986. This densely argued study examines two novels and eighteen stories to show how O'Connor's characters attempt to save themselves by transforming their own grotesqueness. This study should be of interest to those familiar with Mikhail Bakhtin, who supplies much of Gentry's critical vocabulary. **(A)**

Gray, Richard. *Writing the South: Ideas of an American Region.* Cambridge, Cambridge University Press, 1986. Gray begins his examination of southern themes in literature by isolating thematic contrasts—rural versus urban, farm versus factory, paternalism versus populism, region versus tradition. He then demonstrates how writers developed a myth of meaning for the South by exploring those contrasts. The South created these writers, and the writers, in turn, recreated the southern identity. Gray affords the greatest space to Twain and Faulkner. Although Gray discusses many themes, he fails to adequately address the race issue. In all, he presents a strong case that the last "southern novel" has not yet been written. **(A,G)**

Kessler, Edward. *Flannery O'Connor and the Language of the Apocalypse.* Princeton: Princeton University Press, 1986. Kessler's study focuses on O'Connor's use of figurative and metaphorical language and makes a strong comparison with similar tendencies in Eudora Welty's work. Kessler contends that O'Connor's use of language points to a mysterious, hidden realm beyond the visible world of her characters and plot. O'Connor ended her best stories inconclusively because she was interested in opening possibilities for the evolving consciousness rather than providing closure in the "real world." **(A,G)**

Logsdon, Loren, and Charles Mayer, eds. *Since Flannery O'Connor: Essays on the Contemporary American Short Story.* Macomb: Western Illinois University Press, 1987. Of this collection of fourteen essays, only four deal directly with O'Connor or her works. Two essays discuss O'Connor's reworking of "Geranium" into "Judgment Day." Others analyze her influences on Bobbie Ann Mason and Raymond Carver. (A,G)

Paulson, Suzanne Morrow. *Flannery O'Connor: A Study of the Short Fiction.* Boston: Twayne, 1988. One of the Twayne Studies in Short Fiction Series, Paulson's study offers a concise survey of O'Connor's short stories. The first part is a systematic critical analysis of O'Connor's themes, such as death, gender conflict, and the nature of good and evil. The second section provides excerpts from her letters, articles, and interviews that have a bearing on her work. The final section offers a selection of critical reviews and articles. Recommended for students as a solid, one-volume introduction to these works. (A,G)

Spivey, Ted Ray. *Revival: Southern Writers in the Modern City.* Gainesville: University Presses of Florida, 1986. Spivey sets out to correct the belief that southern writers are exclusively steeped in rural culture by selecting a group who came to terms with the modern city. He discusses the attitudes and adaptations of playwright Williams, poets Ransom, Tate, and Aiken, and novelists Faulkner, Wolfe, Ellison, O'Connor, and Percy. Although compelled to address the issues of southern "decadence and decline," Spivey also demonstrates how many of these writers offered a vision of how to integrate old values with new social structures, allowing the past to reanimate the present. (A,G)

Westling, Louise. *Sacred Groves and Ravaged Gardens: The Fiction of Eudora Welty, Carson McCullers, and Flannery O'Connor.* Athens: University of Georgia Press, 1985. Original and provocative interpretations characterize this study of the fiction of three prominent southern women writers. Focusing on problems of identity, relationships with mothers and with men, and the use of symbolism, Westling argues that Welty "celebrates" her feminine identity while both McCullers and O'Connor struggle against it. By accepting her identity, Welty gains access to the depths of her emotional and psychological resources, while McCullers and O'Connor become increasingly disconnected from feminine wholeness. (A,G)

Other Sources
Driggers, Stephen G., and Robert J. Dunn, eds. *The Manuscripts of Flannery O'Connor at Georgia College.* Athens: University of Georgia Press, 1989.

Friedman, Melvin J., and Beverly L. Clark. *Critical Essays on Flannery O'Connor.* Boston: G. K. Hall, 1985.

Giannone, Richard. *Flannery O'Connor and the Mystery of Love.* Champaign: University of Illinois Press, 1989.

Kinney, Arthur F. *Flannery O'Connor's Library: Resources of Being.* Athens: University of Georgia Press, 1985.

Magee, Rosemary M. *Conversations with Flannery O'Connor.* Jackson: University Press of Mississippi, 1987.

Ragen, Brian Abel. *A Wreck on the Road to Damascus: Innocence, Guilt, and Conversion in Flannery O'Connor.* Chicago: Loyola University Press, 1989.

FRANK O'CONNOR
1903-1966

Evaluation of Selected Criticism

Thompson, Richard J. *Everlasting Voices: Aspects of the Modern Irish Short Story*. Troy, NY: Whitston, 1989. Thompson discusses five Irish storytellers: George Moore, James Joyce, Frank O'Connor, Liam O'Flaherty, Sean O'Faolain, and Mary Lavin. Of O'Connor, he says: "O'Connor grew at once too gentle and too sanguine, a self-parodying...as if Yeat's warrant that he was doing for Ireland what Chekhov had done for Russia had finally begun to sink in." Thompson's pronouncements may, themselves, seem too weighted and outdated for contemporary criticism, but he does provide an insider's perspective of the burden which Irish literature has assumed for itself, and how its melancholy has captured the hearts of readers. Includes bibliography, notes, and index. **(A,G)**

Hildebidle, John. *Five Irish Writers: The Errand of Keeping Alive*. Cambridge: Harvard University Press, 1989. After the first tier of influential Irish writers—Yeats and Joyce—comes the second tier, made up, according to Hildebidle, of Liam O'Flaherty, Kate O'Brien, Elizabeth Bowen, Sean O'Faolain, and Frank O'Connor. Hildebidle examines these writers for common themes, such as disillusionment, alienation, and cultural detachment, and builds a strong case that they have been unfairly overshadowed by Yeats and Joyce. **(A)**

Other Sources

Steinman, Michael. *Frank O'Connor at Work*. Syracuse, NY: Syracuse University Press, 1989.

FRANK O'HARA
1926-1966

Evaluation of Selected Criticism

Auslander, Philip. *The New York Poets as Playwrights: O'Hara, Ashbery, Kock, Schuyler, and the Visual Arts.* New York: Peter Lang, 1989. As part of Lang's "Literature and Visual Arts" series, this study offers a critical introduction to the plays of the New York School poets. O'Hara wrote most of his twenty-three plays when he was young, and these works have been relegated to the status of obscure juvenilia. Several of them, however, are fully developed and merit critical attention, including the Noh plays, the "combine" plays, and his final work, *The General Returns from One Place to Another.* The Noh plays were based on Japanese dramatic forms and are considered an important dramatic experiment. Auslander compares the structure and themes of O'Hara's last play with those used by Bertolt Brecht. (A,G)

O. HENRY
1862-1910

Evaluation of Selected Biography and Criticism

Blansfield, Karen Charmaine. *Cheap Rooms and Restless Hearts: A Study of Formula in the Urban Tales of William Sydney Porter.* Bowling Green, OH: Bowling Green State University Popular Press, 1988. This concise study addresses the techniques used by Porter (O. Henry) to structure his short stories. Each of the "tales" is analyzed in turn by Blansfield, who obviously enjoys the task. Porter's works are explicated at face value for the morals and lessons they impart, and no exaggerated claims are made for literary significance. (A,G)

O'Quinn, Trueman E., and Jenny Lind Porter. *Time to Write: How William Sidney Porter Became O. Henry.* Austin, TX: Eakin Press, 1986. This volume does not really explain in biographical terms how Porter became a writer. Instead, it reprints all twelve of O. Henry's "prison stories." The editors provide basic biographical details along with a laudatory assessment of O. Henry's literary contributions. The stories, in many ways, speak for themselves. (G)

Stuart, David. *O. Henry: A Biography of William Sydney Porter.* Briarcliff Manor, NY: Stein & Day, 1987. Critics have never held a high literary opinion of the Porter's work, but his short stories continue to enjoy tremendous popularity. In this biography, Stuart focuses on a pivotal event of Porter's life—his arrest and imprisonment for embezzlement. Porter entered prison a wide-eyed innocent and came out a prematurely aged cynic. Ironically, his prison experiences gave him the insight into human motivations, which he used to create his stories. This is not a deeply penetrating biography, but Stuart provides a sympathetic and readable look at the life of a writer whose stories have reached millions of readers. (A,G)

EUGENE O'NEILL
1888-1953

Autobiographical Sources

Bogard, Travis, and Jackson R. Bryer. *Selected Letters of Eugene O'Neill.*
New Haven: Yale University Press, 1988. This selection of 560 letters spans
the playwright's entire life. O'Neill was an engaging letter writer, and of
particular interest are love letters to girl friends and wives. Many display a
vivacity that runs counter to the playwright's reputation for gloom. Clearly
evident is O'Neill's struggle to balance the demands of his inner muse and
the demands of the people and situations around him. Throughout his correspondence, the use of several "voices" and the rhythms of intimacy and distance directly reflect his power as a dramatist. The selected letters are divided
into sections, each introduced by a biographical essay. Recommended for all
O'Neill enthusiasts. (A,G)

Commins, Dorothy, ed. *Love and Admiration and Respect: The O'Neill-
Commins Correspondence.* Durham, NC: Duke University Press, 1986. Dorothy Commins has edited this selection of letters from O'Neill to her husband,
who was a senior editor at Random House. O'Neill was as close to Saxe
Commins as he was to anyone. These letters, which span the years 1920 to
1951, show O'Neill's need for approval, personal affection, and minute professional attention. This volume will be considered indispensable for any
O'Neill collection and generally makes for interesting reading. (A,G)

Roberts, Nancy, and Arthur Roberts, eds. *As Ever, Gene: The Letters of
Eugene O'Neill to George Jean Nathan.* Madison, NJ: Fairleigh Dickinson
University Press, 1987. O'Neill's letters reveal much about his hopes and
plans for his plays and for the future of American theater. Theater critics like
Nathan could make or break a play. Consequently, O'Neill made every effort
to convince Nathan of his artistic seriousness, often going into great detail
about how and why he composed. Nathan, in turn, seemed to be guiding
O'Neill's work in the direction that he envisioned for American theater. The
Robertses have carefully transcribed and annotated each letter and offer an
overview of the playwright's career. (A,G)

Evaluation of Selected Criticism

Barlow, Judith E. *Final Acts: The Creation of Three Late O'Neill Plays.*
Athens: University of Georgia Press, 1985. Beginning with random notes and
scenarios, Barlow traces O'Neill's last three plays—*The Iceman Cometh, Long
Day's Journey into Night,* and *A Moon for the Misbegotten*—through typescript
to the printed page. Barlow's purpose is to provide a technical analysis of
O'Neill's methods of composition and revision. O'Neill tended to rework too
obvious statements of his themes into more subtle expressions. He often used

374

real names until very late in the writing process, providing valuable insight into the sources and models of his characters. He rearranged scenes to heighten dramatic tension. Barlow's study successfully combines textual history with insightful literary criticism. **(A,G)**

Bogard, Travis. *Contour in Time: The Plays of Eugene O'Neill.* New York: Oxford University Press, 1988. This substantial revision of Bogard's 1972 book of the same title takes into account the important material that has recently become available. Bogard explains the relationship between O'Neill's complex life and his plays, and in the process discusses many of the dramatist's themes. The extensive index and two appendices help locate many details that otherwise might be overlooked. **(A,G)**

Bogard, Travis, ed. *The Unknown O'Neill.* New Haven: Yale University Press, 1988. Bogard has collected the author's little-known published as well as the unpublished works and appended an expansive commentary. Most are early works that show O'Neill's developing style and his experimentation with themes that return in full force in the later plays. **(A)**

Dardis, Tom. *The Thirsty Muse: Alcohol and the American Writer.* New York: Ticknor & Fields, 1989. Dardis applies the results of current addiction research to the lives and careers of American writers. Of eight authors who won the Nobel Prize, five were alcoholics. The popular theory that alcohol liberates the creative impulse, however, is thoroughly debunked. These were addicted men whose addictions got in the way of their creativity. Close-up views of O'Neill, Faulkner, Fitzgerald, Hemingway, and others are fraught with binges, black-outs, wife-beatings, delirium, disease, and untimely death. **(A, G)**

Floyd, Virginia. *The Plays of Eugene O'Neill: A New Assessment.* New York: Ungar, 1985. Floyd's study is a detailed introduction for undergraduates and general readers. She divides the plays into four chronological groups and provides each section with a biographical introduction. Each play is given a synopsis that includes biographical, thematic, and interpretive comments. Written with style and passion, this study reinforces O'Neill's towering position in American drama. **(A,G)**

Murphy, Brenda. *American Realism and American Drama, 1880-1940.* Cambridge: Cambridge University Press, 1987. Murphy clarifies the relationship between literary realism and dramatic realism in this study of the works of Howells and James, culminating in the plays of O'Neill. Several plays by Hamlin Garland and James A. Herne are examined to demonstrate the impact of realistic theory on dramatic practice. Murphy sees the works of Odets and Hellman leading, via the cultural impact of Freud, to O'Neill, who reigns as undisputed master of the American stage. A valuable overview of the antecedents of twentieth-century American drama. **(A,G)**

Shaughnessy, Edward L. *Eugene O'Neill in Ireland: The Critical Reception.* Westport, CT: Greenwood, 1988. This study attempts to document what Irish audiences and critics have thought, and continue to think, about O'Neill. Shaughnessy gathers all the available data on the Irish performances, reviews, and popularity of O'Neill's plays; he then surveys the opinions of fourteen contemporary critics. (A)

Other Sources
Schroeder, Patricia R. *The Presence of the Past in Modern American Drama.* Madison, NJ: Fairleigh Dickinson University Press, 1989.

JOHN OLDHAM
1653-1683

Evaluation of Selected Criticism

Brooks, Harold F., ed. *The Poems of John Oldham*. Oxford: Oxford University Press, 1987. Although immensely popular in his own time, Oldham's poetic reputation has steadily declined. This is the first complete modern edition of the poetry, which was previously available only in seventeenth-century editions or an error-filled reprinted 1854 edition. The introduction is ponderous, but the poems are lovingly edited. (A,G)

CHARLES OLSON
1910-1970

Evaluation of Selected Criticism

Butterick, George F., ed. *The Collected Poems of Charles Olson Excluding the "Maximus" Poems.* Berkeley: University of California Press, 1987. Butterick, curator of the Olson archives, has produced a definitive edition to supplement his recent edition of *The Maximus Poems* (1983). Included are three hundred poems not published during Olson's lifetime. Many defects in chronology and textual accuracy have been clarified. Butterick discusses sources in an excellent introduction and provides annotations that shed light on problematical passages. **(A,G)**

McPheron, William. *Charles Olson: The Critical Reception, 1941-1983; A Bibliographic Guide.* New York: Garland, 1986. This carefully annotated bibliography cites books, essays, articles, interviews, and reviews that refer, even in passing, to Olson's life or works. Sources of significant critical interest are given greater attention by the commentary. **(A)**

Ross, Andrew. *The Failure of Modernism: Symptoms of American Poetry.* New York: Columbia University Press, 1986. Ross examines the works of Eliot, Olson, and Ashberry to conclude that modernism as a poetic movement was an unabashed failure. The cause of this failure, he contends, was a confusion between subjectivism and subjectivity, a confusion that he believes continues to plague the work of critics who address modernist poets. **(A)**

Stein, Charles. *The Secret of the Black Chrysanthemum.* Barrytown, NY: Station Hill Press, 1987. Stein traces the influence of Jung's psychological theories on Olson's poetics, especially his concept of "projective verse." Stein does not, however, undertake a "Jungian analysis" of the *Maximus* poems, but instead tries to show how Olson understood Jung's concepts and reworked them, incorporating influences from Pound, Melville, and Lawrence to make the ideas truly his own. **(A)**

Other Sources

Conniff, Brian. *The Lyric and Modern Poetry: Olson, Creeley, Bunting.* New York: Peter Lang, 1988.

Walker, Jeffrey. *Bardic Ethos and the American Epic Poem.* Baton Rouge: Louisiana State University Press, 1989.

GEORGE ORWELL
1903-1950

Evaluation of Selected Criticism

Alok Rai. *Orwell and the Politics of Despair: A Critical Study of the Writings of George Orwell*. Cambridge: Cambridge University Press, 1989. Alok Rai has studied Orwell's letters, diaries, and published and unpublished works and concludes that Orwell adopted an ordinary persona that served him as "protective coloring." This allowed him to adopt unpopular political attitudes, many generated by his impatience with the propagandistic use of language. Rather than being a proponent of the "Cold War" philosophy, Alok Rai argues that Orwell was far along in an "unfinished radicalism" that resulted from the inherent contradictions of the era. This study is recommended for its original insights and as an alternative view of Orwell and his work. (A,G)

Carter, Michael. *George Orwell and the Problem of Authentic Existence*. Totowa, NJ: Barnes & Noble, 1985. Carter argues that the themes of Orwell's fiction closely parallel the existential thinking of Buber, Heidegger, and Sartre. Carter examines each of Orwell's novels, tracing the development of a theme which he characterizes as the conflict between the private "authentic" individual and the public "inauthentic self." A comprehensive bibliography is divided into books on Orwell and books on philosophy, psychology, and existentialism. (A)

Connelly, Mark. *The Diminished Self: Orwell and the Loss of Freedom*. Pittsburgh: Duquesne University Press, 1987. According to Connelly, Orwell was not a political philosopher but a political reporter. Comparing Orwell's themes with those of Heidegger, Sartre, and Nietzsche, contends Connelly, is not productive. In this study, Connelly proposes another model of comparison —Roderick Seidenberg, who wrote *Posthistoric Man: An Inquiry*. In this scenario, man drifts toward a world dictated by intellect, instinct wanes, and individuality is diminished. The self is "churned into an ever smaller particle." Orwell's love of nature, however, tempered his Seidenbergian pessimism and led him instead to embrace the cause of survival. (A,G)

Meyer, Michael. *Words Through a Windowpane: A Life in London's Literary and Theatrical Scenes*. New York: Grove Weidenfeld, 1989. Meyer's entertaining reminiscences of postwar British literary circles touches upon his association with Shaw, Orwell, Graham Greene, and poet Sidney Keys, among others. The amusing anecdotes seem to spring from an inexhaustible source. (A,G)

Mulvihill, Robert, ed. *Reflections on America 1984: An Orwell Symposium*. Athens: University of Georgia Press, 1986. For this collection of Orwell essays, Mulvihill has attracted a stellar cast of contributers, among them Robert Coles, Sheldon Wolin, James Billington, and Joseph Weizenbaum. Adding to the attractiveness of this collection of twelve critical essays are nearly fifty photographs of Orwell. This is the best of the several *Nineteen Eighty-Four* compilations. (A,G)

Reilly, Patrick. *Nineteen Eighty-Four: Past Present, and Future.* Boston: Twayne, 1989. In Reilly's view, Orwell was a "propagandist" whose chief purpose was to expose falsehood. This study of Orwell's most famous novel fully explores the implications of this insight for understanding the thematic and narrative structures of the book. Milton is fingered as the source for Orwell's fictional theocracy, Oceania, and of his tripartite arrangement which posits an earthly hell. Reilly draws astute comparisons between *Nineteen Eighty-Four* and what he considers to be the "master myth" of Western culture--"Jack the Giant Killer." (A,G)

Rodden, John. *The Politics of Literary Reputation: The Making and Claiming of "St. George" Orwell.* New York: Oxford University Press, 1989. More social commentary than literary analysis, Rodden's study examines how Orwell's reputation was made by critics, other writers, and the general public. Rodden divides Orwell's life and reputation into four phases—rebel, common man, prophet, and saint. He traces the development of each phase, using editorials, criticism, newspaper cartoons, and even songs. The most important ingredient of this work is its methodology, which could be adopted to analyze the reputations of other literary figures. (A)

Slater, Ian. *Orwell: The Road to Airstrip One.* New York: Norton, 1985. This is not merely a biography, but a sensitive analysis of the development of Orwell's political and social thinking, beginning with *Burmese Days* and ending with *Nineteen Eighty-Four.* Slater approaches his material like the social scientist he is and investigates Orwell's themes in terms of their larger social significance. He identifies Orwell's major themes as the negative effects of colonialism on both the exploiter and the exploited, the loss of identity due to social demands, and the power and corruption of language. Slater concludes that Orwell was a better social critic than a political theorist. (A,G)

Wemyss, Courtney T., and Alexej Ugrinsky. *George Orwell.* Westport, CT: Greenwood, 1987. The twenty-two papers collected here were originally presented at an Orwell conference. All but one deal exclusively with *Nineteen Eighty-Four,* and their themes range from Orwell's views on capitalism and political awareness to comparisons of Orwell to G. K. Chesterton, Arthur Koestler, and Jack London. Uneven in both subject matter and treatment, these essays are best used by students to develop a specific topic for further research. (A,G)

West, W. J., ed. *George Orwell: The War Commentaries.* New York: Pantheon, 1986. In this volume, West has collected the commentaries written by Orwell during WWII for a weekly news broadcast. They dwell almost exclusively on topics concerning the war effort. Of interest are Orwell's interaction with the censors that required him to use a brand of "Newspeak." The appendix includes several examples of Axis propaganda broadcasts. Obviously, his work for and with the government influenced many of the ideas ultimately expressed in *Nineteen Eighty-Four.* An interesting addition to the Orwell canon. (A,G)

Other Sources

Buitenhuis, Peter, and Ira B. Nadel, eds. *George Orwell: A Reassessment.* New York: St. Martin's, 1988.

Calder, Jenni. *"Animal Farm" and "Nineteen Eighty-Four."* New York: Open University Press/Taylor & Francis, 1987.

Oldsey, Bernard, and Joseph Browne, eds. *Critical Essays on George Orwell.* Boston: G. K. Hall, 1986.

Plank, Robert. *George Orwell's Guide Through Hell: A Psychological Study of 1984.* San Bernardino, CA: Borgo Press, 1986.

Reilly, Patrick. *George Orwell: The Age's Adversary.* New York: St. Martin's, 1986.

Sandison, Alan. *George Orwell: After "Nineteen Eighty-Four."* Wolfeboro, NH: Longwood, 1986.

Savage, Robert L., *et al.*, eds. *The Orwellian Moment.* Fayetteville: University of Arkansas Press, 1989.

Singh, P. M. *George Orwell: As a Political Novelist.* New York: Amar Prakashan/Advent, 1987.

Smyer, Richard I. *"Animal Farm": Pastoralism and Politics.* Boston: Twayne, 1988.

WILFRED OWEN
1893-1918

Evaluation of Selected Criticism

Hibberd, Dominic. *Owen the Poet.* Athens: University of Georgia Press, 1987. Hibberd uses archival sources to trace the development of Owen's celebrated war poems from the first drafts to their final form. The themes developed in these poems—images of darkness, fire and blood, guilt and desire, an obsession with pain, and lost youth and beauty—are then tracked through the remainder of the canon and are shown to provide an underlying unity. Hibberd ably points to Owen's sources, influences, and literary parallels, and provides particularly strong readings of "Strange Meeting" and "Spring Offensive." (A,G)

Simcox, Kenneth. *Wilfred Owen: Anthem for a Doomed Youth.* Totowa, NJ: Woburn, 1987. Simcox attributes Owen's pervading sense of guilt, his sexual inhibitions, and his voracious desire for independence to a mother whose overarching concern was for conventional respectability. The poet's education and religious training are placed in context of contemporary beliefs and practices. Strongest in his treatment of the development of Owen's personality, Simcox falls short when he tries to focus only on the poetry. Best suited for the general reader. (G)

Other Sources

Giddings, Robert. *The War Poets: The Lives and Writings of Rupert Brooke, Siegfried Sassoon, Wilfred Owen, Robert Graves, Edmund Blunden and the Other Great Poets of the 1914-1918 War.* Durango, CO: Orion Books/Crown, 1988.

WALTER PATER
1839-1894

Evaluation of Selected Criticism

Buckler, William E. *Walter Pater: The Critic and Artist of Ideas.* New York: New York University Press, 1987. Buckler argues that Pater possessed a unique ability to identify and synthesize ideas. Unlike some other biographers who see Pater's importance in intellectual history, Buckler treats Pater's creative sensibilities and argues that they are incorporated into his keen sense of abstract ideas. **(A)**

Buckler, William, ed. *Walter Pater: Three Major Texts--"The Renaissance," "Appreciations" and "Imaginary Portraits."* New York: New York University Press, 1986. Buckler's edition is meant as a popular rather than scholarly offering. Nevertheless, his introduction is useful for understanding Pater's role in literary history. The chronology provided is mostly accurate, and the set of suggestions for further study is invaluable for students. Each text is preceded by a preface that provides background and context. **(A,G)**

Fraser, Hilary. *Beauty and Belief: Aesthetics and Religion in Victorian Literature.* Cambridge: Cambridge University Press, 1986. In this specialized study in intellectual history, Fraser traces the relationship between religion and aesthetic doctrine from Coleridge and Wordsworth through the aestheticism of Walter Pater and Oscar Wilde. Fraser argues that through concepts propounded by Hopkins, Ruskin, Arnold, and the Oxford aesthetes, Christianity is reduced to a merely subjective religion of art. **(A)**

McGrath, F. C. *The Sensible Spirit: Walter Pater and the Modernist Paradigm.* Tampa: University of South Florida Press, 1986. McGrath argues that Pater's contribution to the development of modernism was a finely tuned balance of German idealism and English empiricism. He explores the philosophers—particularly Kant, Hegel, and Hume—who influenced Pater, and in turn he explains how Pater influenced the modernists, especially Yeats, Pound, Eliot, and Joyce. McGrath dissects Pater's intellectual life, and demonstrates his importance as a transitional figure between the Victorian and modern ages. Recommended for scholars. **(A)**

Scott, Nathan A. *The Poetics of Belief: Studies in Coleridge, Arnold, Pater, Santayana, Stevens, and Heidegger.* Chapel Hill: University of North Carolina Press, 1985. This collection of Scott's essays on writers and philosophers explores the power of the imagination for evoking religious awareness and transcendence. Examining each writer in turn—Coleridge, Arnold, Pater, Santayana, and Stevens—Scott finds a commonality of purposes and intentions among them that is best articulated by Heidegger. **(A)**

Other Sources

Barolsky, Paul. *Walter Pater's "Renaissance."* University Park: Pennsylvania State University Press, 1987.

Donoghue, Denis. *England, Their England: Commentaries on English Language and Literature.* New York: Knopf, 1988.

Iser, Wolfgang. *Walter Pater: The Aesthetic Moment.* Translated by David Wilson. New York: Cambridge University Press, 1987.

Keefe, Robert, and Janice A. Keefe. *Walter Pater and the Gods of Disorder.* Columbus: Ohio State University Press, 1988.

Williams, Carolyn. *Transfigured World: Walter Pater's Aesthetic Historicism.* Ithaca, NY: Cornell University Press, 1990.

Wright, Samuel. *An Informative Index to the Writings of Walter H. Pater.* Cornwall, CT: Locust Hill Press, 1988.

COVENTRY PATMORE
1823-1896

Evaluation of Selected Criticism

Dhar, A. N. *Mysticism in Literature*. New Delhi: Atlantic Publishers, 1985. This study of the poetry of Patmore and Frances Thompson examines the spiritual and mystical affinities of their language and themes. By explicating passages of the poems, Dhar identifies the characteristics of a "mystical tradition" in English poetry, comparing these poets' works with those of Yeats, Wordsworth, Blake, and Eliot. (A)

THE *PEARL*-POET (*GAWAIN*-POET)
fl. 1380-1400

Evaluation of Selected Criticism

Lenz, Joseph M. *The Promised End: Romance Closure in the Gawain-poet, Malory, Spenser, and Shakespeare*. New York: Peter Lang, 1986. Lenz examines the particular ways romances end as a defining characteristic of the genre. To do this, he examines *Sir Gawain and the Green Knight*, Malory's *Le Morte Darthur*, and two Renaissance texts, *The Faerie Queen* and *The Winter's Tale*. A limited but useful study for medieval and Renaissance scholars. (A)

Nicholls, Jonathan. *The Matter of Courtesy: Medieval Courtesy Books and the "Gawain" Poet*. Dover, NH: Brewer, 1985. Courtesy books first appeared in the twelfth century in Latin and were later written in French. In the fifteenth century the first courtesy books written in English were introduced and enjoyed relative popularity. Many manuscripts survive, and Nicholls contends that close scrutiny of these works can shed light on the intentions of medieval writers, in particular, the *Gawain*-poet. Nicholls examines scenes where decorum is observed or flouted in both *Sir Gawain and the Green Knight* and *Pearl*. (A,G)

SAMUEL PEPYS
1633-1703

Evaluation of Selected Criticism

Delaforce, Patrick. *Pepys in Love: Elizabeth's Story.* London: Bishopsgate Press, 1986. Delaforce has written a biography of Samuel Pepys' wife of fifteen years in the form of a first-person narrative told from Elizabeth's viewpoint. It is based on episodes related in Pepys' *Diaries* and is more an imaginative reworking of biographical materials than true biography. Students of Pepys will find it of minimal research value. (G)

Taylor, Ivan E. *Samuel Pepys.* Boston: Twayne, 1989. This study describes the historical, social, and cultural background of events recorded in Pepys' famous *Diaries*—for example, the coronation of Charles II, the plague, and the Great Fire of London. In the process, Taylor provides his own reflections on the personality and importance of Pepys. This is a useful "companion" to the *Diaries* for students and the general reader. It contains a detailed chronology and a selected bibliography. (A,G)

Other Sources

Driver, Christopher, and Michelle Berriedale-Johnson, eds. *Pepys at Table.* Berkeley: University of California Press, 1984.

Tanner, J. R. *Samuel Pepys's Naval Minutes.* New York: State Mutual Book, 1985.

SYLVIA PLATH
1932-1963

Evaluation of Selected Biography and Criticism

Annas, Pamela J. *A Disturbance in Mirrors: The Poetry of Sylvia Plath.* Westport, CT: Greenwood, 1988. Annas offers a detailed study of Plath's imagery to demonstrate how Plath turned from natural images in her early work to social images in later poems. Annas argues that this progression resulted from Plath's realization that her life was controlled by social rather than natural events. Annas applies gender criticism in explaining how the poems reflect a patriarchal and capitalistic society. While working out her particular thesis, Annas provides a thorough close reading of many of Plath's famous poems, as well as providing new insights into the lesser-studied "bee poems" and a verse radio play entitled *Three Women: A Poem for Three Voices.* Recommended for both general readers and scholars. **(A,G)**

Bassnett, Susan. *Sylvia Plath.* New York: Barnes & Noble, 1987. This exercise in feminist deconstruction attempts to wrest control of Plath criticism from a field dominated by male critics. In carefully developing the themes of daughterhood, motherhood, and wifehood, Bassnett seeks to stretch what she believes are the limits imposed on Plath's accomplishment by more traditional critics. **(A,G)**

Chainey, Graham. *A Literary History of Cambridge.* Ann Arbor: University of Michigan Press, 1986. This behind-the-scenes look at the literary stories and scandals of Cambridge University makes for enjoyable voyeurism. The gossip is truly on an epic scale—spread over 800 years of Cambridge history and featuring anecdotes on nearly every notable British writer, including Milton, Wordsworth, Macaulay, and Sylvia Plath. Love affairs, drinking habits, duels, rivalries—all are paraded forth in often humorous detail. This is a very entertaining book that in its own way reveals the immense contribution Cambridge has made to the literary world. **(G)**

Stevenson, Anne. *Bitter Fame: A Life of Sylvia Plath.* Boston: Houghton Mifflin, 1989. Stevenson mines a mass of previously unused materials to describe Plath's short and tragic life. Stevenson characterizes the poet's drive to self-destruction as stemming from an inherently contradictory personality fueled by an overweening ambition, neurotic fears of failure, and irrational rages and jealousies. Stevenson skillfully analyzes Plath's poetry as she develops her portrait. **(A)**

Wagner-Martin, Linda. *Sylvia Plath: A Biography.* New York: Simon & Schuster, 1987. Books about Plath since her suicide have polarized both poets and admirers. She has variously been portrayed as self-destructive, or as a helpless victim of her parents, husband, editors, and friends. The recurring themes of victimization that are so poignant in her poems, such as "Daddy" and "Lady Lazarus," have fueled the fires of partisanship. Wagner-Martin attempts a biography that balances the facts, and the Plath who emerges is a strong but vulnerable, ambitious but fallible woman. Best suited for general readers, this account provides an introduction to Plath's life more than it treats her art. (A,G)

Westbrook, Perry D. *A Literary History of New England.* Bethlehem, PA: Lehigh University Press, 1988. Spanning the years 1620 to 1950, this study of literary New England explains how literature mirrored and influenced the religious, political, social, and cultural forces of the region. Besides the most famous authors—Mather, Plath, Frost, Bradstreet—many lesser-known writers, such as Mercy Warren, Catharine Sedgwick, and Lucy Larcom, are also treated. Detailed enough to provide information for scholars, this lively study may also satisfy a more general audience. (A,G)

Other Sources
Ramakrishnan, E. V. *Crisis and Confession: Studies in the Poetry of Theodore Roethke, Robert Lowell and Sylvia Plath.* Columbia, MO: Chanakya India/South Asia Books, 1988.

Tabor, Stephen. *Sylvia Plath: An Analytical Bibliography.* Bronx: Mansell, 1986.

Wagner, Linda. *Critical Essays on Sylvia Plath.* Boston: G. K. Hall, 1984.

EDGAR ALLAN POE
1809-1849

Evaluation of Selected Criticism

Auerbach, Jonathan. *The Romance of Failure: First-Person Fictions of Poe, Hawthorne, and James*. New York: Oxford University Press, 1989. Auerbach examines the first-person narratives of Poe, Hawthorne, and James to better understand the writers' relationship to their works. Auerbach believes the first-person perspective is revealing because it provides less of a grammatical barrier to mediation between author and text. Poe is shown to display a contradiction between his personal and public identities. In *The Blithedale Romance*, Hawthorne preserves his artistic integrity by hiding behind a "clownish" persona. In *The Sacred Fount*, James drives his narrator into madness in order to maintain his own sanity. **(A)**

Carlson, Eric W. *Critical Essays on Edgar Allan Poe*. Boston: G. K. Hall, 1987. The thirty-three essays collected here deal with subjects such as Poe as critic, poet, cosmologist, and tale teller, a historical overview of critical approaches to Poe, and Poe's philosophy and aesthetics. Because of the different aspects of Poe's life and work presented here, this work is a good place to find ideas for further research. **(A,G)**

Dayan, Joan. *Fables of Mind: An Inquiry into Poe's Fiction*. New York: Oxford University Press, 1987. In this study, Dayan combines recent critical theory with an emphasis on philosophy and religion to critique Poe's fiction. According to Dayan, Poe's visionary impulses were held in check by his grounding in the world of physical phenomena. In terms of intellectual history, she places Poe in the line of Locke, St. Augustine, Kant, Calvin, and Edwards. This well-written book provides new insights into Poe's humor, his place in the Gothic tradition, and his use of language to express gender and sexuality. **(A,G)**

Fisher, Benjamin Franklin, ed. *Poe and Our Times: Influences and Affinities*. Baltimore: The Edgar Allan Poe Society, 1986. Much recent Poe scholarship has fallen into a narrow poststructuralist discourse. To remedy this, Poe enthusiast Fisher has compiled fourteen essays that examine the critical reputation of Poe and go further to trace his influence on many modern writers, including Stephen King. Of notable importance are Bruce Weiner's piece on Poe's mysteries, Maurice Bennett's essay on Poe and Borges, and Craig Werner's discussion of the parodies of Ishmael Reed. This collection succeeds admirably in broadening current critical discussion. **(A,G)**

Haggerty, George E. *Gothic Fiction/Gothic Form*. University Park: Pennsylvania State University Press, 1989. In this study in reader-response criticism, Haggerty attempts to lift Gothic fiction into the category of serious literature. To do this, he establishes two categories—Gothic novels and Gothic tales. Gothic *novels* fail because the genre is unsuited to the effects generated in the reader by the Gothic impulse. Gothic *tales*, on the other hand, succeed admirably. Indeed, because Haggerty's conception of the tale is represented by such works as Shelley's *Frankenstein*, Brontë's *Wuthering Heights*, Poe's "The Fall of the House of Usher," Hawthorne's "Rappaccini's Daughter," and James' *Turn of the Screw*, it is difficult to argue with the conclusion. Some have questioned Haggerty's categories of novel and tale as artificial. (A,G)

Kennedy, Gerald J. *Poe, Death, and the Life of Writing*. New Haven: Yale University Press, 1987. Kennedy argues that death is much more than the central theme in Poe's work: rather, the work is the self-conscious reflection of his fundamental response to death. Kennedy believes that death drove Poe to write, and underlies every creative instinct. He groups Poe's works under death themes: premature burials and funeral rights; beautiful women and death; anxieties of death. Scholarly in its methodology, this study draws on various critical theories and attempts to expand them. (A)

Knapp, Bettina L. *Edgar Allan Poe*. New York: Ungar, 1984. In this psychological analysis of Poe, Knapp pursues popular Freudian-Jungian explanations for the thematic and symbolic nature of the works. This study, however, seems deficient in its knowledge of Poe as it pursues a predilection for linking his thought with mysticism and occultism. This is a truly New Age biography that recycles or merely discards many of the reliable Old Facts. (A,G)

Lee, A. Robert, ed. *Edgar Allan Poe: The Design of Order*. New York: Vision/Barnes & Noble, 1987. This critical anthology reexamines many of the staple issues of Poe studies—the extent of his Gothicism, the motif of entombment, and his self-reflexive irony. Notable essays include James Justus on Poe's use of southwestern humor; Lee's discussion of *The Narrative of Arthur Gordon Pym*; David Murray's analysis of the poetry; and Richard Gray on Poe as a southern writer. The scope of this anthology should be most useful to students. (A,G)

Ljungquist, Kent. *The Grand and the Fair: Poe's Landscape Aesthetics and Pictorial Techniques*. Potomac, MD: Scripta Humanistica, 1984. Ljungquist's thesis is that Poe's descriptive writing gradually shifted from spatial openness to enclosure and psychological limitation. He views the works in the critical context of Poe's contemporaries, a perspective shaped by Burke's ideas on the beautiful, the sublime, and the picturesque. Ljungquist's reading of *The Narrative of Arthur Gordon Pym* is particularly revealing. (A,G)

Pahl, Dennis. *Architects of the Abyss: The Indeterminate Fictions of Poe, Hawthorne, and Melville*. Columbia: University of Missouri Press, 1989. Drawing on the theories of Nietzsche, Derrida, and de Man, Pahl explores the nature of the "abyss of signification" generated by a writer's problematic notions of "truth." Using Poe's short stories and *The Narrative of Arthur*

Gordon Pym, Pahl examines categories of "the uncanny," "recuperation," and "authority" as they relate to narration. Using Hawthorne's "Rappaccini's Daughter," he dissects the contradictory nature of the perspective on which the reader is forced to rely. Turning to Melville's "Billy Budd," Pahl develops the full complexity of his theoretical paradigms. This is a specialized study that should be of interest to scholars of critical theory and American literature. (A)

Pollin, Burton, ed. *Writings in the Broadway Journal: Nonfictional Prose.* 2 vols. Staten Island, NY: Gordian, 1986. The third and fourth volumes of Gordian's *Collected Writings* of Poe gather the prolific writer's critical work on the theatre, art, music, and literature. Also included are general observations and commentary on politics and technology. Part 1 contains the original text, while Part 2 provides an insightful overview of Poe's life and career. The text is carefully annotated and reveals the careful scholarship that is the mark of this series. (A)

Sutherland, Judith. *The Problematic Fictions of Poe, James, and Hawthorne.* Columbia: University of Missouri Press, 1984. Sutherland focuses on three texts that "force romantic premises to the breaking point"--*The Narrative of Arthur Gordon Pym, The Sacred Fount,* and *The Marble Faun.* According to Sutherland, each of these works resists thematic interpretation and represents the writer's confrontation with the schism between the world and its representation, a theme developed by the modernist writers who followed. This study in deconstructive methodology provides new insights into the relationship between the modernists and their predecessors. (A)

Thomas, Dwight, and David K. Jackson. *The Poe Log: A Documentary Life of Edgar Allan Poe, 1809-1849.* Boston: G. K. Hall, 1987. The editors record day-by-day events of Poe's life, including letters to and by Poe, newspaper accounts, reviews, lectures, business transactions, and photographs. They also include opinions of Poe by those who knew him. For researchers in need of biographical details, this 919-page compilation has it all. (A)

Varnado, S. L. *Haunted Presence: The Numinous in Gothic Fiction.* Tuscaloosa: University of Alabama Press, 1987. Drawing upon Rudolph Otto's concept of the "numinous," Varnado examines the subjective experience of the supernatural as revealed in the major gothic texts. In Walpole he sees the harmony of contrasts, in Radcliff the sublime raised to numinosity. Lewis presents the demonic, while Stoker evokes the rational-nonrational paradigm. Separate chapters are devoted to Mary Shelley's sacred and profane theme and Poe's mysticism. This is an intriguing application of a useful theory. (A,G)

Walker, I. M., ed. *Edgar Allan Poe: The Critical Heritage.* London: Routledge & Kegan Paul, 1987. Walker has compiled a thorough selection of reviews, prefaces, and letters dating from Poe's first publication. This collection provides a fascinating look at the dramatic fluctuations of Poe's reputation. Particularly strong on reviews before 1850, Walker continues the survey to the present-day in a more telegraphic manner. This book complements Carlson's *The Recognition of Edgar Allan Poe,* which is stronger on the author's reputation after 1850. **(A,G)**

Williams, Michael J. S. *A World of Words: Language and Displacement in the Fiction of Edgar Allan Poe.* Durham, NC: Duke University Press, 1988. As a critic, Poe explained the importance of language in literature; as a practitioner, he was highly aware of the effect that language exerted. Williams explores Poe's poetics, his use of symbol and voice, and his textual control and "interpretative consciousness" to show how the writer elicited reader responses and controlled the author-reader relationship. **(A)**

Other Sources
Carton, Evan. *The Rhetoric of American Romance: Dialectic and Identity in Emerson, Dickinson, Poe, and Hawthorne.* Baltimore: Johns Hopkins University Press, 1985.

Deas, Michael J. *The Portraits and Daguerrotypes of Edgar Allan Poe.* Charlottesville: University Press of Virginia, 1989.

Marsden, Simon. *Visions of Poe: A Selection of Edgar Allan Poe's Stories and Poems.* New York: Knopf, 1988.

Muller, John P., and William J. Richardson, eds. *The Purloined Poe: Lacan, Derrida, and Psychoanalytical Reading.* Baltimore: Johns Hopkins University Press, 1988.

Person, Leland S., Jr. *Aesthetic Headaches: Women and a Masculine Poetics in Poe, Melville, and Hawthorne.* Athens: University of Georgia Press, 1988.

Wiley, Elizabeth. *Concordance to the Poetry of Edgar Allan Poe.* Cranbury, NJ: Susquehanna University Press, 1989.

Wilhelm, James J., and Leroy T. Day, eds. *Narrative Transgression and the Foregrounding of Language in Selected Prose Work of Poe, Valery and Hofmannsthal.* New York: Garland, 1988.

Wuletich-Brinberg, Sybil. *Poe: The Rationale of the Uncanny.* New York: Peter Lang, 1988.

Zayed, George S. *The Genius of Edgar Allan Poe.* Cambridge: Schenkman, 1985.

ALEXANDER POPE
1688-1744

Evaluation of Selected Biography and Criticism

Bloom, Harold, ed. *Alexander Pope: Modern Critical Views.* New York: Chelsea House, 1986. This anthology comprises nine essays on Pope and an introduction by Bloom. The critics are arranged into three chronological "generations," the first consisting of Maynard Mack, W. K. Wimsatt, Jr., and Earl Wasserman. Essays span the years from 1949 to 1984. In his introduction, Bloom positions Pope between the traditions of Milton and Blake, and differs with Samuel Johnson's opinion that Dryden was Pope's primary influence. (A)

Cowler, Rosemary, ed. *The Prose Works of Alexander Pope: Volume 2, 1725-1744.* Hamden, CT: Archon, 1986. This volume completes the task begun by Norman Ault and first published in 1936 (*Prose Works: Volume 1, 1711-1720*). All of the texts in this volume have been meticulously collated, edited, and annotated, with cross-references to the *Letters*. Included are Pope's preface to Shakespeare, his postscript to the *Odyssey*, his masterpiece *Peri Bathous, or The Art of Sinking in Poetry*, and numerous miscellaneous pieces, including his last testament. With this volume, the complete corpus of Pope's known works have now been compiled, indexed, and published. (A,G)

Damrosch, Leopold, Jr. *The Imaginative World of Alexander Pope.* Berkeley: University of California Press, 1987. Damrosch argues that Pope was not the last of the Renaissance poets but the "first modern poet." Damrosch bases his theory on a detailed analysis of why Pope did not achieve the philosophical order that critics have purported, and therefore is closer to modern thought than to that of Milton and Shakespeare. This revisionist appraisal is required reading for Pope scholars and highly recommended for advanced students of eighteenth-century studies. (A)

Ferguson, Rebecca. *The Unbalanced Mind: Alexander Pope and the Rule of Passion.* Philadelphia: University of Pennsylvania Press, 1986. Ferguson examines Pope's interest in theories of the passions. Focusing critical attention on selected passages of Pope's works, she analyzes them for Pope's attitudes toward the interaction of subjective emotion and objective reason. She feels that he developed a rough version of the concepts of modern psychology. (A)

Guilhamet, Leon. *Satire and the Transformation of Genre.* Philadelphia: University of Pennsylvania Press, 1987. Using selected works of Dryden, Pope, and Swift, Guilhamet dissects and analyzes satiric form. He divides satire into three types—demonstrative, deliberative, and judicial—and then shows how these types interact within the complex structures devised by the authors. Great satire, he contends, emerges with the belief that the past is superior to the present and that innovation is destructive of important institutions. **(A)**

Hammond, Brean. *Pope.* Atlantic Highlands, NJ: Humanities Press, 1986. This is an introductory study of Pope that challenges readers to think deeply about his political ideology. Approaching his subject through Marxist criticism, Hammond attempts to reveal the economic and material basis for Pope's value system, which includes a subconscious attitude of class superiority. Organizing chapters around specific poems, Hammond argues that Pope projected the voice of the anxiety-ridden privileged class, compromised by his politics, his gender, and his physique. This intelligent, provocative, readable book will encourage advanced students to explore ideology in the eighteenth century and to read Pope more closely. **(A,G)**

Ingram, Allan. *Intricate Laughter in the Satire of Swift and Pope.* New York: St. Martin's, 1986. This study examines the complex nature of humor as it is employed by eighteenth-century satirists, particularly Pope and Swift. Ingram applies critical ideas derived from a variety of sources, such as Freud, Bergson, and Lange. He examines the opinions of major critical sources of the period—Hobbes, Shaftesbury, Addison, and Steele. Most satire, according to Ingram, employs laughter as a weapon that excludes the victims from human acceptance. Laughter also appears as a means to achieve group identity. This well-written work is recommended for anyone interested in eighteenth-century literature. **(A,G)**

Mack, Maynard. *Alexander Pope: A Life.* New York: W. W. Norton/Yale, 1986. This is the long-awaited biography from the foremost Pope scholar of our time, and it does not disappoint. Through careful scholarship and colorful description, Mack brings Pope and his world to life. In the process, Mack reaffirms the artistic merit and critical significance of Pope's poetry. This definitive biography is essential Pope reading. **(A,G)**

Martin, Peter. *Pursuing Innocent Pleasures: The Gardening World of Alexander Pope.* Hamden, CT: Archon Books, 1984. Written by the garden historian at the Colonial Williamsburg Foundation in Virginia, this is a study of garden design and construction during the first half of the eighteenth century. Pope was an avid gardener during a period when structure and design in all pursuits were greatly admired. Pope's own five-acre garden occupied his attention until his death. Lavishly illustrated, this book is recommended for anyone interested in Pope, eighteenth-century thought, or the history of gardens. **(A,G)**

Pollak, Ellen. *The Poetics of Sexual Myth: Gender and Ideology in the Verse of Swift and Pope.* Chicago: University of Chicago Press, 1985. Pollak contends that "Swift was committed in his poems to exploring certain sexual myths that Pope's verse insistently worked to justify." She views Swift's writing as "one more possible point of departure, one more vantage point . . . in the ongoing project of unraveling—and undoing—the ideological grounds of patriarchy as we know it in the West." Some critics have criticized Pollak's study for the narrowness of its focus and its uncertain grasp of literary history. **(A)**

Rousseau, G. S., and Pat Rogers, eds. *The Enduring Legacy: Alexander Pope Tercentenary Essays.* Cambridge: Cambridge University Press, 1988. This collection of thirteen essays examines subjects ranging from Pope's imaginative perception of women to his villa at Twickenham to his role as translator. Two essays look at the poem "Epistle to a Lady." In conclusion, Donald Greene offers a rousing "An Anatomy of Pope-Bashing" just to ruffle a few critical feathers. **(A,G)**

Other Sources
Atkins, G. Douglas. *Quests of Difference: Reading Pope's Poems.* Lexington: University Press of Kentucky, 1986.

Berry, Reginald. *A Pope Chronology.* Boston: G. K. Hall, 1988.

Brooks-Davies, Douglas. *Pope's "Dunciad" and the Queen of Night: A Study in Emotional Jacobitism.* New York: Manchester University Press/ St. Martin's, 1988.

Brown, Laura. *Alexander Pope.* Cambridge: Basil Blackwell, 1985.

Morris, David B. *Alexander Pope: The Genius of Sense.* Cambridge: Harvard University Press, 1984.

Nicholson, Colin. *Alexander Pope: Essays for the Tercentenary.* Elmsford, NY: Pergamon, 1988.

Nuttall, A. D. *Pope's "Essay on Man."* Winchester, MA: Unwin Hyman, 1984.

O'Grady, Deirdre. *Alexander Pope and Eighteenth-Century Italian Poetry.* New York: Peter Lang, 1986.

Rosslyn, F. *Pope's "Iliad": A Selection with Commentary.* London: Bristol Classical UK, 1985.

Rumbold, Valerie. *Women's Place in Pope's World.* New York: Cambridge University Press, 1989.

Stack, Frank. *Pope and Horace: Studies in Imitation.* New York: Cambridge University Press, 1985.

Wood, Alan G. *Literary Satire and Theory: A Study of Horace, Boileau, and Pope.* New York: Garland, 1985.

KATHERINE ANNE PORTER
1890-1980

Autobiographical Sources

Bayley, Isabel, ed. *Letters of Katherine Anne Porter*. New York: Atlantic Monthly Press, 1990. Porter wrote thousands of letters to such important literary figures as Hart Crane, Caroline Gordon, J. F. Powers, Allen Tate, Robert Penn Warren, and Glenway Wescott. Also included in this selection by Bayley are many of Porter's more personal letters, as well, to family, friends, and lovers. What emerges from these pages is a more gracious, generous, and loving person than is typically presented by biographers. (A,G)

Givner, Joan, ed. *Katherine Anne Porter: Conversations*. Jackson: University Press of Mississippi, 1987. This collection of previously unpublished interviews reveals the charming evasiveness of Katherine Anne Porter. Although no new biographical information is revealed, many facets of Porter's life and career are touched upon. (A,G)

Evaluation of Selected Criticism

Hendrick, Willene, and George Hendrick. *Katherine Anne Porter*. [Rev. ed.] Boston: Twayne, 1988. In this critical study the authors group Porter's short fiction according to setting to demonstrate connecting themes and characters. The stories with settings in Mexico and Texas also reflect the facts of Porter's life at the time, and will encourage student researchers to consult biographical sources. The authors also evaluate Porter's one novel, *Ship of Fools,* and her insightful essays. A good starting point for understanding the fiction. (A,G)

Unrue, Darlene Harbour. *Truth and Vision in Katherine Anne Porter's Fiction*. Athens: University of Georgia Press, 1985. In this examination of Porter's world view, Unrue demonstrates that her works are unified by an underlying impetus toward truth and the difficulty of attaining it. She effectively uses material from Porter's personal papers, housed in the McKeldin Library at the University of Maryland. The overall result is a welcome addition to Porter scholarship. (A,G)

Other Sources

Hilt, Kathryn. *Katherine Anne Porter: A Bibliography*. New York: Garland, 1989.

Unrue, Darlene H. *Understanding Katherine Anne Porter*. Columbia: University of South Carolina Press, 1988.

EZRA POUND
1885-1972

Autobiographical Sources

Materer, Timothy, ed. *Pound-Lewis: The Letters of Ezra Pound and Wyndham Lewis.* New York: New Directions, 1985. Of interest primarily to scholars, this edition of the correspondence between Pound and Lewis has some serious flaws. The selected letters are reproduced accurately but many important letters have been omitted for no apparent reason. Materer chooses to clarify items seemingly by whim and merely skips over many obtuse passages instead of confessing ignorance. While this edition is certainly valuable for the letters it contains, the editorial standards make it less useful than it should be. (A,G)

Scott, Thomas L. *et al.*, eds. *Pound and the "Little Review": The Letters of Ezra Pound to Margaret Anderson.* New York: New Directions, 1988. Pound's correspondence with Margaret Anderson, his editor at the Chicago-based *Little Review*, is obscure, trite, or overly clever, despite the powerful literary events they produced. Together the pair first brought *Ulysses* to the U.S. Anderson's letters, which have mostly been lost, were probably the better part of the dialogue. This collection has proven a disappointment to most scholars. (A)

Evaluation of Selected Biography and Criticism

Brown, Dennis. *The Modernist Self in Twentieth-Century English Literature: A Study in Self-Fragmentation.* New York: St. Martin's, 1989. In this study of major British writers of the twentieth century, Brown develops the thesis that the convention of unitary selfhood was the heart of narrative perspective until challenged by the modernists. Drawing heavily on such writers as Conrad, Joyce, Pound, David Jones, and Ford Madox Ford, Brown masses material from writers who depicted the self as fragmentary and heterogeneous, rather than unitary. He examines the roles of inner conflict and self-deception in shaping the form of the novel. Fragmentation of self, in Brown's view, could be depicted negatively—leading to various forms of disintegration—or positively—allowing a restricted selfhood to expand and diversify. (A,G)

Carpenter, Humphrey. *A Serious Character: The Life of Ezra Pound.* Boston: Houghton Mifflin, 1988. This imposing biography is so rich in detail, scrupulously demanding of its sources, and objectively critical of Pound, the man and artist, that it may well never be supplanted. Carpenter covers Pound's childhood, the Kensington years, summers at Stone Cottage, and Pound's internment at St. Elizabeth's with a carefully detached eye that nevertheless acknowledges Pound's boundless energy and enthusiasm. Julien Cornell, Pound's lawyer, and Dr. Overholser, his "overseer" at the asylum, come off looking very nearly as fascist as the Mussolini regime Pound supported. Carpenter includes the views and opinions of contemporary poets and critics to provide a literary context for Pound's works. A bibliography and an index to the poetry, by title and first line, are included. Recommended for anyone not put off by its 1,000-page length. (A,G)

Carpenter, Humphrey. *Geniuses Together: American Writers in Paris in the 1920s.* Boston: Houghton Mifflin, 1988. Carpenter, who has written biographies of Auden and Tolkien, provides a portrait of expatriate life on the Left Bank in post-WWI Paris and surveys the American writers who flocked there for inspiration and camaraderie, including Pound, Hemingway, Anderson, Fitzgerald, Boyle, Joyce, and Stein. Although the spotlight is on Hemingway, Carpenter does provide a flavor for the times and influences on all the expatriate writers. (A,G)

Casillo, Robert. *The Genealogy of Demons: Anti-Semitism, Fascism, and the Myths of Ezra Pound.* Evanston, IL: Northwestern University Press, 1988. Casillo attacks all those critics, past and present, who are willing to regard Pound's poetry as works of art. Casillo paints a vehement portrait of Pound as devil, and sees the poetry as little more than a vehicle for propaganda. The dogmatic tone of this study will challenge Pound enthusiasts. (A,G)

Childs, John Steven. *Modernist Form: Pound's Style in the Early Cantos.* Cranbury, NJ: Susquehanna University Press, 1986. Childs' study, the first true structuralist treatment of the *Cantos,* is filled with the dense prose and terminology that readers have come to expect from that critical school. The study attempts to connect the poem's "microcontextual and macrocontextual devices." (A)

Coles, Robert. *That Red Wheelbarrow: Selected Literary Essays.* Iowa City: University of Iowa Press, 1988. Harvard professor Coles brings psychiatric insights to bear upon a selection of his favorite authors. Often pedantic in tone, the essays nevertheless are well constructed and erudite. Of interest to Pound critics is a rather clinical assessment of the case for and against Pound's supposed insanity. (A)

Cookson, William. *A Guide to the Cantos of Ezra Pound.* New York: Persea, 1985. This is truly a guide book to one of the most difficult poems in English. Composed over nearly a half century, the *Cantos* changed in style and substance as the world changed. Cookson takes the poem canto-by-canto and explains the themes, translates the non-English phrases, clarifies allusions and references, and provides relevant historical and literary background. Both beginning readers and researchers will find this work indispensable. (A,G)

Dasenbrock, Reed Way. *The Literary Vorticism of Ezra Pound & Wyndham Lewis: Towards the Condition of Painting.* Baltimore: Johns Hopkins University Press, 1985. Dasenbrock traces the influence of painting on the modernist literary imagination as revealed in the work of Pound and Lewis. He concentrates on the Vorticist movement, describing its history and philosophy. He analyzes Lewis' *Enemy of the Stars*, *Tarr*, and the *Apes of God*; and Pound's poetry, including the *Cantos*. A useful study of the modernist imagination. (A)

Dickie, Margaret. *On the Modernist Long Poem*. Iowa City: University of Iowa Press, 1986. Dickie contends that by extending their "personal imagist pieces" into the extended "public" long poem, modernist poets redefined the shape and direction of their movement. In this study, which is, in effect, a history of the development of modernism, Dickie examines the formal problems faced by Eliot (*The Waste Land*), Crane (*The Bridge*), Williams (*Paterson*), and Pound (the *Cantos*). This study would be most useful for teachers and students who are seeking a framework for discussion of these complex works. (A)

Ellmann, Maud. *The Poetics of Impersonality: T. S. Eliot and Ezra Pound*. Cambridge: Harvard University Press, 1987. Eliot and Pound were central to the twentieth-century aesthetic principal which held that the writer must disassociate from his work—that the narrator be impersonal and distinct from the author himself. Ellman attacks this much-heralded theory, arguing that the poets were merely disguising their anti-semitic and fascist politics. She examines the poetry in light of Eliot's own notes about Henri Bergson, and links both Eliot and Pound to Bergsonian ideas of time and memory. Recommended for scholars. (A)

Flory, Wendy Stallard. *The American Ezra Pound*. New Haven: Yale University Press, 1989. Flory's study is a biographical reexamination of Pound's entanglement with fascist politics, anti-semitism, and mental instability. She traces the events of Pound's early life, up to the time he formulates his mature political and philosophical ideals. Her discussion of Pound's incarceration in St. Elizabeth's, in which she develops themes of Pound's denial and self-accusation, is revealing. In all, this is a more balanced biography than several recent "Pound-bashings." (A,G)

Fogelman, Bruce. *Shapes of Power: The Development of Ezra Pound's Poetic Sequences*. Ann Arbor, MI: UMI Research, 1988. Fogelman examines all of Pound's work prior to the *Cantos* to demonstrate how Pound gave coherence to the extended poetic sequence. The study shows the originality of the lyrical sequence and its importance to modern poetry. (A)

Kayman, Martin A. *The Modernism of Ezra Pound: The Science of Poetry*. New York: St. Martin's, 1986. In this sensitive study, informed by contemporary literary theory, Kayman addresses the issue of poetics and politics in the work of Pound. He describes how Pound's poetics developed in stages— Venice, London, Paris, Rapallo, imagism, and vorticism—and relates these developments to Pound's gradual embrace of an "undemocratic hierarchy." More than an analysis of Pound, Kayman offers a look at the critics and readers who partake in the "politics of our literary pleasure." (A)

Laughlin, James. *Pound as Wuz: Essays and Lectures on Ezra Pound*. St. Paul, MN: Graywolf, 1987. Combining memoir with critical analysis, Laughlin offers a unique perspective on Pound's life and work. As founder of New Directions, Laughlin published many writers who went on to become giants of modern literature, most notably his friend Pound. Laughlin's casual style is deceptive in that it gives him the ability to lull readers into the midst of highly sophisticated critical discussions. He talks of Pound's translations of the medieval troubadours, his sources for the *Cantos* and the *Propertius* sequence, his methods of working, and his controversial economic theories. Appended is a previously unpublished story that Pound wrote while in college called "In the Water-Butt." Laughlin has also included a bibliography of Pound's sources for his economics theory. This is an essential read for anyone interested in Pound. (A,G)

Laughlin, James. *Random Essays*. Mount Kisco, NY: Moyer Bell, 1989. Essayist, poet, and publisher Laughlin offers a selection of criticism and personal reminiscences of many of the noted writers of our time, including Pound, William Carlos Williams, Stein, Saroyan, and Merton. Laughlin's opinions are insightful, direct, and useful for the scholar. Robert Giroux provides an introduction. (A)

Longenbach, James. *Stone Cottage: Pound, Yeats, and Modernism*. New York: Oxford University Press, 1988. This study of a literary friendship is the story of how two innovative poets developed their modernist aesthetic. Longenbach presents this famous story in a readable work that should prove useful and enjoyable to serious students. (A)

Pound, Omar, and Robert Spoo, eds. *Ezra Pound and Margaret Cravens: A Tragic Friendship, 1910-1912*. Durham, NC: Duke University Press, 1988. Margaret Cravens was a mysterious American woman who went to Paris, befriended Pound, H. D. (Hilda Doolittle), the pianist Walter Rummel, and became part of their inner circle. In 1912, at age thirty-one, she ended her life with a single shot. There were accusations that Pound might have been the reason for her suicide, although none of the letters in this collection shed any light on the issue. The letters provide some insight into Pound, and much fodder for literary gossip. (A,G)

Raffel, Burton. *Possum and Ole Ez in the Public Eye: Contemporaries and Peers on T. S. Eliot and Ezra Pound, 1892-1972*. Hamden, CT: Archon, 1985. This is a chronological collection of excerpts from reviews, criticism, and commentary on the works of Pound and Eliot by their contemporaries. Particularly telling are Virginia Woolf's comments in 1918, "Not that I've read more than ten words by Ezra Pound but my conviction of his humbug is unalterable." Eliot, on the whole, fares better. Raffel's collection demonstrates once again the volatility of a literary reputation and the fashions of literary criticism. (A,G)

Raffel, Burton. *Ezra Pound: The Prime Minister of Poetry*. Hamden, CT: Archon Press, 1985. Raffel's study is more general, more readable, and more succinct in its presentation of Pound's ideas and influence than most critical studies. Raffel touches briefly on the biography, relating it to the works, then explicates the early works, mature works, and translations. (A,G)

Ricks, Beatrice. *Ezra Pound: A Bibliography of Secondary Works*. Metuchen, NJ: Scarecrow, 1986. Ricks follows the same format here as in her previous bibliographies of Faulkner and T. S. Eliot. The first section lists Pound biographies; the second contains criticism arranged alphabetically by Pound's titles; the third consists of "supplemental works," which are more general critical works. Other sections list interviews, collections of correspondence, and a useful bibliography of bibliographies. Entries are thoroughly indexed by title, topic, and critic's name. This is the most comprehensive and current Pound bibliography. (A)

Smith, Marcel, and William Ulmer, eds. *Ezra Pound: The Legacy of Kulchur*. Tuscaloosa: University of Alabama Press, 1988. This collection of essays includes contributions from noted critics James Laughlin, Hugh Kenner, Alfred Kazin, James Wilhelm, Leslie Fiedler, and Michael North. A full range of critical attitudes is represented in these discussions of Poundian economics, industrial aesthetics, "gut-level" antipathy, and poetic memory. (A)

Stead, Christian Karlson. *Pound, Yeats, Eliot, and the Modernist Movement*. New Brunswick, NJ: Rutgers University Press, 1986. Stead's study surveys the origins of the modernist movement, with particular attention to Pound, Yeats, and Eliot. He argues that Pound's influence on Yeats and Eliot has not been adequately acknowledged. To demonstrate this he scrutinizes the manuscript of *The Waste Land*, pointing out those sections where Pound dominated over Eliot's more conventional approach. In his discussion of politics and modernism, he claims that Eliot's conservative views had a deadening effect on the work, holding "Burnt Norton" an abject failure. The result of Pound's bout with fascism is noted in the structures of the *Cantos*. Stead's study is solid and well-written, and provides an enlightening account of the causes and effects of modernism. (A,G)

Sultan, Stanley. *Eliot, Joyce, and Company*. London and New York: Oxford University Press, 1987. One of the most valuable aspects of this study is Sultan's explanation of the modernist movement. He examines how Eliot, Pound, and Joyce contributed to the movement and argues that Joyce and Pound exerted considerable influence on Eliot, especially in *The Waste Land* and "The Love Song of J. Alfred Prufrock." This readable book will assist anyone researching the development of modern literature. (A,G)

Tytell, John. *Ezra Pound: The Solitary Volcano*. New York: Anchor/Doubleday, 1987. Using a mass of unpublished material and personal interviews with those who knew the poet, Tytell has produced a commendable interpretive biography of Pound. He examines in detail what he calls the "tragic fracture" in Pound's personality—the inharmonious blend of vanity, arrogance, and hatred—that ultimately came to rule his life. That Pound was also capable of forming intensely loyal friendships and performing feats of generosity only highlights the tragedy of his later years. **(A)**

Wilhelm, J. J. *The American Roots of Ezra Pound.* New York: Garland, 1985. This sympathetic treatment of Pound's life and poetry is conceived as a partial response to E. Fuller Torrey's unsympathetic *The Roots of Treason.* Wilhelm does not attempt to excuse Pound's scandalous politics but to explain their genesis and examine why an American turns his back on his native roots and chooses the life of an expatriate. The book ends, unfortunately, with Pound's emigration in 1907 after the scandal at Wabash College. Wilhelm stops with his task only half done. **(A,G)**

Other Sources

Apter, Ronnie. *Digging for the Treasure: Translation after Pound.* New York: Peter Lang, 1984.

Bornstein, George, ed. *Ezra Pound Among the Poets.* Chicago: University of Chicago Press, 1985.

Eder, Doris L. *Three Writers in Exile: Eliot, Pound and Joyce.* Troy, NY: Whitston, 1985.

Froula, Christine. *To Write Paradise: Style and Error in Pound's Cantos.* New Haven: Yale University Press, 1985.

Hoffman, Daniel, ed. *Ezra Pound and William Carlos Williams: The University of Pennsylvania Conference Papers.* Philadelphia: University of Pennsylvania Press, 1984.

Hooley, Daniel M. *The Classics in Paraphrase: Ezra Pound and Modern Translators of Latin Poetry.* Cranbury, NJ: Susquehanna University Press, 1988.

Kappel, Andrew, ed. *Pound: Letters to Tom Carter.* Redding Ridge, CT: Black Swan, 1989.

Kearns, George. *Pound: The Cantos.* New York: Cambridge University Press, 1989.

Korn, Marianne. *Ezra Pound and History.* Orono, ME: National Poet Foundation, 1985.

Lindberg, Kathryne V. *Reading Pound Reading: Modernism after Nietzsche.* New York: Oxford University Press, 1987.

McGann, Jerome J. *Towards a Literature of Knowledge.* Chicago: University of Chicago Press, 1989.

Makin, Peter. *Pound's Cantos.* Winchester, MA: Unwin Hyman, 1985.

Morgan, John H., ed. *Ezra Pound in Memoriam: An Anthology of Contemporary Poetry.* Bristol, IN: Wyndham Hall, 1988.

Nelson, James G. *Elkin Mathews: Publisher to Yeats, Joyce, Pound.* Madison: University of Wisconsin Press, 1989.

Oderman, Kevin. *Ezra Pound and the Erotic Medium.* Durham, NC: Duke University Press, 1986.

Pearce, Donald, and Herbert Schneidau, eds. *Pound: Letters to John Theobald.* Redding Ridge, CT: Black Swan, 1984.

Pound, Ezra. *Ezra Pound and Japan: Letters and Essays.* Redding Ridge, CT: Black Swan, 1987.

Rabate, Jean-Michael. *Language, Sexuality, and Ideology in Ezra Pound's Cantos.* Albany: State University of New York Press, 1986.

Saunders, Jeraldine. *The Cruise Diary.* Los Angeles: Tarcher, 1988.

Schwartz, Sanford. *The Matrix of Modernism: Pound, Eliot, and Early Twentieth Century Thought.* Princeton, NJ: Princeton University Press, 1985.

Singh, Gurbachan. *Transcultural Poetics: Corporative Studies of the Cantos by Ezra Pound and Bachittra Natak.* Columbia, MO: Ajanta/South Asia Books, 1987.

Torrey, E. Fuller. *The Roots of Treason: Ezra Pound and the Secret of St. Elizabeth's.* New York: McGraw-Hill, 1984.

Walker, Jeffrey. *Bardic Ethos and the American Epic Poem: Whitman, Pound, Crane, Williams, Olson.* Baton Rouge: Louisiana State University Press, 1989.

E. J. PRATT
1883-1964

Evaluation of Selected Biography and Criticism

Collins, Robert G. *E. J. Pratt*. Boston: Twayne, 1988. Collins' study presents an overview of the achievement of this much-neglected Canadian poet with special emphasis on his long narrative poems. After an account of Pratt's life, Collins proceeds to treat Pratt's first mature poems. He then discusses the narrative poems with special attention to Pratt's masterpiece, *Brébeuf and His Brethren*. The remainder of the study examines the later narratives which became progressively more experimental in form. Collins concludes with an assessment of Pratt's achievement. The thorough bibliography is annotated. A good introductory study for students and readers new to Pratt's poetry. (A,G)

Djwa, Sandra, and R. G. Moyles. *E. J. Pratt: Complete Poems, Parts 1 & 2*. Toronto: University of Toronto Press, 1989. These are the first two volumes in the publication of Pratt's complete works. Forthcoming volumes will include his prose and correspondence. The high editorial standards, detailed annotations, fine descriptive bibliography, and an appendix of unpublished works make it unlikely that this edition will ever be supplanted. (A,G)

Pitt, David G. *E. J. Pratt: The Master Years, 1927-1964*. Toronto: University of Toronto Press, 1987. Though not as famous abroad as fellow Canadian Northrup Frye, Pratt nonetheless holds a premier place among editors, poets, and critics. He has also led a fascinating life, coming from a poor maritime family to become a minister, psychologist, teacher, and poet. In his first biography, *E. J. Pratt: The Truant Years* (1985), Pitt covered the early life; now he continues with Pratt's professional years, a time when Pratt received the highest distinctions bestowed upon Canadian intellectuals. This readable biography of an interesting subject is appropriate for anyone exploring the literary process or the poet himself. (A,G)

MATTHEW PRIOR
1664-1721

Evaluation of Selected Criticism

  Rippy, Frances Mayhew. *Matthew Prior*. Boston: Twayne, 1986. Prior was extremely important in his own day but little recognized today. By examining Prior's works in detail, Rippy hopes to refurbish his reputation. A lengthy biographical chapter supplies a useful summary of Prior's life and career. In Rippy's assessment Prior's works had a great influence on Swift's writings. (A,G)

ANN RADCLIFFE
1764-1823

Evaluation of Selected Criticism

Cottom, Daniel. *The Civilized Imagination: A Study of Ann Radcliffe, Jane Austen, and Sir Walter Raleigh.* Cambridge: Cambridge University Press, 1985. Cottom explores the role of the educated and refined in defining social aesthetics by examining the writings of Radcliffe, Austen, and Raleigh—three writers, he contends, who represent the epitome of "taste." For these individuals, the perceptions of the uneducated were merely "pseudo-events." Cottom demonstrates how the class values of the eighteenth century were inextricably connected with aesthetic values. (A)

SIR WALTER RALEIGH
1552?-1618

Evaluation of Selected Criticism

Cottom, Daniel. *The Civilized Imagination: A Study of Ann Radcliffe, Jane Austen, and Sir Walter Raleigh.* Cambridge: Cambridge University Press, 1985. Cottom explores the role of the educated and refined in defining social aesthetics by examining the writings of Radcliffe, Austen, and Raleigh—three writers, he contends, who represent the epitome of "taste." For these individuals, the perceptions of the uneducated were merely "pseudo-events." Cottom demonstrates how the class values of the eighteenth century were inextricably connected with aesthetic values. **(A)**

Waller, Gary. *English Poetry of the Sixteenth Century.* White Plains, NY: Longman, 1986. Using the theories of Eagleton, Greenblatt, Sinfield, and Greenberg, Waller's study is a revisionist history of English Renaissance poetry. Waller develops a parallel chronological overview and critical reevaluation. Chapters cover sixteenth-century literary theory, the ideology of the Elizabethan court, Petrarch, and Protestantism. Several authors are given prolonged treatment—Dunbar, Wyatt, Raleigh, Greville, Sidney, Spenser, Shakespeare, and Donne. This book was meant to, but does not, supplant C. S. Lewis' *English Literature of the Sixteenth Century* (1954). **(A)**

Other Sources

Armitage, Christopher M. *Sir Walter Raleigh: An Annotated Bibliography.* Chapel Hill: University of North Carolina Press, 1988.

Miles, Jerry L. *Sir Walter Raleigh: A Reference Guide.* Boston: G. K. Hall, 1986.

JOHN CROWE RANSOM
1888-1974

Autobiographical Sources
Young, Thomas Daniel, and George Core, eds. *Selected Letters of John Crowe Ransom*. Baton Rouge: Louisiana State University Press, 1985. This selection of Ransom's correspondence covers the years 1911 to 1968 and includes letters to his father, mother, sister, and friends, especially Allen Tate and Robert Penn Warren. These 250 letters are grouped by decade, with each section provided with a short biographical and critical introduction. The letters are annotated and a detailed chronology gives a useful overview of Ransom's life. While they acknowledge that Ransom was not among the great American letter writers, the editors rank only Allen Tate as a stronger letter writer among major Southern writers since 1925. (A,G)

Evaluation of Selected Criticism
Quinlan, Kieran. *John Crowe Ransom's Secular Faith*. Baton Rouge: Louisiana State University Press, 1989. This is a study of Ransom's intellectual growth. Quinlan chronicles his early days as an aggressive Catholic convert, his political dabbling in the Southern agrarian movement and flirtation with Marxism, his avid support of the New Deal, his mentorship of the New Critics, his adaptation of psychology and anthropology to literary studies, and his eventual abandonment of the basic tenets of the Christian faith. Quinlan contends that he never lost faith in humankind, however—a point that is demonstrated through close readings of his poetry. (A,G)

JEAN RHYS
1890-1979

Author's Recent Bibliography
Jean Rhys: The Collected Short Stories, 1987.

Evaluation of Selected Biography and Criticism
Angier, Carole. *Jean Rhys*. New York: Viking, 1986. Part of the Lives of Modern Women series, this volume examines the life and career of Dominican-born novelist Jean Rhys. Angier emphasizes the autobiographical elements in Rhys' fiction. **(A,G)**

Gardiner, Judith Kegan. *Rhys, Stead, Lessing, and the Politics of Empathy.* Bloomington: Indiana University Press, 1989. Gardiner compares the biographical similarities between these writers to argue that their fiction served as an outlet for their exile, and finds that their fiction examines the common concerns of "empathy," "history," and "identity." All three women, and their characters, form gender relationships that come from a "mothering theory." As an exile, Rhys was keenly aware of being included or excluded, a theme that is particularly prominent in her autobiographical fiction. Gardiner carefully explicates *Wide Sargasso Sea* for its structure and point of view to argue her point that empathy is a dominant theme. **(A)**

Harrison, Nancy R. *Jean Rhys and the Novel as Women's Text.* Chapel Hill: University of North Carolina Press, 1988. Harrison starts with the assumption that twentieth-century women's novels, including those of Jean Rhys, are more directly autobiographical than men's novels. For Harrison, a woman's novel acts out her life in gestures that are more readily recognized by other women than by men. Only by learning to read women's texts as a "common" rather than "professional" reader can a woman short-circuit the "father-text" of literary criticism. Harrison's analysis of *Wide Sargasso Sea* includes insights derived from Brontë's *Jane Eyre* and Freud's *Interpretation of Dreams*. **(A)**

O'Connor, Teresa F. *Jean Rhys: The West Indian Novels.* Albany: New York University Press, 1986. In this carefully crafted study, O'Connor draws persistent parallels between Rhys' life and art, relying on materials found in the "Black Exercise Book," the letters, and the autobiography (*Smile Please,* 1979). O'Connor examines the many discrepancies that have surfaced in accounts of Rhys' life and then develops a discussion of what are regarded as the finest novels—*Voyage in the Dark* and *Wide Sargasso Sea*. O'Connor contends that Rhys' major themes in these novels are the mother/daughter relationship, racial tension, sexuality, and the dichotomy of nature and culture. **(A,G)**

Other Sources

Emery, Mary Lou. *Jean Rhys at "World's End."* Austin: University of Texas Press, 1990.

Kloepfer, Deborah K. *The Unspeakable Mother: Forbidden Discourse in Jean Rhys and H. D.* Ithaca, NY: Cornell University Press, 1989.

Le Galley, Paula. *The Rhys Women.* New York: St. Martin's, 1990.

Mellown, Elgin W. *Jean Rhys: A Descriptive and Annotated Bibliography of Works and Criticism.* New York: Garland, 1984.

Rumens, Carol. *Jean Rhys.* Savage, MD: Barnes & Noble/Rowman, 1990.

SAMUEL RICHARDSON
1689-1761

Evaluation of Selected Criticism

Brophy, Elizabeth Bergen. *Samuel Richardson*. Boston: Twayne, 1987. This skillful introduction to the life and work of Samuel Richardson emphasizes the major novels—*Pamela*, *Clarissa*, and *Sir Charles Grandison*. Richardson is presented as a radical social critic who prescribed an alternative "good life" in his writings. Brophy reviews the author's critical reputation to reaffirm that he is a significant contributor to fictional theory and technique. **(A,G)**

Erickson, Robert A. *Mother Midnight: Birth, Sex, and Fate in Eighteenth-Century Fiction: Defoe, Richardson, and Sterne*. New York: AMS, 1986. Erickson examines the ambiguous character of the midwife in eighteenth-century fiction to shed light on the philosophical attitudes toward fate prevalent during the period. The "representation of fate," as examined in *Moll Flanders*, *Pamela*, *Clarissa*, and *Tristram Shandy* extends to a discussion of "spiritual midwives" who appear at crisis points in a character's life to assist an emotional and spiritual rebirth. Although the reader may sense that the midwife metaphor is occasionally strained, this in no way undermines the overall value of this book. **(A,G)**

Harris, Joycelyn. *Samuel Richardson*. Cambridge: Cambridge University Press, 1987. This is an introductory critical work on Richardson that will facilitate research for students new to the novelist. Interweaving text with critical observations, Harris extracts the major themes, although he neglects some of Richardson's more interesting, minor themes, such as feminist politics. **(A,G)**

McDermott, Hubert. *Novel and Romance: The "Odyssey" to "Tom Jones."* Totowa, NJ: Barnes & Noble, 1989. This study seeks to isolate the elements that constitute the romance tradition of the eighteenth-century novel and to examine their classical origins. He examines the narrative structures of the *Odyssey* and several Greek romances, then turns his attention to comic Latin works, such as *Satyricon* and *The Golden Ass*, and the medieval romances. He then demonstrates how the novels of Fielding and Richardson continue this tradition. Anyone interested in the origins of the novel and eighteenth-century literature, in particular, should find this study provocative and enlightening. **(A,G)**

McKee, Patricia. *Heroic Commitment in Richardson, Eliot, and James*. Princeton, NJ: Princeton University Press, 1986. This demanding theoretical excursion into the works of Samuel Richardson, George Eliot, and Henry James derives its critical stance from the works of Derrida and the French feminist school. Comparing the structures, characterization, and thematic preoccupations of the authors, McKee offers insightful, open-ended readings of major works, focusing most closely on James' *The Golden Bowl*. Women characters are seen as drawn into relationships of heroic commitment made possible by an indeterminacy that negates the determinacy of power. (A,G)

Myer, Valerie G. *Samuel Richardson: Passion and Prudence*. New York: Barnes & Noble, 1986. Eleven essays, all but one published for the first time, examine Richardson's three great novels—*Clarissa, Sir Charles Grandison*, and *Pamela*. The contributors—Sir Angus Wilson, Pat Rogers, and Margaret Doody, among others—adopt a wide range of critical perspectives, including feminism. (A)

Other Sources

Doody, Margaret A., and Peter Sabor, eds. *Samuel Richardson: Tercentenary Essays*. New York: Cambridge University Press, 1989.

Goldberg, Rita. *Sex and Enlightenment: Women in Richardson and Diderot*. New York: Cambridge University Press, 1984.

Kay, Carol. *Political Constructions: Defoe, Richardson, and Sterne in Relation to Hobbes, Hume, and Burke*. Ithaca, NY: Cornell University Press, 1988.

Marks, Sylvia K. *Sir Charles Grandison: The Compleat Conduct Book*. Lewisburg, PA: Bucknell University Press, 1986.

Smith, Sarah W. *Samuel Richardson: A Reference Guide*. Boston: G. K. Hall, 1984.

Wilhelm, James J., and Richard Saez, eds. *The Seducer As Mythic Figure in Richardson, Laclos, and Kierkegaard*. New York: Garland, 1988.

EDWIN ARLINGTON ROBINSON
1869-1935

Evaluation of Selected Criticism

Bloom, Harold, ed. *Modern Critical Views: Edwin Arlington Robinson.* New York, Chelsea House, 1988. This anthology of nine critical essays offers a close look at many aspects of Robinson's poetry. Bloom introduces the collection by examining Robinson's sources, influence, and poetic development. Contributors include Yvor Winters, Roy H. Pearce, James Dickey, Hyatt Waggoner, Nathan Starr, Irving Howe, and Josephine Miles. Of particular note are Denis Donoghue's assessment of Robinson's continuing relevance, and John Lucas' overview of the poetic works and their place in literary history. (A)

Boswell, Jeanetta, ed. *Edwin Arlington Robinson and the Critics: A Bibliography of Secondary Sources with Selective Annotations.* Metuchen, NJ: Scarecrow, 1988. Boswell has compiled many of the bibliographies in the Scarecrow "Author Bibliographies" series and now turns her attention to a writer who has been long neglected. This listing of books, essays, articles, and reviews—many annotated—provides one of the few research tools available for those interested in Robinson's life and works. (A)

Burton, David H. *Edwin Arlington Robinson: Stages in a New England Poet's Search.* Lewiston, NY: Mellen, 1987. Burton's intention is to stimulate renewed attention to Robinson's responses to the events, personalities, and social forces of his age, which reached from the Gilded Age to the New Deal. Burton contends that Robinson's dilemma as an artist in America is reflective of "the dilemma of America itself." By analyzing passages of the poems, Burton demonstrates that Robinson came to doubt the national destiny, even as he exalted the dignity of mankind. (A)

EARL OF ROCHESTER
1647-1680

Evaluation of Selected Criticism
    Vieth, David M. *Rochester Studies, 1925-1982: An Annotated Bibliography.* New York: Garland, 1984. This bibliography provides annotated assessments of all the published editions of Rochester's writings, and citations for primary and secondary biographical and critical sources. Vieth then turns his attention to published criticism of the poetry, the prose, and the drama, providing annotated entries arranged alphabetically by author. The materials are fully indexed. **(A)**

    Vieth, David M., and Dustin Griffin. *Rochester and Court Poetry.* Los Angeles: William Andrews Clark Memorial Library, University of California, 1988. Vieth's essay examines the role of Erasmus' *Moriae Encomium* as a model for the court literature of Rochester and his contemporaries. Griffin describes Rochester as a writer of "court poetry" and provides a concise definition of the term. **(A)**

    Wasserman, George. *Samuel Butler and the Earl of Rochester: A Reference Guide.* Boston: G. K. Hall, 1986. This reference guide provides selected, annotated citations of writings by and about authors Butler and Rochester. A list of recent dissertations is included. The purpose of this guide is to provide scholars with up-to-date assessments of the available sources. **(A)**

Other Sources
    Notzon, Mark. *The Noise of Reason: Scepticism and the Art of Rochester.* Bloomington, IN: Eastern Press, 1984.

    Walker, Keith. *The Poems of John Wilmot, Earl of Rochester.* Cambridge: Basil Blackwell, 1984.

THEODORE ROETHKE
1908-1963

Evaluation of Selected Criticism

Dalakian, Peter. *Theodore Roethke's Far Fields: The Evolution of His Poetry*. Baton Rouge: Louisiana State University, 1989. Dalakian approaches Roethke's poetry from various directions—metaphysics, religion, psychology, biography—and, by working around his subject, reiterates his themes with ever-increasing clarity and resonance. Dalakian places Roethke squarely within the British romantic tradition but demonstrates how he absorbed American idealism as well as modernism. Too densely structured to serve as an introduction, Dalakian's study is essential for deeper understanding of Roethke and his poetry. **(A)**

Foster, Ann T. *Theodore Roethke's Meditative Sequence: Contemplation and the Creative Process*. Lewiston, NY: Mellen, 1985. This study, one in the publisher's "Studies in Art and Religious Interpretation" series, analyzes the religious ideas and spiritual practices that enabled Roethke to focus his concentration for the creative act. **(A)**

Kalaidjian, Walter B. *Understanding Theodore Roethke*. Columbia: University of South Carolina Press, 1987. Kalaidjian opens this study with an overview of Roethke's life and work, then explicates major poems from all of Roethke's books. This study is particularly good in explaining Roethke's thought and techniques, and is an invaluable resource for beginning readers. **(A,G)**

Stiffler, Randall. *Theodore Roethke: The Poet and His Critics*. Chicago: American Library Association, 1986. Stiffler summarizes over one hundred books, articles, and reviews, relating the critical views to the major groupings of Roethke's poems. This approach allows readers to make quick acquaintance with the diversity of critical opinion about Roethke. This guide does not pretend to replace the critics that are summarized. It is intended to direct interested readers to the right resources. **(A,G)**

Other Sources

Bowers, Neal. *Theodore Roethke: The Journey from I to Otherwise*. Columbia: University of Missouri Press, 1982.

Ramakrishnan, E. V. *Crisis and Confession: Studies in the Poetry of Theodore Roethke, Robert Lowell and Sylvia Plath*. Columbia, MO: Chanakya India/South Asia Books, 1988.

CHRISTINA ROSSETTI
1830-1894

Evaluation of Selected Criticism

Charles, Edna Kotin. *Christina Rossetti: Critical Perspectives, 1862-1982*. Cranberry, NJ: Associated University Presses, 1985. This study describes the critical reception of Christina Rossetti's works from Victorian times to the present day. Charles divides Rossetti's career into three chronological phases that suggest an evolution of reputation from "poet as saint" to "woman as poet" to a "poet psychoanalyzed." This is a broad outline of Rossetti criticism, presented with a minimum of sustained analysis. (A)

Coslett, Tess. *Woman to Woman: Female Friendship in Victorian Fiction*. Brighton: Harvester Press, 1988. Focusing on the Victorian era, Coslett demonstrates how women writers of the time were able to lend special power and significance to female friendships in their fiction. In these works, personal transformation is wrought through "sisterhood," rather than through the conventions of courtship and marriage. Coslett traces the process of individual development in novels by Gaskell, Rossetti, Browning, Eliot, and Charlotte Brontë. (A,G)

Harrison, Anthony H. *Christina Rossetti in Context*. Chapel Hill: University of North Carolina Press, 1988. Harrison provides backgrounds, readings of poems, and surveys of earlier criticism to encourage a reevaluation of Rossetti. He sees her, not as a woman whose life was marked by loneliness, unrequited love, self-suppression, and excessive piety, but as a self-conscious artist in control of her craft. He examines the connection between her secular and religious verse, and analyzes the spareness, repetitiveness, and self-abnegation of her work in an attempt to show how she is a much different writer from others in her time. (A,G)

Kent, David A., ed. *The Achievement of Christina Rossetti*. Ithaca, NY: Cornell University Press, 1988. Until very recently the Rossettis have always been treated collectively, but now it appears that Christina is emerging from Dante's shadow. This collection of fifteen essays makes a significant contribution to Christina Rossetti's literary identity as an important Victorian religious poet. Of particular note are W. David Shaw's essay on mystery in the poetry, and William Witla's deconstruction of the sonnet sequence "Monna Innominata." Anthony Harrison discusses eighteen unpublished early letters. This anthology should accompany Crump's edition of Rossetti's complete poems (1986). (A,G)

Leder, Sharon, and Andrea Abbott. *The Language of Exclusion: The Poetry of Emily Dickinson and Christina Rossetti*. New York: Greenwood. 1987. For much of their critical history, both these poets have been examined with regard to the reclusive, sheltered lives they seem to have led, but revisionist and gender critics have radically altered that perception during the last few years. These two critics set out to prove that Dickinson and Rossetti were "public poets" very aware of and engaging in the issues of their day. They argue that their gender exclusions in historical, economic, and political terms led to their use of complex language to critique the industrial world around them. Specifically, Leder and Abbott discuss these poets' views on war and marriage to demonstrate their interaction with a changing society. This study should inspire new views of both poets, as well as validate the importance of gender criticism. **(A)**

Nathan, Rhoda B. *Nineteenth-Century Women Writers of the English Speaking World.* New York: Greenwood, 1986. This collection of twenty-three essays focuses heavily on Dickinson and George Eliot but includes a strong essay on the work of Christina Rossetti from a feminist perspective. A bibliographical essay offers useful pointers for research. **(A,G)**

Rosenblum, Dolores. *Christina Rossetti: The Poetry of Endurance.* Carbondale: Southern Illinois University Press, 1987. Rosenblum applies feminist criticism to trace the motifs and the female personae in Rossetti's poetry. Since Rossetti plays her themes and forms against the male literary tradition, Rosenblum terms it a "poetry of endurance." Of particular value is Rosenblum's reading of *Goblin Market*. This detailed study is appropriate for Rossetti scholars and advanced students of feminist criticism. **(A)**

DANTE GABRIEL ROSSETTI
1828-1882

Evaluation of Selected Criticism

Faxon, Alicia. *Dante Gabriel Rossetti*. New York: Abbeville Press, 1989. This lavishly illustrated art book combines biography with art criticism as Faxon traces the influences on Rossetti's early art (e.g., Poe), his attraction to the Pre-Raphaelite brotherhood and medievalism, his themes (e.g., the fallen woman), his critical reception, the inevitable bond between Rossetti and Ruskin, and his passionate involvement with Jane Morris, William Morris' wife. This excellent, accessible study provides a fine introduction to the important events in Rossetti's life, as well as his artistic aims and achievements. The color plates greatly enhance the reader's understanding of both his painterly and literary concerns. (A,G)

Hall, N. John, ed. *Max Beerbohm: Rossetti and His Circle*. New Haven: Yale University Press, 1987. Caricaturist Max Beerbohm created a set of humorous portraits of Dante Rossetti and his immediate social circle of painters and poets. Hall has collected these cartoons and presents a lively introduction as to their significance, quoting heavily from Beerbohm's unfinished comic novel, *The Mirror of the Past*. In addition to Dante Rossetti, the personalities captured by Beerbohm include Swinburne, Ruskin, Morris, Christina Rossetti, Browning, Tennyson, and Whistler. (A,G)

Richardson, James. *Vanishing Lives: Style and Self in Tennyson, D. G. Rossetti, Swinburne, and Yeats*. Charlottesville: University Press of Virginia, 1988. In this study, Richardson, noted for his critical work on Thomas Hardy, elaborates on an important, but neglected characteristic that links the works of Tennyson, Dante Rossetti, Swinburne, and Yeats. In his view, these poets may be considered "elegists of the self," who treat life as a fleeting, "ghostly" vapor. Of particular interest is his discussion of how Yeats significantly transformed his Victorian heritage. This study deserves the attention of students of the period but is also suitable for general readers. (A,G)

PHILIP ROTH
1933

Author's Recent Bibliography
The Counterlife, 1986 (novel); *The Facts*, 1988 (autobiography); *Deception*, 1990 (novel).

Autobiographical Sources
Roth, Philip. *The Facts: A Novelist's Autobiography*. New York: Farrar, Straus & Giroux, 1988. A smart, literarily informed, and often tongue-in-cheek treatment of the author by himself with commentary by Nathan Zuckerman, Roth's alter ego. Roth readily admits that "autobiography may indeed be the most manipulative of all literary forms." **(A,G)**

Evaluation of Selected Criticism
Milbauer, Asher Z., and Donald G. Watson, eds. *Reading Philip Roth*. New York: St. Martin's. 1988. The common thread of this collection of thirteen new essays is how readers perceive, or misperceive, certain elements in Roth's fiction, especially Judaism, guilt, homelessness, the influence of Kafka, and comedy. Roth, himself, provides yet another lucid interview, in which he explores reasons why so many different interpretations have been applied to his work. This readable collection is a testimony to the importance and richness of Roth's fiction. **(A,G)**

Searles, George J. *The Fiction of Philip Roth and John Updike*. Carbondale: Southern Illinois University Press, 1984. Searles begins by defining the similarities between these two novelists: in age, urban experience, east coast sensibility, prose style, intelligence, and wit. He then defines their differing religious/ethnic background and establishes Roth as the leading spokesman for modern Jewish thought and Updike as the quintessential WASP chronicler. He concludes with a thorough analysis of how they both deal with religion, cultural assimilation, loss of traditional values, decline of the family, and loss of individuality. This is a lively, provocative analysis that will help readers understand the fiction, as well as generate ideas for research. **(A,G)**

SUSANNA ROWSON
1762-1824

Evaluation of Selected Criticism

Davidson, Cathy N. *Susanna Rowson: "Charlotte Temple."* New York: Oxford University Press, 1987. Davidson deftly includes intellectual and social history in her literary study of Susanna Rowson's *Charlotte Temple*. Continuing the critical exploration of her previous study, *Revolution and the Word: The Rise of the Novel in America*, Davidson provides a refreshing discussion of Rowson's work, placing it in the context of women's struggles to reshape literary creation and criticism. (A,G)

Parker, Patricia L. *Susanna Rowson.* Boston: Twayne, 1986. Parker's is the first full-length study of Rowson in a decade. She divides Rowson's works into those produced in London and America, then subdivides them by genre. Parker discusses Rowson's literary purposes and style, and analyzes each work to display characteristic themes: morality, Christian principles, and the betterment of the lot of women. Recommended for scholars of early American fiction or women's studies. (A,G)

JOHN RUSKIN
1819-1900

Autobiographical Sources

Bradley, John Lewis, ed. *The Correspondence of John Ruskin and Charles Eliot Norton*. Cambridge: Cambridge University Press, 1987. This book collects the voluminous forty-one-year correspondence between two men, decidedly different in both temperament and culture. Norton was a sociable, scholarly American; Ruskin a rich, wayward, lonely, British genius. Of particular interest are the letters dealing with their differences on the American Civil War, their appraisal of the history, politics, and religions of Europe, and Ruskin's love for Rose La Touche. **(A)**

Evaluation of Selected Biography and Criticism

Boris, Eileen. *Art and Labor: Ruskin, Morris, and the Craftsman Ideal in America*. Philadelphia: Temple University Press, 1986. Boris undertakes a general history of the American Arts and Crafts Movement of the late nineteenth century. Using William Morris and Ruskin as the focal points of her discussion, Boris examines the relationship of the movement to education, religion, architecture, the revival of folk traditions, immigration, and the developing factory system of production. This book is probably of most interest to students of social history, although literature is seen as an integral part of the movement. **(A)**

Brooks, Michael W. *John Ruskin and Victorian Architecture*. New Brunswick, NJ: Rutgers University Press, 1987. In this study of Ruskin and his relationship to Victorian architectural theory, Brooks reveals the polarities of architectural style and religious practice in the nineteenth century. This work updates older studies of Ruskin's influence on American styles and attitudes. By comparing Ruskin with his contemporaries, Brooks demonstrates that Ruskin's undeniable superiority led to his success. Valuable bibliographical information is contained in the annotations. **(A,G)**

Cate, George Allan. *John Ruskin, A Reference Guide: A Selective Guide to Significant and Representative Works about Him*. Boston: G. K. Hall, 1988. Ruskin, the widely popular Victorian critic of art and society, suffered a decline in his critical reputation in the twentieth century. Cate's bibliographical guide to secondary sources is designed to rekindle Ruskin studies. Entries, which span the years from 1843 to 1987, have been selected on the basis of their significance and usefulness, and include major studies in German and French. Annotations are generally clear and concise. **(A)**

Hardman, Malcolm. *Ruskin and Bradford: An Experiment in Victorian Cultural History*. Manchester, England: Manchester University Press, 1985.

Ruskin visited the industrial town of Bradford in 1859 and again in 1864 to deliver lectures. Hardman broadens the cultural and social context of these visits by showing how Ruskin's presence influenced the lives of seven common citizens of Bradford. The focus is much more on Bradford than on Ruskin, who plays an offstage but essential role. **(A)**

Hilton, Tim. *John Ruskin: The Early Years, 1819-59.* New Haven: Yale University Press, 1985. Hilton draws on material unavailable to earlier biographers in this chronicle of Ruskin's early life in Scotland and London. Because Ruskin became such an important social critic, Hilton contends, the events that shaped his early perceptions are especially important. Hilton is especially good analyzing Ruskin's art criticism and at defining the relationship between Ruskin and Turner. **(A)**

Kemp, Wolfgang. *The Desire of My Eyes: The Life and Works of John Ruskin.* New York: Farrar, Straus & Giroux, 1989. Noted German art historian Kemp compares Ruskin to his Victorian peers, including Byron and Carlyle, to conclude that Ruskin was a major reformer, educator, and ecologist. As his attention moved from art to social criticism, Ruskin increased his attacks on capitalism, religion, technology, and the destruction of nature. With an eye always trained on Ruskin's art, Kemp explores the sensibilities that enabled Ruskin to transfer his keen sense of structure and detail from painting to social criticism. Illustrated. **(A)**

Landow, George P. *Elegant Jeremiahs: The Sage from Carlyle to Mailer.* Ithaca, NY: Cornell University Press, 1986. Landow contends that Victorian authors Ruskin, Carlyle, and Arnold developed a genre of "secular prophesy" derived from sermons, religious essays, and the Old Testament. He examines the rhetorical devices used by these writers and traces their use into the twentieth century. To establish credibility, the "sage" employs biblical allusion, redefinition and clarification of language, and pronouncement. These devices convince the reader that the writer enjoys a special and privileged view of history. **(A)**

Landow, George. *Ruskin.* New York: Oxford University Press, 1985. Landow focuses on the way Ruskin's prose works rather than on the complexities of cultural or social history. Ruskin's prose is seen as visually acute and experiential. His interpretive methods and rhetorical skills are examined in detail. Landow's introduction offers a concise overview of Ruskin's life and literary output. **(A)**

Proust, Marcel. *On Reading Ruskin: Prefaces to "La Bible d'Amiens" and "Sesame et les Lys" with Selections from the Notes to the Translated Text.* New Haven: Yale University Press, 1987. This translation makes Proust's authoritative criticism of Ruskin available in English, much of it for the first time. These essays and notes reveal the influence Ruskin had on Proust's development. **(A)**

Sawyer, Paul L. *Ruskin's Poetic Argument: The Design of the Major Works.* Ithaca, NY: Cornell University Press, 1985. Sawyer argues that Ruskin's development follows the pattern that characterizes romantic poetry: a movement from innocence to doubt and estrangement, ending in a fusion of mind and nature that returns a state of informed tranquility. Sawyer follows Ruskin's thinking through *Modern Painters II* and *The Seven Lamps of Architecture,* in which Ruskin struggles with "psychic discordance" to *The Stones of Venice,* in which Ruskin was most troubled by the way in which art reflects a nation's moral temper. He then argues that *Unto This Last* blends the idealistic and pragmatic, reaching a tenuous resolution of the burning Victorian questions of honor, fidelity, paternalism, benevolence, and justice. This is a complicated, provocative study for scholars. (A)

Wihl, Gary. *Ruskin and the Rhetoric of Infallibility.* New Haven: Yale University Press, 1985. Wihl argues that Ruskin is as much a man of words and ideas as of visual experience, and that part of the problem in understanding his writing stems from conflicts between his epistemology, rhetoric, and visual sensibility. Wihl believes that modern readers have a skewed view of Ruskin, believing that he attributes to crude images the power of beautiful experiences. Wihl's study seeks to correct this view. (A)

Other Sources

Bradley, Alexander. *Ruskin and Italy.* Ann Arbor: UMI Research Press, 1987.

Bradley, J. L. *Ruskin: The Critical Heritage.* London: Routledge and Kegan Paul, 1984.

Henderson, Heather. *The Victorian Self: Autobiography and Biblical Narrative.* Ithaca, NY: Cornell University Press, 1989.

Kirchhoff, Frederick. *John Ruskin.* Boston: Twayne/G. K. Hall, 1984.

McElroy, Bernard. *Fiction of the Modern Grotesque.* New York: St. Martin's, 1989.

Spear, Jeffrey L. *Dreams of an English Eden: Ruskin and His Tradition in Social Criticism.* New York: Columbia University Press, 1984.

J. D. SALINGER
1919

Evaluation of Selected Biography and Criticism

Bloom, Harold, ed. *J. D. Salinger.* New York: Chelsea House, 1987. Bloom has collected what he considers the best critical opinions on Salinger's work. The essays, written between 1958 and 1984, include those by Alfred Kazin, Helen Weinberg, Gerald Rosen, and Dennis O'Connor. Bloom sees Salinger as a dated writer, whose slim body of work includes two minor classics: *The Catcher in the Rye* and *Nine Stories.* A useful introductory collection for students. **(A,G)**

French, Warren. *J. D. Salinger, Revisited.* Boston: Twayne, 1988. French surveys Salinger's critical reputation—founded as it is on such a slim corpus—and attempts to explain why the author continues to intrigue readers despite a self-imposed exile from the world. French touches on a few points of popular interest, such as John Lennon's assassin's misreading of *Catcher in the Rye.* He scrutinizes the preoccupation with Buddhism that led Salinger to abandon his career as a writer. **(A,G,Y)**

Hamilton, Ian. *In Search of J. D. Salinger: A Writing Life.* New York: Random House, 1988. When Random House announced the planned publication of this biography, Salinger, one of the most reclusive writers in American history, began legal actions to protect his privacy. A Supreme Court ruling prohibited any unauthorized use of his letters or other personal material. This revised product is a competent, if stark, compilation of the important events and works in Salinger's life up to 1965 when he ceased publishing. Very little new biographical information emerges from Hamilton's efforts. **(A)**

Salzberg, Joel, ed. *Critical Essays on "The Catcher in the Rye."* Boston: G. K. Hall, 1990. Salzberg collects the best essays on the novel written over three decades—from publication through the 1980s. This compilation allows readers to understand how critical perceptions have changed as a result of an evolving society, as well as new methodology, such as feminist and Marxist criticism. Valuable for both students and scholars. **(A,G)**

Other Sources

Sublette, Jack R. *J. D. Salinger: An Annotated Bibliography, 1938-1961.* New York: Garland, 1984.

CARL SANDBURG
1878-1967

Autobiographical Sources

Sandburg, Margaret, ed. *The Poet and the Dream Girl: The Love Letters of Lilian Steichen and Carl Sandburg*. Champaign: University of Illinois Press, 1987. During the six months in which Sandburg courted his future wife Lilian, they saw each other only twice. Letters became the means by which they grew to know and love each other. These letters offer a vivid and personal account of two lives, including their political beliefs and ideals. Lilian reveals herself an accomplished letter writer, displaying a ready wit and often penning short essays on topics such as socialism and sexism. Carl's letters are shorter and poetic, and inspire Lilian to respond in full. This readable volume will interest both a general audience and serious students. (A,G)

Evaluation of Selected Biography amd Criticism

Fetherling, Dale, and Doug Fetherling, eds. *Carl Sandburg at the Movies*. Metuchen, NJ: Scarecrow, 1985. Sandburg's poetry, his Lincoln biography, his children's stories, his novel, and his folk song books secured him a place in American literary history, while his work as a film critic has been entirely overlooked. This book collects his film reviews written for the Chicago *Daily News* between 1920 and 1927, when silent films were in their heyday. In a loose, idiomatic, humorous style, Sandburg dealt with screen romances, child stars, props, screenplays, and sex symbols. He was one of the first critics to comment on directorial style, the hokum of Hollywood, and the irresponsibility of filmmakers toward society. In these reviews Sandburg shows himself a socially conscious critic who believed film could be a bridge between different people. For film buffs and Sandburg enthusiasts. (G)

Callahan, North. *Carl Sandburg: His Life and Works*. University Park: Pennsylvania State University Press, 1987. Although Callahan had access to excellent material for this biography, his results are mixed. Sandburg's personal identification with Lincoln and struggle to write a monumental biography of him are well treated. Less satisfying is Callahan's neglect of Sandburg's other historical and biographical studies and of his poetry. Readers should consult this biography only for the chapters on the Lincoln biography. (A,G)

Salwak, Dale. *Carl Sandburg: A Reference Guide*. G. K. Hall, 1988. This chronologically arranged bibliography spans the years 1904 to 1987, citing writings by and about Sandburg. All entries are carefully annotated. (A)

WILLIAM SAROYAN
1908-1981

Author's Recent Bibliography
   The Armenian Trilogy, 1986 (plays); *Man With a Heart in the Highlands and Other Poems,* 1989.

Evaluation of Selected Criticism
   Hamalian, Leo, ed. *William Saroyan: The Man and the Writer Remembered.* Madison, NJ: Fairleigh Dickinson University Press, 1987. This anthology contains thirty essays on Saroyan's life and work, selected to represent a range of attitudes and critical perspectives. In his introduction, Hamalian examines the seeming paradox that Saroyan is viewed as a preeminent immigrant writer-in-exile whose work is inextricably tied to an intimately American setting—Fresno, California. Included among these contributions by noted scholars is a bittersweet memoir of Saroyan by his children. This is an important anthology, published at a time when Saroyan is attracting renewed critical interest. (A,G)

   Kouymjian, Dickran, ed. *William Saroyan: An Armenian Trilogy.* Fresno: California State University Press, 1986. This volume collects three Saroyan plays that were previously unpublished or unavailable—*The Armenians, Bitlis,* and *Haratch.* These late plays, written in the 1970s, mark Saroyan's examination of his Armenian roots. In them he explores such themes as loss of homeland, exile, diaspora, and dual identity. A lengthy introduction provides an informative discussion of Saroyan's life, works, and his significance for American literature. (A,G)

Other Sources
   Foard, Elisabeth C. *William Saroyan: A Reference Guide.* Boston: G. K. Hall, 1988.

   Samuelian, Varaz. *Willie and Varaz: Memories of My Friend William Saroyan.* New York: Pioneer, 1985.

427

MAY SARTON
1912

Author's Recent Bibliography
   The Magnificent Spinster, 1985 (novel); *The Bridge of Years*, 1985 (novel); *The Silence Now: New and Uncollected Earlier Poems*, 1988; *After the Stroke: A Journal*, 1988; *The Education of Harriet Hatfield*, 1989 (novel).

Autobiographical Sources
   Sarton, May. *After the Stroke: A Journal.* New York: Norton, 1988. In both her life and her poetry Sarton has projected a tough-minded New England independence. She is a woman who has struggled against psychological and social adversity and triumphed. But at age seventy-three she suffered a debilitating stroke, which deprived her not only of her health but her ability to write. Through long months of recovery she regained her courage to continue working, and this journal poetically recounts her experience. For anyone wanting to understand the poet behind the poems, this intimate autobiography provides insight and elicits admiration for an inspirational writer. (A,G)

Evaluation of Selected Criticism
   Evans, Elizabeth. *May Sarton, Revisited.* Boston: Twayne, 1989. This brief study, in the Twayne's United States' Authors series, treats Sarton's works by genre. Following an introductory chapter which places her in a cultural context and sketches the facts of her life, Evans devotes separate chapters to the memoirs and journals, the novels, and the poetry. An appendix contains a brief exchange of letters between Sarton and her editor Eric Swenson concerning her novel *Mrs. Stevens Hears the Mermaids Singing*. A good general introduction to Sarton's varied literary career. (A,G)

Other Sources
   Simpson, Marita, and Martha Wheelock, eds. *May Sarton: A Self Portrait.* New York: Norton, 1986.

DOROTHY L. SAYERS
1893-1957

Evaluation of Selected Biography and Criticism

    Reynolds, Barbara. *The Passionate Intellect: Dorothy L. Sayers' Encounter with Dante.* Kent, OH: Kent State University Press, 1989. Dante-scholar Reynolds has written an intellectual biography of Sayers that begins in 1943 with her first critical essay on Dante and ends with her death in 1957. During this period, Sayers translated most of the *Divine Comedy*, wrote two volumes of essays on Dante, outlined a book on Dante's mysticism, and drafted a novel on Dante and his daughter. Reynolds is an apt person to tell Sayers' story as she completed Sayers' translation. Recommended for anyone interested in Sayers or Dante. **(A,G)**

DELMORE SCHWARTZ
1913-1966

Author's Recent Bibliography
The Ego Is Always at the Wheel: Bagatelles, 1986.

Autobiographical Sources
   Pollet, Elizabeth, ed. *Portrait of Delmore: Journals and Notes of Delmore Schwartz, 1939-1959.* New York: Farrar Straus & Giroux, 1986. Although the quality of Schwartz's notebooks and journals depended on his varying mental and physical condition, he kept a record that clearly documents the rise and fall of his career and the depth of his poetic genius. Edited by his second wife from fourteen hundred journal pages, this volume contains different drafts of published poetry, some poem fragments, and miscellaneous writings that provide an intimate portrait of his wit, obsessions, and despair. An indispensable tool for researchers. **(A,G)**

SIR WALTER SCOTT
1771-1832

Evaluation of Selected Criticism

Cottom, Daniel. *The Civilized Imagination: A Study of Ann Radcliffe, Jane Austen, and Sir Walter Raleigh.* Cambridge: Cambridge University Press, 1985. Cottom explores the role of the educated and refined in defining social aesthetics by examining the writings of Radcliffe, Austen, and Raleigh—three writers, he contends, who represent the epitome of "taste." For these individuals, the perceptions of the uneducated were merely "pseudo-events." Cottom demonstrates how the class values of the eighteenth century were inextricably connected with aesthetic values. **(A)**

Dryden, Edgar A. *The Form of American Romance.* Baltimore: Johns Hopkins University Press, 1988. In this study, Dryden undertakes an analysis of the structure and development of American Romanticism. He first examines the origins of the novel and its relationship to romance by discussing *Don Quixote* and Scott's *Waverley.* He views Scott's early novel as a "founding text" in the history of the English novel. Dryden then dissects the narrative structures of five American novels—Hawthorne's *The Marble Faun*, Melville's *Pierre*, James' *The Portrait of a Lady*, Faulkner's *Absalom, Absalom!*, and Barth's *LETTERS*. He sees these American novelists responding directly to narrative problems inherited from Scott. **(A)**

Goslee, Nancy Morre. *Scott the Rhymer.* Lexington: University Press of Kentucky, 1988. Goslee reexamines Scott's "little-read" poetry, stressing its close relation to the oral tradition. Goslee's study shows three critical tendencies: a revaluation of romance, feminist theory, and recent narrative theory. Goslee sees strong romantic elements in Scott, but also detects an inclination to realism. Little else on Scott's poetry is currently in print, making this a useful update and suggesting that the romantic poet's reputation may be overdue for a critical review. **(A,G)**

Millgate, Jane. *Walter Scott: The Making of the Novelist.* Toronto: University of Toronto Press, 1984. Between 1814 and 1819 Scott published nine novels, most of which are among the most famous in English literature. Already one of the most famous and influential poets of his day, he carried on a voluminous correspondence and had personal and professional acquaintances from all walks of life. Millgate draws on this abundance of material and applies it to the composition of the first nine Waverley novels. **(A)**

Wilt, Judith. *Secret Leaves: The Novels of Walter Scott.* Chicago: University of Chicago Press, 1985. Wilt argues that the figure of the outlaw in Scott's Waverley novels is central to the hero's progress. Donald Bean Lean and Robin Hood, for example, have dual identities: one as outlaw, the other as purveyor of moral behavior. The dual identities ultimately lead the outlaws to a rediscovery and redefinition of their roles, thereby developing the themes of moral choice and personal freedom. **(A)**

Other Sources

Kerr, James. *Fiction against History: Scott as Storyteller.* New York: Cambridge University Press, 1989.

Mitchell, Jerome. *Scott, Chaucer, and Medieval Romance: A Study in Sir Walter Scott's Indebtedness to the Literature of the Middle Ages.* Lexington: University Press of Kentucky, 1987.

Sultana, Donald. *The Journey of Sir Walter Scott to Malta.* New York: St. Martin's, 1987.

ANNE SEXTON
1928-1974

Evaluation of Selected Criticism

Colburn, Steven E., ed. *Anne Sexton: Telling the Tale.* Ann Arbor: University of Michigan Press, 1988. This anthology of writing about Sexton begins with a chronology of her life and career, biographical sketches, memoirs and reminiscences. Essays and reviews of her work by M. L. Rosenthal, Diana Hume George, Helen Vendler, and Diane Wood Middlebrook, among others, follow. The bibliography is notable for a listing of recordings of Sexton reading and discussing her poetry. A useful addition to the growing body of critical work on Sexton and her poetry. (A,G)

Colburn, Steven E., ed. *No Evil Star: Selected Essays, Interviews, and Prose.* Ann Arbor: University of Michigan Press, 1985. This volume collects six essays and eight interviews that range in subject matter from Sexton's mentor relationship with Robert Lowell to her friendship with Sylvia Plath and their obsession with suicide. The interviewers often bring out the best in Sexton, especially the one with Sexton's friend and neighbor, poet Maxine Kumin. The portrait that emerges is of a poet whose tragic, almost destined life is as touching and alarming as her poetry. (A,G)

George, Diana Hume. *Oedipus Anne: The Poetry of Anne Sexton.* Champaign: University of Illinois Press, 1987. This is one of the first sustained treatments of Sexton's poetry to appear. George compares Sexton's life to that of Oedipus--driven to confront the truth no matter how horrible. She sees the central preoccupations of Sexton's poetry as the duality of body and spirit, the "family romance," the multiplicity of first-person perspectives, and death. On the subject of Sexton's suicide, George believes she felt powerless in a world presided over by God and elected suicide as a means of regaining control. For George, Sexton's feeling of powerlessness is uniquely feminine, deriving from her worship of her father. Sexton's death was thus a self-fulfilled prophecy whose psychological history is recorded in the poetry. (A,G)

George, Diana Hume. *Sexton: Selected Criticism.* Champaign: University of Illinois Press, 1988. This anthology analyzes the poetry and tries to fix Sexton's place in literary history. Alicia Ostriker argues for a radical reevaluation of her significance. J. D. McClatchy traces Sexton's recurrent theme of endurance. Since many of these essays take differing positions on Sexton, students will encounter a wide range of critical opinion. (A,G)

Hill, Caroline King Barnard. *Anne Sexton.* Boston: Twayne, 1989. Sexton's life and art are inseparable, and Hill convincingly demonstrates how they drew from each other. Sexton entrapped herself with madness, then used her poetry to escape into an even more confined psychic world. Providing a close reading of the work, Hill shows the complexity of both poet and poetry as they were spun into a web that became increasingly mysterious and dangerous. This is a provocative study for beginning students of both literature and psychology. (A,G)

Wagner-Martin, Linda, ed. *Critical Essays on Anne Sexton*. Boston: G. K. Hall, 1989. This anthology presents a rich selection of essays on Sexton's life and poetry. In addition to a section of new and reprinted essays, Wagner-Martin has included a long section of reviews, including those by Joyce Carol Oates, Neil Myers, and Katha Politt. Diana Hume George, Greg Johnson, and Gwen L. Nagel are among those providing longer, more critical essays. A short section of reminiscences, including those by Kathleen Spivack and Maxine Kumin, rounds out the collection. Very useful to students of Sexton and modern poetry. (A,G)

Other Sources

Barnard-King, Caroline H. *Anne Sexton*. Boston: Twayne/G. K. Hall, 1989.

Bixler, Francis. *Original Essays on the Poetry of Anne Sexton*. Conway: University of Central Arkansas Press, 1988.

WILLIAM SHAKESPEARE
1564-1616

Evaluation of Selected Biography and Criticism

Adamson, Jane. *Troilus and Cressida*. Boston: Twayne, 1987. As part of the New Critical Introductions series, this book provides a dependable and detailed reading of Shakespeare's *Troilus and Cressida*. Adamson briefly discusses the stage history and critical reception of the play and devotes the bulk of her study to astute analysis of language and character as related to the play's themes. She demonstrates how conflict within the play's double plot shapes the interaction of characters, scenic design, and use of language. This study is recommended as an accessible introduction for those who have been confused by the play's complexities. (A,G)

Anderson, Linda. *A Kind of Wild Justice: Revenge in Shakespeare's Comedies*. Newark: University of Delaware Press, 1987. Disagreeing with those who claim that revenge has no place in comedy, Anderson demonstrates that revenge is a pervasive theme in Shakespeare's comedies. In her view, many of Shakespeare's intrigues are based upon the idea of getting even. The revenge seeker rights the balance of justice by exposing hypocrisy in an amusing way or embarrassing an errant character. Anderson systematically examines the early comedies, the romance comedies, and the problem comedies in detailing her theme. Includes a useful bibliography. (A,G)

Barber, C. L., and Richard P. Wheeler. *The Whole Journey: Shakespeare's Power of Development*. Berkeley and London: University of California Press, 1986. This study analyzes the types of human conflict Shakespeare chose to dramatize. It concludes that the "family constellation," deprived of any divine outlet, creates the conditions for tragedy. The authors combine psychoanalytical thought with cultural analysis, avoiding hackneyed Freudian readings of the tragedies. The result is a challenging, imaginative case study on the relationship of Shakespeare to his culture. (A,G)

Bate, Jonathan. *Shakespeare and the English Romantic Imagination*. Oxford: Oxford University Press, 1986. In this well-written study, Bate examines the influence of Shakespeare on Byron, Coleridge, Wordsworth, Keats, and Blake. He examines how each poet's critical theory developed either out of or as a reaction to Shakespeare's poetic identity. This is a large field to cover, and Bate's study is a creditable overview that should be useful for anyone studying the English romantics. (A,G)

Bergeron, David M., and Geraldo de Sousa. *Shakespeare: A Study and Research Guide*. Lawrence: University of Kansas Press, 1987. This book is divided into three parts: an outline of scholarship on Shakespeare; a guide to the resources available; and a guide to developing and preparing a topic on

Shakespeare, including documenting the research paper. This is a useful "how-to" book for any student. **(G)**

Boorman, S. C. *Human Conflicts in Shakespeare.* London and New York: Routledge & Kegan Paul. 1987. Boorman starts with Shakespeare's cosmos, its perplexities and joys, then analyzes characters within its context. While hardly definitive, this study establishes a framework for understanding why Shakespeare constructed conflicts, and thus motivations, as he did. **(A)**

Brennan, Anthony. *Onstage and Offstage Worlds in Shakespeare's Plays.* New York: Routledge, 1989. This study continues the analysis of Shakespeare's works begun in Brennan's *Shakespeare's Dramatic Structures.* **(A,G)**

Brennan, Anthony. *Shakespeare's Dramatic Structures.* London: Routledge & Kegan Paul/Methuen, 1986. Using a structuralist approach, Brennan displays the various patterns Shakespeare used for the dramatic presentation of scenes. After isolating such patterns as visual repetition and echo, contrast in body movement and scene development, he relates them to audience response. Recommended not only for its sound theory but for its practical applications. **(A,G)**

Bryant, Joseph Allen. *Shakespeare and the Uses of Comedy.* Lexington: University Press of Kentucky, 1986. Bryant contends that comedy and tragedy are two equally important, complementary forces in the order of the Shakespearean universe. In arguing his case he devotes a chapter to critical readings of each of Shakespeare's comedies through *Twelfth Night.* He examines the characters and "human situations" of the plays, showing how Shakespeare uses plot to transform and revitalize relationships between the sexes. Taken in sequence, says Bryant, the comedies display an increasing concern for the hardships of women and gender injustice, and eventually acknowledge the intellectual and spritual equality women and men. **(A)**

Bulman, J. C., and H. R. Coursen. *Shakespeare on Television: An Anthology of Essays and Reviews.* Hanover, NH: University Press of New England, 1988. This lively study considers how television affects both Shakespeare's plays and the audience. The cultural, social, and intellectual expectations that audiences create for stage and film may be different for television. The authors discuss the successes and failures of performances recorded during the 1950s and how they might be edited for a contemporary audience. This provocative approach requires readers to confront Shakespeare in new and unusual ways. **(A,G)**

Calderwood, James L. *Shakespeare and the Denial of Death.* Amherst: University of Massachusetts Press, 1988. Calderwood argues that Shakespeare's characters attempt to deny their mortality by using money, food, costume, art, and wit to identify themselves with the immortal. The theme of bestiality becomes important as characters are transformed into and out of their bestial identities. **(A)**

Carroll, D. Allen. *"A Midsummer Night's Dream": An Annotated Bibliography*. New York: Garland, 1986. This volume is another in the series of Garland Shakespeare Bibliographies. Coverage is comprehensive since 1940 and all major earlier works are listed. Over 1,600 citations are arranged chronologically within seven thematic sections—"Criticism", "Sources and Background," "Textual Studies," "Bibliographies," "Editions and Translations," "Adaptations," and "Stage History." Annotations range from a few lines to a full page and cross-references are thorough. Recommended for any level of research on *A Midsummer Night's Dream*. **(A,G)**

Champion, Larry S. *The Essential Shakespeare: An Annotated Bibliography of Major Modern Studies*. Boston: G. K. Hall, 1986. Logically organized and easy to use, this bibliography cites more than 1,500 works written between 1900 and 1984. Citations are grouped in sections: general works, poetry, comedies, and tragedies. Each section is preceded by a discussion of the genre and an overview of the state of scholarship. The clarity of the annotations makes this a very useful reference tool. **(A,G)**

Clemen, Wolfgang. *Shakespeare's Soliloquies*. Translated by Charity Scott Stokes. London: Methuen, 1987. Clemen's study examines the relation of the soliloquies to both their immediate dramatic context and the larger shape of the play, as well as the effect that they have upon audiences. Recommended for scholars. **(A)**

Cohen, Derek. *Shakespeare's Motives*. New York: St. Martin's, 1988. Cohen focuses on how Shakespeare's characters imagine their world, and how this conception of character helps shape the plays. The plays Cohen analyzes include *Othello, King Lear, The Merchant of Venice, Henry IV, Richard II, Measure for Measure,* and *Twelfth Night.* **(A,G)**

Cox, John D. *Shakespeare and the Dramaturgy of Power*. Princeton, NJ: Princeton University Press, 1989. According to Cox, Shakespeare inherited a pragmatic, even cynical, view of secular power and its abuses from the stage traditions and ideology of medieval drama. This theory challenges critics who have characterized Shakespeare as a Christian idealist or a philosophical materialist. A useful addition to the debate over Shakespeare's political perspectives. **(A)**

Davies, Anthony. *Filming Shakespeare's Plays: The Adaptations of Laurence Olivier, Orson Welles, Peter Brook, and Akira Kurosawa*. London: Cambridge University Press, 1988. Although Davies' conclusion is that the plays are more successful on stage than on the screen, he deftly analyzes cinematic techniques such as camera movement and positioning, frame composition, and lighting to show how they affect the audience. In discussing the effect of technique on interpretation, he gives close readings of *Othello*, *Macbeth*, *Henry V*, *Richard III*, and *King Lear*. (A)

Dreher, Diane Elizabeth. *Domination and Defiance: Fathers and Daughters in Shakespeare*. Lexington: University of Kentucky Press, 1986. Dreher examines the relationships between fathers and daughters that are central to many of Shakespeare's plays. She draws upon feminism, Renaissance social thought, and modern depth psychology to explore Shakespeare's understanding of the interaction between masculine and feminine principles. Shakespeare's strongest women characters—Rosalind and Portia—seem primarily androgynous. According to Dreher, these characters had come to terms with the masculine principle within themselves and directed their energies toward problem-solving. Traditional patriarchal dominance brings tragedy to weaker personalities, such as Desdemona and Ophelia. More enlightened fathers, such as Prospero, develop a relationship with their daughters that allows them to incorporate the feminine principle. Recommended for students and scholars of Shakespeare and feminist literary theory. (A,G)

Edwards, Philip. *Shakespeare: A Writer's Progress*. Oxford: Oxford University Press, 1986. Written for beginning students but valuable to anyone, this book provides a comprehensive account of Shakespeare's life and works. Edwards begins with a brief biographical sketch, continues with an account of the human relationships in the plays, and concludes with five chapters dealing with individual works. Edwards' wit and lively style make this an excellent overview of Shakespeare's accomplishment. (A,G)

Empson, William. *Essays on Shakespeare*. Cambridge: Cambridge University Press, 1986. Empson is considered one of the foremost Shakespearian critics of the twentieth century, and this collection includes seven of his most insightful essays. Three of these essays—on Falstaff, Hamlet, and Macbeth—are thought to be his most provocative and brilliant. A fourth essay, "The Globe Theatre," appears in print for the first time. The style may sound old-fashioned to those whose critical ear is attuned to semiotics and deconstruction, but Empson's perceptions are founded on solid scholarship, and his influence on subsequent scholarship has been immense. His style, wit, and erudition will delight everyone. (A,G)

Fineman, Joel. *Shakespeare's Perjured Eye: The Invention of Poetic Subjectivity in the Sonnets*. Berkeley: University of California Press, 1986. Fineman's focus is less on the sexuality of the poet/narrator than on the nature of desire and how it is determined by language. He examines the manner in which the moment of passion is recollected in the poem, and how sexuality changes the narrator's world view. This is a difficult work, rewarding for dedicated readers. (A)

Fraser, Russell. *Young Shakespeare*. New York: Columbia University Press, 1988. Surprisingly, this critical biography adds more to an understanding of Shakespeare's life than one might expect. Fraser presents a clear sense of

Elizabethan times, and offers hundreds of intriguing parallels between Shakespeare's background and his art. Although scholarly, the lively writing makes this book appropriate reading for anyone. (A,G)

Frye, Northrop. *Northrop Frye on Shakespeare.* New Haven: Yale University Press, 1986. This study is a revision of a popular lecture series once offered by Frye. In carefully informal language, he surveys the Elizabethan Age, its stage traditions, and Shakespeare's plays. Although Frye is a noted critical theorist, here he holds close to his role as teacher, bringing in theory only incidentally. The result is a compact, entertaining introduction to Shakespeare. (G)

Greenblatt, Stephen. *Shakespearian Negotiations: The Circulation of Social Energy in Renaissance England.* Berkeley: University of California Press, 1988. Greenblatt, considered the leading practitioner of "New Renaissance Historicism," explores the relationship of Shakespeare's works to society. Opening with a personal appreciation of Shakespeare ("the total artist"), Greenblatt describes how he arrived at his current view of "historico-literary relativism," wherein there could be "no single method, no overall picture, no exhaustive and definitive cultural poetics." He then examines Shakespeare's genres—history, comedy, tragedy, and romance—describing each as a particular form of rhetorical "energy" that circulates within society. Each form requires a particular social "negotiation" to facilitate its circulation. Throughout this study, Greenblatt's obvious passion for his subject is contagious. (A)

Greer, Germaine. *Shakespeare.* Oxford: Oxford University Press, 1986. This short study emphasizes a view of the playwright as a pragmatic theorist whose works were influenced by his audience's responses. Among other topics, Greer discusses Shakespeare's view of his art as revealed in *The Tempest,* the conflict of values developed in his tragedies, and the metaphysics of *King Lear.* Of particular interest is her treatment of marriage in the comedies as a "heroic way of life." Well-reasoned and entertaining, this book is one of those rare introductory studies that stimulates new readers yet still delivers insights to scholars. (A,G)

Hapgood, Robert. *Shakespeare the Theatre-Poet.* Oxford: Oxford University Press, 1989. Noted Shakespeare-scholar Hapgood questions the contemporary trend among directors and actors to treat the plays as mere scripts, to be used or departed from at whim. Instead, he argues, direction, staging, choreography, and sequencing are subtly built into the text. He proceeds to examine the elements of stagecraft in *Hamlet, Othello, Macbeth,* and *King Lear.* He further suggests that going with Shakespeare's "flow," rather than against it, is the only way to create the powerful "Shakespearian" rapport among author, actors, and audience. Highly recommended for students of Shakespeare and the theatre. (A,G)

Hassel, R. Chris. *Songs of Death: Performance, Interpretation, and the Text of Richard III.* London and Lincoln: University of Nebraska Press, 1987.

Calling on performance history, historical and literary sources, military manuals, theology, and a close textual reading of the play, Hassel traces various interpretative performances from Colly Cibber to Laurence Olivier. In the process he offers his own reading. **(A)**

Hawkes, Terence. *That Shakespearian Rag: Essays on a Critical Process.* London: Methuen, 1986. This collection of what the author calls "sketches" looks at how Shakespeare has been adopted to serve various social and political purposes. In what amounts to a critique of the critics, Hawkes dissects the ulterior motives of such critics as T. S. Eliot, John Dover Wilson, Sir Walter Raleigh, and A. C. Bradley. It is an entertaining exercise that only serves to reinforce the current critical trend that views the plays as "scripts" rather than as "novels." Hawkes is best in his discussion of the year 1917 when several social-political-critical strands of the Shakespearian image converged. **(A)**

Holderness, Graham, ed. *The Shakespeare Myth.* New York: Manchester/ St. Martin's, 1988. This collection of essays is united around an ideological stance, characterized in the introduction as "cultural materialism." The essayists use Shakespeare to discuss their own views on social exploitation and class conflict, which are similar to Marxist ideological critiques. **(A,G)**

Homan, Sidney. *Shakespeare's Theater of Presence: Language, Spectacle, and the Audience.* Lewisburg, PA: Bucknell University Press, 1986. Homan explores those aspects of drama highlighted in its public performance—the use of language, the presentation of "spectacle," and the interaction of audience, performer, and playwright. He examines the texts of eleven plays to show how the interplay of visual presentation and language allow the internal world of the players to penetrate the external world of the audience. Homan's extensive notes are, in themselves, mini-essays on critical scholarship. Students of Shakespeare will find this an excellent guidebook for applying the principles of performance criticism. **(A)**

Honigmann, E. A. J. *Shakespeare and His Contemporaries: Essays in Comparison.* Manchester: Manchester University Press, 1986. This collection of nine essays examines the relationships between Shakespeare's plays and those of his contemporaries—Marlowe, Jonson, Dekker, Peele, Tourneur, and Ford. The contributors are highly respected names in the field, and each assumes a familiarity with the plays. Honigmann's introduction describes each of the essays and relates the various theoretical approaches of the contributors. A valuable collection of criticism aimed more for the specialist or advanced student. **(A)**

Honigmann, E. A. J. *Myriad-Minded Shakespeare: Essays, Chiefly on the Tragedies and Problem Comedies.* New York: St. Martin's, 1989. Always opinionated and controversial, Honigmann presents Shakespeare as a reclusive, bookish scholar with little time for the active lifestyle suggested by many recent critics. Among his opinions: *King Lear* is an "Oedipus-Everyman" play;

Troilus and Cressida was performed once, then suppressed by Shakespeare; the innovative *All's Well That Ends Well* is a "feminist" play; the Bard's stage directions were timidly suggestive, rather than forcefully directive. Those with serious interest in Shakespeare will find this study challenging. (A,G)

Johnson, Samuel. *Selections from Johnson on Shakespeare.* Edited by Bertrand Bronson. New Haven: Yale University Press, 1986. Johnson remains one of the most respected critics of Shakespeare who ever lived. A selection of his writings on the Bard has been judiciously compiled by Bronson in this one-volume abridgement of a previous Yale collection. Bronson's introduction provides some detail of Johnson's life, but it is too brief to encompass the full significance of his neoclassical critical position. (A)

Kawachi, Yoshiko. *Calendar of English Renaissance Drama, 1558-1642.* New York: Garland, 1986. Compiled from fifteen sources, this work presents a daily record of all the plays and entertainments staged in Renaissance England. Listed in calendar format, each entry includes date, dramatic company, place, title, type of play, author, known texts, and source. For those researching the history of English drama or the origins of a particular play, this compilation is an essential research tool. (A)

Lenz, Joseph M. *The Promised End: Romance Closure in the Gawain-poet, Malory, Spenser, and Shakespeare.* New York: Peter Lang, 1986. Lenz examines the particular ways romances end as a defining characteristic of the genre. To do this, he examines *Sir Gawain and the Green Knight*, Malory's *Le Morte Darthur*, and two Renaissance texts, *The Faerie Queen* and *The Winter's Tale*. This is a limited but useful study for medieval and Renaissance scholars. (A)

Levi, Peter. *The Life and Times of William Shakespeare.* New York: Henry Holt, 1989. Levi, professor of poetry at Oxford, ably dissects the Bard's background and upbringing, his cultural milieu, and the poets, players, and stage managers of the time. In the process, he debunks many of the common myths surrounding Shakespeare. Levi's discussion of the plays is deepened by this carefully constructed context. Where documentation or strong circumstantial evidence is lacking, Levi prefers to leave the picture vague rather than speculate. The facts are more than adequate to sustain the Shakespeare student. (A,G)

McGee, Arthur. *The Elizabethan Hamlet.* New Haven: Yale University Press, 1987. McGee argues that *Hamlet* is a study in evil, but not as has been traditionally interpreted. He argues that for the Elizabethan audience the play was an anti-Catholic satire. This unorthodox, reductive view of a play that has been praised for its complexity seems narrow-minded in its explanation of man's relation to God in institutional terms. (A)

Mehl, Dieter. *Shakespeare's Tragedies: An Introduction.* Cambridge: Cambridge University Press, 1987. This volume, first published in German, claims to be an introductory overview of critical interpretation of Shakespeare's tragedies. Mehl's work, however, overlooks many recent (and some not-so-recent) critical trends, such as the psychoanalytical, feminist, deconstructionist, and new historical schools. As a result the overview is skewed to favor a traditional British perspective. (A,G)

Montano, Rocco. *Shakespeare's Concept of Tragedy: The Bard as Anti-Elizabethan.* Washington, DC: Regnery Gateway, 1986. This study of Shakespeare's concept of tragedy is prefaced by a long discussion of the development of humanism in Italy and England. Montano then argues that Shakespeare held a Christian concept of tragedy that leads his characters to the resignation that the "will of God" prevails. The fact that Montano fails to consider much of the research amassed since the 1950s, however, considerably weakens his argument. (A)

Moore, James A. *Richard III: An Annotated Bibliography.* New York: Garland, 1986. This massive compilation is a comprehensive guide to published and unpublished works (in all languages) published between 1940 and 1981 on Shakespeare's *Richard III.* The annotated citations are grouped into eight sections—criticism, editions (including important pre-1940 texts), textual studies, bibliographies, sources, stage history, influence, and media criticism. The entries are extensively cross-referenced. Moore's introduction surveys the current state of scholarship and criticism on the play. For its intended purpose, this bibliography is currently unsurpassed. (A,G)

Nevo, Ruth. *Shakespeare's Other Language.* London: Methuen, 1988. Using Freudian concepts and the techniques of depth psychology, Nevo attempts to unravel the many inconsistencies of Shakespeare's later plays. Because Shakespeare relies heavily on dream and nightmare in these plays, logical analysis tends to break down. Nevo delves into what she terms a "syntax of unconscious fantasy" to offer plausible interpretations of seemingly illogical events. She pursues the theme of psychic transformation in *Pericles, Cymbeline, The Winter's Tale,* and *The Tempest,* concluding that the characters work their greatest magic on themselves. (A,G)

Nicholls, Graham. *"Measure for Measure": Text and Performance.* New York: Macmillan, 1986. This short study guide for students begins with a discussion of themes and characters, then considers four different performances and how they reveal differing interpretations. The elementary discussion of themes and characters is appropriate for beginning readers while the section on performance will interest theatre students. (G)

Parker, Barbara L. *A Precious Seeing: Love and Reason in Shakespeare's Plays.* New York: New York University Press, 1987. Parker examines the patterns of nonmarital love in Shakespeare's plays to argue against the view that he believed romantic love to be an intuitive force transcending reason, and that rational love comes through marriage. Although more advanced students of Shakespeare will benefit the most from Parker's work, others may discover exciting ideas for additional research. (A)

Pequigney, Joseph. *Such Is My Love: A Study in Shakespeare's Sonnets.* Chicago: University of Chicago Press, 1985. In this controversial, sensational interpretation of the sonnets, Pequigney argues that the sonnet sequence tells the story of an erotic drama in which the bisexual poet/narrator falls in love with a young man, consummates the union, loses his lover to a woman, and eventually takes the woman for himself. In supporting his thesis, Pequigney offers a detailed, intelligent close reading that scholars will find provocative. (A)

Pinciss, G. M. *Literary Creations: Conventional Characters in the Drama of Shakespeare and His Contemporaries.* Wolfeboro, NH: D. S. Brewer, 1988. Using a conventional approach, Pinciss traces five character types through selected texts by Dekker, Kyd, Jonson, Marlowe, Massinger, Middleton, Webster, and Shakespeare. He goes on to describe changes in the character types brought about by the different needs of the authors. Taking his analysis one step further, Pinciss relates these character transformations to changes in society, linking the drama of the theatre with that of history. Recommended for students interested in the English Renaissance. (A,G)

Sanders, Wilbur. *"The Winter's Tale."* Boston: Twayne, 1988. This is a clearly written, informal reader's guide to the themes, characters, and scenes of the play. Sanders explains the jealousy of Leontes, the roles of Paulina and Autolycus, the royal families, and the relationship of this play to *King Lear.* Sanders works all of his ideas through a scene-by-scene analysis. He includes a selective bibliography and an index that references authors, subjects, and plays. (A,G)

Scragg, Leah. *Discovering Shakespeare's Meaning.* New York: Barnes & Noble, 1988. Scragg argues that our difficulty in understanding Shakespeare lies in our lack of understanding of Elizabethan and Jacobean theatre conventions. She sets out to teach the basics in chapters entitled: Verse and Prose, Imagery and Spectacle, The Treatment of Character, and The Use of Soliloquy. Students may find this return to the basics enlightening. (A,G)

Shaheen, Naseeb. *Biblical References in Shakespeare's Tragedies.* Newark: University of Delaware Press, 1987. Shaheen's opening chapters cover the English Bible and Anglican liturgy in Shakespeare's day. He reviews Shakespeare's style and method of composition, the availability of Tudor and Stuart Bibles, and his familiarity with Anglican clerical service and sermons. Shaheen then lists references for three types of allusions: those certain to be related to the Bible; those mistakenly attributed to the Bible, and those that sound like speech patterns in the Bible but which have no biblical reference. A good tool for researchers. (A)

Siegel, Paul N. *Shakespeare's English and Roman History Plays: A Marxist Approach.* Madison, NJ: Fairleigh Dickinson University Press, 1986. Over a third of this Marxist critique of a group of Shakespeare's plays is devoted to establishing the historical context. The remainder links individual plays with political themes, such as "Richard III and the Spirit of Capitalism" or "Falstaff and his Social Milieu." **(A)**

Spenser, Christopher. *The Genesis of Shakespeare's "Merchant of Venice."* Lewiston, NY: E. Mellen, 1989. Writing from a performance-oriented perspective, Spenser analyzes the sources, plot elements, character types, and stage history of the *Merchant of Venice.* Although his conclusions are not particularly new, his approach offers a balance for more theory-oriented criticism. Of particular interest is Spenser's discussion of the dramatic potential of the role of Shylock, which transcends traditional stereotyping. Students can use the notes and bibliography to survey the current status of scholarship relative to the play. **(A,G)**

Stockholder, Kay. *Dream Works: Lovers and Families in Shakespeare's Plays.* Toronto: University of Toronto Press, 1987. Stockholder brings deconstructive and feminist criticism together in this study of sexuality and power in Shakespeare's tragedies. She contends that Shakespeare's women have such erotic power as to "infect the entire cosmos." Masculine terror is contained by the "strategy of reducing the sexually impure woman to a thought in the protagonist's head, balanced by the external 'truth' of her purity." Stockholder's psychoanalysis deals more with the erotic nature of women than with their role in Shakespeare's plays as she demonstrates the psychic structures of patriarchy. **(A)**

Taylor, Gary. *Reinventing Shakespeare: A Cultural History, 1642-1986.* London: Weidenfeld & Nicolson, 1989. Written by a co-editor of the new *Oxford Shakespeare,* this work provides a long view of the Bard's reputation through the centuries and his influence on subsequent writers. Dividing his expansive topic into six literary time periods, Taylor pieces history, politics, economics, and technology into a lively collage that shows what Shakespeare has meant to later generations. **(A)**

Waller, Gary. *English Poetry of the Sixteenth Century.* White Plains, NY: Longman, 1986. Using the theories of Eagleton, Greenblatt, Sinfield, and Greenberg, Waller's study is a revisionist history of English Renaissance poetry. Waller develops a parallel chronological overview and critical reevaluation. Chapters cover sixteenth-century literary theory, the ideology of the Elizabethan court, Petrarch, and Protestantism. Several authors are given prolonged treatment—Dunbar, Wyatt, Raleigh, Greville, Sidney, Spenser, Shakespeare, and Donne. This book was meant to, but does not, supplant C. S. Lewis' *English Literature of the Sixteenth Century* (1954). **(A)**

Warren, Charles. *T. S. Eliot on Shakespeare.* Ann Arbor: UMI Research, 1987. This general bibliographic overview of Eliot's criticism on Shakespeare includes excerpts from BBC interviews with Eliot as well as his published pieces. In Warren's summations of each entry he manages to elucidate Eliot's vision of Shakespeare's art. This volume is more valuable for its insights into Eliot and the influences on his work than for Eliot's insights of Shakespeare. (A,G)

Weiser, David K. *Mind in Character: Shakespeare's Speaker in the Sonnets.* Columbia: University of Missouri Press, 1987. Weiser's study provides a clear, interesting interpretation of the sonnets, comparing the dramatic qualities of the poems to the plays and developing an interesting theory about the narrator as a dramatic character. Weiser argues that the narrator moves through periods of growth, conflict, and final deterioration; and that the sonnets are in fact a story with a beginning, middle, and end. The index is especially useful for cross-referencing the poems. Recommended for anyone reading the sonnets or studying dramatic voice in Shakespeare. (A,G)

Wells, Stanley, ed. *"Twelfth Night": Critical Essays.* New York: Garland, 1986. This compilation of critical essays and reviews of performances provides a useful companion volume to the study or critical viewing of Shakespeare's *Twelfth Night.* Wells' volume is destined to supplant Walter N. King's *Twentieth Century Interpretations of "Twelfth Night"* (1968). (A,G)

Wiles, David. *Shakespeare's Clown: Actor and Text in the Elizabethan Playhouse.* Cambridge: Cambridge University Press, 1987. At the close of every Elizabethan performance, even tragedy, the Clown/Fool had the last words, which sometimes took the form of an extended performance. Wiles examines the performances of three kinds of clowns, played by Dick Tarlton, Will Kemp, and Robin Armin, and analyzes their effect on audiences and their relation to Shakespeare's characters. This is a convincing, interesting discussion for anyone studying Elizabethan times or theatre. (A,G)

Other Sources
Adams, Robert M. *Shakespeare—The Four Romances.* New York: Norton, 1989.

Andrews, John F., ed. *William Shakespeare: His World, His Work, His Influence.* 3 vols. New York: Scribner's, 1985.

Bate, Jonathan. *Shakespearean Constitutions: Politics, Theater, Criticism 1730-1830.* New York: Oxford University Press, 1989.

Berger, Harry, Jr. *Imaginary Audition: Shakespeare on Stage and Page.* Berkeley: University of California Press, 1989.

Bergeron, David M. *Pageantry in the Shakespearean Theater.* Athens: University of Georgia Press, 1985.

Bergeron, David M., and Douglas G. Atkins. *Shakespeare and Deconstruction.* New York: Peter Lang, 1988.

Bermann, Sandra L. *The Sonnet over Time: A Study in the Sonnets of Petrarch, Shakespeare, and Baudelaire.* Chapel Hill: University of North Carolina Press, 1988.

Berry, Edward. *Shakespeare's Comic Rites.* New York: Cambridge University Press, 1984.

Berry, Ralph. *Shakespeare and Social Class.* Atlantic Highlands, NJ: Humanities, 1988.

Berry, Ralph. *Shakespeare and the Awareness of Audience.* New York: St. Martin's, 1985.

Bevington, David. *Action Is Eloquence: Shakespeare's Language of Gesture.* Cambridge: Harvard University Press, 1984.

Birenbaum, Harvey. *The Art of Our Necessities: Form and Consciousness in Shakespeare.* New York: Peter Lang, 1989.

Bowers, Fredson. *Hamlet As Minister and Scourge and Other Studies in Shakespeare and Milton.* Charlottesville: University Press of Virginia, 1990.

Bradshaw, Graham. *Shakespeare's Scepticism.* New York: St. Martin's, 1987.

Bristol, Michael D. *Shakespeare's America, America's Shakespeare: Literature, Institution, Ideology in the United States.* New York: Routledge Chapman & Hall, 1989.

Brockbank, Philip. *On Shakespeare: Jesus, Shakespeare and Karl Marx, and Other Essays.* Cambridge: Basil Blackwell, 1989.

Bulman, James C. *The Heroic Idiom of Shakespearean Tragedy.* Newark: University of Delaware Press, 1985.

Burton, S. H. *Shakespeare's Life and Stage.* New York: Chambers/ Cambridge University Press, 1990.

Cahn, Victor L. *The Heroes of Shakespeare's Tragedies.* New York: Peter Lang, 1988.

Carroll, William C. *The Metamorphoses of Shakespearean Comedy.* Princeton, NJ: Princeton University Press, 1985.

Cavell, Stanley. *Disowning Knowledge: In Six Plays of Shakespeare.* New York: Cambridge University Press, 1987.

Chambers, E. K. *William Shakespeare: A Study of Facts and Problems.* 2 vols. New York: Oxford University Press, 1989.

Charney, Maurice, ed. *Bad Shakespeare: Revaluations of the Shakespeare Canon.* Madison, NJ: Fairleigh Dickinson University Press, 1988.

Coursen, H. R. *The Compensatory Psyche: A Jungian Approach to Shakespeare.* Lanham, MD: University Press of America, 1986.

Cox, C. B., and D. J. Palmer, eds. *Shakespeare's Wide and Universal Stage.* New York: Manchester University Press/St. Martin's, 1988.

Dawson, Anthony B. *Watching Shakespeare: A Playgoer's Guide.* New York: St. Martin's, 1988.

Dessen, Alan C. *Shakespeare and the Late Moral Plays.* Lincoln: University of Nebraska Press, 1986.

Dollimore, Jonathan. *Radical Tragedy: Religion, Ideology, and Power in the Drama of Shakespeare and His Contemporaries.* Chicago: University of Chicago Press, 1986.

Donaldson, E. Talbot. *The Swan at the Well: Shakespeare Reading Chaucer.* New Haven: Yale University Press, 1985.

Donawerth, Jane. *Shakespeare and the Sixteenth-Century Study of Language.* Champaign: University of Illinois Press, 1984.

Dotterer, Ronald, ed. *Shakespeare: Text, Subtext, and Context.* Cranbury, NJ: Susquehanna University Press, 1989.

Dubrow, Heather. *Captive Victors: Shakespeare's Narrative Poems and Sonnets.* Ithaca, NY: Cornell University Press, 1987.

Dutton, Richard. *William Shakespeare: A Literary Life.* New York: St. Martin's, 1989.

Elliott, Martin. *Shakespeare's Invention of Othello.* New York: St. Martin's, 1988.

Elton, W. R., and William B. Long, eds. *Shakespeare and Dramatic Tradition: Essays in Honor of S. F. Johnson.* Newark: University of Delaware Press, 1989.

Erickson, Peter, and Coppelia Kahn, eds. *Shakespeare's Rough Magic.* Newark: University of Delaware Press, 1985.

Erickson, Peter. *Patriarchal Structures in Shakespeare's Drama.* Berkeley: University of California Press, 1985.

Estrin, Barbara L. *The Raven and the Lark: Lost Children in Literature of the English Renaissance.* Lewisburg, PA: Bucknell University Press, 1985.

Evans, B. Ifor. *The Language of Shakespeare's Plays.* Westport, CT: Greenwood, 1985.

Evans, Faith, ed. *Clamorous Voices: Shakespeare's Women Today.* New York: Routledge Chapman & Hall, 1989.

Evans, Malcolm. *Signifying Nothing: Truth's True Contents in Shakespeare's Text.* Athens: University of Georgia Press, 1986.

Everett, Barbara. *Young Hamlet: Essays on Shakespeare's Tragedies.* New York: Oxford University Press, 1989.

Farrell, Kirby. *Play, Death, and Heroism in Shakespeare.* Chapel Hill: University of North Carolina Press, 1989.

Fass, Ekbert. *Shakespeare's Poetics.* New York: Cambridge University Press, 1986.

Fass, Ekbert. *Tragedy and After: Euripides, Shakespeare, and Goethe.* Toronto: McGill Canada/University of Toronto Press, 1986.

Fischer, Susan L., ed. *Comedias del Siglo de Oro and Shakespeare.* Lewisburg, PA: Bucknell University Press, 1989.

Foakes, R. A., ed. *Coleridge's Criticism of Shakespeare.* Detroit: Wayne State University Press, 1989.

Foster, Donald W. *Elegy by W. S.: A Study in Attribution.* Newark: University of Delaware Press, 1989.

Foulkes, Richard, ed. *Shakespeare and the Victorian Stage.* New York: Cambridge University Press, 1986.

Fox, Levi, ed. *The Shakespeare Handbook.* Boston: G. K. Hall, 1987.

Frey, Charles H. *Experience in Shakespeare: Essays on Text, Classroom, and Performance.* Columbia: University of Missouri Press, 1988.

Frey, Charles H., ed. *Shakespeare, Fletcher, and "The Two Noble Kinsmen."* Columbia: University of Missouri Press, 1989.

Frye, Northrop. *A Natural Perspective—Development of Shakespearean Comedy and Romance.* Magnolia, MA: Peter Smith, 1988.

Frye, Roland Mushat. *The Renaissance Hamlet: Issues and Responses in 1600.* Princeton, NJ: Princeton University Press, 1984.

Gallatin, Michael D. *Shakespearean Alchemy: Theme and Variations in Literary Criticism.* Ann Arbor: QED Press, 1986.

Garfield, Leon. *Shakespeare Stories.* New York: Schocken, 1985.

Goldman, Michael. *Acting and Action in Shakespearean Tragedy.* Princeton, NJ: Princeton University Press, 1985.

Gowda, H. H. *Shakespeare's Comedies and Poems.* New York: Envoy Press, 1986.

Halio, Jay. *Understanding Shakespeare's Plays in Performance.* New York: Manchester University Press/St. Martin's, 1988.

Hall, Michael. *The Structure of Love: Representational Patterns and Shakespeare's Love Tragedies.* Charlottesville: University Press of Virginia, 1989.

Harbage, Alfred. *William Shakespeare: A Reader's Guide.* New York: Octagon/Hippocrene Books, 1985.

Hawkins, Harriet. *The Devil's Party: Critical Counter-Interpretations of Shakespearean Drama.* New York: Oxford University Press, 1985.

Hazelton, Nancy J. *Historical Consciousness in Nineteenth-Century Shakespearean Staging.* Ann Arbor: UMI Research Press, 1987.

Hildy, Franklin J. *Shakespeare at the Maddermarket: Nugent Monck and the Norwich Players.* Ann Arbor: UMI Research Press, 1986.

Hobson, Alan. *Shakespeare Looks at Man.* New York: Guild of Pastoral Psychologists/State Mutual Book, 1985.

Hoff, Linda Kay. *Hamlet's Choice: "Hamlet"—A Reformation Allegory.* Lewiston, NY: Edwin Mellen, 1989.

Holderness, Graham, et al. *Shakespeare: The Play of History.* Iowa City: University of Iowa Press, 1987.

Holderness, Graham. *Shakespeare's History.* New York: St. Martin's, 1985.

Holland, Norman. *Shakespeare's Personality.* Berkeley: University of California Press, 1989.

Honigmann, E. A. *The "Lost Years."* Savage, MD: Barnes & Noble, 1985.

Horwich, Richard. *Shakespeare's Dilemmas.* New York: Peter Lang, 1988.

Houston, John P. *Shakespearean Sentences: A Study in Style and Syntax.* Baton Rouge: Louisiana State University Press, 1988.

Howard, Jean, and Marion O'Connor, eds. *Shakespeare Reproduced: The Text in History and Ideology.* New York: Routledge Chapman & Hall, 1988.

Howard-Hill, T. H., ed. *Shakespeare and "Sir Thomas More": Essays on the Play and Its Shakespearean Interest.* New York: Cambridge University Press, 1989.

James, Max H. *"Our House Is Hell": Shakespeare's Troubled Families.* Westport, CT: Greenwood, 1989.

Jorgensen, Paul A. *William Shakespeare: The Tragedies.* Boston: Twayne/ G. K. Hall, 1985.

Kellerman, Faye. *The Quality of Mercy.* New York: Morrow, 1989.

Kimpel, Ben. *Moral Philosophies in Shakespeare's Plays.* Lewiston, NY: Edwin Mellen, 1987.

Knapp, Robert S. *Shakespeare—The Theater and the Book.* Princeton, NJ: Princeton University Press, 1989.

Kolin, Philip C., ed. *Shakespeare and Southern Writers: A Study in Influence.* Jackson: University Press of Mississippi, 1985.

Kott, Jan. *The Bottom Translation: Marlowe and Shakespeare and the Carnival Tradition.* Evanston, IL: Northwestern University Press, 1987.

Leiter, Samuel L., ed. *Shakespeare Around the Globe: A Guide to Notable Postwar Revivals.* Westport, CT: Greenwood, 1986.

Levin, Richard A. *Love and Society in Shakespearean Comedy: A Study of Dramatic Form and Content.* Newark: University of Delaware Press, 1985.

Levith, Murray J. *Shakespeare's Italian Settings and Plays.* New York: St. Martin's, 1989.

Lyon, John. *The Merchant of Venice.* Boston: Twayne, 1988.

MacCary, Thomas W. *Friends and Lovers: The Phenomenology of Desire in Shakespearean Comedy.* New York: Columbia University Press, 1985.

Mackinnon, Lachlan. *Shakespeare the Aesthete: An Exploration of Literary Theory.* New York: St. Martin's, 1988.

Marienstras, Richard. *New Perspectives on the Shakespearean World.* New York: Cambridge University Press, 1985.

McGuire, Philip C. *Speechless Dialect: Shakespeare's Open Silences.* Berkeley: University of California Press, 1985.

Mebane, John S. *Renaissance Magic and the Return of the Golden Age: The Occult Tradition and Marlowe, Jonson, and Shakespeare.* Lincoln: University of Nebraska Press, 1989.

Metz, G. Harold. *Sources of Four Plays Ascribed to Shakespeare: "The Reign of King Edward III," "Sir Thomas More," "The History of Cardenio," "The Two Noble Kinsmen."* Columbia: University of Missouri Press, 1989.

Milward, Peter. *Biblical Influences in Shakespeare's Great Tragedies.* Bloomington: Indiana University Press, 1987.

Morris, Harry. *Last Things in Shakespeare.* Gainesville: University Presses of Florida, 1986.

Muir, Kenneth, ed. *Interpretations of Shakespeare.* New York: Oxford University Press, 1987.

Myers, Jeffrey R. *Shakespeare's Mannerist Canon: "Ut Picturas Poemata."* New York: Peter Lang, 1989.

Nagarajan, S., and S. Viswanathan, eds. *Shakespeare in India.* New York: Oxford University Press, 1987.

Neely, Carol T. *Broken Nuptials in Shakespeare's Plays.* New Haven: Yale University Press, 1985.

Newman, Karen. *Shakespeare's Rhetoric of Comic Character: Dramatic Convention in Classical and Renaissance Comedy.* New York: Routledge Chapman & Hall, 1985.

Ogburn, Charlton. *The Mysterious William Shakespeare: The Myth and the Reality.* New York: Dodd, Mead, 1984.

Ornstein, Robert. *Shakespeare's Comedies: From Roman Farce to Romantic Mystery*. Newark: University of Delaware Press, 1986.

Parker, G. F. *Johnson's Shakespeare*. New York: Oxford University Press, 1989.

Parker, Patricia, and Geoffrey Hartman, eds. *Shakespeare and the Question of Theory*. New York: Routledge Chapman & Hall, 1985.

Patterson, Annabel. *Shakespeare and the Popular Voice*. Cambridge: Basil Blackwell, 1990.

Poole, Adrian. *Tragedy: Shakespeare and the Greek Example*. Cambridge: Basil Blackwell, 1987.

Porter, Peter. *The Great Poets: William Shakespeare*. New York: Potter/Crown, 1987.

Ranald, Margaret L. *Shakespeare and His Social Context: Essays in Osmotic Knowledge and Literary Interpretation*. New York: AMS Press, 1987.

Rhoads, Diana A. *Shakespeare's Defense of Poetry: "A Midsummer Night's Dream" and "The Tempest."* Lanham, MD: University Press of America, 1986.

Rovine, Harvey. *Silence in Shakespeare: Drama, Power and Gender*. Ann Arbor: UMI Research Press, 1987.

Salinger, Leo. *Dramatic Form in Shakespeare and the Jacobeans*. New York: Cambridge University Press, 1986.

Salmon, Vivian, and Edwina Burgess. *A Reader in the Language of Shakespearean Drama*. Philadelphia: John Benjamins, 1987.

Sams, Eric, ed. *Shakespeare's Lost Play: "Edmund Ironside."* New York: St. Martin's, 1986.

Schoenbaum, Marilyn, ed. *A Shakespeare Merriment: An Anthology of Shakespearean Humor*. New York: Garland, 1988.

Schoenbaum, S. *Shakespeare and Others*. Cranbury, NJ: Folger Books, 1985.

Siemon, James R. *Shakespearean Iconoclasm*. Berkeley: University of California Press, 1985.

Smidt, Kristian. *Unconformities in Shakespeare's Early Comedies*. New York: St. Martin's, 1986.

Spain, Delbert. *Shakespeare Sounded Soundly: The Verse Structure and the Language.* Studio City, CA: Players Press, 1989.

Stevens, Paul. *Imagination and the Presence of Shakespeare in "Paradise Lost."* Madison: University of Wisconsin Press, 1985.

Tarlinskaja, Marina. *Shakespeare's Verse.* New York: Peter Lang, 1987.

Taylor, Gary. *To Analyze Delight: A Hedonist Criticism of Shakespeare.* Newark: University of Delaware Press, 1985.

Tennenhouse, Leonard. *Power on Display: The Politics of Shakespeare's Genres.* New York and London: Methuen, 1987.

Thomas, W. V. *The Moral Universe of Shakespeare's Problem Plays.* Savage, MD: Barnes & Noble, 1987.

Thompson, Marvin, and Ruth Thompson, eds. *Shakespeare and the Sense of Performance: Essays in the Tradition of Performance Criticism in Honor of Bernard Beckerman.* Newark: University of Delaware Press, 1988.

Toliver, Harold. *Transported Styles in Shakespeare and Milton.* University Park: Pennsylvania State University Press, 1989.

Trewin, J. C. *Five and Eighty Hamlets.* New York: New Amsterdam Books, 1989.

Van Den Berg, Kent. *Playhouse and Cosmos: Shakespearean Theater As Metaphor.* Newark: University of Delaware Press, 1985.

Vickers, Brian. *Returning to Shakespeare.* New York: Routledge Chapman & Hall, 1989.

Wells, R. Headlam. *Shakespeare, Politics and the State.* Atlantic Highlands, NJ: Humanities Press, 1986.

Wells, Stanley. *The Cambridge Companion to Shakespeare Studies.* New York: Cambridge University Press, 1986.

Wells, Stanley, ed. *Current Approaches to Shakespeare: Language, Text, Theatre, and Ideology.* New York: Cambridge University Press, 1988.

Wells, Stanley, and Gary Taylor. *William Shakespeare: A Textual Companion.* New York: Oxford University Press, 1988.

White, R. S. *Keats as a Reader of Shakespeare.* Norman: University of Oklahoma Press, 1987.

454
William Shakespeare

Wilders, John. *New Prefaces to Shakespeare.* Cambridge: Basil Blackwell, 1988.

Williamson, Marilyn L. *The Patriarchy of Shakespeare's Comedies.* Detroit: Wayne State University Press, 1986.

Woodbridge, Linda. *Shakespeare: A Selective Bibliography of Modern Criticism.* Cornwall, CT: Locust Hill Press, 1988.

Wright, George T. *Shakespeare's Metrical Art.* Berkeley: University of California Press, 1988.

Ziegler, Georgiana, ed. *Shakespeare Study Today: The Horace Howard Furness Memorial Lectures.* New York: AMS Press, 1986.

GEORGE BERNARD SHAW
1856-1950

Autobiographical Sources

Weintraub, Stanley, ed. *Bernard Shaw: The Diaries, 1885-1897, with Early Autobiographical Notebooks and Diaries, and an Abortive 1917 Diary.* University Park: Pennsylvania State University Press, 1986. Shaw's diaries, in most cases, are merely glorified appointment calendars, so the general reader should not expect to find intimate details revealed in this collection. For the scholar of Shaw's life, however, these two volumes are a gold mine: meeting times and places, people and reasons for meeting, expenditures, lecture appointments, eating and sleeping habits, and more. Weintraub has extensively annotated the entries to provide further background and cross-references. (A,G)

Evaluation of Selected Biography and Criticism

Crawford, Fred, ed. *Shaw Offstage: The Nondramatic Writings.* University Park: Pennsylvania State University Press, 1989. Shaw continued to write even in the years when he produced no plays. This collection of Shaw's nondramatic writings fills in the gaps. Included, among others, are "The Best Books for Children," "Orkney and Shetland," "Civilization and the Soldier," and "The Salt of the Earth." Each is introduced by a brief critical essay. Also included are essays on Shaw's ideas about the English language, his anonymous ballads, and The Shaw/Gordon controversy. A fine contribution to the Shavian canon. (A,G)

Holroyd, Michael. *Bernard Shaw: Volume 1, 1856-1898: The Search for Love.* New York: Random House. 1989. This is the first of a projected three-volume, definitive biography based on fifteen years of research into the life of a very private man. This volume chronicles Shaw's Dublin childhood and his first twenty-two years in London. Shaw's childhood was a bitter one, shaped by a stoical, unloving mother and a drunken father. Holroyd follows Shaw through his various incarnations as soap-box orator, vegetarian pacifist, Fabian socialist, boxing aficionado, and struggling novelist, detailing the tempestuous romantic affairs that seemed to accompany these changes. Eventually, Shaw matures into a robust middle age and is "captured" by the wealthy Charlotte Payne-Townsend. This is a splendid work—perhaps the best ever written on Shaw. (A,G)

Holroyd, Michael. *Bernard Shaw: Volume II, 1893-1914: The Pursuit of Power.* New York: Random House, 1989. The second volume of Holroyd's ambitious biography follows Shaw's career from relative obscurity to increasing reputation. It focuses on Shaw's literary productions—*Caesar and Cleopatra, Man and Superman, Pygmalion,* and others—and their reception by the critics and his growing audience. The text is liberally spiced with witty quotes and colorful dialogue from Shaw, his friends, and associates. The three-volume biography is being published without notes, but a fourth volume is anticipated that will provide a comprehensive scholarly apparatus. Holroyd's intent in writing this biography, which enjoys the sanction of the Shaw estate, was to "engage the interest of outsiders" in his subject. He should succeed marvelously. **(A)**

Meyer, Michael. *Words Through a Windowpane: A Life in London's Literary and Theatrical Scenes.* New York: Grove Weidenfeld, 1989. Meyer's entertaining reminiscences of postwar British literary circles touches upon his association with Shaw, Orwell, Graham Greene, and poet Sidney Keys, among others. The amusing anecdotes seem to spring from an inexhaustible source. **(A,G)**

O'Casey, Eileen. *Cheerio, Titan: The Friendship Between George Bernard Shaw, Sean O'Casey, and Eileen O'Casey.* New York: Scribner's, 1989. Octogenarian actress Eileen O'Casey offers a nostalgic account of the relationship between her husband, playwright Sean O'Casey, and Shaw. She relies heavily on their correspondence to provide a framework for her reminiscences. The chatty tone and avoidance of detail convey the impression that what she left out of the account might have been more interesting to the academic than what was included. **(G)**

Wearing, J. P., ed. *G. B. Shaw: An Annotated Bibliography of Writings About Him, Volume 1, 1871-1930; Volume 2, 1931-1956.* De Kalb: Northern Illinois University Press, 1986, 1987. The aim of this bibliographical series is to provide a comprehensive record of everything written about an author. This compilation contains over 3,600 items, each carefully annotated. The entries provide a record of the playwright's critical and popular reception. Arranged chronologically with extensive indexes, this work is an essential tool for students of Shaw. **(A)**

Wisenthal, *G. B. Shaw's Sense of History.* London and New York: Oxford University Press, 1988. Wisenthal attempts to demonstrate how Shaw incorporates history into his plays, especially *Saint Joan, Man and Superman, Major Barbara,* and *Heartbreak House.* He succeeds in defining the historic forces of the times, especially those of pessimism and optimism that mold most of Shaw's themes. Wisenthal provides a good reading of some of Shaw's later, and frequently ignored, plays: *In Good King Charles's Golden Days, The Apple Cart, On the Rocks,* and *The Simpleton of the Unexpected Isles.* **(A,G)**

MARY SHELLEY
1797-1851

Autobiographical Sources

Bennett, Betty T., ed. *The Letters of Mary Wollstonecraft Shelley*. Volume 3: *What Years I Have Spent!* Baltimore: Johns Hopkins University Press, 1988. During the last ten years of Mary Shelley's life covered here, she was plagued by ill-health and concerns over her son. Over a third of the 1,300 letters in this edition have not previously been published or published only in heavily abbreviated form. Scholars now have the opportunity to view these letters in their entirety and in chronological context. The editorial standards are high and annotations are admirable. The index is comprehensive for all three volumes. This entire edition is a highly recommended supplement for recent biographical works. (A,G)

Feldman, Paula R., and Diana Scott-Kilvert, eds. *The Journals of Mary Shelley: 1814-1844*. Oxford: Clarendon Press, 1987. This two-volume edition divides the journals into the years 1814-1822, covering Mary's life with Percy; and 1822-1844 after his death. Volume One includes references to betrayals and quarrels emanating from the Shelleys' *ménage à trois*. Written jointly by both Mary and Percy, this volume is secretive; absent are details about unfaithfulness, loneliness, miscarriages, and death. Conversely, Volume Two releases Mary's personal feelings, which are passionate and compelling. The contrast of the years will fascinate social as well as literary critics. Volume Two is essential reading for understanding Mary Shelley's life. (A,G)

Evaluation of Selected Biography and Criticism

Haggerty, George E. *Gothic Fiction/Gothic Form*. University Park: Pennsylvania State University Press, 1989. In this study in reader-response criticism, Haggerty attempts to lift Gothic fiction into the category of serious literature. To do this, he establishes two categories--Gothic novels and Gothic tales. Gothic *novels* fail because the genre is unsuited to the effects generated in the reader by the Gothic impulse. Gothic *tales*, on the other hand, succeed admirably. Indeed, because Haggerty's conception of the tale is represented by such works as Shelley's *Frankenstein*, Brontë's *Wuthering Heights*, Poe's "The Fall of the House of Usher," Hawthorne's "Rappaccini's Daughter," and James' *Turn of the Screw*, it is difficult to argue with the conclusion. Some have questioned Haggerty's categories of novel and tale as artificial. (A,G)

Homans, Margaret. *Bearing the Word: Language and Female Experience in Nineteenth-Century Women's Writing*. Chicago: University of Chicago Press, 1986. Delving into the Oedipal propositions of psychoanalytic theory, Homans emerges with an insight into the interaction of language acquisition and the formation of gender identity. Building on the ideas of Jacques Lacan and

Nancy Chodorow, she describes a dominant myth of language that identifies the woman with the "literal," and a dominant myth of gender that connects her with nature and matter. To support these theories, she provides close readings of excerpts from Mary Shelley, Dorothy Wordsworth, the Brontë sisters, Elizabeth Gaskell, George Eliot, and Virginia Woolf. Scholars should acquaint themselves with the theoretical framework that Homans develops here. (A)

Mellor, Anne K. *Mary Shelley: Her Life, Her Fiction, Her Monsters.* London: Methuen, 1988. Mellor, a noted feminist critic of the Romantic period, interweaves biography and criticism to reevaluate Mary Shelley and her fiction. She contends that since Shelley was deprived of close family ties, she went on to present an idealized view of the family in her fiction, one which she then proceeded to deflate. Mellor argues that Shelley identified with the motherless "creature" of her most famous novel and that Dr. Frankenstein was a parody of her husband, Percy. *Frankenstein* is seen as a critique of the entire Romantic genre. Recommended to supplement the standard works on Mary Shelley. (A,G)

Poovey, Mary. *The Proper Lady and the Woman Writer: Ideology as Style in the Works of Mary Wollstonecraft, Mary Shelley, and Jane Austen.* Chicago: University of Chicago Press, 1984. This was perhaps the first extended feminist study of eighteenth- and nineteenth-century fiction to introduce a rigorously applied historical dimension to literary analysis. Poovey reveals the underlying ideological contradictions in the Victorian ideal of the "proper lady" through close readings of works by Shelley, Wollstonecraft, and Austen. (A,G)

Spark, Muriel. *Mary Shelley: A Biography.* New York: Dutton, 1987. This biography of Mary Shelley was originally published in England over thirty years ago. In response to a resurgent interest in the author, Spark has revised her work in light of recent scholarship and the availability of Shelley's papers. The first part addresses Shelley's life, while the concluding section provides a critical overview of her work. There is a pirated edition, *Child of Light,* which has been published in the U.S. without the author's permission. (A,G)

St. Clair, William. *The Godwins and the Shelleys: The Biography of a Family.* New York: Norton, 1989. Meeting the highest standards of research and analysis, this biography interweaves the lives and works of four of the most influential literary minds of the nineteenth century. St. Clair examines the origin and impact of William Godwin's *Political Justice,* Mary Wollstonecraft's *Vindication of the Rights of Women,* Mary Shelley's *Frankenstein,* and Percy Bysshe Shelley's poetry. The interplay of radical political beliefs, divergent moral standards, and literary achievement makes for intriguing and thought-provoking reading. This book is highly recommended for the scholar and for the general reader. (A,G)

Sunstein, Emily. *Mary Shelley: Romance and Reality.* Boston: Little, Brown, 1989. Sunstein, author of a biography of Mary Wollstonecraft, has now produced the first full-length biography of her daughter, Mary Shelley. The exhaustive research behind this biography puts to rest many of the falsehoods spread by both admirers and detractors. Shelley's copious writings—many neglected and overdue for reappraisal—are examined in light of the events of her life. Seen against the backdrop of her parents and husband, whose careers and reputations so overshadowed her own, Mary Shelley emerges as a truly remarkable human being. (A, G)

Thornburg, Mary K Patterson. *The Monster in the Mirror: Gender and the Sentimen- tal/Gothic Myth in "Frankenstein."* Ann Arbor: UMI Research, 1987. The first half of this study offers a useful overview of the gothic tradition. Thornburg examines the "gothic" personality and how it relates to sexuality, sensuality, and other nonrational aspects of life. She then turns her attention to Shelley's *Frankenstein* to identify three "circles" of relationship that surround the monster. The book's protagonist is developed as a norm by which to measure other gothic characters, particularly those of Poe. This book could be recommended for general readers who are interested in exploring the gothic mystique. (A,G)

Varnado, S. L. *Haunted Presence: The Numinous in Gothic Fiction.* Tuscaloosa: University of Alabama Press, 1987. Drawing upon Rudolph Otto's concept of the "numinous," Varnado examines the subjective experience of the supernatural as revealed in the major gothic texts. In Walpole he sees the harmony of contrasts, in Radcliff the sublime raised to numinosity. Lewis presents the demonic, while Stoker evokes the rational-nonrational paradigm. Separate chapters are devoted to Mary Shelley's sacred and profane theme and Poe's mysticism. This is an intriguing application of a useful theory. (A,G)

Veeder, William R. *Mary Shelley and Frankenstein: The Fate of Androgyny.* Chicago: University of Chicago Press, 1986. Veeder's study intertwines three themes—the literary-historical context of Mary Shelley's novel, biographical issues of Mary and her husband Percy, and the nature of androgyny as developed in depth psychology and applied to *Frankenstein.* Veeder's breadth of scholarship is impressive. However, he too often assumes that his readers are as informed as he. This unfortunately excludes many students from this fascinating work. (A)

Other Sources
Marshall, David. *The Surprising Effects of Sympathy: Marivaux, Diderot, Rousseau, and Mary Shelley.* Chicago: University of Chicago Press, 1988.

Phy, Allene S. *Mary Shelley.* Mercer Island, WA: Starmont House, 1988.

PERCY BYSSHE SHELLEY
1792-1822

Evaluation of Selected Biography and Criticism

Blank, G. Kim. *Wordsworth's Influence on Shelley: A Study of Poetic Authority.* New York: St. Martin's, 1988. Shelley himself acknowledged his poetic debt to Wordsworth. In the first part of his study Blank examines Shelley's early poetry and argues that the best of it falls clearly into the Wordsworthian school. In the second part he explores the result of one poet influencing another. In addition to arguing his influence thesis, Blank provides excellent close readings of both poets. Clearly written, this study is readable for students at any level, but is most valuable for students familiar with the poetry. (A,G)

Crook, Nora, *et al. Shelley's Venomed Melody.* Cambridge: Cambridge University Press, 1986. This book is built upon a single premise—the possibility that Percy Shelley contracted syphilis during his student years. Other biographers have touched upon his possible infection but left the subject unexplored. Here, the authors leave no stone unturned in their search for evidence. Alternative explanations are often advanced—the possibility that Shelley's infection was psychosomatic rather than actual, for example—but the indications within the poetry itself seem almost irrefutable as the authors develop their case. Difficult to prove, impossible to know for a fact, it appears that syphilis left its mark on Shelley, and the implications for future biographers are immense. (A,G)

Engelberg, Karsten Klejs. *The Making of the Shelley Myth: An Annotated Bibliography of Criticism of Percy Bysshe Shelley, 1822-1860.* Bronx, NY: Mansell, 1988. In Engelberg's view, the Shelley "myth" developed as a sympathetic reaction to the immoral, atheistic, and radical reputation he acquired in his lifetime. This bibliography covers the formative years of that myth, from Shelly's death in 1822 until 1860. Most of the citations are of reviews of Shelley's poetry and articles on him published in London. Four introductory chapters examine the development of Shelley's personal and literary reputation, focusing on the circumstances of his death, his first marriage, his mental stability, and the "myth" as reflected in the poetry. The annotated citations are arranged chronologically. A table of quotations found in the reviews, a list of works consulted, and indexes of sources, reviews, and reviewers are also included. (A,G)

Johnson, Paul. *Intellectuals.* New York: Harper & Row, 1989. Johnson exercises his caustic wit in a critical look at some of the world's most famous, and often self-proclaimed, intellectuals. Coming under the gun are Shelley, Hemingway, Rousseau, Sartre, Brecht, Bertrand Russell, Hellman, and

460

Marx. Although colored by a readily admitted "anti-intellectual" bias, Johnson's profiles are thought-provoking, entertaining, and useful as an antidote to hero worship. **(A,G)**

Keach, William. *Shelley's Style*. New York: Methuen, 1984. Keach begins by analyzing Shelley's ideas about language in *A Defense of Poetry*, continues with his conception of imagery and versification, and concludes with a discussion of the biographical and historical influences on Shelley's style. He argues that Shelley believed that words were an imperfect expression of thought and that, consequently, poetic language was a veil rather than a mirror of nature. This complex, scholarly study illuminates the artistic and philosophical rebellion of the Romantic poets and presents new insights into Shelley's ideas about art and life. **(A)**

O'Neill, Michael. *Percy Bysshe Shelley: A Literary Life*. New York: St. Martin's, 1989. While O'Neill breaks no new ground, he provides a clear account of the circumstances leading to Shelley's publications, his religious and political views, and his personal triumphs and disappointments. This is a good source for beginning and intermediate students. **(A,G)**

Sperry, Stuart M. *Shelley's Major Verse: The Narrative and Dramatic Poetry*. Cambridge: Harvard University Press, 1988. Sperry argues that Shelley's poetry connected his idealized world to the real world. Thus, as exterior events changed, Shelley invented "visionary structures" to accommodate them. In developing this psychoanalytic thesis, Sperry analyzes "Queen Mab," *Alastor, The Revolt of Islam, The Cenci*, "The Witch of Atlas," "Epipsychidion," *The Triumph of Life*, and *Prometheus Unbound*. Whether or not readers finally accept Sperry's thesis, they will certainly appreciate his sensitive reading of the poetry. **(A)**

St. Clair, William. *The Godwins and the Shelleys: The Biography of a Family*. New York: Norton, 1989. Meeting the highest standards of research and analysis, this biography interweaves the lives and works of four of the most influential literary minds of the nineteenth century. St. Clair examines the origin and impact of William Godwin's *Political Justice*, Mary Wollstonecraft's *Vindication of the Rights of Women*, Mary Shelley's *Frankenstein*, and Percy Bysshe Shelley's poetry. The interplay of radical political beliefs, divergent moral standards, and literary achievement makes for intriguing and thought-provoking reading. This book is highly recommended for the scholar and for the general reader. **(A,G)**

Tetreault, Ronald. *The Poetry of Life: Shelley and Literary Form*. Toronto: University of Toronto Press, 1987. This excellent study traces Shelley's intellectual development from youthful confidence to lyric isolation, and finally to a new faith in an aesthetic response to life. As Shelley's outlook changed, so did his literary forms. Tetreault argues that Shelley generates profound meanings and ironies through the subversion of literary form; by breaking the boundaries of conventional systems, he affirms human liberty. **(A)**

Other Sources

Behrendt, Stephen C. *Shelley and His Audiences.* Lincoln: University of Nebraska Press, 1989.

Clark, Timothy. *Embodying Revolution: The Figure of the Poet in Shelley.* New York: Oxford University Press, 1989.

Duerksen, Roland A. *Shelley's Poetry of Involvement.* New York: St. Martin's, 1988.

Goslee, Nancy M. *Uriel's Eye: Miltonic Stationing and Statuary in Blake, Keats, and Shelley.* Tuscaloosa: University of Alabama Press, 1985.

Hoagwood, Terence Allan. *Prophecy and the Philosophy of Mind: Traditions of Blake and Shelley.* Tuscaloosa: University of Alabama Press, 1985.

Hoagwood, Terence Allan. *Skepticism and Ideology: Shelley's Political Prose and Its Philosophical Context from Bacon to Marx.* Iowa City: University of Iowa Press, 1988.

Hodgart, Patricia. *A Preface to Shelley.* White Plains, NY: Longman, 1985.

Hodgson, John A. *Coleridge, Shelley and Transcendental Inquiry: Rhetoric, Argument, Metapsychology.* Lincoln: University of Nebraska Press, 1989.

Hogle, Jerrold E. *Shelley's Process: Radical Transference and the Development of His Major Works.* New York: Oxford University Press, 1989.

O'Neill, Michael. *The Human Mind's Imaginings: Conflict and Achievement in Shelley's Poetry.* New York: Oxford University Press, 1989.

Pirie, David. *Shelley.* New York: Open University Press/Taylor & Francis, 1988.

Shelley, Percy Bysshe. *Shelley's Prose: The Trumpet of a Prophecy.* New York: New Amsterdam Books, 1988.

SIR PHILIP SIDNEY
1554-1586

Evaluation of Selected Criticism

Brennan, Michael. *Literary Patronage in the English Renaissance: The Pembroke Family*. London: Routledge, 1988. Based on extensive study of manuscripts and early printed sources, Brennan's work examines the complex role of literary patronage during the Renaissance. Sidney's sister was countess to the second Earl of Pembroke and was influential in finding support for her brother's work. The wealth of information Brennan provides and his efficient organization of the material enables this book to supplant other treatments of this topic. (A,G)

Dobyns, Ann. *The Voices of Romance: Studies in Dialogue and Character*. Newark: University of Delaware Press, 1989. For Dobyns, an essential element of the romance is the fact that character is of secondary importance and is usually determined by plot necessities. She argues that romance authors use speech characteristics to develop distinct characters that embody themes. In arguing her thesis, she compares parallel characters from Malory's *Le Morte Darthur*, Sidney's *New Arcadia*, and Brontë's *Wuthering Heights*. She demonstrates that although the characters in romance are conventional and sometimes static and abstract, they can at the same time be "complex and richly detailed." Useful to students of the romance. (A)

Duncan-Jones, Katherine, ed. *Sir Philip Sidney*. London: Oxford University Press, 1989. This is an anthology of Sidney's important poetry and prose, fifteen of his letters, thirty pages of new biographical data, excellent notes, bibliography, and scholarly apparatus. This excellent edition is recommended for both scholars and readers of Sidney. (A,G)

Kay, Dennis, ed. *Sir Philip Sidney: An Anthology of Modern Criticism*. Oxford: Clarendon Press, 1987. The contributors to this collection provide informed studies of Sidney's major works from a variety of critical approaches. The volume also includes a chronology, a bibliography of criticism, and an excellent history of Sidney's critical reputation. Kay outlines topics in need of further research. Although all these essays have appeared elsewhere, this volume is a convenient resource for researchers. (A)

McCanles, Michael. *The Text of Sidney's Arcadian World*. Durham, NC: Duke University Press, 1989. According to McCanles' structuralist assessment, Sidney's *New Arcadia* is primarily an exercise in self-reflective discourse. Meaning is generated through a dialectic of syntax, characterization, and plot. Binary oppositions provide the dramatic foundation for Sidney's prose works. McCanles contends that Sidney "deconstructs" Aristotelian ethics and rules of rhetoric in anticipation of literary modernism. (A)

Skretkowicz, Victor. *The Countess of Pembroke's Arcadia: "The New Arcadia."* Oxford: Oxford University Press, 1987. At the time of his death in 1586, Sidney was revising his *Arcadia*. The incomplete revision was first published in 1590 and promptly labeled *The New Arcadia*. This revision is extremely important to Renaissance scholars because it reveals how dramatically Sidney had changed his concept of the romance. Skretkowicz has meticulously collated the existing manuscripts and added extensive notes and commentary. **(A)**

Stillman, Robert E. *Sidney's Poetic Justice: "The Old Arcadia," Its Eclogues, and Renaissance Pastoral Traditions.* Lewisburg, PA: Bucknell University Press, 1986. Stillman's reading of *The Old Arcadia* contends that it argues neither for nor against select systems of values, but instead projects a world based on inward contentment that is secure from the "ravages of misfortune in the iron age." Stillman discusses the creation of a new pastoral mode that fuses classical and Christian traditions. He contends that the dramatic structure of the work fuses audience and singers, prose and poetry, and that Sidney's defense of poetry is embedded in *The Old Arcadia*. A well-written, focused book that will challenge scholars. **(A)**

Other Sources
Heninger, S. K., Jr. *Sidney and Spenser: The Poet as Maker.* University Park: Pennsylvania State University Press, 1990.

Kinney, Arthur F., ed. *Essential Articles for the Study of Sir Philip Sidney.* Hamden, CT: Archon/Shoe String, 1986.

Van Dorsten, Jan, *et al. Sir Philip Sidney: 1586 and the Creation of a Legend.* Leiden, Netherlands: E. J. Brill, 1986.

Waller, Gary F., and Michael D. Moore, eds. *Sir Philip Sidney and the Interpretation of Renaissance Culture: The Poet in His Times and in Ours: A Collection of Critical and Scholarly Essays.* Savage, MD: Barnes & Noble, 1984.

WILLIAM GILMORE SIMMS
1806-1870

Evaluation of Selected Criticism

Guilds, John Caldwell, ed. *Long Years of Neglect: The Work and Reputation of William Gilmore Simms*. Fayetteville: University of Arkansas Press, 1988. Guilds has collected twelve original essays on Simms in the hope that the anthology will arouse a new curiosity about this once-renowned Southern writer. The collection includes essays on Simms' novels *Woodcraft* and *Paddy McGann*, as well as discussions of his life, poetry, historical philosophy, and humor. Appended is a biographical sketch of Thomas Cary Duncan Eaves, the scholar who renewed the study of Simms by carefully editing the six volumes of *The Letters of William Gilmore Simms* during the 1950s. A useful collection for students of Southern literature. (A)

Wimsatt, Mary Ann. *The Major Fiction of William Gilmore Simms: Cultural Traditions and Literary Form*. Baton Rouge: Louisiana State University Press, 1989. This is the first full-length treatment of the fiction of William Gilmore Simms. According to Wimsatt, the three major groupings of Simms' novels relate to the three major geographical regions of the South—Tidewater, the Appalachians, and the Deep South. Attempting to track Simms' personal and literary development within this context, however, proves no easy task. She traces individual strands of literary genealogy back to rather vague regional distinctions. The pivotal "ancestors" never seem to be identified. On the other hand, Wimsatt's readings of the novels, if brief, are nicely interwoven with an awareness of the society and economy that influenced Simms. (A,G)

UPTON SINCLAIR
1878-1968

Evaluation of Selected Criticism
  Mookerjee, R. N. *Art for Social Justice: The Major Novels of Upton Sinclair.* Metuchen, NJ: Scarecrow, 1988. In this partially successful reevaluation of Sinclair's major fiction, Mookerjee examines *The Jungle, King Coal, Oil!, Boston,* and the eleven Lanny Budd books. He succeeds in reminding us that Sinclair pioneered the documentary novel, but he does not clarify what place Sinclair holds or should hold in literary history. Contains an excellent bibliography. (A,G)

ISAAC BASHEVIS SINGER
1904

Author's Recent Bibliography

The Penitent, 1983 (novel); *Stories for Children*, 1984; *The Image and Other Stories*, 1985; *The Death of Methuselah and Other Stories*, 1988; *The King of the Fields*, 1988 (novel).

Autobiographical Sources

Burgin, Richard, ed. *Conversations with Isaac Bashevis Singer*. New York: Doubleday, 1985. Singer is one of the most articulate, witty, charming, and thoughtful contemporary writers, and these conversations reflect those qualities. Topics include Singer's childhood in Poland; his attitudes about literature; his beliefs about God, faith, and the supernatural; and his views on humanity. Singer's provocative ideas stimulate any discussion of his work. (A,G)

Evaluation of Selected Criticism

Farrell-Lee, Grace. *From Exile to Redemption: The Fiction of Isaac Bashevis Singer*. Carbondale: Southern Illinois University Press, 1987. Farrell-Lee examines Singer's fiction in light of the Kabbalah and Scriptures to provide insightful readings of his novels and short stories. She contends that Singer's work is characterized by a secular reworking of many of the images and myths of Jewish tradition. She places Singer in the same literary tradition as Borges, Nabokov, Fowles, and Barth, arguing for a more modern perspective of several works that have been considered conservative. (A,G)

Milbauer, Asher Z. *Transcending Exile: Conrad, Nabokov, I. B. Singer*. Gainesville: University Presses of Florida, 1985. In this narrowly focused study, Milbauer, an emigré himself, examines the issue of literary transplantation in the works of Conrad, Nabokov, and Singer. Each of these authors experienced cultural displacement or created their finest works in a language other than their native tongue. (A)

Other Sources

Friedman, Lawrence S. *Understanding Isaac Bashevis Singer*. Columbia: University of South Carolina Press, 1988.

Miller, David N. *Fear of Fiction: Narrative Strategies in the Works of Isaac Bashevis Singer*. Albany: State University of New York Press, 1985.

Miller, David N. *Recovering the Canon: Essays on Isaac Bashevis Singer*. Leiden, Netherlands: E. J. Brill, 1986.

JOHN SKELTON
1460?-1529

Evaluation of Selected Criticism

Kinney, Arthur F. *John Skelton, Priest as Poet: Seasons of Discovery.* Chapel Hill: University of North Carolina Press, 1987. Skelton's poetics were intimately intertwined with the practices of the priesthood and the fifteenth-century Catholic church. In this study, Kinney examines Skelton's complete works in the historical context of clerical life, the liturgical calendar, and the rich symbolism of Renaissance art and architecture. In the process, the poetry loses much of its "strangeness" and assumes new significance. (A,G)

Walker, Greg. *John Skelton and the Politics of the 1520s.* Cambridge: Cambridge University Press, 1988. Walker's study focuses on Skelton's social and political satire, a small but important portion of his writings. By examining Skelton's access to the court, his shifting political contacts and views, and his attempts to write his way back into the king's favor, Walker challenges conventional opinions about his stature as a court poet and the identity of his patrons. An important contribution to Skelton scholarship. (A)

Other Sources

Fox, Alistair, and Gregory Waite. *A Concordance to the Complete Poems of John Skelton.* Ithaca, NY: Cornell University Press, 1987.

MURIEL SPARK
1918

Author's Recent Bibliography
Mary Shelley: A Biography, 1987; *A Far Cry from Kensington*, 1988 (novel).

Evaluation of Selected Criticism
Bold, Alan. *Muriel Spark.* New York: Methuen, 1987. Bold analyzes Spark's novels from *The Comforters* (1957) to *The Only Problem* (1984), demonstrating that she is a "poetic novelist" whose themes are derived from language. Bold packs a lot of comparative criticism into this short study, and provides excellent interpretations of the individual novels, their place within Spark's canon, and the patterns among them. (A)

Richmond, Velma Bourgeois. *Muriel Spark.* New York: Ungar, 1985. Richmond examines the thesis that Spark's Catholicism is the underlying source of meaning for her novels and stories. She makes overly ambitious claims for Spark's significance, but she draws deserving attention to Spark's wit, humor, and poetic vision. (A,G)

Other Sources
Hynes, Joseph. *The Art of the Real: Muriel Spark's Novels.* Madison, NJ: Fairleigh Dickinson University Press, 1988.

Kane, Richard C. *Iris Murdoch, Muriel Spark, and John Fowles: Didactic Demons in Modern Fiction.* Madison, NJ: Fairleigh Dickinson University Press, 1988.

Walker, Dorothea. *Muriel Spark.* Boston: Twayne/G. K. Hall, 1988.

STEPHEN SPENDER
1909

Author's Recent Bibliography
Journals, 1939-1983, 1986; *Collected Poems, 1928-1985*, 1986; *Oedipus Trilogy: A Play in Three Acts Based on the Oedipus Plays of Sophocles*, 1987; *The Temple*, 1988 (novel).

Autobiographical Sources
Goldsmith, John, ed. *Stephen Spender: Journals, 1939-1983*. New York: Random, 1986. Spender was the last survivor of Auden's famous literary group, whose members included Christopher Isherwood, Cyril Connolly, Louis MacNeice, and C. Day-Lewis. Beginning with meditations on pre-Hitler Germany, Spender recounts his travels, comments on political and social trends, or works out drafts for articles that were later published. Most important are his recollections of his friends, collaborators, and fellow writers, who make up a Who's Who of the twentieth-century literary world. (A,G)

Other Sources
Bhattacharyya, Binay K. *The Oxford Group: Auden and Others*. New York: Associated/Advent, 1989.

EDMUND SPENSER
1552?-1599

Evaluation of Selected Criticism

Bernard, John D. *Ceremonies of Innocence: Pastoralism in the Poetry of Edmund Spenser*. Cambridge: Cambridge University Press, 1989. Bernard adopts a traditional thematic approach to Spenser, while acknowledging recent efforts by other critics to explain Elizabethan pastorals as statements of royal ideology. Bernard examines Spenser's precedents and sources in classical and medieval works. He demonstrates how the conflict between the "active life" and the "contemplative life" is exemplified throughout the pastoral tradition. Scholars will find his discussion of Virgil's influence on Spenser highly rewarding. **(A)**

Bloom, Harold, ed. *Edmund Spenser: Modern Critical Reviews*. New York: Chelsea House, 1986. This is a collection of important essays drawn from over three decades of Spenserian scholarship. Contributors include Northrop Frye, Thomas Green, Harry Berger, Jr., Isabel MacCaffrey, Angus Fletcher, Patricia Parker, and many others. Spenser critics from the 1980s are especially well represented, including Lawrence Manley, John Guillory, and Kenneth Gross. The essays are arranged chronologically and cover a full range of themes, topics, and critical perspectives. Bloom provides an overview of the collection in his introduction. **(A,G)**

Heale, Elizabeth. *The Faerie Queen: A Reader's Guide*. Cambridge: Cambridge University Press, 1987. Anyone coming to *The Faerie Queen* for the first time will find this guide indispensable. Heale frames each of the poem's books with a discussion of Spenser's ideas and attitudes. She concentrates on the poem's meaning as reflected by Spenser's use of the Bible, classical philosophers, legends, epics, and romances, and in the process unravels many of the problems that often frustrate students. **(A,G)**

Johnson, William C. *Spenser's "Amoretti"; Analogies of Love*. Lewisburg, PA; Bucknell University Press, 1990. Johnson convincingly argues that Spenser linked his courtship of Elizabeth Boyle to the Lenten calendar, so that the *Amoretti* contrasts earthly love with the penitent's religious struggle. Johnson goes on to link this sonnet sequence with *The Faerie Queen* to explain Spenser's subtle use of puns, syntax, and biblical allusions, especially Christ's Passion, Crucifixion, and Resurrection. This is an important study for serious readers. **(A)**

Lenz, Joseph M. *The Promised End: Romance Closure in the Gawain-poet, Malory, Spenser, and Shakespeare*. New York: Peter Lang, 1986. Lenz examines the particular ways romances end as a defining characteristic of the genre. To do this, he examines *Sir Gawain and the Green Knight*, Malory's

Le Morte Darthur, and two Renaissance texts, *The Faerie Queen* and *The Winter's Tale.* A limited but useful study for medieval and Renaissance scholars. (A)

Oram, William, ed. *The Yale Edition of the Shorter Poems of Edmund Spenser.* New Haven: Yale University Press, 1989. Although the text of these poems does not radically depart from that of previous editions, the Yale edition does add a detailed chronology, reproductions of title pages, select bibliographies, brief introductions for the poems, and a glossary of technical terms. The book's introduction makes no attempt to put the shorter poems in the context of Spenser's canon, nor to survey the poet's critical reputation. It ably serves its purpose of providing a dependable text. (A,G)

Shepherd, Simon. *Spenser.* Atlantic Highlands, NJ: Humanities Press, 1989. Targeting an undergraduate audience, Shepherd delves into the political and economic underpinnings of Spenser's world view to reveal an irritable civil servant dependent upon the machinations of English imperialism. Spenser's politics, sexual attitudes, and self-definition are all treated in this Marxist analysis. (A,G)

Tonkin, Humphrey. *"The Faerie Queen."* Winchester, MA: Unwin Hyman, 1989. Tonkin applies new methodologies and literary values to Spenser's *The Faerie Queen* in an effort to summarize and extend recent critical scholarship. Drawing upon the observations of previous critics, Tonkin carefully tears apart the complex structure of the epic. He discusses Spenser's influence on his successors and outlines his most important precursors. As an introduction for new students of Spenser, this study would be useful, although the subject matter often plunges deeply into specialized Spenserian concerns. (A,G)

Wall, John N. *Transformations of the Word: Spenser, Herbert, Vaughan.* Athens: University of Georgia Press, 1988. Wall contends that the works of Spenser, Herbert, and Vaughan are best understood within the context of the sixteenth- and seventeenth-century tenets of the Church of England. The post-Reformation Church had distinctive characteristics that have been obscured, causing the modern reader to lose the meaning of these writers' works. This dense book is divided into sections that treat each of the authors individually against a backdrop of theological concepts and liturgical practices. While certainly offering valuable information, the plodding prose makes the argument difficult to follow for the uninitiated. (A)

Waller, Gary. *English Poetry of the Sixteenth Century.* White Plains, NY: Longman, 1986. Using the theories of Eagleton, Greenblatt, Sinfield, and Greenberg, Waller's study is a revisionist history of English Renaissance poetry. Waller develops a parallel chronological overview and critical reevaluation. Chapters cover sixteenth-century literary theory, the ideology of the Elizabethan court, Petrarch, and Protestantism. Several authors are given prolonged treatment—Spenser, Dunbar, Wyatt, Raleigh, Greville, Sidney,

Shakespeare, and Donne. This book was meant to, but does not, supplant C. S. Lewis' *English Literature of the Sixteenth Century* (1954). **(A)**

Other Sources

Berger, Harry, Jr. *Revisionary Play: Studies in the Spenserian Dynamics.* Berkeley: University of California Press, 1988.

Bieman, Elizabeth. *Plato Baptized: Towards the Interpretation of Spenser's Mimetic Fictions.* Toronto: University of Toronto Press, 1988.

Dundas, Judith. *The Spider and the Bee: The Artistry of Spenser's Faerie Queene.* Champaign: University of Illinois Press, 1986.

Gleckner, Robert F. *Blake and Spenser.* Baltimore and London: Johns Hopkins University Press, 1985.

Gross, Kenneth. *Spenserian Poetics: Idolatry, Iconoclasm and Magic.* Ithaca, NY: Cornell University Press, 1985.

Heninger, S. K., Jr. *Sidney and Spenser: The Poet as Maker.* University Park: Pennsylvania State University Press, 1990.

Kane, Sean. *Spenser's Moral Allegory.* Toronto: University of Toronto Press, 1989.

Lockerd, Benjamin G., Jr. *The Sacred Marriage: Psychic Integration in the Fairie Queene.* Lewisburg, PA: Bucknell University Press, 1987.

Logan, George M., and Gordon Teskey, eds. *Unfolded Tales: Essays on Renaissance Romance.* Ithaca, NY: Cornell University Press, 1989.

Moses, Carole. *Melville's Use of Spenser.* New York: Peter Lang, 1989.

Richardson, J. M. *Astrological Symbolism in Spenser's "The Shepheardes Calender": The Cultural Background of a Literary Text.* Lewiston, NY: Edwin Mellen, 1989.

Sacks, Peter M. *The English Elegy: Studies in the Genre from Spenser to Yeats.* Baltimore: Johns Hopkins University Press, 1985.

CHRISTINA STEAD
1902-1983

Author's Recent Bibliography
  An Ocean of Story: The Uncollected Stories of Christina Stead, 1986; *I'm Dying Laughing*, 1986 (novel).

Geering, R. G., ed. *An Ocean of Story: The Uncollected Stories of Christina Stead.* New York: Viking, 1986. The prolific Australian author Christina Stead is best known for her novel *The Man Who Loved Children* published in 1940. Geering has now gathered Stead's previously uncollected short fiction into a single edition. Included are several essays, a play, and twenty-five short stories arranged in categories according to setting and theme. Most of these pieces are unfinished. Of particular interest, however, are "A Harmless Affair" and "The Milk Run," which showcase Stead's considerable talent. (A,G)

Evaluation of Selected Criticism
  Brydon, Diana. *Christina Stead.* Totowa, NJ: Barnes & Noble, 1987. Brydon examines how being a women influenced Stead's style and techniques. In the process, she discusses the eleven novels in the context of biographical events. Stead's antagonism toward lesbianism and her rejection of a feminine aesthetic have made her unpopular with many feminist critics, but Brydon contends that Stead is a political writer who combines the novel of character with the novel of ideas. (A,G)

Gardiner, Judith Kegan. *Rhys, Stead, Lessing, and the Politics of Empathy.* Bloomington: University of Indiana Press, 1989. Gardiner approaches the life and works of three modern women writers—Christina Stead, Jean Rhys, and Doris Lessing—by examining the themes of empathy, history, and identity. Beginning with a discussion of biographical parallels, she then turns to close readings of several of the works, including Rhys' *Wide Sargasso Sea*, Stead's *The Man Who Loved Children*, and Lessing's *The Golden Notebook*. Gardiner reveals the authors' similar conceptions of gender relationships and suggests that these are based on a theory of "mothering." Although Gardiner's prose is often dense and jargon-laden, the insights are worth the effort. (A)

Sheridan, Susan. *Christina Stead.* Bloomington: University of Indiana Press, 1988. Stead considered herself a socialist and a psychological writer, disavowing any connection with feminism, *per se*. In this study, Sheridan demonstrates how feminist and traditional critics must meet head-on when attempting to explicate Stead's fiction. Sheridan contends that Stead's protagonists, far from representing "true voices" of modern women as some critics have claimed, actually display a "robust gift for social conformity and thus survival." (A,G)

SIR RICHARD STEELE
1672-1729

Evaluation of Selected Criticism

Bloom, Edward A., Lillian Bloom, and Edmund Leites. *Educating the Audience: Addison, Steele, and Eighteenth-Century Culture.* Los Angeles: William Andrews Clark Memorial Library, University of California, 1984. The Blooms and Leites presented two papers at a Clark Library Seminar in 1980. The Blooms examine the role of the imagination and contemplation in the life and works of Addison and Steele. Leites focuses on the ethics of Steele on issues of marriage and the civilities of social life. **(A)**

Ketcham, Michael G. *Transparent Designs: Reading, Performance, & Form in the "Spectator" Papers.* Athens: University of Georgia Press, 1985. Ketcham attempts to explain why *The Spectator* was the most successful, polished, and influential periodical of the eighteenth century. Divided into six chapters, this book analyzes *The Spectator* for its style and attitudes, and examines how the periodical's particular readership responded to the editors' social and artistic biases. Although *Transparent Designs* plows some new ground, it is sometimes tedious, sometimes outdated, and demonstrates that additional scholarship is necessary for a full understanding of *The Spectator's* success. Recommended for scholars and advanced students of Addison, Steele, and the period. **(A)**

McCrea, Brian. *Addison and Steele are Dead: The English Department, Its Canon, and the Professionalization of Literary Criticism.* Newark: University of Delaware Press, 1990. This clever book uses the lives, careers, and works of Addison and Steele to develop a devastating critique of how college English departments were established, how they function, and how they fail. He begins with the simple question—How could the two loudest voices of the eighteenth century, Addison and Steele, be now so stilled? The authors lie neglected, untaught, unread. The reasons are bound up with the formation of a "canon" of books that were considered acceptable to teach and in the formation of a professional cadre of critics who employ fashionable theories to dissect susceptible works. **(A)**

GERTRUDE STEIN
1874-1946

Autobiographical Sources

Burns, Edward, ed. *The Letters of Gertrude Stein and Carl Van Vechten, 1913-1946.* New York: Columbia University Press, 1986. This two-volume edition is a record of the friendship between Stein, Van Vechten, and Alice B. Toklas. Stein met Van Vechten at the Paris opera, and soon he became her admirer, supporter, editor, publicity agent, and literary educator. She seldom embarked on any professional course without seeking, and usually following, his counsel. During World War II, when she was in southern France and he was in New York, she sorely missed his correspondence. The letters reveal less about Stein's role in his life than about her need for his friendship—which is especially interesting because Stein made few lasting friends. This edition is complete with references and footnotes that are particularly useful in dating Stein's work. **(A)**

Evaluation of Selected Criticism

Benstock, Shari. *Women of the Left Bank: Paris, 1900-1940.* Austin: University of Texas Press, 1986. Benstock sets out to reshape the conventional perception of pre-World War II literary Paris, arguing that what has been called "the Pound era" was actually "the Gertrude Stein era." Included in Benstock's survey of notable women writers of the period are H.D., Anais Nin, and Djuna Barnes. Many lesser-known female writers are given their proper due, among them: Barney, Beach, Boyle, Colette, Cumard, Flanner, Jolas, Monnier, Solano, Toklas, and Wharton. The result of Benstock's reevaluation of these authors is a redefinition of literary modernism. **(A,G)**

Chessman, Harriet Scott. *The Public is Invited to Dance: Representation, the Body, and Dialogue in Gertrude Stein.* Stanford, CA: Stanford University Press, 1989. This specialized study of deconstructionist/feminist critical methodology deals only incidentally with Stein. The critic's technique has center stage in this rereading of several of Stein's works, including *The Mother of Us All.* The methodology, which pays excruciatingly close attention to surface details, could be adapted for other authors. **(A)**

Kellner, Bruce. *A Gertrude Stein Companion: Content with the Example.* Westport, CT: Greenwood, 1988. This companion gathers together a great deal of information not conveniently found elsewhere. These include recent essays on Stein, a 156-page biographical dictionary of all the people mentioned in Stein's writings, a collection of Stein's famous "pronouncements," and an annotated bibliography of criticism. Kellner has provided all the tools necessary for basic research on Stein. **(A,G)**

Neuman, Shirley, and Ira B. Nadel. *Gertrude Stein and the Making of Literature*. Boston: Northeastern University Press, 1988. This collection of essays features younger Stein scholars who offer fresh interpretations of her works, including "Stanzas in Meditation," "Dr. Faustus Lights the Lights," *Ida,* and *Mother of Us All*. Especially interesting is an analysis of how the highly popular one-character show, *Gertrude Stein, Gertrude Stein, Gertrude Stein* misses the mark in so many ways. This collection provides beginning Stein readers with an excellent introduction, and veteran readers with provocative ideas. **(A,G)**

Wagner-Martin, Linda. *The Modern American Novel, 1914-1945: A Critical History*. Boston: Twayne, 1989. Wagner-Martin presents a densely compact overview of modernist writers that flies in the face of the traditional critique that the modernists were a uniformly angst-ridden lot. Some of the authors treated are Stein, Cather, Hemingway, Faulkner, Norris, and Agee. This study goes beyond the traditional pantheon to treat many writers highly regarded during their times but nearly forgotten now—Nella Larsen, Meridel Le Sueur, Martha Gellhorn, and Henry Brown, among others. Black and women modernists are "dusted off" and given their fair place on the shelf. This study is intended for a scholarly audience. **(A)**

Other Sources

Bennett, Albert S. *Just a Very Pretty Girl from the Country: Letters from Gertrude Stein's Paris*. New York: Paragon House, 1988.

Doane, Janice L. *Silence and Narrative: The Early Novels of Gertrude Stein*. Westport, CT: Greenwood, 1986.

Dubnick, Randa. *The Structure of Obscurity: Gertrude Stein, Language, and Cubism*. Urbana: University of Illinois Press, 1984.

Hoffman, Michael J. *Critical Essays on Gertrude Stein*. Boston: G. K. Hall, 1986.

Walker, Jayne L. *The Making of a Modernist: Gertrude Stein from "Three Lives" to "Tender Buttons."* Amherst: University of Massachusetts Press, 1984.

White, Ray L. *Gertrude Stein and Alice B. Toklas: Reference Guide*. Boston: G. K. Hall, 1984.

JOHN STEINBECK
1902-1968

Autobiographical Sources

DeMott, Robert, ed. *Working Days: The Journals of the "Grapes of Wrath,"* *1938-1941.* New York: Viking, 1989. Although they are sometimes repetitive and bland, these journals reveal much about Steinbeck's hopes, doubts, and work habits. There are references to his wife Carol Henning, agent Elizabeth Otis, publisher Pascal Covici, and others. A thorough introduction and helpful comments, notes, and annotations are provided. (A)

Fensch, Thomas, ed. *Conversations with John Steinbeck.* Jackson: University Press of Mississippi, 1988. This collection of interviews with and reminiscences of the reclusive Steinbeck raises more questions than it can possibly answer. Steinbeck is often at odds with himself—whether due to purposeful obfuscation or to an evolving opinion of himself and his work is unclear. What is clear is that Steinbeck challenged the right and ability of literary critics to practice their trade. Little of his personal life surfaces, but readers will be rewarded with glimpses of his writing methods, his passion for the plight of migrant workers, and his love of Celtic mythology and dogs. (G)

Evaluation of Selected Biography and Criticism

Benson, Jackson J. *Looking For Steinbeck's Ghost.* Norman: University of Oklahoma Press, 1988. This is not a biography of Steinbeck but a witty auto-biographical account of a Steinbeck biographer. In that sense it provides interesting background on how Benson went about researching Steinbeck's life. After all, how does one go about tracking down the unpublished letters and opinions of ex-wives of a noted author? Benson spent fifteen years in the search. Because *Looking for Steinbeck's Ghost* is not intended to be a biography, Benson selects data about Steinbeck that serves his story, and thus this book is not a substitute for the actual biography. Steinbeck's strongly espoused opinions of publishers, lawyers, and editors are of narrow interest, but Steinbeck scholars and others will find the biographical details entertaining. (A,G)

Ditsky, John, ed. *Critical Essays on Steinbeck's "The Grapes of Wrath."* Boston: G. K. Hall, 1989. Four of these nine essays were written expressly for this collection, which also includes early reviews of the novel and useful maps. As a group, the essays bring differing critical perspectives to Steinbeck's motifs of community, family, and cultural geography. The editor's introduction, which summarizes the current status of Steinbeck scholarship, is excellent. (A,G)

Ferrell, Keith. *John Steinbeck: The Voice of the Land.* New York: Evans, 1986. Although it is based on a limited number of secondary sources, this biography is a competent introduction to Steinbeck for the beginning reader. When it errs, it errs on the side of flattery. **(G,Y)**

Gladstein, Mimi Reisel. *The Indestructible Woman in Faulkner, Hemingway, and Steinbeck.* Ann Arbor: UMI Research, 1986. "Indestructible" women are those who are generally defined by men as "other." Because they are essentially unknown quantities, men tend to project upon them idealized traits of strength and perseverance. Such is the case, argues Gladstein, with the few women characters that appear in the fiction of Faulkner, Steinbeck, and Hemingway. This feminist critique is handled with well-balanced precision and lays bare the personal dependencies of a group of male writers who leaned too heavily on the women in their lives. **(A,G)**

Hughes, R. S. *Beyond the "Red Pony": A Reader's Companion to Steinbeck's Complete Short Stories.* Metuchen, NJ: Scarecrow, 1987. Hughes provides a concise and useful introductory guide to Steinbeck's short stories. More than mere plot summaries, the entries discuss themes, characterization, and critical significance. Many of the stories treated here are not readily available in a collected form, which suggests a task for the ambitious publisher. **(A,G)**

Hughes, R. S. *John Steinbeck: A Study of the Short Fiction.* Boston: Twayne, 1988. Hughes' contribution to the Twayne New Studies in Short Fiction series is divided into three parts. The first provides a systematic analysis of each of Steinbeck's short stories. The second gathers statements from the author about the stories, their production, and intent. The final part collects several critical essays. Taken together, these elements provide a solid overview of Steinbeck's short fiction, which in many ways rivals his longer works. **(A)**

Mangelsdorf, Tom. *A History of Steinbeck's Cannery Row.* Western Tanager, 1986. Mangelsdorf has produced a well-researched and literate guide to one of the most famous streets in literature--Cannery Row. Working primarily from newspaper accounts of the era, he brings to life the waxing and waning of the sardine industry that provided the backdrop in Steinbeck's novel. Mangelsdorf delves into the possible real-life character models and settings used by Steinbeck. Much more than just a "tourist guide," this book offers useful, profusely illustrated background material for understanding the novel. Suggested for students and the general reader. **(A,G)**

Mills, Nicolaus. *The Crowd in American Literature.* Baton Rouge: Louisiana State University Press, 1986. Mills explicates the use of "crowds" by American writers from Jefferson to Steinbeck. For colonial writers crowds were a "force for democracy"; for the classical American novelists—Hawthorne, Melville, and Twain—they were a force for national unity. Mills examines the "noble" working-class masses of such writers as Howells,

480 *John Steinbeck*

Dreiser, and Steinbeck. Finally, he turns to Norman Mailer and Ralph Ellison for an examination of postwar crowds, the repository of intellectual and moral power contrasted with brute force. This is a fascinating thematic social history drawn from American literary works. **(A,G)**

Owens, Louis. *John Steinbeck's Re-Vision of America*. Athens: University of Georgia Press, 1985. Owens takes his reader deep into the topography of northern California, Steinbeck country, to explain the degree to which place influenced the fiction. He groups the novels and stories into clusters dealing with themes and symbols. The first chapter deals with mountains, which Steinbeck associates with death; the second, on the valley, discusses stories about the illusionary nature of Eden; the third, on the sea, analyzes the Monterey trilogy, in which the presence of the ocean symbolizes the last hope for psychological renewal. This lucid study provides a sensitive reading of Steinbeck's major works, one that will reward students and challenge scholars. **(A,G)**

Timmerman, John H. *John Steinbeck's Fiction: The Aesthetics of the Road Taken*. Norman: University of Oklahoma Press, 1986. Timmerman freely addresses the subject of Steinbeck's aesthetics. His approach yields valuable insight into *Cup of Gold*, the Monterey trilogy, and *East of Eden*, but is less successful with *The Winter of Our Discontent*. Timmerman's insistence on developing his own theories with little regard for established Steinbeck criticism offers original readings and suggests new directions for understanding Steinbeck. **(A,G)**

Other Sources
Harmon, Robert B. *The Collectible John Steinbeck: A Practical Guide*. Jefferson, NC: McFarland, 1986.

Harmon, Robert B. *Steinbeck Bibliographies: An Annotated Guide*. Metuchen, NJ: Scarecrow, 1987.

Hayashi, Tetsumaro. *A Student's Guide to Steinbeck's Literature: Primary and Secondary Sources*. Muncie, IN: Steinbeck Society, 1986.

Hayashi, Tetsumaro, and Thomas J. Moore, eds. *Steinbeck's "The Red Pony": Essays in Criticism*. Muncie, IN: Steinbeck Society, 1988.

Lewis, Cliff, ed. *Rediscovering Steinbeck: Revisionist Views of His Art, Politics, and Intellect*. Lewiston, NY: Edwin Mellen, 1989.

LAURENCE STERNE
1713-1768

Evaluation of Selected Biography and Criticism

Cash, Arthur H. *Laurence Sterne: The Later Years*. London and New York: Methuen, 1986. The first volume of Cash's biography, published in 1975, covered forty-six years of Sterne's life. This volume covers only eight years, but they are the most important, and in many ways the most interesting of his life. The womanizing Yorkshire parson had taken London by storm with *Tristram Shandy*; the attacks on the "immorality" of his fiction were as lively as Sterne's own high-living. During the last decade of his life, with his ailing wife and frail daughter in Europe for their health, Sterne began searching for true, sentimental love to help him cope with his tuberculosis. Cash portrays Sterne as benevolent, good-natured, and wryly comic, characteristics that have made *Tristram Shandy* an enduring novel. Both scholars and general readers will find much to enjoy. **(A,G)**

Erickson, Robert A. *Mother Midnight: Birth, Sex, and Fate in Eighteenth-Century Fiction: Defoe, Richardson, and Sterne*. New York: AMS, 1986. Erickson examines the ambiguous character of the midwife in eighteenth-century fiction to shed light on the philosophical attitudes toward fate prevalent during the period. The "representation of fate," as examined in *Moll Flanders*, *Pamela*, *Clarissa*, and *Tristram Shandy* extends to a discussion of "spiritual midwives" who appear at crisis points in a character's life to assist an emotional and spiritual rebirth. Erickson's discussion of the governess in *Moll Flanders* is especially rich and provocative. Although the reader may sense that the midwife metaphor is occasionally strained, this in no way undermines the overall value of this book. **(A,G)**

Iser, Wolfgang. *Laurence Sterne: "Tristram Shandy."* Translated by Henry Wilson. Cambridge: Cambridge University Press, 1988. Although not a landmark study, Iser provides a guidebook to the essential passages and subjective elements that characterize the novel. Iser's ideas are complicated and his prose dense, which makes this study appropriate only for scholars. **(A)**

Lamb, Jonathan. *Sterne's Fiction and the Double Principle*. Cambridge: Cambridge University Press, 1990. Lamb begins by explaining Sterne's use of "double arrangements and double effects," then demonstrates how these principles create comic effects. Moving from techniques to meaning, Lamb explains how Sterne adopted the philosophies of Hume and Hartley, and Hogarth's ideas and images. This accomplished, readable study is important for all students of the eighteenth century. **(A)**

Myer, Valerie Grosvenor, ed. *Laurence Sterne: Riddles and Mysteries*. Totowa, NJ: Barnes & Noble, 1984. Reacting to critics that have termed it a "boring" book, editor Myer blames residual Anglo-American puritanism for what she senses as critical neglect of Sterne's *Tristram Shandy*. This collection of critical essays delves into the form, thematic content, and characterization of the maligned book. Several essays focus on Sterne's preoccupation with sex and sexual innuendo. Of special note is Jacques Berthoud's essay, "Shandeism and Sexuality," which illuminates Sterne's use of "sexual disconnexion" with a Lacanian light. (A)

Other Sources

Kay, Carol. *Political Constructions: Defoe, Richardson, and Sterne in Relation to Hobbes, Hume, and Burke*. Ithaca, NY: Cornell University Press, 1988.

Lamb, Jonathan. *Sterne's Fiction and the Double Principle*. New York: Cambridge University Press, 1989.

Matteo, Sante. *Textual Exile: The Reader in Sterne and Foscolo*. New York: Peter Lang, 1985.

New, Melvyn, ed. *Approaches to Teaching Sterne's "Tristram Shandy."* New York: Modern Language Association, 1989.

Quennell, Peter. *Four Portraits: Boswell, Gibbon, Sterne and Wilkes*. North Pomfret, VT: David & Charles, 1988.

WALLACE STEVENS
1879-1955

Autobiographical Sources

Coyle, Beverly, and Alan Filreis, eds. *Secretaries of the Moon: The Letters of Wallace Stevens and Jose Rodriquez Feo*. Durham, NC: Duke University Press, 1986. Feo first wrote to Stevens in 1944, asking permission to translate one of his poems for a Cuban literary journal. This initiated a lively correspondence that continued for over ten years. This edition contains all 98 extant letters, which document both sides of the exchange. A continuing theme of these letters is the often contradictory claims of art and life. Those familiar with Stevens' formal side might be surprised at his informal tone when addressing Feo. This is a useful primary source for the study of Stevens. **(A,G)**

Evaluation of Selected Biography and Criticism

Bates, Milton J. *Wallace Stevens: A Mythology of Self*. Berkeley: University of California Press, 1985. Bates' focus in this critical biography is on exploring how Stevens' imagination is reconciled in the seemingly opposed pursuits of law and poetry. By establishing the dichotomy, Bates is able to illustrate the complexity of the man and his work. **(A)**

Beehler, Michael. *T. S. Eliot, Wallace Stevens, and the Discourses of Difference*. Baton Rouge: Louisiana State University Press, 1987. Beehler relates the work of both Eliot and Stevens to a single theme—the need of the human mind for unity in a pluralistic world. Chapters alternate between Eliot and Stevens, as Beehler attempts to define how each poet treats diversity and the instinct for wholeness. **(A)**

Berger, Charles. *Forms of Farewell: The Late Poetry of Wallace Stevens*. Madison: University of Wisconsin Press, 1985. Berger contends that Stevens wrote his own elegy over and over in his final poetry in an effort to secure a place in "the afterlife of literary history." To support this thesis he traces Stevens' meditations on survival in "The Auroras of Autumn," "An Ordinary Evening in New Haven," "Credences of Summer," and "The Owl in the Sarcophagus." **(A,G)**

Brogan, Jacqueline V. *Stevens and Simile: A Theory of Language*. Princeton, NJ: Princeton University Press, 1986. Brogan provides a fresh view of Stevens' poetic development while simultaneously reexamining the linguistic role of simile. For Brogan, simile sustains language's contradictory intentions, while metaphor often stultifies it because metaphors are more often used to identity images than to show their similarity. Stevens' poetry often takes a back seat in this detailed discussion of language theory. **(A)**

Byers, Thomas. *What I Cannot Say: Self, Word, and World in Whitman, Stevens, and Merwin.* Champaign: University of Illinois Press, 1989. Byers examines the aesthetic, epistemological, metaphysical, and religious implications of the poetics of Whitman, Stevens, and Merwin. For Whitman poetry not only defines but constitutes a relation to the world. Stevens has less faith in the power of the word but affirms the human ability to create fictions within which to rejoice. Merwin reacts against Whitman's celebration of the self over the world by painting a bleaker portrait of relationship in *The Lice.* Byers combines a close reading of the poetry with an intertextuality influenced by phenomenology and semiotics. (A)

Carroll, Joseph. *Wallace Stevens' Supreme Fiction: A New Romanticism.* Baton Rouge: Louisiana State University Press, 1987. Although Carroll's close readings of some of Stevens' poems are useful, he sets out in this study to prove a larger thesis. For Carroll, the "supreme fiction" is Stevens' quest to develop "a poem equivalent to the idea of God." He thinks Stevens failed his quest but fails to establish why such a quest existed for Stevens. (A)

Cook, Eleanor. *Poetry, Word-Play, and Word-War in Wallace Stevens.* Princeton, NJ: Princeton University Press, 1988. To demonstrate Stevens' mastery of language Cook closely examines the poetry to discover countless riddles, puns, and other plays on the sounds and meanings of words. She also tracks down the sources of Stevens' literary allusions, from Homer, Milton, Wordsworth, and the Bible. This clearly written book will help readers to approach Stevens' work with confidence. (A,G)

Leggett, B. J. *Wallace Stevens and Poetic Theory: Conceiving the Supreme Fiction.* Chapel Hill: University of North Carolina Press, 1987. Leggett claims that four books heavily influenced Stevens' concept of the imagination: I. A. Richards' *Coleridge on Imagination,* Charles Mauron's *Aesthetics and Psychology,* H. P. Adams' *The Life and Writings of Giambattista Vico,* and Henri Focillon's *The Life of Forms in Art.* Leggett proposes that Stevens' concept of reality underwent significant change in his later poetry. (A)

Lensing, George S. *Wallace Stevens: A Poet's Growth.* Baton Rouge: Louisiana State University Press, 1986. Stevens led a singularly uneventful life, so tracing his poetic growth requires a different approach than with most writers. Unlike William Wordsworth, for example, whose poetic art and philosophy radically changed when his brother drowned, Stevens led the serene life of a business executive. Lensing does connect life events to the poet's sensibilities: relations with his father, school friends, literary friends, wife and daughter. He demonstrates that the remarkable growth of this poet was a function of a brilliant imagination, and not the result of external events. Recommended for anyone interested in the details of Stevens' life. (A,G)

Leonard, J. S., and C. E. Wharton. *The Fluent Mundo: Wallace Stevens and the Structure of Reality.* Athens: University of Georgia Press, 1988. The authors address the wide sources of philosophical influence that make their way into Stevens' poetry, from Nietzsche and Heidegger to Blake and Carlyle. They also analyze the philosophical male-female forces surrounding Stevens' work. (A)

Patke, Rajeev S. *The Long Poems of Wallace Stevens: An Interpretative Study.* New York: Cambridge University Press, 1985. Stevens' longer poems best reflect his sense of the world and the imagination. Seven of these poems—*The Comedian as the Letter C, Owl's Clover, The Man with the Blue Guitar, Notes Toward a Supreme Fiction, Esthetique du Mal, The Auroras of Autumns,* and *An Ordinary Evening in New Haven*—are analyzed in this study of Stevens' techniques and themes. Patke provides a wealth of detail for the reader, often delving into obscure word origins or less obvious sources and models for the poetry. His penchant for classification, however, is less satisfying. He fits categories of activity, mode, environment, and self-identity over the poems like a restrictive grid. (A)

Rehder, Robert. *The Poetry of Wallace Stevens.* New York: St. Martin's. 1988. This is an excellent introduction to Steven's poetry, with fine explications of all the major works. A long biographical sketch traces Stevens' life from his boyhood, through his college days at Harvard, his courtship and marriage, and his successful career as a business executive. Recommended for all general readers, this study is ideal for new students of Stevens. (A,G)

Richardson, Joan. *Wallace Stevens: The Early Years, 1879-1923.* New York: William Morrow, 1986. Part biography, part psychoanalysis, part literary criticism, this valuable study by Richardson explores the relationship of his "real" life with his "written" life. Stevens acknowledged a large distinction between the self he commanded through his writing and the self he presented in his everyday life. In this look at the early years, Richardson examines the nature of these two "selves" and how the schism developed. The poems are brilliantly explicated with allusions to Hardy, Goethe, Tennyson, Stevensen, and Schopenhauer. Based on much previously unavailable material, this biography builds logically and powerfully to its sequel, *The Later Years,* and offers the possibility that Stevens will be able to "heal the rift" in himself toward the end of his life. (A,G)

Richardson, Joan. *Wallace Stevens: The Later Years, 1923-1955.* New York: Morrow. 1988. This is the conclusion of Richardson's two-volume biography. Here she portrays Stevens' desire to become the "platonic man" amid social upheavals and family squabbles. Richardson speculates on the effects that a slavishly dependent wife and angrily rebellious daughter might have had on his belief in the supremacy of the imagination. She gives excellent close readings of the poems and demonstrates their dependence on Freud, Plato, and Nietzsche. (A,G)

Schaum, Melita. *Wallace Stevens and the Critical Schools.* Tuscaloosa: University of Alabama Press, 1988. Schaum's study is more of a critique of twentieth-century critical schools than an examination of Stevens' poetry. In the process of talking about Stevens, Schaum gives a systematic overview of the New Humanism (1920s), the New Criticism (1930-1950), and more recent critical schools: deconstruction, "Bloomism," hermeneutic criticism, and historicism. The ideas are clearly and concisely presented. Recommended for students of literary criticism. (A,G)

Scott, Nathan A. *The Poetics of Belief: Studies in Coleridge, Arnold, Pater, Santayana, Stevens, and Heidegger.* Chapel Hill: University of North Carolina Press, 1985. This collection of Scott's essays on writers and philosophers explores the power of the imagination for evoking religious awareness and transcendence. Examining each writer in turn—Coleridge, Arnold, Pater, Santayana, and Stevens—Scott finds a commonality of purposes and intentions among them that is best articulated by Heidegger. (A)

Steinman, Lisa M. *Made in America: Science, Technology, and American Modernist Poets.* New Haven: Yale University Press, 1987. This study examines how modernist poets—specifically, Williams, Moore, and Stevens—set out to rejuvenate poetry by redefining its relationship with the developing world of technology and commerce. To justify the virtues of "genteel verse," modernists stressed poetry's "technical" structure and virtues (its efficiency, for example) or associated poetry with the values of pure scientific research. This study is a valuable contribution to understanding the modernists, their cultural context, and their theories of poetics. (A,G)

Other Sources
Arensberg, Mary, ed. *The American Sublime.* Albany: State University of New York Press, 1986.

Axelrod, Steven G., and Helen Deese, eds. *Critical Essays on Wallace Stevens.* Boston: G. K. Hall, 1988.

Bates, Milton J., ed. *Sur Plusieurs Beaux Sujects: Wallace Stevens' Commonplace Book, a Facsimile and Transcription.* Palo Alto, CA: Stanford University Press, 1989.

Bevis, William. *Mind of Winter: Wallace Stevens, Meditation, and Literature.* Pittsburgh: University of Pittsburgh Press, 1989.

Doyle, Charles. *Wallace Stevens: The Critical Heritage.* New York: Routledge Chapman & Hall, 1985.

Fisher, Barbara M. *Wallace Stevens: The Intensest Rendezvous.* Charlottesville: University Press of Virginia, 1990.

Gelpi, Albert, ed. *Wallace Stevens: The Poetics of Modernism.* New York: Cambridge University Press, 1985.

Holmes, Barbara. *The Decomposer's Art: Ideas of Music in the Poetry of Wallace Stevens.* New York: Peter Lang, 1989.

Lentricchia, Frank. *Ariel and the Police: Michel Foucault, William James, Wallace Stevens.* Madison: University of Wisconsin Press, 1987.

Prasad, Veena R. *Wallace Stevens: Symbolic Dimensions in His Poetry.* Atlantic Highlands, NJ: Arnold Heinemann India/Humanities, 1986.

Vendler, Helen. *Wallace Stevens: Words Chosen Out of Desire.* Knoxville: University of Tennessee Press, 1984.

Wilhelm, James J. *Wounded Fiction: The Deconstruction of the "Proper" in Vallejo, Stevens, and Char.* New York: Garland, 1988.

Wilhelm, James J., and Richard Saez, eds. *A History That Includes the Self: Essays on the Poetry of Stefan George, Hugo von Hofmannsthal, William Carlos Williams, and Wallace Stevens.* New York: Garland, 1988.

ROBERT LOUIS STEVENSON
1850-1894

Evaluation of Selected Criticism

Knight, Alanna. *The Robert Louis Stevenson Treasury.* New York: St. Martin's, 1986. Following an encyclopedic format, Knight presents a full range of information on Stevenson. She has compiled over 200 books that were written about the man or his writings. Also provided are biographical sketches of influential figures in Stevenson's life, such as Henry James and Sidney Colvin. There is a short entry on Samoa, where Stevenson spent the last years of his life. Other entries examine Stevenson's fictional characters and places, his correspondence, poems, music, and even the films, radio, and television shows produced about him. For scope, there is no better compilation of Stevenson information. For depth of analysis the reader would be better served by J. R. Hammond's *Robert Louis Stevenson Companion,* published in 1984. (A,G)

Noble, Andrew, ed. *From the Clyde to California: Robert Louis Stevenson's Emigrant Journey.* Aberdeen, TX: Aberdeen University Press, 1985. Noble compares Stevenson's earlier works with those he produced after emigrating to California in 1880. Noble claims that the American works, which are collected in this edition, surpassed anything else, fiction or nonfiction, that he wrote. Be that as it may, the reader is encouraged to accompany Stevenson through a time in his life that was unsettled and in many ways miserable. (A,G)

Treglown, Jeremy, ed. *The Lantern-Bearers and Other Essays,* by Robert Louis Stevenson. New York: Farrar, Straus, Giroux, 1988. Like most Victorian writers, Stevenson produced voluminous letters and essays, written in eloquent, often convoluted language, with numerous references in Latin. Although formal in tone, the thirty essays collected here depict a man who was witty, argumentative, and at times funny. He provides clear insights into his work, travels, attitudes about other writers, health, politics, and more. For the serious researcher, these essays are excellent autobiographical materials. (A)

Veeder, William, and Gordon Hirch, eds. *"Dr. Jekyll and Mr. Hyde" after One Hundred Years.* Chicago: University of Chicago Press, 1988. This collection of essays is divided into sections focusing on thematic aspects of the novel. These sections—voice, repression, genre, and context—deal with such topics as homosexuality, the use of science fiction, and reader response. The essays serve to provide modern critical readings of this popular novel and show its continuing vibrancy. (A)

Other Sources
Hillier, Robert I. *The South Seas Fiction of Robert Louis Stevenson.* New York: Peter Lang, 1989.

Menikoff, Barry. *Robert Louis Stevenson and "The Beach of Falesa": A Study in Victorian Publishing with the Original Text.* Palo Alto, CA: Stanford University Press, 1984.

Rankin, Nicholas. *Dead Man's Chest: Travels after Robert Louis Stevenson.* Winchester, MA: Faber & Faber, 1987.

HARRIET BEECHER STOWE
1811-1896

Evaluation of Selected Biography and Criticism

Gossett, Thomas F. *"Uncle Tom's Cabin" and American Culture*. Dallas: Southern Methodist University Press, 1985. Gossett's study describes the social history of Harriet Beecher Stowe's masterwork *Uncle Tom's Cabin*. Beginning with the cultural and social atmosphere surrounding the novel's writing, Gossett examines the furor created by its publication in 1852. He examines the historical context of the popularity of the subsequent dramatic version and the play's adaptation for silent films. In each of its incarnations, *Uncle Tom's Cabin* served as a focus for debate over slavery, racial attitudes, and stereotypes. Gossett continues his survey through the Civil Rights movement of the 1960s, when "Uncle Tom" was adopted as a pejorative term by black activists. Highly recommended for anyone interested in the history of race relations in nineteenth- and twentieth-century America. (A,G)

Hovet, Theodore R. *The Master Narrative: Harriet Beecher Stowe's Subversive Story of Master and Slave in "Uncle Tom's Cabin" and "Dred."* New York: University Press of America, 1989. Hovet examines *Uncle Tom's Cabin* and *Dred* from historical, religious, and feminist perspectives. He contends that these novels follow a pattern exemplified by the mystical Gnostic "master narrative," in which humankind's fall is caused by the descent of the spirit into matter. In this fall, the primal human being was separated into masculine and feminine forms. The individual seeks salvation first by suppressing the feminine "material" principle. In *Uncle Tom's Cabin*, Tom adopts an attitude of the "suffering servant" on a journey of return to spiritual wholeness. Hovet reads *Dred* in the same light, finding an underlying structural unity in a work that has heretofore been described as scattered and incomplete. (A,G)

Jakoubek, Robert E. *Harriet Beecher Stowe*. New York: Chelsea House, 1989. Quoting heavily from her letters and other personal writings, Jakoubek presents an engaging and informative biography of Stowe. The issue of slavery is examined from both northern and southern viewpoints, providing a necessary context for understanding the impact of *Uncle Tom's Cabin* on the American public. Jakoubek frankly addresses literary critics who have been less than kind in their pronouncements on Stowe's writing style. (A,G)

Reynolds, Moira Davison. *"Uncle Tom's Cabin" and Mid-Nineteenth Century United States: Pen and Conscience*. Jefferson, NC: McFarland, 1985. Reynolds explores the moral atmosphere of antebellum America that influenced Stowe's composition of *Uncle Tom's Cabin* and the novel's public reception. Those interested in this subject should also refer to Gossett's *"Uncle Tom's Cabin" and American Culture* (1985). (A,G)

Sundquist, Eric, ed. *New Essays on "Uncle Tom's Cabin."* Cambridge: Cambridge University Press, 1987. In an opening essay, Sundquist, the editor of this collection of essays, reexamines this novel's critical reception and its influence on subsequent antislavery fiction. Other essays deal with a variety of subjects. Karen Halttunen explores Stowe's uses of the "haunted house" metaphor, Robert Stepto examines the sources for her black characters, and Richard Yarborough analyzes the fictional characterizations. Elizabeth Ammons examines how Stowe's work influenced later women writers, and Jean Yellin shows the power of Christian morality when harnessed to outrage. The essays complement one another nicely and provide an overview of a newly reconstructed period of literary history. (A)

Thomas, Brook. *Cross-Examinations of Law and Literature: Cooper, Hawthorne, Stowe, and Melville.* Cambridge: Cambridge University Press, 1987. In this specialized study in cultural history, Thomas examines the early nineteenth-century tradition of combining the study of law and literature. He uses selected works of writers of the American Renaissance—Stowe, Cooper, Hawthorne, and Melville—to define the fictional presentation of legal issues of the times. He pairs these writers with prominent contemporary lawyers with whom they had a personal or professional connection. For example, he relates Stowe's work to litigation over slavery. (A)

Other Sources
Van Why, Joseph S., and Earl French, eds. *Harriet Beecher Stowe in Europe: The Journal of Charles Beecher.* Hartford, CT: Stowe-Day, 1986.

JESSE STUART
1907-1984

Author's Recent Bibliography
Foretaste of Glory, 1986 (novel); *Cradle of the Copperheads*, 1988 (novel).

Evaluation of Selected Biography
Stuart, Jane. *Transparencies: Remembrances of My Father, Jesse Stuart.* Lynnville, TN: Archer Editions Press, 1985. Stuart has dedicated this loose collection of prose and poetry to the memory of her father, Jesse Stuart. Her memories of her father are presented in a manner of free association and through subjective images. Although pleasant to peruse, this volume will probably disappoint researchers looking for biographical details. **(G)**

JONATHAN SWIFT
1667-1745

Evaluation of Selected Biography and Criticism

Guilhamet, Leon. *Satire and the Transformation of Genre*. Philadelphia: University of Pennsylvania Press, 1987. Using selected works of Dryden, Pope, and Swift, Guilhamet dissects and analyzes satiric form. He divides satire into three types—demonstrative, deliberative, and judicial—and then shows how these types interact within the complex structures devised by the authors. Great satire, he contends, emerges with the belief that the past is superior to the present and that innovation is destructive of important institutions. (A)

Hinnant, Charles H. *Purity and Defilement in "Gulliver's Travels."* New York: St. Martin's, 1987. Hinnant applies Mary Douglas' views on purity, pollution, and defilement to Swift's imaginative cultures—Laputa, Lilliput, Brobdingnag, and Houyhnhnmland. The result is a serious anthropological evaluation of fictional settings that Swift used as a backdrop for satire. In this critique, even the Yahoos possess a complex social and political organization. This study would probably have been more productive and enjoyable if Hinnant hadn't taken the project so seriously. (A)

Ingram, Allan. *Intricate Laughter in the Satire of Swift and Pope*. New York: St. Martin's, 1986. This study examines the complex nature of humor as it is employed by eighteenth-century satirists, particularly Pope and Swift. Ingram applies critical ideas derived from a variety of sources, such as Freud, Bergson, and Lange. She examines the opinions of major critical sources of the period—Hobbes, Shaftesbury, Addison, and Steele. Most satire, according to Ingram, employs laughter as a weapon that excludes the victims from human acceptance. Laughter also appears as a means to achieve group identity. This well-written work is recommended for anyone interested in eighteenth-century literature. (A,G)

Kelly, Ann Cline. *Swift and the English Language*. Philadelphia: University of Pennsylvania Press, 1988. Drawing on Swift's many pronouncements on the "English tongue," Kelly provides an overview of his theories and attitudes toward the language. She examines Swift's linguistic theories in the context of the ferment caused by publication of the King James Version of the Bible, Bacon's *Novum Organum*, and Johnson's *Dictionary*. Swift's concept of "proper words in proper places" is further related to his expectations of the social structure and his role within it. (A,G)

Nokes, David. *Jonathan Swift, a Hypocrite Reversed: A Critical Biography*. Oxford: Oxford University Press, 1986. Nokes' sensitive portrayal of Swift is more plausible than the misanthropic, lecherous portrait presented by others.

Nokes does an excellent job re-creating the eighteenth-century context needed to understand Swift's multifaceted and contradictory personality. Well-researched and well-written, this biography is the definitive treatment for the general reader. (A,G)

Pollak, Ellen. *The Poetics of Sexual Myth: Gender and Ideology in the Verse of Swift and Pope*. Chicago: University of Chicago Press, 1985. Pollak contends that "Swift was committed in his poems to exploring certain sexual myths that Pope's verse insistently worked to justify." She views Swift's writing as "one more possible point of departure, one more vantage point ... in the ongoing project of unraveling—and undoing—the ideological grounds of patriarchy as we know it in the West." Some critics have criticized Pollak's study for the narrowness of its focus and its uncertain grasp of literary history. (A)

Rembert, James A. W. *Swift and the Dialectical Tradition*. New York: St. Martin's, 1988. Rembert argues that Swift's philosophy is based on opposites and that, within the literary tradition of questioner and answerer, his questions establish the basis for his satire. (A)

Tippett, Brian. *"Gulliver's Travels."* Atlantic Highlands, NJ: Humanities Press, 1989. In this study Tippett presents an overview of the criticism of *Gulliver's Travels*. He has grouped the critical approaches into categories: author-centered, formal and rhetorical, and historical and contextual. In each section he gives an extended bibliographical survey of important books and essays. His overview neglects ideological approaches such as Althusser and feminist critics, such as Ellen Pollak. In many ways, this study amounts to "study-notes" of Gulliver criticism. (G)

Wood, Nigel. *Swift*. Atlantic Highlands, NJ: Humanities Press, 1986. Poststructuralist Wood examines Swift's works for manifestations of uncertainty, indeterminacy, and inconclusiveness. Wood finds Swift's critical significance to be rooted in his hermeneutic procedures. This is a specialized study written for other specialists who (it is assumed) are already convinced of the primacy of their point of view. (A)

Wyrick, Deborah Baker. *Jonathan Swift and the Vested Word*. Chapel Hill: University of North Carolina Press, 1988. This study relies on phenomenology, structuralism, post-structuralism, and new historicism to explain Swift's struggle with language. For scholars only. (A)

Other Sources
Acworth, B. *Swift*. Brunswick, ME: Bern Porter, 1985.

Backscheider, Paula R. *A Being More Intense: A Study of the Prose Works of Bunyan, Swift, and Defoe*. New York: AMS Press, 1984.

Davis, Herbert, and L. Landa, eds. *Jonathan Swift: Miscellaneous and Autobiographical Pieces, Fragments and Marginalia.* Cambridge: Basil Blackwell, 1986.

Fischer, John I., *et al.,* eds. *Swift and His Contexts.* New York: AMS Press, 1990.

Hammond, Brean. *"Gulliver's Travels."* New York: Open University Press/ Taylor & Francis, 1988.

Rawson, Claude. *Order from Confusion Sprung: Studies in Eighteenth Century Literature from Swift to Cowper.* Winchester, MA: Unwin Hyman, 1985.

Ross, Angus. *Jonathan Swift.* Oxford and New York: Oxford University Press, 1984.

Vieth, David M., ed. *Essential Articles for the Study of Jonathan Swift's Poetry.* Hamden, CT: Archon/Shoe String, 1985.

ALGERNON CHARLES SWINBURNE
1837-1909

Evaluation of Selected Criticism

Harrison, Antony H. *Swinburne's Medievalism: A Study in Victorian Love Poetry*. Baton Rouge: Louisiana State University Press, 1988. Of the many Victorian writers who used medieval themes, Swinburne was one of the few to refrain from over-romanticizing the medieval past. In almost 50 works that dealt with the period, Swinburne portrayed medieval culture in a way that emphasized "universal truths." His heroes were finely wrought individuals who courageously defied the cruelties of fate and expressed qualities common to all ages. In Harrison's view, *Tristram of Lyonese* is Swinburne's masterwork. He discusses it in detail and provides illumination as to its sources and influences. (A,G)

Richardson, James. *Vanishing Lives: Style and Self in Tennyson, D. G. Rossetti, Swinburne, and Yeats*. Charlottesville: University Press of Virginia, 1988. In this study, Richardson, noted for his critical work on Thomas Hardy, elaborates on an important, but neglected, characteristic that links the works of Tennyson, Dante Rossetti, Swinburne, and Yeats. In his view, these poets may be considered "elegists of the self," who treat life as a fleeting, "ghostly" vapor. Of particular interest is his discussion of how Yeats significantly transformed his Victorian heritage. This study deserves the attention of students of the period but is also suitable for general readers. (A,G)

ALLEN TATE
1899-1979

Autobiographical Sources

Young, Thomas Daniel, and Elizabeth Sarcone. *The Lytle-Tate Letters: The Correspondence of Andrew Lytle and Allen Tate.* Jackson: University of Mississippi Press, 1987. These two writers survived four decades of friendship. The letters, which are annotated and prefaced by the editors, follow their friendship from 1927 through the Fugitive decade, multiple marriages, and old age. They provide amusing and sometimes enlightening reading for researchers interested in American letters between 1930 and 1960. (A)

Evaluation of Selected Criticism

Brinkmeyer, Robert H., Jr. *Three Catholic Writers of the Modern South.* Jackson: University Press of Mississippi, 1985. Brinkmeyer has selected three Southern writers who were converts to Catholicism—Allen Tate, Caroline Gordon, and Walker Percy—to examine what he sees as the particular dilemma of the Southern writer. He argues that although many Southern writers revel in the freedom of a self-imposed exile, they eventually find the modern world lacking in a sense of community and moral vision. Unable to fully accept the modernist position that sees no purpose beyond art, they are often led to religious conversion in a search for larger meaning. (A,G)

Sullivan, Walter. *Allen Tate: A Recollection.* Baton Rouge: Louisiana State University Press, 1988. Sullivan, a distinguished novelist and critic, offers a beautifully written, penetrating portrait of his friend and colleague of thirty-five years. Although not a biography, this memoir combines the facts of Tate's life with Sullivan's keen eye for character development. The result is an intimate reflection on the achievements and spirit of an important poet. (A,G)

EDWARD TAYLOR
1645?-1729

Evaluation of Selected Criticism

Gatta, John. *Gracious Laughter: The Meditative Wit of Edward Taylor.* Columbia: University of Missouri Press, 1989. Gatta describes Taylor's wit as the mediating force between his art and his spirituality. By closely examining the poetry, Gatta reveals the nature of Taylor's humor and shows how it ties directly to his perceptions of divinity. Of particular note is his explication of Taylor's *God's Determinations Touching His Elect.* An appendix provides a chronology of significant events in Taylor's life. (A)

Grabo, Norman S. *Edward Taylor.* Rev. ed. Boston: Twayne, 1988. The original edition (1961) laid the foundation for many of the critical studies that followed. The purpose of the revised edition is to expand Grabo's original theory and update the overview of criticism. The revised edition is considerably shorter since detailed discussions of some poems have been reduced. Although this makes it more readable, advanced students will still want to consult the original. The most important new feature is Grabo's discussion of *God's Determinations*, which he thinks might be seen "more usefully in terms of musical models than literary ones," specifically the rhapsody, the cantata, and the chamber opera. In a final chapter Grabo surveys the major Taylor studies. This section is especially useful for guiding researchers to areas in need of further study. (A,G)

Rowe, Karen E. *Saint and Singer: Edward Taylor's Typology and the Poetics of Meditation.* New York: Cambridge University Press, 1986. This clearly written study of the traditions expressed in Edward Taylor's poetry expertly guides the reader through the complexities of seventeenth-century typological exegesis and meditative conventions. Relying heavily on the work of Thomas and Nina Davis and Charles Mignon—in particular, the recently discovered typology sermons—Rowe provides a definitive explication of the poetry. This is one of the most valuable contributions to Taylor scholarship in recent years. (A)

White, Peter, ed. *Puritan Poets and Poetics: Seventeenth-Century American Poetry in Theory and Practice.* University Park: Pennsylvania State University Press, 1985. This collection of twenty-two essays examines the nature and vocabulary of Puritan poetry during the seventeenth century. Separate essays are devoted to the works of Bradstreet, Taylor, and others. Bradstreet's poetry is examined for its biblically derived prophetic rhetoric; Taylor is examined in the context of his contemporaries. A closing group of essays provides an overview of the various poetic forms of the period. (A)

SARA TEASDALE
1884-1933

Evaluation of Selected Criticism

Schoen, Carol B. *Sara Teasdale*. Boston: Twayne, 1986. Schoen's study is especially astute at discussing Teasdale's use of poetic devices—rhythm, assonance, alliteration, and rhyme. She skillfully interweaves biographical details with close readings of the poems, finding evidence in the poetry of Teasdale's ill health and trying marriage, while keeping the focus on the poetry. Teasdale's style was considered "old-fashioned" even in her day, but scholars, who have recently been looking more closely, have found innovations in her later works. (A,G)

ALFRED, LORD TENNYSON
1809-1892

Autobiographical Sources

Lang, Cecil Y., and Edgar F. Shannon, eds. *The Letters of Alfred Lord Tennyson, Vol. 2, 1851-1870.* Cambridge: Harvard University Press, 1987. This second volume of the complete letters contains the correspondence of the mature poet at the height of his career. His topics, which range from the stillbirth of his son to an explication of *Maud*, reveal a great deal about Tennyson the family man and poet. His excellence as a letter-writer makes this volume enjoyable reading for the general reader as well as an essential scholarly tool. The editors have provided excellent footnotes, an index of correspondents, a general index, and several useful appendices. **(A,G)**

Evaluation of Selected Criticism

Albright, Daniel. *Tennyson: The Muse's Tug of War.* Charlottesville: University Press of Virginia, 1986. Albright examines the struggle between the real and the ideal in Tennyson's imagery, revealing what he describes as a schism between the poet's interest in life and his commitment to art. Albright ably supports his thesis with critical readings of the poems, but often allows his argument to stray into unsupported realms. These digressions often distract the reader and mar what is otherwise a solid critical work. Suited for advanced students and scholars. **(A)**

Chapman, Raymond. *The Sense of the Past in Victorian Literature.* New York: St. Martin's, 1986. Chapman wittily surveys Victorian concepts and uses of history in the works of Thackery, Morris, Disraeli, Tennyson, and others. Victorians often looked to the past to frame solutions for their own problems. Each chapter introduces a period of English history, beginning with the Norman conquest, then examines how that period was portrayed by Victorian historians, artists, and writers. Chapman's study is a spirited introduction to the temper of the times. The well-arranged notes and bibliography are a helpful aid to further study. **(A,G)**

Goslee, David. *Tennyson's Characters: Strange Faces, Other Minds.* Iowa City: University of Iowa Press, 1989. Goslee applies a modern Freudian approach to Tennyson's poetry, arguing that there are usually three components at work: the narrator, an antagonist, and a mediator, roughly corresponding to the *id, ego,* and *superego.* This highly specialized study will delight some Tennyson critics and appear old-fashioned to others. In any case Goslee provides lively, intelligent observations. **(A)**

Hughes, Linda K. *The Many-Faced Glass: Tennyson's Dramatic Monologues.* Athens: Ohio University Press, 1987. Hughes uses unpublished

500

manuscripts to examine Tennyson's poetry from an unusual angle—a comparison of the technique of the dramatic monologue as used by Tennyson and Browning. The significance of monologues within works—as in *In Memoriam*—is then related to their importance within the entire body of poetry. Over one-fifth of Tennyson's poems are written as, or contain, dramatic monologues, and close analysis shows a number of connections with the other poems. (A)

Richardson, James. *Vanishing Lives: Style and Self in Tennyson, D. G. Rossetti, Swinburne, and Yeats.* Charlottesville: University Press of Virginia, 1988. In this study, Richardson, noted for his critical work on Thomas Hardy, elaborates on an important, but neglected, characteristic that links the works of Tennyson, Dante Rossetti, Swinburne, and Yeats. In his view, these poets may be considered "elegists of the self" who treat life as a fleeting, "ghostly" vapor. Of particular interest is his discussion of how Yeats significantly transformed his Victorian heritage. This study deserves the attention of students of the period but is also suitable for general readers. (A,G)

Schulz, Max F. *Paradise Preserved: Recreations of Eden in Eighteenth and Nineteenth-Century England.* Cambridge: Cambridge University Press, 1986. Schulz's study explores the idealized gardens and landscapes of the English nobility and relates these miniature Edens to the work of painters and poets of the era. Schulz discusses the work of Blake and Coleridge and provides insightful parallels with landscape artists such as Constable and Turner. He also considers Tennyson's view of Eden and anti-Eden within the context of Whistler and the mid-Victorians. Selected illustrations help amplify many of Schulz's points. This is an important study that seeks to interrelate areas of scholarship that are too often compartmentalized. Highly recommended. (A,G)

Shatto, Susan, ed. *Tennnyson's "Maud": A Definitive Edition.* Norman: University of Oklahoma Press, 1986. This edition of *Maud* collates all known manuscripts, proofs, the trial issue, and subsequent editions up to 1889. Shatto's introduction discusses the history of the poem's composition and describes its literary and biographical influences. She also describes Tennyson's work habits in valuable detail. The commentary that follows the text contains Shatto's notes and summaries of other critics' views and opinions. In all, the editorial standards of this work are difficult to surpass. The word "definitive" certainly belongs in the title. (A,G)

Sinfield, Alan. *Alfred Tennyson.* London: Blackwell, 1986. Instead of arguing from specific texts to discover a more "universal" social significance in the poetry, Sinfield starts with the social and historical milieu and, working backward, analyzes Tennyson's work as an "interpretation" of the prevailing ideology. After establishing the socio-historical context, Sinfield explains that poetry interacts with established structures in one of three ways: relegation, incorporation, or marginalization. Tennyson was able to adapt his poetry to these three roles as required by the conditions of the times. This provocative critical study turns many accepted interpretations of Tennyson's poetry inside out. (A)

Thomson, Alastair W. *The Poetry of Tennyson*. New York: Methuen, 1987. Thomson's approach to Tennyson's poetry is non-doctrinaire. His readings of the shorter poems, such as "Recollections of the Arabian Nights," are straightforward and convincing. However, he is too quick to resort to generalities when confronted with the complexities of the longer works, such as *In Memoriam*. This book was intended as an introduction for younger readers and, as such, amply discusses a variety of critical approaches to Tennyson. (G)

Timko, Michael. *Carlyle and Tennyson*. Iowa City: University of Iowa Press, 1988. Timko's study traces the complex history of mutual influence between Carlyle and Tennyson. Carlyle opened Tennyson's eyes to the multitude of Victorian social problems. Tennyson envisioned solutions that were gradualist, while Carlyle became apocalyptic in his outlook. As a result, Tennyson was more generally received, while Carlyle became increasingly more isolated. Unfortunately, this edition is an example of good ideas put into a shoddy package. Careless proofreading has left the text laced with errors that even distort the integrity of the quotations. (A,G)

Tucker, Herbert F. *Tennyson and the Doom of Romanticism*. Cambridge: Harvard University Press, 1988. In this massive critical study, Tucker contends that "Romanticism was the destiny dealt Tennyson . . . and he sought less to escape his confinement than to explore the prison in which he found himself." According to Tucker, Tennyson's unavoidable inheritance was the romantic proclivity for subjectivity, and he self-consciously, and less successfully, pursued romantic themes. Tucker explains why. Recommended for scholars. (A)

Other Sources
Beetz, Kirk H. *Tennyson: A Bibliography, 1827-1982*. Metuchen, NJ: Scarecrow, 1984.

Buckler, William E. *Man and His Myths: Tennyson's "Idylls of the King" in Critical Context*. New York: New York University Press, 1984.

Harris, Daniel A. *Tennyson and Personification: The Rhetoric of "Tithonus."* Ann Arbor: UMI Research Press, 1986.

Jordan, Elaine. *Alfred Tennyson*. New York: Cambridge University Press, 1988.

McKay, Kenneth M. *Many Glancing Colours: An Essay in Reading Tennyson, 1809-1850*. Toronto: University of Toronto Press, 1988.

Peltason, Timothy. *Reading "In Memoriam."* Princeton, NJ: Princeton University Press, 1985.

Peters, Robert, ed. *Letters to a Tutor: The Tennyson Family Letters to Henry Graham Dakyns with the Audrey Tennyson Death-Bed Diary.* Metuchen, NJ: Scarecrow, 1988.

Platizky, Roger S. *A Blueprint of His Dissent: Madness and Method in Tennyson's Poetry.* Lewisburg, PA: Bucknell University Press, 1989.

Schur, Own. *Victorian Pastoral: Tennyson, Hardy, and the Subversion of Forms.* Columbus: Ohio State University Press, 1989.

Shaw, Marion. *Alfred Lord Tennyson.* Atlantic Highlands, NJ: Humanities Press, 1988.

Shaw, Marion, ed. *An Annotated Critical Bibliography of Tennyson.* New York: St. Martin's, 1988.

Waller, John O. *A Circle of Friends: The Tennysons and the Lushingtons of Park House.* Columbus: Ohio State University Press, 1987.

WILLIAM MAKEPEACE THACKERAY
1811-1863

Evaluation of Selected Biography and Criticism

Harden, Edgar F. *Thackeray's "English Humorists" and "Four Georges."* Newark: University of Delaware Press, 1985. This study examines Thackeray's lectures in terms of his compositional process, his interest in his subjects as people, and their introspective value. Harden argues that the lectures are important in understanding Thackeray's concept of humor and that this is essential for understanding his work in general. Humor, for Thackeray, had a moral and social function. Harden analyzes each of the lectures, and while he does not draw parallels to Thackeray's fiction, he has done much of the groundwork for such a project. (A)

Lund, Michael. *Reading Thackeray.* Detroit: Wayne State University Press, 1988. Many of the great nineteenth-century novels were being serially published as they were being written. The development of plots and characters were often decided by the reading public's response to the various installments. In this interesting study, Lund examines how readers influenced *Vanity Fair, Pendennis,* and *The Newcomers.* This readable study will interest most readers. (A,G)

McKay, Carol, ed. *The Two Thackerays: Anne Thackeray Ritchie's Centenary Biographical Introduction to the Works of William Makepeace Thackeray.* New York: AMS Press, 1988. One of Thackeray's last requests was that his daughter, Anne, make certain that no one write his biography. McKay's introduction and the ensuing account by Anne Thackeray Ritchie explain how Anne came to break her promise and accept the task of chronicling the life of this great novelist. These two volumes contain all the material on Thackeray that Anne compiled and published in the centenary edition of his work. (A)

Peters, Catherine. *Thackeray's Universe: Shifting Worlds of Imagination and Reality.* Oxford: Oxford University Press, 1987. Primarily biographical, Peters' study is a discussion of Thackeray's life and writings for a more general audience than that addressed by previous scholarly biographies. Her intimate acquaintance with Thackeray allows her to speak to the reader with confident simplicity. This book is recommended as an accurate but readily accessible introduction. (A,G)

DYLAN THOMAS
1914-1953

Autobiographical Sources

Ferris, Paul, ed. *The Collected Letters of Dylan Thomas.* New York: Macmillan, 1986. This definitive collection of Thomas' correspondence chronicles the tragic decline of a young genius into chronic self-pity. Full of gossipy tales and abundant evidence of his boredom, the later letters reveal few glimpses of the brilliance that characterized his best work. Taken together, these unabridged epistles could serve as a morality tale if not for the evident unvoiced plea for help. If anyone needed further evidence that Thomas destroyed what talent he had, it is contained here. The high editorial standards and careful notations make this the definitive edition. (A,G)

Evaluation of Selected Biography and Criticism

Davies, Walford. *Dylan Thomas.* Philadelphia: Open University Press, 1986. This "pedagogical" introduction to Thomas' poetry offers a tutorial exchange between the critic, the text, and the reader. Instructions are given in the text about selecting the most appropriate Thomas poem to read. This is followed by questions to the reader on the poem and a discussion of some aspect of it. Davies provides the reader with relevant biographical, historical, and cultural information that bears upon the given poem. The close reading approach taken in this study makes this a valuable introduction to the skills of reading poetry in general and to Thomas' work in particular. Its goal is not to present an interpretation but to lead the reader into doing that for himself. (A,G)

Deane, Sheila. *Bardic Style in the Poetry of Gerard Manley Hopkins, W. B. Yeats, and Dylan Thomas.* Ann Arbor: UMI Research Press, 1989. Deane examines the poetry of Hopkins, Yeats, and Thomas in terms of the poets' use of traditional bardic sources and rhetorical devices. Deane finds close parallels among these authors who were "suspicious" of one another during their lifetimes. Each thought the other "obscure" due to the "subjective haze" of their romantic and metaphysical affectations—all of which, according to Deane, derive from a "bardic style." (A)

Gaston, Georg, ed. *Critical Essays on Dylan Thomas.* Boston: G. K. Hall, 1989. This collection of six long essays (including ones by John Berryman, Conrad Aiken, and William Empson) and fifteen shorter articles examines Thomas' life and works from a variety of critical perspectives. Alfred Kazin discusses the growth of Thomas' reputation since his death; Richard Morton analyzes his use of imagery; William Moynihan compares Thomas' rhythms to the cadence of Biblical prose. Most of these articles have been printed elsewhere but are collected here for the first time with an introduction by

Gaston that surveys the highs and lows of Thomas' reputation. There is an index but no bibliography. (A,G)

Gittins, Rob. *The Last Days of Dylan Thomas*. London: Macdonald, 1986. Gittins narrates the tragic events of Thomas' final trip to the United States. In 1953 Thomas found himself suffering from continued financial troubles, a fractious relationship with his wife, and difficulties keeping his mind on his poetry. Additionally, he wanted to reestablish contact with his new American lover. Gittins' narration is straightforward, but has the limitation of being without notes, bibliography, or index. (A,G)

Peach, Linden. *The Prose Writing of Dylan Thomas*. Totowa, NJ: Barnes & Noble, 1988. Peach analyzes Thomas' prose to illuminate the "surrealism" of his early stories and poetry and account for his avoidance of social themes. He argues that Thomas used his prose to address his concerns about Wales and that he was torn by a love-hate relationship with the country. He despised its parochialism but sentimentalized its rural charm. In a concluding chapter Peach discusses the poetry of R. S. Thomas and compares it to Dylan Thomas' poetry in the attitude taken toward Wales. Suitable for the student or researcher. (A,G)

Thomas, Caitlin, and George Tremlett. *Caitlin: Life with Dylan Thomas*. New York: Holt, 1987. Caitlin, Thomas' wife, offers her second memoir of their life together. More frank than her previous volume, *Leftover Life to Kill*, Caitlin here reveals her own flaws as well as those of her emotionally addled husband. Caitlin brought her own set of problems into the marriage, and they only intensified. Both shared a fondness for alcohol. However, the bond between them was strong enough to survive most of the harrowing experiences. The details are often unpleasant, but what emerges is a reevaluation of the poet's life. Required reading for students of Thomas. (A,G)

HENRY DAVID THOREAU
1817-1862

Evaluation of Selected Biography and Criticism

Adams, Stephen, and Donald Ross. *Revising Mythologies: The Composition of Thoreau's Major Works*. Charlottesville: University Press of Virginia, 1989. The "New Scholarship" seeks to blend facts about composition and revision of texts with relevant biographical evidence and textual criticism. In this case, Adams and Ross have applied these principles to the major writings of Thoreau. Utilizing the authoritative Princeton edition of the works, significant critical studies, and biographies, the authors trace Thoreau's journal ideas through their various revisions to finished product. In the process, such works as *Walden* undergo complex changes. The study contends that Thoreau did not become a romantic and transcendentalist until the early 1850s. Until then he was principally influenced by classical ideals, and unable to fully understand the direction that *Walden* was taking. Romanticism, however, caused him to realize that his manuscript was about "a quest for unity in the world." As his interest in romanticism waned, Thoreau's focus turned to politics and natural history. The authors are thorough in their coverage of the earlier works; Thoreau's later works are treated as an anticlimax to *Walden*. This study is sophisticated and impressive. Highly recommended. **(A)**

Bonner, Willard H., and George Levine. *Harp on the Shore: Thoreau and the Sea*. Albany: State University of New York Press, 1985. According to this study, the pervasive influence of the ocean on Thoreau is often overlooked. Bonner and Levine discuss the power of the sea over the lives of nineteenth-century residents of Concord, Massachusetts. They analyze the numerous sea images in Thoreau's writings and then turn to his inner voyage. Of particular interest is their discussion of Thoreau's admiration for the character of Robinson Crusoe, who provided a "rough prototype" for his Walden Pond experiment. **(A,G)**

Burbick, Joan. *Thoreau's Alternative History: Changing Perspectives on Nature, Culture, and Language*. Philadelphia: University of Pennsylvania Press, 1987. Burbick argues that Thoreau rejected accounts of history based on "civilized progress"; that is, histories that focus on the progress of societies rather than on the changing political and social conditions or restrictions. Burbick then applies this theory to Thoreau's journals. Although difficult, Burbick's reading of Thoreau as a historian offers a fascinating argument, especially as she attempts to link Thoreau's literary strategy with social change in the nineteenth century. **(A)**

Cameton, Sharon. *Writing Nature: Henry Thoreau's "Journal."* New York: Oxford University Press, 1985. The central argument of this well-conceived study is that Thoreau's *Journal* was his primary literary achievement. In it,

Cameton argues, he sees nature with "clearer eyes" and more squarely addresses the central romantic issues than in his published works. The "Journal" deserves to be examined for its own merits, rather than being seen as background material or as a "draft" of the published works. Cameton bogs down in an attempt to reduce the value of the other writings to make her premise look better, however. She is also guilty of misreading passages of Thoreau to fit her conclusions. Although not altogether satisfying, students of Thoreau should find an impetus here to pursue further work in the same direction. **(A,G)**

Dombrowski, Daniel A. *Thoreau the Platonist.* New York: Peter Lang, 1986. The quirky forthrightness of this study is best displayed in a discussion of Thoreau's vegetarianism and his "Higher Laws." Although it does not succeed in establishing Thoreau's indebtedness to Plato, it does succeed in suggesting that Thoreau's own eccentricities have been too readily dismissed by modern critics. **(A,G)**

Donoghue, Denis. *Reading America: Essays on American Literature.* New York: Knopf, 1987. Noted Irish literary critic Donoghue turns his critical eye on American writers in this collection of nine essays and seventeen book reviews. Each of the longer pieces—on Thoreau, Dickinson, Trilling, Whitman, Henry Adams, Emerson, Henry James, and Stevens—is prefaced by a discussion of the writer's moral and rhetorical intentions. Donoghue has a dedicated following of serious-minded readers who swear by his awesome insights. Others may have difficulty working through the details to reach the payoff. **(A)**

Johnson, Linck C. *Thoreau's Complex Weave: The Writing of "A Week On the Concord and Merrimack Rivers" with the Text of the First Draft.* Charlottesville: University Press of Virginia, 1986. *A Week on the Concord and Merrimack Rivers* is one of the more under-appreciated works of a major American author. Its subtle interplay of themes led to its commercial failure. But it is just this quality which now attracts Johnson's critical admiration. In addition to providing an excellent thematic analysis of the text, he has collected all but four pages of Thoreau's original 117-page manuscript of the first draft. This manuscript is printed with a detailed scholarly apparatus and is an invaluable primary resource. **(A)**

Myerson, Joel, ed. *Critical Essays on Henry David Thoreau's "Walden."* Boston: G. K. Hall, 1988. This three-part collection focuses primarily on opinions about Thoreau. The first section reprints early reviews of his work; the second and third sections are essays that evaluate Thoreau's reputation, including Lowell's notorious attack. Intended to focus on the man rather than the works, these essays confirm the view that Thoreau remains one of the most controversial American writers. **(A)**

Richardson, Robert D. *Henry Thoreau: A Life of the Mind.* Berkeley: University of California Press, 1986. Richardson focuses on the inner Thoreau in this treatment of his ideas, aspirations, and achievements. As such, it is an excellent complement to Walter Harding's biography of the outer man—*The Days of Henry Thoreau* (1966). Read together, these two biographies seem to have captured the complete man. Richardson is adept at finding connections between Thoreau's reading and his writings, such as his reading Goethe and writing *A Week on the Concord and Merrimack Rivers*. An intriguing view of a college boy growing into intellectual maturity and acquiring late-in-life wisdom. Highly recommended. (A,G)

Sattelmeyer, Robert. *Thoreau's Reading: A Study in Intellectual History with Bibliographical Catalogue*. Princeton, NJ: Princeton University Press, 1988. Listing fifteen hundred books, articles, and pamphlets quoted or referred to by Thoreau, and examining Thoreau's library and required reading lists as a student at Harvard, Sattelmeyer convincingly details how Thoreau's reading influenced his work. This study is particularly valuable in light of recent criticism that blames Thoreau's late career decline on ideological influences. (A)

Schneider, Richard J. *Henry David Thoreau*. Boston: Twayne, 1987. Building on recent scholarship, Schneider provides a convincing reassessment of the significance of Henry David Thoreau, whom he considers one of America's most misunderstood writers. Schneider summarizes Thoreau's developing attitudes toward nature, philosophy, society, and writing and provides in-depth readings of the most important works: *A Week on the Concord and Merrimack Rivers, Walden, The Maine Woods, Cape Cod, Journal*, and *Reform Papers*. Taken together, these materials provide an ideal introduction for those new to the study of Thoreau's works. (A,G)

Steele, Jeffrey. *The Representation of the Self in the American Renaissance*. Chapel Hill: University of North Carolina Press, 1987. Steele draws on modern psychological theories to explore the concept of the self as portrayed in major works of the American Renaissance. He makes illuminating comparisons between the orientations of writers and psychologists/philosophers—for example, Emerson and Jung, Thoreau and Medard Boss, Hawthorne and Freud, and Melville and Nietzsche. (A,G)

Other Sources
Borst, Raymond R. *Henry David Thoreau: A Reference Guide, 1835-1899*. Boston: G. K. Hall, 1987.

Dillman, Richard. *Thoreau's Comments on the Art of Writing*. Lanham, MD: University Press of America, 1987.

Fleck, Richard F. *Henry Thoreau and John Muir Among the Indians*. Hamden, CT: Archon/Shoe String, 1985.

Friesen, Victor C. *The Spirit of the Huckleberry: Sensuousness in Henry Thoreau*. Lincoln: University of Nebraska Press, 1984.

Lebeaux, Richard. *Thoreau's Seasons*. Amherst: University of Massachusetts Press, 1984.

Neufeldt, Leonard N. *The Economist: Henry Thoreau and Enterprise*. New York: Oxford University Press, 1989.

Pillai, A. K. *Transcendental Self: A Comparative Study of Thoreau and the Psycho-Philosophy of Hinduism and Buddhism*. Lanham, MD: University Press of America, 1985.

Sattelmeyer, Robert, ed. *Henry David Thoreau—Journal Two: 1842-1848*. Princeton, NJ: Princeton University Press, 1984.

Thoreau, Henry David. *Consciousness in Concord: The Text of Thoreau's Hitherto "Lost Journal," 1840-1841*. New York: AMS Press, 1985.

JAMES THURBER
1894-1961

Autobiographical Sources

Fensch, Thomas, ed. *Conversations with James Thurber*. Jackson: University Press of Mississippi, 1989. Fensch has collected a wide range of Thurber's newspaper and magazine interviews. Although the shorter entries often repeat basic biographical information, the longer ones reveal his serious mind and spontaneous wit. Thurber is in top form with his tongue-in-cheek pontificating on relations between the sexes. Full of useful details for the scholar, these interviews also provide a pleasant introduction to Thurber for the uninitiated reader. (A,G)

Evaluation of Selected Biography Criticism

Long, Robert Emmett. *James Thurber*. New York: Ungar, 1988. This straightforward study combines Thurber's biography with a survey of his comic art, including fiction, cartoons, and fables. Long places Thurber in the context of both his times and the comic tradition, and compares his work with that of other humorists. This introductory overview provides new readers with a primer on the life and works of one of America's finest humorists. (G)

Rosen, Michael, ed. *Collecting Himself: James Thurber on Writing and Writers*. New York: Harper, 1989. Rosen has collected a potpourri of lesser-known works by Thurber to display the humorist's range and eccentricity. Interspersed with these pieces are previously unpublished drawings, interviews, and random examples of wit. Included is Thurber's unusual critique of the writings of Henry James. The interviews provide useful commentary on the more well known works. Recommended for those with previous experience of Thurber's world. (A)

Other Sources

Tibbetts, Robert A. *James Thurber: A Guide to Research*. New York: Garland, 1989.

Toombs, Sarah E. *James Thurber: An Annotated Bibliography of Criticism*. New York: Garland, 1987.

J. R. R. TOLKIEN
1892-1973

Author's Recent Bibliography

The Lays of Beleriand, 1985; *The Shaping of Middle Earth: The Quenta, the Ambrakanta, and the Annals*, 1986; *The Lost Road and Other Writings: Language and Legend Before the Lord of the Rings*, 1987; *Tree and Leaf*, 1989; *The Return of the Shadow: The History of the Lord of the Rings, Part 1*, 1989. *The Treason of Isengard: History of the Lord of the Rings, Part 2*, 1989. (All are nonfiction journals by Tolkien edited posthumously by his son.)

Evaluation of Selected Criticism

Crabbe, Katharyn W. *J. R. R. Tolkien*. New York: Continuum, 1988. This "revised and expanded" version of Crabbe's 1981 study adds a new chapter that discusses Tolkien's manuscripts. Tolkien's son Christopher has been editing his father's papers and publishing them under the general title *The History of Middle Earth*. Crabbe's new chapter gives interesting close readings to these newly published versions. Unfortunately neither the bibliography nor the index has been updated from the 1981 edition. **(A,G)**

Johnson, Judith Anne. *J. R. R. Tolkien: Six Decades of Criticism*. Westport, CT: Greenwood, 1986. This comprehensive bibliography of Tolkien criticism covers the years 1922 through 1984. The citations are divided into four sections on: *The Hobbit* and earlier writings, *The Lord of the Rings*, the resulting controversy, and finally the posthumous works and criticism. Each section has an introductory essay summarizing the period and works covered. All of Tolkien's writings are listed—scholarly, poetic, and literary. Critics and titles are thoroughly indexed. Johnson's annotations are excellent. **(A,G)**

Sammons, Martha C. *A Better Country: The Worlds of Religious Fantasy and Science Fiction*. Westport, CT: Greenwood, 1988. Sammons begins with an analytical discussion of the fantasy works of Tolkien and C. S. Lewis and pursues the religious themes revealed there through a range of modern science fiction/fantasy writers. She examines the nature and depiction of evil, the description of the struggle between good and evil, and Tolkien's suggestion that evil ultimately may be overcome. Of particular note is her discussion of the biblical and mythological sources of these works. **(A,G)**

Tolkien, Christopher, ed. *"The Lost Road" and Other Writings: Language and Legend before "The Lord of the Rings."* Boston: Houghton Mifflin, 1987. Tolkien kept voluminous notes and manuscript revisions, which Christopher Tolkien continues to edit. This is the fifth volume, in which he analyzes the mythologies and legends that inspired *The Lord of the Rings*. Included are

512

early versions of "The Fall of Numenor," "The Lost Road," "The Later Annals of Valinor," and "The Later Annals of Beleriand." A useful feature of this volume is a dictionary explaining the history and vocabulary of the Elvish tongues. The fourth volume, entitled *The Shaping of Middle-Earth: the Quenta, the Ambrakanta, and the Annals* (1986), includes fragments of *Lost Tales,* the earliest version of *The Silmarillon,* a history of the gnomes, the first Silmarillon map, and the "Earliest Annals of Valinor and Beleriand." These volumes offer important insights into Tolkien's imagination and provide excellent primary material for scholars. (A)

Other Sources
Purtill, Richard L. *J. R. R. Tolkien: Myth, Morality, and Religion.* New York: Harper & Row, 1984.

JEAN TOOMER
1894-1967

Evaluation of Selected Biography and Criticism

Baker, Houston A. *Afro-American Poetics: Revisions of Harlem and the Black Aesthetic.* Madison: University of Wisconsin Press, 1988. This is the second volume in a projected three-volume reassessment of postmodernist Afro-American writers. Baker examines conceptions of history and the self as they relate to Afro-American culture. Individual essays examine the significance of works by Jean Toomer, Contée Cullen, Amiri Baraka, Larry Neal, and Hoyt Fuller. In the conclusion he analyzes the sources and expressions of black creativity. Although he has included useful notes, Baker appears to have put off a bibliography until the final volume of the trilogy is published. (A,G)

Callahan, John F. *In the African-American Grain: The Pursuit of Voice in Twentieth-Century Black Fiction.* Champaign: University of Illinois Press, 1988. This thematic study of narrative voice links aspects of folk culture to the works of several generations of black writers. Callahan focuses on the folk tradition of call and response and how it influenced the narrative voice. Callahan explores the lyrical qualities of Jean Toomer's *Cane*, which is expressed in a "musical" rather than a rhetorical voice. Examining Zora Neale Hurston's *Their Eyes Were Watching God* and the *Autobiography of Jane Pittman,* he shows how the conventions of storytelling are used to establish an interactive relationship with the reader. Callahan stresses the essential "Americanness" of these works, placing them in the line of Emerson and democratic idealism. (A,G)

Kerman, Cynthia Earl, and Richard Eldridge. *The Lives of Jean Toomer: A Hunger for Wholeness.* Baton Rouge: Louisiana State University Press, 1987. Relying heavily on Freudian concepts, this important biography attempts to clarify Jean Toomer's inner turmoil over defining or avoiding a racial identity for himself and others. He expounded his views in various "incarnations" as a writer, a follower of Gurdjieff, and a Quaker leader. Toomer's masterwork, *Cane,* which touched off the Harlem Renaissance, is discussed only where passages seem to illuminate biographical events. (A,G)

O'Daniel, Therman B., ed. *Jean Toomer: A Critical Evaluation.* Washington, DC: Howard University Press, 1988. These forty-six essays provide a comprehensive look at Jean Toomer's achievement and place in literary history. A biographical introduction describes the development of Toomer's career, his views on race, his embrace of philosophy and mysticism, and his refusal to accept the label "Negro novelist." The remaining essays are grouped according to theme, such as his views of women, interest in Gurdjieff, relationships with other writers, and critical reputation. (A,G)

THOMAS TRAHERNE
1637-1674

Evaluation of Selected Criticism

Deneff, A. Leigh. *Traherne in Dialogue: Heidegger, Lacan, and Derrida.* Durham, NC: Duke University Press, 1988. Deneff's ambitious study seeks to break the objective "myth" of established historical criticism of Traherne's poetry. He evaluates the poetry in light of post-structuralist theories derived from Heidegger, Lacan, and Derrida. His strategy is to establish a dialogue between Traherne's poetry and each of these thinkers. A chapter on Heidegger seeks to allow "some of the key issues of the philosopher to disclose significant verbal and ideational centers of the poet." In later chapters Deneff turns to Lacan to explore Traherne's psychology and to Derrida to trace the poet's discursive logic. This is an ambitious attempt to make practical application of post-structuralist literary theory. An engaging book for literary theorists and Traherne scholars. (A)

Dickson, Donald R. *The Fountain of Living Waters: The Typology of the Waters of Life in Herbert, Vaughan, and Traherne.* Columbia: University of Missouri Press, 1987. Dickson traces the use of water by medieval writers and theologians to explain the process of salvation. Dickson then applies these theories to the three poets. Good footnotes, index, and bibliography make this study especially useful to scholars. (A)

ANTHONY TROLLOPE
1815-1882

Evaluation of Selected Biography and Criticism

Hamer, Mary. *Writing by Numbers: Trollope's Serial Fiction*. London: Cambridge University Press, 1987. Hamer argues that Trollope's novels before *Framley Parsonage* were "mechanical and primitive," and that the process of writing serialized novels opened his imagination. Writing in installments forced him to reveal his characters more directly and to create more drama for his plot. Hamer's introduction outlines the historical background of serial publication. She then examines six novels in detail: *Orley Farm, The Small House at Allington, Can You Forgive Her?, The Claverings, Phineas Finn,* and *The Last Chronicle*. This is a readable study appropriate for any interested student or reader. (A,G)

Herbert, Christopher. *Trollope and Comic Pleasure*. Chicago: University of Chicago Press, 1987. Strictly an exercise in critical methodology, this extended essay is notable for its almost complete disregard for biography. Herbert, in the vanguard of the New Critical movement, examines Trollope's novels in terms of the sensibilities of Jacobean drama and is generally successful. Recommended as a strong critical introduction to this significant Victorian author. (A,G)

MacDonald, Susan Peck. *Anthony Trollope*. Boston: Twayne, 1987. MacDonald provides a general overview of Trollope's life, reputation, themes, and techniques, combined with brief but useful interpretations of his novels. She attempts to argue why Trollope changed his political views between 1866 and 1870, a topic student researchers might well pursue. (A,G)

McMaster, Rowland. *Trollope and the Law*. New York: St. Martin's, 1986. This study is a clear treatment of Trollope's depiction of the law and the legal profession. McMaster examines works such as *Is He Popinjoy?, Mr. Scarborough's Family, Lady Anna,* and *Orley Farm* to develop an understanding of Trollope's ambiguous attitude toward the law. On the one hand, law must be respected as it maintains the continuity of English culture; on the other hand, the law is a human product that is not free from error and thus should be mistrusted. Lawyers are seen as "slaves" of the legal system, employed to maintain the privilege of the English nobility. This is the definitive study on the topic and is highly recommended. (A,G)

Morse, Deborah D. *Women in Trollope's Palliser Novels*. Ann Arbor: UMI Research, 1987. The five Palliser novels, according to Morse, fully reveal Trollope's ambivalent attitudes toward the role of women in Victorian society. In depicting strong, ambitious women struggling for identity in a male-dominated society, Trollope undermines the traditional assumption that women should be fulfilled by love, marriage, and childbirth. At the same time, he subverts the woman's attempts at self-actualization through plot and character, often in a way that points to broader social ironies. Close readings of the novels perceptively trace the development and expression of these attitudes. Occasionally heavy-handed but never dogmatic, this study is recommended for all students of Trollope and those concerned with the condition of women in Victorian culture. (A,G)

Nardin, Joan. *He Knew She Was Right*. Carbondale: University of Southern Illinois Press, 1989. Analyzing Trollope's rhetorical strategies and structural unity, Nardin offers a feminist argument that Trollope was "affirming the Victorian ideal" of women while, at the same time, promoting women's rights. The tensions and contradictions between the two are best realized in the subplots, where Trollope's true intentions can be discovered. This interesting, intelligent analysis demonstrates Trollope's modernity and timeliness for contemporary readers. (A)

Super, R. H. *The Chronicler of Barsetshire: A Life of Anthony Trollope*. Ann Arbor: University of Michigan Press, 1988. Super's biography is a painstaking effort to set the record straight on the life of Anthony Trollope. His familiarity with Trollope's public career, his surroundings, his social life, and personal preferences in dress, food, and drink provide a vivid background for discussing the novels. While Super's approach at times verges on adulation, his accumulation of facts and details make this biography important for anyone studying Trollope's life and fiction. (A,G)

Terry, R. C., ed. *Trollope: Interviews and Recollections*. New York: St. Martin's, 1987. Terry has collected anecdotes, conversations, and impressions from a wide variety of people who knew Trollope: E. B. Browning, Carlyle, Hawthorne, James, George Eliot, Thackeray, and Twain. The introduction presents a balanced view of Trollope's personality, and Terry's annotations are useful for understanding the significance of the entries. Appropriate for all levels of serious readers. (A,G)

Other Sources
Epperly, Elizabeth R. *Patterns of Repetition in Trollope*. Washington, DC: Catholic University of America, 1989.

Terry, R. C. *A Trollope Chronology*. London: Macmillan UK, 1988.

Trollope, Anthony. *Anthony Trollope: An Illustrated Autobiography*. New York: Hippocrene Books, 1989.

Wall, Stephen. *Trollope: Living with Character*. New York: Henry Holt, 1989.

MARK TWAIN
1835-1910

Autobiographical Sources

Branch, Edgar, ed. *Mark Twain's Letters, Volume 1: 1853-1866*. Berkeley: University of California Press, 1988. Projected to be one of the most important collections of letters by an American author, the first volume admirably meets the expectations. Beginning with a seventeen-year-old Sam Clemens, this collection follows him through adventures from Missouri to the East Coast, Nevada, Hawaii, and finally to California, where he is firmly entrenched in the persona of Mark Twain. The letters themselves are sprightly, spontaneous, and immensely enjoyable for those familiar with the author's works. The editors' extensive notes and annotations are efficiently arranged and accessible even to the general reader. Literary students will have a field day with the appendices, which include genealogies, maps, manuscript facsimiles, and a full commentary. (A,G)

Evaluation of Selected Biography and Criticism

Beaver, Harold. *"Huckleberry Finn."* Boston: Allen & Unwin, 1987. Beaver surveys the immense scholarship inspired by the novel and summarizes what he believes are the questions awaiting further research. Included are a glossary of colloquialisms, selected bibliography, and index. This study is clearly written, and although the subject is more appropriate for advanced students and scholars, it contains an excellent overview and term paper ideas for any serious student. (A,G)

Bloom, Harold, ed. *Mark Twain*. New York: Chelsea House, 1986. An introduction by Bloom places Twain's works in critical context and describes the themes and concerns of the twenty essays in this anthology. The essays discuss important themes and issues in Twain's works and represent a range of theories and perspectives. This collection is useful as an introduction to Twain's critical reputation. (A,G)

Bridgman, Richard. *Traveling in Mark Twain*. Berkeley: University of California Press, 1987. Twain wrote seven books based on his travels. Given Twain's wit and propensity to weave yarns, few critics read these adventures as either pure autobiography or pure fiction. Bridgman's thesis is that Twain's accounts of his travels reflect the exploration of his tortured psyche. Bridgman contends that during each of his extended travels, Twain focused on specific interests: *Innocents Abroad* takes him to the roots of Judeo-Christian culture; *Roughing It* charts a course through frontier America back to its roots in Eden; *Following the Equator* develops his sexual interests. Bridgman does not address the possibility that the narrator of the travel books could be a fictional character, but allows the reader to think that the psychological quests of the narrator are those of Twain himself. (A)

Brown, Caroline S. *The Tall Tale in American Folklore and Literature.* Knoxville: University of Tennessee Press, 1987. The tall tale is the single genre of humor whose essential features remain markedly similar whether it is expressed in oral or literary form. Drawing equally from folklore study and literary criticism, Brown surveys the historical development of the American oral tradition, then examines the rise of nineteenth-century written humor, focusing on T. B. Thorpe, George Washington Harris, and Mark Twain. By examining Twain's *Roughing It* and the *Autobiography*, for example, Brown establishes that the relationship between narrator and reader is structurally identical to that of the speaker and audience in oral presentation. (A,G)

Clemens, Susy. *Papa: An Intimate Biography of Mark Twain.* Edited by Charles Neider. New York: Doubleday, 1985. When Twain's daughter Susy was thirteen, she wrote a biography of her father, in which she describes family life and her relationship with her father, and demonstrates an intelligent understanding of his importance. Twain himself cribbed sections of Susy's book for his autobiography, though he colored her account with his own interpretation of events. Never published in its entirety, this charming biography by a little girl is complete with Neider's authoritative scholarship. This book is important not only for what it says about Twain, but also for the portrait it paints of Susy, who died an untimely death at age twenty-four. (A,G)

Cummings, Sherwood. *Mark Twain and Science: Adventures of the Mind.* Baton Rouge: Louisiana State University Press, 1988. Cummings contends that Twain drew upon four incompatible intellectual heritages: Calvinistic, deistic, evangelical Christian, and Darwinian. Cummings explains each philosophy with regards to Twain's fiction, but focuses particularly on his scientific responses to Darwin. For example, Cummings believes that the interplay between Darwin's ideas and Twain's concept of his ideas resulted in "a fiction (in *Pudd'nhead Wilson*) of race and bloodlines—about the poisonous way it classifies people as inferior or superior, about its enormous social authority and about its persistence in the face of contrary evidence." Cummings also argues that there are five works that profoundly influenced Twain: Paine's *The Age of Reason*; Darwin's *The Descent of Man*; Holmes' *Autocrat of the Breakfast-Table*; Lecky's *History of European Morals*; and Taine's *The Ancient Regime*. This is an interesting study for any serious student of Twain. (A,G)

David, Beverly R. *Mark Twain and His Illustrators: Volume 1, 1869-1875.* Troy, NY: Whitston, 1986. Mark Twain worked closely with the illustrators of his books to try to ensure a favorable reception in a mass "backwoods" market. As a result, the illustrations are not mere representations of scenes, but often extend the meaning of passages in the books. Most of the major works, such as *Huckleberry Finn*, will be treated in the second and concluding volume of the study. A solid groundwork has been established with David's meticulous analysis of Twain's relationship with his illustrators. (A,G)

Eble, Kenneth E. *Old Clemens and W. D. H.: The Story of a Remarkable Friendship.* Baton Rouge: Louisiana State University Press, 1985. In this thorough study, Eble traces the forty-one-year friendship of two transplanted midwesterners—Mark Twain and William Dean Howells. The two met in 1869 when both men were in their early thirties; they remained close friends until Twain's death in 1910. As both grew older they suffered the gradual loss of those closest to them and turned increasingly to each other for support. Their relationship is offered here as a model friendship. Eble provides a biographical perspective that sheds light on the career and writings of both men. (A,G)

Garcia, Wilma. *Mothers and Others: Myths of the Females in the Works of Melville, Twain, and Hemingway.* New York: Peter Lang, 1984. Garcia's study of female characters in Melville, Twain, and Hemingway promises a complex archetypal analysis of feminine imagery. It delivers significantly less, however. Although the study contains a useful overview of archetypal theory and criticism, it is flawed by a confusion over the differences between "archetype" and "stereotype." (A,G)

Gerber, John C. *Mark Twain.* Boston: Twayne, 1988. This volume in the ongoing Twayne series is offered as a general introduction to the major writings of Twain. Gerber's criticisms of the works are clearly and carefully reasoned and appropriately aimed at the intended audience. Plot summaries are quite detailed and could nearly serve as "study notes." Only a bibliography of Twain's works is included; secondary sources or criticism are not cited. Recommended for the general reader or student who wants a reliable introduction to the works of Twain. (G)

Gillman, Susan. *Dark Twins: Imposture and Identity in Mark Twain's America.* Chicago: University of Chicago Press, 1989. By focusing on *Pudd'nhead Wilson*, the "transvestite tales," and the dream writings, Gillman reveals a side of Twain that is rarely expressed in his more popular fiction. Twain explored the mystery of identity through his many personal obsessions (including Siamese twins and murder trials) as detailed by Gillman, who supplies the appropriate cultural context. In his stories of cross-dressing and transvestism, such as "Feud Story and the Girl Who Was Ostensibly a Man," Twain questioned the legitimacy of culturally defined racial and gender identities. Gillman isolates and analyzes Twain's use of metaphors, including what he considered the "dark twin," the unconscious force that thwarts the conscious motivation. Gillman examines Twain's attitudes toward creativity and writing. This is an important contribution to Twain scholarship, more for the questions it raises than for the conclusions it reaches. (A,G)

Gray, Richard. *Writing the South: Ideas of an American Region.* Cambridge: Cambridge University Press, 1986. Gray begins his examination of southern themes in literature by isolating thematic contrasts—rural versus urban, farm versus factory, paternalism versus populism, region versus tradition. He then demonstrates how writers developed a myth of meaning for the South by exploring those contrasts. The South created these writers, and the writers, in turn, recreated the Southern identity. Gray affords the greatest space to Twain and Faulkner. Excluded from the numerous themes Gray discusses is the race issue. In all, he presents a strong case that the last "southern novel" has not yet been written. (A,G)

Hoffman, Andrew Jay. *Twain's Heroes, Twain's Worlds: Mark Twain's "Adventures of Huckleberry Finn," "A Connecticut Yankee in King Arthur's Court," and "Pudd'nhead Wilson."* Philadelphia: University of Pennsylvania Press, 1988. Basing his insights on theories of the "hero" as espoused by Lord Raglan and Joseph Campbell, Hoffman reexamines Twain's most famous protagonists—Huckleberry Finn, Hank Morgan, and David "Pudd'nhead" Wilson. Lord Ragland's famous critical study purported that heroes in the world's literature possess twenty-two similar characteristics: unusual circumstances of birth, threatened death at infancy, a mysterious childhood, divine parents, death on a hill or on a tree, and so on. Ragland's heroic model has often been applied to popular heroes, such as cowboys. In this study, Huck is viewed as a hero of "Jacksonian democracy" cast out of a more "civilized," authoritarian or industrial world. Hank is the technological hero who almost destroys the world through his "imperialism." Wilson is portrayed as an existential hero in a universe gone crazy. The approach is fresh and innovative, and Hoffman's insights go far in explaining why Twain's characters still have such appeal for a modern audience. (A,G)

Lauber, John. *The Inventions of Mark Twain.* New York: Hill & Wang, 1990. This authoritative and well-written biography describes Twain's preoccupations and achievements during the 1880s when he was writing *Huckleberry Finn.* Lauber places much of his emphasis on Twain's life as celebrity and *bonvivant.* Readily accessible to the general reader, this book will also provide Twain scholars with pleasurable reading and a few new insights into the novelist. (A,G)

Lauber, John. *The Making of Mark Twain.* New York: American Heritage, 1985. In this readable, engrossing biography, Lauber focuses on the life of young Sam Clemens to demonstrate how Clemens' own experiences later inspired those of his famous boy characters, Huck Finn and Tom Sawyer. In arguing his case, Lauber skillfully matches quotations from Twain's writings to the facts of Clemens' life. This study is an excellent biography enhanced by impeccable scholarship. For all readers and researchers. (A,G)

Mills, Nicolaus. *The Crowd in American Literature.* Baton Rouge: Louisiana State University Press, 1986. Mills explicates the use of "crowds" by American writers from Jefferson to Steinbeck. For colonial writers crowds were a "force for democracy;" for the classical American novelists— Hawthorne, Melville, and Twain—they were a force for national unity. Mills

522 Mark Twain

examines the "noble" working-class masses of such writers as Howells, Dreiser, and Steinbeck. Finally, he turns to Norman Mailer and Ralph Ellison for an examination of postwar crowds, the repository of intellectual and moral power contrasted with brute force. This is a fascinating thematic social history drawn from American literary works. (A,G)

Neider, Charles, ed. *The Outrageous Mark Twain: Some Lesser-Known but Extraordinary Works.* New York: Doubleday, 1987. In his usual fashion, Twain attacks what he believes are misinformed or stupid concepts about God and heaven. This may not be Twain at his best, but even at his second-best he cannot be ignored. These essays provide good material for Twain scholars and general readers alike. (A,G)

Robinson, Forrest G. *In Bad Faith: The Dynamics of Deception in Mark Twain's America.* Cambridge: Harvard University Press, 1986. This book is primarily a study of the theme of deception in *Tom Sawyer* and *Huckleberry Finn.* Tom is so successful at deception that he fails to develop a sense of guilt because he is never forced to confront his actions. Huck's deceptions, on the other hand, are self-deceptions. He denies his relationship to civilization, his responsibility for certain actions and attitudes, and his moral complicity in the ideology of slavery and racism. Most readers are eager to forgive Huck, explains Robinson, because they are eager to overlook their own self-deceptions. This important study reevaluates Twain's intentions and forces readers to scrutinize their own "bad faith" agreements. (A,G)

Schulman, Robert. *Social Criticism and Nineteenth-Century American Fictions.* Columbia: University of Missouri Press, 1987. Schulman examines the political psychology of capitalism and its influence on the lives and works of some of the most famous American authors—Twain, Franklin, Melville, Hawthorne, Chesnutt, Whitman, Wharton, Howells, and Dreiser. His study pursues three main themes—the fragmentation of community, the impact of social change, and the styles of American individualism. This is a truly new and refreshing reevaluation of nineteenth-century American literature. (A,G)

Sewell, David R. *Mark Twain's Language. Discourse, Dialogue, and Linguistic Variety.* Berkeley: University of California Press, 1987. Throughout his career Twain considered language a barometer of social development, subcribing to the theory that a decline in a society's use of language paralleled its general decline. In this study, Sewell divides Twain's view into three stages. During his western period (to 1872) language evoked laughter; in the second stage (1873-1894), during which *Huckleberry Finn* was composed, language served as an index to social status, moral values, and failures in communication. In the final stage, language explained thought, an idea that finally led Twain to reject the notion that any real communication between people is possible. Sewell provides a close reading of Twain's fiction, and demonstrates how these stages of language use can help explicate Twain's themes. Recommended for all serious students of Twain or linguistics. (A)

Shillingsburg, Miriam Jones. *At Home Abroad: Mark Twain in Australasia.* Jackson: University Press of Mississippi, 1988. In 1895, Mark Twain embarked on a lecture tour of Australia and New Zealand. In this study, Shillingsburg provides the details of Twain's less-than-adventurous adventure, including even the price of his train tickets. Twain's powerful lecturing style, however, is barely described and nothing new is added to Paul Fatout's *Mark Twain on the Lecture Circuit* (1960). Twain was very popular on this tour, however, and readers who want to know what the Australian papers thought of him or where he spent the night, should consult this book. **(A,G)**

Sloane, David E. E. *"Adventures of Huckleberry Finn": American Comic Vision.* Boston: G. K. Hall, 1988. In this short study Sloane addresses the novel's structure and themes to explain the roots of its humor and irony. This useful approach for the general reader and student provides a good basis for understanding the nuances of Twain's masterpiece. However, Sloane elects not to discuss some of the incidents that have led some scholars to read *Huckleberry Finn* as a "dark" rather than comic work. For a quick introduction to the novel, Sloane's reading is lively and engaging, but Twain's novel requires further investigation. **(A,G)**

Wilson, James D. *A Reader's Guide to the Short Stories of Mark Twain.* Boston: G. K. Hall, 1987. This introductory guide to Twain's short fiction is arranged alphabetically by title. Each plot summary is prefaced by information about the story's composition, publication history, sources, influences, and critical reception. Extensive appendices summarize Twain's short stories according to chronological sequence and provide useful bibliographical information. This title is strongly recommended as an introduction for new readers and students of Twain's critical significance. **(A,G)**

Other Sources

Budd, Louis J., ed. *New Essays on "Adventures of Huckleberry Finn."* New York: Cambridge University Press, 1985.

Giddings, Robert, ed. *Mark Twain: A Sumptuous Variety.* Savage, MD: Barnes & Noble, 1985.

Hays, John Q. *Mark Twain and Religion: A Mirror of American Eclecticism.* New York: Peter Lang, 1989.

Inge, M. Thomas, ed. *Huck Finn Among the Critics: A Centennial Selection.* Westport, CT: Greenwood, 1985.

Kinch, J. C. *Mark Twain's German Critical Reception, 1875-1986: An Annotated Bibliography.* Westport, CT: Greenwood, 1989.

Machlis, Paul, ed. *Union Catalog of Clemens Letters.* Berkeley: University of California Press, 1986.

Mailloux, Steven. *Rhetorical Power*. Ithaca, NY: Cornell University Press, 1989.

Marotti, Maria O. *The Duplicating Imagination: Twain and the Twain Papers*. University Park: Pennsylvania State University Press, 1990.

Rich, Janet A. *The Dream of Riches and the Dream of Art: The Relationship Between Business and the Imagination in the Life and Major Fiction of Mark Twain*. New York: Garland, 1987.

Sattelmeyer, Robert, and J. Donald Crowley, eds. *One Hundred Years of "Huckleberry Finn": The Boy, His Book and American Culture*. Columbia: University of Missouri Press, 1985.

Williams, George J. III. *Mark Twain: His Adventures at Aurora and Mono Lake*. Riverside, CA: Tree by River, 1986.

Williams, George J. III. *Mark Twain: His Life in Virginia City, Nevada*. Riverside, CA: Tree by River, 1986.

JOHN UPDIKE
1932

Author's Recent Bibliography

Facing Nature, 1985 (poetry); *Roger's Version*, 1986 (novel); *Trust Me*, 1987 (stories); *S.*, 1988 (novel); *Just Looking: Essays on Art*, 1989; *Self-Consciousness*, 1989 (memoirs).

Autobiographical Sources

Updike, John. *Self-Consciousness: Memoirs*. New York: Knopf, 1989. Not quite fiction and not quite autobiography, Updike looks back on his life and holds a colloquium of his previous incarnations. He writes insightfully of his hometown, his parents, politics, and religion. He examines how each of his previous selves responded to his surroundings, to events, and to the people who filled his life. This memoir was obviously written with the audience in mind, but there are a surprising number of frank admissions. (A,G)

Evaluation of Selected Criticism

Campbell, Jeff H. *Updike's Novels: Thorns Spell a Word*. Wichita Falls, TX: Midwestern State University Press, 1987. In 1969 Updike composed *Midpoint*, a long, philosophical poem. Campbell uses the themes of the poem as a map to the underlying preoccupations of the novels: the reality of the world, the dual nature of life, the mystery of that which transcends the world, and the affirmation of those qualities that remain within it. After obtaining initial good results with his readings, Campbell begins to feel the straitjacket of his thesis. Updike's often divergent tendencies resist reduction to these few basic themes. (A)

Greiner, Donald J. *Adultery in the American Novel: Updike, James, and Hawthorne*. Columbia: University of South Carolina Press, 1985. This narrowly focused study examines the relationship between the depiction of adultery in Updike's novels and the narrative models provided by his predecessors, Hawthorne and James. Greiner believes that Updike's essentially religious outlook inhibits a full development of the adultery theme, and his work suffers in comparison with the past masters. (A)

Greiner, Donald J. *John Updike's Novels*. Athens: Ohio University Press, 1984. Master critic Greiner provides a close reading of the novels, identifies themes, and discusses Updike's concerns and artistic development. Greiner offers many insights useful to both general readers and researchers. (A,G)

Newman, Judie. *John Updike*. New York: St. Martin's, 1988. Opening with a short biography, Newman proceeds with a fresh reading of all Updike's novels published through 1988. In contrast to previous studies, which concentrate on themes such as myth, religion, or adultery, Newman explores the social and cultural issues as they relate to particular novels: social conformity, work, the aesthetics of society, and "the politics of the imagination." This is a highly readable and valuable study for all readers of Updike. (A,G)

Ristoff, Dilvo I. *Updike's America: The Presence of Contemporary American History in John Updike's Rabbit Trilogy.* New York: Peter Lang, 1988. Ristoff's study demonstrates the importance of recent history in John Updike's Rabbit trilogy. Of particular value for researchers is the preface, which describes the Updike material at Harvard's Houghton Library. This material should be useful for studying Updike's methods of research, composition, and revision. (A)

Searles, George J. *The Fiction of Philip Roth and John Updike.* Carbondale: Southern Illinois University Press, 1984. Searles begins by defining the similarities between these two novelists: in age, urban experience, east coast sensibility, prose style, intelligence, and wit. He then defines their differing religious/ethnic background and establishes Roth as the leading spokesman for modern Jewish thought and Updike as the quintessential WASP chronicler. He concludes with a thorough analysis of how they both deal with religion, cultural assimilation, loss of traditional values, decline of the family, and loss of individuality. This is a lively, provocative analysis that will help readers understand the fiction, as well as generate ideas for research. (A,G)

Shinn, Thelma J. *Radiant Daughters: Fictional American Women.* Westport, CT: Greenwood, 1986. In this provocative study, Shinn analyzes fictional women characters in a variety of novels from the 1940s through the 1960s. Maintaining that fictional females often reflect "common human social concerns," Shinn extrapolates from her analysis to characterize a changing social climate. The novels of Updike, Bellow, Calisher, Shirley Jackson, and McCullers present a series of female characters slowly moving from fragmented identities toward greater maturity. For Shinn, both men and women are searching for community in a "dehumanized" society. This study is a good example of the recent feminist literary critique. Highly recommended. (A,G)

Other Sources
Gearhart, E. A. *John Updike Bibliography.* Brunswick, ME: Bern Porter, 1985.

HENRY VAUGHAN
1622-1695

Evaluation of Selected Biography and Criticism

Dickson, Donald R. *The Fountain of Living Waters: The Typology of the Waters of Life in Herbert, Vaughan, and Traherne.* Columbia: University of Missouri Press, 1987. Dickson traces the use of water by medieval writers and theologians to explain the process of salvation. Dickson then applies these theories to the three poets. Good footnotes, index, and bibliography make this study especially useful to scholars. **(A)**

Rudrum, Alan, ed. *Essential Articles for the Study of Henry Vaughan.* Hamden, CT: Archon Books, 1987. These twenty-one critical essays offer a variety of perspectives on Vaughan's works. As one of the metaphysical poets, Vaughan's reputation has fluctuated wildly through the years. These essays explore his sources in hermetic and religious writings, his influences, his use of imagery and symbolism, and his impact on his contemporaries. **(A)**

Thomas, Noel Kennedy. *Henry Vaughan: Poet of Revelation.* Worthing, England: Churchman, 1986. Thomas offers a reappraisal of Vaughan's religious poetry, placing his work firmly in the context of its tumultuous century. He contends that it is impossible to understand the poems without understanding the impact of the English Civil War on Vaughan. Vaughan's was a voice of compassion and sanity in the midst of bitter persecution. Thomas examines the influence of biblical prophesy on the young Vaughan and argues that political strife pushed him into an apocalyptic state of mind in his later years. His later works rely heavily for imagery on the Book of Revelation. **(A)**

Wall, John N. *Transformations of the Word: Spenser, Herbert, Vaughan.* Athens: University of Georgia Press, 1988. Wall contends that the works of Spenser, Herbert, and Vaughan are best understood within the context of the sixteenth- and seventeenth-century tenets of the Church of England. The post-Reformation Church had distinctive characteristics that have been obscured, causing the modern reader to lose the meaning of these writers' works. This dense book is divided into sections that treat each of the authors individually against a backdrop of theological concepts and liturgical practices. While certainly offering valuable information, the plodding prose makes the argument difficult to follow for the uninitiated. **(A)**

Other Sources

Clements, Arthur. *Poetry of Contemplation: John Donne, George Herbert, Henry Vaughan, and the Modern Period.* Albany: State University of New York Press, 1989.

KURT VONNEGUT, JR.
1922

Author's Recent Bibliography
Galapagos, 1985; *Bluebeard*, 1987; *Hocus Pocus*, 1990 (all novels).

Autobiographical Sources
Allen, William Rodney, ed. *Conversations with Kurt Vonnegut*. Jackson: University of Mississippi Press, 1988. This collection reprints twenty-one interviews from the *New York Times* and *Playboy*, among other sources, as well as offering transcripts of TV and radio interviews. The interviews are arranged chronologically and span the years from 1969 to 1987. (A,G)

Evaluation of Selected Criticism
Broer, Lawrence R. *Sanity Plea: Schizophrenia in the Novels of Kurt Vonnegut*. Ann Arbor: UMI Research, 1989. In an approach that straddles psychoanalytical theory and social analysis, Broer offers the first comprehensive guide to Vonnegut's works. He explores all the novels from *Player Piano* (1952) to *Bluebeard* (1987) and provides a substantial amount of insight along the way. Broer suggests that Vonnegut is a barometer of society's trend toward isolation and dehumanization and explores the author's "several selves." An interesting study for all Vonnegut readers. (A,G,Y)

Klinkowitz, Jerome. *Slaughterhouse-Five: Reforming the Novel and the World*. Boston: Twayne, 1990. Klinkowitz draws on Vonnegut's commentaries, essays, and biography, as well as historical documentation about World War II, to show how he created a new form of the novel in order to record human responses to absurdity. This lucid study is valuable to both scholars pursuing the sources of Vonnegut's imagination, critics of modern fiction, and students at all levels. (A,G)

Merrill, Robert. *Critical Essays on Kurt Vonnegut*. Boston: G. K. Hall, 1989. These essays and reviews cover a wide assortment of topics, from Vonnegut's philosophy of life and society to his use of myth and literary devices. Merrill provides a long introduction that traces the critical reception, while the essays cover the entirety of Vonnegut's career as soldier and writer. There are many ideas here for further research. (A,G)

Peratt, Asa B. Jr. *et al. Kurt Vonnegut: A Comprehensive Bibliography*. Hamden, CT: Archon Books, 1987. This is a comprehensive bibliography of works by and about Vonnegut, including dissertations and film adaptations. The primary entries are listed descriptively while secondary sources are supplied with brief annotations. (A)

IZAAK WALTON
1593-1683

Evaluation of Selected Criticism

Bevan, Jonquil. *Izaak Walton's "The Compleat Angler": The Art of Recreation*. New York: St. Martin's Press, 1988. Bevan, who edited the Clarendon Press edition of *The Compleat Angler*, turns a critical eye on one of the few seventeenth-century books of this genre to enjoy a current distribution in paperback. Bevan describes the rhetorical devices Walton uses to "conceal his art," that is, to make the writing seem spontaneous and unstructured, while in actuality being thoroughly premeditated. In his conclusion, Bevan describes Walton's contributions to literary history and stresses the continued importance of *The Compleat Angler* for the modern audience. (A,G)

ROBERT PENN WARREN
1905-1989

Author's Recent Bibliography
New and Selected Poems, 1985; *Portrait of a Father*, 1988 (memoir); *New and Selected Essays*, 1989.

Autobiographical Sources
Warren, Robert Penn. *Portrait of a Father*. Lexington: University Press of Kentucky, 1988. In this book, written when he was eighty-three years old, Warren takes us into his family's past with stories of his grandmother, mother, and especially his father. In tracing his family history, Warren provides a poetic statement on the elusiveness of history, memory, and the facts of one's life. This memoir contains five poems that Warren wrote upon the death of his father in 1952 which, in this autobiographical context, become even more powerful. Highly recommended for anyone wishing to study Warren or his work in depth. (A,G)

Evaluation of Selected Criticism
Burt, John. *Robert Penn Warren and American Idealism*. New Haven: Yale University Press, 1988. Warren's work as a critic has provided ideas that can be applied to his own work. Drawing on Warren's criticism of Lincoln, Hawthorne, Melville, Emerson, and others, Burt explores the conflicting ideals and realities embodied in Warren's poetry and fiction. For Burt, the visionary power of the ideal forces Warren's characters to seek reconciliation as their response to reality. Burt establishes his thesis in the first three chapters by exploring certain American ideals; he then connects the historical setting to Warren's works. Although the thesis is clear and interesting, the book is unnecessarily vague in places, and is best suited for scholars and advanced students. (A)

Grimshaw, James, *et al.*, eds. *Time's Glory: Original Essays on Robert Penn Warren*. Conway: University of Central Arkansas Press, 1986. This collection of essays is most useful for Richard Law's long article on *World Enough and Time*, one of Warren's novels that has been largely overlooked by critics. Law examines Warren's sources and explores the theme of dualism as embodied in the novel's central character. Grimshaw contributes an up-to-date annotated bibliography that compiles much of the criticism that has recently been published on Warren. (A)

Young, Thomas Daniel, ed. *Modern American Fiction: Form and Function*. Baton Rouge: Louisiana State University Press, 1989. Young has collected thirteen essays that he believes represent the best criticism on the modes of expression of American novelists. The essays examine novels by such authors as Warren (*All the King's Men*), Crane (*The Red Badge of Courage*), Barth (*The Floating Opera*), and James (*The Wings of the Dove*). The form of each novel is examined and related to the particular author's "vision of life." Many of these essayists remark that American authors are much more likely to allow the action to unfold without the commentary of an omnipresent narrator than most British and European authors. This collection provides a thoughtful overview for students of nineteenth- and twentieth-century American literature. (A)

EVELYN WAUGH
1903-1966

Evaluation of Selected Biography and Criticism

Carens, James F., ed. *Critical Essays on Evelyn Waugh.* Boston: G. K. Hall, 1987. These essays cover Waugh's ideas about sociology, religion, nostalgia, values, vision, and style. Other essays cover his life and works and his autobiography. This study is most valuable for readers familiar with several of Waugh's novels. **(A)**

Carpenter, Humphrey. *The Brideshead Generation: Evelyn Waugh and His Friends.* Boston: Houghton Mifflin/Davidson, 1990. Carpenter, who has authored books on Tolkien, Auden, and Pound, provides a new perspective on Waugh's life, built from rich detail and astute literary criticism. Although given the leading role, Waugh shares the stage with other Bloomsbury notables. Carpenter is particularly insightful in his discussion of Waugh's later years when he appeared to parody his staunchly Catholic, right-wing invective. Waugh, who had little use for the common man, chose to mire his uncommon talents in bitter ranting fueled by the drugs and alcohol that contributed heavily to his death. **(A,G)**

Crabbe, Katharyn. *Evelyn Waugh.* New York: Frederick Ungar, 1988. Although Waugh continued to publish into the 1960s, he is best known for the satires he produced before World War II. In this timely retrospective, Crabbe revives many of the works that have slipped into obscurity. Her analysis of *The Ordeal of Gilbert Pinfold,* for example, reveals Waugh's prescription for the social "wasteland" his satires exposed. More than a simple application of Catholicism, as some critics have suggested, Waugh's solution was a complex blend of faith, conservative values, and application to creative work. In his later years, though, Waugh's confidence in "old-fashioned" faith and values seems to have been shaken and with it his self-confidence as a writer. Crabbe examines Waugh's falling away and suggests that he became absorbed by a comfortable materialism that sapped his creative energies. In many ways Waugh came to embody what he mercilessly pilloried in his youth. This fascinating character study is recommended both for students and a more popular audience. **(A,G)**

McCartney, George. *Confused Roaring: Evelyn Waugh and the Modernist Tradition.* Bloomington: Indiana University Press, 1987. McCartney argues that, while Waugh flaunted his disdain for modernism, his works reflect the freedom it championed. Tracing the influence of Nietzsche, Bergson, Spengler, Picabia, Futurism, and Bauhaus aesthetics on Waugh, McCartney postulates that at every turn the novelist pays "parodic tribute to modernist art and literature." McCartney even applies his theory to film conventions. Scholars may not find McCartney's discussion convincing because of the premises of his argument, but it may open the way for new views on Waugh. (A)

McDonnell, Jacqueline. *Waugh on Women.* New York: St. Martin's, 1986. McDonnell plays the role of detective in "identifying" the real-life women who served as models for the characters in Waugh's fiction. McConnell comments that most of the women characters display limited intelligence and that the attractive females are portrayed as "bitches." It is further revealed that Lady Marchmain's eyes are so blue that "she doesn't need eyeshadow." This is good bedside reading for Waugh lovers. (A,G)

Stannard, Martin. *Evelyn Waugh: The Early Years, 1903-1939.* New York: Norton, 1987. In this first volume of a projected two-volume study, Stannard covers the life up to *Brideshead Revisited.* He draws on letters, interviews, and diaries to add much firsthand information. This is a readable account that will interest the casual reader as much as the serious student. (A,G)

Other Sources
Davis, Robert M. *Evelyn Waugh, Apprentice.* Norman, OK: Pilgrim, 1985.

Davis, Robert M., *et al.,* eds. *A Bibliography of Evelyn Waugh.* Troy, NY: Whitston, 1986.

Doyle, Paul A. *A Reader's Companion to the Novels and Short Stories of Evelyn Waugh.* Norman, OK: Pilgrim, 1989.

McDonnell, Jacqueline. *Evelyn Waugh.* New York: St. Martin's, 1988.

Morris, Margaret, and D. J. Dooley. *Evelyn Waugh: A Reference Guide.* Boston: G. K. Hall, 1984.

Stannard, Martin, ed. *Evelyn Waugh: The Critical Heritage.* New York: Routledge Chapman & Hall, 1984.

H. G. WELLS
1866-1946

Evaluation of Selected Biography and Criticism

Anderson, Linda R. *Bennett, Wells, and Conrad: Narrative in Transition.* New York: St. Martin's, 1988. Anderson maintains that between 1890 and 1910 ideas about the nature of fiction were undergoing a major change, which led Bennett, Wells, and Conrad to redefine the relationship of the novel to reality. One result of this change was the incorporation of many of the unsavory aspects of life into the novel; another was a growing moral concern over the effects of confronting the darker side of life. Anderson develops this theme through her discussions of the major novels of these writers. This is a valuable study to those interested in the transition from the Victorian to the modern novel. (A,G)

Batchelor, John. *H. G. Wells.* Cambridge: Cambridge University Press, 1985. Batchelor argues that, although Wells' initial success and lasting reputation are based on his early science fiction novels, he was seriously interested in fiction as social critique. Batchelor contends that Wells' fiction falls into three distinct periods: science fiction (*The Time Machine, The Island of Dr. Moreau,* and *The War of the Worlds*), novels that set out to contribute to the art of fiction (*Love and Mr. Lewisham* and *Kipp*), and novels of social criticism (*Tono-Bungay, Ann Veronica,* and *The History of Mr. Polly*). Batchelor believes that *Mr. Polly* is one of the best works of the Edwardian decade. (A,G)

Draper, Michael. *H. G. Wells.* New York: St. Martin's, 1988. This 132-page general introduction to Wells begins with a biographical sketch, then moves to an overview of his philosophy of life and his concept of utopia. Draper characterizes Wells as a "philosophical desperado" whose influences included Plato; the anti-Christian periodical, *Freethinker;* and the classics, *Gulliver's Travels, Candide,* and *Rasselas.* Draper sees Wells' short stories as the early working out of his disillusionment with society before recreating a more acceptable social system in his science fiction novels. This slight study moves at break-neck pace through Wells' canon and leaves the reader with the impression that a comet just whizzed by. (G)

Hammond, J. R. *H. G. Wells and the Modern Novel.* New York: St. Martin's, 1988. Wells' reputation has risen and fallen many times. He has been hailed as one of the first modernists, as well as criticized for being an old-fashioned realist. Hammond, who has written three books on Wells, argues here that Wells was an experimental writer who broke new ground with "didactic fictions" in a sub-genre that Hammond terms the "dialogue novel." Hammond argues that Wells was better informed, cleverer, and more intelligent than most of his peers, including Kipling, Joyce, and Lawrence.

Readers may heartily disagree with Hammond's laudatory analysis of an out-of-fashion writer, but they will also find fresh ideas for a reappraisal. (A,G)

Seymour, Miranda. *A Ring of Conspirators: Henry James and His Literary Circle, 1895-1915*. Boston: Houghton Mifflin, 1989. The godfather of literature during the opening decades of the twentieth century, James attracted the best and the brightest writers to his estate in Rye. He especially attracted Americans who were either expatriates or temporarily enchanted by the wonders of the European intelligentsia. Seymour recreates this world and the band of gypsy writers who inhabited it, including Joseph Conrad, H. G. Wells, Ford Madox Ford, Edith Wharton, and Stephen Crane. This delightful and readable biography is sound in scholarship and is valuable to anyone studying any of these writers, the period, or the development of modern fiction. (A,G)

Smith, David C. *H. G. Wells: Desperately Mortal—A Biography*. New Haven: Yale University Press, 1986. Fifteen years in the making, this is probably the most important critical biography of Wells to appear in recent years. Smith brings a massive amount of information to bear on his subject and discusses everything of importance that Wells produced. Smith's judgments of Wells and his writings are often provocative and "beyond the pale" of accepted criticism. But he cannot be accused of avoiding the issues, and all future Wells scholarship must take his opinions into consideration, whether in agreement or dissent. Recommended for scholars and for the general reader. (A,G)

Other Sources

Crossley, Robert. *Reader's Guide to H. G. Wells*. Mercer Island, WA: Starmont House, 1986.

Geduld, Harry M. *The Definitive Time Machine: A Critical Edition of H. G. Wells's Scientific Romance with Introduction and Notes*. Bloomington: Indiana University Press, 1987.

Scheick, William, and J. Randolph Cox. *H. G. Wells: A Reference Guide*. Boston: G. K. Hall, 1988.

Stableford, Brian. *Scientific Romance in Britain Eighteen Ninety to Nineteen Fifty*. New York: St. Martin's, 1985.

West, Anthony. *H. G. Wells: Aspects of a Life*. New York: Random House, 1984.

EUDORA WELTY
1909

Author's Recent Bibliography
Photographs, 1989 (photographs).

Evaluation of Selected Criticism
Bloom, Harold, ed. *Eudora Welty*. New York: Chelsea House, 1986. An introduction by Bloom places the works of Eudora Welty in critical context and describes the themes and concerns of the twenty essays in this anthology. These essays discuss important themes and issues in Welty's works and represent a range of theories and perspectives. This collection is useful as an introduction to Welty's critical reputation. (A,G)

Devlin, Albert, ed. *Welty: A Life in Literature*. Jackson: University Press of Mississippi, 1987. This collection of essays, reminiscences, and interviews provides a new look at Welty's life and the significance of her art. Devlin examines several well-known novels in detail—*Delta Wedding, The Golden Apples*, and *The Optimist's Daughter*. Most useful are essays that examine lesser-known short stories, such as "Powerhouse," "Old Mr. Marblehall," and "At the Landing." The quality of the material and the range of critical approaches, together with excellent bibliographies of primary and secondary sources, make this anthology the best that is currently available. (A,G)

Manning, Carol S. *With Ears Opening Like Morning Glories: Eudora Welty and the Love of Storytelling*. Westport, CT: Greenwood, 1985. Recent criticism has tended to place more emphasis on Welty's essential "southerness" than was previously acknowledged. This study examines, in particular, her fondness for the grand old southern tradition for storytelling and reveals how various storytelling techniques inform her works. Manning also looks at how Welty uses her stories to analyze regional attitudes and to interpret the "southern myth." (A,G)

Trouard, Dawn, ed. *Eudora Welty: Eye of the Storyteller*. Kent, OH: Kent State University Press, 1990. This is a collection of sixteen essays presented at conferences during 1987. They are grouped roughly into four general headings: "Language and Culture," "Women," "Visible Connections," and "Endurance and Change." Woven into the various topics are analyses of Welty's stories. Those on some of the lesser known stories are the only ones in print. Though generally a weak collection, these essays do provide some new ideas for insiders who know Welty's work. (A)

Turner, W. Craig, and Lee Harding, eds. *Critical Essays on Eudora Welty*. Boston: G. K. Hall, 1989. This collection ranges from brief reviews to analyses of individual works. All nine of Welty's fictional works are discussed, most by more than one critic. Of particular value is Robert Penn Warren's "The Love and the Separateness in Miss Welty." The introduction provides an overview of current Welty scholarship and an assessment of her critical reputation. Recommended as an introductory study. **(A,G)**

Vande Kieft, Ruth M. *Eudora Welty*. Boston: Twayne, 1987. This revised and enlarged edition of a study originally published in 1962 provides excellent explications of Welty's short stories and novels. Vande Kieft identifies the controlling themes and techniques and illustrates how Welty employs recurring motifs. This exemplary piece of scholarship and criticism will greatly assist advanced students and researchers. **(A)**

Westling, Louise. *Sacred Groves and Ravaged Gardens: The Fiction of Eudora Welty, Carson McCullers, and Flannery O'Connor*. Athens: University of Georgia Press, 1985. Original and provocative interpretations characterize this study of the fiction of three prominent southern women writers. Focusing on problems of identity, relationships with mothers and with men, and the use of symbolism, Westling argues that Welty "celebrates" her feminine identity while both McCullers and O'Connor struggle against it. By accepting her identity, Welty gains access to the depths of her emotional and psychological resources, while McCullers and O'Connor become increasingly disconnected from feminine wholeness. **(A,G)**

Other Sources

Marrs, Suzanne. *The Welty Collection: A Guide to the Eudora Welty Manuscripts and Documents at the Mississippi Department of Archives and History*. Jackson: University Press of Mississippi, 1988.

Westling, Louise. *Eudora Welty*. Savage, MD: Barnes & Noble, 1989.

NATHANAEL WEST
1903-1940

Evaluation of Selected Criticism

Bloom, Harold, ed. *Nathanael West's "Miss Lonelyhearts."* New York: Chelsea House, 1987. This terrifying novel published in 1933 has evoked critical responses ranging from Freudianism to nihilism. The eminent scholars whose essays are collected here provide a lively interpretation of the psychological, social, and stylistic forces that shape West's masterpiece. A convenient volume for students reading the novel. (A,G)

Bloom, Harold, ed. *Nathanael West.* New York: Chelsea House, 1986. This anthology collects a wide range of critical opinion on West's fiction. Bloom considers the novels as a "wild medley of magnificent writing and inadequate writing, except in *Miss Lonelyhearts,* which excels *The Sun Also Rises, The Great Gatsby,* and even *Sanctuary* as the perfected instance of a negative vision in modern American fiction." Bloom's collection contains fourteen essays, including those by W. H. Auden, R. W. B. Lewis, T. R. Steiner, Max Appel, and James Light. A good introduction for students of West. (A,G)

Gorak, Jan. *God the Artist: American Novelists in a Post-Realist Age.* Champaign: University of Illinois Press, 1987. Gorak's study attempts to trace the idea of the artist as a "godly" maker of worlds in the work of three twentieth-century novelists: West, Hawkes, and Barth. He argues that the ubiquity of this conception among artists has weakened its force and rendered it little more than an excuse for linguistic gamesmanship. Gorak argues that West's fiction shows the predicament of the artist in modern society: he is "trapped in illusion-making machinery he can no longer control." A valuable critical study for students of the modern novel. (A,G)

Long, Robert Emmet. *Nathanael West.* New York: Frederick Ungar, 1985. West died young, leaving a slender body of work, including four novels. Long provides a biographical introduction, then examines each of the novels in turn—*The Dream Life of Balso Snell, Miss Lonelyhearts, A Cool Million,* and *The Day of the Locust.* Long offers detailed plot summaries and examines West's themes and techniques in view of his literary precedents. This volume includes extensive notes and a selected bibliography. (A,G)

EDITH WHARTON
1862-1937

Autobiographical Sources

Lewis, R. W. B., and Nancy Lewis. *The Letters of Edith Wharton.* New York: Scribner, 1988. Compiled by one of the most revered scholars of our time, these four hundred of the four thousand extant letters, many never-before published, span five decades and three continents. The letters are divided chronologically into seven sections and include many directed to such literary notables as Henry James, William Dean Howells, Sarah Orne Jewett, and Sinclair Lewis. The picture of Wharton that emerges is that of a prolific writer who battled social disapproval and emerged as a courageous intellectual whose emerging, improving literary reputation is well deserved. R. W. B. Lewis won a Pulitzer Prize in 1975 for his biography of Wharton. (A,G)

Powers, Lydall H. *Henry James and Edith Wharton: Letters 1900-1915.* New York: Scribner, 1990. In periods of deep depression in 1909 and again in 1915, a year before his death, James burned his personal papers, including much of his voluminous correspondence. Wharton, however, kept hers, and of the estimated four hundred letters that passed between them, the 180 that are known to exist are collected in this volume. The subjects range from literary analysis of James' novels to Wharton's seeking advice about her ill-fated marriage to William Morton Fullerton. The letters display a rich and complex exchange of frank views and tempered passions. James played the confidant for Wharton, who provided the writer with sustained and intimate friendship. Here is a glimpse of the mutually supportive relationship that existed between these two expatriates. (A,G)

Evaluation of Selected Criticism

Donovan, Josephine. *After the Fall: The Demeter-Persephone Myth in Wharton, Cather, and Glasgow.* University Park: The Pennsylvania State University Press, 1989. Donovan contends that the "Demeter-Diana-Persephone script" is preeminent in the literature of American women writers of the late nineteenth and early twentieth centuries. For Donovan, Persephone represents the "daughters" (feminine consciousness) that are whisked away into "patriarchal captivity." The Demeter-Diana world is related to the women's culture of the Victorian era, characterized by a marginal, segregated, "male-less" web of romantic female friendships. Donovan explores her thesis by devoting a section on each of the writers she feels most fully expresses the myth —Wharton, Cather, and Glasgow. (A)

Fryer, Judith. *Felicitous Space: The Imaginative Structures of Edith Wharton and Willa Cather.* Chapel Hill: University of North Carolina Press, 1986. The concept of "imaginative space" is derived from French phenomenologists

Gaston Bachelard and Maurice Meleau-Ponty. In this study, Fryer examines the types of spatial ordering that "rendered comfort and security" to Edith Wharton and Willa Cather. Wharton preferred ordered space as reflected by the function-defined rooms of a house. Cather preferred "geographical" spaces, a more loosely related set of landmarks related by a mental-imaginative map. This insightful work is a good introduction to a French critical approach that has only recently managed to cross the Atlantic. (A,G)

Goodwyn, Janet. *Edith Wharton: Traveller in the Land of Letters.* New York: St. Martin's, 1990. Goodwyn groups Wharton's novels by the country of their settings: Italy, France, and the U.S.—and discusses the cultural context of each. Novels receiving full treatments are *The House of Mirth, The Mother's Recompense, A Backward Glance,* and *The Age of Innocence.* Although not a ground-breaking approach, this lucid study provides a very useful context for understanding Wharton's cosmopolitan sensibilities. (A,G)

Kaplan, Amy. *The Social Construction of American Realism.* Chicago: University of Chicago Press, 1988. In this study of American realists, Kaplan focuses on the works of Howells, Wharton, and Dreiser and stresses their relation to the social changes of the late-1800s. Kaplan challenges recent feminist criticism by describing Wharton as a professional writer in conflict with women writers with a more popular appeal. She examines Dreiser's conception of art as commodity. Kaplan's arguments are well-documented and persuasively developed. (A,G)

Schulman, Robert. *Social Criticism and Nineteenth-Century American Fictions.* Columbia: University of Missouri Press, 1987. Schulman examines the political psychology of capitalism and its influence on the lives and works of some of the most famous American authors—Wharton, Franklin, Twain, Melville, Hawthorne, Chesnutt, Whitman, Howells, and Dreiser. His study pursues three main themes—the fragmentation of community, the impact of social change, and the styles of American individualism. In his discussion of Franklin's *Autobiography,* Schulman describes the costs of success and upward mobility as emotional deadening, increased isolation, and personal fragmentation. A truly new and refreshing reevaluation of nineteenth-century American literature. (A,G)

Seymour, Miranda. *A Ring of Conspirators: Henry James and His Literary Circle, 1895-1915.* Boston: Houghton Mifflin, 1989. The godfather of literature during the opening decades of the twentieth century, James attracted the best and the brightest writers to his estate in Rye. He especially attracted Americans who were either expatriates or temporarily enchanted by the wonders of the European intelligentsia. Seymour recreates this world and the band of gypsy writers who inhabited it, including Joseph Conrad, H. G. Wells, Ford Madox Ford, Edith Wharton, and Stephen Crane. (A,G)

PHILLIS WHEATLEY
1753-1784

Evaluation of Selected Criticism
Shields, John C., ed. *The Collected Works of Phillis Wheatley.* New York: Oxford University Press, 1988. Wheatley's importance as a black American writer and her influence on the women's literary tradition has been underestimated, partly because the context of her achievements has been obscured by shifting literary sensibilities. Phillis Wheatley's *Poems on Various Subjects, Religious and Moral* was published in 1773, making it the first imaginative work published by a black in North America. For this edition Shields has augmented the small body of extant poetry with several recently discovered poems. All known texts and variants of fifty-five poems, twenty-two letters, and a prose prayer are included with appropriate annotation. An introductory essay discusses Wheatley's critical reception and the political context of her writing. **(A,G)**

Other Sources
Mason, Julian D. ed. *The Poems of Phillis Wheatley.* Chapel Hill: University of North Carolina Press, 1989.

WALT WHITMAN
1819-1892

Evaluation of Selected Biography and Criticism

Byers, Thomas. *What I Cannot Say: Self, Word, and World in Whitman, Stevens, and Merwin.* Champaign: University of Illinois Press, 1989. Byers examines the aesthetic, epistemological, metaphysical, and religious implications of the poetics of Whitman, Stevens, and Merwin. For Whitman poetry not only defines but constitutes a relation to the world. Stevens has less faith in the power of the word but affirms the human ability to create fictions within which to rejoice. Merwin reacts against Whitman's celebration of the self over the world by painting a bleaker portrait of relationship in *The Lice.* Byers combines a close reading of the poetry with an intertextuality influenced by phenomenology and semiotics. **(A)**

Cady, Edwin, and Louis Budd, eds. *On Whitman.* Durham, NC: Duke University Press, 1987. This anthology is the first in a series entitled "The Best from *American Literature*," which will reprint important critical articles from past issues of that magazine. These sixteen judiciously selected articles —many published more than twenty years ago—are still full of insights and witticisms and purport to offer the final word on Whitman and his works. **(A,G)**

Cavitch, David. *My Soul and I: The Inner Life of Walt Whitman.* Boston: Beacon, 1985. In this psycho-biographical study of *Leaves of Grass,* Cavitch examines Whitman's power and ability to "interpret the world." Following a summary of Whitman's childhood and early education, Cavitch analyzes the poetry in the light of Whitman's biography. He considers each of the poems of the cycle in turn, often drawing new insights. He contends that Whitman's poetry declined precipitously after 1859. **(A,G)**

Donoghue, Denis. *Reading America: Essays on American Literature.* New York: Knopf, 1987. Noted Irish literary critic Donoghue turns his critical eye on American writers in this collection of nine essays and seventeen book reviews. Each of the longer pieces—on Dickinson, Thoreau, Trilling, Whitman, Henry Adams, Emerson, Henry James, and Stevens—is prefaced by a discussion of the writer's moral and rhetorical intentions. Donoghue has a dedicated following of serious-minded readers who swear by his awesome insights. Others may have difficulty working through the details to reach the payoff. **(A)**

Hutchinson, George B. *The Ecstatic Whitman: Literary Shamanism and the Crisis of the Union.* Columbus: Ohio State University Press, 1986. Hutchinson applies a cross-cultural analysis to Whitman's life and works, comparing his personality and visionary ecstasies with the character and roles of a Siberian shaman. The theory is intriguing and well-presented, although not all of the analogies are convincing. He has shown that shamanism can be invoked to account for the blend of styles in Whitman's poetry, his preoccupation with death, his identification with the sick and wounded, and his desire to heal the rift of the Civil War. This is more of a study, however, of shamanistic impulses continuing in modern man than a rigorous analysis of Whitman's work. (A,G)

Killingsworth, M. Jimmie. *Whitman's Poetry of the Body: Sexuality, Politics, and the Text.* Chapel Hill: University of North Carolina Press, 1989. In this thorough and challenging study, Killingsworth addresses the complex issue of sexuality in Whitman's life and works. Whitman's use of sexual imagery has been variously interpreted as immature lust and as a sophisticated metaphor of social and political interactions. To examine the complexity, Killingsworth establishes a nineteenth-century context for Whitman's attitudes toward homosexuality and heterosexuality. Although certainly not the last word on the subject, this study is the finest existing treatment of Whitman's sexuality and poetics. (A,G)

Larson, Kerry C. *Whitman's Drama of Consensus.* Chicago, University of Chicago Press, 1988. Working from literary history seen through the lens of poststructuralist theory, Larson develops a "unified field" theory to explain the themes and motifs of Whitman's *Leaves of Grass.* He sees Whitman as "transacting" with the reader, alternately reaching out to forge a group identity and withdrawing to maintain an individual identity. The poet's personal tensions and oppositions reflect a national conflict of unity and dissolution. Whitman strives for "consensus" on all levels. This hope for agreement and acceptance turns to despair in Whitman's later writings. (A,G)

Orvell, Miles. *The Real Thing: Imitation and Authenticity in American Culture, 1880-1940.* Chapel Hill: University of North Carolina Press, 1989. With a notable depth and breadth of scholarship, Orvell examines the inter-relationships between material culture, photography, and literature during a sixty-year period of American history. This study is especially strong in three areas: the cultural importance of Walt Whitman, the impact of photography on literature, and the changing perception of the machine and its role in society. Whitman is seen as the progenitor of a generation of modern creative artists who are intent on reflecting authentic American life. (A,G)

Schulman, Robert. *Social Criticism and Nineteenth-Century American Fictions.* Columbia: University of Missouri Press, 1987. Schulman examines the political psychology of capitalism and its influence on the lives and works of some of the most famous American authors—Whitman, Franklin, Twain, Melville, Hawthorne, Chesnutt, Wharton, Howells, and Dreiser. His study pursues three main themes—the fragmentation of community, the impact of social change, and the styles of American individualism. In his discussion of Franklin's *Autobiography,* Schulman describes the high costs of success and upward mobility as emotional deadening, increased isolation, and personal fragmentation. A truly new and refreshing reevaluation of nineteenth-century American literature. **(A,G)**

Thomas, M. Wynn. *The Lunar Light of Whitman's Poetry.* Cambridge: Harvard University Press, 1987. Welsh scholar Thomas brings an objective eye to Whitman's vision of America and its ideals. Whitman was profoundly influenced by his experiences with the "common man" during the Civil War. In individual acts of long-suffering heroism, he saw the true promise of what America could and should become after the war to save the Union was won. In consequence, he became obsessed with unearthing the flaws of the national character, the darker side of American reality. This dichotomy, according to Thomas, provided the impetus for some of Whitman's greatest poetry. Thomas does not dwell on Whitman's inner struggle but emphasizes the strength of his poetry and its ability to capture the essence of his vision. Considered the best Whitman study to appear in years, this study is highly recommended. **(A,G)**

Other Sources
Allen, C. W. *Walt Whitman Poet, Philosopher.* Brunswick, ME: Bern Porter, 1985.

Allen, C. W. *Walt Whitman Abroad.* Brunswick, ME: Bern Porter, 1985.

Allen, Gay W. *The New Walt Whitman Handbook.* New York: New York University Press, 1987.

Berthold, Dennis, and Kenneth M. Price, eds. *Dear Brother Walt: The Letters of Thomas Jefferson Whitman.* Kent, OH: Kent State University Press, 1984.

Erkkila, Betsy. *Whitman the Political Poet.* New York: Oxford University Press, 1989.

Gardner, Thomas. *Discovering Ourselves in Whitman: The Contemporary American Long Poem.* Champaign: University of Illinois Press, 1989.

Kreig, Joan P., ed. *Walt Whitman: Here and Now.* Westport, CT: Greenwood, 1985.

Kuebrich, David. *Minor Prophecy: Walt Whitman's New American Religion.* Bloomington: Indiana University Press, 1989.

Miller, Edwin Haviland, ed. *Walt Whitman's "Song of Myself": A Mosaic of Interpretations.* Iowa City: University of Iowa Press, 1989.

Moore, Geoffrey. *The Great Poets: Walt Whitman.* New York: Potter Books/Crown, 1987.

Porter, Peter, and Geoffrey Moore, eds. *Walt Whitman.* New York: Potter/Crown, 1988.

Pucciani, Oreste F. *The Literary Reputation of Walt Whitman in France.* New York: Garland, 1987.

Tapscott, Stephen. *American Beauty: William Carlos Williams and the Tradition of the Modernist Whitman.* New York: Columbia University Press, 1984.

Walker, Jeffrey. *Bardic Ethos and the American Epic Poem: Whitman, Pound, Crane, Williams, Olson.* Baton Rouge: Louisiana State University Press, 1989.

OSCAR WILDE
1854-1900

Autobiographical Sources

Smith, Philip E., and Michael S. Helfand, eds. *Oscar Wilde's Oxford Notebooks: A Portrait of the Mind in the Making.* London: Oxford University Press, 1988. The title reflects the editors' belief that these journals provide an important source for tracing the development of Wilde's literary imagination. But to do this, one must extrapolate and conjecture from Wilde's pompously academic musings, quotations, paraphrases of other writers, and random observations. The editors' commentary is valuable in putting the notebook into perspective, and will be of some use to scholars. **(A)**

Evaluation of Selected Biography and Criticism

Ellman, Richard. *Oscar Wilde.* New York: Knopf, 1988. Veteran biographer Ellman (*James Joyce*) reexamines and practically dismantles the reigning Wilde legends, building his case on heretofore unearthed facts and anecdotes. The man that is revealed turns out to be more interesting than the legends. The life-events are well selected and vividly described. The image that emerges of Wilde is that of a towering, but tragically flawed individual. This work has been praised by critics and scholars and surely will be the definitive Wilde biography for some time to come. **(A,G)**

Ellmann, Richard. *Four Dubliners: Wilde, Yeats, Joyce, and Beckett.* New York: Braziller, 1987. With his usual elegance and clarity, Ellmann discusses the lives and works of four Irish writers who shaped the character of twentieth-century literature. Although these authors have significant differences, Ellmann concentrates on their commonalities: the desire to transform language and literature, the need to establish autonomy, a preoccupation with inner conflicts, and an insistence on remaining Irish in spite of living as expatriates. This is a splendid introduction for new readers to their lives and works. Highly recommended. **(A,G)**

Gagnier, Regenia. *Idylls of the Marketplace: Oscar Wilde and the Victorian Public.* Stanford, CA: Stanford University Press, 1986. Moving away from personal psychology and textual autonomy, this study dissects the social institutions within which Wilde developed his art forms. According to Gagnier, discerning the relevant "historical discourse" of Wilde's works allows one to relate the works to discernible audiences. This approach does provide many stunning insights, particularly in terms of Wilde's prose styles. He used two such styles—one of wit and critique for a general audience, a second of "jeweled seduction" to attract a more specialized audience. Special attention is paid to the scandal provoked by *The Picture of Dorian Gray.* Gagnier does an excellent job in analyzing the forms of expression in *Salome* and *The Ballad of Reading Gaol.* **(A)**

Raby, Peter. *Oscar Wilde*. Cambridge: Cambridge University Press, 1988. This is a solid, comprehensive introduction to the life and works of Wilde, providing a balanced assessment of his achievements and scandals. Emphasizing the drama, Raby interweaves the works with the life while providing background on the stage history of the famous plays. A good beginning for general readers and students. **(A,G)**

THORNTON WILDER
1897-1975

Autobiographical Sources

Gallup, Donald. *The Journals of Thornton Wilder, 1939-1961*. New Haven: Yale University Press, 1985. This selection, culled from over a thousand manuscript pages in two journals, provides an intimate look at the thoughts and preoccupations of Wilder during the most productive period of his career. Throughout these entries, Wilder discourses on the psychological motivations of people, offers critical observations of literary works, discusses sex, religion, and politics, among numerous topics. The influence of Freud is pervasive. Although Wilder rarely used these journals to work out drafts of his plays, these materials do include two scenes from an unfinished play, entitled *The Emporium*. Wilder's sister, Isabel, provides a biographical introduction, and Gallup provides annotations when necessary. This is an essential primary source for anyone interested in the life and writings of Wilder. (A,G)

Evaluation of Selected Criticism

Castronovo, David. *Thornton Wilder*. New York: Crossroad/Ungar/ Continuum, 1986. Castronovo's study follows the format of Ungar's American writers series: chronology, brief biography, a discussion of major works and themes, and a bibliographical selection. This is a useful book for the student or general reader who wants a quick and fair overview of the life and works of a complex and ambitious writer. (A,G)

Other Sources

Newlin, Jeanne T. *Our Town on Stage: The Original Promptbook in Facsimile*. Cambridge: Harvard University Press, 1988.

TENNESSEE WILLIAMS
1911-1983

Autobiographical Sources

Devlin, Albert J. *Conversations with Tennessee Williams*. Jackson: University Press of Mississippi, 1986. This collection of conversations by such feisty reviewers as Rex Reed, Tom Buckley, William Burroughs, and William Inge, reveals less about Williams' art and life than about his personality. Although not a valuable research tool, this volume will surely add to the mystique surrounding Williams' controversial life. (G)

Evaluation of Selected Criticism

Boxill, Roger. *Tennessee Williams*. New York: St. Martin's, 1987. This study tracks patterns of thematic interrelatedness among Williams' plays and other writings. Following the concepts of Eric Bentley, Boxill provides objective summaries of important works that produce implicit insights and analysis. Boxill is strongest when searching out highly original connections between seemingly disparate passages and weakest when discussing Williams' sexual orientation in terms of stereotypes. (A,G)

Norse, Harold. *Memoirs of a Bastard Angel*. New York: William Morrow, 1989. In this no-holds-barred autobiography, Harold Norse describes his acquaintance and encounters with many of the major figures of twentieth century "bohemian" literature—Tennessee Williams, W. H. Auden, James Baldwin, William Burroughs, Anais Nin, Ezra Pound, and others. This is arresting reading for students of the period. (A,G)

Presley, Delma E. *The Glass Menagerie: An American Memory*. Boston: Twayne, 1990. This enthusiastic appreciation of the durability and achievement of Williams' most-performed play provides insights into the American theatrical psyche. This is a good source for beginning students learning about Williams or theatre. (G)

Rader, Dotson. *Tennessee: Cry of the Heart*. New York: Doubleday. Long-time friend and companion of Williams', Rader recounts the lively, wild times as well as the period of Williams' physical and artistic decline. He captures an intimate portrait of Williams' torment, and if this biography revels in sensational details, it nonetheless explains much about Williams' obsessions and motivations. (A,G)

Rasky, Harry. *Tennessee Williams: A Portrait in Laughter and Lamentation*. New York: Dodd, Mead, 1986. Rasky has produced a personal memoir that details his encounters with Williams while the two worked together on the film, *Tennessee Williams' South*. Rasky was obviously profoundly influenced by Williams, but his view adds little more than anecdotes to our understanding of the playwright. (G)

Spivey, Ted Ray. *Revival: Southern Writers in the Modern City.* Gainesville: University Presses of Florida, 1986. Spivey sets out to correct the belief that southern writers are exclusively steeped in rural culture by selecting a group who came to terms with the modern city. He discusses the attitudes and adaptations of playwright Williams, poets Ransom, Tate, and Aiken, and novelists Faulkner, Wolfe, Ellison, O'Connor, and Percy. Although compelled to address the issues of southern "decadence and decline," Spivey also demonstrates how many of these writers offered a vision of how to integrate old values with new social structures, allowing the past to reanimate the present. (A,G)

Thompson, Judith. *Tennessee Williams' Plays: Memory, Myth, and Symbol.* Lawrence: University of Kansas, 1988. Thompson's fascinating thesis is that Williams established a pattern of memory that is transformed into myth and enacted as ritual. Her introduction explains the pattern and ensuing chapters apply the theory. This study is highly recommended for readers or playgoers, as well as drama students and directors. (A,G)

Vannatta, Dennis. *Tennessee Williams: A Study of the Short Fiction.* Boston: Twayne, 1988. For the first book-length study of Williams' short fiction, Vannatta has selected what appear to be the most significant works. He carefully summarizes the plots, characterization, and major themes of each piece. Williams is characterized as a "southern gothic homosexual writer," but Vannatta is so out of touch with the issues of the gay community that he can only generalize about Williams' contributions. On the "gothic" portion of the description, he does a better job of showing how Williams stands in that tradition. (A,G)

Other Sources
Bigsby, C. W. *A Critical Introduction to Twentieth-Century American Drama, Volume 2: Tennessee Williams, Arthur Miller, Edward Albee.* New York: Cambridge University Press, 1985.

Schroeder, Patricia R. *The Presence of the Past in Modern American Drama.* Madison, NJ: Fairleigh Dickinson University Press, 1989.

Shaland, Irene. *Tennessee Williams on the Soviet Stage.* Lanham, MD: University Press of America, 1987.

Spoto, Donald. *The Kindness of Strangers: The Life of Tennessee Williams.* Boston: Little, Brown, 1985.

Windham, Donald. *Lost Friendships: A Memoir of Truman Capote, Tennessee Williams and Others.* New York: Morrow, 1987.

WILLIAM CARLOS WILLIAMS
1883-1963

Evaluation of Author's Recent Bibliography

MacGowan, Christopher, ed. *The Collected Poems of William Carlos Williams, Volume 1: 1909-1939*. New York: New Directions, 1986. This series represents the first full collection of Williams' poetry and contains at least one hundred poems that had not been previously compiled. The poems are arranged chronologically, rather than thematically, which allows a sense of context and continuity to develop. Modernist scholars Litz and MacGowan provide nearly eighty pages of useful annotations, which are essential for any student of Williams' poetry. **(A)**

MacGowan, Christopher, ed. *The Collected Poems of William Carlos Williams. Vol. 2: 1939-1962*. New York: New Directions, 1988. With eighty-nine pages of annotations, notes, textual variations, and biographical notes related to the poems, this final edition of the collected works is an essential reference for any student of Williams. **(A)**

Autobiographical Sources

Witemeyer, Hugh. *William Carlos Williams and James Laughlin: Selected Letters*. New York: Norton, 1989. Laughlin's New Directions Press provided an outlet for experimental work beginning in 1936, publishing such authors as Pound and Williams. This collection of letters between author and publisher documents the growth of mutual respect between two strong-willed personalities. Also revealed are Williams' developing views of his poetry, its intention and purpose. The collection is fully annotated by Witemeyer who provides information on people and events in the poet's life. **(A)**

Evaluation of Selected Biography and Criticism

Baldwin, Neil. *To All Gentleness: William Carlos Williams, the Doctor-Poet*. New York: Atheneum, 1984. Written in a novelistic style, Baldwin's imaginative biography of Williams attempts to reconstruct crucial events and scenes of his life. Some will be put off by what often seems to be sheer "mind-reading," and it is difficult to know which vignettes are invented and which are documented because only the quotes are footnoted. The poems are quoted profusely but only as a backdrop for the hectic events of the doctor's life. This style of biography seems aimed at the young adult reader. Students will demand more methodological rigor than Baldwin provides. **(G,Y)**

Breslin, E. B., ed. *Something to Say: William Carlos Williams on Younger Poets*. New York: New Directions, 1985. Williams was exceedingly generous in his efforts to help younger poets, and he frequently provided criticism and wrote letters of introduction, recommendations, prefaces, and reviews. In his enthusiasm to help, he often inflated a poet's achievement, and he was more favorably disposed toward poetry that sounded like his own, but for whatever demerits he earned for nepotism, these writings say much about his sense of contemporary poetry and his love of the art form. (A)

Coles, Robert. *That Red Wheelbarrow: Selected Literary Essays.* Iowa City: University of Iowa Press, 1988. Harvard professor Coles brings psychiatric insights to bear upon a selection of his favorite authors. Often pedantic in tone, the essays nevertheless are well constructed. Several pieces examine the anti-intellectual tendencies that were shared by Flannery O'Connor, William Carlos Williams, and James Agee. Also included is a rather clinical assessment of Ezra Pound's supposed insanity. (A)

Cushman, Stephen. *William Carlos Williams and the Meanings of Measure.* New Haven: Yale University Press, 1985. Williams' own pronouncements on the topic of metrics were contradictory and murky at best. In this specialized study, Cushman attempts to tease out the facts of Williams' metrics. He analyzes Williams' use of enjambment, typographical experimentation, and tropes. Cushman also establishes a closer link between the works of Williams and Emerson than has previously been acknowledged. (A)

Dickie, Margaret. *On the Modernist Long Poem.* Iowa City: University of Iowa Press, 1986. Dickie contends that by extending their "personal imagist pieces" into the extended "public" long poem, modernist poets redefined the shape and direction of their movement. In this study, which is, in effect, a history of the development of modernism, Dickie examines the formal problems faced by Williams (*Paterson*), Eliot (*The Waste Land*), Crane (*The Bridge*), and Pound (*The Cantos*). This study would be most useful for teachers and students who are seeking a framework for discussion of these complex works. (A)

Driscoll, Kerry. *William Carlos Williams and the Maternal Muse.* Ann Arbor: UMI Research Press, 1987. Although Williams' view of women has been explored by numerous biographers and critics, Driscoll discovers a wealth of previously unexamined material in the poetry that reflects Williams' conflicting attitudes towards women. She postulates that Williams' difficult relationship with his mother created sexual identity problems. She argues that the polarities of their relationship are reflected in his dual portrayal of women as wholesome or tainted. Driscoll provides enlightening readings of some of the poetry, particularly *Kora in Hell* and *Paterson*. (A)

Duffey, Bernard. *A Poetry of Presence: The Writing of William Carlos Williams.* Madison: University of Wisconsin Press, 1986. Basing much of his analysis on the critical work of Kenneth Burke, Duffey examines William Carlos Williams' ability to evoke the immediacy of the moment. Works are explicated in terms of five interlocking concepts—scenes, agents, agencies, purposes, and acts. At times unnecessarily abstract, Duffey is at his best when examining specific poems. (A,G)

Gish, Robert. *William Carlos Williams: A Study of the Short Fiction.* Boston: Twayne, 1989. Although Williams published four collections of fine short stories, his impact on redefining American poetry has overshadowed his prose achievement, and until now no full-length study of the fiction existed. Gish applies Williams' theory of language to representative stories in all four collections. The book reprints Williams' fascinating *Paris Review* interview, and concludes with a few essays by prominent Williams critics. Includes a chronology and selected bibliography. (A)

Kallet, Marilyn. *Honest Simplicity in William Carlos Williams' "Asphodel, That Greeny Flower."* Baton Rouge: Louisiana State University Press, 1985. Kallet examines Williams' later poetry in order to reveal the poet's underlying humanity. The core of the study is an explication of "Asphodel, That Greeny Flower." Kallet approaches her subject with a sentimentality that is often at odds with her critical method. She focuses closely on Williams' personal and physical weaknesses and their influence on the poetry, often to the detriment of broader issues of historical and literary context. The result is a study that offers a sensitive appreciation of the poem but contributes less to a critical understanding of it. (A,G)

Laughlin, James. *Random Essays.* Mount Kisco, NY: Moyer Bell, 1989. Essayist, poet, and publisher Laughlin offers a selection of criticism and personal reminiscences of many of the noted writers of our time, including Pound, William Carlos Williams, Stein, Saroyan, and Merton. Laughlin's opinions are insightful, direct, and useful for the scholar. Robert Giroux provides an introduction. (A)

Liebowitz, Herbert. *Fabricating Lives: Explorations in American Autobiography.* New York: Knopf, 1989. Liebowitz unearths unexpected character traits and suspect motivations in his examination of eight noted autobiographers, ranging from Benjamin Franklin to William Carlos Williams, whom he calls a "tricky equivocator." This study gets beneath the surface of what the autobiographer intended for his audience to perceive by closely comparing actions with words. (A)

Rapp, Carl. *William Carlos Williams and Romantic Idealism.* Hanover, NH: University Press of New England, 1984. Basing his premise on early poems and on the essay "Vortex," Rapp argues that Williams was an heir to the philosophical tradition of romantic idealism. Examining the poet's sources and influences from Keats to Whitman, Rapp describes a poet that is more contemplative, more philosophical, and less naive than is presently accepted. Although Rapp's terms are sometimes vaguely defined, his perspective sheds light on the later poems. (A)

554   William Carlos Williams

Rodgers, Audrey T. *Virgin and Whore: The Image of Women in the Poetry of William Carlos Williams.* Jefferson, NC: McFarland, 1987. Feminist readings of Williams' attitudes toward women have clearly established that while he liked and admired women, and while they became a primary element in his work, he nevertheless feared them. Rodgers sets out to understand Williams' conflicting and complex views of women, which she does by tracing the literary and historical figures of the virgin and the whore. Eventually, she connects these archetypes with Williams' mother and grandmother, and the dichotomy of imagination versus experience. This is an especially interesting study for readers interested in revisionist criticism. (A)

Schmidt, Peter. *William Carlos Williams, The Arts, and Literary Tradition.* Baton Rouge: Louisiana State University Press, 1988. Most recent criticism on Williams has been divided between two approaches: those critics who relate science and technology to his poetry and those who link him to modernism through painting. Schmidt attempts to broaden these narrowly focused approaches by showing more complex historical influences on Williams and his work. This is a thoroughly documented, scholarly work, but it also contains very accessible readings of some of the poems. Besides furthering the scope of Williams scholarship, this study is also appropriate for serious students. (A)

Steinman, Lisa M. *Made in America: Science, Technology, and American Modernist Poets.* New Haven: Yale University Press, 1987. This study examines how modernist poets—specifically, Williams, Moore, and Stevens—set out to rejuvenate poetry by redefining its relationship with the developing world of technology and commerce. To justify the virtues of "genteel verse," modernists stressed poetry's "technical" structure and virtues (its efficiency, for example) or associated poetry with the values of pure scientific research. This study is a valuable contribution to understanding the modernists, their cultural context, and their theories of poetics. (A,G)

Other Sources

Fisher-Wirth, Ann W. *William Carlos Williams and Autobiography: The Woods of His Own Nature.* University Park: The Pennsylvania State University Press, 1989.

Frail, David. *The Early Politics and Poetics of William Carlos Williams.* Ann Arbor: UMI Research Press, 1987.

Kutzinski, Vera M. *Against the American Grain: Myth and History in William Carlos Williams, Jay Wright and Nicholas Guillen.* Baltimore: Johns Hopkins University Press, 1986.

Mariani, Paul. *A Usable Past: Essays on Modern and Contemporary Poetry.* Amherst: University of Massachusetts Press, 1984.

Movius, Geoffrey H. *The Early Prose of William Carlos Williams, 1917-1925*. New York: Garland, 1987.

Tapscott, Stephen. *American Beauty: William Carlos Williams and the Tradition of the Modernist Whitman*. New York: Columbia University Press, 1984.

Walker, Jeffrey. *Bardic Ethos and the American Epic Poem: Whitman, Pound, Crane, Williams, Olson*. Baton Rouge: Louisiana State University Press, 1989.

Wilhelm, James J., and Richard Saez, eds. *A History That Includes the Self: Essays on the Poetry of Stefan George, Hugo von Hofmannsthal, William Carlos Williams, and Wallace Stevens*. New York: Garland, 1988.

SIR ANGUS WILSON
1913

Author's Recent Bibliography
Diversity and Depth in Fiction, 1984 (criticism); *Reflections in a Writer's Eye*, 1986 (travel).

Evaluation of Selected Criticism
Gardner, Averil. *Angus Wilson*. Boston: Twayne, 1985. Gardner provides a concise and objective analysis of the novels and short stories of Angus Wilson. She does not shy away from pointing out the flaws that she finds in Wilson, which makes this a more valuable book than other, more adulatory, efforts. This study should be examined in conjunction with Jay Halio's *Critical Essays on Angus Wilson* (1985). (A)

Kums, Guido. *Fiction, or the Language of Our Discontent: A Study of the Built-in Novelist in Novels by Angus Wilson, Lawrence Durrell, and Doris Lessing*. New York: Peter Lang, 1985. Kums contends that the use of the novelist as a character in a novel allows the author to comment theoretically on the process of writing in a way that is unique. He examines three works that feature novelist characters—Wilson's *No Laughing Matter*, Durrell's *Alexandria Quartet*, and Lessing's *The Golden Notebook*—finding parallels in the authors' perspectives on writing. This is a specialized study that attempts a radical reevaluation of the form and definition of the modern novel. (A)

Stape, J. H., and Anne Thomas. *Angus Wilson: A Bibliography, 1947-1987*. New York: Mansell Publishing, 1988. This bibliography of primary and secondary sources features a brief forward by Wilson himself. Over 1,200 reviews alone are listed. Dissertations are cataloged. None of the entries are annotated. (A)

Other Sources
McSweeney, Kerry, ed. *Diversity and Depth in Fiction: Selected Critical Writings of Angus Wilson*. New York: Viking, 1984.

THOMAS WOLFE
1900-1938

Evaluation of Selected Biography and Criticism

Doll, Mary A., and Clara Stites, eds. *In the Shadow of the Giant, Thomas Wolfe: Correspondence of Edward C. Aswell and Elizabeth Nowell, 1949-1958.* Athens: Ohio University Press, 1988. Elizabeth Nowell was Thomas Wolfe's literary agent and biographer. Edward Aswell was his last editor and became the executor of his estate. After Wolfe's death in 1938, these two individuals were immersed in resolving the issues of his life and work. Arranged chronologically, these letters provide an inside look at Wolfe's reputation and achievement. (A,G)

Donald, David Herbert. *Look Homeward: A Life of Thomas Wolfe.* New York: Little, Brown, 1987. Donald, winner of a Pulitzer prize for his history, *Charles Sumner and the Coming of the Civil War*, has written copiously on history and the South. For his biography of Wolfe, he had full access to Wolfe's papers, diaries, and letters, which are at the Houghton Library and the University of North Carolina. Details of Wolfe's personal life are inter-woven with an account of the author's artistic development. According to Donald, Wolfe wrote a ton of bad prose. But buried within the hundreds of thousands of "excess" words were gems that rank him among the greatest American authors. With such a "shotgun" approach to the novel, however, the importance of the editor's task was significantly magnified. Donald scrutinizes Wolfe's relationship with his editors and devotes a chapter to the role of Edward Aswell in shaping the last novels, which he finds little short of reprehensible. Donald provides succinct portraits of Wolfe's mistress Aline Bernstein and his first editor Maxwell Perkins. An annotated bibliography is included. (A,G)

Field, Leslie. *Thomas Wolfe and His Editors: Establishing a True Text for the Posthumous Publications.* Norman: University of Oklahoma Press, 1987. It is said that Wolfe wrote so prolifically and furiously that at the end of the day he would dump loose sheets of paper into a large trunk. When he died, thousands of manuscripts pages were turned over to his editor, Edward Aswell, who reconstructed them into three novels, *The Web and the Rock, You Can't Go Home Again,* and *The Hills Beyond.* Field compares these published texts with available manuscript evidence to study the exact nature of Aswell's editing in an effort to show that these are, indeed, Wolfe's novels and not the creation of an insensitive editor. (A)

Idol, John. *A Thomas Wolfe Companion.* New York: Greenwood, 1987. More a scholar's companion than reader's guide, this work contains chapters on Wolfe's themes, his editors and critics, a glossary of fictional places in the work, a list of characters and the page of their first appearance, genealogical charts, an annotated bibliography, a list of special collections on Wolfe, and a good index. (A)

Skipp, Francis E. *The Complete Short Stories of Thomas Wolfe*. New York: Scribner, 1987. This is the only truly comprehensive edition of Wolfe's shorter fiction, including even such pieces as "Angel on the Porch," published in *Scribner Magazine* in 1929. The introductory material, unfortunately, is not as comprehensive. Each story's publication history, for example, is not provided, only a general overview. The reward is having all of these stories between two covers. Wolfe's expansive, "rambling" style suffered at the hands of the New Criticism, which emphasized concise formulation and artistic control. This collection may well stimulate a reappraisal of Wolfe's contribution to American literature. (A,G)

Spivey, Ted Ray. *Revival: Southern Writers in the Modern City*. Gainesville: University Presses of Florida, 1986. Spivey sets out to correct the belief that southern writers are exclusively steeped in rural culture by selecting a group who came to terms with the modern city. He discusses the attitudes and adaptations of playwright Williams, poets Ransom, Tate, and Aiken, and novelists Faulkner, Wolfe, Ellison, O'Connor, and Percy. Although compelled to address the issues of southern "decadence and decline," Spivey also demonstrates how many of these writers offered a vision of how to integrate old values with new social structures, allowing the past to reanimate the present. (A,G)

Other Sources
Johnston, Carol. *Thomas Wolfe: A Descriptive Bibliography*. Pittsburgh: University of Pittsburgh Press, 1987.

McCormick, John. *Wolfe, Malraux, Hesse: A Study in Creative Vitality*. New York: Garland, 1987.

Magi, Aldo P., and Richard Walser, eds. *Thomas Wolfe Interviewed, 1929-1938*. Baton Rouge: Louisiana State University Press, 1985.

Phillipson, John S. *Critical Essays on Thomas Wolfe*. Boston: G. K. Hall, 1985.

MARY WOLLSTONECRAFT
1759-1797

Evaluation of Selected Biography and Criticism

Poovey, Mary. *The Proper Lady and the Woman Writer: Ideology as Style in the Works of Mary Wollstonecraft, Mary Shelley, and Jane Austen.* Chicago: University of Chicago Press, 1984. This was perhaps the first extended feminist study of eighteenth and nineteenth-century fiction to introduce a rigorously applied historical dimension to literary analysis. Poovey reveals the underlying ideological contradictions in the Victorian ideal of the "proper lady" through close readings of works by Wollstonecraft, Shelley, and Austen. (A,G)

St. Clair, William. *The Godwins and the Shelleys: The Biography of a Family.* New York: Norton, 1989. Meeting the highest standards of research and analysis, this biography interweaves the lives and works of four of the most influential literary minds of the nineteenth century. St. Clair examines the origin and impact of William Godwin's *Political Justice*, Mary Wollstonecraft's *Vindication of the Rights of Women*, Mary Shelley's *Frankenstein*, and Percy Bysshe Shelley's poetry. The interplay of radical political beliefs, divergent moral standards, and literary achievement makes for intriguing and thought-provoking reading. This book is highly recommended for the scholar and for the general reader. (A,G)

VIRGINIA WOOLF
1882-1941

Autobiographical Sources

Banks, Joanne T. *Congenial Spirits: The Selected Letters of Virginia Woolf.* Orlando, FL: Harcourt Brace Jovanovich, 1990. This collection of Woolf's letters is distilled from the comprehensive six-volume *Letters* co-edited by Banks. She offers an astute introduction that looks at Woolf's dependence upon relationships to define herself. The letters themselves, selected primarily for their strength of composition, reveal all of the charm, wit, breadth, and vivacious intelligence of the author. Twelve previously unpublished letters have been added to this collection. In addition, Banks has written an introduction to each section to relate Woolf's life events to the contents of the letters. Footnotes have been added to clarify obscure names and situations. Banks' selection is recommended for a more general audience or as a stepping off point for study of the full six volumes. **(A,G)**

Spotts, Frederick, ed. *Letters of Leonard Woolf.* Orlando, FL: Harcourt Brace Jovanovich, 1989. Spotts has collected over six hundred letters written by Woolf's husband, who was a distinguished publisher and author in his own right. Arranged thematically, the letters provide insights into his wife's spells of madness and touch upon the careers of other authors—E.M. Forster, Eliot, Wells, and Sylvia Townsend Warner. The editor offers a concise and useful introduction. **(A)**

Evaluation of Selected Biography and Criticism

Baldwin, Dean. *Virginia Woolf: A Study of the Short Fiction.* Boston: Twayne, 1989. This volume in the Twayne Short Fiction Series fills a surprising gap in current scholarship by critically examining Woolf's short fiction. The book is arranged chronologically and reads more like biography than undiluted criticism. Several of Woolf's essays on the craft of writing are appended, as are other critics' views of her fiction. In all, the clarity of Baldwin's study makes it valuable for the scholar and accessible to the more general reader. **(A, G)**

Bowlby, Rachael. *Virginia Woolf. Feminist Destinations.* London: Basil, Blackwell, 1988. Applying a feminist reading to Woolf's major works, Bowlby attempts to show the relationship between feminism, modernism, and realism. Because this study is incohesive and badly written, it loses the impact of what might have been a valuable thesis. **(A)**

Bradbury, Malcolm. *The Modern World: Ten Great Writers.* New York: Viking, 1989. Bradbury's study consists of essays on ten modern writers who he believes have shaped twentieth-century literature—Woolf, Eliot, Conrad,

Joyce, Kafka, Pirandello, Mann, Proust, Ibsen, and Dostoevsky. He examines these writers' underlying themes of alienation, rage, and disaffection and describes how their work influenced contemporary authors. (A)

Briggs, John. *Fire in the Crucible: The Alchemy of Creative Genius.* St. Martin's, 1988. Briggs adopts alchemy as a metaphor for the transformation of emotions and ideas into products of the creative genius. Against this backdrop, he examines the creative processes of scientists, artists, and authors, among them Emily Dickinson and Virginia Woolf. This study is recommended for those who are generally interested in the author's creative act. (A, G)

DeSalvo, Louise. *Virginia Woolf: The Impact of Childhood Sexual Abuse on Her Life and Work.* New York: Beacon, 1989. DeSalvo's study examines the labyrinth of abusive sexual and homoerotic relations that influenced Woolf's childhood and development. Especially valuable are DeSalvo's analyses of selected works in light of Woolf's later feminism. This study is recommended as required reading for fans of Woolf. (A)

Gordon, Lyndall. *Virginia Woolf: A Writer's Life.* New York: Norton, 1985. In a harmonious blend of biography and literary criticism, Gordon examines Woolf's novels in light of selected biographical events. The tone is personal and engaging. As such, this study becomes a meditation about art and womanhood. The thesis is developed through extensive quotations and reflexive analysis that illuminates passages of fiction and the inner recesses of Woolf's motivations and accomplishments. Gordon assumes that the reader has a reasonable familiarity with the novels. (A,G)

Homans, Margaret. *Bearing the Word: Language and Female Experience in Nineteenth-Century Women's Writing.* Chicago: University of Chicago Press, 1986. Delving into the Oedipal propositions of psychoanalytic theory, Homans emerges with an insight into the interaction of language acquisition and the formation of gender identity. Building on the ideas of Jacques Lacan and Nancy Chodorow, she describes a dominant myth of language that identifies women with the "literal," and a dominant myth of gender that identifies her with nature and matter. To support these theories, she provides close readings of excerpts from Dorothy Wordsworth, Mary Shelley, the Brontë sisters, Elizabeth Gaskell, George Eliot, and Virginia Woolf. Scholars should acquaint themselves with the theoretical framework that Homans develops here. (A)

Hussey, Mark. *The Singing of the Real World: The Philosophy of Virginia Woolf's Fiction.* Columbus: Ohio State University Press, 1986. This attempt to define the indefinable—Woolf's philosophy of life—ultimately fails for lack of a good editor. Hussey's prose is mired in repetition, circular reasoning, and confusing constructions. (A)

Kelley, Alice van Buren. *"To the Lighthouse": The Marriage of Life and Art.* Boston: Twayne, 1988. Kelley argues that Woolf used this novel to come to terms with her parents, her childhood, and the society that demanded so much of her. Carefully developing the analogies between the novel and Woolf's biography, Kelley shows how Woolf used art to resolve emotional conflicts. Although this approach could be speculative and sensational, Kelley's careful scholarship and lucid prose provide convincing insights into both the novel and the life. **(A)**

Marcus, Jane. *Art & Anger: Reading Like a Woman.* Columbus: Miami University Press/Ohio State University Press, 1988. Noted feminist critic Marcus offers a series of essays on Virginia Woolf and her circle. The stated purpose of this study is to "change the subject," that is, to change the idea of the appropriate audience for Woolf's literature. This is done through innovative interpretation and an injection of feminist theory. In the process, she provides an insightful view of Oscar Wilde's *Salome* and George Meredith's *Diana of the Crossways.* Women's issues are foremost in this very readable study. **(A,G)**

Marcus, Jane. *Virginia Woolf and the Languages of Patriarchy.* Bloomington: Indiana University Press, 1987. This is a collection of eight of Marcus' previously published essays analyzing gender politics in Woolf's novels. *Night and Day* and *To the Lighthouse* are viewed from a variety of perspectives, including Marxist and lesbian, as well as the more mainstream feminist angle. Of particular note is her comparison of the handling of male violence and rape in the works of Woolf and Colette. According to Marcus, Woolf's socialist and feminist politics are revealed in her use of language and her ability to weave political perspectives into her literature. **(A,G)**

Marcus, Jane, ed. *Virginia Woolf and Bloomsbury: A Centenary Celebration.* Bloomington: Indiana University Press, 1987. This collection of fifteen essays reflects critical perspectives ranging from traditional to feminist. Marcus contributes a fine essay, "Taking the Bull by the Udders;" Nigel Nicolson describes the world of the "Bloomsberries;" and Noel Annan takes on the parochial Leavis and his cult. Anthologies typically suffer from inconsistent quality, but here the standard is high. This collection is highly recommended as an overview of current critical opinion on Woolf. **(A)**

McNeillie, Andrew, ed. *The Essays of Virginia Woolf: Volume 1, 1904-1912.* Orlando, FL: Harcourt Brace Jovanovich, 1987. This compilation of essays and book reviews provides a further complement to the collected letters and diaries. McNeillie has gathered an unprecedented number of short works with the help of recent advances in Woolf scholarship which enabled identification of many unsigned pieces. The scholarly apparatus of this edition is sizeable, well-arranged, and knowledgeable. Many cross-references are provided to guide the reader to appropriate passages in the *Letters* or *Diaries.* **(A,G)**

McNeillie, Andrew, ed. *The Essays of Virginia Woolf: Volume 2, 1912-1918.* Orlando, FL: Harcourt Brace Jovanovich, 1988. Almost all of the ninety-eight essays collected in volume two of this edition originally appeared in the *Times Literary Supplement* and consist primarily of her literary views and criticism. She expounds freely upon Edwardian and nineteenth-century poets and novelists, such as Conrad, James, Galsworthy, Brooke, and Charlotte Brontë. Besides recording Woolf's considerable reading, this collection allows the scholar to document the development of her literary and aesthetic opinions. Only four articles represent 1912-1915, which was the period of Woolf's severe mental breakdown. The annotations are meticulous and useful. (A,G)

Minow-Pinkney, Makiko. *Virginia Woolf and the Problem of the Subject.* New Brunswick, NJ: Rutgers University Press, 1987. Examining such works as *The Waves, Between the Acts, The Years,* and *Three Guineas,* Minow-Pinkney suggests how Woolf achieved a remarkable convergence of modernism and feminism. Supposedly, Woolf's feminism was "suppressed" in the 1920s by her experimentation with language and form. Minow-Pinkney demonstrates how her feminist convictions were intertwined with her aesthetic innovations. (A,G)

Paul, Janis M. *The Victorian Heritage of Virginia Woolf: The External World in Her Novels.* Norman, OK: Pilgrim, 1987. This cultural-historical exploration of Woolf's Victorian roots enables the reader to better understand the thrust of her modernism. Paul establishes the historical context of the first five novels—*The Voyage Out, Night and Day, Jacob's Room, Mrs. Dalloway,* and *To the Lighthouse.* (G)

Rosenblatt, Aaron. *Virginia Woolf for Beginners.* New York: Writers and Readers, 1987. In this introduction to the works of Virginia Woolf for the younger reader, Rosenblatt offers a popular version of her life but introduces many sexual ambiguities that may not be considered appropriate for his intended audience. The tongue-in-cheek presentation is meant more as entertainment than scholarship. It is indeed entertaining, but the Woolf who is portrayed may be only a parody of the real thing. (G)

Rosenman, Ellen Bayuk. *The Invisible Presence: Virginia Woolf and the Mother-Daughter Relationship.* Baton Rouge: Louisana State University Press, 1986. Rosenman's feminist critique of Woolf's writings offers new insight into her underlying perceptions and motivations. Rosenman examines the literal and metaphorical ways in which Woolf projected the "psychological experience of daughterhood" and discovers a surprising consistency of theme in such diverse works as *The Waves, Night and Day, Three Guineas,* and *Between the Acts.* The closing chapter examines her attitudes toward other women writers that focuses on *A Room of One's Own.* Frequent use of correspondance and diaries provides a useful grounding in the author's life. This analysis is useful for advanced students and those interested in tracing themes of motherhood in literature. (A)

Ruotolo, Lucio. *The Interrupted Moment: A View of Virginia Woolf's Novels.* Stanford, CA: Stanford University Press, 1986. In this study of eight of Woolf's novels, Ruotolo skillfully blends biography and analysis. He traces the roots of Woolf's rejection of social authoritarianism in all its forms to an over-riding confidence in reason and a distrust of hierarchies. Gleaning information from letters and diaries to support his views, Ruotolo examines Woolf's characters in terms of their "openness to interruption." Into each life, Woolf seems to be saying, some chaos must fall. Out of chaos come the energies that can transform the rigidity of structure. Although this same insight has been applied to individual works in previous essays, this is the first book to examine the novels as a whole. It is highly recommended for Woolf scholars and will undoubtedly influence future scholarship. (A)

Transue, Pamela J. *Virginia Woolf and the Politics of Style.* Albany: State University of New York Press, 1986. Transue's insistence on describing the development of Woolf's narrative style entirely in terms of feminism ultimately does her subject an injustice. Certainly Woolf's style cannot be examined without considering feminist themes, yet there seems little reason to disregard parallel studies from such critics as Dorothy Richardson, James Joyce, and D. H. Lawrence. This work is more valuable when considered in conjunction with other interpretations. (A,G)

Warner, Eric. *Virginia Woolf: "The Waves."* Cambridge: Cambridge University Press, 1987. This is a volume in the Cambridge Landmarks of World Literature Series, designed to introduce students to classic works of literature. *The Waves* is considered one of Woolf's more complex works, but Warner's clear analysis and concise presentation makes it readily accessible to newcomers to Woolf's fiction. An introductory chapter places *The Waves* within the context of Woolf's canon. Warner then examines Woolf's methods of creation, techniques, and use of themes and images. As a narrator, Woolf strove to remove the ego from the product, to reveal underlying structures that outlasted the individual, and to free unconscious drives and urges from the ego's control. (A,G)

Wilson, Jean Moorcroft. *Virginia Woolf: Life and London; A Biography of Place.* New York: Norton, 1988. Wilson contends that London inspired and invigorated the writings of Woolf and attempts to portray the city that she loved and experienced. This book is of interest primarily to the Woolf aficionado who plans a vacation in London. Several London walks are outlined that highlight buildings and places that were known to Woolf or featured in her works. (G)

Zwerdling, Alex. *Virginia Woolf and the Real World.* Berkeley: University of California Press, 1986. Using a social history approach, Zwerdling attacks the assumptions that Woolf isolated herself from the "real world" and that her fiction can be understood without appealing to her social context. The first half of this book scrutinizes a thousand details of society during Woolf's lifetime--attitudes toward money, class, family, even feminism and warfare. The discussion of details is interesting enough in itself as social history. Zwerdling then examines how Woolf's personality, opinions, and values merged or clashed with the cultural milieu. Context, argues Zwerdling, is the only way to generate meaning. Those who project late twentieth-century ideologies and political agendas onto Woolf are roundly criticized for confusing eras and cultures and thus negating the significance of Woolf's life and work. Recommended for all audiences. (A,G)

Whiteley, Patrick J. *Knowledge and Experimental Realism in Conrad, Lawrence, and Woolf.* Baton Rouge: Louisiana State University Press, 1987. Whiteley offers a good analysis of all three writers' works as he explains how each writer thought people perceived reality, and how they embodied this perceptual process in their fiction. The quest for self-knowledge and its implications for people's relationships is, in Whiteley's opinion, the important thread that ties these three writers together and established the groundwork for the modern psychological novel. (A)

Other Sources

Abel, Elizabeth. *Virginia Woolf and the Fictions of Psychoanalysis.* Chicago: University of Chicago Press, 1989.

Beja, Morris. *Critical Essays on Virginia Woolf.* Boston: G. K. Hall, 1985.

Bishop, Edward. *A Virginia Woolf Chronology.* Boston: G. K. Hall, 1988.

Bond, Alma H. *Who Killed Virginia Woolf? A Psychobiography.* New York: Human Sciences Press, 1989.

Broe, Mary Lynn and Angela Ingram, eds. *Women's Writing in Exile.* Chapel Hill: University of North Carolina Press, 1989.

D'Aquila, Ulysses L. *Bloomsbury and Modernism.* New York: Peter Lang, 1989.

Dick, Susan. *Virginia Woolf.* New York: Routledge Chapman & Hall, 1989.

Dowling, David. *Bloomsbury Aesthetics and the Novels of Forster and Woolf.* New York: St. Martin's, 1985.

Hyman, Virginia. *To the Lighthouse and Beyond: Transformations in the Narratives of Virginia Woolf.* New York: Peter Lang, 1989.

Kushen, Betty. *Virginia Woolf and the Nature of Communion.* West Orange, NJ: Raynor Press, 1985.

Maika, Patricia. *Virginia Woolf's "Between the Acts" and Jane Harrison's Con-Spiracy.* Ann Arbor: UMI Research Press, 1987.

McCluskey, Kathleen. *Reverberations: Sound and Structure in the Novels of Virginia Woolf.* Ann Arbor: UMI Research Press, 1985.

McNichol, Stella. *Virginia Woolf and the Poetry of Fiction.* New York: Routledge Chapman & Hall, 1988.

Miller, C. Ruth. *Virginia Woolf: The Frames of Art and Life.* New York: St. Martin's, 1988.

Panken, Shirley. *Virginia Woolf and the "Lust of Creation": A Psychoanalytic Exploration.* Albany: State University of New York Press, 1987.

Rhein, Donna E. *The Handprinted Books of Leonard and Virginia Woolf at the Hogarth Press, 1917-1932.* Ann Arbor: UMI Research Press, 1985.

Schwarz, Daniel R. *The Transformation of the English Novel, 1890-1930.* New York: St. Martin's, 1989.

Squier, Susan M. *Virginia Woolf and London: The Sexual Politics of the City.* Chapel Hill: University of North Carolina Press, 1985.

Steele, Elizabeth. *Virginia Woolf's Rediscovered Essays: Sources and Allusions.* New York: Garland, 1987.

Velicu, A. *Unifying Strategies in Virginia Woolf's Experimental Literature.* Stockholm: Almquist & Wiksell/Coronet Books, 1985.

Wheare, Jane. *Virginia Woolf: Dramatic Novelist.* New York: St. Martin's, 1989.

WILLIAM WORDSWORTH
1770-1850

Evaluation of Selected Biography and Criticism

Bate, Jonathan. *Shakespeare and the English Romantic Imagination.* Oxford: Oxford University Press, 1986. In this well-written study, Bate examines the influence of Shakespeare on Byron, Coleridge, Wordsworth, Keats, and Blake. He examines how each poet's critical theory developed either out of or as a reaction to Shakespeare's poetic identity. This is a large field to cover, and Bate's study is a creditable overview that should be useful for anyone studying the English romantics. **(A,G)**

Bewell, Alan. *Wordsworth and the Enlightenment: Nature, Man, and Society in the Experimental Poetry.* New Haven: Yale University Press, 1989. Bewell's study is a radically new interpretation of many of Wordsworth's greatest poems. Works such as *Lyrical Ballads* and *The Prelude*, Bewell contends, were written to challenge Enlightenment concepts of how humans were able to make the transition from nature to culture. These poems, which have long been relegated personal and psychological significance, are reread as an imaginative history of humanity's development from savagery to civilization. Related to Wordsworth and his works are eighteenth-century encounters with feral children, origin myths, hysteria, witchcraft, and concepts of death. The arguments are persuasive and well-documented. Highly recommended. **(A,G)**

Blank, G. Kim. *Wordsworth's Influence on Shelley: A Study of Poetic Authority.* New York: St. Martin's, 1988. Shelley himself acknowledged his poetic debt to Wordsworth. In the first part of his study Blank examines Shelley's early poetry and argues that the best of it falls clearly into the Wordsworthian school. In the second part he explores the result of one poet influencing another. In addition to arguing his influence thesis, Blank provides excellent close readings of both poets. Clearly written, this study is readable for students at any level, but is most valuable for students familiar with the poetry. **(A,G)**

Chainey, Graham. *A Literary History of Cambridge.* Ann Arbor: University of Michigan Press, 1986. This behind-the-scenes look at the literary stories and scandals of Cambridge University makes for enjoyable voyeurism. The gossip is truly on an epic scale—spread over eight hundred years of Cambridge history and featuring anecdotes on nearly every notable British writer, including Wordsworth, Milton, Macaulay, and Sylvia Plath. Love affairs, drinking habits, duels, rivalries—all are paraded forth in often humorous detail. This is a very entertaining book that in its own way reveals the immense contribution Cambridge has made to the literary world. **(G)**

Fraser, Hilary. *Beauty and Belief: Aesthetics and Religion in Victorian Literature*. Cambridge: Cambridge University Press, 1986. In this specialized study in intellectual history, Fraser traces the relationship between religion and aesthetic doctrine from Coleridge and Wordsworth through the aestheticism of Walter Pater and Oscar Wilde. Fraser argues that through concepts propounded by Hopkins, Ruskin, Arnold, and the Oxford aesthetes, Christianity is reduced to a merely subjective religion of art. (A)

Galperin, William H. *Revision and Authority in Wordsworth: The Interpretation of Career*. University Park: University of Pennsylvania Press, 1989. Galperin suggests that Wordsworth's later work did not represent a decline in the author's powers but rather a studied reaction to his earlier romantic vision. Wordsworth systematically questions the assumptions underlying the romantic creation of self. Borrowing from such theorists as Thompson, Paul de Man, Bloom, and Derrida, Galperin forges a new interpretation of *The Excursion*, selected sonnets, and other late poetry. (A)

Gill, Stephen. *William Wordsworth: A Life*. New York: Oxford University Press, 1989. Armed with a cache of recently discovered family papers in the Wordsworth Library, Gill has produced a fresh and controversial view of the English visionary and poet. He focuses primarily on the writer and his works, but describes the poetry against a background that emphasizes the poet's hardships. A year after its publication in England, this biography continued to generate letters in the press from critics and scholars who felt compelled to attack or defend Gill's assessments. The controversy was generated partly by Wordsworth's personality and reputation and partly by Gill's ability to bring the ethereal poet down to earth. In particular, Gill's examination of the mutual influences of Wordsworth and Coleridge galvanized opposing camps championing each poet. The biography successfully deflates Wordsworth the Legend, while revealing a Wordsworth of human strengths and flaws. He provides capable and sensitive commentary on the poetry—particularly on *Lyrical Ballads* and *The Prelude*. (A)

Greenberg, Martin. *The Hamlet Vocation of Coleridge and Wordsworth*. Iowa City: University of Iowa Press, 1986. The separation of mind and action, according to Greenburg, represents the current situation of modern civilization. Shakespeare's Hamlet is described as the prototypical character whose attitude revealed a preoccupation with the inner world that worked to defeat the outer man. Both Coleridge and Wordsworth were "called" to adopt inward lives of reflection unsuited to the practical life. Thus, the work of both poets—through inner reflection and outward "defeat"—provides insight into the current human condition. (A)

Harvey, Geoffrey. *The Romantic Tradition in Modern English Poetry: Rhetoric and Experience*. New York: St. Martin's, 1986. Harvey fashions a framework of rational sympathy and rhetorical balance to gather Wordsworth, Hardy, Betjeman, and Larkin within a single poetic tradition. He then discusses the complex relationship between the "native English tradition" and emerging modernism. (A,G)

Kelley, Theresa M. *Wordsworth's Revisionary Aesthetics.* London and New York: Cambridge University Press, 1988. This complex critical thesis explains how Wordsworth uses language to first establish those momentous occasions in which he and nature became one and then to transcend poetic and natural beauty to capture the moment in what Wordsworth called "spots of time." Kelley works with revisions as well as related poems to illustrate the system of aesthetics she is arguing. (A)

Leask, Nigel. *The Politics of Imagination in Coleridge's Critical Thought.* New York: St. Martin's, 1988. In the prefaces to each edition of the *Lyrical Ballads* Coleridge and Wordsworth addressed the power of poetry to shape social awareness and action. Both poets drew on social change for the subject matter of their work, but Coleridge went on to develop his ideas about art, knowledge, and the imagination in his mammoth, unfinished *Biographia Literaria.* In this study, Leask begins by examining Wordsworth's developing aesthetics and how Coleridge altered or modified them. He goes on to explain the impact of Kant and Schelling on Coleridge's thought and to define the relationship between Coleridge's politics and imagination. (A)

Magnuson, Paul. *Coleridge and Wordsworth: A Lyrical Dialogue.* Princeton: Princeton University Press, 1988. Magnuson's assumption is that it is more important to see the connections between the poems of these two poets than it is to study the integral unity of individual poems. He argues that Wordsworth and Coleridge were so influenced by each other that their poems result in a dialogue that reveals a process of negation, interrogation, and interruption. Individual poems, therefore, are most revealingly seen as fragments of a long lyrical sequence. Magnuson argues his points carefully, and the result is an intriguing study for scholars and students of romanticism. (A)

Meisenhelder, Susan Edwards. *Wordsworth's Informed Reader: Structures of Experience in His Poetry.* Nashville, TN: Vanderbilt University Press, 1988. Meisenhelder sets out to recreate Wordsworth's intentional impact on his readers by examining the nature and contextual structure of 250 poems in the 1815 edition. To build her case she quotes at length from individual poems, creating an intrusive critical buffer between the very meanings she attempts to identify. Although she generates occasional insights through this methodology, the effect is not cumulative. The reader tends to pay more and more attention to the poems themselves and less to the critical commentary. (A)

Metzger, Lore. *One Foot in Eden: Modes of Pastoral in Romantic Poetry.* Chapel Hill: University of North Carolina Press, 1986. In this study, Metzger traces the influence of classical pastoralism on the works of some of the major romantics—Blake, Coleridge, Wordsworth, and Keats. In the process, she provides an important overview of English romanticism. Drawing upon Schiller's thesis that pastoral innocence must be put to a more practical test,

Metzger examines the question of whether individuality and ideality can be truthfully expressed in the same work of art. For the most part, she concludes, the English romantics only intensified the dissonance between the ideal and the real world. This book is recommended for scholars and students of the romantic period. **(A)**

Newlyn, Lucy. *Coleridge, Wordsworth, and the Language of Allusion.* Oxford: Oxford University Press, 1986. Newlyn examines the early poetry of Coleridge and Wordsworth to reveal an intricate structure of echoes of and allusions to one another. According to Newlyn's reading, Coleridge dominated Wordsworth intellectually and artistically, particularly in the first six months of their association. Her assessment of the relationship is part of an ongoing critical controversy that shows little sign of waning. Although this is primarily a book for scholars, the style and tone are accessible to any student of English romanticism. **(A,G)**

Roe, Nicholas. *Wordsworth and Coleridge: The Radical Years at Oxford.* London and New York: Oxford University Press, 1988. From 1789 to 1798 the winds of revolution were so strong in England and France that Wordsworth and Coleridge moved to Germany. Roe's detailed research focuses on romanticism as a political and social movement, rather than a literary response to nature, and places these poets squarely in the center of political upheaval. This is an exciting narrative of two fascinating men. **(A,G)**

Rzepka, Charles J. *The Self as Mind: Vision and Identity in Wordsworth, Coleridge, and Keats.* Cambridge: Harvard University Press, 1986. This award-winning study of the romantic mind examines Coleridge, Wordsworth, and Keats as they struggled to create a place for their "visionary selves" in the external world. Rzepka examines the nature of the visionary self, its expression, and the role of the reading public in providing external affirmation of the internal experience. A thorough overview of relevant scholarship is provided through extensive documentation. **(A)**

Sale, Roger. *Closer to Home.* Cambridge: Harvard University Press, 1988. Sale, a critic at home in many literary periods, addresses the treatment of place in the works of five English authors, including Wordsworth, Austen, Clare, and Crabbe. The local landscape and society strongly influenced all five writers and became became a principal theme and structural device for their art. Sale contends that these authors broke away from the established pictorial treatment of landscape to produce a psychological response to place and time. This, in turn, set the stage for the realism that would emerge in the writings of the Victorians, especially Hardy, Dickens, and Eliot. For serious students, Sale offers fresh and provocative ideas for interpreting each of these writers. **(A,G)**

Simpson, David. *Wordsworth's Historical Imagination: The Poetry of Displacement.* New York: Metheun, 1987. Simpson argues that Wordsworth explored the tensions between his private imagination and social forces. Using close readings of *Home at Grasmere, The Prelude, The Excursion*, and others, Simpson places Wordsworth within a socio-historical context to discuss the poet's ideas of urbanization, the economy, and the ideals of nature. (A)

Stein, Edward. *Wordsworth's Art of Allusion*. University Park: Pennsylvania State University Press, 1988. This study carefully breaks down into categories Wordsworth's allusions to earlier writers. Stein's methodology sheds light on about a hundred poems and draws interesting parallels with the works of such poets as Homer, Spenser, Drayton, Milton, Pope, Cowper, and Coleridge. Wordsworth is shown to have had a propensity for assimilating the concepts and images of other poets, rather than for indulging in formal imitation. Several figures are included that chart the frequency with which Wordsworth draws on other poets for source materials. This study in intertextuality is lucidly written and has been highly recommended. (A,G)

Other Sources

Abrams, M. H. *The Correspondent Breeze: Essays on English Romanticism*. New York: Norton, 1984.

Austin, Frances. *The Language of Wordsworth and Coleridge*. New York: St. Martin's, 1989.

Bialostosky, Don H. *Making Tales: The Poetics of Wordsworth's Narrative Experiments*. Chicago: University of Chicago Press, 1984.

Brennan, Matthew C. *Wordsworth, Turner, and Romantic Landscape: A Study of the Traditions of the Picturesque and the Sublime*. Columbia, SC: Camden House, 1987.

Cappon, Alexander P. *Action, Organism and Philosophy in Wordsworth and Whitehead*. New York: Philosophy Library, 1985.

Cave, Richard A., ed. *The Romantic Theatre: An International Symposium*. Savage, MD: Barnes & Noble, 1987.

Chandler, James K. *Wordsworth's Second Nature: A Study of the Poetry and Politics*. Chicago: University of Chicago Press, 1984.

Ellis, David. *Wordsworth, Freud and the Spots of Time: Interpretation in "The Prelude."* New York: Cambridge University Press, 1985.

Hagstrum, Jean H. *The Romantic Body: Love and Sexuality in Keats, Wordsworth, and Blake*. Knoxville: University of Tennessee Press, 1986.

Hamilton, Paul. *Wordsworth: A Critical Introduction*. Atlantic Highlands, NJ: Humanities Press, 1986.

Hartman, Geoffrey. *The Unremarkable Wordsworth*. Minneapolis: University of Minnesota Press, 1987.

Harvey, Geoffrey. *The Romantic Tradition in Modern English Poetry: Rhetoric and Experience*. New York: St. Martin's, 1986.

Hill, Alan G., ed. *The Letters of William Wordsworth: A New Selection*. New York: Oxford University Press, 1985.

Jacobus, Mary. *Romanticism, Writing, and Sexual Difference: Essays on "The Prelude."* New York: Oxford University Press, 1989.

Johnston, Kenneth R. *Wordsworth and "The Recluse."* New Haven: Yale University Press, 1984.

Johnston, Kenneth R., and Gene Ruoff, eds. *The Age of William Wordsworth: Critical Essays on the Romantic Tradition*. New Brunswick: Rutgers University Press, 1987.

Jones, Alun R., ed. *Wordsworth's Poems of 1807*. Atlantic Highlands, NJ: Humanities Press, 1987.

Kneale, J. Douglas. *Monumental Writing: Aspects of Rhetoric in Wordsworth's Poetry*. Lincoln: University of Nebraska Press, 1988.

Levinson, Marjorie. *Wordsworth's Great Period Poems: Four Essays*. New York: Cambridge University Press, 1986.

Liu, Alan. *Wordsworth, the Sense of History*. Palo Alto: Stanford University Press, 1989.

McCracken, David. *Wordsworth and the Lake District: A Guide to the Poems and Their Places*. New York: Oxford University Press, 1985.

McEahern, Patricia A., and Thomas F. Beckwith. *A Complete Concordance to the Lyrical Ballads of Samuel Taylor Coleridge and William Wordsworth: 1789 and 1800 Editions*. New York: Garland, 1987.

Pinion, F. B. *A Wordsworth Chronology*. Boston: G. K. Hall, 1988.

Ruoff, Gene W. *Wordsworth and Coleridge: The Making of the Major Lyrics, 1802-1804*. New Brunswick: Rutgers University Press, 1989.

Spiegelman, Willard. *Wordsworth's Heroes*. Berkeley: University of California Press, 1985.

Talbot, John H. *The Nature of Aesthetic Experience in Wordsworth*. New York: Peter Lang, 1989.

Thomas, Gordon Kent. *Wordsworth and the Motions of the Mind.* New York: Peter Lang, 1989.

Thomas, Keith G. *Wordsworth and Philosophy: Empiricism and Transcendentalism in the Poetry.* Ann Arbor: UMI Research Press, 1988.

Thomas, W. K., and Warren Ober. *A Mind Forever Voyaging: Wordsworth at Work Portraying Newton and Science.* Edmonton: University of Alberta Press, 1989.

Ward, J. P. *Wordsworth's Language of Men.* Savage, MD: Barnes & Noble, 1984.

Williams, John. *Wordsworth: Romantic Poetry and Revolution Politics.* Manchester: University of Manchester Press, 1989.

Wolfson, Susan. *The Questioning Presence: Wordsworth, Keats and the Interrogative Mode in Romantic Poetry.* Ithaca, NY: Cornell, 1986.

Wordsworth, Dorothy. *The Grasmere Journal.* Edited by Jonathan Wordsworth. New York: Henry Holt, 1987.

RICHARD WRIGHT
1908-1960

Evaluation of Selected Biography and Criticism

Bradley, David, ed. *Eight Men: Stories.* New York: Thunder's Mouth, 1987. Until this edition, Richard Wright's last work, *Eight Men*, has survived only in anthologies where it shows up piecemeal. The book comprises five stories, two radio plays, and an autobiographical essay, which hang together only very loosely. In his introduction, Bradley recounts how Wright struggled to publish these pieces, often revising and rerevising to achieve a market. He persisted with little success against the entrenched racist attitudes of editors, publishers, and the marketplace. The two best stories in this collection, "The Man Who Lived Underground," and "The Man Who Was Almost a Man" stand out against the fitful qualities of the other pieces. **(A,G)**

Fabre, Michel. *The World of Richard Wright.* Jackson: University Press of Mississippi, 1985. The barrier-breaking black American novelist, Richard Wright, continued to write with powerful purpose and controlled rage until his death in 1960. Since the publication of *Native Son* in 1940, Wright's reputation has undergone several transformations. His initial popular acclaim faded too swiftly. Social critics of the 1960s considered him politically naive. Theoreticians had trouble fitting him into a developing black aesthetic framework. In many ways, Michel Fabre's biography *The Unfinished Quest of Richard Wright* (1973) saved him from premature obscurity. This collection of twelve essays continues Fabre's scholarly resuscitation of Wright's critical reputation. **(A,G)**

Joyce, Joyce Ann. *Richard Wright's Art of Tragedy.* Iowa City: University of Iowa Press, 1986. This is the first study of Richard Wright's work to focus exclusively on *Native Son*, the book that forged his reputation. The book's protagonist, Bigger Thomas, is a hulking, violent man whom many critics have viewed as barely human. Joyce examines the character as a tragic hero who is as much a victim of fate as a victimizer of others. In arguing her case, Joyce strongly attacks the sociological approach that dominates the criticism of Afro-American literature. Although controversial in its approach, this study brings out subtleties of Wright's plot and characterization that have been previously overlooked. **(A,G)**

Kinnamon, Kenneth, ed. *A Richard Wright Bibliography: Fifty Years of Criticism and Commentary, 1933-1982.* New York: Greenwood, 1988. This labor-of-love may well be the most massive bibliography ever compiled for an American writer. It consists of over 13,100 entries, referring the researcher to essays, reviews, interviews, and articles, domestic and foreign, that address Wright or his works. The editor had an ulterior motive for producing this awesome compilation—to "expand current notions of what constitutes a total literary reputation." He has certainly expanded what constitutes "comprehensive" for a bibliography. (A)

Miller, Eugene E. *Voice of a Native Son: The Poetics of Richard Wright.* Jackson: University Press of Mississippi, 1990. Miller's aim is to define Wright's critical self-perceptions and "to bring into relief an often semiconscious, often seemingly abeyant pattern of his conceptualizations and justifications for what he wanted to do as a writer." Miller examines Wright's essays that preface his own work, unpublished fragments of fiction and nonfiction, the novels themselves, and the disparity Wright experienced between his Afro-American heritage and the refinement of European culture that influenced his aesthetics. In individual chapters Miller treats various forms, conventions, and philosophies that appear in Wright's work: political, folk, surrealistic, and archetypal. He explains how Kenneth Burke's treatise on political dialectics (*Permanence and Change*), which Wright read in the late 1930s, and Burke's successive papers on surrealism and power, affected Wright's social and personal views. This erudite, readable study is the most serious recent critical work on Wright. To some readers it might seem like theoretical overkill of a writer who spoke so directly to his readers. (A)

Urban, Joan. *Richard Wright.* New York: Chelsea House, 1989. This is another in the series entitled Black Americans of Achievement, whose purpose is to provide a sense of the struggle which its subjects overcame on the way to greatness. Complete with a generic introduction by Coretta Scott King and an abundance of period photographs, this appreciative biography is suited for younger students of social history or literature. (G,Y)

Walker, Margaret. *Richard Wright, Daemonic Genius: A Portrait of the Man, A Critical Look at His Work.* New York: Dodd Mead, 1987. Walker believes that all previous critical biographies of Wright have been inadequate, inaccurate, or misguided. Having known Wright intimately over many years, she is a first-hand witness to the events that molded his writing, to his artistic development, and to the unfolding of his personality. Walker's study manages to capture the torment of Wright's life and work, and, if her own biases sometimes intrude, they serve to emphasize the ideas that made Wright's work so powerful. (A,G)

Other Sources

Evans, James H., Jr. *Spiritual Empowerment in Afro-American Literature: Frederick Douglass, Rebecca Jackson, Booker T. Washington, Richard Wright, Toni Morrison.* Lewiston, NY: Edwin Mellen, 1987.

Fabre, Michel. *Richard Wright.* Jackson: University Press of Mississippi, 1990.

Trotman, James C. *Richard Wright: Myths and Realities.* New York: Garland, 1989.

SIR THOMAS WYATT
1503-1542

Evaluation of Selected Criticism

Mason, H. A. *Sir Thomas Wyatt: A Literary Portrait. Selected Poems, with Full Notes, Commentaries, and a Critical Introduction.* Bristol, England: Bristol Classical Press, 1986. This lively, wide-ranging study offers a well-documented reading of Wyatt's poetry. Mason brings to his discussion the backgrounds and influences on Wyatt's life and imagination. He gives the reader everything needed to appreciate the poetry, from simple definitions to classical allusions. Advanced students and scholars will find Mason's work refreshingly old-fashioned. (A,G)

Ross, Diane M. *Self-Revelation and Self-Protection in Wyatt's Lyric Poetry.* New York: Garland, 1988. This study of Wyatt's poetry explores the poet's "stand-offishness toward the reader, which balances his pleas or longing for mutual understanding." Ross examines the ways in which the lyrics resemble narratives, Wyatt's use of proverbs as a formal model, and his interest in fables. Originally presented as a doctoral thesis, Ross's study should be of interest to advanced students of Wyatt's poetry. (A)

WILLIAM BUTLER YEATS
1865-1939

Autobiographical Sources

Domville, Eric, and John Kelly, eds. *The Collected Letters of W. B. Yeats: Volume 1, 1865-1895.* Oxford: Clarendon Press, 1986. This is the first volume of a projected ten-volume series of Yeats' correspondence. Beginning with an eleven-year-old Yeats, this collection of over 350 copiously footnoted letters ends when the fledgling author has left home for good and embarked in earnest on his career. Included is a detailed chronology of the events in Yeats' life, as well as a biographical and historical appendix containing entries on people important to Yeats. This is a priceless treasure of information about Yeats, his family, his associates, and his times. (A,G)

Evaluation of Selected Biography and Criticism

Dawson, Carl. *Prophets of Past Time: Seven British Autobiographers, 1880-1914.* Baltimore: Johns Hopkins University Press, 1988. This group of essays on seven autobiographers—Yeats, W.H. White, George Tyrell, Samuel Butler, Edmund Goss, George Moore, and Ford Madox Ford—goes beyond the typical concerns of nonfictional and fictional presentation of the self. It also examines the nature of memory, its role in creativity, its unconscious influences, and the anxiety of forgetting. Dawson draws upon these autobiographies to explore the interplay of past, present, and future in literary lives. He quotes extensively from philosophers, psychologists, and authors to enhance the context of his approach. A major contribution to the history of turn-of-the-century thought. (A,G)

Deane, Seamus. *A Short History of Irish Literature.* South Bend, IN: University of Notre Dame Press, 1986. Noted Irish scholar Deane develops a number of themes in this survey of Irish literature: the allegiance of Irish literature to history and politics, the struggle of authors to champion acceptance of Irish ideals, and the interplay of art and political polemic. The approach is primarily historical, but Deane offers concise and useful readings of works by Joyce, Yeats, and others. The volume is divided into chronological sections: Gaelic background, Anglo-Irish tradition, Celtic revival, nineteenth-century fiction and drama, and Irish modernism. This book is recommended as a supplement to McHugh's *Short History of Anglo-Irish Literature.* (A,G)

Deane, Sheila. *Bardic Style in the Poetry of Gerard Manley Hopkins, W. B. Yeats, and Dylan Thomas.* Ann Arbor: UMI Research Press, 1989. Deane examines the poetry of Hopkins, Yeats, and Thomas in terms of the poets' use of traditional bardic sources and rhetorical devices. Deane finds close parallels among these authors who were "suspicious" of one another during their lifetimes. Each thought the other "obscure" due to the "subjective haze" of their romantic and metaphysical affectations—all of which, according to Deane, derive from a "bardic style." (A)

Ellmann, Richard. *Four Dubliners: Wilde, Yeats, Joyce, and Beckett.* New York: Braziller, 1987. With his usual elegance and clarity, Ellmann discusses the lives and works of four Irish writers who shaped the character of twentieth-century literature. Although these authors have significant differences, Ellmann concentrates on their commonalities: the desire to transform language and literature, the need to establish autonomy, a preoccupation with inner conflicts, and an insistence on remaining Irish in spite of living as expatriates. This is a splendid introduction for new readers to their lives and works. Highly recommended. (A,G)

Finneran, Richard, ed. *Critical Essays on W. B. Yeats.* Boston: G. K. Hall, 1986. This collection of essays by leading Yeats scholars examines his critical reputation. Although not the best anthology—there have been eight over the past thirty years—it is of generally high quality and should complement Pritchard's *W. B. Yeats: A Critical Anthology* (1972). (A,G)

Fletcher, Ian. *W. B. Yeats and His Contemporaries.* New York: St. Martin's, 1987. This collection of eleven of Fletcher's essays ably covers the subject of English aestheticism of the 1890s. Fletcher has a talent for picking out the unnoticed detail or neglected event and revealing its significance. The opening essays discuss Yeats' literary and aesthetic context. Six essays follow on the importance of the earlier works. He then examines the curious interactions between Yeats and his book cover designer, Althea Byles. The closing essays examine sources and influences, such as Arthur Symons, John Gray, and Lionel Johnson. Although primarily recommended for advanced students, Fletcher's prose would be pleasingly accessible to a more general audience. (A,G)

Garratt, Robert F. *Modern Irish Poetry: Tradition and Continuity from Yeats to Heaney.* Berkeley: University of California Press, 1986. Beginning with the romanticism of Yeats, Garratt follows the developing themes of Irish poets since the grudging acceptance of Joyce's modernism. Following an introductory chapter that establishes the poetic tradition of Yeats, Garrett examines in turn the revivalists, Joyce, Austin Clarke, Patrick Kavanagh, Thomas Kinsella, John Montague, Seamus Heaney, and some of the other Ulster poets, such as Tom Paulin, Paul Muldoon, and Derek Mahon. This book is indispensable for anyone with an interest in twentieth-century Irish poetry, especially as the war between northern and southern Ireland has affected literature. (A,G)

Good, Maeve. *W. B. Yeats and the Creation of A Tragic Universe.* Totowa, NJ: Barnes & Noble, 1987. Good applies insights from a close reading of *A Vision* and the essays to Yeats' plays—*Calvary, The Words Upon the Window Pane, Purgatory,* and *The Resurrection.* While quite readable, Good covers her ground quickly, making numerous references that a newcomer to Yeats would find obscure. Some familiarity with Yeats' work is necessary. This book should be read in conjunction with Ure's *Yeats the Playwright*, Skene's *The Cuchulain Plays of W. B. Yeats*, and Vendler's *Yeats's Vision and the Later Plays*. (A,G)

Harper, George Mills. *The Making of Yeats's "A Vision": A Study of the Automatic Script*. Carbondale: Southern Illinois University Press, 1987. Yeats believed he communicated with spirits through the medium of automatic writing. This massive, two-volume study presents the evidence supplied by over 3,600 obscure pages of automatic writing text produced in 450 sessions over a period of thirty months. The sessions are presented chronologically, and each chapter reveals a new facet of the unfolding revelation. Yeats interpreted and reworked these materials to compose his text of *A Vision*. Much of the subject matter of the revelation revolves around sexuality and guilt. Yeats made much use of Freud's ideas when framing his questions for the "spiritual instructors," which reveals an advanced acquaintance with psychoanalysis for the year 1917. (A)

Jeffares, A. Norman. *W. B. Yeats: A New Biography*. New York: Farrar, Straus & Giroux, 1990. Jeffares has already written an excellent, if dated, biography of Yeats (*W. B. Yeats: Man and Poet*, 1948). Instead of revising it in light of recent scholarship, he has chosen to write a completely new work. Focusing primarily on the development and ultimate deterioration of Yeats' contradictory personality, he gives an excellent portrayal of the creative act as Yeats experienced it. Although the thrust of this book is biographical rather than critical, insights into Yeats' works emerge as a matter of course. (A)

Keane, Patrick J. *Yeats's Interactions with Tradition*. Columbia: University of Missouri Press, 1987. Keane provides a critical survey of Yeats' works stressing his sources and his attitude toward poetic tradition. In the process, he pays homage to the established critics—Ellmann, Rosenthal, Bloom, Unterecker, and Vendler. The study is admirably organized. Poems are presented in clusters that illuminate one another. The clusters, in turn, are grouped to shed light on a larger theme, such as paradoxes of earth and spirit, self and soul. Keane's overall goal is to reveal Yeats' relation to romanticism. Recommended as an excellent introduction to Yeats criticism. (A,G)

Kuch, Peter. *Yeats and A. E.: The Antagonism That Unites Dear Friends*. Totowa, NJ: Barnes & Noble, 1986. In volume one of a projected two-volume work, Kuch examines in detail the relationship between Yeats and his friend George Russell (A. E.). Kuch treats their artistic, political and social connections, their influence on the Irish literary movement, and related literary and religious involvements. This volume ends in 1907 as the two friends drifted apart after arguments over the Abbey Theatre. (A,G)

Leeming, Glenda. *Poetic Drama*. New York: St. Martin's, 1988. This concise look at twentieth-century British poetic drama is a useful introductory study. Significant portions of the book are devoted to Yeats, Eliot, and Christopher Fry. Little attention is paid to American or other influences. **(A,G)**

Loizeaux, Elizabeth Bergmann. *Yeats and the Visual Arts.* New Brunswick, NJ: Rutgers University Press, 1987. Loizeaux offers a well-developed assessment of the relationship between Yeats' poetics and his ideas about poetry and sculpture. Finding the source of his aesthetics in the tradition of the pre-Raphaelite artists, Loizeaux contends that Yeats gradually abandoned his sense of the "poem as picture" for a concept of the "poem as sculpture." The thesis is explored through an examination of many of the major poems and through commentary on an ample number of illustrations. **(A)**

Longenbach, James. *Stone Cottage: Pound, Yeats, and Modernism.* New York: Oxford University Press, 1988. This study of a literary friendship is the story of how two innovative poets developed their modernist aesthetic. Longenbach presents this famous story in a readable work that should prove useful and enjoyable to serious students. **(A)**

Martin, Heather C. *W. B. Yeats: Metaphysician as Dramatist.* Atlantic Highlands, NJ: Laurier/Humanities, 1986. This is not a Yeats study to be approached lightly. Martin's aim is to study Yeats' private metaphysics with a view to clarifying the content of the plays. She moves quickly through the plays, and it is difficult for the uninitiated to keep up. Newcomers to Yeats who are interested in this subject may want to begin with Vendler's 1963 study, *Yeats's Vision and the Later Plays.* **(A)**

O'Donnell, William H. *The Poetry of William Butler Yeats: An Introduction.* New York: Crossroad/Ungar/Continuum, 1986. Noted Yeats scholar O'Donnell provides a concise and useful survey of thirty-six poems. The introductory material offers a biographical sketch and a summary of Yeats' major themes and influences. He then analyzes the poems for matters of style, structure, thematic content, and critical reception. Although rather limited in scope, O'Donnell's work serves its purpose—to provide full readings of selected poems for new readers. **(A,G)**

Richardson, James. *Vanishing Lives: Style and Self in Tennyson, D. G. Rossetti, Swinburne, and Yeats.* Charlottesville: University Press of Virginia, 1988. In this study, Richardson, noted for his critical work on Thomas Hardy, elaborates on an important, but neglected characteristic that links the works of Tennyson, Dante Rossetti, Swinburne, and Yeats. In his view, these poets may be considered "elegists of the self," who treat life as a fleeting, "ghostly" vapor. Of particular interest is his discussion of how Yeats significantly transformed his Victorian heritage. This study deserves the attention of students of the period but is also suitable for general readers. **(A,G)**

Stead, Christian Karlson. *Pound, Yeats, Eliot, and the Modernist Movement.* New Brunswick, NJ: Rutgers University Press, 1986. Stead's study surveys the origins of the modernist movement, with particular attention to Pound, Yeats, and Eliot. He argues that Pound's influence on Yeats and Eliot has not been adequately acknowledged. To demonstrate this he scrutinizes the manuscript of *The Waste Land,* pointing out those sections where Pound dominated over Eliot's more conventional approach. In his discussion of politics and modernism, he claims that Eliot's conservative views had a deadening effect on the work, holding "Burnt Norton" an abject failure. The result of Pound's bout with fascism is noted in the structures of *The Cantos.* Stead's study is solid and well-written, and provides an enlightening account of the causes and effects of modernism. (A,G)

Young, David. *Troubled Mirror: A Study of Yeats's "The Tower."* Iowa City: University of Iowa Press, 1987. Young's study of Yeats's *The Tower* is an admirably clear analysis of the poem's structure and content. Young manages to discuss Yeats's technique of "intertextual process and juxta- position" in clear, jargon-free language that makes the concepts readily accessible. This volume is recommended as a readable introduction to one of Yeats's most complex works. (A,G)

Other Sources
Adams, Hazard. *The Book of Yeats's Poems.* Gainesville: University Presses of Florida, 1990.

Adams, Joseph. *Yeats and the Masks of Syntax: A Study in Connections.* New York: Columbia University Press, 1984.

Brunner, Larry. *Tragic Victory: The Doctrine of Subjective Salvation in the Poetry of W. B. Yeats.* Troy, NY: Whitston, 1986.

Cavanaugh, Catherine. *Love and Forgiveness in Yeats' Poetry.* Ann Arbor: UMI Research Press, 1985.

Croft, Barbara L. *Stylistic Arrangements: A Study of William Butler Yeats' "A Vision."* Lewisburg, PA: Bucknell University Press, 1987.

Faulkner, Peter. *Yeats: The Tower and the Winding Stair.* New York: Open University Press/Taylor & Francis, 1987.

Finneran, Richard J., ed. *Yeats: A Special Issue on Yeats and Modern Poetry.* Ithaca, NY: Cornell University Press, 1985.

Gardner, Joann. *Yeats and the Rhymers' Club: A Nineties' Perspective.* New York: Peter Lang, 1989.

Hassett, Joseph. *Yeats and Poetics of Hate.* New York: St. Martin's, 1986.

Helmling, Steven. *The Esoteric Comedies of Carlyle, Newman, and Yeats.* New York: Cambridge University Press, 1988.

Hough, Graham. *The Mystery Religion of W. B. Yeats.* Savage, MD: Barnes & Noble, 1984.

Jordan, Carmel. *A Terrible Beauty: The Easter Rebellion and Yeats's "Great Tapestry."* Lewisburg, PA: Bucknell University Press, 1987.

Keane, Patrick J. *Terrible Beauty: Yeats, Joyce, Ireland, and the Myth of the Devouring Female.* Columbia: University of Missouri Press, 1988.

Kinahan, Frank. *Yeats, Folklore and Occultism: Contexts of the Early Work and Thought.* Winchester, MA: Unwin Hyman, 1988.

Komesu, Okifumi. *The Double Perspective of Yeats's Aesthetic.* Savage, MD: Barnes & Noble, 1984.

Nelson, James G. *Elkin Mathews: Publisher to Yeats, Joyce, Pound.* Madison: University of Wisconsin Press, 1989.

Oppel, Frances N. *Mask and Tragedy: Yeats and Nietzsche, 1902-1910.* Charlottesville: University Press of Virginia, 1987.

Putzel, Steven. *Reconstructing Yeats: "The Secret Rose" and "The Wind among the Reeds."* Savage, MD: Barnes & Noble, 1986.

Sacks, Peter M. *The English Elegy: Studies in the Genre from Spenser to Yeats.* Baltimore: Johns Hopkins University Press, 1985.

Siegel, Sandra F., ed. *"Purgatory": Manuscript Materials Including the Author's Final Text.* Ithaca, NY: Cornell University Press, 1985.

Smith, Peter A. *W. B. Yeats and the Tribes of Danu: Three Views of Ireland's Fairies.* Savage, MD: Barnes & Noble, 1986.

Stanfield, Paul S. *Yeats and Politics in the 1930s.* New York: St. Martin's, 1988.

Steinman, Michael. *Yeats' Heroic Figures: Wilde, Parnell, Swift, Casement.* Albany: State University of New York Press, 1984.

Taylor, Richard H. *A Reader's Guide to the Plays of W. B. Yeats.* New York: St. Martin's, 1984.

Wright, David G. *Yeats's Myth of Self: The Autobiographical Prose.* Savage, MD: Barnes & Noble, 1987.

CONTENTS FOR THE RESEARCH GUIDE TO BIOGRAPHY AND CRITICISM: WORLD DRAMA (VOLUME III)

CONTENTS FOR THE RESEARCH GUIDE TO BIOGRAPHY AND CRITICISM: VOLUME V

CUMULATIVE INDEX FOR VOLUMES I-II AND THE 1990 UPDATE (VOLUME IV)

The italicized page number is the first page of *1990 Update* entry; the Roman page number is the first page of the original article in Volumes I-II. "Drama" indicates that an article is also included in the *Research Guide to Biography and Criticism: World Drama* (Volume III).